COINS
OF
CANADA

by J.A.Haxby and R.C.Willey

2016

Editor – Serge Pelletier

Pricing and Editorial – Steve Woodland

Cover Design by – Steven Dobbing

THE UNITRADE PRESS

99 FLORAL PARKWAY, TORONTO, ON M6L 2C4

Copyright © 2016, 2015, 2014, 2013, 2012, 2011, 2010, 2009, 2008, 2007, 2006, 2005, 2004, 2003, 2002, 2001, 1999, 1998, 1997, 1996, 1995, 1994, 1993, 1992, 1990, 1988, 1987, 1986, 1985, 1984, 1983
The Unitrade Press
Copyright © 1982, 1977, 1972, 1971 Western Publishing Co.

IMPORTANT NOTICE

The editors have attempted to provide the most accurate, up-to-date retail prices for all Canadian coins, tokens and paper money. Our pricing is based on information from across the country. Collectors should note that the prices shown in any catalogue should be taken as a guide only.

While every care has been taken to ensure accuracy, the publisher cannot accept responsibility for typographical errors. Please forward any such errors to the Editor.

ACKNOWLEDGEMENTS

The authors wish to express their sincere thanks and appreciation to the following individuals for their assistance and contributions, both direct and indirect, to this and past volumes.

Walter D. Allan, Larry Becker, R.C. Bell, G.H. Bishop, R.F. Blandford, George Blenker, Al Bliman, Fred Bowman, Bill Boynton, K.E. Bressett, Patrick Brindley, Major Sheldon S. Carroll, Freeman Clowery, Myron Cook, Marcel Cool, Brian Cornwell, Michael Curry, Earl Davis, R.H.M. Dolley, Mark Drake, Stephen Dushnick, Graham Dyer, Harry Eisenhauer, Wayne Etmanskie, J. Douglas Ferguson, R.P. Findley, Guy Gibbons, Andrèe Good, Robert J. Graham, E.C. Grandmaison, Friederich D. Grosse, Leslie C. Hill, Klaas Hirsch, Dr. Douglas D. Hunter, Dr. J.P.C. Kent, James D. King, Andrew Kossman, Robert Kril, Glen Lacey, Daniel Langlais, Wilf Latta, Michael Levy, Yvon Marquis, C.F. Martin, Ruth McQuade, Michele Menard, Charles Moore, Eric P. Newman, Walter Ott, Gary Patterson, Alfred E.H. Petrie, Major Fred Pridmore, R.K. Robertson, Douglas Robins, Dick Robinson, K.S. Sargent, Neil Shafer, Thomas Shingles, Thomas S. Shipman, Ed Solski, F. Stewart Taylor, Donald Thomas, Richard Thompsen, Pierre Van Wissen, Don Wainwright, Holland Wallace, Randy Weir, Harold Whiteneck, Warren X, G. Gordon Yorke

Special thanks to the Royal Canadian Mint for illustrations and technical information.

Suggested Retail: $22.95
Spiral Bound
ISBN 978-1-894763-54-7
1-894763-54-8
Printed in China

THE UNITRADE PRESS
99 FLORAL PARKWAY, TORONTO, ON M6L 2C4

TABLE OF CONTENTS

INTRODUCTION

Historical Outline for British
North American Colonies

England was the first European power to explore the North American area, following John Cabot's discovery of the rich fishing regions off Newfoundland in 1497. The promise of good fishing drew other Europeans, including the French, during the early years of the next century. The French initially concentrated on the area around the Gulf of St. Lawrence, founding settlements in Acadia (later Nova Scotia) in 1605 and Quebec City in 1608. During the next 150 years, France and England fought over the North American possessions. Gradually, England took control. The Hudson Bay region was ceded in 1713. In the 1750s most of the Acadians moved out and New Englanders moved in. Quebec and Montreal fell in 1759–60 and British control of the entire Maritimes region was confirmed by the Peace of Paris in 1763.

The area along the St. Lawrence River, formerly called New France, was renamed Quebec under English rule. The American Revolution (1775–83) had an important effect upon the northern colonies. About 50,000 Tories (English sympathizers) from the 13 colonies migrated to Canada, to the east and west of the French area. Most went to the Nova Scotia region, where the separate colony of New Brunswick was formed in 1784. Those who migrated to the west did not like the lack of democracy inherent in the old French order of Quebec and agitated for separation. This was effected by the Constitutional Act of 1791 in which Quebec became Lower Canada and the western region Upper Canada. Each was provided with its own governing body, consisting of a governor, executive council and legislative council appointed by the home government and a legislative assembly elected by the people. The seeds were thus sown for later conflicts. Similar situations existed in the Maritime colonies.

The War of 1812 was a temporary interlude in Canadian history. It was essentially a successful defense by the British against American expansionists. The battlegrounds lay in Upper Canada for the most part.

The Canadian constitutional conflicts continued rising in intensity after the war, especially in Lower Canada, where the Catholic French-Canadians bitterly resented their tyrannical domination by a few Protestant English-speaking officials. The Lower Canadian power movement was fundamentally a "radical conservatism"; the desire was to keep life as it had always been by obtaining the power to assure it. The leader of this movement was Louis Joseph Papineau.

In Upper Canada, under William Lyon Mackenzie, the power movement was more directed toward change. In 1837 armed rebellions broke out in both the Canadas, but they were not well coordinated and were easily put down. Following these rebellions, Lord Durham was dispatched from England to examine the situation. His 1839 report is one of the most famous documents in British Imperial history. His two fundamental suggestions for correcting the causes of the uprising were to reunite the Canadas and to provide the British North American colonies with "responsible" government: the executives would hold office at the discretion of colonial representative assemblies. Sovereignty was to be divided without disintegration of the colonial empire. This new system of responsible government was first applied in 1848 to Nova Scotia and to the Province of Canada (formed from Upper and Lower Canada in 1841) and by 1855 was in operation in the other colonies.

Confederation was slow in coming. Prior to 1864 the Colonial Office favored a union of the Maritime provinces, but feared a larger union involving Canada. They secretly backed a conference of Maritime delegates in Charlottetown, P.E.I., in September 1864. Meanwhile, Canada was increasingly encumbered by a constitution dictating equal representation in the legislature for Canada West and Canada East (the new designations for what were formerly Upper and Lower Canada). Canada West wanted representation by population, and a federation of the two Canadas was sought by Canada West liberals. When word of the impending P.E.I. conference was received in Canada, the Canadians asked to be unofficially included. A formal conference to consider the union of all the provinces was held in Quebec in October 1864 (unknown to the Colonial Office) and a series of resolutions set forth. The resolutions were received well only in Canada West. In Canada East, Nova Scotia and New Brunswick they were contested and in Newfoundland and Prince Edward Island the resolutions were soundly defeated in the legislatures. The union movement was saved by the potential economic boons of such a union and by increasing fears of possible fresh American attempts to annex British North America. The BNA Act was passed by the English Parliament and took effect on July 1, 1867. Newfoundland and Prince Edward Island did not participate in the initial union, but joined later with the more western areas.

The Pre-Confederation Coinages of Canada

One of the greatest hindrances to trade during the early days of the settlements in North America was a lack of coined money. What coins were used trickled in from all over the world. Prior to the English conquest in the 1700s, France endeavored to keep her colonies in coins with special colonial issues and some French Imperial issues, but the balance of trade always caused a net loss of coin from the colonies. The situation was not much better under the British.

One of the major coins circulating in the British North American colonies was the Spanish milled dollar, which was being produced in considerable quantities in several mints to the south. These coins gained wide acceptance and the colonial monetary systems came to be expressed in terms of them. The value of the Spanish dollar varied from colony to colony; in New York it was rated at 8 shillings and in Nova Scotia it was worth 5s. The New York rating was called York Currency and the Nova Scotia rating was called Halifax Currency. Halifax Currency was extended to old Quebec in 1777 during the American Revolution and to Upper Canada, superseding York Currency, in 1822. In English money (sterling) the Spanish dollar was worth 4s, 2d.

The local non-sterling ratings of the Spanish dollar had a profound effect upon the colonial copper currency. While it was possible for British shillings to circulate at the lowered ratings (by giving them a value in local currency of 1 shilling and a certain number of pence, and then giving coppers in change), the smaller valued pieces could not pass for more than their face (sterling) value. There was no way to make change for their additional increment of value in local currency. Thus the importer of British regal coppers incurred a significant loss while the exporter incurred a significant profit. Obviously, the net flow of these coins had to be out of the colonies.

As the situation grew worse, local merchants decided to import tokens from England. They were usually of halfpenny size, with a smaller number of penny pieces and a few farthings. Some tokens were anonymously issued. Others had the name of the issue, for example, PAYABLE AT THE STORE OF J. BROWN. Soon there were a number of attractive, generally well made, coppers in circulation.

However, the element of profit caused some to import lightweight pieces and in time the copper currency became too voluminous. New laws were passed to deal with the problem. In 1817, the Nova Scotia government forbade importation of private copper pieces and directed that the ones already in circulation be withdrawn within three years. In the Canadas an 1825 law was passed to prohibit the private issues, but it had no clause for the withdrawal of those in circulation and was worded so that the importation of tokens dated 1825 or earlier was not illegal. Hence the appearance of private coppers, many of light weight, and antedated, continued in the Canadas.

Meanwhile, the Nova Scotian government stepped in and assumed the responsibility for providing that colony's copper currency. Semi-regal pence and halfpence were issued in 1823 and intermittently until 1856. The people were thereby spared the deluge of metallic trash that was to continue to harass the Canadas, particularly Lower Canada.

The continued and growing presence of spurious coppers, many of which were struck locally, finally forced Lower Canada to take steps to correct the situation. In the absence of action on the part of the government, the Bank of Montreal issued one sou pieces in 1835, followed in 1837 by

Banque du Peuple sous. These were of mediocre quality, however, and were immediately buried under an avalanche of counterfeits.

In 1837, four major Lower Canada banks participated in the issue of the habitant one- and two-sous pieces. After the Canadas reunited in 1841, three banks issued copper pence and half-pence. All four of these later bank coinages were of high quality and were not counterfeited to any significant degree. Gradually, the low quality pieces disappeared from circulation.

The semi-regal and bank issues paved the way for regal issues, based upon a decimal system of dollars and cents. They were struck at the Royal Mint in London or its prime sub-contrac-tor, Heaton's Mint in Birmingham, England. Just as there had been individual colony's currency pounds, each colony's dollar was rated in its own particular way.

The province of Canada, New Brunswick and Prince Edward Island all set their dollar equal to the U.S. gold dollar, so the £ sterling was worth $4.86. Nova Scotia set its currency at $5.00 to the £ sterling and Newfoundland's dollar was initially equal to the Spanish dollar, which made the £ sterling worth $4.80. The first decimal coins were for the Province of Canada in 1858, fol-lowed by issues for Nova Scotia and New Brunswick in 1861, Newfoundland in 1865 and Prince Edward Island in 1871.

Coinages for the Dominion of Canada

Following the formation of the Dominion of Canada, decimal coins were issued in 1870. The British North American colonies which had entered into the Confederation ceased to issue their own distinctive coins and a single coinage was issued for all. Newfoundland's coinage continued until 1947 and Prince Edward Island had a single issue of cents in 1871 prior to its entry into the Dominion in 1873.

Mints, Mint Marks and Quantities Of Coins Struck

The pre-decimal colonial issues (tokens) were struck at many different mints. Most of the better quality pieces emanated from private mints in England, the foremost of which were Boulton and Watt, and Ralph Heaton and Sons. The bank tokens of 1837 (habitants) to 1857 all were struck at one or the other of these mints. Another prominent producer of tokens, Thomas Halliday, of Birmingham, struck the Tiffin pieces (Nos. 115–120), and many of the SHIPS, COLONIES & COMMERCE and Wellington tokens.

The only tokens to bear mint marks are the 1846 Rutherfords of Newfoundland (No. 4), which have RH (for Ralph Heaton) above the date, and some SHIPS, COLONIES & COMMERCE tokens which were struck with an additional incuse H (for Heaton) on the water (No. 14c). When-ever known, the maker of each token issue is indicated in the text. Prior to 1908, all decimal issues for British North America were struck in England. The matrices, punches and dies were prepared at the Royal Mint in London and, when time permitted, the coins were struck there. As the Mint's workload increased, it was necessary to sometimes send the dies to the Heaton Mint (after 1889 called The Mint, Birmingham), where coins were struck on contract.

Except for the 1871 Prince Edward Island cent, all Heaton-struck coins bear a small H mint mark. The last Heaton issue for British North America was the Canadian cent of 1907. Locations of the H are as follows: Canada: 1¢ (1876–90, 1907): below date; (1898, 1900): below bottom leaf; 5–50¢ (1871–1903): below bow of wreath; Newfoundland: 1¢ (1872–1904): below bow of wreath: 5–50¢ (1872–76): below bust; (1882): below the date; $2. (1882): below date.

Late in the 19th century, the Canadians began agitating for a domestic mint with the power to coin sovereigns. Such an institution was authorized by the Ottawa Mint Act of 1901. However, construction was not begun until 1905 and was finally completed in time for commencement of coinage on 2 January 1908.

The name of the new mint was The Royal Mint, Ottawa Branch, but this was changed to The Royal Canadian Mint on 1 December 1931 when it became part of the Canadian government's

Department of Finance, and has been a Crown Corporation since 1969, reporting to parliament through the Minister of Supply and Services. In November of 1973 the Mint's preparatory facility at Hull, Quebec received satellite mint status with the striking of the first Olympic coins. A completely new and separate mint at Winnipeg, Manitoba became operational in the Spring of 1975 to relieve some of the increasing demands for domestic coinage at Ottawa.

Certain 20th century Newfoundland coinages were struck at the Ottawa Mint; and are designated with a C (Canada) mint mark on the reverse: 1¢ (1917–20): below the bow of the wreath; (1941–47): above the T of CENT; 5–50¢ (1917–47): at bottom reverse below oval. In addition, Ottawa-struck British type sovereigns of 1908–19 have a raised C mint mark centred on the base of the design above the date.

In many cases the mintages of tokens are not known, but when known are indicated in the text. The reader should be cautioned that, since many of the tokens were eventually melted, mintages are not necessarily reliable guides to scarcity today.

The quantities struck for the decimal coins are known with more certainty; nevertheless, those for the period 1858–1907 must, for the most part, be considered approximate. This is because the Royal Mint often attempted to use up all good dies, even if they bore the previous year's date. Hence, while the reported number of coins struck in a given year may be quite correct, one cannot be certain what proportion actually bore that date. A good example of the problem is the Canadian ten cents issue for 1889. Research results have pointed to the scarcity of that date (reported mintage 600,000) because 1888 dies were used to strike most of the pieces.

The reliability of mintage figures for the decimal coins is further complicated by the fact that portions of some issues were officially melted. This has turned what would otherwise be a readily available issue into a scarce or rare one. Where it is known or strongly suspected that such a melt has occurred, we have preceded the figure for quantity minted with word originally: and placed the whole in parentheses.

The Manufacture of Coinage Dies

Working punch and die

Collectors have long been interested in differences between coins of the same date or series. There can be variations in the precise details of portraits, the style or size of lettering or date, and so on. Such items have become increasingly popular, and a study of varieties can transform an otherwise placid series into an exciting one.

Together with the rise in variety interest has come a group of terms to describe these differences. Two coins are different types if their designs show some basic difference. For example, the Elizabeth II 1953–64 and 1965–89 obverses represent separate types. The critical distinction is the presence of a laureated bust on the former and a diademed bust on the latter. Conversely, the "broad leaves" and "small leaves" Canadian 10¢ reverses of George V are of the same type. The designs certainly differ in fine details; however, the basic appearance was unchanged.

The above mentioned George V 10¢ examples are major varieties, meaning that there is an obvious and deliberate alteration without changing the basic design. Less apparent varieties are termed minor varieties or variants. When the difference was actually prepared in the dies, the resulting coins will show variations called die varieties. There can also be non-die varieties. Examples in this category include deliberate changes in the planchet composition or thickness.

Not all coins that differ from each other are varieties. The latter designation is reserved for coins differing as a result of some deliberate action by the issuing mint. Any variations arising from such causes as deterioration of dies or malfunction of mint machinery are not true varieties. They are known by names such as freaks, mint errors or irregularities. The term mint error, however, is usually inappropriate and its use in most cases should be avoided.

In order to understand varieties and the place they hold in numismatics, it is important to have at least a casual knowledge of how they came into being; that is, of how coinage dies are made.

Development of the Matrix-Punch-Die System

The usual method of making coins is to place a flat metal disc (the planchet or blank) between two dies bearing the designs and impart the designs to the blank with a sharp blow. A die has at its top the flat or slightly convex surface that will become the field of the struck coin. The design elements (e.g., portrait), which are cameo (raised) on the coin are incuse (sunken) and face the opposite direction in the die. If the reader has difficulty grasping this concept, he should press a coin onto a piece of clay. The image left in the clay is a model of what the top of the die which struck that side of the coin looked like.

In the beginning and for many years thereafter, dies were individually hand engraved. This system was extremely laborious, and once any given die wore out, its precise design was lost for future coinages. Gradually, more complex systems arose, with the ultimate result of preserving a design for an essentially indefinite period.

The first refinement in die-making technique was to engrave the device (e.g., the portrait) in the form of a punch. A punch is a steel intermediate that has its design in cameo, in the same sense as on a coin. The design of the punch would then be impressed into blocks of steel, each of which would become a die. All secondary details (legends, rim beads, etc.) were hand engraved into each die, as previously. The effect of the punch-die system was to extend the life of those parts of the design borne on the punches, because each punch could make (sink) multiple dies.

The transition to the period of modern die-making occurred in the 1600s with the introduction of a third kind of intermediate, the matrix. A matrix has its design in the same sense as a die; however, it is used to make (raise) punches instead of to strike coins. The addition of the matrix step offered two advantages over the previous system. First, a design could be better preserved (a matrix can be used to raise several punches). Second, instead of adding the legend and rim heads at the die stage, these details could be incorporated into the matrix. With only slight modifications, the matrix-punch-die system of die making has persisted to this day.

Initiation of a New Coinage Design

In modern die-making one of the fundamental problems is how to produce a matrix for a new design. The most direct way, but also the most difficult, is to engrave it by hand. After the outlines are scratched on the face of a steel block, the design elements are painstakingly hand cut to the exact size they are to appear on the finished coins. Lettering and other secondary features are often engraved as individual hand punches and punched into the matrix. Only a highly skilled engraver is capable of hand engraving a matrix, and this once common practice has largely disappeared today. The Canadian issues produced by this method are the Victory 5¢ of 1943–45 and the Newfoundland commemorative dollar of 1949. Both were by Thomas Shingles, formerly the chief engraver at the Royal Canadian Mint.

The alternative method for making a matrix of a new design is to use a "reducing machine." This machine was invented around the beginning of the 19th century by a Frenchman, Contamin, and was first used in London's Royal Mint in 1824. While initially rather crude, reducing machines have gradually evolved into a very important part of the engraver's tools. Briefly, it functions as follows: An 8" diameter three dimensional model of the design is produced in some hard substance such as plaster or plastic (formerly electroplated metals). At one end of the arm is a rapidly revolving cutter that faithfully duplicates the movements of the tracer, cutting the design on a reduced scale into a steel block. The reduction from the 8" model to coin size is usually made in two steps. Using the 8" model as a pattern, a steel intermediate model (about 3" in diameter) is made using the machine. This intermediate model is then similarly used to make a second reduction to coin scale. The second product of the machine is almost always a punch, called the reduction punch. The perfected reduction punch is placed in a powerful press and its design used to sink the matrix. Any details absent from the original model are then punched into the matrix. During the Victorian period reduction punches bore only the portrait or reverse device; now only the rim denticles are lacking.

Alteration of Existing Designs

The creation of a partially new design from one already used for coinage can be accomplished by a number of methods. During the Victorian and Edwardian periods, the most common means was to re-engrave a punch or matrix bearing the old design. In some cases the change was slight, in others very pronounced. The Victorian portrait modifications are elegant examples of such a process.

In the George VI and Elizabethan series, changes have been made more often by re-engraving at some point prior to the matrix stage. For example, the famous 1953 modification of the Canadian obverses was made by re-engraving the intermediate model for the reducing machine (see above section).

Dating of Coinage Dies

The dating of dies for the decimal coins has been accomplished by two methods. During the Victorian period it was common practice to employ reverse punches which had only a portion of the date (the first two or three digits). Dies sunk from such punches would then be finished by punching in, one digit at a time, the missing portion of the date. Occasionally, the date was completed at matrix stage.

Post-Victorian dies have usually been prepared from fully dated matrices. Notable exceptions, however, are the 50¢ and dollars for part of the 1940s and the early 1950s, where the date was once again completed in the dies.

Chromium Plating of Coinage Dies

During World War II, an attempt was made to increase die life. The most important advance was the development of an electrolytic process whereby a thin coating of pure chromium was deposited on the die faces. This gave the desired increase in die life and imparted a better finish to the coins. Following limited use in 1942–44, chromium plating was finally adopted for all coinage dies in 1945.

The process, for all its advantages, has also led to the creation of two kinds of trivial differences between coins. First, it sometimes happens that tiny pieces of the plating chip away, leaving pits in the die faces. Such pits are manifested on the struck coins as tiny, irregular "dots," (e.g., the 1947 "dot" coins). Second, during the late 1940s and part of the 1950s, serviceable dies with degenerated plating were replated and put back in the presses. One danger of this was the inadvertent removal of delicate design details when the dies were repolished. The 50¢ 1950 "no lines in 0" and 1955 and other so-called "Arnprior" dollars are doubtless traceable to this practice. Dies are no longer replated at the Mint.

Grading Canadian Coins

Conditions of Coins

In very general terms, the condition of a coin indicates the amount of wear it has sustained since the time it was minted. Coin conditions are distinguished from each other by a series of coin grades. A coin's grade is important to know because it determines the coin's value; the better a coin's grade, the higher will be its value. Coins are classified as belonging to one of two groups, that is, circulated or uncirculated coins. Each of these groups is further divided into many grades.

To properly understand the factors which influence a coin's grade, it is first necessary to appreciate that older coins were manufactured to be used quite simply as money in the world of commerce. Secondly, these business or production strike coins were made on high speed presses, run through counting machines, and dumped into bags where they were scraped with other coins as they were being shipped to various banks across the country. Needless to say, they were handled with little regard to their numismatic posterity. Consequently it is the rule, not the exception, that these coins had marks and other signs of coin-to-coin contact even before they were placed into circulation and used as money. These marks show on the surface of the coin as bright spots or streaks against the soft sheen of the coin's mint lustre. They are called bag marks or bag scratches and are easily distinguished from ordinary wear. Once placed into circulation, all coins begin to show signs of physical wear, i.e., a gradual destruction of the fine details that were originally present on a new coin.

Those coins that were used the most tended to have the fewest details remaining. Today the Mint makes many coins specifically for the collector. These coins are carefully handled and packaged in plastic holders by trained Mint personnel. Unless they are removed from their holders, it is unlikely their grade will change over time.

Until the mid 1970s, coin grades were described by adjectives such as Very Good, Fine, and Uncirculated. Since then the industry has adopted an alternative grading system using a numerical scale from 1 to 70. This system was originally attributed to Dr. Wm. Sheldon who devised it as a means of grading and relating prices for early U.S. copper cents. In his numerical scheme, the circulated grades use the range from one to 59; the uncirculated range begins with 60 and progresses to a perfect coin which is 70. In general, the higher the number assigned, the better the grade or quality of the coin. While the numerical scale is a continuous one, not all of its numbers are used. Grading simply is not that precise, but rather a mixture of both science-like methods and human judgements. Today it is quite common to see coins described using both the adjectival and numerical systems as in the example Extremely Fine-40.

Grading Uncirculated Coins

An uncirculated coin must show absolutely no signs of wear or loss of detail (due to wear) when examined by the naked eye. To properly grade an uncirculated coin, it is necessary to assess three different qualities of the coin in relation to the typical mint state characteristics seen on a coin of that particular type. These three factors are the qualities of the coin's lustre, surfaces, and strike. A coin that has lustre that is dazzling and "alive" is much to be preferred to lustre that is dull and lifeless. A coin that has surfaces that are free, or nearly so, of marks is preferable to one that shows obvious marks that are very distracting to the overall appeal of the coin. A well-struck coin that shows all of the detail intended by the coin's designer is preferable to one that is very poorly struck with the resultant loss of detail in some area of the coin. Each of these factors are equally important in determining the grade of an uncirculated coin. In some cases, one of the factors may be so superior to that normally seen in a particular series that it can make up for a slight deficiency in the quality of one of the remaining factors which by itself would lower the grade.

There are currently five recognized grades used to describe uncirculated coins. These, along with their numerical designations, are: Typical Uncirculated (Mint State-60), Select Uncirculated (MS-63), Choice Uncirculated (MS-65), Gem Uncirculated (MS-67), and Perfect Uncirculated (MS-70). A brief description of each follows:

Perfect Uncirculated-70: The finest quality available. Such a coin under 4X magnification will show no marks, lines or other evidence of handling or contact with other coins. The lustre quality will be of the highest quality possible, with no impairment of any sort. The strike will be perfectly sharp and of a quality very unusual for that series. The strike will show all of the detail intended by the coin's designer/engraver.

Gem Uncirculated-67: A more select example of a Choice Uncirculated coin by virtue of the coin's overall qualities of lustre, surfaces, and strike. The coin is essentially perfect in all respects to the naked eye. Only after extensive study is there likely to be any fault or criticism of the coin.

Choice Uncirculated-65: This grade is reserved for coins that have an overall unquestionable quality look to them. Each of the factors of lustre, surfaces, and strike will be well above average for that normally seen on a typical mint-state coin of the series. The strike will be nearly full except for a slight weakness in a very localized area, the lustre will be almost completely free from impairments, and the surfaces generally free of marks except on the largest coins and those made of softer metals such as gold. Any slight imperfections present in no way distract from the overall beauty of the coin.

Select Uncirculated-63: A more select example of a typical uncirculated coin but lacking the quality appeal of a full Choice Uncirculated-65. Any faults with the surfaces, lustre or strike may be readily seen with the naked eye but they collectively are not a major distraction to the overall appearance of the coin.

Typical Uncirculated-60: Shows absolutely no signs of wear on any part of the coin's surface. This grade refers to a typically seen uncirculated coin and is expected to have a moderate but not excessive number of bagmarks or rim nicks, although none of a serious nature. The coin's lustre may be somewhat impaired by spotting or dullness. The strike may be weak enough to show a generalized weakness in detail in several areas. Usually the impairments to any of these three factors will be obvious at first glance and will continue to be distracting to the overall appeal of the coin.

Grading Circulated Coins

Once a coin enters circulation, it begins to show physical wear on its surfaces. As time goes on the circulating coin becomes more and more worn until, after many decades, only a few of its original details remain. The extent of this wear is the primary factor that determines the grade of circulated coins. There are ten regularly used grades for circulated coins. A brief description of each, along with its numerical grade assignment, follows:

Choice About Uncirculated-55 (AU-55): Only a small, localized trace of wear, at the highest relief points of the coin's design, is visible to the naked eye.

About Uncirculated-50 (AU-50): Traces of wear on nearly all the highest areas. Much of the original mint lustre is still present.

Choice Extremely Fine-45 (EF-45): Light wear can be seen on the highest parts of the coin. All design details are very sharp. Mint lustre is usually seen only in sheltered areas between the inscription letters and around the edges.

Extremely Fine-40 (EF-40): With only slight wear but more extensive than the preceding, the coin still has excellent overall sharpness. Traces of mint lustre may still show.

Choice Very Fine-30 (VF-30): With light even wear on the surface: design details on the highest points are lightly worn, but with all lettering and major features still sharp.

Very Fine-20 (VF-20): As preceding but with moderate wear on the high parts.

Fine-12 (F-12): Moderate to considerable even wear. Entire design is bold. All lettering is visible but with some weaknesses.

Very Good-8 (VG-8): Well worn. Most of the fine details of the hair and leaves are worn nearly smooth.

Good-4 (G-4): Heavily worn. Major designs remain visible but are faint in some areas. Other major features visible only in outline form without the central details.

About Good-3 (AG-3): Very heavily worn with portions of the lettering, date, and legends being worn smooth. The date is barely readable.

While these general definitions of grades are quite useful for most coins, the exact descriptions of circulated grades vary widely from coin type to coin type.

The use of intermediate grades such as EF-42, EF-43, and so on is not encouraged. Grading is not that precise, and using such finely split intermediate grades is imparting a degree of accuracy which probably cannot be verified consistently by other numismatists.

Toning

Often a coin will develop a toning or tarnish on its surfaces. This toning can be particularly colourful and attractive on uncirculated coins because they tend to be free of dirt and grime that will surround the surface of a circulated coin. Silver coins may tarnish in blues, purples, reds, greens, and other colours of the rainbow. Copper or bronze coins may develop dull red, purplish-brown, olive, and chocolate brown toning. However, just because a coin has attractive toning, it should not be concluded that the coin is necessarily a strictly uncirculated example. Numismatists have often fallen into this trap.

These toning features, while an integral part of a coin's price, do not form part of its grade assignment. That is, a coin is first graded as if it were a fully brilliant example and the quality of the toning present, if any, is described by a separate adjective. For example, a Choice Uncirculated-63 coin that is fully brilliant, or possibly with just a hint of toning, may be called Choice BU for Choice Brilliant Uncirculated. On the other hand, that same coin with very dark toning is referred to as being Choice Toned Uncirculated. Some toning descriptions are prefaced by the word "Original" as in Original Toned Choice Unc. This additional adjective refers to those coins that are thought never to have been cleaned (i.e., dipped) since the time they were first minted. As a result, the quality of the toning has a very special pristine look to it which is of considerable appeal to certain connoisseur collectors.

Toned coins must be considered with caution, especially if high price premiums are being demanded. Toning that is darker can obscure very fine marks on the coin's surfaces and therefore make it appear in better condition than it really is. Toning can also hide the fact that a coin has very slight signs of wear and in fact is not the uncirculated coin that it at first appeared to be. The best protection when examining toned coins is to ensure adequate lighting, lots of study time, and use of a magnifying glass. Because collectors have begun to pay premiums for toned coins, it has spawned an increase in the number of people attempting to "artificially" tone coins through chemical reactions. Most specialists in the colour field can tell artificial toning from that of Mother Nature. When in doubt, it would be wise to seek the opinion of one of these specialists.

Marks on Coins

There are many, many adjectives that are used to describe the various marks and other imperfections seen on coins. These descriptions tend to be confusing and make it difficult to properly describe the condition of a coin to others. The following scheme is simple and recommended for describing all marks, rim nicks, and other coin imperfections whether man made or caused by the minting process.

Major: Immediately obvious at first glance to the naked eye. Very distracting.

Minor: Still immediately noticed on first glance to the naked eye but not a major distraction considering the other qualities of the coin.

Slight: Can be seen by the naked eye but usually discovered only after a more detailed study (more than just a glance). Not distracting.

Very Slight: Really only clearly discernable when using low power magnification (4–5 power). Have to search to find it.

Very, Very Slight: Likely not even observable with the naked eye after the closest of study. Details will become clearly defined only under stronger magnification of 8–10 power.

Some Useful Grading Caveats

A grading caveat is, in simple terms, a warning of something to be sensitive to, or careful about, when evaluating the condition of a coin. A healthy respect for each of the following caveats is as important to being a consistently successful grader as is a knowledge of the rules that distinguish a VF coin from an EF and so on.

1. Scarcer dates within a coin series are graded no differently than the more common dates of the same series.

2. There is no such grade as "commercial" grade. Coins are either strictly graded or they are sliders.

3. Expect the largest coins to have more and larger bagmarks than the smallest ones. Also expect to see larger and more numerous marks on coins made of softer metals such as gold.

4. The higher the grade of a coin, the greater the amount of time that should be taken to arrive at that conclusion.

5. Toned coins must always be studied more carefully to see what problems are being obscured.

6. Grading uncirculated coins requires an assessment of three of the coin's factors: the lustre, surfaces, and strike. On the other hand, grading a circulated coin basically involves only one factor, that being, the amount of wear of the surfaces of the coin.

7. There is a natural human tendency for the owner of a coin to overgrade his coin and for the purchaser to undergrade someone else's coin.

8. While a coin's grade and price are inter-related, a coin can only be priced once its grade has been determined. Furthermore a coin cannot be reliably graded by only knowing its price.

9. It is impossible to accurately grade an uncirculated coin of a given series without first understanding the typical mint state characteristics for coins of that series.

10. Grading is not, and never will be, an exact science. It involves a great deal of human judgement too.

11. It is the rule, not the exception, that business or production strike coins will have bag marks and other possible manufactured imperfections.

12. Grading only by "eye appeal" is not really grading at all. Eye appeal grading can be deceptively inaccurate because the grader is tricked into overlooking the problems that may exist on the coin.

Rarity and Value

When one inquires as to the rarity of a coin, it is not really sufficient to specify merely the date and denomination. Varieties exist for several issues, and where they are particularly noteworthy, they are often widely collected as distinct entities—that is, as if they were separate dates. It is also best to specify the condition of the coin. There is always a marked difference between the rarity of earlier issues in uncirculated and well-circulated conditions. Compare values for the various conditions of the Canadian 50¢ piece of 1911. In Very Good (well circulated) it lists at $15, but in uncirculated it jumps to $5,500!

Because determining rarity by examining a large number of coins is often impractical, it is usually deduced by other means. A common practice is to compare prices. This method, while certainly a reasonable starting point, can sometimes be very misleading. For example, the Canadian 1921 50¢ in uncirculated condition lists for $75,000 while the 1870 50¢ without the designer's initials has been valued at nearly $60,000 in the same condition. The mint state 1870 is in fact twice as rare as the 1921. Why the price relationship? Because the 1870 is part of a series not widely collected by date and variety, its rarity is much less appreciated than that of the famous 1921.

The other usual way to ascertain rarity is by comparing mintage figures. Here too, caution is in order. First, reported figures especially for the Victorian period (see above), are not always reliable. Second, in the case of varieties, the mints rarely know what proportion of a given year's issue was of a particular variety. And third, mint figures tell one nothing about the number of pieces preserved in the better conditions. Example: the mintages for the Canadian 1937 and 1938 50¢ are almost identical, yet the uncirculated valuation for the 1937 is $90 while that for the 1938 is $450. The 1937s were saved in quantity because they were the first date of a new series. On the other hand, most of the 1938s were put into circulation.

The value of a coin is determined by the law of supply and demand. Some very scarce items change little in value from year to year because they are not widely collected, whereas commoner dates that are part of a very popular series can show great differences.

The approximate market values listed in this catalog are only indications of probable average worth. In an individual transaction a coin may sell for more or less than what is indicated here. Every attempt has been made to quote values that realistically reflect the market. These values were determined by a panel of several individuals, most of whom are in close contact with retail sales. In some instances, particularly for previously unpublished varieties, the prices are either theoretical or omitted.

The Scope of Listings In This Catalogue

Pre-decimal Colonial Issues

The well-known reference on Canadian tokens, Breton's 1894 work, is a hodgepodge of several different kinds of items which can be divided into seven basic categories:

1. Items that are not really Canadian.
2. Patterns.
3. Merchant and other advertising cards, tickets, etc.
4. Trade tokens, redeemable in goods and services only (e.g., transportation tokens) and only to a very limited extent money.
5. Fabrications made to deceive collectors.
6. Pieces that were used as money, with relatively unrestricted validity throughout the colony issue.
7. Contemporary counterfeits of (6).

The approach used in this catalog is to list only those pieces falling in classes (6) and (7). Careful note should be made of the distinction between contemporary counterfeits and those made to deceive collectors. Contemporary counterfeits, or imitations as they are often called in the listings, are of the same period as the production and circulation of the originals. They were made to circulate and serve as money along with the originals. Being of lighter weight and often containing less pure copper, the imitations brought a tidy profit to their purveyors. The contemporary counterfeits have traditionally been collected along with the originals and some can even command a higher premium today. The inclusion of contemporary imitations in this catalog is quite logical, for they, too, for at least a while, served as Canada's money.

The collectors' forgeries or concoctions are another matter. They are usually made long after the originals circulated, with the intent to deceive coin collectors into paying substantial premiums for them. These items are not worthy of listing in a catalog of this kind.

Over the years, many token die varieties and freaks have been described. Men like Lees and Courteau have devoted considerable energy to the study of varieties in this series. An important reason why such studies are possible has to do with how the dies were made. Most (but not all) of the token dies, including the devices, were engraved entirely by hand. This made every such die distinct from each of the others, creating a large number of die varieties. In a general catalog it is not desirable to list every known difference, even when true die varieties are involved. Therefore, we have surveyed the varieties and have selected for separate listing those that seem to be the most interesting and easy for the average collector to recognize.

Decimal Issues

Although most pattern pieces have been excluded from the listings (see the comments above on token patterns), two decimal coins that might be called "semi patterns" are included: the 1965 medium beads dollar obverse and 1967 flat dies dollar. These coins are the products of trial production runs of several thousand each and are from regular dies. True patterns are almost always proof and are struck in very small quantities.

Varieties in the decimal series have been very popular with collectors and traditionally have been included in Canadian catalogs. Unfortunately, the treatment of varieties has not always been consistent; some have been listed while others, at least as important, have been omitted. In this work an effort has been made to list all noteworthy varieties, regardless of how rare they might be.

It has also been deemed necessary to include a small number of items that are either trivial varieties or not varieties at all. That is because the particular items involved have been touted as differences of importance (through advertising campaigns, etc.) for so long that many collectors have been misled into thinking they really are important. At this date it would seem unwise to remove such things as the "Arnprior" dollars from the catalogue. Each of these "objectionable" listings is explained in the appropriate place in the main body of the catalogue.

As a final comment regarding those varieties which have been listed, it is stressed that this book is only a guide. By the inclusion of a given item the authors do not necessarily suggest that it should be part of a "complete" set. Each collector is urged to decide for himself the extent of his interest in the sub listings.

Local and National Numismatic Organizations

Throughout Canada and the U.S. are located many local coin clubs that include in their memberships those interested in any and all phases of numismatics. Becoming involved in such an organization offers important advantages to beginner and more experienced collector alike. One can acquire needed coins, dispose of extras, gain valuable knowledge and enjoy the good fellowship of others with like interests.

Similarly, anyone seriously interested in Canadian numismatics should join and support Canada's national numismatic organization, The Royal Canadian Numismatic Association. Its members have access by mail to the association's impressive library and receive the official monthly periodical, the Canadian Numismatic Journal. The Journal provides a medium for publishing and disseminating numismatic knowledge, so important for progress in the hobby. Those interested in membership should contact:

Royal Canadian Numismatic Association
General Secretary
Suite 432, 5694 Hwy 7 East
Markham, ON L3T 1B4 Canada
www.rcna.ca

There is also an organization for those interested in paper money:

Canadian Paper Money Society
P.O. Box 562
Pickering, ON L1V 2R7 Canada
www.cpmsonline.ca

The principal national U.S. numismatic association (the largest in the world) is:

The American Numismatic Association
P.O. Box 2366
Colorado Springs, CO 80901 USA
www.money.org
(Membership inquiries should be directed to the General Secretary)

Numismatic Publications

Weekly and bi-weekly (every two weeks) tabloid-type publications fill another need for the collector, that of providing an up-to-date view of hobby activity. Dealer advertising offering coins, paper money and related numismatic items can be found in abundance, as well as special sections devoted to features and events of interest. Many coin shops carry these informative periodicals, or subscriptions may be entered by writing directly to the publications listed below:

Canadian Coin News
PO BOX 28103 LAKEPORT PO 600 Ontario St.
St. Catharines, ON L2N 7P8 Canada
(Bi-Weekly)
www.canadiancoinnews.ca
Write for a sample copy.

World Coin News
700 East State Street
Iola, WI 54990 USA
(Weekly, sample copy $1.00)

CANADIAN DECIMAL COINS

Although the early 19th century coinage of commerce in all the British North American colonies was ostensibly that of England, the actual coins were scarce and issues of a number of countries were used. They were primarily those of France, Portugal, Spain, Mexico and the United States. Furthermore, as outlined in other chapters, large numbers of privately issued base metal pieces circulated for pennies and halfpennies. The need for unified currencies was clear-cut. The final result was a distinctive decimal currency for each of the colonies.

The principal leader in the Province of Canada's struggle for its own coinage was Sir Francis Hincks, Inspector General (1848–54), Prime Minister (1851–54) and later Minister of Finance for the Dominion of Canada. Legislation establishing the Province's decimal coinage consisted of several steps that took almost a decade. Initially there was strong British opposition.

In 1850 an act was passed that empowered the provincial government to have its own distinctive coinage, struck in denominations of pounds, shillings and pence. The British government disallowed the act, however, partly because it was felt that the regulation of coinage was the prerogative of the Sovereign and the use of English currency facilitated trade with the Mother Country.

In a second act passed in 1851, the Canadians continued the fight for control of their own currency. For the first time a decimal system was suggested; public accounts were to be kept in dollars, cents and mils. The English Treasury also viewed the second act with disfavour, but did not disallow it. Instead, it was proposed that the province have its own pound and that it could be divided into decimal units if necessary.

The 1851 act paved the way for an act of 1853, which established a Canadian currency consisting of pounds-shillings-pence and dollars-cents-mils, the public accounts being kept in the latter. The striking of coins was left to the Queen's prerogative and none was issued under this act.

Finally, in 1857, the dollar alone was established as the unit of money and all accounts, public and government, were to be kept in dollars and cents. The Canadian dollar was given the same intrinsic value as the U.S. dollar; the English sovereign (pound sterling) was worth $4.86. An issue of decimal coins followed in 1858–59.

LARGE CENTS
Victoria, Province of Canada, 1858–1859

Diameter: 25.40 mm; weight: 4.54 grams; composition: .950 copper, .040 tin, .010 zinc; edge: plain

The basic obverse design, a bust separated from the legend by a beaded circle, is said to have been

G:	Braid worn through
VG:	No detail in braid around ear
F:	Segments of braid begin to merge into one another
VF:	Braid is clear but not sharp
EF:	Braid is slightly worn but generally sharp and clear

copied from the Napoleon III bronze coinages of France (1853–70). The Canadian obverse shows a very youthful Victoria with a laurel wreath in her hair and was designed and engraved by the Royal Mint's famed engraver, Leonard C. Wyon.

The reverse was also by L.C. Wyon and has a serpentine vine with 16 maple leaves. There are numerous slight variations involving recutting of some of the leaf stems or the vine stalk.

The coins were conceived to be used also as convenient units of measure; the diameter is exactly 1 inch and 100 (unworn) pieces weigh 1 avoirdupois pound. Nevertheless, they were not very popular at first and were discounted, sometimes by as much as 20%, to get them into circulation.

| Wide, bold 9 over 8 | Early form   Late form Narrow 9 | No. 1   No. 2 Double-punched narrow 9 (No. 1 is often erroneously called a narrow 9 over 8) |

1859 date varieties. Although the Province of Canada placed its single order for cents in 1858, insufficient time forced the Royal Mint to strike the bulk of the coins in 1859. Two distinctly different 9 punches were used for dating the dies. A number of dies (at least 11) were originally dated 1858 and have the final 8 altered by overpunching with a wide, bold 9, this 9 was apparently used only for overdating (we cannot confirm the claims that the wide 9 occurs on a non overdate). A second figure, used for non-overdates, is narrow and initially rather delicate. Some narrow 9 specimens have the 9 somewhat broadened; these are thought to be from dies dated late in the issue when the narrow 9 punch had distorted from extensive use (rather than two different styles of narrow 9 punches being used). Both the delicate and broadened narrow 9s are illustrated because the latter is sometimes confused with the wide, bold 9. The so-called "narrow 9 over 8" is not a true overdate but a double-punched narrow 9 with a small piece out of the die at the lower front of the 9s. A second double-punched narrow 9 has traces of the original 9 to the left of the second figure. The latter double-punchings are considered trivial by these cataloguers; however, they are included because of the current wide acceptance by collectors.

DATE	QTY. (000)	G-4	VG-8	F-12	VF-20	EF-40	AU-50	BROWN UNC-60	RED† BU-63
1858 421		50.00	80.00	100.00	140.00	235.00	350.00	600.00	2,275
1859 (incl. all var.) 9,579									
9 over 8, wide 9		30.00	50.00	70.00	100.00	175.00	275.00	550.00	2,275
narrow 9, all forms		2.50	4.50	5.50	8.00	12.00	25.00	75.00	270.00
double-punch, narrow 9 . . . . No. 1		200.00	300.00	400.00	550.00	800.00	1,350	2,250	7,500
double-punch, narrow 9 . . . . No. 2		55.00	90.00	135.00	185.00	275.00	500.00	900.00	4,500
1859 . . Brass . . . . .rare		12,000	20,000	25,000	35,000	—	—	—	—

† 70% Lustre

Victoria, Dominion of Canada, 1876–1901

Diameter: 25.40 mm; weight: 5.67 grams; composition: .955 copper, .030 tin, .015 zinc; edge: plain

G:	Hair over ear worn through
VG:	No details in hair over the ear
F:	Strands of hair over the ear begin to run together
VF:	Hair and jewels are clear but no longer sharp
EF:	Hair over the ear is sharp and clear. Jewels

Because of the large issue of 1858–59 cents by the Province of Canada and later the Dominion of Canada governments, this denomination was not issued again until nearly ten years after Confederation. The Provincial cents had been unpopular because of their weight, so the Dominion cents were struck in the same weight as the British halfpenny.

The obverse type of the Dominion cents was changed to one with a diademed Queen, although a pattern piece with the 1876 reverse and 1858–59 obverse suggests that the laureated type may have been considered. The diademed obverse type is composed of four distinctive portrait varieties, differing in the facial and certain other details. The portrait for the initial obverse (Obv. 1) was created by modifying one of those used for the Jamaican halfpenny. Later obverses were revisions to those previously used: Obv. 2 being derived from Obv. 1, while Obv. 3 and 4 were derived from Obv. 2. All designs were by L.C. Wyon except for Obv. 4, which was probably by G.W. de Saulles. The portraits are distinguished as follows:

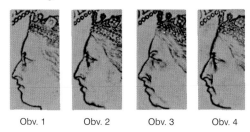

Obv. 1   Obv. 2   Obv. 3   Obv. 4

Obverse 1: Generally youthful appearance: rounded chin and prominent lips.

Obverse 2: Somewhat aged facial features: double chin and repressed upper lip.

Obverse 3: Even more aged features: double chin with a square front and depression over the eye.

Obverse 4: Smooth chin restored, but has repressed upper lip.

In addition to the portrait differences there are also several variations of lettering style, the most obvious of which occurs in association with Obv. 3. When the obverse was used in 1890, it had a normal (or nearly so) legend; however, the 1891–92 Obv. 3s all have a legend with more coarse style letters punched over the original.

Three major reverse varieties exist. The first (1876–82) is identical to the 1858–59 issues, except for some re-cutting of the leaf stems and vine stalk. The second has a new vine containing wider leaves with less venation. The third (1891–1901) has yet another vine containing narrow leaves with incuse venation. Each reverse was from a separate reducing machine model; the first two were by L.C. Wyon and the third is thought to be by G.W. De Saulles. There are numerous re-cuttings of the stems and stalks of the vines on the first and third reverses.

DATE	QTY. (000)	G-4	VG-8	F-12	VF-20	EF-40	AU-50	BROWN UNC-60	RED† BU-63
Provincial Leaves Reverse (1876–1882)									
1876H.....obv. 1..........	4,000	2.50	5.00	6.00	8.00	16.00	35.00	70.00	250.00
1881H.....obv. 1..........	2,000	3.00	6.00	9.00	15.00	25.00	50.00	100.00	360.00
1882H.....obv. 1, 2........	4,000	2.50	5.00	6.00	8.00	14.00	30.00	65.00	250.00
† 70% Lustre									

Large Leaves Reverse 1884–1891   Small Leaves Reverse 1891–1901

Large date | Small date

DATE	QTY. (000)	G-4	VG-8	F-12	VF-20	EF-40	AU-50	BROWN UNC-60	RED† BU-63
Large Leaves Reverse (1884–1891)									
1884 .. obv. 1, 2	2,500	3.00	5.00	7.00	10.00	17.00	40.00	95.00	270.00
1886 .. obv. 1, 2	1,500	4.00	7.50	11.00	18.00	35.00	70.00	160.00	550.00
1887 .. obv. 2	1,500	3.25	5.00	7.00	11.00	22.00	45.00	100.00	270.00
1888 .. obv. 2	4,000	3.00	4.00	5.00	7.00	12.00	25.00	60.00	200.00
1890H obv. 3	1,000	6.00	10.00	15.00	15.00	40.00	75.00	150.00	400.00
1891 .. obv. 2, 3									
large date	1,452	5.00	10.00	15.00	25.00	50.00	90.00	175.00	550.00
small date . . . . inc. above		60.00	100.00	140.00	200.00	325.00	575.00	1,100	5,400
Small Leaves Reverse (1891–1901)									
Note: All large cents with small leaves reverse, including those dates 1891, have a small date.									
1891 .. obv. 2, 3 . . . . incl. above		40.00	70.00	95.00	135.00	200.00	300.00	450.00	1,575
1892 .. obv. 2,3,4	1,200	4.00	7.00	12.00	18.00	30.00	50.00	100.00	315.00
1893 .. obv. 4	2,000	2.00	5.00	6.50	9.00	15.00	30.00	75.00	225.00
1894 .. obv. 4	1,000	8.00	17.00	22.00	30.00	50.00	80.00	150.00	400.00
1895 .. obv. 4	1,200	4.00	8.00	12.00	20.00	30.00	50.00	100.00	340.00
1896 .. obv. 4	2,000	2.00	5.00	6.00	9.00	15.00	30.00	65.00	225.00
1897 .. obv. 4	1,500	2.00	5.00	6.00	9.00	15.00	35.00	75.00	270.00
1898H obv. 4	1,000	6.00	9.00	14.00	22.00	35.00	65.00	130.00	400.00
1899 .. obv. 4	2,400	3.00	4.00	5.00	8.00	14.00	30.00	60.00	180.00
1900 .. obv. 4	1,000	7.00	11.00	16.00	25.00	45.00	90.00	175.00	585.00
1900H obv. 4	2,600	3.00	4.00	5.00	7.00	12.00	25.00	50.00	110.00
1901 .. obv. 4	4,100	3.00	4.00	5.00	7.00	12.00	25.00	50.00	120.00

On the 1898 and 1900 Heaton issues, the H mark is below the bottom leaf in the wreath.

Edward VII, 1902–1910

Diameter: 25.40mm; weight 5.67 grams; composition; .955 copper, .030 tin, .015 zinc; edge: plain

G: Band of crown worn through
VG: Band of crown worn through at highest point
F: Jewels in band of crown will be blurred
VF: Band of crown is still clear; no longer sharp
EF: Band of crown is slightly worn but generally sharp and clear

A single obverse, designed and engraved by G.W. De Saulles (DES below bust), was employed for the entire series.

The reverse was a continuation of the small leaves Victorian variety.

	QTY. (000)	G-4	VG-8	F-12	VF-20	EF-40	AU-50	BROWN UNC-60	RED† BU-63
1902	3,000	1.50	2.50	3.50	5.00	9.00	15.00	30.00	80.00
1903	4,000	1.50	2.50	3.50	5.00	9.00	17.00	35.00	100.00
1904	2,500	1.75	3.50	4.50	7.00	12.00	25.00	50.00	120.00
1905	2,000	3.50	5.00	7.00	10.00	15.00	30.00	60.00	160.00
1906	4,100	1.50	2.50	3.50	5.00	9.00	20.00	45.00	180.00
1907	2,400	2.00	3.00	4.00	6.00	11.00	22.00	45.00	180.00

† 70% Lustre

On the 1907 Heaton issue
the mint mark is below the date.

DATE	QTY. (000)	G-4	VG-8	F-12	VF-20	EF-40	AU-50	BROWN UNC-60	RED† BU-63
1907H	800	10.00	15.00	23.00	35.00	60.00	100.00	200.00	630.00
1908	2,402	2.00	4.00	5.00	7.00	13.00	25.00	50.00	135.00
1909	3,973	1.25	2.25	3.25	4.50	8.00	17.00	35.00	110.00
1910	5,146	1.25	2.00	2.75	4.00	7.00	15.00	35.00	90.00

George V, 1911–1920

Diameter: 25.40 mm; weight 5.67 grams; composition: .955 copper, .030 tin, .015 zinc; edge: plain

G:	Band of crown worn through
VG:	Band of crown worn through at highest point
F:	Jewels in band of crown will be blurred
VF:	Band of crown is still clear; no longer sharp
EF:	Band of crown is slightly worn but generally sharp and clear

The original obverse, used for the 1911 issues of the 1¢ to 50¢, bore a legend lacking the words DEI GRATIA ("by the grace of God") or some abbreviation for them. The public complained, calling these coins 'Godless', and in 1912 a modified legend containing DEI GRA was introduced. Both varieties were derived from a portrait model of the King by Sir E.B. MacKennal (initials B.M on truncation).

The reverse, although resembling previous designs, is completely new. The engraver was W.H.J. Blakemore.

Godless Obverse (1911)

1911	4,663	1.00	1.50	2.00	3.00	5.00	15.00	30.00	75.00

Modified Obverse Legend (1912–1920)

1912	5,108	.80	1.50	2.00	4.00	6.00	15.00	35.00	80.00
1913	5,735	.80	1.25	2.00	3.00	6.00	15.00	40.00	100.00
1914	3,406	1.10	1.50	2.50	3.50	7.00	120.00	50.00	110.00
1915	4,932	.90	1.25	2.00	3.00	6.00	15.00	40.00	100.00
1916	11,022	.70	1.00	1.50	2.00	4.00	10.00	25.00	75.00
1917	11,899	.70	1.00	1.50	2.00	4.00	7.00	18.00	60.00
1918	12,971	.70	1.00	1.50	2.00	4.00	7.00	17.00	60.00
1919	11,280	.70	1.00	1.50	2.00	4.00	7.00	17.00	60.00
1920	6,762	.70	1.00	1.50	2.00	4.00	9.00	25.00	90.00

† 70% lustre

SMALL CENTS
George V, 1920–1936

Diameter: 19.05 mm; weight: 3.24 grams; thickness: 1.65 mm;
composition: .955 copper, .030 tin, .015 zinc; edge: plain

In order to conserve copper, the large cent was replaced in 1920 with one of smaller size, like that of the United States. The obverse bust was MacKennal's familiar design and the reverse was a new design by Fred Lewis. The matrices were prepared in London by W.H.J. Blakemore.

DATE	MILLIONS MINTED	G-4	VG-8	F-12	VF-20	EF-40	AU-50	BROWN UNC-60	RED† BU-63
1920	15	.20	.25	.50	1.00	2.00	7.00	17.00	60.00
1921	8	.25	.50	1.00	2.00	7.00	15.00	40.00	300.00
1922	1	13.00	20.00	22.00	35.00	60.00	120.00	250.00	1,500
1923	1	24.00	35.00	40.00	50.00	80.00	175.00	350.00	2,500
1924	2	4.50	8.00	10.00	15.00	25.00	65.00	150.00	1,000
1925	1	20.00	28.00	32.00	40.00	65.00	120.00	250.00	1,300
1926	2	3.00	5.00	6.00	10.00	20.00	50.00	100.00	700.00
1927	4	.90	1.50	2.00	4.00	10.00	25.00	50.00	275.00
1928	9	.20	.25	.50	1.00	2.50	10.00	25.00	110.00
1929	12	.20	.25	.50	1.00	2.50	10.00	25.00	90.00
1930	3	1.50	2.50	3.50	6.00	12.00	30.00	65.00	275.00
1931	4	.50	1.00	1.50	3.00	8.00	25.00	50.00	225.00
1932	21	.10	.20	.30	.75	2.00	6.00	20.00	75.00
1933	12	.10	.20	.40	.75	2.00	6.00	20.00	60.00
1934	7	.20	.25	.50	1.00	2.00	6.00	20.00	75.00
1935	8	.20	.25	.50	1.00	2.00	6.00	20.00	65.00
1936	9	.20	.25	.50	1.00	2.00	6.00	17.00	50.00

† 70% lustre

George VI Issue Struck in Name of George V

King George V died early in 1936 and was succeeded by his son Edward VIII, whose portrait was planned for introduction on 1937 coinage. Edward abdicated late in 1936 and his younger brother was crowned as George VI. The Royal Mint in London did not have time to prepare new Canadian George VI obverse matrices and punches for shipment to Ottawa by the beginning of 1937. This led to an emergency situation because of a pressing demand for 1-, 10- and 25-cent coins, and in order to meet the emergency, these were struck using George V dies dated 1936. To denote that the coins were actually struck in 1937 a small round depression was punched into each die, causing a raised dot to appear in that position on the coins. On the cent the dot is centered below the date.

Of the three denominations thus made, only the 25¢ is readily available (in circulated condition), while the two others are known only in mint state and are very rare. Obviously if all had been released they would be known in greater quantity today; therefore it seems reasonable to explain the situation in one of two ways: (a) the 1¢ and 10¢ were not struck with the dots (it has often been suggested that the depression in these dies filled with extraneous matter or that they were never punched into the dies in the first place), or (b) they were made with dots but not issued. The first explanation is quite doubtful because (1) a former mint employee who worked in the press room in early 1937 maintains that all three denominations were struck with dots, (2) the known 10¢ specimens have a dot larger than that on the 25¢, yet the "clogging" theory would require that the 25¢ dies did not fill up while all the rest did, and (3) one of the dot cents was found in the pyx, a container where coins taken at random from production runs are reserved for assay.

In view of the above, these authors suggest serious consideration of the possibility that the dot 1¢ and 10¢ pieces were struck but never issued (i.e., melted).

The physical specifications are the same as the George V issues.

DATE	QUANTITY MINTED		
1936 raised dot below date	(originally: 678,823)	Rare	5 known

Pittman sale, 21 October 1997 – $121,000 US ($170,000 CAD)
Krause sale, January, 2004 – $207,000 US ($280,000 CAD) resold Canadiana sale, 2010 – $300,000.00 CAD

George VI, 1937–1952

Diameter: 19.05 mm; weight: 3.24 grams; thickness: 1.65 mm; composition: (1937–41) .955 copper, .030 tin, .015 zinc; (1942–52) .980 copper, .005 tin, .015 zinc; edge: plain

The obverses of the George VI issues are unique in that the monarch is bareheaded. The original obverse legend contains the phrase ET IND : IMP : (for Et Indiae Imperator, meaning "and Emperor of India"). Beginning with coins dated 1948, the phrase was omitted from the King's titles, India having gained independence from England during the previous year. Both varieties were derived from a portrait model by T.H. Paget (H.P. under bust).

In keeping with a government decision to modernize the designs, the simple but compelling "maple twig" design by G.E. Kruger-Gray (K.G under the right leaf) was adopted for the cent.

1947 maple leaf. Some specimens of all denominations dated 1947 have a tiny maple leaf after the date, to denote that they were actually struck in 1948. Later that year, while the Royal Canadian Mint was awaiting arrival of the new obverse matrices and punches bearing the modified legend from the Royal Mint in London, a pressing demand for all denominations arose. In order to meet the demand, coins were struck with 1947 obverse and reverse dies, with the leaf added to indicate the incorrect date. After the new obverse punches and matrices arrived later in the year, normal 1948 coins were put into production.

DATE	MILLIONS MINTED	VG-8	F-12	VF-20	EF-40	AU-50	BROWN UNC-60	RED† BU-63
"ET IND : IMP :" Obverse (1937–1947)								
1937	10	.40	.50	.75	1.00	2.00	3.00	15.00
1938	18	.15	.25	.35	1.00	2.00	3.00	15.00
1939	22	.15	.25	.35	.75	1.50	2.50	10.00
1940	86	.01	.10	.35	.75	1.00	3.00	10.00

† 70% lustre

DATE	MILLIONS MINTED	VG-8	F-12	VF-20	EF-40	AU-50	BROWN UNC-60	RED† BU-63
1941	56	.01	.15	.35	1.00	2.50	10.00	55.00
1942	76	.01	.15	.35	.75	2.00	8.00	55.00
1943	89	.01	.15	.35	.50	1.50	4.00	25.00
1944	44	.01	.15	.35	1.00	2.50	12.00	75.00
1945	77	.01	.15	.25	.50	1.00	3.00	23.00
1946	57	.01	.15	.25	.50	1.00	3.00	15.00
1947	31	.01	.15	.25	.50	1.00	3.00	12.00
1947 maple leaf	44	.01	.15	.25	.50	1.00	3.00	12.00

Modified Obverse Legend (1948–1952)

DATE	MILLIONS MINTED	VG-8	F-12	VF-20	EF-40	AU-50	BROWN UNC-60	RED† BU-63
1948	26	.15	.20	.35	1.00	1.50	5.00	30.00
1949	33	.01	.01	.25	.50	1.00	3.00	12.00
1950	60	.01	.01	.20	.35	.75	2.00	12.00
1951	80	.01	.01	.20	.35	.50	2.00	18.00
1952	68	.01	.01	.20	.35	.50	1.50	12.00

† 70% lustre

Elizabeth II, Laureate, 1953–1964

Diameter: 19.05 mm; weight: 3.24 grams; thickness: 1.65 mm;
composition: .980 copper, .005 tin, .015 zinc; edge: plain

F: *Leaves worn almost through;*
    shoulder fold indistinct
VF: *Leaves considerably worn;*
    shoulder fold must be clear
EF: *Laurel leaves somewhat worn*

No shoulder fold   Note style of letters, relation to denticles.
1953-55   The 'I' points between two denticles.

The initial obverse for the 1953 issue had a high relief, laureate portrait of the Queen by Mary Gillick (M.G. on truncation) which did not strike up well on the coins. Later in the year, the relief was lowered and the hair and shoulder detail re-engraved by Thomas Shingles, chief engraver of the Royal Canadian Mint. Two lines at the shoulder, representing a fold in the gown, are clear on the second variety but almost missing on the first. (There has been a tendency to erroneously term them "shoulder strap" and "no shoulder strap", respectively, but even on the original portrait the ridge representing the top of the gown can be seen high above the shoulder). The two varieties also differ in the positioning of the legend relative to the rim denticles and in the styles of some of the letters.

The reverse device for the 1953–64 period was basically the same as for George VI.

1954, 1955 No shoulder fold. Through an oversight, a small number of 1954 prooflike sets included cents struck from the rejected no shoulder fold obverse. An even smaller number of regular 1955 cents were also struck with this obverse.

With shoulder fold   Note style of letters, relation to denticles
1953–64   The 'I' points to a denticle.

DATE	MILLIONS MINTED	F-12	VF-20	EF-40	AU-50	BROWN UNC-60	RED† BU-63
1953 .. no shoulder fold 68		.01	01	.30	.50	1.00	3.00
...... with shoulder fold included above		1.50	2.00	4.00	8.00	15.00	75.00
1954 .. no shoulder fold 22				(proof-like only)		700.00	1,000
1954 .. with shoulder fold included above		.15	.25	.50	1.00	2.00	8.00
1955 .. no shoulder fold 56		180.00	225.00	325.00	500.00	800.00	2,500
with shoulder fold included above		.01	.01	.20	.25	.50	4.00
1956 79		.01	.01	.20	.25	.35	3.00
1957 101		.01	.01	.01	.01	.15	1.50
1958 59		.01	.01	.01	.01	.15	1.50
1959 84		.01	.01	.01	.01	.01	.75
1960 76		.01	.01	.01	.01	.01	.75
1961 140		.01	.01	.01	.01	.01	.75
1962 227		.01	.01	.01	.01	.01	.50
1963 279		.01	.01	.01	.01	.01	.50
1964 485		.01	.01	.01	.01	.01	.50

Elizabeth II, Tiara, 1965–1978

In 1965, an obverse with a new style portrait by Arnold Machin was introduced. The Queen has more mature facial features and is wearing a tiara. Two obverse varieties exist for 1965: the first has a flat field and small rim beads, while the second has a concave field (sloping up toward the rim) and large rim beads. The second obverse was instituted because of the unacceptably short die life with the first. The large beads obverse was replaced because of the tendency for the rim detail in the dies to wear too rapidly. So, starting in 1966, the obverse has a less concave field and small rim beads. As with the 1953 issues, the 1965–66 varieties can be distinguished by the positioning of the legend relative to the rim beads.

Small beads   Large beads   Pointed 5 (at top)   Blunt 5
Detail at "A" in "REGINA"

1965 date and combinational varieties. Coupled with the two 1965 obverses in all combinations were two reverses, having trivially different 5s in the dates. The varieties of 5 have become popular, but the authors of this catalogue do not consider them significant.

DATE	MILLIONS MINTED	BROWN UNC-60	RED† BU-63
1965	small beads, pointed 5 (Variety 1) 304	1.50	7.00
	small beads, blunt 5 (Variety 2) .... incl. above	.01	.50
	large beads, blunt 5 (Variety 3) .... incl. above	.01	.50
	large beads, pointed 5 (Variety 4) .... incl. above	22.00	60.00
1966	 184	.01	.50

† 70% Lustre

Confederation Centennial, 1967

All denominations for 1967 bore special reverses to commemorate the 1867 confederation of the provinces of Canada, Nova Scotia and New Brunswick to form the Dominion of Canada. The designer was Alex Colville. The 1-cent reverse shows a rock dove in flight.

DATE	MILLIONS MINTED	BROWN UNC-60	RED† BU-63
1967 Confederation Centennial	345	.01	.50

Maple Twig Resumed, 1968 –

1968	330	.01	.50
1969	335	.01	.50
1970	311	.01	.50
1971	298	.01	.50
1972	451	.01	.50
1973	457	.01	.50
1974	692	.01	.50
1975	642	.01	.50
1976	701	.01	.50
1977	453	.01	.50

Reduced Thickness, 1978–1979

Diameter: 19.05 mm; weight: 3.24 grams; thickness: 1.52 mm; composition: .980 copper, .0175 zinc, .0025 other; edge: plain

1978	911	.01	.50

Elizabeth II, Modified Obverse, 1979–1989

Beginning with 1979, the portrait of the Queen was made smaller to standardize our coinage, making the effigy proportional to the diameter of the coin, regardless of denomination.

1979	754	.01	.50

Reduced Weight, 1980–1981

Diameter: 19.00 mm; weight 2.80 grams; thickness: 1.45 mm; composition: .980 copper, .0175 zinc, .0025 other; edge: plain

Pattern pieces dated 1979 were struck in 1978 with a reduced weight and a diameter of 16 mm. This action was in response to the rising cost of copper which was causing the 1-cent coin to be produced at a loss. The 16 mm cent was cancelled when it was found that this was the same diameter used for tokens by the Toronto Transit Commission. The 1979 cent was of the old weight and diameter. In 1980, a decreased diameter, thickness and weight were introduced.

1980	912	.01	.50
1981	1,209	.01	.50

† 70% lustre

Elizabeth II, 12-Sided Cent, 1982–1996

Diameter: 19.1 mm; weight: 2.50 grams; thickness: 1.45 mm;
composition: .980 copper, .0175 zinc, .0025 other; edge: plain

Beginning in 1982 the shape of the 1-cent coin was changed from round to 12-sided to make it easier for the blind to identify. The new shape also meant a reduction in weight.

DATE		MILLIONS MINTED	BROWN UNC-60	RED† BU-63
1982	 911		.01	.50
1983	 976		.01	2.00
1984	 838		.01	.50
1985	blunt 5 783		.01	.50
1985	pointed 5 .... included above		15.00	35.00
1986	 740		.01	.50
1987	 919		.01	.50
1988	 483		.01	.50
1989	 1,077		.01	.50

† 70% lustre

Elizabeth II, Crowned, 1990–2003

The first effigy designed by a Canadian for use on Canadian coins was introduced on the obverse of all Canadian issues for 1990. The design depicts a more contemporary portrait of the Queen wearing a necklace and earrings. The elaborate crown, last seen on Victorian issues, replaced the tiara used on previous issues. The obverse was designed by Dora de Pédery-Hunt.

1990	 218		.01	.50
1991	 831		.01	.50

125th Anniversary of Confederation, 1992

To celebrate the 125th anniversary of Confederation, all circulation coins issued in 1992 bear the date "1867–1992".

DATE		MILLIONS MINTED	BROWN UNC-60	RED BU-63
1992	(1867–1992) 674		.01	.50
1993	 809		.01	.50
1994	 614		.01	.50
1995	 625		.01	.50
1996	 446		.01	.50

New Material, Round Cent, 1997–

Diameter: 19.05 mm; weight: 2.25 grams; thickness: 1.45 mm;
material: copper-plated zinc; edge: plain

DATE		MILLIONS MINTED	BROWN UNC-60	RED BU-63
1997	 550		.01	.50
1998	 1,000		.01	.50
1999	 1,090		.01	.50
2000	 772		.01	.50
2001	 919		.01	.50

New Material, 2002 –

Diameter: 19.05 mm; weight: 2.35 grams; thickness: 1.45 mm;
material: .94 steel, .045 copper, .015 nickel; edge: plain

During 2002 the mint began splitting the production of one-cent coins between copper-plated zinc and copper-plated steel. The copper-plated steel coins bear the material mark "P" below the obverse effigy and are attracted by a magnet; the others are not. In 2006, a number of planchets of both types were inadvertently struck as wrong planchet types. The RCM's corporate mark (M) was phased in during 2006 and appears on both zinc and steel types.

Elizabeth II, Golden Jubilee (1952–2002)

To celebrate the 50th anniversary of the reign of Queen Elizabeth II, all circulation coins issued in 2002 bear the double date "1952-2002" on the obverse.

DATE		MILLIONS MINTED	BROWN UNC-60	RED BU-63
2002	(1952–2002)	716	.01	.25
2002P	(1952–2002)	114	.01	.50
2003	Diadem obverse	92	.01	.25
2003P	Diadem obverse	236	.01	.25

Elizabeth II, Bareheaded, 2003 –

Corporate mark (M)

The new uncrowned effigy of Queen Elizabeth, designed by Susanna Blunt, was introduced in 2003 in celebration of the jubilee year of her reign.

DATE		MILLIONS MINTED	BROWN UNC-60	RED BU-63
2003	Bareheaded	56.9	.01	.25
2003P	Bareheaded	591	.01	.25
2004		653	.01	.25
2004P	Steel	135	.01	.25
2005		759	.01	.25
2005P	Steel	30.5	.01	.25
2006	Zinc	866	.01	.25
2006	Steel	included above	25.00	100.00
2006P	Steel	233 Thousand	.01	10.00
2006P	Zinc	included above	100.00	300.00
2006L	Steel	138	2.00	6.00
2006L	Zinc	176	.01	.25
2007	Steel	938	.01	.25
2007	Zinc	10	.01	8.00
2008	Steel	820	.01	.25
2009	Steel	419	.01	.25
2009	Zinc	37	2.00	3.00
2010	Zinc	486	.01	.25
2011	Steel	361	.01	.25
2011	Zinc	301	.01	.25
2012	Steel	111	.01	.25
2012	Zinc	88	.01	.25

The last 1-cent coin was minted at the RCM's Winnipeg, Manitoba plant on May 4, 2012. The 1-cent was withdrawn from circulation on February 4, 2013.

5 CENTS SILVER
Victoria, 1858–1901

Diameter: 15.494 mm; weight: 1.167 grams;
composition: .925 silver, .075 copper; edge: reeded

G: *Braid around ear worn through*
VG: *No detail in braid around ear*
F: *Segments of braid begin to merge into one anoher*
VF: *Braid is clear but not sharp*
EF: *Braid is slightly worn but generally sharp and clear*

Five different portraits of Victoria were employed for this denomination, each differing from the others in some facial features and in certain other respects. Except for the initial portrait, all varieties were designed and engraved by L.C. Wyon. None of these was a serious attempt to accurately portray the Queen as she looked at the time.

In some years two obverses were used. These are most easily distinguished as follows:

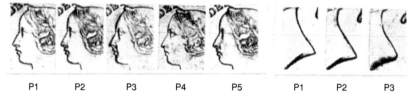

| P1 | P2 | P3 | P4 | P5 | P1 | P2 | P3 |

P1 vs P2: P1 has a convex lower rear neck profile and an incuse hairline above the eye, while P2 has a straight lower rear neck profile and lacks the incuse hairline.

P2 vs P3: P2 has a prominent forehead, a smooth chin and a slightly rounded point at the lower right corner of the neck, while P3 has a recessed forehead, a slight double chin and a very blunted lower right neck corner.

P2 vs P5: P2 has a prominent upper lip and a smooth chin, while P5 has a repressed upper lip, generally "droopy" mouth and an irregular chin.

The basic reverse device consists of crossed maple boughs, tied at the bottom by a ribbon, and separated at the top by St. Edward's crown. Three major reverse varieties exist. The first (1858, 1870) has an unusually wide rim, long denticles and a crown with both bottom corners protruding. The second (1870–81, 1890–1901), derived from the first, has somewhat altered leaves, a narrow rim, short rim denticles and a crown on which only the left lower corner protrudes. The third variety (1882-89) is like the second, with an additional (22nd) maple leaf added to the lower right of the wreath. Sub varieties of all three reverses are known; for example, the 22nd leaf on the 1882 issue differs from and was added independently of that on the 1883-89 issues. The major, and most of the minor varieties were designed and engraved by L.C. Wyon.

Wide rim,
long denticles

Small date

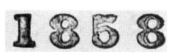

Re-engraved large date

DATE..	QTY. (000)	G-4	VG-8	F-12	VF-20	EF-40	AU-50	MS-60	MS-63
Wide Rim Reverse (1858, 1870)									
1858 small date P1 1,460		12.00	28.00	42.00	70.00	120.00	190.00	365.00	900.00
re-engraved lg. date... P1 . incl. above		110.00	200.00	300.00	500.00	900.00	1,500	2,500	5,500
1870.............. P1 2,800		12.00	25.00	40.00	65.00	125.00	200.00	400.00	1,150

Narrow rim,
short denticles

21 leaves
1870–81, 1890–1901

Narrow Rim, 21-Leaf Reverse (1870–1881)									
1870.............. P2 . incl. above		12.00	25.00	40.00	65.00	125.00	200.00	400.00	1,000
1871.............. P2 1,400		12.00	25.00	40.00	65.00	125.00	200.00	400.00	1,000
1872H P2 2,000		9.00	18.00	32.00	55.00	115.00	250.00	550.00	1,600

Plain 4,
small date   Crosslet 4,
large date

1874H plain 4 .... P2 .... 1.800		15.00	35.00	75.00	150.00	250.00	375.00	700.00	1,600
1874Hcrosslet 4 ..... P2 . incl. Above		12.00	30.00	65.00	125.00	250.00	400.00	800.00	1,800

Small
date   Large
date

1875H small date .... P2 . incl. above		110.00	235.00	365.00	650.00	1,000	1,750	3,500	10,000
1875H large date ..... P2 . incl. above		225.00	400.00	600.00	1,000	2,000	4,000	8,000	—
1880H P2,3 3,000		5.00	10.00	18.00	40.00	100.00	225.00	450.00	1,100
1881H P3 1,500		6.00	12.00	20.00	45.00	110.00	250.00	550.00	1,250

Note: 1874H and 1875H mintage figures were combined through a mint error.

22nd leaf added
1882–1889

Narrow Rim, 22-Leaf Reverse (1882–1889)									
1882H.............. P4 1,000		8.00	16.00	27.00	55.00	120.00	250.00	550.00	1,250
1883H.............. P5 600		15.00	35.00	65.00	135.00	300.00	650.00	1,500	4,000
1884.............. P5 200		100.00	185.00	300.00	550.00	1,250	2,500	5,500	15,000

Large tail 5   Small tail 5   Small 6   Large 6

1885 Large tail 5 ..... P5 1,000		12.00	25.00	45.00	90.00	200.00	500.00	1,200	4,500
1885 small tail 5 ..... P5 incl. above		10.00	20.00	40.00	80.00	200.00	550.00	1,200	4,000
1886 small 6 .... P5 1,700		8.00	18.00	30.00	60.00	110.00	275.00	600.00	2,000
1886 large 6 .... P5 incl. above		7.00	15.00	25.00	50.00	100.00	250.00	600.00	2,000
1887.............. P5 500		15.00	30.00	60.00	100.00	225.00	350.00	700.00	1,600
1888.............. P5 1,000		5.00	10.00	18.00	38.00	80.00	125.00	275.00	750.00
1889.............. P5 1,200		20.00	40.00	65.00	120.00	275.00	450.00	850.00	2,500

DATE..	QTY. (000)	G-4	VG-8	F-12	VF-20	EF-40	AU-50	MS-60	MS-63
21-Leaf Reverse Resumed (1890–1901)									
1890H	P5 1,000	6.00	12.00	20.00	40.00	100.00	175.00	350.00	750.00
1891	P5,2 1,800	5.00	9.00	13.00	25.00	50.00	115.00	250.00	700.00
1892	P5,2 860	5.00	11.00	20.00	40.00	100.00	200.00	500.00	1,250
1893	P2 1,700	5.00	9.00	13.00	25.00	50.00	115.00	275.00	700.00
1894	P2 500	12.00	25.00	50.00	100.00	200.00	350.00	700.00	2,000
1896	P2 1,500	5.00	9.00	13.00	25.00	55.00	125.00	300.00	700.00
1897	P2 1,319	5.00	9.00	13.00	25.00	50.00	125.00	275.00	650.00
1898	P2 581	10.00	20.00	30.00	65.00	150.00	275.00	550.00	1,500
1899	P2 3,000	4.00	8.00	11.00	20.00	40.00	90.00	200.00	550.00

1900 large date	P2 1,800	17.00	35.00	65.00	100.00	250.00	400.00	700.00	1,600
1900 small date	P2 . incl. above	4.00	8.00	11.00	20.00	40.00	100.00	225.00	600.00
1901	P2 2,000	4.00	8.00	11.00	20.00	40.00	90.00	200.00	550.00

Edward VII, 1902–1910

Diameter: 15.494 mm; weight: 1.167 grams; composition: .925 silver, .075 copper; edge: reeded

G: *Band of crown worn through*
VG: *Band of crown worn through at highest point*
F: *Jewels in band of crown will be blurred*
VF: *Band of crown is still clear but no longer sharp*
EF: *Band of crown slightly worn but generally sharp and clear*

A single obverse, designed and engraved by G.W. De Saulles (DES. below bust), was used for the entire reign.

With the initiation of a new series, two basic changes were to be made in the reverse designs. First, the word CANADA was to be transferred from the obverse to the reverse legend. Second, the heraldic St. Edward's crown (depressed arches), used on English coinages throughout most of the 19th century and on the Victorian Canadian issues, was to be replaced with the Imperial State crown (raised arches). These objectives were realized on all silver denominations except the five cents, where a shortage of time at the Royal Mint forced a compromise. The 1902 design (London and Heaton) utilized the unaltered crown and wreath from the second variety Victorian reverse, with the date and modified legend added. The presence of the outmoded St. Edward's crown caused the public to surmise that an error had been made and the 1902 coinage was consequently hoarded.

Beginning with the 1903 Heaton issue, the Imperial State crown was incorporated into the five cent reverse design. Again the wreath was derived from the second variety of the Victorian reverse, in this instance with slight retouching of some of the leaves. The designer and engraver for the 1902 and probably the 1903H reverses was G.W. De Saulles.

A third major reverse variety, introduced for the 1903 London issue, is from a new reducing machine model, and as such represents the first completely new reverse since 1858. The designer is presumably W.H.J. Blakemore. This design, with 22 leaves, was used every year from 1903 through the conclusion of the reign. However, in 1909–10 a major variety derived therefrom was also used. This modification is characterized by the presence of a "+" cross cut over the original "bow tie" cross atop the crown, and by sharp points along the leaf edges. The fourth variety is presumably by Blakemore, modifying his previous design.

		Large H		Small H				
DATE	MILLIONS MINTED	G-4	VG-8	F-12	VF-20	EF-40	AU-50	MS-60	MS-63

St. Edward's Crown Reverse (1902)

DATE	MILLIONS MINTED	G-4	VG-8	F-12	VF-20	EF-40	AU-50	MS-60	MS-63
1902	2	1.50	3.00	4.00	6.00	12.00	22.00	50.00	75.00
1902H large H	2	1.75	3.00	4.50	8.00	16.00	30.00	60.00	90.00
small H	incl. above	7.50	12.00	20.00	35.00	65.00	100.00	160.00	275.00

Imperial crown
21 leaves
1903H only

Imperial Crown, 21-Leaf Reverse (1903 Heaton)

DATE	MILLIONS MINTED	G-4	VG-8	F-12	VF-20	EF-40	AU-50	MS-60	MS-63
1903H	3	2.00	3.00	5.00	12.00	25.00	75.00	150.00	450.00

Imperial crown	Leaves with	Leaves with
22 leaves	rounded edges	pointed edges
1903–1910	1903–1910	1909–1910

Rounded Leaves Reverse (1903–1910)

DATE	MILLIONS MINTED	G-4	VG-8	F-12	VF-20	EF-40	AU-50	MS-60	MS-63
1903	1	3.00	7.00	12.00	25.00	60.00	135.00	275.00	600.00
1904	2	3.50	4.00	6.00	13.00	35.00	100.00	275.00	800.00
1905	3	2.00	3.00	5.00	11.00	25.00	60.00	150.00	350.00
1906	3	2.00	3.00	4.00	8.00	18.00	50.00	135.00	400.00
1907	5	2.00	3.00	4.00	7.00	14.00	35.00	90.00	200.00

Note shape of inner circles   Cross at top of crown

   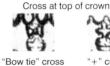

Large 8	Small 8	"Bow tie" cross	"+" cross

1908 varieties: The normal reverse (bow tie cross atop crown) for 1908 has a large 8; a second variety has a "+" cross cut over the bow tie, as on the 1909–1910 reverse, with sharp leaf points and a small date.

DATE	MILLIONS MINTED	G-4	VG-8	F-12	VF-20	EF-40	AU-50	MS-60	MS-63
1908 large 8	1	25.00	50.00	85.00	150.00	275.00	400.00	750.00	1,500
1908 small 8	incl. above	4.00	8.00	15.00	35.00	65.00	100.00	150.00	250.00

Pointed Leaves Reverse (1909–1910)

DATE	MILLIONS MINTED	G-4	VG-8	F-12	VF-20	EF-40	AU-50	MS-60	MS-63
1909 round leaves	2	4.00	5.00	9.00	18.00	45.00	110.00	300.00	850.00
1909 pointed leaves	incl. above	11.00	20.00	30.00	65.00	150.00	300.00	800.00	2,000
1910 round leaves	6	10.00	20.00	30.00	55.00	135.00	275.00	650.00	2,000
1910 pointed leaves	incl. Above	2.00	3.00	4.00	7.00	14.00	30.00	75.00	150.00

George V, 1911–1921

Diameter: 15.494 mm; weight: 1.167 grams;
composition: (1911–19) .925 silver, .075 copper, (1920–21) .800 silver, .200 copper; edge: reeded

G:	Band of crown worn through
VG:	Band of crown worn through at highest point
F:	Jewels in band of crown will be blurred
VF:	Band of crown is still clear but no longer sharp

Two obverse varieties exist; the first (1911) lacks the phrase DEI GRATIA or an abbreviation thereof, while the second (1912–21) has DEI GRA : incorporated into the legend. Both obverses were derived from a portrait model by Sir E.B. MacKennal (B.M. on truncation). See text on the 1-cent issue for more details.

The reverse is identical to Blakemore's rounded leaves design introduced in the Edward VII series. On May 3, 1921, the government passed an act authorizing the substitution of a larger nickel 5-cent piece to replace the small silver coin. Consequently, almost the entire coinage of the silver 5-cent pieces dated 1921 was melted. About 400 specimens of this date are known, most or all of which were (a) regular strikes sold by the mint in 1921 to visitors, or (b) specimen strikes sold or given to individuals as part of 1921 specimen sets.

DATE	MILLIONS MINTED	G-4	VG-8	F-12	VF-20	EF-40	AU-50	MS-60	MS-63
"Godless" Obverse (1911)									
1911	4	1.50	3.00	5.00	8.00	15.00	45.00	90.00	150.00
Modified Obverse Legend (1912–1921)									
1912	6	2.00	3.00	4.00	7.00	12.00	35.00	80.00	225.00
1913	6	2.00	3.00	4.00	6.00	10.00	20.00	40.00	85.00
1914	4	2.00	3.00	4.00	7.00	12.00	35.00	80.00	225.00
1915	1	8.00	18.00	25.00	40.00	80.00	200.00	400.00	850.00
1916	2	3.00	5.00	8.00	15.00	30.00	75.00	150.00	350.00
1917	6	1.50	2.50	3.50	5.00	10.00	25.00	50.00	125.00
1918	6	1.50	2.50	3.50	5.00	9.00	20.00	45.00	100.00
1919	(Orig.: 7,835,400)	1.50	2.50	3.50	5.00	9.00	20.00	45.00	100.00
1920	(Orig.: 10,649,851)	1.50	2.50	3.50	5.00	9.00	20.00	40.00	85.00
1921	(Orig.: 2,582,495)	3,500	5,000	6,500	8,500	11,500	15,000	20,000	35,000

5 CENTS, NICKEL
George V, 1922–1936

Diameter: 21.21 mm; weight: 4.54 grams; thickness: 1.70 mm; composition: .99 nickel; edge: plain

G: *Band of crown worn through*
VG: *Band of crown worn through at highest point*
F: *Jewels in band of crown will be blurred*
VF: *Band of crown is still clear but no longer sharp*
EF: *Band of crown slightly worn*
but generally sharp and clear

To provide a 5-cent piece of more manageable size, and "because nickel is essentially a Canadian metal" the Canadian government introduced a coin of pure nickel in 1922, similar in size to the 5-cent coins of the United States.

The obverse was derived from the MacKennal portrait model (initials B.M. on truncation); the reverse was engraved by W.H.J. Blakemore. Mint records do not clearly specify the designer; it was either W.H.J. Blakemore or Fred Lewis.

DATE	QTY. (000)	G-4	VG-8	F-12	VF-20	EF-40	AU-50	MS-60	MS-63
1922	4,763	.30	.35	1.00	2.50	12.00	35.00	70.00	150.00
1923	2,475	.40	.50	2.00	7.00	25.00	70.00	175.00	400.00
1924	3,067	.30	.50	1.50	5.00	18.00	45.00	125.00	325.00
1925	200	45.00	80.00	100.00	160.00	350.00	800.00	2,000	6,000

6 near leaf   6 far from leaf

1926 date varieties. Most of the 1926 issue was derived from a matrix in which the tip of the 6 is very close to the right-hand maple leaf. A second matrix (or perhaps individual die) had the 6 punched in a lower position, so that it appeared farther from the leaf. Such digit spacing and position differences are considered trivial by these cataloguers, and these 1926 varieties are included only because their listing in previous catalogues has led to their widespread acceptance by collectors.

DATE	QTY. (000)	G-4	VG-8	F-12	VF-20	EF-40	AU-50	MS-60	MS-63
1926 near 6	934	3.00	4.50	9.00	25.00	90.00	250.00	600.00	2,000
1926 far 6	incl. above	105.00	165.00	200.00	375.00	800.00	1,300	2,500	7,000
1927	5,286	.30	.50	1.00	4.00	15.00	40.00	90.00	210.00
1928	4,589	.30	.50	1.00	4.00	15.00	40.00	80.00	150.00
1929	5,562	.30	.50	1.00	4.00	15.00	40.00	100.00	250.00
1930	3,686	.30	.50	1.50	5.00	20.00	55.00	120.00	350.00
1931	5,101	.30	.50	1.50	6.00	25.00	80.00	225.00	900.00
1932	3,199	.30	.50	1.50	6.00	22.00	60.00	175.00	600.00
1933	2,598	.40	.50	2.50	8.00	30.00	90.00	300.00	1,000
1934	3,827	.30	.50	1.50	5.00	22.00	65.00	185.00	850.00
1935	3,900	.30	.50	1.50	5.00	20.00	60.00	150.00	550.00
1936	4,400	.30	.50	1.00	3.00	12.00	35.00	75.00	175.00

George VI, Beaver, 1937–1942

Diameter: 21.21 mm, weight: 4.54 grams; thickness: 1.70 mm; composition: .99 nickel, edge: plain

VG: *No detail in hair above the ear*
F: *Only slight detail in hair above the ear*
VF: *Where not worn, hair is clear but not sharp*
EF: *Slight wear in hair over the ear*

Both obverses (for the round and 12-sided issues) display a bare-headed portrait of the King designed by T.H. Paget (H.P. below bust).

In keeping with the decision to modernize the new George VI reverses, the now-familiar beaver motif was chosen for the 5-cent piece (after first being considered for the 10-cent piece). The 1937 issue has a period after the date to balance the design, but after 1937 the period was omitted. The design was by G.E. Kruger-Gray (K•G to the left of the log).

Period after date, 1937 only   No period after date, 1938–1942

DATE . .	MILLIONS MINTED	VG-8	F-12	VF-20	EF-40	AU-50	MS-60	MS-63
Nickel Issues (1937–1942)								
1937 (period after date) 5		.25	.35	1.50	3.00	6.00	15.00	30.00
1938 4		.35	1.00	4.00	15.00	45.00	100.00	200.00
1939 6		.25	.50	2.00	8.00	25.00	65.00	110.00
1940 14		.25	.35	1.50	4.00	10.00	25.00	65.00
1941 9		.25	.35	1.50	5.00	15.00	35.00	85.00
1942 7		.25	.35	1.50	4.00	10.00	25.00	60.00

12-Sided Coinage, 1942–1962
George VI, Tombac, 1942–1943

Diameter: 21.23-21.29 mm (opposite corners), 20.88-20.93 mm (opposite sides); weight: 4.54 grams; thickness: 1.70 mm; composition: .880 copper, .120 zinc; edge: plain

Because nickel was needed for Second World War, its use for coinage was suspended late in 1942. The substitute first used was a brass alloy commonly called tombac. This alloy quickly tarnished to the brownish hue acquired by bronze, so the new coins were made 12-sided to avoid their confusion with the cents. Due to lack of time, the new matrices (obverse and reverse) were made without the conventional rim denticles.

1942 (12 sided) 3		.65	1.00	1.50	2.00	3.00	5.00	20.00

Victory, 1943–1945

Composition (1944-45): steel, coated with .0127 mm layer of nickel and
.0003 mm plating of chromium.
Other specifications as for 1942 tombac issue

This design was introduced with the aim of furthering the war efforts. The obverse used was as the 1942 tombac issue, except that rim denticles were added.

The torch and "V" on the reverse symbolize sacrifice and victory (the V also indicates the denomination, the idea coming from the U.S. Liberty 5-cent pieces of 1883–1912). Instead of rim denticles, a Morse code (dot-dash) pattern reading WE WIN WHEN WE WORK WILLINGLY was used. The designer was the chief engraver of the Royal Canadian Mint, Thomas Shingles (T.S. at right of torch), who cut the master matrix entirely by hand – a feat few present-day engravers can accomplish.

The 1943 issue was struck in tombac. This alloy was replaced with chromium-plated steel in 1944-45 because copper and zinc were needed for the war effort.

DATE	MILLIONS MINTED	VG-8	F-12	VF-20	EF-40	AU-50	MS-60	MS-63
Tombac Issue (1943)								
1943 25		.35	.35	.50	1.00	2.00	4.00	15.00
Chromium-Plated Steel Issue (1944–1945)								
1944 12		.20	.25	.50	1.00	1.50	3.00	7.00
1945 19		.20	.25	.50	1.00	1.50	3.00	7.00

Beaver Resumed, 1946–1950

Diameter: 21.234 mm (opposite corners), 20.878 mm (opposite sides); weight: 4.54 grams;
thickness: 1.70 mm; composition: .999 nickel; edge: plain

After the conclusion of World War II the 5-cent piece was again struck in nickel, but the 12-sided shape had become popular and was retained. The initial obverse was identical to the 1943-45 issues. A second variety, introduced in 1948, incorporates the modified titles of the King (see 1-cent text). This second obverse was used for the 1948-50, 1951 commemorative, and a portion of the 1951 beaver issues. A third variety was coupled with most of the 1951 beaver and all of the 1952 issues. This variety is distinguishable by the lower relief of the portrait and the different positioning of the legend relative to the rim denticles.

Two major reverse varieties are known. The first (1946-50) differs from the 1942 tombac issue only in having rim denticles. The second variety (1951-52), introduced simultaneously with the change to steel composition, has a slightly larger beaver and is perhaps slightly lower in relief.

1947 "dot"
(deteriorated die)

1947 maple leaf
(official issue)

1947 "dot" This item is apparently the product of a deteriorated die and hence is not a true die variety. Some have suggested that this was an official issue because of the fact that the 25-cent and dollar (pointed 7) issues dated 1947 are also known with a "dot" after the date. The alternative explanation, currently favoured by most students of decimal coins, is that the "dots" resulted from small pieces chipping out of the chromium plating and leaving pits in individual dies. These pits would appear as raised "dots" on struck coins. It is conceded, however, that if the latter were true it would be a remarkable coincidence. In any case, the 1947 "dot" coins are probably not official because (a) the dots are irregular and of poor quality, and (b) the engravers who would have prepared such dies are quite certain that they did not do so.

1947 maple leaf variety This was an official issue struck in 1948, which is explained in the text for the 1-cent issue.

DATE	MILLIONS MINTED	VG-8	F-12	VF-20	EF-40	AU-50	MS-60	MS-63
Small Beaver Reverse (1946–1950)								
1946 7		.25	.30	.75	3.00	9.00	20.00	50.00
1947 normal date. 8		.25	.30	.75	2.00	6.00	14.00	30.00
1947 "dot" .... incl. above		22.00	30.00	45.00	95.00	200.00	275.00	465.00
1947 maple leaf 10		.25	.30	.50	2.00	6.00	14.00	30.00

Modified legend,
high relief portrait
1948–1952

High relief portrait
Last 'A' of 'GRATIA'
points to denticle

Modified Legend (1948–1952)								
1948 2		.75	1.00	1.50	5.00	12.00	25.00	45.00
1949 14		.20	.30	.50	1.50	4.00	8.00	20.00
1950 12		.20	.30	.50	1.50	4.00	8.00	20.00

Isolation of Nickel Bicentennial, 1951

As Canada is the world's largest single producer of nickel, it seemed appropriate to issue a commemorative piece on the 200th anniversary of the isolation and naming of the element by the Swedish chemist A.F. Cronstedt. The obverse was as on the 1948-50 issues; the reverse, showing a nickel refinery, was designed by Stephen Trenka (ST monogram at lower right).

1951 commemorative 8		.20	.30	.35	.50	1.00	2.50	10.00

Beaver Resumed, Steel Coinage, 1951–1952

Because nickel was needed for the Korean War, the use of nickel was suspended near the end of 1951. The beaver reverse was resumed for the balance of 1951 5-cent pieces with the composition changed to steel. New lower relief dies had to be prepared for both the obverse and reverse since the harder steel surface did not strike well with the higher relief dies the mint had been using. By error, a small quantity of 1951 pieces were struck with a high relief obverse die, creating two varieties for 1951. As mentioned above, the two dies are distinguishable by the difference in relief of the portraits and the different positioning of the legend relative to the rim denticles.

Low relief,
last 'A' of 'GRATIA'
points between denticles

Low relief portrait
1951–1952

Large beaver
reverse

DATE	MILLIONS MINTED	VG-8	F-12	VF-20	EF-40	AU-50	MS-60	MS-63
Large Beaver Reverse (1951–1952)								
1951 high relief obverse 4		450.00	650.00	900.00	1,500	2,250	3,000	4,000
1951 low relief obverse .... incl. above		.20	.25	.50	1.00	2.00	4.00	12.00
1952 (low relief obverse) 11		.20	.25	.50	1.00	2.00	4.00	10.00

Elizabeth II, Laureate, 1953–1964

Physical specifications for 1953–1954 remain the same as the previous issue;
composition (1953–54) steel coated with a .0127 mm layer of nickel and chromium plated, (1955-64): .999 nickel

The initial obverse for the 1953 issue, a laureate portrait of the Queen by Mary Gillick (M.G. on truncation) was engraved in high relief and did not strike up well on the coins. Later in the year the relief was lowered and the hair and shoulder detail re-engraved. The re-engraving included sharpening two lines which represent a fold in, not a shoulder strap on, the Queen's gown. The two varieties also differ in the positioning of the legend relative to the rim denticles and the styles of some of the letters. (See 1-cent text for more details.) The second portrait was not modified when the shape of the 5-cent piece was changed back to round in 1963.

No
shoulder
fold
1953

Note style of
letters, relation
to denticles

DATE	MILLIONS MINTED	F-12	VF-20	EF-40	AU-50	MS-60	MS-63
"No Shoulder Fold" Obverse (1953)							
1953 no shoulder fold 17		.25	.50	1.00	2.00	4.00	8.00
"Shoulder Fold" Obverse (1953–1964)							
1953 shoulder fold .... incl. above		.25	.50	1.00	2.50	6.00	10.00
1954 7		.35	.75	1.50	3.00	7.00	15.00

With
shoulder
fold
1953–1962

Note style of
letters, relation
to denticles

Four noteworthy reverse varieties appeared during the 1953–64 period. The first is associated with the 1953 "no shoulder fold" obverse and is identical to the 1951–52 George VI beaver design. The second reverse variety has the design elements placed closer to the rim denticles than before, and was used for the 1953 "shoulder fold" and 1954 issues. The third variety was introduced with the resumption of nickel composition in 1955 when the smaller beaver, last used in 1950, was restored. The fourth variety occurred when the beaver was readapted with the change in shape to round in 1963 because of continuing difficulties with the 12-sided collars.

Small beaver
1955–1962

Design far
from rim, 1953

Design near rim,
1953–1954

DATE	MILLIONS MINTED	F-12	VF-20	EF-40	AU-50	MS-60	MS-63
Small Beaver Reverse, 12-sided (1955–1962)							
1955	5	.20	.50	1.00	2.00	4.00	8.00
1956	9	.20	.50	.75	1.50	3.00	6.00
1957	7	.20	.35	.50	.75	1.50	4.00
1958	8	.20	.35	.50	.75	1.50	4.00
1959	12	.05	.20	.25	.30	.50	2.00
1960	37	.05	.20	.25	.30	.50	2.00
1961	48	.05	.20	.25	.30	.50	1.50
1962	46	.05	.05	.05	.25	.50	1.50

Round Coinage Resumed 1963 –

Extra
waterline
1964

DATE	MILLIONS MINTED	EF-40	AU-50	MS-60	MS-63
1963	44	.05	.20	.35	1.00
1964	78	.05	2.0	.35	1.00
1964 (extra waterline)	incl. above	30.00	35.00	50.00	150.00

Elizabeth II, Tiara, 1965–1978

Diameter: 21.21 mm; weight: 4.54 grams; thickness: 1.70 mm;
composition: (1965–1981) .999 nickel; edge: plain

In 1965 an obverse with a new style portrait by Arnold Machin was introduced. The Queen has more mature facial features and is wearing a tiara.

DATE	MILLIONS MINTED	MS-60	MS-63
1965	85	.35	1.00
1966	28	.35	1.00

Confederation Centennial, 1967

All denominations for 1967 bore special reverses to commemorate the 1967 confederation of the province of Canada, Nova Scotia and New Brunswick to the Dominion of Canada. The 5 cents reverse device depicts a hopping rabbit. Designer: Alex Colville. The obverse and physical specifications are as for the 1956-1966 issues.

DATE	MILLIONS MINTED	MS-60	MS-63
1967 Confederation commemorative	37	.35	1.00

Beaver Resumed, 1968–1978

The obverse, the reverse and technical data are the same as the emissions from 1965

DATE	MILLIONS MINTED	MS-63	DATE	MILLIONS MINTED	MS-63
1968	99	1.00	1974	95	1.00
1969	28	1.00	1975	139	1.00
1970	6	2.00	1976	55	1.00
1971	27	1.00	1977	89	5.00
1972	62	1.00	1978	137	1.00
1973	54	1.00			

Modified Obverse, 1979–1989

Beginning with the 1979 issue, the portrait of the Queen was made smaller. This was done to standardize our coinage, making the size of the portrait proportional to the diameter of the coin, regardless of denomination.

DATE	MILLIONS MINTED	MS-63
1979	187	1.00
1980	135	1.00
1981	99	1.00

Cupro-nickel alloy, 1982–1999

Diameter: 21.20 mm; weight: 4.6 grams; thickness: 1.76 mm;
composition: .75 copper, .25 nickel; edge: plain

In 1982, the five-cent piece was first coined in cupro-nickel, an alloy of 75% copper and 25% nickel. This is the same alloy used in United States coinage.

DATE	MILLIONS MINTED	MS-63	DATE	MILLIONS MINTED	MS-63
1982	65	1.00	1986	156	1.00
1983	73	1.00	1987	106	1.00
1984	84	1.00	1988	75	1.00
1985	127	1.00	1989	142	1.25

Elizabeth II, Crowned, 1990–2003

The first effigy designed by a Canadian for use on Canadian coins was introduced on the obverse of all Canadian issues for 1990. The design depicts a more contemporary portrait of the Queen wearing a necklace and earrings. The elaborate crown, last seen on Victorian issues, replaced the tiara used on previous issues. The obverse was designed by Dora dePédery-Hunt.

DATE	MILLIONS MINTED	MS-63
1990	43	1.00
1991	11	1.50

125th Anniversary of Confederation, 1992

To celebrate the 125th anniversary of Confederation, all circulation coins issued in 1992 bear the double date "1867–1992".

DATE		MILLIONS MINTED	MS-63
1992	(1867–1992)	54	1.00
1993		87	1.00
1994		99	1.00
1995		79	1.00
1996		37	1.00
1997		27	1.00
1998		157	1.00
1999		125	1.00

Nickel-plated Steel, 1999–

Diameter: 21.20 mm; weight: 3.95 grams;
composition: nickel plated steel; edge: plain

In 1999, test coins composed of nickel plated steel were struck to test vending machines. In December 2000, the Royal Canadian Mint issued approximately 5 million 5¢ coins for circulation. All of the new plated coins bear a "P" material mark on the obverse, below the effigy of the queen. Finished blanks for the new nickel-plated coins are produced at the new plating facility in Winnipeg. Both Winnipeg and Ottawa mints are capable of striking coins from these blanks.

DATE		MILLIONS MINTED	MS-63
1999P	test coin	N/A	
2000		106	10.00
2000P		5	1.00
2001		30	1.50
2001P		137	.75
2003P		33	1.00

Elizabeth II, Golden Jubilee (1952–2002)

Elizabeth II, Golden Jubilee (1952–2002)

To celebrate the 50th anniversary of the reign of Queen Elizabeth II, all circulation coins issued in 2002 bear the double date "1952-2002" on the obverse.

DATE		MILLIONS MINTED	MS-63
2002P	(1952–2002)	134	.75

Elizabeth II, Bareheaded, 2003–

Corporate mark (M)

The new bareheaded effigy of Queen Elizabeth, designed by Susanna Blunt, was introduced in 2003 in celebration of the jubilee year of her reign. The corporate mark of the RCM (M) was phased in during 2006 replacing the "P" mark.

DATE		MILLIONS MINTED	MS-63
2003P		61	1.00
2004P		132	.75
2005P		89.6	.75
2006P		94	.75
2006L		45	.75
2006	Nickel.	43	.75
2007		221	.75
2008		279	.75
2009		266	.75
2010		127	.75
2011		230	.75
2012		203	.75
2013		78	.75
2014		66	.75
2015		N/A	.75

Victory Anniversary, 2005

The Victory reverse, designed by Thomas Shingle, was displayed on the Canadian five-cent coins of 1943–1945. The dated areas on the original reverse have been replaced by the double dates "1945 2005".

DATE		MILLIONS MINTED	MS-63
2005P	(1945 2005)	59	.75

10 CENTS SILVER
Victoria, 1858–1901

Diameter: 18.034 mm; weight: 2.32 grams;
composition: .925 silver, .075 copper; edge: reeded

G: *Braid near ear worn through*
VG: *No details in braid around ear*
F: *Segments of braid begin to merge into one another*
VF: *Braid is clear but not sharp*
EF: *Braid is slightly worn but generally sharp and clear*

In all, six different portrait varieties of Victoria were used for this denomination. Each differs from the others in some of the facial features and in certain other respects. Except for the initial portrait, all subsequent varieties were created by re-engraving a previous design; these modifications were probably the work of the original designer, L.C. Wyon. None of them represent a serious attempt to accurately portray Victoria as she looked at the time.

In some years two busts were coupled with a given date reverse. Such varieties are most easily distinguished as follows:

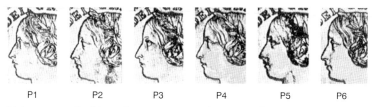

P1   P2   P3   P4   P5   P6

P1 vs P2: P1 has a smooth chin and a narrow truncation, extending almost the entire length of the lower neck, while P2 has a slightly "double" chin and a wide truncation, restricted to the rear half of the lower neck.

P4 vs P5: P4 has a rounded forehead, smooth chin and much hairline detail above the eye, while P5 has a flat forehead, slightly double chin and very little hair detail above the eye.

P5 vs P6: P5 is as described above, P6 has the general characteristics of P4.

The basic reverse device consists of crossed maple boughs tied at the bottom by a ribbon. At the top is St. Edward's crown. Two major device varieties exist; the first has a wreath with 21 leaves and the second, derived from the first, has a 22nd leaf added to the lower right. Numerous subvarieties of both reverses are known; for example, the 22nd leaf on the 1882 issue differs from, and was added independently to that on the 1883–1901 issues. Both of the major and most of the minor varieties were designed and engraved by L.C. Wyon.

1871H Newfoundland / Canada mule. See Newfoundland 10 Cents Silver.

DATE	QTY. (000)	G-4	VG-8	F-12	VF-20	EF-40	AU-50	MS-60	MS-63
21-Leaf Reverse (1858–1881, 1891)									
1858 .... P1 1,216		15.00	30.00	550.00	100.00	175.00	275.00	475.00	1,350
1870 .... P1 1,600		15.00	30.00	60.00	120.00	200.00	300.00	550.00	1,800
1871 .. .. P1 800		20.00	45.00	80.00	175.00	325.00	550.00	1,000	3,500
1871H P1 1,870		25.00	55.00	100.00	200.00	350.00	600.00	1,000	3,500
1872H P1 1,000		110.00	220.00	350.00	600.00	900.00	1,650	2,800	5,800
1874H P1 1,600		11.00	22.00	40.00	80.00	180.00	300.00	550.00	1,750
1875H ..... P1 .... incl. above		275.00	500.00	850.00	1,500	3,000	4,500	9,000	20,000
1880H P1,2 1,500		15.00	30.00	50.00	100.00	200.00	325.00	575.00	1,700
1881H P1,2 950		17.00	35.00	55.00	110.00	225.00	375.00	650.00	2,000

21 leaves
1858–1881, 1891

22 leaves
1882–1901

DATE	QTY. (000)	G-4	VG-8	F-12	VF-20	EF-40	AU-50	MS-60	MS-63
22-Leaf Reverse (1882–1901)									
1882H P3 1,000		17.00	35.00	55.00	110.00	225.00	375.00	700.00	2,400
1883H P3 300		50.00	100.00	200.00	400.00	750.00	1,200	2,000	4,500
1884 .... P4 150		200.00	425.00	750.00	1,400	2,750	5,000	10,000	25,000
1885 .... P4,5 400		50.00	100.00	200.00	400.00	800.00	1,750	3,650	10,000

Small 6   Large over small 6   Large knobbed 6

DATE	QTY. (000)	G-4	VG-8	F-12	VF-20	EF-40	AU-50	MS-60	MS-63
1886 small 6 ... P4,5 800		25.00	50.00	100.00	200.00	450.00	1,000	2,250	5,500
large over small 6 P5 incl. above......		50.00	100.00	200.00	400.00	850.00	1,800	3,500	7,500
large pointed 6 .. P5 ...... incl. above		85.00	175.00	325.00	600.00	1,200	2,000	4,000	—
large knobbed 6 P5 .... incl. above		32.00	65.00	130.00	250.00	550.00	1,200	2,400	6,500
1887 .... P5 350		45.00	100.00	175.00	350.00	750.00	1,300	2,750	6,000
1888 .... P5 500		12.00	25.00	45.00	85.00	180.00	300.00	550.00	1,500
1889 .... P5 600		700.00	1,250	2,000	3,300	6,500	11,000	20,000	50,000
1890H P5 450		18.00	35.00	70.00	150.00	300.00	450.00	800.00	1,750

Small date   Large date

DATE	QTY. (000)	G-4	VG-8	F-12	VF-20	EF-40	AU-50	MS-60	MS-63
1891 21 lvs., sm. date P5..... 800,000		18.00	35.00	70.00	150.00	300.00	450.00	800.00	2,000
22 lvs., lg. date . P5........ incl. above		18.00	35.00	70.00	150.00	300.00	450.00	800.00	2,000

2 over 1, large 9   Normal date, small 9

DATE	QTY. (000)	G-4	VG-8	F-12	VF-20	EF-40	AU-50	MS-60	MS-63
1892 2 over 1, lg. 9 P5 520		200.00	400.00	650.00	1,100	2,250	4,000	—	—
norm. date, sm. 9 P5,6 ..... incl. above		15.00	30.00	55.00	110.00	225.00	375.00	700.00	2,000

Flat top 3   Round top 3

DATE	QTY. (000)	G-4	VG-8	F-12	VF-20	EF-40	AU-50	MS-60	MS-63
1893 flat top 3 .. P5,6 500		30.00	65.00	110.00	225.00	450.00	800.00	1,600	3,750
1893 round top 3 P5,6 incl. above		900.00	1,500	2,200	4,000	7,500	12,000	20,000	50,000
1894 .... P5,6 500		25.00	55.00	95.00	175.00	325.00	500.00	900.00	2,250
1896 .... P5,6 650		11.00	22.00	40.00	75.00	150.00	275.00	500.00	1,250
1898 .... P6 720		11.00	22.00	40.00	75.00	150.00	275.00	500.00	1,250

Small 9s   Large 9s

DATE	QTY. (000)	G-4	VG-8	F-12	VF-20	EF-40	AU-50	MS-60	MS-63
1899 small 9s ... P6 1,200		9.00	18.00	35.00	65.00	125.00	200.00	375.00	1,000
1899 large 9s ... P6 incl. above......		20.00	40.00	75.00	140.00	250.00	425.00	800.00	2,000
1900 .... P6 1,100		8.00	15.00	30.00	55.00	110.00	175.00	300.00	900.00
1901 .... P6 1,200		8.00	15.00	30.00	55.00	110.00	175.00	300.00	1,000

Edward VII, 1902–1910

Diameter: 18.034 mm; weight: 2.32 grams; composition: .925 silver, .075 copper; edge: reeded

G: *Band of crown worn through*
VG: *Band of crown worn through at highest point*
F: *Jewels in band of crown will be blurred*
VF: *Band of crown is still clear but no longer sharp*
EF: *Band of crown slightly worn but generally sharp and clear*

A single obverse was employed, designed and engraved by G.W. De Saulles (DES. below bust). The initial reverse was partially by De Saulles; the wreath was taken unaltered from Wyon's 22-leaf Victorian variety and a new legend and the Imperial State crown added. The leaves of the wreath have moderate venation, with all of the veins raised. A second variety, from a new reducing machine model, has broader leaves with extensive, incuse venation. It was designed and engraved by W.H.J. Blakemore (copying the previous design).

Victorian leaves, 1902–1909   Broad leaves, 1909–1910

DATE	QTY. (000)	G-4	VG-8	F-12	VF-20	EF-40	AU-50	MS-60	MS-63
Victorian Leaves Reverse (1902–1909)									
1902	720	5.00	10.00	20.00	50.00	125.00	225.00	525.00	1,500
1902H	1,100	3.00	7.00	13.00	25.00	60.00	100.00	175.00	400.00
1903	500	10.00	20.00	45.00	110.00	325.00	700.00	1,500	3,500
1903H	1,320	5.00	10.00	20.00	50.00	110.00	180.00	400.00	1,000
1904	1,000	8.00	15.00	32.00	75.00	160.00	250.00	555.00	1,200
1905	1,000	6.50	12.00	32.00	85.00	185.00	350.00	750.00	1,750
1906	1,700	4.00	9.00	18.00	45.00	100.00	180.00	400.00	1,100
1907	2,620	4.00	8.00	16.00	40.00	75.00	150.00	350.00	750.00
1908	777	8.00	15.00	32.00	80.00	165.00	225.00	375.00	750.00
1909 Victorian leaves	1,697	5.00	10.00	25.00	60.00	150.00	275.00	600.00	1,500
Broad Leaves Reverse (1909–1910)									
1909 broad leaves	incl. above	7.00	15.00	35.00	80.00	180.00	400.00	900.00	2,200
1910	4,468	3.00	6.00	12.00	25.00	55.00	90.00	180.00	450.00

George V, 1911–1936

Diameter: 18.034 mm; weight: 2.33 grams; composition: (1911–19) .925 silver, .075 copper, (1920-36) .800 silver, .200 copper; edge: reeded

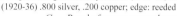

G: *Band of crown worn through*
VG: *Band of crown worn through at highest point*
F: *Jewels in band of crown will be blurred*
VF: *Band of crown is still clear but no longer sharp*
EF: *Band of crown slightly worn but generally sharp and clear*

Two obverse varieties exist; the first (1911) lacks the phrase DEI GRATIA or an abbreviation for it and the second (1912-36) has DEI GRA: incorporated into the legend. Both obverses were derived from a portrait model by Sir. E.B. MacKennal (B.M. on truncation). See the 1-cent text for more details.

    The series began with the broad leaves design introduced late in the Edward VII series. However, this was replaced in 1913 with another Blakemore design (from a new model) in which the maple leaves are distinctly smaller and have less venation.

Obverse
1912–1936

Broad leaves
1911–1913

DATE	QTY. (000)	G-4	VG-8	F-12	VF-20	EF-40	AU-50	MS-60	MS-63
Broad Leaves Reverse (1911–1913)									
1911 (no DEI GRA:)	2,738	4.00	8.00	15.00	30.00	65.00	90.00	165.00	350.00
1912	2,236	1.75	4.00	6.00	12.00	40.00	100.00	275.00	700.00
1913 broad leaves	3,614	75.00	150.00	250.00	550.00	1,400	3,500	9,000	32,000

Small leaves
1913–1936

Small Leaves Reverse (1913–1936)									
1913 (small leaves) ...... incl. above		2.00	4.00	5.50	10.00	35.00	90.00	225.00	550.00
1914	2,550	2.00	5.00	6.00	10.00	35.00	85.00	200.00	600.00
1915	688	5.00	8.00	20.00	50.00	150.00	275.00	550.00	1,100
1916	4,218	2.00	3.00	4.00	7.00	22.00	55.00	110.00	235.00
1917	5,012	2.00	3.00	4.00	5.00	15.00	45.00	80.00	150.00
1918	5,134	2.00	3.00	4.00	7.00	12.00	40.00	70.00	120.00
1919	7,878	2.00	3.00	4.00	5.00	12.00	40.00	70.00	120.00
1920	6,306	2.00	3.00	4.00	5.50	15.00	50.00	85.00	150.00
1921	2,470	2.00	3.00	4.00	7.00	25.00	60.00	110.00	250.00
1928	2,459	2.00	3.00	4.00	6.00	20.00	45.00	95.00	200.00
1929	3,254	2.00	3.00	4.00	6.00	20.00	45.00	90.00	145.00
1930	1,831	2.00	3.00	4.00	7.00	25.00	55.00	100.00	200.00
1931	2,067	2.00	3.00	4.00	6.00	20.00	45.00	85.00	150.00
1932	1,154	2.00	3.00	5.00	15.00	40.00	70.00	140.00	275.00
1933	672	3.00	4.00	6.00	20.00	60.00	100.00	250.00	500.00
1934	409	4.00	5.00	10.00	30.00	90.00	175.00	400.00	800.00
1935	384	4.00	5.00	10.00	30.00	90.00	175.00	400.00	750.00
1936	2,461	2.00	3.50	4.00	5.00	12.00	40.00	70.00	120.00

George VI Issue Struck in the Name of George V

A portion of the 1-, 10- and 25-cent pieces dated 1936 have a small raised dot on the reverse, denoting that they were actually struck in 1937 for George VI. On the 10-cent coins, the dot is below the bow in the wreath. There is some question whether all of the dot 1- and 10-cent pieces reported to have been struck exist today (see the 1-cent text).

DATE		QTY. MINTED
1936 raised dot below wreath .... (orig.: 191,237)		5 known
... (Specimen)		220,000

George VI, 1937–1952

Diameter: 18.034 mm; weight: 2.33 grams; composition: .800 silver, .200 copper; edge: reeded

VG: No detail in hair above ear
F: Only slight detail in hair above ear
VF: Where not worn, hair is clear but not sharp
EF: Slight wear in hair over ear

The first obverse for this series has a legend containing the phrase ET IND: IMP: for Et Indiae Imperator (and Emperor of India). Beginning with coins dated 1948 the phrase was omitted from the King's titles, as India had gained independence from England the previous year. Both varieties were derived from a portrait model by T.H. Paget (initials H.P. under bust). The obverses of this series are unique in that the monarch is bare-headed.

A government decision was made to modernize the reverse designs for the George VI series, and the popular fishing schooner motif was selected for this denomination. The design was first considered for the 25 cents, with the beaver design to be used for the 10 cents. Although the government proclamation stated that a "fishing schooner under sail" is shown, it is clear that the designer, Emanuel Hahn, used the Canadian racing yacht Bluenose as his model. Hahn's initial H appears above the waves to the left. The small date on the 1937 issue wore badly in circulation so, beginning in 1938, the date was enlarged and placed higher in the field. Some coins dated 1947 have a tiny maple leaf after the date to denote that they were actually struck in 1948. For more information see text on the 1-cent.

Small low date 1937 only   Large high date, 1938–1952

DATE	MILLIONS MINTED	VG-8	F-12	VF-20	EF-40	AU-50	MS-60	MS-63
"ET IND : IMP :" Obverse (1937–1947)								
1937 (small date)	3	*	3.50	4.50	5.50	9.00	20.00	30.00
1938	4	*	3.50	6.00	15.00	35.00	75.00	125.00
1939	6	*	3.50	5.00	10.00	25.00	60.00	95.00
1940	17	*	*	3.50	5.00	10.00	25.00	45.00
1941	9	*	*	4.50	12.00	25.00	60.00	125.00
1942	10	*	*	3.50	7.00	20.00	45.00	75.00
1943	21	*	*	3.50	5.00	10.00	25.00	40.00
1944	9	*	*	3.50	6.00	14.00	35.00	55.00
1945	11	*	*	3.50	5.00	10.00	25.00	40.00
1946	6	*	3.50	4.50	8.00	17.00	35.00	50.00
1947	4	*	4.00	5.50	10.00	20.00	45.00	75.00
1947 maple leaf	10	*	*	3.50	5.00	8.00	18.00	25.00

Obverse 1948–1952

Modified Obverse Legend (1948–1952)								
1948	(coins minted: 422,741)	4.00	6.00	13.00	25.00	40.00	70.00	100.00
1949	11	*	*	3.50	5.00	7.00	15.00	22.00
1950	18	*	*	3.50	4.50	6.00	12.00	18.00
1951	15	*	*	*	3.50	4.50	8.00	15.00
1952	10	*	*	*	3.50	4.50	7.00	12.00

Elizabeth II, Laureate, 1953–1964

Diameter: 18.034 mm; weight: 2.33 grams; composition: .800 silver, .200 copper; edge: reeded

F: *Leaves almost worn through; shoulder fold indistinct*
VF: *Leaves worn considerably; shoulder fold must be clear*
EF: *Laurel leaves on head somewhat worn*

The initial obverse for the 1953 issue had a high relief, laureate portrait of the Queen by Mary Gillick (M.G. on truncation) which did not strike up well on the coins. Later in the year, the relief was lowered and the hair and shoulder detail re-engraved. The re-engraving included sharpening two lines which represented a fold in the Queen's gown. The two varieties also differ in the positioning of the legend relative to the rim denticles and the styles of some of the letters. See the text on the 1-cent for more details.

The reverse remained basically the same as that introduced in the previous series.

 With shoulder fold 1953–1964

 Note style of letters, relation of 'I' to denticles

 No shoulder fold, 1953

DATE	MILLIONS MINTED	VG-8	F-12	VF-20	EF-40	AU-50	MS-60	MS-63
"No Shoulder Fold" Obverse (1953)								
1953 (no fold) 18		*	*	*	3.50	4.00	5.00	10.00
"Shoulder Fold" Obverse (1953–1964)								
1953 (with fold) . . . . incl. above		*	*	3.50	4.50	5.00	7.00	15.00
1954 4		*	*	3.50	5.50	8.00	15.00	25.00
1955 12		*	*	*	3.50	4.00	5.00	10.00
1956 17		*	*	*	*	4.00	4.50	7.00
1956 dot . . . . (incl. above)		*	4.00	5.00	8.00	11.00	18.00	30.00
1957 16		*	*	*	*	3.50	4.00	5.00
1958 11		*	*	*	*	3.50	4.00	5.00
1959 20		*	*	*	*	*	3.50	4.50
1960 45		*	*	*	*	*	3.50	4.50
1961 27		*	*	*	*	*	3.50	4.50
1962 42		*	*	*	*	*	3.50	4.50
1963 42		*	*	*	*	*	3.50	4.50
1964 50		*	*	*	*	*	3.50	4.50

*Common silver coins (marked with *) are worth a premium only for their silver content. This price may vary according to prevailing market value of silver bullion.

Elizabeth II, Tiara, 1965–1978

In 1965 an obverse with a new style portrait by Arnold Machin was introduced. The Queen has more mature facial features and is wearing a tiara. The reverse and physical specifications for the 1965-66 period remain as before.

DATE	MILLIONS MINTED	VG-8	F-12	VF-20	EF-40	AU-50	MS-60	MS-63
1965 57		*	*	*	*	*	*	4.00
1966 34		*	*	*	*	*	*	4.00

Confederation Centennial, 1967

All denominations for 1967 bore special reverses to commemorate the 1867 confederation of Nova Scotia, New Brunswick and the Province of Canada, to form the Dominion of Canada. The design for this denomination, by Alex Colville, shows a mackerel. During the issue, the alloy was changed to .500 silver, .500 copper. The alloy varieties are not distinguishable by eye, so only a single catalogue value is given below.

DATE	MILLIONS MINTED	MS-60	MS-63
1967 .800 silver 32		*	3.50
.500 silver 31		*	3.50

Schooner Resumed, 1968 –

Diameter: 18.034 mm; weight: (silver) 2.33 grams, (nickel) 2.07 grams; thickness: (nickel) 1.16 mm; composition: (1968) .500 silver, .500 copper, (1968–1977) .999 nickel, edge: reeded

Two major reverse varieties have appeared since the 1968 resumption of the fishing schooner design. The first is as the previous issue; the second, by Myron Cook (but still bearing Emanuel Hahn's initial H), has the size of the device reduced and a smaller date placed lower in the field.

1968 varieties The earlier portion of the 1968 issue was in silver. Later, the composition was changed to nickel. The nickel specimens are slightly darker in color and are attracted to a magnet. Due to lack of time, the Royal Canadian Mint made arrangements with the United States Mint at Philadelphia to strike many of the nickel 10-cent pieces for 1968. The Ottawa and Philadelphia strikings differ only in the number of reeds on the edge and shape of the slots between them.

Large high date, 1968–1969

Ottawa Mint
V-shaped grooves
(reeded edge)

Philadelphia Mint
flat-bottomed grooves
(serrated edge)

DATE	MILLIONS MINTED	MS-63
Large Schooner Reverse (1968–1969)		
1968 .500 silver 70		2.50
nickel, Ottawa 87		.50
nickel, Philadelphia 85		.50

Small schooner, small low date, 1969

DATE	MILLIONS MINTED	EF-40	MS-60	MS-63
1969 large date (rarity not yet known) . . . . incl. below		20,000	25,000	—

Small Schooner Reverse (1969–)

DATE	MILLIONS MINTED	MS-63
1969 (small date)	56	1.00
1970	5	2.00
1971	41	1.00
1972	60	1.00
1973	168	1.00
1974	211	1.00
1975	208	1.00
1976	95	1.00
1977	128	1.00

Increased Thickness, 1978

Diameter: 18.03 mm; weight: 2.07 grams; thickness: 1.19 mm; composition: .999 nickel; edge: reeded

DATE	MILLIONS MINTED	MS-63
1978	170	1.00

Modified Obverse, 1979–1989

Diameter: 18.03 mm; weight: 2.07 grams; thickness: 1.22 mm; composition: .99 nickel; edge: reeded

Beginning with 1979, the portrait of the Queen was made smaller. This was done to standardize our coinage, making the size of the portrait proportional to the diameter of the coin, regardless of denomination.

DATE	MILLIONS MINTED	MS-63
1979	237	1.00
1980	170	5.00
1981	123	1.00
1982	93	1.00
1983	111	1.00
1984	122	1.00
1985	143	1.00
1986	169	1.00
1987	147	1.00
1988	163	1.00
1989	199	1.25

Elizabeth II, Crowned, 1990–2003

The first effigy designed by a Canadian for use on Canadian coins was introduced on the obverse of all issues for 1990. The obverse, designed by Dora de Pédery-Hunt, depicts a more contemporary portrait of the Queen wearing a necklace and earrings. An elaborate crown, last seen on Victorian issues, replaced the tiara displayed on previous issues.

DATE	MILLIONS MINTED	MS-63
1990	75	1.00
1991	50	1.50

125th Anniversary of Confederation, 1992

To celebrate the 125th anniversary of Confederation, all circulation coins issued in 1992 bear the date "1867–1992".

DATE	MILLIONS MINTED	MS-63
1992 (1867–1992)	174	1.00
1993	136	1.00
1994	146	.1.00
1995	124	1.00
1996	52	1.00
1997	43	1.00
1998	204	.1.00
1999	258	1.00
2000	161	.75

New material, 2000 –

Diameter: 18.03 mm; weight: 1.75 grams; thickness: 1.22 mm;
composition: nickel-plated steel; edge: reeded

The new plating facility of the Royal Canadian Mint, in Winnipeg went into full production of nickel-plated steel blanks for all Canadian 5-, 10-, 25- and 50-cent coins in 2001. These blanks can be struck at either Ottawa or Winnipeg. The coins produced from the blanks bear a "P" mint mark on the observe, below the effigy of the queen.

DATE	MILLIONS MINTED	MS-60	MS-63
2000P	N/A	1,000	1,350

International Year of Volunteers, 2001

Issued to commemorate the 7.5 million Canadian volunteers who work towards making this country a better place for all. Design by Stan Witten.

Early in 2001, the well-known Schooner reverse was used. Most of the production of circulation 10-cent pieces displayed the Year of the Volunteer reverse shown above.

DATE		MILLIONS MINTED	MS-63
2001P	Schooner reverse	46	75
2001P	Volunteers reverse	225	.75

Elizabeth II, Golden Jubilee (1952–2002)

To celebrate the 50th anniversary of the reign of Queen Elizabeth II, all circulation coins issued in 2002 bear the double date "1952-2002" on the obverse.

DATE		MILLIONS MINTED	MS-63
2002P	(1952–2002)	251	.75
2003P		164	1.00

Elizabeth II, Bareheaded, 2003–

Corporate mark (M)

The new uncrowned effigy of Queen Elizabeth, designed by Susanna Blunt, was introduced in 2003 in celebration of the jubilee year of her reign. The RCM's corporate mark (M) was phased in during 2006 replacing the "P" material mark.

DATE	MILLIONS MINTED	MS-63
2003P		1.00
2004P	214	.75
2005P	212	.75
2006P	312	.75
2006L	included above	.75
2007	304	.75
2008	467	.75
2009	371	.75
2010	252	.75
2011	292	.75
2012	335	.75
2013	105	.75
2014	153	.75
2015	N/A	.75

20 CENTS SILVER
Victoria, 1858

Diameter: 23.27 mm; weight: 4.67 grams; composition: .925 silver, .075 copper; edge: reeded

G: *Braid around ear worn through*
VG: *No details in braid around ear.*
F: *Segments of braid begin to merge into one another*
VF: *Braid is clear but not sharp*
EF: *Braid is slightly worn but generally sharp and clear*

The English shilling being valued at slightly over 24 cents and the Halifax currency shilling valued at 20 cents (there was no actual coin in the latter instance), the Province of Canada decided to issue a 20-cent instead of a 25-cent coin.

This move proved unpopular because of the ease of confusion of the coin with U.S. and later Canadian 25-cent pieces. Consequently, the 20-cent coin was never again issued for circulation.

In 1870, when the Dominion of Canada issued its first coins, the 25-cent piece was selected and by a proclamation dated 9 September, 1870, the old 20-cent pieces were withdrawn. More than half the issue was returned to the Royal Mint at various times between 1885 and 1906, melted and the silver recoined into 25-cent pieces.

DATE	QTY. MINTED	G-4	VG-8	F-12	VF-20	EF-40	AU-50	MS-60	MS-63
1858 .. (Originally 730,392) 60.00		90.00	120.00	170.00	340.00	600.00	1,200	3,250

25 CENTS SILVER
Victoria, 1870–1901

Diameter: 23.62 mm; weight: 5.81 grams; composition: .925 silver, .075 copper; edge: reeded

G: *Hair over ear worn through*
VG: *No details in hair over the ear; jewels in diadem are partly worn away*
F: *Strands of hair over the ear begin to merge together; jewels slightly blurred*
VF: *Hair and jewels are clear but not sharp*
EF: *Hair over ear and jewels in diadem are slightly worn but generally sharp and clear*

A total of five minor varieties of the Queen's portrait were used for this denomination, each differing in some of the facial features and in certain other respects. Each successive variety was created by re-engraving one of those used previously. The initial and probably all later portraits were designed and engraved by L.C. Wyon and only on the final variety was he probably attempting to portray Victoria as she appeared in real life.

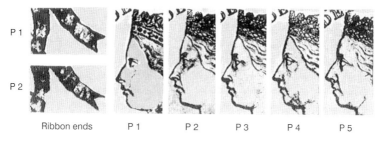

P 1
P 2

Ribbon ends   P 1   P 2   P 3   P 4   P 5

In some instances two portraits are coupled with a given date reverse. Such portraits are most easily differentiated as follows:

P1 vs P2: The ribbon end extending toward the rear has a relatively constant width on P1 but gradually narrows on P2.

P4 vs P5: The P5 face has much more aged features and a larger nose.

The reverse device shows crossed boughs of maple, tied at the bottom with a ribbon and separated at the top by St. Edward's crown. Although there were several modifications of this design, the most noteworthy came in 1886 and was derived from the first. It has longer cut ends to the maple boughs, slight re-cutting of other portions of the wreath and the design elements generally closer to the rim denticles. Both reverses were by L.C. Wyon.

Short bough ends
1870-1886

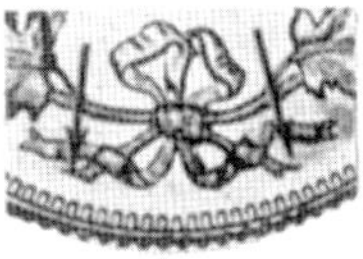

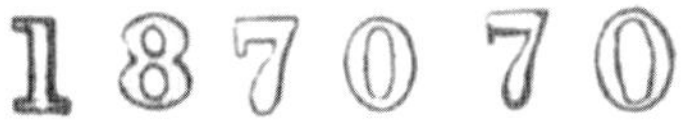

1 8 7 0 7 0

Narrow 0   Wide 0

DATE	QTY. (000)	G-4	VG-8	F-12	VF-20	EF-40	AU-50	MS-60	MS-63
Short Bough Ends Reverse (1870-1886)									
1870 narrow 0 ......P1 900		20.00	38.00	65.00	140.00	300.00	550.00	1,200	3,200
wide 0 ....P2 .. incl. above		150.00	300.00	600.00	1,200	—	—	—	—
1871..............P1, 2 400		25.00	45.00	80.00	175.00	400.00	750.00	1,600	4,000
1871H P1, 2 748		30.00	55.00	110.00	235.00	525.00	850.00	1,600	3,300
1872H ....P1, 2 .. 2,240		12.00	20.00	35.00	70.00	175.00	350.00	900.00	2,750
1874H P2 1,600		12.00	20.00	35.00	70.00	170.00	340.00	750.00	2,250
1875H ....P2......1,000		300.00	600.00	1,100	2,500	4,500	9,500	22,000	—

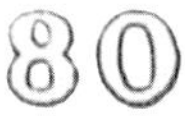

8 0   8 0   8 0

Wide 0 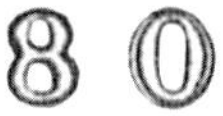   Narrow 0 over wide 0 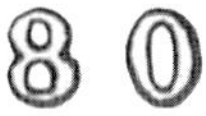   Narrow 0

1880H wide 0 ....P2 400		125.00	250.00	550.00	1,000	2,200	3,500	7,000	—
narrow over wide 0...P2 .. incl. above		100.00	200.00	380.00	900.00	1,650	2,500	4,500	12,000
narrow 0 ....P2 .. incl. above		45.00	90.00	200.00	400.00	850.00	1,400	2,600	5,500
1881H P2 820		25.00	45.00	90.00	200.00	450.00	850.00	2,000	5,500
1882H P3 600		28.00	50.00	100.00	200.00	450.00	850.00	1,900	4,750
1883H P4 960		18.00	32.00	65.00	140.00	300.00	500.00	1,000	2,700
1885..............P2 192		100.00	250.00	490.00	950.00	1,700	3,000	6,000	16,500
1886 short b. ends P2, 4, 5 540		35.00	75.00	160.00	340.00	700.00	1,250	2,750	6,000

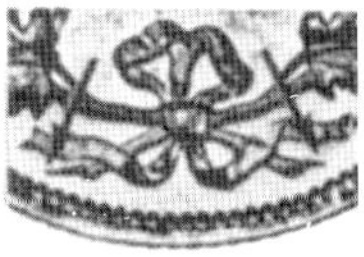

Long bough ends
1886-1901

Long Bough Ends Reverse (1886-1901)

1886 long b. ends ....P5 .. incl. above		50.00	100.00	200.00	400.00	800.00	—	—	—
1887..............P5 100		125.00	265.00	465.00	950.00	1,900	3,800	—	—

Narrow 8s   1 8 8 8   1 8 8 8   Wide 8s

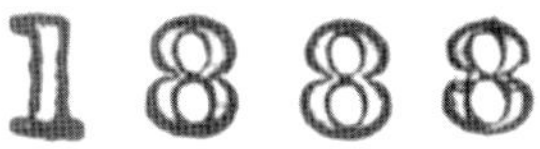

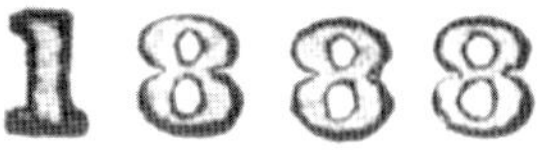

1888 narrow 8s P5 400		18.00	45.00	80.00	170.00	350.00	550.00	1,200	3,000
wide 8s ....P5 . incl. above		18.00	45.00	80.00	170.00	325.00	550.00	1,200	3,000
1889..............P5 66		125.00	300.00	600.00	1,100	2,200	3,500	7,500	—
1890H P5 200		25.00	50.00	100.00	225.00	500.00	850.00	1,600	3,750

DATE		QTY. (000)	G-4	VG-8	F-12	VF-20	EF-40	AU-50	MS-60	MS-63
1891	P5	120	85.00	190.00	375.00	600.00	1,200	1,650	3,000	5,500
1892	P5	510	18.00	32.00	65.00	130.00	325.00	600.00	1,200	3,250
1893	P5	100	125.00	250.00	500.00	850.00	1,400	1,650	3,250	5,500
1894	P5	220	25.00	50.00	110.00	225.00	450.00	700.00	1,350	3,000
1899	P5	416	12.00	20.00	40.00	100.00	225.00	450.00	1,000	2,500
1900	P5	1,320	12.00	18.00	30.00	70.00	185.00	350.00	650.00	1,500
1901	P5	640	12.00	18.00	30.00	80.00	225.00	400.00	800.00	1,650

Edward VII, 1902–1910

Diameter: 23.62 mm; weight: 5.81 grams; composition: .925 silver, .075 copper; edge: reeded

G: Band of crown worn through
VG: Band of crown worn through at highest point
F: Jewels in band of crown will be blurred
VF: Band of crown still clear but no longer sharp
EF: Band of crown slightly worn but generally
     sharp and clear

A single obverse, designed and engraved by G.W. De Saulles (DES below bust), was used for the entire series.

For the first reverse, De Saulles used the almost unaltered wreath from the second Victorian reverse and coupled it with the Imperial State crown and a new legend. A major modification, presumably by W.H.J. Blakemore, appeared in 1906. It has a larger crown and many of the leaves are re-engraved. A specimen dated 1906 with the small crown reverse has been documented. The issues of 1908-10 to have thickened stems.

Small Crown Reverse (1902-1906)

	QTY. (000)	G-4	VG-8	F-12	VF-20	EF-40	AU-50	MS-60	MS-63
1902	464	8.00	20.00	40.00	100.00	300.00	500.00	1,100	2,800
1902H	800	5.00	13.00	25.00	75.00	160.00	250.00	400.00	750.00
1903	846	8.00	22.00	45.00	120.00	350.00	600.00	1,200	3,000
1904	400	12.00	35.00	90.00	290.00	600.00	1,100	2,500	8,250
1905	800	8.00	22.00	50.00	175.00	425.00	900.00	2,250	6,500
1906	238	1,800	4,000	6,500	12,000	20,000	30,000	—	—

Large Crown Reverse (1906-1910)

	QTY. (000)	G-4	VG-8	F-12	VF-20	EF-40	AU-50	MS-60	MS-63
1906	1,238	6.00	17.00	40.00	90.00	300.00	500.00	1,000	2,500
1907	2,088	5.00	13.00	25.00	75.00	200.00	380.00	720.00	1,800
1908	495	10.00	30.00	65.00	125.00	300.00	450.00	650.00	1,250
1909	1,336	8.00	17.00	45.00	115.00	300.00	500.00	1,000	2,250
1910	3,578	5.00	12.00	25.00	60.00	115.00	225.00	420.00	1,000

George V, 1911–1936

Diameter: 23.62 mm; weight: 5.83 grams; composition: (1911-19) .925 silver, .075 copper,
(1920-36) .800 silver, .200 copper; edge: reeded

G: Band of crown worn through
VG: Band of crown worn through at highest point
F: Jewels in band of crown will be blurred; (CAN
     of CANADA worn but readable on 1936 dot.)
VF: Band of crown still clear but no longer sharp
EF: Band of crown slightly worn but generally
     sharp and clear

As in the case of all other Canadian denominations, the 1911 legend did not include the phrase
DEI GRATIA (by the grace of God). Public objection to this break with tradition resulted in the
addition of the abbreviation DEI GRA: the following year. Both varieties were based on the design
of Sir E.B. MacKennal, whose initials B.M. appear on the truncation of the bust. The reverse is
identical to that used for 1908–1910 issues.

DATE	QTY. (000)	G-4	VG-8	F-12	VF-20	EF-40	AU-50	MS-60	MS-63
"Godless" Obverse (1911)									
1911 1,721		6.00	14.00	25.00	60.00	135.00	200.00	400.00	800.00

Modified Obverse Legend (1912–1936)									
1912 2,544		6.00	11.00	16.00	35.00	90.00	225.00	550.00	1,750
1913 2,214		6.00	11.00	16.00	35.00	90.00	200.00	400.00	1,400
1914 1,215		6.00	12.00	18.00	50.00	110.00	300.00	800.00	2,250
1915 242		10.00	35.00	80.00	280.00	750.00	1,7500	4,200	9,000
1916 1,463		6.00	8.00	13.00	30.00	65.00	125.00	275.00	900.00
1917 3,366		6.00	8.00	10.00	20.00	50.00	75.00	165.00	350.00
1918 4,176		6.00	8.00	10.00	15.00	40.00	65.00	130.00	280.00
1919 . . . . (coins struck: 5,852,262)		6.00	8.00	10.00	15.00	40.00	60.00	140.00	280.00
1920 1,975		6.00	8.00	11.00	22.00	50.00	100.00	225.00	600.00
1921 597		10.00	20.00	40.00	140.00	350.00	850.00	1,800	4,000
1927 468		20.00	45.00	75.00	150.00	320.00	750.00	1,350	2,500
1928 2,114		6.00	8.00	10.00	20.00	60.00	100.00	200.00	500.00
1929 2,691		6.00	8.00	10.00	20.00	55.00	100.00	180.00	450.00
1930 969		6.00	8.00	11.00	30.00	75.00	110.00	300.00	700.00
1931 538		6.00	8.00	11.00	35.00	85.00	135.00	325.00	800.00
1932 538		6.00	8.00	13.00	35.00	85.00	135.00	325.00	800.00
1933 421		6.00	8.00	15.00	40.00	100.00	165.00	275.00	500.00
1934 384		6.00	8.00	15.00	50.00	110.00	190.00	400.00	800.00
1935 538		6.00	8.00	15.00	40.00	100.00	140.00	225.00	425.00
1936 1,126		6.00	8.00	10.00	15.00	40.00	65.00	120.00	250.00

George VI Issue, Struck in the Name of George V

A portion of the 1-, 10- and 25-cent pieces dated 1936 have a small raised dot on the reverse, denoting that they were actually struck in 1937 for George VI. On the 25-cent pieces the dot is below the ribbon of the wreath. See text on the 1-cent piece for more details.

This issue seems to be particularly liable to "ghosting," thus the CAN of CANADA often will be much weaker than the rest of the legend. Nevertheless, the entire CANADA must still be readable for any specimen to grade at least Very Good. Otherwise, the grading and physical specifications are exactly as for the regular George V issues.

DATE	QTY. (000)	G-4	VG-8	F-12	VF-20	EF-40	AU-50	MS-60	MS-63
1936 raised dot under wreath .... incl.		20.00	45.00	110.00	250.00	550.00	850.00	1,350	3,000

George VI, 1937–1952

Diameter: 23.62 mm; weight: 5.83 grams; composition: .800 silver, .200 copper; edge: reeded

VG: No detail in hair above the ear
F: Only slight detail in hair above the ear
VF: Hair above ear and side of head is clear
     but not sharp
EF: Slight wear in the hair over the ear

Three obverse varieties are known for this series. The first two have in common a high relief bust of the King by T.H. Paget (H.P. below bust); the second variety has the ET IND : IMP : omitted from the legend (see the 1-cent text). The third has a low relief modification of the original portrait. The latter variety, the work of Thomas Shingles, was made to improve the overall appearance and the clarity with which the design could be struck up. In addition to the relief of the portraits, the second and third varieties can be differentiated by the position of the legend relative to the rim denticles and by the style of some of the letters.

Because of the government decision to modernize the reverse designs, the caribou motif was selected for the 25-cent piece. At one time the fishing schooner had been considered for this denomination. The designer was Emanuel Hahn (H under caribou's neck).

1947 "dot" This item is apparently the product of a deteriorated die. See text on the 5-cent piece for more details.

1947 maple leaf variety This is an official issue struck in 1948. See text on the 1-cent piece for details.

DATE	MILLIONS MINTED	VG-8	F-12	VF-20	EF-40	AU-50	MS-60	MS-63
"ET IND : IMP : " Obverse (1937–1947)								
1937 3		*	8.00	9.00	11.00	15.00	22.00	45.00
1938 3		*	8.00	13.00	23.00	40.00	85.00	175.00
1939 4		*	8.00	11.00	16.00	30.00	70.00	140.00
1940 10		*	*	8.00	10.00	12.00	25.00	50.00
1941 7		*	*	8.00	10.00	12.00	28.00	55.00
1942 7		*	*	8.00	10.00	12.00	30.00	50.00
1943 14		*	*	8.00	10.00	12.00	28.00	55.00
1944 7		*	7.00	9.00	12.00	17.00	35.00	70.00
1945 5		*	*	8.00	10.00	12.00	28.00	60.00
1946 2		*	8.00	10.00	20.00	35.00	60.00	125.00
1947 normal date 2		*	8.00	10.00	20.00	40.00	70.00	120.00
1947 dot	incl. above	80.00	110.00	150.00	250.00	380.00	650.00	1,100
1947 maple leaf 4		*	*	8.00	12.00	13.00	22.00	35.00

High relief	Low relief
High relief 1948-1952	Low relief 1951-1952

Note style of letters, relation of "A" to denticles

Modified Legend, High Relief Bust (1948–1952), Low Relief Bust (1951–1952)

DATE	MILLIONS MINTED	VG-8	F-12	VF-20	EF-40	AU-50	MS-60	MS-63
1948 3		*	8.00	10.00	13.00	35.00	75.00	150.00
1949 8		*	*	8.00	10.00	12.00	16.00	35.00
1950 10		*	*	8.00	10.00	12.00	15.00	28.00
1951 high relief bust 8		*	*	8.00	9.00	10.00	12.00	20.00
1951 low relief bust	PL grades only (any MS grades are mis-attributed)					120.00	160.00	250.00
1952 high relief bust 9		*	8.00	10.00	13.00	20.00	40.00	75.00
1952 low relief bust	incl. above	*	*	8.00	9.00	10.00	12.00	20.00

Elizabeth II, Laureate, 1953–1964

Diameter: (1953 large date) 23.62 mm, (1953 small date to 1964) 23.88 mm; weight: 5.83 grams; composition: .800 silver, .200 copper; edge: reeded

F: *Leaves worn almost through; shoulder fold indistinct*

VF: *Leaves considerably worn; shoulder fold must be clear*

EF: *Laurel leaves on the head are somewhat worn*

The initial obverse for the 1953 issue had a high relief, laureate portrait of the Queen by Mrs. Mary Gillick (M.G. on truncation) which did not strike up well on the coins. Later in the year, the rim width and coin diameter were increased, the obverse relieve lowered and the hair and shoulder detail re-engraved. The re-engraving included sharpening two lines which represented the fold in (not a shoulder strap on) the Queen's gown. The two varieties also differ in the positioning of the legend relative to the rim denticles and the style of some of the letters.

The reverse coupled with the "no shoulder fold" obverse in 1953 is exactly as that for the George VI issues. Together with the obverse change, however, came a new reverse with a smaller date, wider rim and modified caribou (note the change in the contour of the lower neck). After 1953, the reverse design was not significantly altered until 1967.

No shoulder fold, high
relief, narrow rim, 1953

Large date, narrow rim, 1953

DATE	MILLIONS MINTED	F-12	VF-20	EF-40	AU-50	MS-60	MS-63
Large Date, No Shoulder Fold (1953)							
1953 large date	10	*	*	8.00	9.00	10.00	16.00

Shoulder fold,
low relief, wide rim,
1953-1964

Small date, wide rim,
modified caribou, 1953-1964

Small Date, Shoulder Fold (1953-1964)							
1953 small date	incl. above	*	8.00	9.00	10.00	13.00	30.00
1954	2	8.00	9.00	12.00	20.00	35.00	65.00
1955	10	*	*	8.00	9.00	11.00	18.00
1956	11	*	*	*	8.00	10.00	15.00
1957	13	*	*	*	8.00	9.00	12.00
1958	9	*	*	*	8.00	9.00	12.00
1959	14	*	*	*	*	8.00	10.00
1960	23	*	*	*	*	8.00	10.00
1961	18	*	*	*	*	8.00	10.00
1962	30	*	*	*	*	8.00	10.00
1963	21	*	*	*	*	*	9.00
1964	36	*	*	*	*	*	9.00

*Common silver coins (marked with *) are worth a premium
only for their silver content.*

Elizabeth II, Tiara, 1965–1978

In 1965 an obverse with a new style portrait by Arnold Machin was introduced. The Queen has
more mature facial features and is wearing a tiara. The reverse was continued as before, and
physical specifications are as on the previous issues.

DATE	MILLIONS MINTED	MS-60	MS-63
1965	45	*	9.00
1966	25	*	9.00

Confederation Centennial, 1967

All denominations for 1967 bore special reverses to commemorate the 1867 confederation of Nova Scotia, New Brunswick and the Province of Canada, to form the Dominion of Canada. The design for this denomination, by Alex Colville, shows a bobcat as its device. During 1967 the alloy was changed to .500 silver, .500 copper.

DATE		MILLIONS MINTED	MS-60	MS-63
1967	.800 silver	49	*	7.00
	.500 silver	incl. above	*	7.00

Elizabeth II, Caribou Resumed, Nickel, 1968–2001

Diameter: 23.88 mm; weight: (silver) 5.83 grams (nickel) 5.05 grams; thickness (nickel): 1.60 mm; composition: (1968 silver) .500 silver, .500 copper, (nickel) .999 nickel; edge: reeded

During 1968, the composition was changed to pure nickel. The nickel specimens are slightly darker in color and are attracted to a magnet.

1968	.500 silver	71	*	5.00
	pure nickel	89	.50	1.00
1969		133	.50	1.00
1970		10	1.25	2.50
1971		48	.50	1.00
1972		44	.50	1.00

Royal Canadian Mounted Police Centennial, 1973

large bust   small bust

The 25-cent pieces for 1973 bear a special reverse designed by Paul Cedarberg (PC behind horse) marking the centenary of the Royal Canadian Mounted Police. The initial circulation strikes bear a smaller obverse effigy engraved from Patrick Brindley's modification of the Machin bust of Queen Elizabeth. The smaller effigy has more hair detail and the obverse has fewer beads, pulled in farther from the edge. The Brindley obverse was used only in 1973.

DATE		MILLIONS MINTED	F-12	VF-20	EF-40	AU-50	MS-60	MS-63
1973	small bust	135	—	—	—	—	.75	1.50
	large bust	incl. above	120.00	150.00	185.00	215.00	350.00	800.00

Caribou Reverse Resumed, 1974–1977

DATE	MILLIONS MINTED	MS-63
1974	192	1.25
1975	141	1.25
1976	87	1.25
1977	100	1.25

Increased Thickness, 1978

Diameter: 23.88 mm; weight: 5.10 grams; thickness: 1.58 mm; composition: .999 nickel; edge: reeded

DATE	MILLIONS MINTED	MS-63
1978	176	1.25

Modified Obverse, 1979–1989

Beginning with 1979, the portrait of the Queen was made smaller. This was done to standardize our coinage, making the size of the portrait proportional to the diameter of the coin, regardless of denomination.

DATE	MILLIONS MINTED	MS-63
1979	131	1.25
1980	77	1.50
1981	131	1.50
1982	172	1.50
1983	13	3.00
1984	122	1.50
1985	159	1.50
1986	132	1.50
1987	53	2.00
1988	80	1.50
1989	120	1.50

Elizabeth II, Crowned, 1990–2003

The first effigy designed by a Canadian for use on Canadian coins was introduced on the obverse of all Canadian issues for 1990. The design depicts a more contemporary portrait of the Queen wearing a necklace and earrings. The elaborate crown, last seen on Victorian issues, replaced the tiara used on previous issues. The obverse was designed by Dora de Pédery-Hunt.

DATE	MINTED (000)	MS-63
1990	31,258	1.50
1991	459	15.00

125th Anniversary of Confederation, 1992

For the 125th anniversary of Confederation, circulation 25-cent pieces in 1992 bear the date "1867-1992" on the obverse, below the Dora de Pédery-Hunt effigy of the queen. Ten million pieces each of twelve reverse designs were struck, one for each province and territory, with a different reverse design released each month during 1992. The sequence of the release dates was determined by random draw.

The "CANADA 125" program of special commemorative issues for 1992 includes the 12 different 25-cent pieces and a commemorative aureate dollar released on July 1st. The 25-cent pieces were also struck in sterling silver and released as individually cased proof coins. A cased proof set consisting of the commemorative aureate dollar and the twelve sterling silver 25-cent pieces was also issued.

New Brunswick	Northwest Territories	Newfoundland	Manitoba
Covered Bridge, Newton	Inuit "inukshuk"	Fisherman in Grandy Dory	Lower Fort Garry
Ronald Lambert	*Ms. Beth McEachen*	*Christopher Newhook*	*Murriel E. Hope*

Yukon	Alberta	Prince Edward Island	Ontario
Kaskawalsh Glacier	Hoodoos	Cousins Shore	Jack Pines
Elizabeth (Libby) Dulac	*Melvin (Mel) Heath*	*Nigel Graham Roe*	*Greg Salmela*

Nova Scotia	Quebec	Saskatchewan	British Columbia
Lighthouse, Peggy's Cove	Percé Rock	Prairie symbols	Natural Beauty of B.C.
Bruce Wood	*Romualdus Bukauskas*	*Brian E. Cobb*	*Carla Herrera Egan*

DATE	MILLIONS MINTED	MS-63
1992	Total of 12 different designs 133	1.50
1993	74	1.25
1994	78	1.25
1995	89	1.25
1996	28	1.25

The mint did not strike 25-cent pieces for circulation in 1997 or 1998.

Millennium, 1999

The end of the second millennium was celebrated by striking a different circulating 25-cent design for each month during 1999 and 2000. The designs were chosen from those submitted from across Canada. The coins were also offered individually and as complete proof sets in sterling silver. The well known Caribou reverse was not used on circulating coins in 1999 and 2000 but appears on the 25-cent pieces in all five collectors' sets for these years.

January	February	March	April
A Country Unfolds	Etched in Stone	The Log Drive	Our Northern Heritage
Peter Ka-Pin Poon	*Lonnie Springer*	*Marjolaine Lavoie*	*Konojuak Ashevak*

May	June	July	August
The Voyageurs	From Coast to Coast	A Nation of People	The Pioneer Spirit
Sergiy Minenok	*Gordon Ho*	*Maria H. Sarkany*	*Alzira Botelho*

September	October	November	December
Canada Through	A Tribute to First Nations	The Airplane Opens the	This is Canada
a Child's Eye	*James Edward Read*	North Brian R. Bacon	*J.L. Pierre Provencher*
Claudia Bertrand			

DATE	MILLIONS MINTED	MS-63
1999 259		1.00

Millennium, 2000

January	February	March	April
Pride	Ingenuity	Achievement	Health
Donald Warkentin	*John Jaciw*	*Daryl Ann Dorosz*	*Amy Wassef*

May	June	July	August
Natural Legacy	Harmony	Celebration	Family
Randy Trantau	*Haver Demirer*	*Laura Paxton*	*Wade Stephen Baker*

September	October	November	December
Wisdom	Creativity	Freedom	Community
Cezar Serbanescu	*Eric (Kong Tat) Hui*	*Kathy Vinish*	*Michelle Thibodeau*

DATE	MILLIONS MINTED	AU	MS-60	MS-63
2000	436			1.00
2000P	.... included above	—	10,000	15,000

Caribou Resumed, Nickel-plated steel, 2001–

Diameter: 23.88 mm; weight: 4.4 grams;
material: nickel-plated steel; edge: reeded

The new plating facility of the Royal Canadian Mint, in Winnipeg, went into full production of nickel-plated steel blanks for all Canadian 5-, 10-, 25- and 50-cent coins in 2001. These blanks can be struck at either Ottawa or Winnipeg. The coins produced from the blanks bear a "P" material mark on the observe, below the effigy of the queen.

DATE	MILLIONS MINTED	AU	MS-60	MS-63
2001	8			5.00
2001P	....			1.00
2003P	88			2.00

Elizabeth II, Golden Jubilee (1952–2002)

To celebrate the 50th anniversary of the reign of Queen Elizabeth II, all circulation coins issued in 2002 bear the double date "1952-2002" on the obverse.

DATE	MILLIONS MINTED	MS-63
2002P (1952–2002)	31	1.00

Canada Day, 2002

This coin, issued on Canada Day, 2002, celebrates Canada's 135th anniversary. The reverse was designed by Judith Chartier.

DATE	MILLIONS MINTED	MS-63
2002P Canada Day reverse	156	1.00

Elizabeth II, Bearheaded, 2003–2004

Caribou Resumed

Designed by Susanna Blunt, a new uncrowned effigy of Queen Elizabeth, was introduced in 2003 in celebration of the jubilee year of her reign.

DATE	MILLIONS MINTED	MS-63
2003P	incl.	1.00
2004P	177	.75

Poppy, 2004, 2008 & 2010

On October 21, 2004, The Royal Canadian Mint, in partnership with the Royal Canadian Legion, unveiled the world's first coloured circulation coin. The coin features a red poppy, the symbol of remembrance for our war dead. The reverse was designed by Cosme Saffioti

DATE	MILLIONS MINTED	MS-63
2004P Coloured Poppy reverse	28.5	1.00
2008 Coloured Poppy reverse	11	1.00
2010 Remembrance Day	11	1.00

Ile Sainte-Croix, 2004

In 1604, Samuel de Champlain and Pierre du Gua, sieur de Monts, established the first french settlement in North America at Ile Sainte-Croix. The settlement was relocated, but the historic impact of this small island would endure for centuries to come. The reverse design is the work of Robert Ralph Carmichael,

DATE	MILLIONS MINTED	MS-63
2004P	15.5	1.00

Province of Alberta Centennial, 2005

Two special coins were struck in celebration of the Alberta's 100th anniversary as a province. The special reverse was designed by Michelle Grant and also adorns the special Alberta Centennial five dollar coin

Province of Saskatchewan Centennial, 2005

Saskatchewan's centennial is being celebrated by the issue of two special coins. The special reverse, designed by Paulett Sapergia, also appears on the special Saskatchewan Centennial five dollar coin

DATE		MILLIONS MINTED	MS-63
2005P	Alberta Centennial	20.6	1.00
2005P	Saskatchewan Centennial	19	1.00

Year of the Veteran, 2005

Designed by Ottawa-based artist Elaine Goble, the coin depicts the profiles of two veterans from different generations, joined by their love of country.

DATE	MILLIONS MINTED	MS-63
2005P	15.5	1.00

Caribou Reverse Resumed

RCM's corporate mark (M)

DATE	MILLIONS MINTED	MS-63
2005P	206	1.00
2006P	423	1.00
2006(M)	Include above	1.00
2007	275	1.00
2008	286	1.00
2009	156	1.00
2010	134	1.00
2011	188	1.00
2012	153.5	1.00
2013	118.5	1.00
2014	97	1.00
2015	N/A	1.00

Breast Cancer Awareness, 2006

Features the iconic pink ribbon, the symbol of hope and awareness in the effort to create a future without breast cancer. Design by Christie Paquet.

DATE		MILLIONS MINTED	MS-63
2006P	Coloured Ribbon reverse	30	1.00

Medal of Bravery, 2006

Medal of Bravery coin pays tribute to everyday Canadians who risk their lives to save or protect others. Design by Cosme Saffioti.

DATE	MILLIONS MINTED	MS-63
2006P 20		1.00

Vancouver 2010 Olympic Winter Games

Fifteen different quarters will be released up to the year 2010. Release dates for different designs are indicated below each coin. Two special Paralympic issues are included, Wheelchair Curling and Ice Sledge Hockey, these have a different logo on the Obverse.

2007 Obverse

Curling
February 23, 2007

Ice Hockey
April 4, 2007

Wheelchair Curling
July 11, 2007

Biathlon
September 12, 2007

Alpine Skiing
October 24, 2007

2008 Obverse

Snowboarding
February 20, 2008

Freestyle Skiing
April 16, 2008

Figure Skating
September 10, 2008

Bobsleigh
October 29, 2008

2009 Obverse

Speed Skating
February 18, 2009

Cross Country Skiing
April 15, 2009

Paralympic Obverse

Ice Sledge Hockey
June 17, 2009

DATE	MINTED	MS-63
2007 - 2009 - Circulation - each issue	22,400,000	1.00
2007 - 2009 - Rolls - each issue	10,000	Issue price 16.95
2007 - 2009 - First day covers - each issue	10,000	Issue price 15.95
2007 - 2009 - Sports card (with red coloured edging on maple leaf) - each issue	N/A	Issue price 7.95
2008 - Mule - Sports card - Alpine Skiing	40,000	25.00
2007 - 2009 - Bookmark & Pin - each issue.	N/A	Issue price 15.95
2007 - 2009 - Magnetic Pin - each issue	N/A	Issue price 14.95

Vancouver 2010 Olympic Winter Games - Top 3 Moments

Canada's top 3 Olympic moments finish off this series of 25 cent coins. Canada's favourite three Canadian Winter Olympic Medals Moments with Men's Hockey, 2002 as the top moment followed by Women's Hockey 2002 and then Speed Skating 2006. Each coin has a mintage of 22 million, with three million of each with red colour and white border on the maple leaf background on the reverse. Designs by Jason Bouwman with obverse design by Susanna Blunt.

Obverse   **Men's Hockey - 2002**

Men's Hockey   **Men's Hockey**
Incused 2   **Raised 2**

Men's Hockey, Colour
Die Varieties

Two distinct varieties exist with the last digit of the date 2002 on the reverse of the colour issue. An incused 2 that appears inset in the right leg of the player being one type. The raised 2 type appears to be on top of the leg. (Non colour Men's Hockey are similar to the raised 2 type.)

Women's Hockey - 2002   **Speed Skating - 2006**

DATE	MILLIONS MINTED	MS-63
2009	Men's Hockey 19	1.00
2009	Men's Hockey, colour - incused 2. 3	2.50
2009	Men's Hockey, colour - rasied 2 . . . . Included Above	12.00
2009	Women's Hockey 19	1.00
2009	Women's Hockey, colour 3	2.50
2009	Cindy Flassen. 19	1.00
2009	Cindy Flassen, colour 3	2.50

Legendary Nature

These circulating coins dated 2011, were actually released in 2012. Designs by Jason Bouwman with obverse design by Susanna Blunt.

	Obverse		Wood Bison	
	Orca Whale		Peregrine Falcon	

DATE		MINTAGE	MS-63
2011	Wood Bison	12,500,000	1.00
2011	Wood Bison, colour	incl.	1.00
2011	Orca Whale	450,000	1.00
2011	Orca Whale, colour.	incl.	1.00
2011	Peregrine Falcon.	12,500,000	1.00
2011	Peregrine Falcon, colour.	incl.	1.00

Heroes of 1812, 2012–2013

	Tecumseh		Brock	
	de Salaberry		Secord	

DATE		MINTAGE	MS-63
2012	Chief Tecumseh	12,500,000	1.00
2012	Chief Tecumseh, colour	incl.	1.00
2012	Sir Isaac Brock.	12,500,000	1.00
2012	Sir Isaac Brock, colour.	incl.	1.00
2012	Charles Michel de Salaberry.	12,500,000	1.00
2012	Charles Michel de Salaberry, colour	incl.	1.00
2013	Laura Secord	12,500,000	1.00
2013	Laura Secord, colour	incl.	1.00

Canadian Arctic Expedition

Celebrating the 100th anniversary of the 1913 Canadian Arctic Expedition, as well as the cultures and traditions which continue to thrive in our Arctic regions.

DATE		MINTAGE	MS-63
2013	Arctic Expedition, by Bonnie Ross.	12,500,000	1.00
2013	Bowhead whale, by Tim Pitsiula	12,500,000	1.00

Each coin was available in two different frostings. They were released November 22, 2013.

50 CENTS, SILVER
Victoria, 1870–1901

Diameter: 29.72 mm; weight: 11.62 grams; composition: .925 silver, .075 copper; edge: reeded

G: Hair over ear worn through
VG: No details in hair over ear; jewels in
    diadem are partly worn away
F: Strands of hair over ear begin to merge
    together; jewels slightly blurred
VF: Hair and jewels clear but not sharp
EF: Hair over ear and jewels of diadem
    slightly worn but generally sharp and clear

In all, four portraits were used for this denomination. Except for the first two varieties, which have the same face, the portraits differ in the facial features as well as certain other respects. Each variety after the first was created by re-engraving an earlier one. The first and probably all later portraits were designed and engraved by L.C. Wyon but only on the final one or two varieties could he have been attempting to portray Queen Victoria as she appeared at the time. In some instances two portraits were coupled with a given date reverse. These are most easily differentiated as follows:

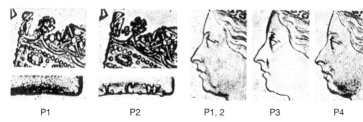

P1   P2   P1, 2   P3   P4

P1 vs P2: P1 has no initials on the truncation, a blank space immediately behind the front cross in the crown and a break in the left-hand ribbon end; P2 has L.C.W. on the truncation, a shamrock behind the front cross in the crown and no breaks in the ribbon ends.

P3 vs P4: P3 has a rounded chin front, and the lower front corner of the crown is in front of the forehead; P4 has a flat chin front and the lower front corner of the crown is even with the forehead.

The reverse device consists of crossed maple boughs, tied at the bottom by a ribbon and separated at the top by St. Edward's crown. Although there were several slight modifications, the most noteworthy occurred in 1871. This variety (1871–1901), derived from the first, has parts of both the crown and the wreath re-engraved. Both reverse varieties were by L.C. Wyon.

DATE	QTY. (000)	G-4	VG-8	F-12	VF-20	EF-40	AU-50	MS-60	MS-63
First Reverse Design (1870)									
1870 no LCW ...P1 450		850.00	1,600	2,350	4,200	8,000	15,000	—	—
1870 LCW on obw P2 .... incl. above		35.00	75.00	125.00	250.00	550.00	1,300	5,000	—

Normal 2

Short base 2

Specimens of the 1872H often have part
or all of the reverse legend repunched.

1872H, inverted A over V

DATE	QTY. (000)	G-4	VG-8	F-12	VF-20	EF-40	AU-50	MS-60	MS-63
Modified Reverse Design (1871–1901)									
1871 . . . . .P2	200	50.00	110.00	230.00	500.00	1,000	2,300	8,500	—
1871H P2	45	85.00	175.00	350.00	750.00	1,750	3,200	11,000	—
1872H normal 2 . . . .P2	80	35.00	75.00	140.00	300.00	700.00	1,500	5,500	—
short base 2 . . . . . .P2 . . . incl. above									
inv. A over V . . . . . . .P2 . . . incl. above		275.00	500.00	1,000	2,000	6,000	12,000	—	—
1881H P3	150	50.00	100.00	175.00	375.00	900.00	2,350	8,000	—
1888 . . . . .P2, 3, 4	60	175.00	375.00	600.00	1,200	2,200	4,500	13,500	—
1890H P3, 4	20	1,000	2,100	3,000	5,000	9,000	16,000	50,000	—
1892 . . . . .P4	151	55.00	110.00	200.00	500.00	1,000	2,800	11,000	—
1894 . . . . .P4	29	375.00	650.00	1,100	2,000	4,000	8,000	20,000	—
1898 . . . . .P4	100	60.00	120.00	250.00	550.00	1,200	3,200	13,500	—
1899 . . . . .P4	50	150.00	300.00	550.00	1,100	2,500	6,000	22,000	—
1900 . . . . .P4	118	40.00	85.00	150.00	325.00	800.00	2,000	7,000	—
1901 . . . . .P4	80	45.00	95.00	175.00	375.00	900.00	2,250	8,500	—

Edward VII, 1902–1910

Diameter: 29.72 mm; weight: 11.62 grams; composition: .925 silver, .075 copper; edge: reeded

G: *Band of crown worn through*
VG: *Band of crown worn through at highest point*
F: *Jewels blurred in band of crown*
VF: *Band of crown still clear but no longer sharp*
EF: *Band of crown slightly worn; generally sharp and clear*

A single obverse, designed and engraved by G.W. De Saulles (DES below bust), was used for the entire series.

For the initial reverse (1902–10) De Saulles utilized the unmodified wreath from the later Victorian reverse with a new legend and the Imperial State crown. A modification of the first variety (probably by W.H.J. Blakemore) appeared in 1910; several leaves and the cross atop the crown differ. The most noticeable change is in the two leaves at the far right opposite CANADA. On the first variety the leaves have long, pointed corners, whereas they are much shorter on the second.

Victorian leaves
1902–1910

Edwardian leaves
1910

Note 3 leaf tips near rim

DATE	QTY. (000)	G-4	VG-8	F-12	VF-20	EF-40	AU-50	MS-60	MS-63
Victorian Leaves Reverse (1902–1910)									
1902	120	20.00	35.00	65.00	170.00	425.00	750.00	2,000	5,000
1903H	140	20.00	40.00	80.00	250.00	600.00	950.00	2,200	6,000
1904	60	90.00	210.00	400.00	900.00	1,650	3,000	6,000	16,500
1905	40	120.00	250.00	500.00	1,200	2,350	4,500	10,000	—
1906	350	15.00	30.00	50.00	170.00	450.00	900.00	2,000	5,000
1907	300	15.00	30.00	55.00	140.00	440.00	800.00	2,000	5,500
1908	128	25.00	50.00	100.00	300.00	650.00	950.00	1,600	3,000
1909	203	20.00	35.00	100.00	250.00	800.00	1,800	3,500	12,500
1910 (Victorian leaves)	650	20.00	40.00	75.00	200.00	600.00	1,200	2,500	8,000
Edwardian Leaves Reverse (1910)									
1910 (Edwardian leaves)	incl. above	15.00	25.00	45.00	125.00	425.00	750.00	1,750	5,500

George V, 1911–1936

Diameter: 29.72 mm; weight: (1911–1919) 11.62 grams, (1920–1936) 11.66 grams;
composition: (1911–19) .925 silver, .075 copper, (1920–36) .800 silver, .200 copper; edge: reeded

G: *Band of crown worn through*
VG: *Band of crown worn through*
     at highest point
F: *Jewels blurred in band of crown*
VF: *Band of crown clear but*
     no longer sharp
EF: *Band of crown slightly worn; but*
     generally sharp and clear

Two obverse varieties exist. The first (1911) lacks the phrase DEI GRATIA or an abbreviation for it and the second (1912–36) has DEI GRA incorporated into the legend. Both obverses were derived from a portrait model by Sir E.B. MacKennal (B.M. on truncation). See the 1-cent text for more details. The reverse is identical to the Edwardian leaves variety, introduced in the previous series.

1921 During the late teens and early 1920s far more 50-cent pieces were struck than were needed. Many of them remained in the Mint with only about 24,000 pieces being issued in 1921–28. In 1929 a sizable demand for this denomination arose. The Mint, however, fearing the public would doubt the authenticity of new coins bearing "old" dates, melted the 500,000 50-cent pieces in stock and struck new ones with the current date (1929). It seems very likely that most of the original 1921 mintage of 206,398 was included in this melt. Only about 100 of the 1921 issue survive today; most of these are business strikes, but a few specimen strikes (originally issued as part of specimen sets) are known.

"Godless" Obverse (1911)

DATE	QTY. (000)	G-4	VG-8	F-12	VF-20	EF-40	AU-50	MS-60	MS-63
1911	210	15.00	25.00	45.00	125.00	425.00	750.00	2,200	4,500

DATE	QTY. (000)	G-4	VG-8	F-12	VF-20	EF-40	AU-50	MS-60	MS-63
Modified Obverse Legend (1912–1936)									
1912 286		*	20.00	50.00	175.00	400.00	750.00	1,700	4,500
1913 266		*	20.00	50.00	200.00	450.00	900.00	2,000	7,000
1914 160		*	45.00	120.00	350.00	850.00	2,000	4,500	12,000
1916 459		*	15.00	30.00	90.00	225.00	450.00	1,000	3,000
1917 752		*	14.00	27.00	60.00	175.00	350.00	750.00	1,800
1918 855		*	14.00	25.00	45.00	150.00	300.00	650.00	1,500
1919 1,113		*	14.00	25.00	45.00	150.00	275.00	600.00	1,500
1920 585		*	20.00	30.00	65.00	225.00	450.00	900.00	2,200
1921 . . . . (originally 206,328)	25,000	38,000	50,000	55,000	60,000	65,000	75,000	—
1929 228		*	14.00	27.00	60.00	175.00	350.00	750.00	1,700
1931 58		*	30.00	50.00	120.00	350.00	700.00	1,250	2,500
1932 19	100.00	175.00	275.00	550.00	1,200	2,500	5,500	12,000
1934 40		*	35.00	55.00	135.00	350.00	650.00	1,000	2,000
1936 39		*	30.00	50.00	120.00	340.00	525.00	800.00	1,500

George VI, 1937–1952

Diameter: 29.72 mm; weight: 11.66 grams; composition: .800 silver, .200 copper, edge: reeded

VG: No detail in hair above the ear
F: Only slight detail in hair above ear
VF: Where not worn, hair is clear but not sharp
EF: Slight wear in hair over ear

There are two obverses the bare-headed portrait of the King by T.H. Paget (H.P. below). The later variety (1948–52) incorporates the change in the King's titles which ensued when India was granted independence from England. See text on the 1-cent series for details.

In keeping with a Government decision to modernize all reverses, a simplified Canadian coat of arms was chosen for this denomination. The simplification involved omission of the crest, helmet and mantling, motto and floral emblems; in addition, no attempt was made to heraldically colour the shield and banners. The shield consists of the arms of England (three lions), Scotland (rearing lion), royalist France (three fleurs-de-lis) and Ireland (a harp) and is surmounted by a stylized Imperial crown. At the left is the English lion holding a lance with the Union flag; on the right is a Scottish unicorn holding a lance with the flag of royalist France. The whole is resting upon a layer of serried clouds. The initials KG flanking the crown indicate the designer, George Kruger-Gray.

The position of the final digit in the date varies because, during most of the 1940s, it was punched separately into each die. Such varieties are too minor to include in a catalogue of this kind.

DATE	QTY. (000)	VG-8	F-12	VF-20	EF-40	AU-50	MS-60	MS-63
"ET IND : IMP :" Obverse (1937–1947)								
1937	192	*	12.00	17.00	22.00	28.00	45.00	100.00
1938	192	*	17.00	25.00	50.00	95.00	200.00	550.00
1939	288	*	15.00	18.00	35.00	70.00	125.00	350.00
1940	1,997	*	*	*	16.00	22.00	40.00	90.00
1941	1,715	*	*	*	16.00	22.00	40.00	90.00
1942	1,974	*	*	*	16.00	22.00	40.00	90.00
1943	3,110	*	*	*	16.00	22.00	40.00	100.00
1944	2,460	*	*	*	16.00	22.00	40.00	100.00
1945	1,960	*	*	*	16.00	22.00	40.00	100.00

1946 and 1949 "hoof" These items are apparently the products of damaged dies and as such are not true die varieties. (See Introduction for further comments on such items.)

1946 normal 6	950	*	*	16.00	22.00	40.00	85.00	200.00
"hoof" in 6	incl. above	35.00	55.00	80.00	250.00	700.00	2,000	5,500

Tall 7	Short 7	Tall 7	Short 7
Without maple leaf		With maple leaf after date	

1947 maple leaf and 7 varieties The 1947 (no maple leaf) issue comes with two styles of 7 in the date. One is a rather tall figure, the bottom of which points to the left and the other is a shorter 7 with the bottom curving back to the right. Both 7s were also used for the maple leaf issue struck in 1948. See text for the l-cent series.

1947 tall 7	425	*	*	16.00	25.00	50.00	100.00	300.00
1947 short 7	incl. above	*	*	16.00	32.00	75.00	150.00	400.00
1947 maple leaf, tall 7	38	35.00	45.00	60.00	110.00	175.00	300.00	500.00
1947 maple leaf, short 7	incl. above	1,800	2,300	2,600	3,600	4,600	7,000	15,000

Obverse
1948–1952

Modified Obverse Legend (1948–1952)

1948	38	110.00	140.00	170.00	200.00	250.00	350.00	500.00
1949 normal 9	859	*	*	*	16.00	25.00	60.00	150.00
"hoof" over 9	incl. above	25.00	30.00	55.00	110.00	225.00	550.00	1,400

1950 no lines in 0 In 1950, the 50-cent dies were derived from a single, fully dated matrix in which the 0 of the date had 4 horizontal lines in its centre. Depending upon the amount of polishing or repolishing of each individual die, the lines in the 0 ranged from completely present to partially missing to entirely absent. Previous cataloguers have chosen to list as a separate entry those pieces that lack the lines. For further comments see Introduction.

DATE	QTY. (000)	VG-8	F-12	VF-20	EF-40	AU-50	MS-60	MS-63
1950 lines in 0 2,384		*	*	*	15.00	17.00	20.00	50.00
1950 no lines in 0 .... incl. above		17.00	20.00	25.00	50.00	100.00	210.00	350.00
1951 2,422		*	*	*	*	15.00	17.00	35.00
1952 2,596		*	*	*	*	15.00	17.00	25.00

Elizabeth II, Laureate, 1953–1964

Diameter: 29.72 mm; weight: 11.66 grams; composition: .800 silver, .200 copper; edge: reeded

VF: *Leaves considerably worn, shoulder fold must show*

EF: *Laurel leaves on head somewhat worn*

AU: *Trace of wear on laurel leaves*

The initial obverse for the 1953 issue had a high relief portrait by Mary Gillick (M.G. on truncation) which did not strike up well on the coins. Later in the year the relief was lowered and the hair and shoulder detail re-engraved. On the second variety two lines at the shoulder, representing a fold in the Queen's gown, are clear, while on the first variety they are almost missing. The obverses also differ in the shape of some letters and in positioning of the legend relative to the rim denticles. See the 1-cent series for more details.

The first reverse for the 1953 issue, used only on the high relief "no shoulder fold" obverse, is identical to that used for the 1950–52 George VI coinages, both in the device and the style and size of the date. Later in the year a new reverse with a larger date and with design elements positioned closer to the rim denticles was introduced. The second reverse is associated with both the high and low relief obverses, the former combination being a mule.

To reduce the "ghosting" that had been so common in the past, a third modification was introduced in 1955. It is characterized by smaller design elements.

No shoulder fold, 1953   Small date, 1953

DATE	QTY. (000)	F-12	VF-20	EF-40	AU-50	MS-60	MS-63
Small Date Reverse (1953)							
1953 no shoulder fold 1,630		*	*	*	15.00	16.00	25.00

*Common silver coins (marked with *) are worth a premium only for their silver content. This price may vary according to prevailing market value of silver bullion.

With shoulder fold, 1953–1964   Large date, 1953–1964

DATE	QTY. (000)	F-12	VF-20	EF-40	AU-50	MS-60	MS-63
Large Date Reverse (1953–1954)							
1953 no shoulder fold . . . . incl. above		*	15.00	22.00	50.00	100.00	250.00
with shoulder fold . . . . incl. above		*	*	15.00	17.00	30.00	60.00
1954 506		*	*	17.00	22.00	35.00	60.00

Modified Reverse, 1955–1958

Smaller Coat of Arms (1955–1958)							
1955 754		*	*	15.00	17.00	20.00	35.00
1956 1,379		*	*	*	*	15.00	22.00
1957 2,172		*	*	*	*	14.00	18.00
1958 2,957		*	*	*	*	14.00	16.00

Complete Coat of Arms, 1959–1966

The obverse for the 1959–64 issues continued to be the shoulder fold variety.

In 1957 the Canadian coat of arms, as described by the Royal proclamation of 21 November, 1921, was approved for all government purposes (except for the replacement of the Imperial crown with the St. Edward's crown). The complete coat of arms was modelled and engraved for this denomination by Thomas Shingles (TS flanking lower part of the shield). As far as was practical, heraldic colouring of the arms and flags was attempted: blue being represented by horizontal lines, while white or silver was left unshaded. On the 1959 issue, the background of the lower section of the shield (the Canadian emblem) was coloured blue, instead of the correct white or silver. The lines were removed beginning with the 1960 issue and no further changes were made in the reverse until 1967.

Horizontal lines in lower shield, 1959 (Blue)			No lines in lower shield, 1960–1966 (White)	

DATE	MILLIONS MINTED	EF-40	AU-50	MS-60	MS-63
"Blue" Lower Panel Reverse (1959)					
1959 3		*	*	*	15.00
"White" Lower Panel Reverse (1960–1966)					
1960 3		*	*	*	15.00
1961 4		*	*	*	15.00
1962 5		*	*	*	15.00
1963 8		*	*	*	15.00
1964 9		*	*	*	15.00

Elizabeth II, Tiara, 1965–1966

In 1965 an obverse with a new style portrait by Arnold Machin was introduced. The Queen has more mature facial features and is wearing a tiara.

The reverse and physical specifications continued as previously.

DATE	MILLIONS MINTED	AU-50	MS-60	MS-63
1965 13		*	*	15.00
1966 8		*	*	15.00

Confederation Centennial, 1967

All denominations for 1967 bore special reverses to commemorate the 1867 confederation of Nova Scotia, New Brunswick and the Province of Canada, to form the Dominion of Canada. The design, by Alex Colville, shows a howling wolf.

1967 Confederation commemorative . .	4	*	*	15.00

Common silver coins (marked with *) are worth a premium only for their silver content. This price may vary according to prevailing market value of silver bullion.

50 CENTS, NICKEL
Elizabeth II, Tiara, 1968–1989

Diameter: 27.13 mm; weight 8.10 grams; thickness: (1968–1979) 1.93 mm, (1980 –) 2.00 mm;
composition: .99 nickel (min.); edge: reeded

With the resumption of the regular reverse design in 1968, two significant changes were made.
The diameter and weight were reduced, and the composition was changed to nickel.

DATE	MILLIONS MINTED	MS-63
1968	4	1.50
1969	7	1.50
1970	2	1.50
1971	2	1.50
1972	3	1.50
1973	3	1.50
1974	3	1.50
1975	4	1.50
1976	3	1.50

Modified Obverse and Reverse (1977)

DATE	QTY. (000)	MS-63
1977	710	3.00

Modified Obverse (1978–1989) and Reverse (1978–1996)

Square beads Round beads

1978 square beads in crown	2,960	2.00
1978 round beads in crown	included above	108.00
1979	3,425	2.00
1980	1,574	2.00

DATE	QTY. (000)	MS-63
1981	2,131	2.00
1982	2,237	2.00
1983	1,177	2.00
1984	1,503	2.00
1985	2,188	2.00
1986	781	2.00
1987	373	2.50
1988	220	4.00
1989	266	2.00

Elizabeth II, Crowned, 1990–2002

The first effigy designed by a Canadian for use on Canadian coins was introduced on the obverse of all Canadian issues for 1990. The design depicts a more contemporary portrait of the Queen wearing a necklace and earrings. The elaborate crown, last seen on Victorian issues, replaced the tiara used on previous issues. The obverse was designed by Dora de Pédery-Hunt.

DATE	QTY. (000)	MS-63
1990	207	5.00
1991	490	2.00

125th Anniversary of Confederation, 1992

To celebrate the 125th anniversary of Confederation, all circulation coins issued in 1992 bear the date "1867–1992."

DATE	QTY. (000)	MS-63
1992 (1867–1992)	248	5.00
1993	393	2.00
1994	987	2.00
1995	626	2.00
1996	458	2.00

Modified Reverse, 1997

DATE	QTY. (000)	MS-63
1997	387	2.00
1998	308	2.00
1999	496	2.00
2000	573	2.00

Nickel-plated Steel, 2000–

Diameter: 27.13 mm; weight: 6.9 grams; composition: nickel-plated steel; edge: reeded

The new plating facility of the Royal Canadian Mint, in Winnipeg went into full production of nickel-plated steel blanks for all Canadian 5-, 10-, 25- and 50-cent coins in 2001. These blanks can be struck at either Ottawa or Winnipeg. The coins produced from the blanks bear a "P" mint mark on the observe, below the effigy of the queen. The RCM's corporate mark (M) was phased in during 2006 replacing the "P" material mark.

DATE	QTY. (000)	MS-60	MS-63
1999P	. . . . .N/A		10.00
2000P	. . . . .N/A	3,500	4,500
2001P	389		2.00

Elizabeth II, Golden Jubilee (1952–2002)

This Golden Jubilee 50¢ coin bears the same obverse as was used on the 1953 Coronation Medallion. The reverse features the coat of arms with the double date "1952–2002".

2002P (1952–2002). 14.4			2.00

The mint did not issue circulation 50-cent pieces during 2003 or 2004.
These were only available in the collectors' sets.

Elizabeth II, Bearheaded, 2005–

Corporate mark (M)

2005P	 200		3.00
2006P	 98		4.00
2006L	. . . . Included above		4.00
2007	 250		4.00
2008	 211		3.00
2009	 150		3.00
2010	 150		3.00
2011	 175		3.00
2012	 250		3.00
2013	 375		3.00
2014	 500		3.00
2015	. . . . .N/A		3.00

Since 2007, 50 cent pieces have only been issued as "special wrap" collectors' rolls of 25 pieces or in collectors' sets.

1 DOLLAR SILVER
George V, Silver Jubilee, 1935

Diameter: 36.06 mm; weight: 23.3 grams; thickness: 2.84 mm;
composition: .800 silver, .200 copper; edge: reeded

F:	Jewels in band of crown will be blurred
V.F.:	Band of crown still clear but no longer sharp
EF:	Band of crown slightly worn but generally sharp and clear
AU:	Trace of wear in band of crown

The first Canadian dollar issued for circulation had a special obverse to mark the 25th anniversary of the accession of George V. The portrait was from a model by Percy Metcalfe, used previously for the obverses of certain Australian and New Zealand coinages of 1933–35. The Latin legend is translated: "George V, King, Emperor; Regnal year 25."

The reverse device consists of a canoe manned by an Indian and a voyageur (travelling agent of a fur company), behind which is an islet with two trees. In the sky are lines representing the northern lights. On the front bundle in the canoe are the incuse initials HB; these signify Hudsons' Bay Co., which played an important role in Canadas' early history. The designer was Emanuel Hahn (EH at left under canoe).

DATE	QTY. (000)	F-12	VF-20	EF-40	AU-50	MS-60	MS-63	MS-64	MS-65
1935	429	25.00	33.00	38.00	42.00	47.00	75.00	125.00	350.00

George V, 1936

The obverse for 1936 had the regular design for George V, first seen on the 1-cent through 50-cent business strikes in 1912. The designer was Sir E.B. MacKennal (B.M. on truncation). The master matrix from which the 1936 obverse dies were prepared was that made in 1911 for the dollar proposed at that time.

The reverse, physical specifications and grading are as for the 1935 issue.

DATE	QTY. (000)	F-12	VF-20	EF-40	AU-50	MS-60	MS-63	MS-64	MS-65
1936	306	28.00	32.00	36.00	40.00	60.00	120.00	225.00	850.00

George VI, 1937–1952

Diameter: 36.06 mm; weight: 23.3 grams; thickness: 2.84 mm;
composition: .800 silver, .200 copper; edge: reeded

F: Only slight detail in hair above ear
VF: Where not worn, hair is clear but not sharp
EF: Slight wear in hair over ear
AU: Trace of wear in hair

The obverse has the conventional bare-headed portrait of the King by T.H. Paget (H.P. under rear of neck), as used for the lower denominations.

The reverse remains unchanged from the George V issues.

DATE	QTY. (000)	F-12	VF-20	EF-40	AU-50	MS-60	MS-63	MS-64	MS-65
1937 241		28.00	32.00	36.00	40.00	50.00	100.00	275.00	
1938 90		40.00	55.00	75.00	90.00	120.00	300.00	750.00	5,000

Royal Visit Commemorative, 1939

In 1939 a special reverse was used on the dollar to mark the visit of George VI and Queen Elizabeth to Canada. The design shows the centre block of the Parliament buildings in Ottawa. Above is the Latin phrase Fide Suorum Regnat, meaning "he reigns by the faith of his people." The designer was Emanuel Hahn; his initials EH flanked the building on the original model, but were removed by government decision prior to the manufacture of the dies. Because of lack of demand, about 150,000 specimens were returned to the Mint and melted in 1940.

The obverse design and physical specifications are as for the 1937–38 issues.

DATE	QTY. (000)	F-12	VF-20	EF-40	AU-50	MS-60	MS-63	MS-64	MS-65
1939 1,364		*	*	18.00	22.00	28.00	40.00	100.00	600.00

Voyageurs Resumed, 1945–1948

During 1945–48 two major obverse varieties appeared on this and all lower denominations. The first has the usual legend containing ET IND : IMP : ("and Emperor of India") and the second has this phrase deleted. (See text on the 1-cent for more details).

| Pointed 7 | Blunt 7 | Maple leaf (blunt 7 only) |

1947 varieties The 1947 issue of the dollar has two styles of 7 in the date, which differ mainly in the lower tip of the 7. The 1947 maple leaf coins of 1948 have only one of these 7s. See the 1-cent text for details.

DATE	QTY. (000)	F-12	VF-20	EF-40	AU-50	MS-60	MS-63	MS-64	MS-65
"ET IND : IMP :" Obverse (1945–1947)									
1945 38		145.00	200.00	275.00	325.00	400.00	900.00	2,000	15,000
1946 93		32.00	45.00	65.00	85.00	125.00	450.00	1,500	10,000
1947 pointed 7 66		100.00	150.00	200.00	275.00	450.00	2,500	6,500	
1947 blunt 7 . . . . included above		75.00	110.00	150.00	175.00	200.00	500.00	1,250	8,000
1947 maple leaf 21		165.00	225.00	300.00	350.00	450.00	1,000	2,000	8,000

Modified Obverse Legend, 1948–1952

DATE	QTY. (000)	F-12	VF-20	EF-40	AU-50	MS-60	MS-63	MS-64	MS-65
1948 19		900.00	1,150	1,350	1,500	1,800	3,200	5,500	17,500

Newfoundland, 1949

On December 31, 1949, Newfoundland became a province of the Dominion of Canada. To mark this event a special reverse appeared on the dollar for that year. The Matthew, the ship in which John Cabot is thought to have discovered Newfoundland, is depicted. Below is the Latin phrase FLOREAT TERRA NOVA. "May the new found land flourish." Thomas Shingles was the designer and engraver, engraving the master matrix entirely by hand. (T.S. above horizon at right) The obverse is as the 1948 issue, and the physical specifications remain unchanged.

DATE	QTY. (000)	F-12	VF-20	EF-40	AU-50	MS-60	MS-63	MS-64	MS-65
1949 672		15.00	22.00	26.00	30.00	33.00	40.00	50.00	100.00

Voyageurs Resumed, 1950–1952

The obverse for the final George VI Voyageurs is as on the 1948–49 issues. There are two note-worthy reverse varieties. The first is the usual "water lines" variety, used for all Voyageurs prior to 1950. The second is the so-called "no water lines" reverse of 1952. On this interesting variety the water lines on both sides of the canoe have been removed and the right-hand tip of the islet re-engraved so that it is both wider and longer than before. There can be no question that the "no water lines" was a deliberate issue; furthermore, unlike the "Arnpriors", it was created by the alteration of a matrix — not simply an individual die or dies. For some reason the modification was apparently not acceptable because it was used only during the one year.

"Arnprior" dollars of 1950 and 1955. In 1955 a firm in Arnprior, Ontario ordered and received 2,000 silver dollars for use as Christmas bonuses. It was later discovered that these coins had only 1½ water lines (instead of the normal 3) to the right of the canoe. This difference became popular and was collected separately from the "normal" counterpart. Further study revealed that some dollars of 1950, 1951 and perhaps 1952–53 have a similar water line configuration. Only the 1950 and 1955s are currently included in the major listings. These items are the result of inadvertent overpolishing of individual dies and as such are not true die varieties. In fact, for 1950, 1955 and certain other years there is a whole gamut of water line differences, ranging from 3 full lines to parts of all 3 to 1½. Collectors and cataloguers have tended to deem all partial water lines greater than 1½ as normal. Whether items like this have any place in a more general catalogue is very questionable; they are included here only because of their current popularity. For further comments on such issues, see — Introduction. Physical specifications are as for the previous issues.

3 water lines, small islet tip (1935–1952)	1½ water lines 1950	No water lines 1952

DATE	QTY. (000)	F-12	VF-20	EF-40	AU-50	MS-60	MS-63	MS-64	MS-65
"Water Lines" Reverse (1950–1952)									
1950 normal water lines	261	*	22.00	28.00	31.00	35.00	70.00	120.00	300.00
1½ lines "Arnprior" incl. above		28.00	35.00	42.00	45.00	60.00	150.00	400.00	2,500
1951 normal water lines	416	*	*	20.00	25.00	29.00	45.00	100.00	750.00
1½ lines "Arnprior" incl. above		45.00	65.00	100.00	150.00	250.00	500.00	1,100	7,500
1952	406	*	*	15.00	27.00	29.00	40.00	80.00	550.00
"No Water Lines" Reverse (1952)									
1952	incl. above	*	20.00	27.00	28.00	32.00	65.00	150.00	1,000

Elizabeth II, Laureate, 1953–1964

Diameter: 36.06 mm; weight: 23:3 grams; thickness: 2.84 mm
composition: .800 silver, .200 copper; edge: reeded

VF: Leaves considerably worn,
      shoulder fold must show
EF: Laurel leaves on head
      somewhat worn
AU: Trace of wear on laurel leaves

The first obverse for 1953 had a high relief, laureate portrait of the Queen by Mary Gillick (M.G. on truncation) which did not strike up well on the coins. Later in the year the rim width and coin diameter were increased, the relief lowered, and the hair and shoulder detail re-engraved. The re-engraving included sharpening two lines representing a fold in the Queen's gown. The two varieties also differ in the positioning of the legend relative to the rim denticles and the styles of some letters.

The reverse used with the 1953 "no shoulder fold" obverse was the "water lines" George VI variety. This has a very narrow rim and the triangular islet tip, extending to the canoe's right, ends about half way to the rim denticles. Together with the obverse change came a slightly modified reverse, the most distinctive features of which are a wider rim and a right-hand islet tip extending almost to the rim denticles.

1955 Arnprior See previous series.

1957, 1 water line This item had the same cause as the "Arnpriors" (see previous series) and is therefore not a true die variety.

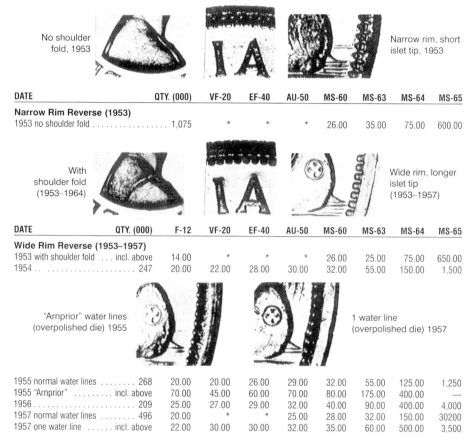

No shoulder fold, 1953

Narrow rim, short islet tip, 1953

DATE	QTY. (000)	VF-20	EF-40	AU-50	MS-60	MS-63	MS-64	MS-65
Narrow Rim Reverse (1953)								
1953 no shoulder fold	1,075	*	*	*	26.00	35.00	75.00	600.00

With shoulder fold (1953–1964)

Wide rim, longer islet tip (1953–1957)

DATE	QTY. (000)	F-12	VF-20	EF-40	AU-50	MS-60	MS-63	MS-64	MS-65
Wide Rim Reverse (1953–1957)									
1953 with shoulder fold . . . incl. above		14.00	*	*	*	26.00	25.00	75.00	650.00
1954	247	20.00	22.00	28.00	30.00	32.00	55.00	150.00	1,500

"Arnprior" water lines (overpolished die) 1955

1 water line (overpolished die) 1957

	QTY. (000)	F-12	VF-20	EF-40	AU-50	MS-60	MS-63	MS-64	MS-65
1955 normal water lines	268	20.00	20.00	26.00	29.00	32.00	55.00	125.00	1,250
1955 "Arnprior" . . . . incl. above		70.00	45.00	60.00	70.00	80.00	175.00	400.00	—
1956	209	25.00	27.00	29.00	32.00	40.00	90.00	400.00	4,000
1957 normal water lines	496	20.00	*	*	25.00	28.00	32.00	150.00	30200
1957 one water line . . . . . . incl. above		22.00	30.00	30.00	32.00	35.00	60.00	500.00	3,500

British Columbia, 1958

To commemorate the gold rush centenary and the establishment of British Columbia as an English Crown colony, a special reverse by Stephen Trenka was employed. (ST at right bottom of totem) British Columbia is the only area in Canada where the Indians constructed totem poles, so the design is very appropriate. It was rumored that this issue was unpopular with the coastal Indians because it contained an element which to them signified death.

The physical specifications for the coin remained unchanged.

DATE	MILLIONS MINTED	VF-20	EF-40	AU-50	MS-60	MS-63	MS-64	MS-65
1958 3		*	20.00	24.00	28.00	32.00	75.00	500.00

Voyageurs Resumed, 1959–1963

There are two major varieties of the Voyageur reverse during this period. The first is the wide rim design, introduced in late 1953. The second has re-engraved water lines and northern lights.

Reverse of 1953–1957 (1959)

1959 1		*	*	18.00	23.00	29.00	125.00	2,200

Recut Water Lines and Northern Lights (1960–1963)

1960 1		*	*	*	20.00	27.00	100.00	1,200
1961 1		*	*	*	*	27.00	125.00	2,000
1962 2		*	*	*	20.00	27.00	80.00	1,000
1963 4		*	*	*	*	27.00	100.00	1,500

Pre-Confederation Meetings, 1964

To mark the 100th anniversary of the meetings at Charlottetown, Prince Edward Island and Qué-bec, Quebec which paved the way for Confederation, a special reverse was used for the 1964 dollar coin. The device is a circle within which are the conjoined French fleur-de-lis, Irish shamrock, Scottish thistle and English rose. The model was prepared by Thomas Shingles (chief engraver at the Royal Canadian Mint) from a sketch by designer Dinko Vodanovic. The initials of both men (D.V. and T.S.) appear along the inner circle.

The effigy on the obverse of this issue was re-engraved by Myron Cook, modifying Thomas Shingles' alteration of the original Gillick design. The revised features consist mostly of sharpened gown details.

DATE	MILLIONS MINTED	EF-40	AU-50	MS-60	MS-63	MS-64	MS-65
1964 7		*	*	*	27.00	100.00	1,500

Elizabeth II, Tiara, 1965–1989

In 1965 a new obverse portrait by Arnold Machin was introduced. The Queen has more mature features and is depicted wearing a tiara. Three obverse varieties exist for 1965. The first has a flat field and small rim beads, and was replaced because of unacceptably short die life. The second variety has a slightly concave field, medium sized rim beads and slight changes in the portrait. Most distinctive is a very thin support to the rear most jewel on the tiara. This variety was struck from a single "test die", made to determine whether a concave field would give better die life. The experiment was successful and a new matrix, punches and dies were prepared. Coins from these dies have the concave field and rim beads even larger than on the "test" variety. In addition, the medium and large beads varieties differ in the positioning of the legend relative to the rim beads.

The 1965–66 reverse is similar but not identical to the earlier Voyageurs. Physical specifications remain unchanged.

1965 date and combinational varieties Coupled with the small and large beads obverses were

Small beads   Medium beads   Large beads
Details of NA in REGINA; note bead size and position relative to apex of A

| Pointed
5 | Blunt
5 | Small and large
bead obverses | Medium bead
obverse |

Detail of rear jewel in tiara

two reverses, having trivially different 5s in the dates. The medium beads obverse is coupled with only one of the 5s.

DATE		MILLIONS MINTED	EF-40	AU-50	MS-60	MS-63	MS-64	MS-65
1965	small beads, pointed 5 . . . . Variety 1	11	*	*	*	29.00	60.00	850.00
	small beads, blunt 5 . . . . Variety 2 incl. above		*	*	*	29.00	125.00	1,600
	large beads, blunt 5 . . . . Variety 3 incl. above		*	*	*	29.00	60.00	750.00
	large beads, pointed 5 . . . . Variety 4 incl. above		*	*	28.00	35.00	80.00	750.00
	med. beads, pointed 5 . . . . Variety 5 incl. above		25.00	28.00	32.00	50.00	200.00	2,000
1966	large beads obverse	10	*	*	*	29.00	60.00	650.00
1966	small beads obverse . . . . incl. above			3,200	3,600	4,500	5,500	

Confederation Centennial, 1967

All denominations of 1967 coins bore Confederation commemorative reverses designed by Alex Colville. During 1966, trial production runs were made with dies of the new designs. Those for the dollar had flat fields and the coins did not strike up well, so new dies with convex fields (giving concave or dished fields to the coins) were prepared. Almost all of the flat field dollars were apparently melted. Apart from the fields, the initial designs can be distinguished from the adopted ones by the positioning of the legends relative to the rim beads.

Flat fields   Concave fields

Note size and spacing of beads

DATE	MILLIONS MINTED	AU-50	MS-60	MS-63	MS-64	MS-65
1967 flat fields* 7**						Rare
concave fields . . . . incl. above		*	20.00	26.00	50.00	450.00

*Rarity not yet known.
**Originally 6,909,237, but 141,741 pieces were re-coined in 1967.

1 DOLLAR, NICKEL
Elizabeth II, 1968–1986

Diameter: 32.13 mm; weight: 15.62 grams; thickness: (1968–82) 2.62 mm, (1983–86) 2.55mm;
composition: .99 nickel; edge: reeded

With the decision to eliminate silver from all circulating coins in 1968, the circulating dollar was reduced in size to achieve better striking on the hard nickel blanks. The obverse bearing Machin's effigy of the Queen was used throughout this series, with Hahn's voyageur reverse appearing on all issues except special commemoratives.

Voyageurs Resumed, 1968–1976

| Typical obverse
1968–1971 | Voyageur reverse
1968, 1969, 1972, 1975, 1976 | Typical obverse
1972–1976 |

DATE	MILLIONS MINTED	MS-63
1968	 6	3.00
1969	 5	3.00

Manitoba, 1970

The reverse device, depicting the prairie crocus, celebrates the centennial of Manitoba's entry into Confederation and was designed was by Raymond Taylor (RT to the right of the centre stem). The obverse was the same as for 1968–69.

British Columbia, 1971

The circulating dollar for 1971 uses a reverse designed by Thomas Shingles (TS below shield), incorporating both the B.C. provincial arms and the flowering dogwood, official flower of British Columbia. The obverse remained the same as for the previous issues.

1970 Manitoba 4		4.00
1971 British Columbia 4		4.00
1972 Voyageur 2		4.00

> In 1971 the mint began issuing collectors' dollars struck in .500 silver. These are not considered circulating coinage and are sold by the mint at a premium over the face value. All .500 silver dollars from 1971 to the present are listed in the section titled Collectors' Issues.

Prince Edward Island, 1973

The obverse of the 1973 circulating dollar features Patrick Brindley's modification of the Machin effigy of Queen Elizabeth II (as used on the collectors' silver dollar in 1971). The reverse design depicts the PEI Provincial Legislature building and was modelled by Walter Ott (WO at right) from a sketch by Terry Manning (TM at left).

Winnipeg, 1974

The reverse design, modelled by Patrick Brindley (B at top) from a sketch by Paul Pederson (PP at bottom), features a large "100" with Winnipeg's main street as it appeared in 1874 depicted in the first "0" and the 1974 equivalent in the second "0".

The same centennial design was used for the 1974 collectors' silver dollar.

DATE	MILLIONS MINTED	MS-63
1973 Prince Edward Island	3	4.00
1974 Winnipeg (nickel)	3	5.00
1975 Voyageur	3	4.00
1976 Voyageur	2	10.00

Modified Voyageurs Reverse, 1977

In 1977 Emanuel Hahn's voyageur reverse was altered. The device was made smaller and the legend reduced in size and placed farther from the rim of the coin. The rim denticles were replaced by beads.

DATE	MILLIONS MINTED	MS-63
1977	1	9.00

Modified Obverse and Reverse, 1978–1986

In 1978 both sides of the circulating dollar were modified to appear more like the issues prior to 1977. The unmodified Machin portrait was restored to the obverse and the reverse returned to the pre-1977 voyageur design with rim denticles restored.

DATE	MILLIONS MINTED	MS-63
1978	3	4.00
1979	3	4.00
1980	3	5.00
1981	2	5.00

Constitution, 1982

The first year in which two circulating nickel dollars were issued was 1982: a voyageur dollar and the commemorative Constitution dollar. The obverse of the latter bears a reduced version of the Machin design, with the 1982 date incorporated into the legend. The reverse features the well known painting of the Fathers of Confederation. This dollar was also issued encapsulated and cased, in select uncirculated condition, for collectors.

1982 Constitution commemorative	12	3.00
1982 Voyageur	1	5.00
1983 Voyageur	2	5.00

Jacques Cartier, 1984

Issued to commemorate Cartier's landing at Gaspé in 1534, this dollar bears the same obverse as the 1982 commemorative dollar with the date changed. The reverse design is by Hector Greville. An encapsulated, cased collectors' version of this dollar was also issued in proof quality only.

1984 Jacques Cartier commemorative	6	4.00
1984 Voyageur	1	5.00
1985 Voyageur	3	5.00
1986 Voyageur	3	5.00

Aureate Bronze, Loon, 1987–

Diameter: 26.72 mm (11-sided); weight: 7.0 grams; thickness: 1.95 mm;
composition: aureate bronze plated on pure nickel; edge: plain

To overcome the high production cost of the dollar note, a new circulating dollar coin was introduced in 1987. Significantly smaller than previous dollar and 50-cent coins which did not circulate well because of their large size and weight, the new circulating dollar is only slightly larger than the 25-cent piece. To simplify identification of the new coin by the visually handicapped and by machine, its shape was changed from round to 11-sided, and the colour changed from white nickel to yellow gold.

The obverse bears the Arnold Machin effigy of Queen Elizabeth II, while the reverse device, designed by Robert Carmichael, depicts a Canadian Loon.

Although the loon dollar was the only circulation dollar issued during 1987, the familiar Voyageur nickel dollar was used in lieu of the loon in all three numismatic sets issued in 1987. The loon dollar was also issued singly in proof quality in 1987.

The one dollar note was not issued after July 1st, 1988.

DATE	MILLIONS MINTED	MS-63
1987 Loon	199	4.00
1988 Loon	139	4.00
1989 Loon	185	6.00

Elizabeth II, Crowned, 1990–2003

The first effigy designed by a Canadian for use on Canadian coins was introduced on the obverse of all Canadian issues for 1990. The design depicts a more contemporary portrait of the Queen wearing a necklace and earrings. The elaborate crown, last seen on Victorian issues, replaced the tiara used on previous issues. The obverse was designed by Dora de Pédery-Hunt.

DATE	MILLIONS MINTED	MS-63
1990 Loon	68	4.00
1991 Loon	23	4.00

125th Anniversary of Confederation, 1992

A commemorative aureate dollar coin was released on July 1 to celebrate the 125th anniversary of Confederation. The reverse, designed by Rita Swanson of Churchbridge, Saskatchewan, depicts three children with a Canadian flag, seated before the centre block of the Parliament Buildings. The obverse bears the dates 1867–1992 below the Dora de Pédery-Hunt effigy of the queen. The commemorative aureate dollar was also struck in proof finish and sold as part of the "CANADA 125" proof set. For more information see – *Canadian Collectors' Issues*.

DATE	MILLIONS MINTED	MS-63
1992 125th anniversary of Confederation	23	4.00

Loon Resumed, 1992

DATE	MILLIONS MINTED	MS-63
1992 Loon (dated 1867–1992)	4	4.00
1993 Loon	34	4.00
1994 Loon	40	4.00

National War Memorial, 1994

A remembrance aureate dollar was issued in 1994. The National War Memorial in Ottawa is depicted on the reverse. A proof version of this dollar was also struck and sold singly and as part of the Special Edition 1994 Proof Set. (See Chapter 3—*Canadian Collectors' Issues*.)

DATE	MILLIONS MINTED	MS-63
1994 National War Memorial	15	4.00

Peacekeeping Monument, 1995

A portion of the Peacekeeping Monument, The Reconciliation, is featured on a circulating dollar commemorating the 50th anniversary of the United Nations and honours the Canadian men and women who have served as United Nations peacekeepers. A proof version of this dollar was also sold singly. (See Chapter 3—*Canadian Collectors' Issues*.)

DATE	MILLIONS MINTED	MS-63
1995 Loon	42	4.00
1995 Peacekeeping Monument	included above	4.00
1996 Loon	17	4.00

The mint did not issue one dollar circulation coinage 1997–2001.
The loon dollars for these years can be found in Uncirculated Sets.

Elizabeth II, Golden Jubilee (1952–2002)

To celebrate the 50th anniversary of the reign of Queen Elizabeth II, all circulation coins issued in 2002 bear the double date "1952-2002" on the obverse.

DATE	MILLIONS	MS-63
2002 .. Loon (1952–2002)	2.3	4.00

Elizabeth II, Diadem Obverse, 2003

DATE	MILLIONS MINTED	MS-63
2003 Loon	5	4.00

Elizabeth II, Bareheaded, 2003–

The new uncrowned effigy of Queen Elizabeth II, designed by Susanna Blunt, was introduced on Canada's coins in 2003 in celebration of the jubilee year of her reign.

DATE	MILLIONS MINTED	MS-63
2003 Loon	Incl.	4.00
2004 Loon	3.4	4.00
2005 Loon	32	4.00

Lucky Loonie, 2004

The Lucky Loonie was issued to support Canada's Olympic Athletes through the Go Canada Go Program. The reverse was designed by R. R. Carmichael.

DATE	MILLIONS MINTED	MS-63
2004 Lucky Loonie	6.5	4.00
2004 Royal Canadian Mint (Mint roll of 25)	incl. above	35.00
2004 Special Edition (housed in a folder, Retail Price $14.95)	34 thousand	15.00

Terry Fox, 2005

Composition: bronze on nickel; diameter: 26.50 mm (11-sided)
weight: 7 grams; edge: plain; finish: circulation

Celebrating the 25th anniversary of the first Marathon of Hope, when Terry Fox attempted to walk across Canada and gather funds to help eliminate cancer. The Marathon of Hope has spread far beyond Canada and thousands of people now walk for cancer relief each year in the name of Terry Fox. Terry Fox is the first Canadian hero featured on a circulation Canadian coin. The reverse design is by Stan Witten.

DATE		MILLIONS MINTED	MS-63
2005	Terry Fox	13	3.00
2005	Fox Mint Roll (Mint roll of 25)	incl. above	35.00
2005	Royal Canadian Mint (Mint roll of 25)	incl. above	35.00
2005	First Strike (Retail Price $14.95)	20,000 pieces	15.00

Lucky Loonie 2006, 2008 & 2010

These coins will serve as a good luck charms for Canadian athletes competing at the Olympic and Paralympic Winter Games.

DATE		MILLIONS MINTED	MS-63
2006	Flying Loon - Design by RCM Engravers	8	2.50
2008	Olympic Loon - Design by Jean-Luc Grodin	11	2.50
2010	Olympic Logo - Design by RCM Engravers	10	3.00

Elizabeth II, Bareheaded, 2006–

RCM's corporate mark (M)

DATE		MILLIONS MINTED	MS-63
2006	Loon	37	2.50
2006L	Loon	Included Above	2.50
2007	Loon	38	2.50
2008	Loon	19	2.50

Montreal Canadiens (1909–2009)

Issued to celebrate the centennial of the Montreal Canadiens hockey team. Founded on December 4, 1909, eight years prior to the formation of the NHL, the Montreal Canadiens are the oldest and most successful franchise in professional hockey history.

DATE	MILLIONS MINTED	MS-63
2009	Montreal Canadiens Centennial. 10	2.50
2009	Loon 29	2.50

Canadian Navy (1910–2010)

This coin celebrates the Canadian Navy's first century at sea. Designed by Bonnie Ross.

Saskatchewan Roughriders (1910–2010)

Issued to celebrate a century of the Saskatchewan Roughrider CFL Football team. These custom designed $1 coins were circulated all across Canada. Designed by the RCM Engravers.

Parks Canada 1911 - 2011

This coin celebrates Canada Parks 100th Anniversary. This coin features stylized land, air , flora and fauna with a silhouette of a hiker. Designed by Nolin BBDO Montreal.

DATE	MILLIONS MINTED	MS-63
2010	Loon 4	2.50
2010	Canadian Navy Centennial 7	2.50
2010	Saskatchewan Roughriders Centennial 3.1	2.50
2011	Loon 20	2.50
2011	Parks Canada Centennial 5	3.00

ONE DOLLAR — BRONZE PLATED STEEL, 2012

diameter: 26.50 mm; composition: bronze plated steel;
weight: 6.27 grams; edge: plain 11 sided.

In April 2012, the RCM announced that a new generation of one-dollar and two-dollar circulation coins, which incorporate advanced security features and are manufactured with the Mint's patented multi-ply plated steel technology, would begin circulating. More cost-effective than their predecessors and unprecedented in their security, this new coin retains the familiar "Common Loon" designs and physical appearance. The new coin is slightly lighter in weight.

DATE	MILLIONS MINTED	MS-63
2012 Loon	N/A	2.50

Grey Cup, 2012

One hundredth playing of the Canadian Football League's *The Grey Cup*.

DATE	MILLIONS MINTED	MS-63
2012 Grey Cup	5	3.00

Lucky Loonie, 2012–2014

DATE	MILLIONS MINTED	MS-63
2012 Lucky Loonie	5	3.00
2012 Loon, micro-laser security mark	107	3.00
2013 Loon	120	3.00
2014 Loon	26	3.00
2015 Lucky Loonie	N/A	

BIMETALLIC 2 DOLLARS

Diameter: 28.0 mm; weight: 7.3 grams; thickness: 1.80 mm; interrupted serration;
composition (outer ring): nickel, (centre): aluminum bronze,
.92 copper, .06 aluminum, .02 nickel; (diameter: 16.8 mm)

The first two dollar circulation coin was issued on February 19, 1996 to replace the two dollar note which ceased production on February 16, 1996. The bimetallic coin has an aluminum-bronze centre featuring a polar bear on an early summer ice floe. The gold-coloured centre is set within a nickel outer ring. The reverse was designed by Campbellford, Ontario artist Brent Townsend. The obverse features the Dora de Pédery-Hunt effigy of the queen.

Nunavut, 1999

Canada's first commemorative circulating two dollar coin was released in 1999 to celebrate the end of the second millennium. The reverse was designed by Inuit artist Germaine Arnaktauyok and depicts an Inuit performing the historic Drum Dance. The coin also celebrates the creation of Nunavut, Canada's newest territory.

The Nunavut coin was included in the 1999 Uncirculated and Specimen sets. The coin was also available singly in proof (cased) in .925 silver and also in 22 karat gold.

Path of Knowledge, 2000

Celebrating the end of the second millennium and looking forward to the beginning of a new era of knowledge, the two dollar coin for the year 2000 displays a mother polar bear and her two cubs on an early spring ice floe. The reverse, designed by Tony Bianco, suggests the importance of knowledge passed from generation to generation.

Elizabeth II, Golden Jubilee (1952–2002)

To celebrate the 50th anniversary of the reign of Queen Elizabeth II, all circulation coins issued in 2002 bear the double date "1952-2002" on the obverse.

DATE	MILLIONS MINTED	MS-63
1996 Polar Bear	375	6.00
1997 Polar Bear	17	6.00
1998 Polar Bear	5	6.00
1999 Nunavut	25	6.00
2000 Path of Knowledge	30	6.00
2001 Polar Bear	12	6.00
2002 (1952–2002)	27	6.00
2003 Polar Bear	7	6.00

Elizabeth II, Bareheaded, 2003–

RCM's corporate mark (M)

2006: 10th anniversary

The new uncrowned effigy of Queen Elizabeth, designed by Susanna Blunt, was introduced in 2003 in celebration of the jubilee year of her reign.

10th Anniversary of $2 Dollar coin, 2006

Issued to celebrate the 10th anniversary of the bimetallic two dollar coin. Reverse design by Tony Bianco. A stylized RCM Logo (L) was phased in during 2006.

Québec City, 2008

Designed to celebrate the 400th anniversary of Quebec, the dual date 1608 - 2008 appears on the reverse designed by Geneviève Bertrand.

Boreal Forest, 2011

Designed to celebrate the boreal forest of Canada, by Nolin BBDO Montreal.

DATE		MILLIONS MINTED	MS-63
2003	Polar Bear	4	6.00
2004	Polar Bear	13	6.00
2005	Polar Bear	38	6.00
2006	Polar Bear	37	6.00
2006(M)	10th anniversary	5	6.00
2007	Polar Bear	39	6.00
2008	Polar Bear	12	6.00
2008	(1608-2008) 400th anniversary of Quebec	6	6.00
2009	Polar Bear	38	6.00
2010	Polar Bear	8	6.00
2011	Polar Bear	22	6.00
2011	Boreal Forest	5	4.00

2 DOLLARS — PLATED STEEL

Diameter: 28.0 mm; weight: 6.92 grams; edge; interrupted serration over lettering;
composition (ring): nickel plated steel, (core): bronze plated steel (core diameter: 16.8 mm)

In April 2012, the RCM announced that a new generation of one-dollar and two-dollar circulation coins, which incorporate advanced security features and are manufactured with the Mint's patented multi-ply plated steel technology begins circulating. More cost-effective than their predecessors and unprecedented in their security, this new coin retains the familiar "Polar Bear" designs and physical appearance. The new coin is slightly lighter in weight and has segmented reeding over edge lettering. (2 DOLLARS CANADA)

DATE		MILLIONS MINTED	MS-63
2012	Polar Bear 1.531		15.00
2012	Polar Bear, Micro-laser security engraving. 82.86		4.00
2013	Polar Bear, Micro-laser security engraving. 12.39		6.00
2014	Polar Bear, Micro-laser security engraving. 16.31		6.00
2014	Wait for me, Daddy. . . . . incl.		4.00
2015	Polar Bear, Micro-laser security engraving. 16.31		6.00
2014	Sir John A. Macdonald . . . . incl.		4.00

The War of 1812 – HMS *Shannon*, 2012

Depicts the Leda-class frigate, HMS *Shannon*.

DATE		MILLIONS MINTED	MS-63
2012	HMS *Shannon* (The War of 1812) 5		4.00

5 DOLLARS
George V, 1912–1914

Diameter: 21.59 mm; weight: 8.36 grams; thickness: 1.82 mm;
composition: .900 gold, .100 copper; edge: reeded

VF: Band of crown still clear but no longer sharp
*EF: Band of crown slightly worn but generally
       sharp and clear*
AU: Trace of wear on band of crown

The obverse device is from a portrait model by Sir E.B. MacKennal (B.M. on truncation) and the reverse design remains one of the most beautiful on Canadian coins, showing the shield from the Canadian coat of arms with crossed boughs of maple behind.

DATE	QTY. (000)	VF-20	EF-40	AU-50	MS-60	MS-63
1912	155	440.00	450.00	465.00	495.00	800.00
1913	94	440.00	450.00	465.00	495.00	950.00
1914	29	475.00	525.00	700.00	1,100	3,500

10 DOLLARS
George V, 1912–1914

Diameter: 26.92 mm; weight: 16.72 grams; thickness: 2.08 mm;
composition: .900 gold, .100 copper; edge: reeded

The obverse and the reverse, by W.H.J. Blakemore, are very similar to those on the five dollars.

DATE	QTY. (000)	VF-20	EF-40	AU-50	MS-60	MS-63
1912	71	840.00	860.00	900.00	1,000	2,750
1913	142	840.00	860.00	900.00	1,050	3,500
1914	135	850.00	880.00	950.00	1,250	3,500

OTTAWA MINT SOVEREIGNS

As a branch of the Royal Mint, the Ottawa Mint struck gold sovereigns during the period 1908–19. These were identical to those struck at the Royal Mint except for a C (for Canada) mint mark, just above the date. Sovereigns struck in London had no mint mark while pieces with mint marks I, M, P, S and SA were from the mints in India, Australia and South Africa.

During WWI, these coins were used to help pay for war materials purchased by England from the United States, saving England the risk of sending gold across the Atlantic.

Such 'branch mint' sovereigns are generally considered to form part of the coinage of the country in which they were struck, and so are included here.

Edward VII, 1908–1910

Diameter: 22.05 mm; weight: 7.988 grams; composition: .917 gold, .083 copper; edge: reeded

Position of C mint mark
for Ottawa Mint

The obverse was derived from a portrait model by G.W. De Saulles (DES below neck) and the reverse is a slight modification of the original 1816 St. George and the dragon design by Benedetto Pistrucci (B.P. at lower right).

DATE	QTY.	VF-20	EF-40	AU-50	MS-60	MS-63
1908C*	636	3,000	4,000	4,500	5,000	6,500
1909C	16,237	420.00	475.00	550.00	800.00	2,500
1910C	28,012	420.00	425.00	500.00	800.00	3,000

*Originally struck in specimen only; however, some circulated.

George V, 1911–1919

VF: Wear on head spreads near the ear and there is slight wear on the beard

EF: Hair over ear is only slightly worn; beard is still sharp

The obverse was derived from a portrait model by Sir E.B. MacKennal (B.M. on truncation) and the reverse is the same as on the Edward VII issues.

1916C. Despite the reported mintage of more than 6,000, specimens of this date are rare, with only about 20 known today. Most were probably melted, as undoubtedly happened with the 1917 London issue and some Australian issues.

DATE	QTY. (000)	VF-20	EF-40	AU-50	MS-60	MS-63
1911C	256	350.00	420.00	430.00	450.00	495.00
1913C	4	1,000	1,300	1,600	2,200	4,000
1914C	15	450.00	500.00	600.00	800.00	1,400
1916C	6	18,000	22,500	25,000	30,000	45,000
1917C	59	375.00	420.00	430.00	440.00	750.00
1918C	106	375.00	420.00	430.00	440.00	1,250
1919C	136	375.00	420.00	430.00	440.00	1,000

CANADIAN GOLD COINS
25 CENTS, PROOF

Diameter: 11 mm; weight: 0.5 gram; edge: serrated. Composition: .9999 gold; finish; proof; illustrations x 2.

Actual size

DATE		QTY.	ISSUE PRICE	VALUE
2010	25¢ Caribou, design by Emanuel Hahn 10,000		74.95	100.00
2011	25¢ Cougar, design by Emily Damstra........................ 8,622		79.95	100.00
2014	25¢ Rocky Mountain Bighorn Sheep, design by Emily Damstra 10,000		79.95	80.00
2015	25¢ Grizzly Bear, design by Emily Damstra 10,000		79.95	80.00

Small Animals Series, 2013–

Diameter: 11mm; weight: 0.5g; composition: .9999 gold; bullion weight: 0.016 troy ounces; illustrations x 2.

Canada is home to a rich biodiversity, with different ecosystems that support a vast number of animal species.

DATE		QTY.	ISSUE PRICE	VALUE
2013	25¢ Hummingbird, design by Claudio D'Angelo 10,000		79.95	80.00
2014	25¢ The Eastern Chipmunk, design by Tony Bianco.............. 10,000		79.95	80.00
2015	25¢ Rock Rabbit, design by Derek C. Wicks 10,000		79.95	80.00

50 CENTS, PROOF

Diameter: 13.92 mm; weight: 1.27 grams; edge: serrated.
Composition: .9999 gold; finish; proof; illustrations x 1.5.

Legendary Nature, 2011

Celebrated First Nation's artist Corrine Hunt has used her distinctive vision of traditional Kwakwaka'wakw and Tlingit forms to create these special editions.

DATE		QTY.	ISSUE PRICE	VALUE
2011	50¢ Boreal Forest, by Corrine Hunt	1,859	139.95	175.00
2011	50¢ Wood Bison, by Corrine Hunt	1,686	139.95	175.00
2011	50¢ Orca Whale, by Corrine Hunt	1,729	139.95	175.00
2011	50¢ Peregrine Falcon, by Corrine Hunt	1,678	139.95	175.00

150th Anniversary of the Cariboo Gold Rush, 2012

Diameter: 13.92mm; weight: 1.27g; composition: .9999 gold; bullion weight: 0.04 troy ounces

In this coin's reverse image design, Canadian artist Tony Bianco portrays the elemental image that inspired gold fever throughout the 1860s: a rusty, smoke-blackened tin pan, just lifted from the river's waters, filled with gleaming gold dust and nuggets of purest water-filtered gold.

DATE		QTY.	ISSUE PRICE	VALUE
2012	50¢ Cariboo Gold Rush		129.95	130.00

Canadian Inuit Art, 2013

The reverse features an intricate reproduction of Joanassie Nowkawalk's original sculpture that he carved out of serpentinite in 1962.

DATE		QTY.	ISSUE PRICE	VALUE
2013	50¢ Canadian Inuit Art	10,000	129.95	130.00

Birds of Prey, 2013–2015

Diameter: 13.92mm; weight: 1.27grams; composition: .9999 gold; finish: proof; edge: serrated; illustrations x 1.5.

DATE		QTY.	ISSUE PRICE	VALUE
2013	50¢ Bald Eagle, by Trevor Tenant	10,000	129.95	130.00
2014	50¢ Osprey, by Arnold Nogy	7,500	129.95	130.00
2015	50¢ Owl, by Arnold Nogy	7,500	129.95	130.00

300th Anniversary of Louisbourg, 2013

The reverse image by Canadian artist Peter Gough features a cod fish and ship as well as the Frédéric Gate. This beautiful symbolic design highlighting the historic connection between Louisbourg and the sea.

DATE		QTY.	ISSUE PRICE	VALUE
2013	50¢ Louisbourg	10,000	129.95	130.00

Sea Creatures, 2013–2014

Diameter: 13.92mm; weight: 1.27grams; composition: .9999 gold; finish: proof; edge: serrated; illustrations x 1.5.

Designer: Emily Damstra.

DATE		QTY.	ISSUE PRICE	VALUE
2013	50¢ Starfish, Leather Star	10,000	129.95	130.00
2014	50¢ Seahorse	7,500	129.95	130.00

Canada's Classic Beaver, 2014

Diameter: 13.92mm; weight: 1.27grams; composition: .9999 gold; finish: proof; edge: serrated
bullion weight: 1/25 troy ounces; illustrations x 1.5.

The beaver has been the cherished star of Canada's five-cent coin for more than 75 years. This affordable gold coin features a design inspired by the 5-cent circulation coin designed in 1937 by G.E. Kruger Gray, which has been adapted for the small surface.

DATE		QTY.	ISSUE PRICE	VALUE
2014	50¢ Canada's Classic Beaver 7,500		129.95	130.00

150th Anniversary of Québec and Charlottetown Conferences, 2014

Diameter: 13.92mm; weight: 1.27g; composition: 99.99% pure gold; finish: proof; edge: serrated

Celebrate the 150th Anniversary of the Charlottetown and Québec Conferences—important steps on Canada's path to nationhood. Designer: Matthew Bowen.

DATE		QTY.	ISSUE PRICE	VALUE
2014	50¢ 150th Anniversary of Québec and Charlottetown Conferences. . . .7,500		129.95	130.00

TORONTO 2015™ Pan Am and Parapan Am Games: Celebrating Excellence, 2015

Diameter: 42.0mm; weight: 32.5g; composition: gold plated copper; finish: proof; edge: serrated

After years of rigorous training, fuelled by determination, passion and unwavering dedication to their sport, more than 7,500 athletes will compete in the TORONTO 2015™ Pan American and Parapan American Games. Each athlete will strive to perform their personal best in the hopes of winning the greatest symbol of athletic excellence—a gold medal. Designer: Christi Belcourt.

DATE		QTY.	ISSUE PRICE	VALUE
2015	50¢ TORONTO 2015™ Pan Am and Parapan Am Games: Celebrating Excellence. 15,000		44.95	45.00

Maple Leaf, 2015

Diameter: 13.92mm; weight: 1.27g; composition: 99.99% pure gold; finish: proof; edge: serrated; illustrations x 1.5.

Since it was first raised in 1965, the National Flag of Canada has come to symbolize many of the values and opportunities that have defined Canada and its people. To Canadians at home and abroad, the red maple leaf unites us and instills a sense of belonging regardless of our different cultures, languages and beliefs. Designer: Pierre Leduc.

DATE		QTY.	ISSUE PRICE	VALUE
2015	50¢ Maple Leaf	7,500	129.95	130.00

1 DOLLAR, PROOF

Diameter: 14.1 mm; weight: 1.555 grams; edge: serrated.
Composition: .9999 gold; finish; proof: illustrations x 1.5.

Louis d'or, 2006 – 2008

These historically inspired coins features the designs of the rare gold coins recovered from the fortunes that were lost when the Auguste sank off the coast of Cape Breton in 1761.

DATE		QTY. (000)	ISSUE PRICE	VALUE
2006	Gold $1 Louis d'or, designed by the RCM engravers 6		102.95	120.00
2007	Gold $1 Louis d'or, designed by the RCM engravers 4		104.95	120.00
2008	Gold $1 Louis d'or, designed by the RCM engravers 4		104.95	120.00

2 DOLLARS, PROOF

Diameter: 28.0 mm; weight: 11.4 grams; thickness: 1.80 mm; edge: interrupted serration.; finish; proof.
Composition (outer ring): .172 gold, .776 silver, (centre): .917 gold, (diameter: 16.8 mm); Overall: .504 gold, .447 silver.

A special limited edition of the bi-metallic two dollar coins are struck in precious metals for sale worldwide. Each coin is housed in a blue ultrasuede case and is accompanied by a numbered certificate of authenticity.

DATE		QTY. (000)	ISSUE PRICE	VALUE
1996	$2 Polar Bear, in presentation folder 5		299.95	275.00
1999	$2 Nunavut, in presentation folder 4		299.95	275.00
2000	$2 Path of Knowledge, in presentation folder 6		299.95	275.00

2 DOLLARS, 2006

Diameter: 28.0 mm; weight: 14.02 grams; edge: interrupted serration; finish; proof.
Composition (outer ring): 22k yellow gold, (centre): 4.1k white gold; (diameter: 16.8 mm).

DATE		QTY. (000)	ISSUE PRICE	VALUE
2006	$2 10th Anniversary of the Two Dollar coin, in presentation case 2		399.95	400.00

5 DOLLARS
75th anniversary of the world's first mobile blood transfusion unit - 1/10-Ounce Gold Coin - 2011

Diameter: 16.0 mm; weight: 3.13 grams; edge: serrated; finish; proof.
Composition: .9999 gold; illustrations x 1.5.

Celebrates the 75th Anniversary of the creation of the world's first mobile blood transfusion vehicle by Canadian physician and medical inventor Dr. Norman Bethune. Design by Harvey Chan.

DATE		QTY.	ISSUE PRICE	VALUE
2011	$5 75th anniv. of the world's first mobile blood transfusion unit 1,457		319.95	320.00

The Queen's Diamond Jubilee - Royal Cypher
2012 marks the Diamond Jubilee of Queen Elizabeth II—a celebration of the 60th anniversary of Her Majesty's accession to the throne in 1952. Design by the RCM engravers.

Year of the Dragon
The design features a four-clawed dragon that stretches along the outer edge of the coin; its lines and contours full of fiery character; with a Chinese character and clouds representing its good fortune. Design by Three Degrees Creative Group Inc.

Maple Leaf Forever
The design is based on the maple leaf design that has graced Canada's one-cent circulation coin since 1937. Design by Luc Normandin.

DATE		QTY.	ISSUE PRICE	VALUE
2012	$5 The Queen's Diamond Jubilee - Royal Cypher 1,500		259.95	260.00
2012	$5 Year of the Dragon.................................... 3,900		229.95	260.00
2012	$5 Maple Leaf Forever 2,500		229.95	260.00

O Canada 5-coin series, 2013

Diameter: 16mm; weight: 3.13g; composition: .9999 gold; bullion weight: 0.1 troy ounces

O Canada series focusing on iconic Canadian animals.

DATE		QTY.	ISSUE PRICE	VALUE
2013	$5 O Canada – The Beaver	4,000	279.95	280.00
2013	$5 O Canada – The Polar Bear	4,000	279.95	280.00
2013	$5 O Canada – The Wolf	4,000	279.95	280.00
2013	$5 O Canada – The Caribou	4,000	279.95	280.00
2013	$5 O Canada – Orca	4,000	279.95	280.00

Devil's Brigade, 2013

Diameter: 20.0mm; weight: 7.8grams; composition: .9999 gold; finish: proof; edge: serrated
bullion weight: 1/4 troy ounce

During World War II, Canada joined forces with the United States to create the First Special Service Force—the first and only time both nations would be seamlessly combined in training, equipment and uniform. Although it was only operational for two years, this elite combat unit demonstrated the power of united national forces against a common foe—and consequently became the forerunner to distinguished Canadian and U.S. units including Canada's Joint-Task-Force 2 and the United States' Navy Seals, Delta Force and Green Berets. Design by Ardell Bourgeois.

DATE		QTY.	ISSUE PRICE	VALUE
2013	$5 Devil's Brigade	2,000	649.95	650.00

O Canada Pure Gold 4–Coin Series, 2014

Diameter: 16.0mm; weight: 3.14grams; composition: .9999 gold; finish: proof; edge: serrated
bullion weight:1/10 troy ounces

Canada is a country of incredible diversity—its landscapes, its fauna and flora, its people. And while most Canadians live in urban centres, images and icons of this land's wild nature resonate with each and every one of us. An exciting O Canada series featuring iconic images celebrating all that makes Canada unique.

DATE		QTY.	ISSUE PRICE	VALUE
2014	$5 The Grizzly Bear (February) design by Glen Loates 4,000		279.95	280.00
2014	$5 The Moose (April) design by Trevor Tennant 4,000		279.95	280.00
2014	$5 The Canada Goose (June) design by Jean-Charles Daumas 4,000		279.95	280.00
2014	$5 The Bison (August)			

Bald Eagle, 2014

Diameter: 16.0mm; weight: 3.13grams; composition: .9999 gold; finish: proof; edge: serrated
bullion weight:1/10 troy ounces

The great Bald Eagle is an amazing predator whose image has become synonymous with the notions of freedom, majesty, strength and individualism in North America. Designer: Derek Wicks.

DATE		QTY.	ISSUE PRICE	VALUE
2014	$5 Bald Eagle 3,000		279.95	280.00

Portrait of Nanaboozhoo, 2014

Diameter: 16.0mm; weight: 3.14grams; composition: .9999 gold; finish: proof; edge: serrated

Storytelling has long been a rich oral tradition for Aboriginal cultures. It is said that from the first snowfall to the first clap of thunder, elders impart history, traditions and life lessons to the younger generation through rich narratives filled with allegories and imagery. For the Anishinaabe, an important cultural character is Nanaboozhoo; as a shape-shifting spirit, he teaches right from wrong through his adventures while offering lessons on how to live in harmony with the natural world. Designed by Cyril Assiniboine, a renowned self-taught Ojibwa artist and a pow-wow dancer.

DATE		QTY.	ISSUE PRICE	VALUE
2014	$5 Portrait of Nanaboozhoo 3,000		279.95	280.00

Prehistoric Animals Series, 2104–

Diameter: 16.0mm; weight: 3.14grams; composition: .9999 gold; finish: proof; edge: serrated

Despite the species' extinction 10,000 years ago, the woolly mammoth continues to inspire and intrigue many who identify it with the last glacial period. Design by Michael Skrepnik.

DATE		QTY.	ISSUE PRICE	VALUE
2015	$5 Woolly Mammoth, design by Michael Skrepnik (from a set) 3,000			

Only available as a subscription with the $20 Woolly Mammoth fine silver coin at $369.90 per set.

| 2015 | $5 American Scimitar Sabre-Tooth Cat, design by Julius Csotonyi . . . .3,000 |

Only available as a subscription with the $20 American Scimitar Sabre-Tooth Cat fine silver coin at $369.90 per set.

Five Blessings, 2014

Diameter: 16.0mm; weight: 3.14grams; composition: .9999 gold; finish: proof; edge: serrated

Blessings are an integral element of Chinese culture. This coin features a beautifully engraved design conferring upon its owner blessings of happiness, success, long life, joy, and good fortune.

DATE		QTY.	ISSUE PRICE	VALUE
2014	$5 Five Blessings 2,000		279.95	280.00

Overlaid Majestic Maple Leaves

Diameter: 16.0mm; weight: 3.14g; composition: 99.99% pure gold; finish: proof; edge: serrated

The inspiring elegance of Canada's national symbol with a beautiful design of a sprig of leaves from the sugar maple, one of ten maple species indigenous to Canada and which is the focal point of Canada's National Flag. Pierre Leduc (reverse), Susanna Blunt (obverse)

DATE		QTY.	ISSUE PRICE	VALUE
2014	$5 Overlaid Majestic Maple Leaves 3,000		279.95	280.00

2014 Cougar

Diameter: 16.0mm; weight: 3.14g; composition: 99.99% pure gold; finish: proof; edge: serrated

The cougar is one of Canada's most powerful, elusive and beautiful predators. The animal's powerful, intimidating golden eyes ringed in dark tones, blunt muzzle spiked with long whiskers, short round ears, and dense fur are presented in full detail, bringing the intensity of the moment fully to life. Glen Loates (reverse), Susanna Blunt (obverse)

DATE		QTY.	ISSUE PRICE	VALUE
2014	$5 Cougar.		279.95	280.00

2015 Year of the Sheep

Diameter: 16.0mm; weight: 3.14g; composition: 99.99% pure gold; finish: specimen; edge: serrated

The creative Sheep personality embodies wealth, warmth and loveliness. Good things seem to come to the Sheep naturally because of its irresistibly good nature. The Sheep rarely speaks its mind. It will go with the flow and only object when things aren't going its way. Push too hard and it will react—decisively! The gregarious Sheep is an eternal romantic. It adores being showered with love and attention. Simon Ng (reverse), Susanna Blunt (obverse)

DATE		QTY.	ISSUE PRICE	VALUE
2015	$5 Year of the Sheep 2,888		278.88	279.00

Commemorative $5 and $10 Gold, 2002

$5 - Diameter: 21.59 mm; weight: 8.36 grams; thickness: 1.82mm; composition: .900 gold, .100 copper; edge: reeded
$10 - Diameter: 26.92 mm; weight: 16.72 grams; thickness: 2.08mm; composition: .900 gold, .100 copper; edge: reeded

Commemorating the ninetieth anniversary of the first domestic gold coins issued in Canada, the reverses for the new two-coin set replicate those of the original coins of 1812. Only the obverse device (the Dora de Pédery-HUNT effigy of Queen Elizabeth II), the legend and date differ from the original.

DATE		QTY.	ISSUE PRICE	VALUE
2002	1912 Commemorative $5 and $10 gold coin set	2,000	741.95	975.00

10 DOLLARS
War of 1812, 2012

Diameter: 16.0 mm; weight: 3.13 grams; edge: serrated; finish; proof.
Composition: .9999 gold; illustrations x 1.5.

A commemoration of the bicentennial of a pivotal moment in Canadian, British, and American history. Design by Cathy Bursey-Sabourin.

DATE		QTY.	ISSUE PRICE	VALUE
2011	$10 War of 1812	2,000	569.95	570.00

Maple Leaves with Queen Elizabeth II, laureate obverse (1953)

Diameter: 20.0mm; weight: 7.8g; composition: 99.99% pure gold; finish: reverse proof; edge: serrated

The glorious Canadian maple and our beloved Sovereign, Her Majesty Queen Elizabeth II, Queen of Canada – two icons that for more than sixty years have symbolized our country and our collective sense of identity. Image by Canadian artist Celia Godkin (reverse), Mary Gillick (obverse).

DATE		QTY.	ISSUE PRICE	VALUE
2014	$10 Maple Leaves with Queen Elizabeth II Effigy from 1953	1,500	649.95	650.00

Maple Leaves with Queen Elizabeth II, tiara obverse (1965)

Diameter: 20.0mm; weight: 7.8g; composition: 99.99% pure gold; finish: reverse proof; edge: serrated

The glorious Canadian maple and our beloved Sovereign, Her Majesty Queen Elizabeth II, Queen of Canada – two icons that for more than sixty years have symbolized our country and our collective sense of identity. Image by Canadian artist Celia Godkin (reverse), Arnold Machin (obverse).

DATE		QTY.	ISSUE PRICE	VALUE
2015	$10 Maple Leaves with Queen Elizabeth II Effigy from 1965	1,500	649.95	650.00

Polar Bear and Cub 2015

Diameter: 20.0mm; weight: 7.8g; composition: 99.99% pure gold; finish: proof; edge: serrated

A symbol of the power and vastness of Canada's northern landscape, the Polar Bear is an iconic animal for Canadians. In a nation dominated by weather extremes, the Polar Bear's ability to survive and thrive in the harshest climate reflects Canadians' stalwart pragmatism and spirit of adventure. Designer: Germaine Arnaktauyok.

DATE		QTY.	ISSUE PRICE	VALUE
2015	$10 Polar Bear and Cub	2,000	649.95	650.00

20 DOLLARS
Confederation Centennial 1967

Diameter: 27.05 mm; weight: 18.27 grams; thickness: 2.43mm; composition: .900 gold, .100 copper; edge: reeded

This denomination was struck only for the special specimen set of Confederation Centennial coins (in a black leather box), originally sold to collectors for $40. This is the only coin in the set which does not bear the commemorative dates: 1867–1967. The obverse bears Arnold Machin's design, introduced on regular denominations in 1965. The reverse is an adaptation of the Canadian coat of arms by Myron Cook, using Thomas Shingles' model for the 50¢ type of 1959.

DATE		QTY.	VALUE
1967	$20 Confederation commemorative	334,000	750.00

25 DOLLARS
Untamed Canada Fine Gold Series, 2013–

Diameter: 20mm; weight: 7.797g; composition: .9999 gold; bullion weight: 0.25 troy ounces

Every day, the dramatic tales of the untamed wilderness are played out across Canada's vast landscape—as they have been for untold millennia.

DATE		QTY.	ISSUE PRICE	VALUE
2013	$25 Arctic Fox by Tivadar Bote	1,500	649.95	650.00
2013	$25 The Pronghorn by Laurie McGaw	1,500	649.95	650.00
2014	$25 Wolverine by Tivadar Bote	1,500	649.95	650.00

Canada: An Allegory, 2013

The reverse image by Canadian artist Laurie McGaw features an iconic rendering of a new Canada allegory for modern-day Canada. Seated on the "throne" of the Canadian Shield, this classically dressed, seated female figure occupies the centre of the reverse field.

DATE		QTY.	ISSUE PRICE	VALUE
2013	$25 Canada: An Allegory	2,000	649.95	650.00

Pope John Paul II, 2014

Diameter: 20.0mm; weight: 7.8grams; composition: .9999 gold; finish: proof; edge: serrated

Since the birth of the Holy Roman Church nearly 2,000 years ago, the Roman Catholic pope has been a powerful political influencer on the world stage. Unlike any leader of the Roman Catholic Church before him, the 264th pope, Pope John Paul II took proactive control of this global influence in order to criticize and combat political oppression. Design is an artist reference by Trevor Tennant.

DATE		QTY.	ISSUE PRICE	VALUE
2014	$25 Pope John Paul II	1,500	649.95	650.00

50 DOLLARS
60th Anniversary,
the End of the Second World War, 2005

Diameter: 27 mm; weight: 12 grams; thickness: 2.08 mm;
composition: .5833 gold, .4167 silver (14k); edge: serrated

The reverse of this commemorative coin was designed by Peter Mossman and incorporates the Maple Leaf, a victorious V and three images representing our navy, army and air force. The same reverse is shown on a Canadian five dollar coin for this year.

DATE		QTY.	ISSUE PRICE	VALUE
2005	$50 End of WWII	4,000	349.95	450.00

The Queen's Portrait – Ultra High Relief, 2012

Diameter: 30 mm; weight: 33.13 grams;
composition: .99999 gold; edge: serrated

This is the world's first 99.999% gold ultra-high relief coin. Design by Laurie McGaw.

DATE		QTY.	ISSUE PRICE	VALUE
2012	$50 The Queen's Portrait	500 coins	2,999.95	3,000.00

Five Blessings, 2014

Diameter: 30 mm; weight: 31.16 grams; composition: .9999 gold; finish: proof; edge: serrated

Blessings are an integral element of Chinese culture. This coin features a beautifully engraved design conferring upon its owner blessings of happiness, success, long life, joy, and good fortune.

DATE		QTY.	ISSUE PRICE	VALUE
2014	$50 Five Blessings	350	2,699.95	2,700.00

UNESCO at Home and Abroad, 2015

Diameter: 20.0mm; weight: 7.8g; composition: 99.99% pure gold; finish: proof; edge: serrated

Some of Canada's most stunning World Heritage properties, with other properties around the world, to illustrate how two sites of global importance share similarities while being so different. Designer: Trevor Tennant.

DATE		QTY.	ISSUE PRICE	VALUE
2015	$50 Mount Fuji & The Canadian Rockies	2,000	649.95	650.00

75 DOLLARS
Pope John Paul II (1920–2005)

Diameter: 36.07 mm; weight: 31.44 grams;
composition: .4166 gold (10kt), .5834 silver; edge: serrated

One of two coins struck by the Royal Canadian Mint to honour the memory of the first and only Pope ever to visit Canada. Both the silver and gold coins bear the same obverse and reverse designs. The obverse features the uncrowned effigy of Queen Elizabeth II, designed by Susanna Blunt; the reverse design, by Susan Taylor, features the signature wave of Ioannes Paulus PP.II.

DATE		QTY.	ISSUE PRICE	VALUE
2005	$75 Pope John Paul II, Proof	1,721	499.00	675.00

VANCOUVER 2010 OLYMPIC WINTER GAMES
75 DOLLARS — 14 KARAT GOLD

Diameter: 27 mm; weight: 12 grams;
composition: .5833 gold (14kt), .4167 silver; edge: serrated, finish: coloured proof.

2007 Obverse	RCMP *Cecily Mok*	Athletes' Pride *Shelagh Armstrong*	Canada Geese Kerri Burnett

2008 Obverse	Four Host First Nations *RCM Engravers*	Home of Winter Games *Shelagh Armstrong*	Inukshuk *Catherine Deer*

2009 Obverse	Wolf *Arnold Nogy*	Olympic Spirit *Shelagh Armstrong*	Moose *Kerri Burnett*

2007	$75 Dollars Proof	8,000	389.95	400.00
2008	$75 Dollars Proof	8,000	389.95	400.00
2009	$75 Dollars Proof	8,000	389.95	400.00

Four Seasons Maple Leaf, 2010

Summer   Fall

Winter   Spring

One of the great gifts of living in Canada is the ever evolving landscape generated by its four seasons. As spring transforms into summer and autumn surrenders to the dormacy of winter, the maple adapts in perfect rhythm with the changing climate and environment.

DATE		QTY.	ISSUE PRICE	VALUE
2010	$75 - Summer - Reverse design by Michelle Grant	136	589.95	600.00
2010	$75 - Fall - Reverse design by Claudio D'Angelo	162	589.95	600.00
2010	$75 - Winter - Reverse design by Celia Godkin	136	589.95	600.00
2010	$75 - Spring - Reverse design by Arnold Nogy	130	589.95	600.00

World Baseball Classic, 2013

DATE		QTY.	ISSUE PRICE	VALUE
2013	$75 Baseball diamond and bats	3,500	899.95	900.00
2013	$75 Hardball	3,500	899.95	900.00

Superman™: The Early Years, 2013

Diameter: 27.0mm; weight: 12.0grams; composition: 58.33% gold, 41.67% silver; finish: proof; edge: serrated

Featuring the iconic 1939 cover of Superman #1 that was drawn by Superman co-creator Canadian Joe Shuster. Set to an engraved background displaying the fortress of solitude, the last son of Krypton flies above the city of Metropolis. Designer: Joe Shuster, DC Comics.

DATE		QTY.	ISSUE PRICE	VALUE
2013	$75 Superman: The Early Years	2,000	750.00	1,800.00

Allied Gold, 2015

Diameter: 20.0mm; weight: 7.8g; composition: 99.99% pure gold; finish: proof; edge: serrated

The harrowing 1940 rescue of Norway's national treasury from the grasp of Nazi invaders to safe-keeping in Canada is one of the most intriguing escape stories of the Second World War. Image by Canadian artist Joel Kimmel.

DATE		QTY.	ISSUE PRICE	VALUE
2015	$75 Allied Gold 1,500		649.95	650.00.

100 DOLLARS
Olympics 1976

Uncirculated (with beads): diameter: 27.00 mm; weight: 13.337 grams; thickness: 2.15 mm;
composition: .583 gold, .313 copper; .064 zinc; edge: reeded

Proof (without beads): diameter: 25.00 mm; weight: 16.965 grams; thickness: 1.962 mm;
composition: .9166 gold, .010 silver, .0734 copper; edge: reeded

Two coins were issued in 1976 to commemorate the XXI Olympiad. Both obverses bear the Arnold Machin effigy of Queen Elizabeth II and are similar to the silver $5 and $10 olympic issues. The reverse device was designed by Dora de Pédery-HUNT, and depicts an athlete of ancient Greece being crowned with a laurel wreath. The larger uncirculated edition, struck in 14k gold, has beads around the perimeter of both sides. The 22k version was struck in proof quality only and has no beads.

DATE		QTY. (000)	ISSUE PRICE	VALUE
1976	$100 Olympic, uncirculated, 14k, with beads	650	105.00	365.00
1976	$100 Olympic, proof, 22k, without beads	350	150.00	750.00

1977   1978

Silver Jubilee Commemorative, 1977

Diameter: 27.00 mm; weight: 16.965 grams; thickness: 2.393 mm;
composition: .9167 gold, .0833 silver; edge: reeded

The 1977 reverse features a bouquet of the official flowers of the provinces and territories designed by Raymond Lee. The obverse bears the Arnold Machin effigy of the Queen.

Canadian Unity, 1978

The reverse design, by Roger Savage, depicts twelve Canada Geese flying in formation to represent the unity of Canada's provinces and territories. The obverse is by Arnold Machin.

DATE		QTY. (000)	ISSUE PRICE	VALUE
1977	$100 Silver Jubilee	180	140.00	750.00
1978	$100 Unity	200	150.00	750.00

1979   1980   1981

International Year of the Child, 1979

Designed by Carola Tietz, the reverse depicts children playing beside a globe and commemorates the International Year of the Child. The obverse bears the Machin effigy of Queen Elizabeth II.

Arctic Territories, 1980

Arnold Machin's obverse design was used again in 1980. The reverse device, by Arnaldo Marchetti, bears no legend. Issued for the centenary of the transfer of the Arctic islands from Britain to Canada.

"O Canada" Commemorative, 1981

Diameter: 27.0 mm; weight: 16.965 grams; thickness: 2.393 mm;
composition: .9167 gold, .0833 silver; edge: reeded

This proof issue commemorates the adoption of O Canada as the Canadian national anthem on July 1, 1980. The reverse design is by Roger Savage and the obverse by Arnold Machin.

DATE		QTY. (000)	ISSUE PRICE	VALUE
1979	$100 Year of the Child	250	185.00	750.00
1980	$100 Arctic Territories	130	430.00	750.00
1981	$100 "O Canada"	101	300.00	750.00

1982   1983

Canadian Constitution, 1982

Diameter: 27.0 mm; weight: 16.965 grams; thickness: 2.25 mm;
composition: .9167 gold, .0833 silver; edge: reeded

This issue celebrates the patriation of the Canadian Constitution. The reverse was designed by Friedrich Peter, obverse by Arnold Machin.

St. John's Newfoundland, 1983

The 400th anniversary of Sir Humphrey Gilbert's landing in Newfoundland is commemorated by the 1983 issue. The obverse is by Arnold Machin and the reverse by John Jaciw. The word CANADA appears on the edge.

DATE		QTY. (000)	ISSUE PRICE	VALUE
1982	$100 Canadian Constitution	122	285.00	750.00
1983	$100 St. John's Nfld.	83	310.00	750.00

1984   1985   1986

Jacques Cartier, 1984

The 450th anniversary of Cartier's landing at Gaspé in 1534 is the subject of this issue. The reverse is by Carola Tietz and the obverse by Arnold Machin. The edge security lettering of 1983 was not repeated for 1984.

National Parks, 1985

The 100th anniversary of the establishment of Canada's National Parks is commemorated by this issue. The reverse was designed by Hector Greville.

International Year of Peace, 1986

Celebrating the International Year of Peace, the reverse device was both designed and modelled by Dora de Pédery-HUNT. The obverse bears the Arnold Machin effigy of Queen Elizabeth.

DATE		QTY. (000)	ISSUE PRICE	VALUE
1984	$100 Jacques Cartier	68	325.00	750.00
1985	$100 National Parks	61	325.00	750.00
1986	$100 Peace	76	325.00	750.00

1987   1988

XVth Winter Olympic Games, 1987

1987–1992: Diameter: 27.00 mm; weight: 13.338 grams; thickness: 2.18 mm;
composition: .5833 gold, .4167 silver; edge: (1987) lettered, (1988–1992) reeded

Commemorating the winter olympic games held in Calgary in 1988, the reverse device was designed by Friedrich Peter. The obverse is again by Arnold Machin. The legend XV OLYMPIC WINTER GAMES – XVES JEUX OLYMPIQUES D'HIVER appears on the edge of the coin.

Bowhead Whale, 1988

The 1988 issue was intended to bring public attention to environmental issues. The Bowhead whale is a protected species. The reverse was designed by Robert Ralph Carmichael and the obverse, again, is by Arnold Machin.

DATE		QTY. (000)	ISSUE PRICE	VALUE
1987	$100 Olympics	106	255.00	375.00
1988	$100 Bowhead whale	53	255.00	375.00

1989

1990

Sainte-Marie Among the Hurons, 1989

The reverse, designed by David Craig, commemorates the 350th anniversary of the first european settlement in Ontario. Arnold Machin's effigy of the Queen is on the obverse.

International Literacy Year, 1990

The 1990 issue celebrates the United Nations Literacy Year, and bears a reverse design by John Mardon. The obverse bears the new effigy of the Queen by Dora de Pédery-HUNT.

DATE		QTY. (000)	ISSUE PRICE	VALUE
1989	$100 Sainte-Marie Among the Hurons	64	245.00	375.00
1990	$100 United Nations Literacy Year	50	245.00	375.00

1991

1992

1993

Empress of India Centennial, 1991

Diameter: 27.0 mm; weight: 13.338 grams; thickness: 2.15 mm;
composition: .5833 gold, .4167 silver; edge: reeded

Commemorating the beginning of the era of the "Great White Empresses," three Canadian Pacific ships which provided passenger and cargo service across the Pacific at record speeds. The reverse, designed by Karsten Smith, depicts the arrival of the Empress of India at the Port of Vancouver on her maiden voyage from Japan in 1891.

350th Anniversary of Montreal, 1992

Issued to celebrate the 350th anniversary of the founding of Montreal (then Ville-Marie), the reverse design was by Ontario artist Stewart Sherwood. The date appears on the obverse.

The Featherstonhaugh, 1993

The reverse, by John Mardon, celebrates 100 years of the automobile and features the Featherstonhaugh, Canada's first electric car, built in 1893.

DATE		QTY. (000)	ISSUE PRICE	MS-65 PROOF
1991	$100 Empress of India Centennial	37	245.00	375.00
1992	$100 Montreal	28	239.85	375.00
1993	$100 Featherstonhaugh	26	239.85	375.00

1994   1995

The Home Front, 1994

The reverse, an excerpt from a painting by Paraskevo Clark depicts a woman working as an aircraft mechanic during WWII.

Louisbourg, Cape Breton, 1995

This issue commemorates the building of Louisbourg in 1720. The reverse, depicting the elaborately carved Porte Dauphine with the harbour in the background, was designed by Lewis Parker. The obverse again features the Dora de Pédery-HUNT effigy of the queen.

DATE		QTY. (000)	ISSUE PRICE	VALUE
1994	$100 The Home Front	18	249.95	375.00
1995	$100 Louisbourg	18	249.95	375.00

1996   1997   1998

Klondike Centennial, 1996

Diameter: 27.0 mm; weight: 13.338 grams; thickness: 2.15 mm;
composition: .5833 gold, .4167 silver; edge: reeded.

The $100 coin for 1996 was struck in 14-Karat gold to commemorate the discovery of gold in the Klondike on 16 August 1896. The reverse was designed by John Mantha.

Alexander Graham Bell, 1997

The reverse, by Donald H. Curley, celebrates the 150th anniversary of the birth of the inventor of the telephone, features a mature effigy of the famous inventor and teacher.

Discovery of Insulin, 1998

The 14 karat gold coin for 1998 celebrates the 75th anniversary of the Nobel prize for Physiology and Medicine presented to Frederick Banting and John MacLeod for their work towards the discovery of insulin and the treatment of diabetes. The award, unfortunately, overlooked the efforts of co-workers Best and Kollip. The reverse was designed by Robert Ralph Charmichael of Ontario.

DATE		QTY. (000)	ISSUE PRICE	MS-65 PROOF
1996	$100 Klondike	20	259.95	375.00
1997	$100 Alexander Graham Bell	15	259.95	375.00
1998	$100 Discovery of Insulin	10	259.95	375.00

1999 2000

Newfoundland, 50th Anniversary, 1999

The reverse, designed by Jackie Gale-Vaillancourt, depicts an iceberg with a puffin and a Pitcher plant in the foreground. All symbolic of the Province.

The Search for the Franklin Expedition, 2000

The 14 karat gold coin for 2000 commemorates the 150th anniversary of Robert McClure's attempt to locate the Franklin expedition. The attempt failed, but McClure succeeded in unlocking the final link of the Northwest Passage by sledge. The reverse, designed by John Mardin, depicts McClure's sledging party in the foreground and his ship, HMS Investigator icebound in the distance.

DATE		QTY. (000)	ISSUE PRICE	VALUE
1999	$100 Puffin, Pitcher plant and iceberg 10		269.95	375.00
2000	$100 The Search for the Franklin Expedition 11		269.95	375.00

2001 2002 2003

Library of Parliament, 2001

Diameter: 27.0 mm; weight: 13.338 grams; thickness: 2.15 mm;
composition: .5833 gold, .4167 silver; edge: reeded.

An interior view of the Library of Parliament is depicted on the reverse to celebrate the Library's 125th anniversary. The reverse was designed by Robert-Ralph Carmichael.

Alberta Strikes Oil, 2002

Celebrating the discovery of the Leduc oil field in 1947 and the importance of oil to the Canadian economy. The reverse design is by John Mardon.

Marquis Wheat, 2003

Issued for the 100th anniversary of Marquis Wheat, developed by Dr. William Saunders of the Central Experimental Farm and his sons. The reverse was designed by Thom Nelson and the obverse features the Dora de Pédery-HUNT effigy of the queen.

DATE		QTY. (000)	ISSUE PRICE	VALUE
2001	$100 Library of Parliament 8		260.95	375.00
2002	$100 Gushing oil well above the Leduc oil field. 10		260.95	425.00
2003	$100 Wheat field with large sheaf of wheat in foreground 10		289.95	375.00

New Obverse Effigy

2004 2005

St. Lawrence Seaway, 2004

For the 50th anniversary of the start of the St. Lawrence Seaway, the 2004 issue bears the uncrowned effigy of the queen, by Susanna Blunt. The reverse was designed by Susan Taylor.

Supreme Court of Canada, 2005

Issued for the 130th anniversary of the Supreme Court, the reverse was designed by Suzanne Duranceau.

DATE		QTY. (000)	ISSUE PRICE	VALUE
2004	$100 St. Lawrence Seaway 7		277.95	375.00
2005	$100 Supreme Court of Canada 5.092		329.95	375.00

2006 2007 2008

75th Game, World's Longest Hockey Series, 2006

Issued for the 75th face-off between Canada's Royal Military College and the United States Military Academy at West Point. The reverse was designed by Tony Bianco.

140th Anniversary of the Dominion of Canada, 2007

This coin features Queen Victoria's coat of arms as it appeared in the British North America Act. The reverse was designed by Bonnie Ross.

200th Anniversary of Descending the Fraser River, 2008

Commemorates explorer Simon Fraser's descent down the river that bears his name. The reverse was designed by John Mantha.

DATE		QTY.	ISSUE PRICE	VALUE
2006	$100 World's Longest Hockey Series 5,439		329.95	400.00
2007	$100 140th Anniversary of the Dominion of Canada 4,453		369.95	375.00
2008	$100 200th Anniversary of Descending the Fraser River 3,089		386.95	375.00

| 2009 | 2010 | 2011 |

10th Anniversary of Nunavut, 2009

Coin commemorates the 10th Anniversary of Nunavut, 1999 - 2009. The reverse was designed by Andrew Qappi.

400th Anniversary of the Discovery of Hudson's Bay, 2010

Commemorates the 400th anniversary of Henry Hudson's important discovery of Hudson's Bay. The Reverse was designed by John Mantha.

175th Anniversary of Canada's First Railway, 2011

The story of Canada's railway, a gargantuan feat of engineering, was the culmination of a 49-year long romance with the iron road that began with Canada's first public railway in 1836. Reverse was designed by Royal Canadian Mint engravers.

DATE		QTY.	ISSUE PRICE	VALUE
2009	$100 10th Anniversary of Nunavut	2,308	509.95	550.00
2010	$100 400th Anniversary of the Discovery of Hudson's Bay	2,431	589.95	590.00
2011	$100 175th Anniversary of Canada's First Railway	5,000	589.95	590.00

150th Anniversary of the Cariboo Gold Rush, 2012

Diameter: 27.0 mm; weight: 12 grams;
composition: .5833 gold, .4167 silver (14K); edge: reeded.

This coin features an intricate design that depicts prospectors as they pan and sluice for gold in a river. In the background, a man sits astride one of the infamous Laumeister camels surrounded by the rugged terrain that gives evidence of the challenging conditions prospectors faced during the Cariboo Gold Rush. The reverse was designed by Toni Bianco.

DATE		QTY.	ISSUE PRICE	VALUE
2012	$100 150th Anniversary of the Cariboo Gold Rush	2,500	599.95	600.00

Arctic Expedition (1913–2013)

Diameter: 27.0 mm; weight: 12 grams; composition: .5833 gold.

In 1913, an international crew of scientists, sailors, guides and crewmen—called the Canadian Arctic Expedition (CAE)—set sail on a remarkable voyage of discovery in Canada's High Arctic. Designed by Canadian artist Bonnie Ross and depicts several key images representative of the Canadian Arctic Expedition, including a survey team atop an ice floe taking research measurements and, in the background, a stylized globe of the Canadian Arctic.

DATE		QTY.	ISSUE PRICE	VALUE
2013	$100 Arctic Expedition 2,500		599.95	600.00

150th Anniversary Of The Charlottetown & Quebec Conferences, 2014

Diameter: 27.0mm; weight: 12.ograms; composition: .9999 gold; finish: proof; edge: serrated; 14 karat gold

This stunningly engraved, finely finished $100 gold coin celebrates the 150th anniversary of the Charlottetown and Québec conferences—important steps on Canada's path to nationhood. The Charlottetown and Québec Conferences were the critical catalysts that propelled the vision for "Canada" forward. Designer: Luc Normandin.

DATE		QTY.	ISSUE PRICE	VALUE
2014	$100 150th Anniversary of the Charlottetown & Quebec Conferences .	2,500	599.95	600.00

200th Anniversary of the Birth of Sir John A. Macdonald, 2015

Diameter: 27.0mm; weight: 12.0g; composition: 14-karat gold; finish: proof; edge: serrated

Celebrating the 200th anniversary of the birth of the nation's primary architect and first Prime Minister: Sir John A. Macdonald. Designer: Glen Green.

DATE		QTY.	ISSUE PRICE	VALUE
2015	$100 200th Anniversary of the Birth of Sir John A. Macdonald 1,500		599.95	600.00

Iconic Superman™ Comic Book Covers: Superman #4 (1940), 2015

Diameter: 27.0mm; weight: 12.0g; composition: 14-karat gold; finish: proof; edge: serrated

Superman comes to the rescue in the issue's first story, Superman versus Luthor, after Metropolis is rocked by its first ever earthquake! Design by Warner Bros. as seen on the iconic cover of Superman #4 (1940).

DATE		QTY.	ISSUE PRICE	VALUE
2015	$100 Iconic Superman™ Comic Book Covers: Superman #4 (1940) . 2,000		750.95	751.00

150 DOLLARS GOLD HOLOGRAM
Chinese Lunar Calendar
Diameter: 28.0 mm; weight: 13.61 grams, thickness: 1.81 mm;
composition: .750 gold, .250 silver; edge: reeded. All reverse designs by Harvey Chan

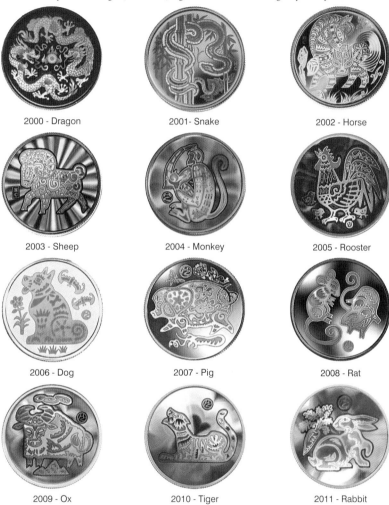

2000 - Dragon	2001- Snake	2002 - Horse
2003 - Sheep	2004 - Monkey	2005 - Rooster
2006 - Dog	2007 - Pig	2008 - Rat
2009 - Ox	2010 - Tiger	2011 - Rabbit

DATE		QTY. (000)	ISSUE PRICE	VALUE
2000	Year of the Dragon	9	388.88	1,250.00
2001	Year of the Snake	7	388.88	500.00
2002	Year of the Horse	6.5	388.88	500.00
2003	Year of the Sheep	4	398.88	500.00
2004	Year of the Monkey	3	398.88	600.00
2005	Year of the Rooster	3.7	398.88	600.00
2006	Year of the Dog	2.6	448.88	575.00
2007	Year of the Pig	1	498.88	575.00
2008	Year of the Rat	.6	508.88	600.00
2009	Year of the Ox	.5	638.88	600.00
2010	Year of the Tiger	.4	555.55	600.00
2011	Year of the Rabbit - (Last coin in this series)	.5	638.88	640.00

150 DOLLARS PURE GOLD
Blessings
Diameter: 22.5 mm; weight: 10.4 grams; finish: proof;
composition: .99999 gold; edge: plain; shape; scallope.

DATE		QTY.	ISSUE PRICE	PROOF MS-65
2009	$150 Blessing of Wealth, by Harvey Chan.	1,273	799.95	800.00
2010	$150 Blessing of Strength, by Harvey Chan.	765	939.95	940.00
2011	$150 Blessing of Happiness, by Harvey Chan	880	988.88	1,000.00
2012	$150 Blessing of Good Fortune	880	988.88	1,000.00
2013	$150 Blessing of Peace, by Aries Cheung	880	988.88	1,000.00
2014	$150 Blessings of Longevity, by Charles Vinh	888	988.88	989.00
2015	$150 Blessings of Prosperity, by Simon Ng	888	988.88	989.00

150 DOLLARS 18K GOLD

Diameter: 28 mm; weight: 11.84 grams; finish: proof;
composition: .750 gold, .250 silver; edge: reeded.

Design by Aries Cheung.

DATE		QTY.	ISSUE PRICE	PROOF MS-65
2010	$150 Year of the Tiger	1,507	555.55	560.00
2011	$150 Year of the Rabbit	2,500	638.88	640.00
2012	$150 Year of the Dragon	1,430	688.88	700.00
2013	$150 Year of the Snake	2,500	688.88	689.00
2014	$150 Year of the Horse	2,500	688.88	689.00
2015	$150 Year of the Sheep	2,500	688.88	689.00

2013 World Baseball Classic Tournament – Celebration

Diameter: 25mm; weight: 15.59g; composition: .9999 gold; bullion weight: 0.5012 troy ounces

The *World Baseball Classic™* tournament brings the best professional baseball players from around the world to one exciting international tournament. Designed by Canadian artist Steve Hepburn and features a stylized baseball player layered over an abstract circling form that symbolizes the event's speed, skill, and global appeal.

DATE		QTY.	ISSUE PRICE	PROOF MS-65
2013	$150 Baseball player	3,500	1,549.95	1,500

175 DOLLARS
IOC Issue, 1992

Diameter: 28.0 mm; weight: 16.97 grams, thickness: 2.00 mm;
composition: .9167 gold, .084 copper; edge: lettered

To celebrate the centennial of the modern olympics, the IOC commissioned five national mints to produce a fifteen-piece set of gold and silver commemorative coins from 1992 to 1996, the centennial year. All fifteen coins in the set will bear the five olympic rings and the dates 1896–1996, with the olympic motto CITIUS, ALTIUS, FORTIUS on the coin edge.

The Royal Canadian Mint issued the first series THE OLYMPIC VISION in 1992, consisting of one gold $175 coin and two silver $15 coins. Each obverse bears the Dora de Pédery-HUNT effigy of the queen. The reverse was designed by Stewart Sherwood.

DATE		QTY. (000)	ISSUE PRICE	VALUE
1992	$175 Gold, Olympics (IOC issue), proof	22	429.75	700.00

200 DOLLARS

Diameter: 29 mm; weight: 17.106 grams;
composition: .916 gold, .0833 silver; edge: reeded

Silver Jubilee of Canadian Flag, 1990

The first in a series of five $200 gold coins celebrating the spirit and promise of Canadian youth commemorates the 25th anniversary of the Canadian flag. The reverse was designed by Stewart Sherwood and illustrates a multicultural group of Canadian children carrying the flag of Canada.

The common obverse features the Dora de Pédery-HUNT effigy of the queen.

DATE		QTY. (000)	ISSUE PRICE	VALUE
1990	$200 Gold, Jubilee of Canadian Flag	21	395.00	700.00

| 1991 | 1992 | 1993 |

Hockey, a National Passion, 1991

The reverse, designed by Stewart Sherwood, pays tribute to the game of hockey.

Niagara Falls, 1992

The reverse of the third issue in the series features two children playing near the Niagara Falls and was designed by Ontario artist John Mardon.

Royal Canadian Mounted Police, 1993

Designed by Toronto artist Stewart Sherwood, the reverse of the 1993 coin shows an RCMP officer alongside his horse, talking with three children.

DATE		QTY. (000)	ISSUE PRICE	MS-65 PROOF
1991	$200 Gold, Hockey, a National Passion	10	425.00	750.00
1992	$200 Gold, Niagara Falls	9	389.65	750.00
1993	$200 Gold, RCMP	11	389.65	750.00

| 1994 | 1995 | 1996 |

Anne of Green Gables, 1994

The 1994 coin pays tribute to the famous characters created by Lucy Maud Montgomery. The reverse, designed by Phoebe Gilman, depicts a young girl in a gazebo who has been reading Anne of Green Gables.

The Sugar Bush, 1995

Diameter: 29 mm; weight: 17.135 grams; thickness: 2 mm;
composition: .9167 gold, .0833 silver; edge: reeded

This coin commemorates the traditional spring tapping of the Maple trees, as taught to the colonists by the First People of Canada. The reverse, designed by Canadian artist John D. Mantha, depicts a typical sugar bush scene at the turn of the century.

Canadian Pacific Railway, 1996

The $200 gold coin for 1996 recognizes the role of the transcontinental railroad in Canadian history. The reverse was designed by Montreal artist Suzanne Duranceau.

DATE		QTY. (000)	ISSUE PRICE	VALUE
1994	$200 Gold, Anne of Green Gables	11	389.65	750.00
1995	$200 Gold, The Sugar Bush	10	399.95	750.00
1996	$200 Gold, Canadian Pacific Railway	8	414.95	750.00

CANADIAN NATIVE CULTURES AND TRADITIONS

1997   1999

Raven Bringing Light to the World, 1997

This is the first in a series of four issues featuring contemporary native art, The reverse was designed by Haida artist Robert Davidson. The only legend, 200 DOLLARS • CANADA [DATE] • ELIZABETH II encircles the Dora de Pédery-HUNT effigy of the queen on the obverse.

Legend of the White Buffalo, 1998

The obverse remains the same as the previous issue. The reverse features a rendition of the rare white buffalo and was designed by Alex Janvier.

1999   2000

Mi'kmaq Butterfly, 1999

The traditional Mi'kmaq double curve symbol representing the balance between the physical and spiritual worlds was expressed as a butterfly by Mi'kmaq artist Alan Syliboy.

Mother and Child, 2000

The reverse of the final coin in the four-coin Native Cultures and Traditions series depicts a mother's love in the gaze that passes from an Inuit woman to her child and was designed by Germaine Arnaktauyok.

DATE		QTY. (000)	ISSUE PRICE	PROOF MS-65
1997	$200 Gold, Raven Bringing Light to the World, encapsulated	12	409.95*	900.00
1998	$200 Gold, Legend of the White Buffalo, encapsulated	6	409.95*	750.00
1999	$200 Gold, Mi'kmaq Butterfly*	7	409.95	750.00
2000	$200 Gold, Mother and Child	11	409.95	750.00

*Available in metal trimmed case and protective box for $5 more.

CANADIAN ART

Diameter: 29 mm; weight: 17.135 grams; thickness: 1.93 mm;
composition: .9167 gold, .0833 silver; edge: reeded

2001   2002

Cornelius Krieghoff, 2001

Cornelius Krieghoff (1815–1872) was one of Canada's greatest artists and specialized in painting Les Habitants, the citizens of Quebec and their daily life.

Tom Thompson, 2002

Tom Thompson (1877–1917) was one of the famous Group of Seven Canadian artists who painted landscapes in Algonquin Park and other locations around Ontario.

2003   2004

Lionel LeMoine FitzGerald, 2003

Lionel LeMoine FitzGerald (1890–1956) created this oil painting of houses on a prairie farm in 1929 and called it simply Houses.

Alfred Pellan, 2004

Recognized as one of the most avant garde artists of his time, Alfred Pellan's vision was perfect for this final issue in the series.

DATE		QTY. (000)	ISSUE PRICE	PROOF MS-65
2001	$200 Gold, The Habitant Farm by Cornelius Krieghoff	5	412.95	700.00
2002	$200 Gold, The Jack Pine by Tom Thompson	6	412.95	700.00
2003	$200 Gold, Houses by Lionel LeMoine FitzGerald	4	412.95	700.00
2004	$200 Gold, Alfred Pellan	4	412.95	700.00

Historical Commerce, 2005–2011

Diameter: 29 mm; weight: 16 grams; thickness: 1.93 mm;
composition: .9167 gold, .0833 silver; edge: reeded; finish: proof.

| 2005 - Fur Traders | 2006 - Timber Trade | 2007 Obverse | 2007 - Fishing Trade |

| 2008 - Agriculture Trade | 2009 - Coal Trade | 2010 - Oil Trade | 2011 - SS Beaver |

This series of coins were issued to commemorate historic trade in early Canada. The reverse designs are by John Mardon and obverse by Susanna Blunt.

DATE		QTY.	ISSUE PRICE	PROOF MS-65
2005	$200 Gold, Fur Traders, proof..........................	3,699	489.95	700.00
2006	$200 Gold, Timber Trade, proof	3,218	564.95	700.00
2007	$200 Gold, Fishing Trade, proof	2,137	579.95	700.00
2008	$200 Gold, Agriculture Trade, proof	1,951	619.95	700.00
2009	$200 Gold, Coal Mining Trade, proof, colourised........	2,241	849.95	850.00
2010	$200 Gold, Oil Trade, proof, colourised................	1,732	999.95	1,000.00
2011	$200 Gold, SS Beaver, proof, laser effect	2,800	1,079.95	1,100.00

First Gold Won, 2010

This coin commemorates the first gold medal won on Canadian soil and captures the occasion by featuring a design of four athletes in various celebratory poses. Designed by Bonnie Ross.

DATE		QTY.	ISSUE PRICE	PROOF MS-65
2010	$200 Gold, First Gold, proof................................	1,999	989.95	990.00

Diameter: 29 mm; weight: 16 grams; composition: .9167 gold, .0833 silver; edge: reeded

Wedding Celebration of the Duke and Duchess, 2011

This coin features a portrait of the bride and groom with maple leaves and a stylized Tudor rose on the outer edge of the design. Designed by Laurie McGaw.

Wayne & Walter Gretzky, 2011

This coin depicts the Wayne Gretzky in action with his father, Walter Gretzky, as a cameo. Designed by Glen Green.

DATE		QTY.	ISSUE PRICE	PROOF MS-65
2011	$200 Wedding Celebration, proof with Swarovski crystal	760	1,199.99	1,200.00
2011	$200 Wayne & Walter Gretzky, proof with laser of number 99	471	1,299.99	1,300.00

Great Explorers Series, 2012–

Diameter: 29 mm; weight: 15.43 grams; composition: .9167 gold, .0833 silver; edge: reeded

Vikings   Cartier   Champlain

Hudson

DATE		QTY.	ISSUE PRICE	PROOF MS-65
2012	$200 Vikings, proof, designed by Yves Bérubé	3,000	1,199.99	1,200.00
2013	$200 Jacques Cartier, designed by Laurie McGaw.	2,000	1,199.95	1,200.00
2014	$200 Samuel de Champlain, designed by Glen Green.	2,000	1,199.95	1,200.00
2015	$200 Henry Hudson, designed by Laurie McGaw.	2,000	1,199.95	1,200.00

The Challenge – Robert Bateman, 2012

Diameter: 30mm; weight: 31.1g; composition: .99999 gold; bullion weight: 1 troy ounces

The year 2012 marks the 50th anniversary of the Canadian Wildlife Federation (CWF), an organization that has achieved exceptional results in conserving Canadian wilderness and Canadians about environmental issues that concern us all. Robert Bateman, the coin designer, is a world-renowned wildlife artist and an unflagging proponent of wildlife conservation and education. The reverse image features a detail from Robert Bateman's painting, *The Challenge*.

DATE		QTY.	ISSUE PRICE	PROOF MS-65
2012	$200 The Challenge	750	2,699.95	2,700.00

Grandmother Moon Mask, 2013

Diameter: 30mm; weight: 33.33g; composition: .99999 gold; bullion weight: 1.07 troy ounces

The reverse design is a faithful reproduction of the wooden mask that Richard Cochrane carved from a 58.4 cm (23 in) piece of old-growth Red Cedar retrieved from Stanley Park after the 2006 windstorm.

Matriarch Moon Mask, 2014

Diameter: 30.0mm; weight: 33.17grams; composition: .99999 gold; finish: proof; edge: serrated

First Nations culture is rich with profound wisdom that eloquently expresses the inter-connectedness between humanity and all of nature. The terms "Mother Earth" and "Grandmother Moon" clearly reflect the similarities that First Nations people see between these two spheres and the foundational and nourishing role women play in their communities. Reproduced from a wooden carving by Haida artist Carol Young.

DATE		QTY.	ISSUE PRICE	PROOF MS-65
2013	$200 Grandmother Moon Mask	500	2,995.00	3,000.00
2014	$200 Matriarch Moon Mask.	500	2,999.95	3,000.00

Bald Eagle Protecting The Nest, 2014

Diameter: 30.0mm; weight: 31.6grams; composition: .9999 gold; finish: proof; edge: serrated

The bald eagle fiercely defends its territory during breeding season, readily confronting predators as large as a bear to protect its young. Designer: Claudio D'Angelo.

DATE		QTY.	ISSUE PRICE	VALUE
2014	$200 Bald Eagle Protecting the Nest	350	2,699.95	2,700.00

The Howling Wolf, 2014

Diameter: 30.0mm; weight: 31.6grams; composition: .9999 gold
finish: proof; edge: interrupted serrations; bullion weight: 1 troy ounce

The eerie sound of a wolf's howl can pierce the air for miles around. It can be a lone voice in the darkness, or multiple calls echoing from the distance. A wolf's howl can send shivers down the most stalwart spine, when in truth there is nothing to fear. Designer: Pierre Leduc.

DATE		QTY.	ISSUE PRICE	VALUE
2014	$200 The Howling Wolf	2,000	2,799.95	2,800.00

75th Anniversary of the First Royal Visit, 2014

Diameter: 30.0mm; weight: 33.17grams; composition: .9999 gold; finish: proof; edge: serrated

History was made when King George VI and Queen Elizabeth visited Canada in 1939. It was the first time a reigning monarch had ever traveled to North America, and for a young nation eager to flex its muscles of independence, the royal tour provided the perfect opportunity.

DATE		QTY.	ISSUE PRICE	VALUE
2014	$200 75th Anniversary of the First Royal Visit	500	2,999.95	3,000.00

The Bison at Home on the Plains, 2014

Diameter: 30.0mm; weight: 31.16g; composition: 99.99% pure gold; finish: proof ; edge: serrated

Until the late 1800s, the bison reigned as the dominant land-grazing animal throughout Canada's grassland regions, from Manitoba to Alberta. Its unique shoulder hump and shaggy mane are just some of the physical attributes that contribute to the bison's reputation as a symbol of strength. Moving across the landscape in large herds, the plains bison (Bison bison bison) is a social animal. Together, they are highly protective of one another – often reacting as a group to a perceived threat – and will go to great lengths to protect calves. Designer: Claudio D'Angelo.

DATE		QTY.	ISSUE PRICE	VALUE
2014	$200 The Bison at Home on the Plains	350	2,699.95	2,700.00

Interconnections Series, 2014

Diameter: 29.0mm; weight: 15.43g; composition: 99.99% pure gold; finish: proof; edge: serrated

Canada's three natural realms of land, sky, and sea mingle in a landscape of unmatched grandeur. Similarly, its people—First Nations and modern inhabitants alike—though culturally distinct, overlap within this landscape in a unique experience of shared history and nationhood. Designer: Andy Everson.

DATE		QTY.	ISSUE PRICE	VALUE
2014	$200 Interconnections: Land - The Beaver	1,500	1,299.95	1,300.00
2014	$200 Interconnections: Air - The Thunderbird	1,500	1,299.95	1,300.00
2014	$200 Interconnections: Sea - Orca	1,500	1,299.95	1,300.00

White Tailed Deer: Quietly Exploring, 2014

Diameter: 30.0mm; weight: 31.16g; composition: 99.99% pure gold; finish: proof; edge: serrated

The white-tailed deer—a Canadian symbol of nature's still and constant presence. Odocoileus virginianus is the smallest member of the deer family in North America but also the most wide-spread. In fact, the white-tailed deer is the most common of all North American large mammals. Designer: Trevor Tennant.

DATE		QTY.	ISSUE PRICE	VALUE
2014	$200 White Tailed Deer: Quietly Exploring	350	2,699.95	2,700.00

Royal Generations: Her Majesty Queen Elizabeth II, Prince Charles, Prince William and Prince George, 2014

Diameter: 30.0mm; weight: 31.16g; composition: 99.999% pure gold: proof; edge: interrupted serrations

On July 22, 2013, His Royal Highness Prince George Alexander Louis became the newest member of Canada's royal family. Third in line for the throne, and prince of the hearts of royal watchers everywhere, young George's birth was met with all of the joy and fanfare that accompanies such a happy event. Canadian artist Cathy Sabourin's interpretation of a photograph by Camera Press and features a portrait of Her Majesty Queen Elizabeth II with three generations of heirs to the throne: Prince Charles, Prince William and Prince George.

DATE		QTY.	ISSUE PRICE	VALUE
2014	$200 Royal Generations	350	2,799.95	2,800.00

The Fierce Canadian Lynx, 2014

Diameter: 30.0mm; weight: 33.17g; composition: 99.999% pure gold; finish: proof; edge: serrated

Native to the boreal forests that stretch from Yukon to Newfoundland, the Canada lynx (Lynx canadensis) is one of the most common wild cats in Canada. Yet, encounters with this stealthy, agile predator remain rare. Designer: Pierre Leduc.

DATE		QTY.	ISSUE PRICE	VALUE
2014	$200 The Fierce Canadian Lynx............................. 500		2,999.95	3,000.00

Growling Cougar, 2015

Diameter: 30.0mm; weight: 31.16g; composition: 99.999% pure gold: proof; edge: interrupted serrations

Few would contest the cougar's reputation as a stealthy hunter that relies on its keen senses to survive in remote areas of western Canada. Its exceptional vision is uniquely adapted to allow the cougar to hunt its prey during any time of day. Designer: Pierre Leduc.

DATE		QTY.	ISSUE PRICE	VALUE
2015	$200 Growling Cougar 250		2,799.95	2,800.00

Singing Moon Mask, 2015

Diameter: 30.0mm; weight: 33.17g; composition: 99.999% pure gold; proof; edge: serrated

Singing is an integral part of First Nations cultures throughout North America—so integral in fact, that many Aboriginal languages don't have a word for "music." Designer: Andy Everson.

DATE		QTY.	ISSUE PRICE	VALUE
2015	$200 *Singing* Moon Mask 300		2,999.95	3,000.00

Largemouth Bass, 2015

Diameter: 30.0mm; weight: 31.16g; composition: 99.99% pure gold: proof; edge: serrated

The largemouth bass (Micropterus salmoides) is a native North American species of black bass that inhabits lakes and rivers in southern British Columbia, eastern Saskatchewan, southern Manitoba, Ontario, and western and southern Quebec. Often the apex predator among its fish brethren in its local habitat, it is a strong and adaptable species whose ability to thrive makes it not only one of the continent's most widespread fish, but at times an invasive threat to ecosystems. Because of its popularity among anglers, the largemouth is now found around the world. Designer: Curtis Atwater.

DATE		QTY.	ISSUE PRICE	VALUE
2015	$200 Largemouth Bass	300	2,699.95	2,700.00

Maple Leaf Reflection, 2015

Diameter: 30.0mm; weight: 31.16g; composition: 99.99% pure gold: proof; edge: serrated

From coast to coast, Canada's natural landscape offers up endless possibilities where one can find beauty and tranquility—even in the smallest of movements In a moment that could be easily overlooked while surrounded by the grandeur of the forest the leaf's graceful descent reminds us that Mother Nature marks the passage of time in her own unhurried way. Designer: Lilyane Coulombe.

DATE		QTY.	ISSUE PRICE	VALUE
2015	$200 Maple Leaf Reflection	350	2,699.95	2,700.00

250 DOLLARS
Dogsled, 2006

Diameter: 40 mm; weight: 45 grams; finish: proof;
composition: .5833 (14 k) gold, .4167 silver; serrated: edge

The energy and eagerness of the Husky Dog is evident in this design that shows a dog team pulling a sled across a snowbound landscape. Designer: Arnold Nogy.

DATE		QTY.	ISSUE PRICE	VALUE
2006	$250 Dogsled	1,252	1,089.95	1,300.00

Canadian Contemporary Art, 2014

Diameter: 42.0mm; weight: 62.34grams; composition: .9999 gold;
finish: proof; edge: serrated; bullion weight: 2 troy ounces

Explore Canada as you've never seen it before with this captivating coin that draws you in to discover more than 50 images that are Canadian icons in their own right, or reflective of the artist's personal Canadian experiences—like time spent under the Yukon's midnight sun, as shown within the centre of this coin. Designed by renowned Canadian artist Tim Barnard and is titled "Canada Through the Eyes of Tim Barnard."

DATE		QTY.	ISSUE PRICE	VALUE
2014	$250 Canadian Contemporary Art	300	5,199.95	5,200.00

Canadian Machine Gunner in Training - 75th Anniversary of the Declaration of the Second World War, 2014

Diameter: 42.0mm; weight: 62.34g; composition: 99.999% pure gold; finish: proof; edge: serrated

Thanks to a national recruitment drive, over 58,000 men and women enlisted by the month's end. Coastal defences were reinforced, militia regiments were mobilized and the British Commonwealth Air Training Plan (BCATP)–which would eventually train nearly half of the Commonwealth's air crews on Canadian soil–was implemented. In December, units of the 1st Canadian Infantry Division set sail from Halifax to Britain–the first wave of Canadians who would serve overseas until the war's end in 1945. Designer: Silvia Pecota.

DATE		QTY.	ISSUE PRICE	VALUE
2014	$250 Canadian Machine Gunner in Training 200		5,199.95	5,200.00

Grand Trunk Pacific Railway, 2014

Diameter: 42.0mm; weight: 62.34g; composition: 99.99% pure gold; finish: proof; edge: serrated

A century ago, the transcontinental railway enabled the settlement of western Canada. Commemorate the 100th anniversary of the completion of the Grand Trunk Pacific Railway—a massive early twentieth-century engineering feat that linked eastern Canada to the Pacific. Designer: Joel Kimmel.

DATE		QTY.	ISSUE PRICE	VALUE
2014	$250 Grand Trunk Pacific Railway 300		5,199.95	5,200.00

300 DOLLARS

Diameter: 50 mm; weight: 60 grams;
composition: .925 silver proof cameo and 14 karat gold (33.67grams) Images reduced by 50%

Queen Elizabeth II, Triple Cameo Portraits, 2002

Struck to commemorate the Golden Jubilee of Queen Elizabeth II, the obverse features triple sterling silver cameos, one each of the obverse effigies used to date on Canadian Coins. The reverse features a central Victorian rose surmounted by a Royal Crown lying between the dates 1952 and 2002.

Great Seal of Canada, 2003

Diameter: 50 mm; weight: 60 grams; Finish: proof;
composition: 14 karat gold (.5833 gold, .4167 silver); edges: serrated

The Royal Seal of Canada, the official stamp used to bring The Queen's authority to any documents produced on her behalf is depicted on the reverse. The Susanna Blunt effigy appears on the obverse. This coin concludes the Royal Canadian Mint's commemorative issues marking the Golden Jubilee of Queen Elizabeth II.

Queen Elizabeth II, Four Cameo Portraits, 2004

All four effigies of Queen Elizabeth II used on Canadian coins appear as silver cameos on the obverse of the third coin in this series. The reverse, designed by Christie Paquet, displays the Canadian Coat of Arms.

DATE		QTY.	ISSUE PRICE	PROOF MS-65
2002	$300 Triple Cameo, proof................................999		1,099.95	2,000.00
2003	$300 Great Seal of Canada, proof..........................998		1,099.95	1,800.00
2004	$300 Quadruple Cameos, proof 995		1,099.95	1,800.00

120th Anniversary of Standard Time, 2005

On January 1, 1885, celebrated Canadian engineer Sir Sanford Fleming's system of standard time was implemented worldwide thus dividing the world into 24 time zones. These are the first coins in the Achievements series. The clock hands are blackened by laser enhancement. The design was created by Bonnie Ross and the obverse features the Susanna Blunt effigy of the queen.

DATE		QTY.	ISSUE PRICE	PROOF MS-65
2005	$300 120th Anniversary of Standard Time - 4:00, proof	200	999.95	1,800.00
2005	$300 120th Anniversary of Standard Time - 5:00, proof	200	999.95	1,800.00
2005	$300 120th Anniversary of Standard Time - 6:00, proof	200	999.95	1,800.00
2005	$300 120th Anniversary of Standard Time - 7:00, proof	200	999.95	1,800.00
2005	$300 120th Anniversary of Standard Time - 8:00, proof	200	999.95	1,800.00
2005	$300 120th Anniversary of Standard Time - 8:30, proof	200	999.95	1,800.00

Britannia, 2005 -2007

This series commemorates the 25-cent (shinplaster) issues of 1870, 1900 and 1923 respectively. The reverse designs by Robert Ralph Carmichael, recreates the effigy's of Britannia as she appeared on those notes. The obverse features the Susanna Blunt effigy of the queen.

DATE		QTY.	ISSUE PRICE	PROOF MS-65
2005	$300 The 1870 Shinplaster - Britannia, proof	990	1,099.95	1,800.00
2006	$300 The 1900 Shinplaster - Britannia, proof	940	1,414.95	1,800.00
2007	$300 The 1923 Shinplaster - Britannia, proof	1,250	1,440.95	1,800.00

Queen Elizabeth II, 80th Birthday, 2006

Images reduced by 50%

The Imperial State Crown with the Second Star of Africa, the Black Prince's Ruby and the Sapphire of King Edward the Confessor enhanced with an enamel effect. Designer: Cosme Saffioti.

Snowflake, 2006

This is the first coin that features imbedded Swarovski Crystals. Designer: Konrad Wachelko.

Crystal Snowflake, 2010

A six-sided dendrite ice crystal overlaid with Swarovski Elements. Designer: Konrad Wachelko.

DATE		QTY.	ISSUE PRICE	PROOF MS-65
2006	$300 QEII 80th birthday, proof	1,000	1,520.95	1,800.00
2006	$300 Snowflake with crystals, proof	998	1,520.95	1,800.00
2010	$300 Crystal Snowflake, proof	305	2,295.95	2,300.00

Provincial Coat of Arms Series, 2008–2009

This series features the coat of arms of each Province. Designed by the RCM Engravers.

DATE		QTY.	ISSUE PRICE	PROOF MS-65
2008	$300 Newfoundland and Labrador Coat of Arms	472	1,541.95	1,800.00
2008	$300 Alberta Coat of Arms	344	1,631.95	1,800.00
2009	$300 Yukon Coat of Arms	325	1,659.95	1,800.00
2009	$300 Prince Edward Island Coat of Arms	236	1,949.95	1,950.00

Provincial Coat of Arms Series, 2010–2014

DATE		QTY.	ISSUE PRICE	PROOF MS-65
2010	$300 British Colombia Coat of Arms	421	1,949.95	1,950.00
2010	$300 New Brunswick Coat of Arms	233	2,249.95	2,250.00
2011	$300 Manitoba Coat of Arms	472	2,429.95	2,530.00
2011	$300 Nova Scotia Coat of Arms	238	2,649.95	2,650.00
2012	$300 Quebec Coat of Arms	500	2,649.95	2,650.00
2012	$300 Nunavut Coat of Arms	500	2,649.95	2,650.00
2013	$300 Ontario Coat of Arms	500	2,649.95	2,650.00
2013	$300 Northwest Territories Coat of Arms	500	2,649.95	2,650.00
2014	$300 Saskatchewan Coat of Arms	500	2,649.95	2,650.00
2014	$300 Canada Coat of Arms	500	2,649.95	2,650.00

Moon Mask Series, 2008–2009

These coins were inspired by an original red cedar mask carved by renowned Canadian artist Jody Broomfield of the Squamish Nation, Coast Salish people.

DATE		QTY.	ISSUE PRICE	PROOF MS-65
2008	$300 Four seasons mask by Jody Broomfield	236	1,559.95	1,800.00
2009	$300 Summer mask by Jody Broomfield	308	1,723.95	1,800.00

CANADIAN ACHIEVEMENTS SERIES - 14 KT GOLD

Diameter: 40 mm; weight: 45 grams; finish: proof;
composition: .5833 gold, .4167 silver; edge: reeded

2005 -Totem Pole
Design - Dr. Richard Hunt

2006 - Canadarm
Design - Cecily Mok

2007 - Rocky Mountains
Design - Chris Jordison

Obverse
Design - Sunna Blunt

2008 - Imax
Design - Chris Jordison

DATE		QTY.	ISSUE PRICE	PROOF MS-65
2005	$300 Totem Pole 948		1,199.95	1,375.00
2006	$300 Canadarm and Col. Chris Hadfield 581		999.95	1,250.00
2007	$300 Panoramic Photography in Canada - Rocky Mountains 551		1,119.95	1,250.00
2008	$300 Imax - Final in the series 252		1,226.95	1,400.00

The Queen's Diamond Jubilee, 2012

Diameter: 25 mm; weight: 22 grams; finish: proof;
composition: .99999 gold; edge: reeded

This coin features a 0.11-0.14ct round brilliant cut real Canadian diamond viewable from both sides to maximize clarity and sparkle. Designed by Laurie McGaw

DATE		QTY.	ISSUE PRICE	PROOF MS-65
2012	$300 The Queen's Diamond Jubilee	684	1,999.95	2,000.00

VANCOUVER 2010 OLYMPIC WINTER GAMES

Diameter: 50 mm; weight: 60 grams;
composition: .5833 gold (14kt), .4167 silver; edge: serrated, finish: bullion

These three coins will be released one at a time during 2007, 2008 and 2009. Ring of faces by Laurie McGaw. Interior design by David Craig.

2007 Obverse

Olympic Ideals
February 24, 2007

Competition
February 20, 2008

Friendship
February 18, 2009

DATE		QTY.	ISSUE PRICE	VALUE
2007	$300 Olympic Ideals	1,049	1,499.95	1,750.00
2008	$300 Competition	417	1,499.95	1,750.00
2009	$300 Friendship	986	1,499.95	1,750.00

350 DOLLARS

Diameter: 34 mm; weight: 38.05 grams (weight reduced to 35 grams in 2007);
thickness: 2.7 mm; composition: .99999 gold; edge: reeded, finish: proof.

For its 90th anniversary the Royal Canadian Mint introduced a new $350 coin. The obverse features the familiar Dora de Pédery-HUNT effigy of the queen circumscribed by the legend ELIZABETH II CANADA D.G. REGINA FINE GOLD 350 DOLLARS OR PUR. The year of issue and 99,999 appear to either side of the effigy.

| 1998 | 1999 | 2000 |

| 2001 | 2002 | 2003 |

| 2004 | 2005 | 2006 |

DATE	QTY. (000)	ISSUE PRICE	MS-65 PROOF
1998	$350 gold, The Flowers of Canada's Coat of Arms, Pierre Leduc . . 664 only	999.99	1,750.00
1999	$350 gold, The Golden Slipper of P.E.I., by Henry Purdy 2	999.99	1,750.00
2000	$350 gold, The Pacific Dogwood of British Columbia, by Caren Heine. . . . 2	999.99	1,750.00
2001	$350 gold, The Mayflower of Nova Scotia, by Bonnie Ross. 2	999.99	1,750.00
2002	$350 gold, The Wild Rose of Alberta, by Dr Andreas Kare Hellum 2	999.99	1,750.00
2003	$350 gold, The White Trillium of Ontario, by Pamela Stagg 2	1,099.99	1,750.00
2004	$350 gold, The Fireweed of Yukon, by Catherine Ann Deer 2	1,099.99	1,750.00
2005	$350 gold, The Western Lily of Saskatchewan, by Chris Jordison 1.6	1,295.95	1,750.00
2006	$350 gold, Iris Versicolor of Quebec, by Susan Taylor. 2	1,489.95	1,750.00

| 2007 | 2008 Obverse | 2008 |

| 2009 | 2010 | 2011 |

DATE		QTY.	ISSUE PRICE	MS-65 PROOF
2007	$350 gold, Purple Violet of New Brunswick, by Sue Rose	1,392	1,520.95	1,800.00
2008	$350 gold, Purple Saxifrage of Nunavut, by Celia Godkin	1,313	1,520.95	1,800.00
2009	$350 gold, Pitcher Plant of Newfoundland, by Julie Wilson	1,003	2,149.95	1,900.00
2010	$350 gold, Prairie Crocus of Manitoba, by Celia Godkin	775	2,149.95	2,200.00
2011	$350 gold, Mountain Avens of NWT, by Caren Heine	1,300	2,799.95	2,800.00

Sir Isaac Brock, The Hero of Upper Canada, 2012

Diameter: 34mm; weight: 35g; composition: .99999 gold; bullion weight: 1.125 troy ounces

Sir Isaac Brock was born at St Peter Port on the Channel Island of Guernsey, the eighth son of John Brock (1729-1777), a midshipman in the Royal Navy, and Elizabeth de Lisle, daughter of Daniel de Lisle, then Lieutenant-Bailiff of Guernsey. Brock was assigned to Canada in 1802. He was promoted to major general, and became responsible for defending Upper Canada. Brock's actions, particularly his success at Detroit, earned him a knighthood, membership in the Order of the Bath, accolades and the sobriquet "The Hero of Upper Canada".

DATE		QTY.	ISSUE PRICE	MS-65 PROOF
2012	$350 Sir Isaac Brock	1,000	2,799.95	2,800.00

Polar Bear, 2013

Diameter: 34.0mm; weight: 35.0grams; composition: .9999 gold; finish: proof; edge: serrated

The majestic polar bear is a fitting icon for a nation that, like Ursus martimus itself, has been shaped by the forces of ice, wind, water and stone. Stoic and strong, adaptable and clever, the polar bear has long captivated the Canadian imagination and been held up as a symbol of the northern spirit. Design by Glen Loates.

DATE	QTY.	ISSUE PRICE	VALUE
2013 $350 Polar Bear 600		2,799.95	2,800.00

The Majestic Moose, 2014

Diameter: 34.0mm; weight: 35.0grams; composition: .9999 gold; finish: proof; edge: serrated

Found in forests across Canada–from the Alaskan border to Newfoundland and Labrador–this "gentle giant" is known for its easy-going nature.

DATE	QTY.	ISSUE PRICE	VALUE
2014 $350 The Majestic Moose 600		2,799.95	2,800.00

500 DOLLARS

Diameter: 60 mm; weight: 155.5 grams;
composition: .9999 gold; edge serrated; finish: proof
Images reduced by 25%

Queen's Diamond Wedding 60th Anniversary, 2007

This 5 ounce fine gold coin was issued in commemoration of the Queens diamond wedding 60th anniversary, with design by Steve Hepburn.

DATE		QTY.	ISSUE PRICE	VALUE
2007	$500 Diamond Wedding Anniversary.	198	5,999.95	8,000.00

100th Anniversary of the RCM, 2008

This 5 ounce fine gold coin was issued in commemoration 100th anniversary of the Royal Canadian Mint, with reverse design by the RCM engravers.

DATE		QTY.	ISSUE PRICE	VALUE
2008	$500 100th Anniversary of the RCM	248	8,159.95	8,000.00

150th Anniversary — Construction of the Parliament Buildings Begins, 2009

Issued in commemoration of the 150th Anniversary of the start of construction of the Parliament buildings, with reverse design by the RCM engravers.

75th Anniversary of the First Bank Notes, 2010

The Bank of Canada's inaugural notes were introduced on March 11, 1935 and included denominations of $1, $2, $5, $10, $20, $50, $100, $500 and $1,000 with a $25 note issued later that year to commemorate the silver jubilee of King George V. Reverse design by the RCM engravers.

DATE		QTY.	ISSUE PRICE	VALUE
2009	$500 150th Anniversary - Construction of the Parliament Buildings 200		10,199.95	8,000.00
2010	$500 75th Anniversary of the First Bank Notes. 191		9,495.95	9,500.00

100th Anniversary of the First Canadian Gold Coins, 2012

Diameter: 60.15 mm; weight: 156.05 grams; composition: .9999 gold; edge serrated; finish: proof. Images reduced by 25%

In 1912, the Mint produced the first distinctly Canadian gold coins in denominations of five and ten dollar. Reverse by the RCM engravers.

DATE		QTY.	ISSUE PRICE	VALUE
2012	$500 100th Anniversary of the First Canadian Gold Coins 115		12,274.95	12,300.00

Maple Leaf Forever, 2012

Diameter: 60mm; weight: 156.05g; composition: .99999 gold; bullion weight: 5 troy ounces

The maple leaf today appears on the penny. However, between 1876 and 1901, it appeared on all Canadian coins. The modern one-cent piece has two maple leaves on a common twig, a design that has gone almost unchanged since 1937.

Calgary Stampede Centennial (1912–2012)

Celebrating 100 years of the Calgary Stampede.

DATE	QTY.	ISSUE PRICE	VALUE
2012 . . $500 Maple Leaf Forever 200		11,999.95	12,000.00
2012 . . $500 Calgary Stampede Centennial 200		11,999.95	12,000.00

HMS Shannon & USS Chesapeake, 2013

The reverse image depicts the final moments of the famous battle of HMS Shannon, pictured on the right, and the battle-worn USS Chesapeake, pictured on the left with its decks ablaze and gun-ports destroyed.

DATE	QTY.	ISSUE PRICE	VALUE
2013 . . $500 HMS Shannon & USS Chesapeake 200		11,999.95	12,000.00

An Aboriginal Story, 2013

Diameter: 60.15mm; weight: 156.05grams; composition: .9999 gold; finish: proof; edge: plain

Part of the Atikamekw First Nation's artistic cooperative, artist Raymond Weizineau of Obedji-wan, Quebec, takes his inspiration from the culture and traditions of his nation.

As with many Inuit and First Nations cultures, the Atikamekw First Nation peoples living in the Mauricie and Lanaudière regions of Quebec pass on their teachings through storytelling. A major element of their oral tradition is tales from the animal world in a mythical time when animals could speak, characters could change shape at will, creatures could die and return to life and one being could inhabit multiple forms. Even today, the Atikamekw like to describe a person with the characteristics of an animal. In Nerosiw Matcisowin, we see the elements of this tradition as it has been passed down from generation to generation among the Atikamekw.

DATE		QTY.	ISSUE PRICE	VALUE
2013	$500 An Aboriginal Story	100	12,000.00	12,000.00

The Legend of the Spirit Bear, 2014

Diameter: 60.15mm; weight: 156.05grams; composition: .9999 gold; finish: proof; edge: plain

Spirit Bear is a great source of intrigue, as is the First Nations legend how this unique bear came to be. When Raven first created the world, everything was white. After some time, Raven decided the world needed colour, but as the ice began to melt, people started fighting over the land that appeared. Years passed, more and more animals changed colour and the world became more beautiful than ever, but the people kept fighting over everything. So, Raven decided to remind them where they came from by turning one in every ten bears white. An original work by Coast Salish First Nation's artist Darlene Gait.

DATE		QTY.	ISSUE PRICE	VALUE
2014	$500 The Legend of the Spirit Bear	50	12,000.00	12,000.00

1,000 DOLLARS
100th Anniversary of the Declaration of the First World War, 2014

Diameter: 76.1mm; weight: 311.5g; composition: 99.99% pure gold; finish: proof; edge: serrated; image reduced by 50%

During the First World War, the final view that tens of thousands of soldiers had after leaving port in the city of Québec was the soaring cliffs of the Gaspe Peninsula. A similar sight awaited those who departed from Halifax (Nova Scotia); they too would watch Canada's rugged coastline disappear behind the horizon. Designer: Yves Bérubé.

DATE		QTY.	ISSUE PRICE	VALUE
2014	$1,000 100th Anniversary of the Declaration of the First World War 40		21,000.00	21,000.00

1,250 DOLLARS
Growling Cougar, 2015
Diameter: 85.0mm; weight: 500.0g; composition: 99.99% pure gold; finish: proof; edge: serrated; image reduced by 50%

Across the wilds of western North and South America stalks the world's fourth-largest cat: the cougar. Found in remote areas from southern Canada to Patagonia, the elusive Puma concolor enjoys the greatest range of any large wild animal in the entire Western hemisphere. This massive tawny cat—about the size of a leopard—stalks the landscapes where its prey lives: from the seaside to the Rocky Mountains, from deserts to boreal forests. Designer: Pierre Leduc.

DATE		QTY.	ISSUE PRICE	VALUE
2015	$1,250 Growling Cougar	25	32,000.00	32,000.00

Howling Wolf, 2014
Diameter: 85.35mm; weight: 500.0g; composition: 99.99% pure gold; finish: proof; edge: serrated
image reduced by approx 50%

Four subspecies of Canis lupus are found across northern and western Canada and in the region around the Great Lakes Some experts believe that howling—that eerie hallmark of this unique species—is a key element of territory establishment, acting both as a warning to other packs and a call to gathering among pack members. Designer: Pierre Leduc.

DATE		QTY.	ISSUE PRICE	VALUE
2014	$1,250 Howling Wolf.	25	32,000.00	32,000.00

2,500 DOLLARS — ONE KILO GOLD

Diameter: 101.6 mm; weight: 1000 grams; finish: proof;
composition: .9999 gold; edge: plain; images reduced by 50%

Vancouver 2010 Olympic Winter Games, 2007 - 2010

These coins are struck in ultra high relief and are the first series of one kilo gold coins ever produced by the RCM.

2007 - Early Canada

2008 - Towards Confederation

— 173 —   2009 - The Canada of Today

2009 - Surviving the Flood   2010 - The Eagle

125th Anniversary of Banff National Park, 2010

2010 - Banff

A montage depicting the history and development of Banff National Park set among the park's majestic mountains and lakes. Reverse design by the RCM engravers.

DATE		QTY.	ISSUE PRICE	VALUE
2007	$2,500 Early Canada, by Stanley Witten.	20	36,000	50,000
2008	$2,500 Towards Confederation, by Susan Taylor	20	49,000	50,000
2009	$2,500 Surviving the Flood, by Xwa Lack Tun	50	54,000	50,000
2009	$2,500 The Canada of Today, by Vancouver Org. Com.	49	54,000	50,000
2010	$2,500 The Eagle, by Xwa lack tun (Rick Harry).	20	54,000	50,000
2010	$2,500 125th Anniversary of Banff National Park.	20	57,000	57,000

2011 - Maple Leaf Forever   2011 - Lacrosse

Maple Leaf Forever, 2011

The design features a trilogy of maple leaves inspired by the airy design that has graced Canada's one-cent circulation coin since 1937.

375th Anniversary of Lacrosse, 2011

To the First Nations people, lacrosse was much more than play. Countless tribes engaged in "The Creator's Game", firm in the belief the Creator invented the game for his own amusement. Players took to the field with the highest ideals. Lacrosse was a training ground for young warriors and was a non-warring means to settle tribal disputes.

Year of the Dragon, 2012

2012 - Year of the Dragon

A stylized dragon character, surrounded by lotus flowers and dark thunderclouds, which are an omen of prosperity and often associated with dragons.

DATE		QTY.	ISSUE PRICE	VALUE
2011	$2,500 Maple Leaf Forever, by Debbie Adams	35	59,995.95	60,000
2011	$2,500 375th Anniversary of Lacrosse, by Steve Hepburn	29	69,000	70,000
2012	$2,500 Year of the Dragon, by Three Degrees Creative Group Inc.	38	69,000	70,000

Maple Leaf Forever, 2012

DATE		QTY.	ISSUE PRICE	VALUE
2012	$2,500 Maple Leaf Forever, by Luc Normandin 30		69,000.00	70,000

The Challenge – Robert Bateman, 2012

The year 2012 marks the 50th anniversary of the Canadian Wildlife Federation (CWF), an organization that has achieved exceptional results in conserving Canadian wilderness and Canadians about environmental issues that concern us all. Robert Bateman, the coin designer, is a world-renowned wildlife artist and an unflagging proponent of wildlife conservation and education. The reverse image features a detail from Robert Bateman's painting, *The Challenge.*

Canadian Arctic Landscape, 2013

Mapped by Canadian explorers such as those of the 1913 Canadian Arctic Expedition, the lands, waterways, and continental shelves extending from the Northwest Passage to the nearer North are sovereign Canadian territories that play an important role in the heritage of Canada's people, geography, and environment.

DATE		QTY.	ISSUE PRICE	VALUE
2012	$2,500 The Challenge 30		69,000.00	70,000
2013	$2,500 Canadian Arctic Landscape 30		69,000.00	70,000

250th Anniversary of the end of the Seven Years War

Canadian artist Luc Normandin designed the reverse which features a period map inspired by Didier Robert de Vaugondy, a renowned map maker of the mid 1700's. The map shows the region where the Seven Years War was fought in North America.

Battle of Chateauguay and Battle of Crysler

Royal Canadian Mint engravers faithfully reproduced portions of historical works by Canadian artists to create the reverse design in commemoration of two key battles from the War of 1812.

DATE		QTY.	ISSUE PRICE	VALUE
2013	$2,500 Seven Years War	30	69,000.00	70,000
2013	$2,500 Battle of Chateauguay and Battle of Crysler	30	69,000.00	70,000

The Caribou, 2013

Diameter: 101.6mm; weight: 1,000.0grams; composition: .9999 gold; finish: proof; edge: serrated

With about 2.4 million caribou roaming freely through the vast Canadian wilderness, our nation is home to one of the world's largest populations. As exceptional travelers, caribou cover more ground in their migrations than any other land animal: in fact, some of Canada's caribou populations travel up to 5,000 kilometres each year. Designer: Trevor Tennant.

DATE		QTY.	ISSUE PRICE	VALUE
2013	$2,500 The Caribou	20	69,000.00	70,000

In the Eyes of the Snowy Owl, 2014

Diameter: 101.6mm; weight: 1,000.0grams; composition: .9999 gold; finish: proof; edge: serrated

Few animals can match the owl for the intensity of its gaze. Unlike other birds, an owl's eyes are located on the front of its head, an adaptation that heightens its depth perception for targeting prey, which it can spot over tremendous distances. Designer: Arnold Nogy.

DATE	QTY.	ISSUE PRICE	VALUE
2014 $2,500 In the Eyes of the Snowy Owl 10		69,000.00	70,000

Year of the Horse, 2014

Diameter: 101.6mm; weight: 1,000.0grams; composition: .9999 gold; finish: proof; edge: serrated

The year 2014 is ruled by the Horse. The Horse personality embodies life, liberty and happiness. He's amazingly agile, physically and mentally; a master problem-solver. Designed by Three Degrees Creative Group.

DATE	QTY.	ISSUE PRICE	VALUE
2014 $2,500 Year of the Horse. 18		69,000.00	70,000

The Battle of Lundy's Lane, 2014

Diameter: 101.6mm; weight: 1,000g; composition: 99.99 % pure gold; finish: proof ; edge: serrated

As the War of 1812 waged on, American and British North American forces continued to battle one another for territorial gains. On July 25, 1814, troops from both sides came face-to-face in an explosive encounter that would bring an end to one last attempted invasion of Upper Canada. Designed by Bonnie Ross.

DATE		QTY.	ISSUE PRICE	VALUE
2014	$2,500 The Battle of Lundy's Lane 10		69,000.00	70,000

In the Eyes of the Cougar, 2015

Diameter: 101.6mm; weight: 1,000.0g; composition: 99.99% pure gold; finish: proof; edge: serrated

Few would contest the cougar's reputation as a stealthy hunter that relies on its keen senses to survive in remote areas of western Canada. Its exceptional vision is uniquely adapted to allow the cougar to hunt its prey during any time of day. Designer: Glen Loates.

DATE		QTY.	ISSUE PRICE	VALUE
2015	$2,500 In the Eyes of the Cougar. 10		69,000.00	69,000

Year of the Sheep, 2015

Diameter: 101.6mm; weight: 1,000.0g; composition: 99.99% pure gold; finish: proof; edge: serrated

The year 2015 is ruled by the Sheep. The creative Sheep personality embodies wealth, warmth and loveliness. Good things seem to come to the Sheep naturally because of its irresistibly good nature. The Sheep rarely speaks its mind. It will go with the flow and only object when things aren't going its way. Push too hard and it will react—decisively! The gregarious Sheep is an eternal romantic. It adores being showered with love and attention. Designer: Three Degrees Creative Group.

DATE		QTY.	ISSUE PRICE	VALUE
2015	$2,500 Year of the Sheep	10	69,000.00	69,000

Maple Leaf Forever (Hologram), 2015

Diameter: 101.6mm; weight: 1,000.0g; composition: 99.99% pure gold; finish: proof; edge: serrated

For over a hundred years, the mighty maple leaf has been used as a beloved symbol for Canada—one that has been immortalized in songs and artwork, and featured on everything from pins, badges and backpacks to banknotes and the flag. While several different maple species are native to Canada, the general outline of their leaves is instantly recognizable, and has become synonymous with national pride and identity. Designer: Celia Godkin.

DATE		QTY.	ISSUE PRICE	VALUE
2015	$2,500 Maple Leaf Forever	10	69,000.00	69,000

100,000 Dollars Gold Maple Leaf

Diameter: 180 mm; weight: 10 kilos;
composition: .99999 gold; finish: proof; images reduced by 75%

The Spirit of Haida Gwaii, 2011

The bold contours of the sculpture commissioned in 1985 for the Canadian Embassy in Washington, D.C., are precisely captured in an ultra-high relief engraving, unique in the world of numismatic art for its sculptural quality. This is the first ever Canadian coin to bear a $100,000 face value. Design by Bill Reid and engraved by Cosme Saffioti.

DATE		QTY.	ISSUE PRICE	VALUE
2011	$100,000 The Spirit of Haida Gwaii......................... 2 pieces		BV	525,000

CANADIAN COLLECTORS' COINS

This section includes items and sets of special quality or unique design and sold directly to collectors at a premium over the face value of the coins. These are produced by the mint as collectors' issues and not released as circulating coinage. Some sets issued in proof-like, specimen or proof condition have been broken by dealers or collectors to acquire higher-quality samples of the year's circulating coinage, although these coins were never released in these conditions individually. In these instances, this catalogue lists only the value of the complete sets as issued. Where, however, a coin from a set was also released singly, the coin has been listed as an individual collectors' item as well.

The quality of strike on collectors' issues varies from series to series and care must be exercised in determining the quality of the strike.

PROOF-LIKE: This term is commonly used to describe select uncirculated coins produced by the mint for collectors. These coins have been struck more slowly than regular circulating coinage, using well-polished dies and selected blanks, to produce a superior finish. Sometimes collectors mistake them for specimen or proof but, they are not double struck and the edges in particular are not as sharp and crisp as the superior specimen and proof strikes.

SPECIMEN: Specimen sets and singles were produced prior to 1973, because the Royal Canadian Mint was incapable of producing true proof-quality coins. These were double-struck under higher pressure than circulating coins and possess sharper details and squarer edges than the proof-like quality, but do not come up to the quality of proof coins.

PROOF: This is the highest quality in which coins are minted. Struck on selected blanks, they are the result of multiple, slow strikes under extreme pressure, using specially-prepared dies. The first proof-quality coins struck by the Royal Canadian Mint were those of the Olympic series, beginning in 1973. Proof coins usually exhibit a frosted relief with polished mirror fields and have sharp crisp edges. A proof coin should have no marks or abrasions.

1 CENT SELECTIVE GOLD PLATING PROOF

Diameter: 19.05 mm; weight: 2.25 grams; edge: plain;
composition: copper-plated zinc, selective gold plating

Issued with the 2003 Annual mint report, this coin is the first in a series of five in a countdown to the 2008 centennial of the Royal Canadian Mint.

DESCRIPTION	QTY. (000)	ISSUE PRICE	VALUE
2003 1¢ Maple Leaves - Selective gold plating 10		19.95	60.00

3 CENTS STERLING SILVER PROOF
3d Red Beaver Postage Stamp, 2001

Diameter: 21.20 mm; weight: 5.39 grams; edge: plain;
composition: .925 silver, 24-karat gold covered

Issued for the 150th anniversary of the first Canadian postage stamp, the 3d Beaver, was designed by Sir Sandford Fleming and issued April 23, 1851.

DESCRIPTION	QTY. (000)	ISSUE PRICE	VALUE
2001 3¢ Beaver 60		39.95*	22.00

The coin was issued in a clam-style package which included a medallion replica of the original red beaver stamp and the 2001 Canada Post commemorative stamp.

5 CENTS STERLING SILVER PROOF

Diameter: 21.20 mm; weight: 5.35 grams; edge: plain;
composition: .925 silver, .075 copper

2000    2001

Les Voltigeurs de Québec, 2000

Issued to honour Les Voltigeurs de Québec, the first French-Canadian regiment, which has distinguished itself in war and peace since 1863. The reverse device depicts a baton, drums and a sash, each of which features the insignia of the regiment.

Royal Military College, 2001

Issued in honour of the 125th anniversary of the Royal Military College of Canada, at Kingston, Ontario. The RMC is the only national military college in Canada.

DESCRIPTION	QTY. (000)	ISSUE PRICE	VALUE
2000 5¢ Les Voltigeurs de Québec	34	16.95	25.00
2001 5¢ Royal Military College	26	16.95	25.00

Vimy Ridge, 2002

Honouring the brave Canadians who fought at the Battle for Vimy Ridge during World War I. The reverse features Canada mourning her dead with the Vimy Ridge Memorial in the background.

DESCRIPTION	QTY. (000)	ISSUE PRICE	VALUE
2002 5¢ Vimy Ridge	23	16.95	40.00

60th Anniversary of D-Day, 2004

Issued in honour of the 60th anniversary of D-Day. 12-sided coin.

60th Anniversary of VE-Day, 2005

Issued in honour of the 60th anniversary of VE-Day. 12-sided coin. The selective gold plated coin was issued with the 2005 Mint Report. This coin is the third in a series of five in a countdown to the 2008 centennial of the Royal Canadian Mint.

DESCRIPTION	QTY. (000)	ISSUE PRICE	VALUE
2004 5¢ D-Day, 1944–2004	20	N/A	45.00
2005 5¢ VE-Day, 1945–2005	42	N/A	25.00
2005 5¢ VE-Day, 1945–2005, selective gold plating	6	29.95	70.00

Legacy of the Canadian Nickel, 2015

Diameter: 40.0mm; weight: 31.83g; composition: 99.99% pure silver; finish: proof; edge: serrated

Throughout its history, each of the nickel's transformations provides a glimpse of a young nation that was seeking to define itself, and a Mint that would quickly come into its own. This Legacy of the Canadian Nickel is a retrospective look at the history of 5-cent coins minted by the Royal Canadian Mint.

DATE		QTY.	ISSUE PRICE	VALUE
2015	5¢ Crossed Maple Bough	8,500	109.95	110.00
2015	5¢ Two Maple Leaves	8,500	109.95	110.00
2015	5¢ The Victory	8,500	109.95	110.00
2015	5¢ The Identification of Nickel	8,500	109.95	110.00
2015	5¢ The Centennial 5-cent coin	8,500	109.95	110.00
2015	5¢ The Beaver	8,500	109.95	110.00

2015 Big Coin Series

Diameter: 65.25mm; weight: 157.6g; composition: 99.99% pure silver; finish: proof with selective gold plating; edge: serrated; ; images reduced by 50%

Part of a six-coin set featuring 5¢, 10¢, 25¢, 50¢, $1, and $2 values.

DATE		QTY.	ISSUE PRICE	VALUE
2015	5¢ Beaver (March 2015) - G.E. Kruger-Gray	1,500	549.95	550.00

10 CENTS STERLING SILVER

Diameter: 18.03 mm; weight: 2.4 grams; thickness: 1.2 mm; edge: reeded;
composition: .925 silver, .075 copper

1997    2000

John Cabot, 1997

Issued to commemorate the 500th anniversary of the first voyage of discovery by John Cabot (born Giovanni Caboto) from Bristol, England in 1497. This was the first Canadian 10¢ piece to be issued expressly as a commemorative coin in proof quality only.

Canadian Credit Unions, 2000

In the year 2000 a second 10¢ coin was struck only in proof quality for collectors. The coin celebrates the centenary of credit unions in Quebec.

DESCRIPTION	QTY. (000)	ISSUE PRICE	VALUE
1997 10¢ Cabot's ship Matthew, proof	50	10.95	20.00
2000 10¢ Centenary of Credit Unions in Quebec, proof	70	14.95	10.00

Year of the Volunteer, 2001

This sterling silver proof version of the circulation 10 cent coin for 2001 was issued individually to collectors. The coins were intended to recognize the contribution of our many volunteers and also to help celebrate the United Nations Year of the Volunteer.

DESCRIPTION	QTY. (000)	ISSUE PRICE	VALUE
2001 10¢ Year of the Volunteer, proof	41	14.95	10.00
2001 10¢ Year of the Volunteer, uncirculated	incl. above	4.95	3.00

10 CENTS .9999 PURE SILVER

Open Championship of Canada, 2004

Features the exclusive RCGA medallion and 99.99% silver five-dollar coin (The Driver) that are only available with this frame. Also includes the special edition 10-cent coin (The Putter) and two round, golf ball-sized stamps with an image of the Glen Abbey Golf Course.

In collaboration with Canada Post. Open Championship of Canada—Canadian Open 100th Anniversary (1904-2004).

DESCRIPTION	QTY. (000)	ISSUE PRICE	VALUE
2004 Open Championship of Canada, proof	37	19.95	25.00

2015 Big Coin Series

Diameter: 65.25mm; weight: 157.6g; composition: 99.99% pure silver; finish: proof with selective gold plating; edge: serrated; ; images reduced by 50%

Part of a six-coin set featuring 5¢, 10¢, 25¢, 50¢, $1, and $2 values.

DATE		QTY.	ISSUE PRICE	VALUE
2015	10¢ Bluenose (May 2015) - Emanuel Hahn 1,500		549.95	550.00

25 CENTS STERLING SILVER PROOF

Diameter: 23.88 mm; weight: 6.0 grams; edge: reeded;
composition: .925 silver, .075 copper

125th Anniversary of Confederation, 1992

New Brunswick
Covered Bridge, Newton

Northwest Territories
Inuit "Inukshuk"

Newfoundland
Fisherman in Grandy Dory

Manitoba
Lower Fort Garry

Yukon
Kaskawalsh Glacier

Alberta
Hoodoos

Prince Edward Island
Cousins Shore

Ontario
Jack Pines

Nova Scotia
Lighthouse

Quebec
Percé Rock

Saskatchewan
Prairie symbols

British Columbia
Natural Beauty of B.C

To celebrate the 125th anniversary of Confederation, the mint issued a different 25-cent piece each month during 1992 to represent Canada's ten provinces and two territories. These sterling silver 25-cent pieces were offered in individual display cases.

DATE		QTY. (000)	ISSUE PRICE	VALUE
1992	Commemorative 25¢ (each) proof	65	129.45	95.00

Millennium, 1999

Diameter: 23.88 mm; weight: 6.0 grams; edge: reeded;
composition: .925 silver, .075 copper

| January | February | March |
| A Country Unfolds | Etched in Stone | The Log Drive |

| April | May | June |
| Our Northern Heritage | Les Voyageurs | From Coast to Coast |

| July | August | September |
| A Nation of People | The Pioneer Spirit | Canada Through a Child's Eye |

October	November	December
A Tribute to	The Airplane	This is
First Nations	Opens the North	Canada

The end of the second millennium was celebrated by striking a different 25 cent design for each month during 1999 and 2000. The reverse designs were chosen from entries submitted from across Canada.

DATE		QTY. (000)	ISSUE PRICE	VALUE
1999	Millennium silver proof 25¢, singles	115	each 14.95	10.00
1999	Millennium silver proof 25¢, set of 12	incl. above	149.95	95.00
1999	Millennium nickel 25¢, set of 12,	1,500	24.95	12.00

Millennium, 2000

Diameter: 23.88 mm; weight: 6.0 grams; edge: reeded;
composition: .925 silver, .075 copper

| January | February | March |
| Pride | Ingenuity | Achievement |

| April | May | June |
| Health | Natural Legacy | Harmony |

| July | August | September |
| Celebration | Family | Wisdom |

| October | November | December |
| Creativity | Freedom | Community |

DATE		QTY. (000)	ISSUE PRICE	VALUE
2000	Millennium 25¢, silver proof 85		each 14.95	10.00
2000	Millennium 25¢, set of 12, silver proof ....inc. above		149.95	95.00
2000	Millennium 25¢, set of 12, nickel, uncirculated 876		24.95	10.00

Vancouver 2010 Olympic Winter Games
Silver 25 Cents Coins

Diameter: 23.88 mm; weight: 6.0 grams; edge: reeded;
composition: .925 silver, .075 copper

This Vancouver 2010 set includes twelve 25-cent sports-themed coins in sterling silver and is accompanied by a wafer engraved with the Vancouver 2010 Olympic and Paralympic Winter Games emblems. All reverse designs by Glen Green with obverse design by Susanna Blunt.

| 2007 Obverse | Curling | Ice Hockey | Wheelchair Curling |

| Biathlon | Alpine Skiing | 2008 Obverse | Snowboarding |

| Freestyle Skiing | Figure Skating | Bobsleigh | 2009 Obverse |

| Speed Skating | Cross Country Skiing | Paralympic Obverse | Ice Sledge Hockey |

DATE		QTY. (000)	ISSUE PRICE	VALUE
2007 - 2009	25¢ Vancouver 2010 Olympic silver proof set . . . . N/A		199.95	200.00
2007 - 2009	25¢ Vancouver 2010 Olympic circulation collection 14 coin NBS . . N/A		29.95	30.00

COLOURISED 25 CENTS

Diameter: 23.88 mm; weight: 6.0 grams; edge: reeded; composition: .999 nickel; finish: uncirculated.

Pride, 2000

The 25-cent coin for January 2000, called *Pride*, was also re-issued colourised. The ribbon and the three maple leaves in the reverse device are red and represent the date 2000.

DATE		QTY. (000)	ISSUE PRICE	VALUE
2000	Millennium 25¢ Pride 50		8.95	75.00

Canada Day, 2000–2009

Diameter: 23.88 mm; weight: 4.4 grams; edge: reeded; finish: uncirculated
composition: (2000) nickel, (2001 –) nickel plated steel.

DATE		QTY. (000)	ISSUE PRICE	VALUE
2000	25¢ Celebration, reverse by Laura Paxton 26		8.95	15.00
2001	25¢ Spirit, reverse by Silke Ware. 96		9.95	15.00
2002	25¢ People holding Maple Leaf, reverse by Judith Chartier. 50		9.95	15.00
2003	25¢ Polar Bear, Maple Leaves, reverse by Jade Pearen 64		9.95	20.00
2004	25¢ Maple Leaf in a spiral, reverse by Cosme Saffioti 45		9.95	20.00
2005	25¢ Beaver, reverse by Stan Witten 58		9.95	20.00
2006	25¢ Flag, reverse by Stan Witten 30		9.95	20.00
2007	25¢ RCMP Saluting. 28		9.95	15.00
2008	25¢ Moose with sunglasses 19		9.95	15.00
2009	25¢ Four cartoon animals sailing boat. 17		14.95	20.00

COLOURISED CHRISTMAS DAY 25 CENTS, 2004–

| 2004 | 2005 | 2006 | 2007 |

| 2008 | 2009 | 2010 |

DATE		QTY. (000)	ISSUE PRICE	VALUE
2004	25¢ Santa Claus	63	19.95	35.00
2005	25¢ Christmas Stocking	73	19.95	20.00
2006	25¢ Santa sled and Reindeer	99	19.95	20.00
2007	25¢ Christmas Tree	66	19.95	20.00
2008	25¢ Santa photo	42	19.95	20.00
2009	25¢ Santa with 3 maple leaves	33	19.95	20.00
2010	25¢ Santa with tree and ribbon	42	19.95	20.00

COLOURISED 25 CENTS, 2004–2007

| 2004 | 2005 | 2006 | 2007 |

| 2007 | 2007 | 2007 | 2007 |

DATE		QTY. (000)	ISSUE PRICE	VALUE
2004	25¢ Poppy, RCM Annual Report, proof	13	29.95	30.00
2005	25¢ Poppy	30	N/A	30.00
2006	25¢ Quebec Winter Carnival	8	19.95	20.00
2007	25¢ Wedding Bouquet (From Wedding Gift Set)	11	19.95	20.00
2007	25¢ Fireworks (From Congratulations Gift Set)	10	19.95	20.00
2007	25¢ Maple Leaf (From Oh! Canada! Gift Set)	24	19.95	20.00
2007	25¢ Balloons (From Birthday Gift Set)	13	19.95	20.00
2007	25¢ Rattle (From Baby Gift Set)	31	19.95	150.00

SPECIAL ISSUES 25 CENTS, 2004–2005

2004   2005

DATE		QTY. (000)	ISSUE PRICE	VALUE
2004	25¢ Moose, Canada Day, bundle set, designed by Nick Wooster 45		9.95	30.00
2005	25¢ 60th Year of Liberation 4		N/A	125.00

COLOURISED 25 CENTS, 2008–2009

2008   2008   2008   2008

2008   2008   2009   2009

2009   2009   2009   2009

DATE		QTY. (000)	ISSUE PRICE	VALUE
2008	25¢ Cake (From Wedding Gift Set) 7		19.95	20.00
2008	25¢ Trophy (From Congratulations Gift Set) 7		19.95	20.00
2008	25¢ Flag (From Oh! Canada! Gift Set) 31		19.95	20.00
2008	25¢ Party Hat (From Birthday Gift Set) 11		19.95	20.00
2008	25¢ Teddy Bear (From Baby Gift Set) 30		19.95	30.00
2008	25¢ Poppy (From 90th Anniversary of the end of WWI Set) 10		19.95	20.00
2009	25¢ Birds (From Wedding Greeting Card and Coin) 11		19.95	20.00
2009	25¢ Fireworks (From Congratulations Greeting Card and Coin) 8		19.95	20.00
2009	25¢ Night time Teddy Bear (From Baby Gift Set) 25		19.95	100.00
2009	25¢ Flower (From Thank You Greeting Card and Coin) 10		19.95	20.00
2009	25¢ Party Favours (From Birthday Greeting Card and Coin) 14		19.95	20.00
2009	25¢ Gold Maple Leafs (From Oh! Canada! Gift Set) 25		19.95	20.00

COLOURISED 25 CENTS, 2010

DATE		QTY.	ISSUE PRICE	VALUE
2010	25¢ Heart (From Wedding Greeting Card and Coin) 8,194		19.95	20.00
2010	25¢ 4 Stars (From Congratulations Greeting Card and Coin). 5,693		19.95	20.00
2010	25¢ Stroller (From Baby Gift Set). 27,048		19.95	30.00
2010	25¢ Flowers (From Thank You Greeting Card and Coin) 5,932		19.95	20.00
2010	25¢ Gift Box (From Birthday Greeting Card and Coin) 8,751		19.95	20.00
2010	25¢ Three Maple Leafs (From Oh! Canada! Gift Set) 19,769		19.95	20.00

SPECIAL ISSUES 25 CENTS, 2011–2012

2011	25¢ Wedding Bands (From Wedding Gift Set) 20,461		19.95	20.00
2011	25¢ Tooth Fairy (From Tooth Fairy Gift Card) 38,200		9.95	10.00
2011	25¢ Baby Feet (From Baby Gift Set). 38,576		19.95	20.00
2011	25¢ Ballons (From Birthday Gift Set) 21,173		19.95	20.00
2011	25¢ Small Maple Leaf (From O Canada Gift Set) 22,475		19.95	20.00
2011	25¢ Snowflake (From Holiday Gift Set) by RCM Engravers. 41,666		19.95	20.00
2012	25¢ Wedding Bands (From Wedding Gift Set) by Gary Taxali . . . . N/A		19.95	20.00
2012	25¢ Tooth Fairy (From Tooth Fairy Gift Card) by Gary Taxali . . . . N/A		9.95	10.00
2012	25¢ Toy (From Baby Gift Set) by Gary Taxali . . . . N/A		19.95	20.00
2012	25¢ Cake (From Birthday Gift Set) by Gary Taxali. . . . . N/A		19.95	20.00
2012	25¢ Maple Leafs (From O Canada Gift Set) by Gary Taxali . . . . N/A		19.95	20.00

COLOURISED HOCKEY 25 CENTS, 2006

DATE		QTY.	ISSUE PRICE	VALUE
2006	25¢ Montreal Canadians, from gift set 70,000		24.95	25.00
2006	25¢ Ottawa Senators, from gift set . . . . included above		24.95	25.00
2006	25¢ Toronto Maple Leafs, from gift set . . . . included above		24.95	25.00

COLOURISED HOCKEY 25 CENTS, 2007

DATE		QTY.	ISSUE PRICE	VALUE
2007	25¢ Calgary Flames, from gift set 1,082		24.95	25.00
2007	25¢ Edmonton Oilers, from gift set 2,214		24.95	25.00
2007	25¢ Montreal Canadians, from gift set 4,091		24.95	25.00
2007	25¢ Montreal Canadians, from gift set (French text) 687		24.95	25.00
2007	25¢ Ottawa Senators, from gift set 2,474		24.95	25.00
2007	25¢ Toronto Maple Leafs , from gift set 5,365		24.95	25.00
2007	25¢ Vancouver Canucks, from gift set 1,526		24.95	25.00

VANCOUVER 2010 25 CENTS - MASCOT COINS, 2008

DATE		QTY.	ISSUE PRICE	VALUE
2008	25¢ 2010 Paralympic Mascot coin "Sumi" 22,067*	15.95**	15.00
2008	25¢ 2010 Olympic Mascot coin "Miga" 21,742*	15.95**	15.00
2008	25¢ Olympic Mascot coin "Quatchi" 25,386*	15.95**	15.00

*Quantity includes those issued in "pucks" . . . . **Issue Price was reduced in 2009 to 9.95

ENLARGED COLOURISED 25 CENTS, 2006–2007

Diameter: 35 mm; weight: 12.61 grams; edge: plain;
composition: nickel plated steel; finish: specimen

Anniversary Issues of Queen Elizabeth II

DATE		QTY. (000)	ISSUE PRICE	VALUE
2006	25¢ Queen Elizabeth II 80th birthday, Artist - Cosme Saffioti 25		19.95	25.00
2007	25¢ Queen Elizabeth II 60th Wedding anniv. Coach 15		21.95	25.00

ENLARGED 25 CENTS, 2008

90th Anniversary of the end of World War I (1918–2008)

The reverse design is the work of David Craig. This coin was packaged and sold with the 2008 25 cents Poppy coin as a commemorative set. This is the first of the enlarged 25 cents type that has not been coloured.

DATE		QTY. (000)	ISSUE PRICE	VALUE
2008	25¢ 90th Anniversary of the end of World War I. .10		24.95	25.00

ENLARGED COLOURISED 25 CENTS, 2008–2009

DATE		QTY. (000)	ISSUE PRICE	VALUE
2008	25¢ 100th Anniv. Anne of Green Gables, Artist - Ben Stahl. 33		19.95	20.00
2009	25¢ Notre Dame du Saguenay, From photo by - Alain Dumas. 25		14.95	25.00

Birds of Canada Series 2007–2015

This series was originally a four coin issue that has been extended due to popular demand. All designs by Arnold Nogy except noted.

DATE		QTY. (000)	ISSUE PRICE	VALUE
2007	25¢ Ruby throated Hummingbird	17	24.95	125.00
2007	25¢ Red breasted Nuthatch	12	24.95	400.00
2008	25¢ Downy Woodpecker	14	24.95	200.00
2008	25¢ Northern Cardinal	13	24.95	300.00
2010	25¢ Gold Finch	14	24.95	150.00
2010	25¢ Blue Jay	14	24.95	90.00
2011	25¢ Barn Swallow	14	24.95	50.00
2011	25¢ Black Capped Chickadee	14	25.95	50.00
2012	25¢ Rose-Breasted Grosbeak	20	29.95	35.00

Birds of Canada Series 2007–2015, continued

DATE		QTY.	ISSUE PRICE	VALUE
2012	25¢ Evening Grosbeak	20,000	29.95	40.00
2013	25¢ American Robin	17,500	29.95	30.00
2013	25¢ Barn Owl, Artist - Trevor Tennant	17,500	29.95	30.00
2014	25¢ Eastern Meadowlark, Artist - Tony Bianco	17,500	29.95	30.00
2014	25¢ Scarlet Tanager, Artist - Pierre Leduc	17,500	29.95	30.00

ENLARGED 25 CENTS

75th anniversary of CBC/Radio-Canada, 2011

For 75 years, Canada's public broadcaster has contributed to the nation's identity by broadcasting the diverse stories of this country's people. Design by the RCM Engravers.

DATE		QTY.	ISSUE PRICE	VALUE
2011	25¢ 75th anniversary of CBC/Radio-Canada	7,777	29.95	30.00

Flowers and Little Creatures Series, 2011–2014

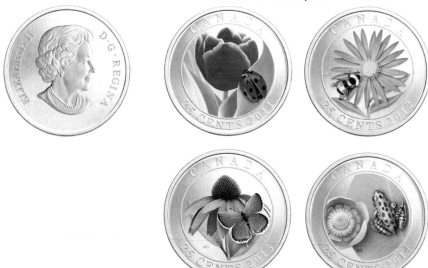

This natural wonders series featrures insects on beautifully engraved and painted flowers native to Canada. Designer: Maurice Gervais.

DATE		QTY.	ISSUE PRICE	VALUE
2011	25¢ Tulip with Ladybug	59,585	24.95	40.00
2012	25¢ Aster with Bumble Bee	20,000	29.95	30.00
2013	25¢ Purple Coneflower and Eastern Tailed Blue Butterfly	20,000	29.95	30.00
2014	25¢ Water Lily and Leopard Frog	17,500	29.95	30.00

H.R.H. Prince William of Wales
and Miss Catherine Middleton, 2011

The design features a portrait of the young couple with Prince William's profile in the foreground and his bride Catherine Middleton at his side. Image is the property of Canadian Press.

DATE		QTY.	ISSUE PRICE	VALUE
2011	25¢ H.R.H. Prince William of Wales and Miss Catherine Middleton	15,777	24.95	25.00

MYTHICAL CREATURES

Sasquatch, 2011

Design features an aerial perspective of Sasquatch walking among snow covered trees, leaving behind a trail of large footprints in the snow.

Mishepishu, 2011

For centuries, Ojibwe legends have described a mysterious creature lurking in the depths of Lake Superior. They call it Mishepishu, which means "Great Lynx", to describe its wildcat shape.

Memphré, 2011

Memphré's dragon-like head peers from the waves as its serpentine body propels it through the waters of Lake Memphremagog, Quebec.

DATE		QTY.	ISSUE PRICE	VALUE
2011	25¢ Sasquatch, by Emily S. Damstra	12,321	24.95	25.00
2011	25¢ Mishepishu, by Emily S. Damstra	5,831	24.95	25.00
2011	25¢ Memphré, by Emily S. Damstra	5,811	24.95	25.00

ENLARGED COLOURISED GOLD PLATED 25 CENTS

Diameter: 35 mm; weight: 12.61 grams; edge: plain;
composition: gold plated nickel plated steel; finish: specimen

Wayne Gretzky, 2011

A portion of these coins sold will be donated to the Wayne Gretzky Foundation where the mission is to provide less fortunate youth with the opportunity to experience the sport of hockey. Design by Glen Green.

DATE		QTY.	ISSUE PRICE	VALUE
2011	25¢ Wayne Gretzky	13,263	34.99	35.00

R.M.S. Titanic, 2012

The Titanic was the grandest passenger liner ever to grace an ocean. Design by the Three Degrees Creative Group.

DATE	QTY.	ISSUE PRICE	VALUE
2012 25¢ R.M.S. Titanic . . . . N/A		25.95	26.00

Calgary Stampede
(1912–2012)

The Stampede is known around the world as "The Greatest Outdoor Show on Earth".

DATE	QTY.	ISSUE PRICE	VALUE
2012 25¢ Calgary Stampede (from gift set)		29.95	30.00

Canadian Coast Guard
(1962–2012)

Stylized image of vessels from the Canadian Coast Guard's fleet.

DATE	QTY.	ISSUE PRICE	VALUE
2013 25¢ Canadian Coast Guard (from gift set)		24.95	25.00

Dinosaur – Glow-in-the-dark Coin, 2012–2014

The Pachyrhinosaurus lakustai dinosaur coin is the first in a 4-coin Prehistoric Creature glow-in-the-dark (photo-luminescent) series. Design by Julius T. Csotonyi.

Across the plains and highlands of the Western Interior Seaway that covered the centre of the North American continent more than 65 million years ago soared one of the largest animals ever to take to the air: Quetzalcoatlus.

DATE		QTY.	ISSUE PRICE	VALUE
2012	25¢ Pachyrhinosaurus lakustai	25,000	29.95	30.00
2013	25¢ Quetzalcoatlus	30,000	29.95	30.00
2013	25¢ Tylosaurus Pembinensis	30,000	29.95	30.00
2014	25¢ Tiktaalik	30,000	29.95	30.00

CFL Teams, 2012

DATE		QTY.	ISSUE PRICE	VALUE
2012	25¢ British Columbia Lions (from gift set)		25.95	26.00
2012	25¢ Edmonton Eskimos (from gift set)		25.95	26.00
2012	25¢ Calgary Stampeders (from gift set)		25.95	26.00
2012	25¢ Saskatchewan Roughriders (from gift set)		25.95	26.00
2012	25¢ Winnipeg Blue Bombers (from gift set)		25.95	26.00
2012	25¢ Hamilton Tiger-Cats (from gift set)		25.95	26.00
2012	25¢ Toronto Argonauts (from gift set)		25.95	26.00
2012	25¢ Montreal Alouettes (from gift set)		25.95	26.00

SPECIAL ISSUES 25 CENTS, 2013

DATE		QTY.	ISSUE PRICE	VALUE
2013	25¢ Baby feet (from Baby Gift Set) . . . . N/A		19.95	20.00
2013	25¢ Cake (from Birthday Gift Set) . . . . N/A		19.95	20.00
2013	25¢ Maple Leaf (from O Canada Gift Set) . . . . N/A		19.95	20.00
2013	25¢ Wedding Bands (from Wedding Gift Set). . . . . N/A		19.95	20.00

Her Majesty Queen Elizabeth II Coronation, 2013

The year 2013 marks the 60th anniversary of the Coronation of Queen Elizabeth II. This stunning coloured coin captures the spirit of Phil Richards' renowned Diamond Jubilee portrait of Her Majesty Queen Elizabeth II, with Queen Victoria in the background.

DATE		QTY.	ISSUE PRICE	VALUE
2013	25¢ Coronation. 15,000		24.95	25.00

The Eastern Prickly Pear Cactus, 2013

The eastern prickly pear is a low-spreading cactus with large, round pads that are covered with long, sharp spines and tiny, hard-to-see barbs. Its name is inspired by its green, pear-shaped fruit that turn red as they ripen in autumn. From June to August, the eastern prickly pear is also covered with large, yellow and orangey-red flowers that are so attractive people take the cactus home to plant in their own gardens. This practice, plus habitat loss are the greatest threats to this endangered plant. Cacti are rarely associated with Canada, but there are a few winter-hardy species that grow here. Designer: Claudio D'Angelo.

DATE		QTY.	ISSUE PRICE	VALUE
2013	25¢ The Eastern Prickly Pear Cactus 17,500		24.95	25.00

Ducks of Canada Series, 2013–

These coins capture in great detail the most beautiful traits of some of North America's most stunning waterfowl.

DATE		QTY.	ISSUE PRICE	VALUE
2013	25¢ Mallard Ducks - Trevor Tennant. 17,500		29.95	30.00
2013	25¢ Wood Duck - Trevor Tennant. 17,500		29.95	30.00
2014	25¢ The Northern Pintail - Trevor Tennant .17,500		29.95	30.00
2014	25¢ Harlequin Duck - Trevor Tennant. 17,500		29.95	30.00
2015	25¢ Cinnamon Teal - Denis Mayer Jr.. 17,500		29.95	30.00

Birth of the Royal Infant, 2013

Elements taken from the Duke and Duchess' ciphers proudly announce this historic birth, while the royal crowns also declare that every baby is one parent's little prince or princess.

DATE		QTY.	ISSUE PRICE	VALUE
2013	25¢ Royal Infant Carriage (from Birth of Royal Infant Gift Set) 17,500		29.95	30.00

Canadian NHL Teams, 2014

DATE		QTY.	ISSUE PRICE	VALUE
2014	25¢ Vancouver Canucks (from coin and stamp gift set) 6,000		29.95	30.00
2014	25¢ Calgary Flames (from coin and stamp gift set) 6,000		29.95	30.00
2014	25¢ Edmonton Oilers (from coin and stamp gift set) 6,000		29.95	30.00
2014	25¢ Winnipeg Jets (from coin and stamp gift set) 6,000		29.95	30.00
2014	25¢ Toronto Maple Leafs (from coin and stamp gift set) 6,000		29.95	30.00
2014	25¢ Ottawa Senators (from coin and stamp gift set) 6,000		29.95	30.00
2014	25¢ Montreal Canadiens (from coin and stamp gift set) 6,000		29.95	30.00

2014 FIFA World Cup

Considered the world's most popular sport, soccer has also taken hold of Canadians young and old. Although the Dominion of Canada Football Association has been a FIFATM/MC member since its formation in 1913 it is largely since the 1980s that soccer's popularity in Canada has soared, particularly among youth. Beginning in the 1980s, soccer became the Canadian sport with the highest number of registered players, surpassing even hockey. Designer: Steve Hepburn.

DATE		QTY.	ISSUE PRICE	VALUE
2014	25¢ 2014 FIFA World Cup 20,000		29.95	30.00

Haunted Canada Ghost Bride, 2014

Legend has it that a bride has made the Fairmont Banff Springs Hotel her eternal home since the 1930s when, upon stepping onto the staircase, she suddenly stumbled and tragically fell to her death! Since then, some claim to have seen an apparition dancing in the hotel's ballroom or walking down the staircase, as she did on that fateful day when death brought a tragic end to her love story – "Till death do us part." Tilt the coin and the bride's eyes suddenly open while behind her, the once-black background is filled with lit candles – the same candles that lined the staircase on her wedding day. But tilt the coin again... and the eyes close shut!

DATE		QTY.	ISSUE PRICE	VALUE
2014	25¢ Haunted Canada Ghost Bride 15,000		29.95	30.00

2015 Big Coin Series

Diameter: 65.25mm; weight: 157.6g; composition: 99.99% pure silver; finish: proof with selective gold plating;
edge: serrated; ; images reduced by 50%

Part of a six-coin set featuring 5¢, 10¢, 25¢, 50¢, $1, and $2 values.

DATE		QTY.	ISSUE PRICE	VALUE
2015	25¢ Caribou (November 2014) - Emmanuel Hahn 1,500		549.95	550.00

50 CENTS STERLING SILVER PROOF

Diameter: 27.13 mm; weight: 9.3 grams; edge: reeded; thickness: 2.08 mm;
composition: .925 silver, .075 copper

DISCOVERING NATURE (1995–2000)

Four-coin sets were issued annually. Each set features a different bird or animal theme. Each coin was encapsulated and held in a card holder, protected by a matching sleeve. The annual set of four encapsulated coins has been issued in a velvet-lined tray, protected by a sleeve. Each set is accompanied by a descriptive booklet.

Birds of Canada, 1995

| Atlantic Puffins | Whooping Crane | Gray Jays | White-tailed Ptarmigans |

Each of the four coins in this wildlife set shows a native bird of Canada. The reverse designs are by Quebec artist Jean-Luc Grondin. Each encapsulated coin is sold in a folder protected by an illustrated pocket.

Available in sets of 2 or 4 coins.

DATE		QTY. (000)	ISSUE PRICE	VALUE
1995	Birds of Canada, 2-coin set 86		29.95	30.00
1995	Birds of Canada, 4-coin set . . . . included above		56.95	85.00

Nature's Playground, 1996

The woodland babies depicted on the reverse of the 1996 proof set coins were designed by Dwayne Harty.

| Moose Calf | Wood Ducklings | Cougar Kittens | Black Bear Cubs |

DATE		QTY. (000)	ISSUE PRICE	VALUE
1996	Little wild ones, single 50¢ coin 207		19.95	30.00
1996	Little wild ones, 4-coin set . . . . included above		59.95	85.00

Canada's Best Friends, 1997

| Nova Scotia | Labrador Retriever | Newfoundland | Canadian |
| Duck Tolling Retriever | | | Eskimo Dog |

Designed by Canadian wildlife artist Arnold A. Nogy, each reverse features one of Canada's favourite canine companions.

DATE		QTY. (000)	ISSUE PRICE	VALUE
1997	Canadian Dogs, single 50¢ coin 185		19.95	25.00
1997	Canadian Dogs, 4-coin set .... included above		59.95	60.00

Canada's Ocean Giants, 1998

| Killer Whale | Humpback Whale | Beluga Whale | Blue Whale |

The reverse designs for the 1998 set in the Discovering Nature series of 50¢ pieces are by Quebec artist and biologist Pierre Leduc. Each reverse represents a different species of whale commonly seen in the waters off Canada's shores.

1998	Whales, single 50¢ coin ....,,,,,,,,, 133		10.05	25.00
1998	Whales, 4-coin set .... included above		59.95	60.00

Cats of Canada, 1999

| Tonkinese | Lynx | Cymric | Cougar |

Cats, both domestic and wild, are depicted on the 1999 set of 50-cent pieces. The reverse designs are by Ontario artist John Crosby.

1999	Cats of Canada, single 50¢ coin 83		19.95	50.00
1999	Cats of Canada, 4-coin set .... included above		59.95	125.00

Canada's Birds of Prey, 2000

| Bald Eagle | Osprey | Great Horned Owl | Red-Tailed Hawk |

Coin 1 designed by Jean-Luc Grondin, features Canada's largest bird of prey, the Bald Eagle. **Coin 2** by Pierre Leduc, displays the Osprey. **Coin 3** is also by Jean-Luc Grondin and features the head of a Great Horned Owl. **Coin 4** is again designed by Pierre Leduc and features a Red-Tailed Hawk.

DATE		QTY. (000)	ISSUE PRICE	VALUE
2000	Birds of Prey, single 50¢ coin, proof 124		19.95	20.00
2000	Birds of Prey, 4-coin set, proof . . . . included above		59.95	100.00

CANADIAN FIRSTS IN SPORTS (1998–2000)

Specification and composition are the same as the previous set.

1998 Issues

| Figure Skating | Skiing | "Soccer" | Auto Racing |

This three-year series of proof 50¢ pieces commemorates important dates in the history of sports, with four coins produced in each of the three years (1998–2000). The common obverse features the familiar Dora de Pédery-HUNT effigy of the Queen.

The reverse designs for the first four coins in the series are by Friedrich G. Peter, RCA. The coins represent: **Coin 1** First Official Amateur Figure Skating Championship (1888), **Coin 2** First Canadian Ski Running and Ski Jumping Championships (1898), **Coin 3** First Overseas Canadian Soccer Tour (1888). **Coin 4** Gilles Villeneuve's victory in the Grand Prix of Canada for F1 Auto Racing (1978).

DATE		QTY. (000)	ISSUE PRICE	VALUE
1998	Sports Firsts, single 50¢ coin, proof 56		19.95	20.00
1998	Sports Firsts, 4-coin set, proof . . . . included above		59.95	100.00

1999 Issues

| Canadian Open | International Yachting | The Grey Cup | Basketball |

The 1999 reverse designs are by Donald H, Curley and commemorate the First Canadian Open Golf Championship in 1904, the First International Yacht Race between Canada and the U.S.A. in 1874, The First Grey Cup in Canadian Football and the invention of the game of Basketball by Canadian James Naismith.

DATE		QTY. (000)	ISSUE PRICE	VALUE
1999	Sports Firsts, single 50¢ coin, proof 52		19.95	20.00
1999	Sports Firsts, 4-coin set, proof . . . . included above		59.95	100.00

2000 Issues

| Hockey | Curling | Steeplechase | Bowling |

Reverse designs for the year 2000 are by Brian Hughes and celebrate: **Coin 1** First Recorded Hockey Game in (1875), **Coin 2** introduction of curling to North America (1760), **Coin 3** First Steeplechase Race in British North America (1840) and **Coin 4** the inception of the First 5-Pin Bowling League in 1910.

DATE		QTY. (000)	ISSUE PRICE	VALUE
2000	Sports Firsts, single 50¢ coin, proof 50		19.95	20.00
2000	Sports Firsts, 4-coin set, proof . . . . included above		59.95	100.00

CANADIAN FESTIVALS (2001–2003)

Diameter: 27.13 mm; weight: 9.30 grams; thickness: 2.08 mm;
composition: .925 silver, .075 copper; edge: reeded

This series of 13 proof coins commemorates a festival from each of the provinces and territories of Canada. The coins will be issued individually throughout the year, with four coins being released during each year 2001, 2003 and five coins during 2002.

2001 Issues

| Quebec | Nunavut | Newfoundland | Prince Edward Island |

Coin 1 designed by Sylvie Daigneault celebrates The Quebec Winter Carnival. **Coin 2** by John Mardin depicts the Toonik Tyme Festival held each Spring in Nunavut. **Coin 3** by Brenda Whiteway represents the Newfoundland and Labrador Folk Festival. **Coin 4** by David Craig celebrates the Festival of the Fathers in PEI.

DATE		QTY. (000)	ISSUE PRICE	VALUE
2001	50¢ Festivals, single	58	21.95	20.00

2002 Issues

| Nova Scotia | Ontario | Manitoba |

| British Columbia | Alberta |

Coin 1 designed by Bonnie Ross celebrates the Apple Blossom Festival in Annapolis Valley, NS. **Coin 2** by Laurie McGaw represents the Stratford Festival of Canada in Stratford, ON **Coin 3** by Andrew Valko represents Folklorama, a multicultural extravaganza held in Winnipeg and celebrates the 100th anniversary of Manitoba as a province. **Coin 4** depicts the Squamish Days Logger Sports Festival held in Squamish, BC and was designed by Steve Hepburn. **Coin 5** by Michelle Grant celebrates the Calgary Stampede, held in Calgary, AB.

2002	50¢ Festivals, single	59	21.95	20.00

2003 Issues

| Yukon | New Brunswick | Saskatchewan | Northwest Territories |

Coin 1 designed by Ken Anderson, celebrates the Yukon International Storytelling Festival.
Coin 2 by David Hannan, celebrates the Saskatchewan Métis festival.
Coin 3 by Hudson Group Design, represents the New Brunswick Festival acadien de Caraquet.
Coin 4 by Dawn Oman represents the Great Northern Arts Festival, in the Northwest Territories.

DATE		QTY. (000)	ISSUE PRICE	VALUE
2003	50¢ Festivals, single..26		21.95	20.00

FOLKLORE AND LEGENDS (2001–2002)
2001 Issues

| The Sled | Maiden's Cave | Le petites Sauteux |

Coin 1 Valentina Hotz-Entin designed *The Sled.*
Coin 2 *The Maiden's Cave* was designed by Miyuki Tanobe
Coin 3 Peter Kiss interprets *Les petites Sauteux.*

2001   50¢ Folklore and Legends, single 29   24.95   20.00

2002 Issues

Coin 1 Laua Jolicoeur illustrated *The Pig That Wouldn't Get Over the Style.*
Coin 2 Francine Gravel designed *The Shoemaker in Heaven.*
Coin 3 Colette Boivin illustrated *le Vaisseau Fantome.*

| 2002 | 50¢ Folklore and Legends, single.............................19 | 24.95 | 20.00 |

PROOF SILVER FLOWERS
SELECTIVELY GOLD PLATED, 2002 – 2007

Diameter: 27.13 mm; weight: 9.30 grams; thickness: 2.11 mm;
composition: .925 silver, .075 copper; edge: reeded

| 2002 | 2003 |

The Golden Tulip, 2002

After the Dutch royal family had stayed in Ottawa during WWII, The Princess (now Queen) Juliana presented Canada with 20,000 tulip bulbs. The gift became an annual bequest and led to the Canadian Tulip Festival, held in Ottawa each year. In recognition of the Dutch generosity and to celebrate the 50th anniversary of the Canadian Tulip Festival, the Royal Canadian Mint issued this silver coin with the selectively gold-plated tulip device. The reverse was designed by Anthony Testa.

The Golden Daffodil, 2003

The reverse was designed by Christie Paquet, an engraver at the Royal Canadian Mint. The mint remitted two dollars to the Canadian Cancer Society for every Golden Daffodil coin purchased.

DATE		QTY. (000)	ISSUE PRICE	VALUE
2002	50¢ Golden Tulip, proof................................. 20		24.95	75.00
2003	50¢ Golden Daffodil, proof.............................. 35		34.95	40.00

| 2004 | 2005 | 2006 | 2007 |

The Golden Easter Lily, 2004

The new uncrowned effigy of the queen, designed by Susanna Blunt appears on the obverse. The reverse was designed by Christie Paquet.

The Golden Rose, 2005

The Golden Rose plant was first discovered in China in 1899. The Reverse was designed by Christie Paquet.

DATE		QTY.	ISSUE PRICE	VALUE
2004	50¢ Golden Easter Lily............................. 24,500		34.95	40.00
2005	50¢ Golden Rose.................................. 17,771		34.95	40.00
2006	50¢ Golden Daisy, Designed by Christie Paquet............. 13,106		36.95	45.00
2007	50¢ Golden Forget-me-not, Designed by Christie Paquet...... 10,845		38.95	50.00

CANADIAN BUTTERFLIES, 2004–

Tiger Swallowtail   Clouded Sulphur

Tiger Swallowtail Butterfly, 2004

This is the first 50-cent coin ever to feature a hologram. The obverse features the Susanna Blunt effigy of the queen. The reverse was designed by Susan Taylor.

Clouded Sulphur Butterfly, 2004

Also called the "Mud Puddle Butterfly" the Clouded Sulphur can be seen in every province and as far north as the Yukon and Northwest Territories. The reverse was designed by Susan Taylor.

DATE		QTY. (000)	ISSUE PRICE	VALUE
2004	50¢ Tiger Swallowtail Butterfly, hologram 20		39.95	70.00
2004	50¢ Clouded Sulphir Butterfly, selective gold plating. 20		39.95	70.00

Monarch   Great Spangled Fritillary   Swallowtail   Silvery Blue

Monarch Butterfly, 2005

The well known Monarch Butterfly can be seen in every province and is known from Canada to Mexico. The reverse was designed by Susan Taylor.

Great Spangled Fritillary Butterfly, 2005

This is the second Butterfly coin to feature a hologram. The reverse was designed by Jianping Yan.

Short-tailed Swallowtail, 2006

The Short-tailed Swallowtail butterfly can only be found in the Maritimes. The reverse was designed by Susan Taylor.

Silvery Blue Butterfly, 2006

The Silvery Blue butterfly is seen in every province and territory as far north as Tuktoyaktuk (Northwest Territories) but is rarely seen in southwestern Ontario. The reverse was designed by Jianping Yan.

DATE		QTY.	ISSUE PRICE	VALUE
2005	50¢ Monarch Butterfly, coloured 35,690		39.95	60.00
2005	50¢ Great Spangled Fritillary Butterfly, hologram . . . . included above		39.95	60.00
2006	50¢ Short-tailed Swallowtail, coloured. 24,568		39.95	50.00
2006	50¢ Silvery Blue, hologram . . . . included above		39.95	70.00

50 CENTS STERLING SILVER PROOF
Expressions of Nationhood, 2004

Diameter: 27.13 mm; weight: 9.30 grams; finish: Proof;
composition: .925 silver, .075 copper; edge: serrated

1953 Obverse by Mary Gillick

1965 Obverse by Arnold Machin

1990 Obverse by Dora de Pedery-Hunt

2003 Obverse by Susanna Blunt

In a world of ancient symbols, Canada's Coat of arms is surprisingly young. Having being pro-
claimed by King George V in 1921, it promptly emerged as the design of choice for the fifty cent
coin. And like the Queen's effigy, it was bound to evolve with time. Since its introduction 83 years
ago, Canada has had 3 different Coats of Arms.

DATE		QTY. (000)	ISSUE PRICE	VALUE
2004	50¢ 1953 Obverse by Mary Gillick...................20		79.95(set of 4)	65.00
2004	50¢ 1965 Obverse by Arnold Machin...................20			
2004	50¢ 1990 Obverse by Dora de Pedery-Hunt...................20			
2004	50¢ 2003 Obverse by Susanna Blunt...................20			

60th Anniversary of
The End of the Second World War, 2005

Battle of Britain
Liberation of the Netherlands
Conquest of Sicily
Battle of the Scheldt
Raid on Dieppe
Battle of the Atlantic

This six-coin set chronicles six areas that Canadians participated in during the Second World War.
The illustration represents the first coin in the set. The coins were sold as a complete set, with a
limit of 20,000 worldwide. The set was designed by Peter Mossman.

DATE		QTY. (000)	ISSUE PRICE	VALUE
2005	Set of six 50 cent coins - Specimen 20		149.95/set	200.00

NHL Hockey Legends, 2005

Beliveau   Lafleur   Plante   Richard

Bower   Horton   Keon   Sittler

Royal Canadian Mint engravers adapted images graciously provided by the Hockey Hall of Fame.

DATE		QTY.	ISSUE PRICE	VALUE
2005	50¢ Jean Beliveau			30.00
2005	50¢ Guy Lafleur			30.00
2005	50¢ Jacques Plante			30.00
2005	50¢ Maurice Richard			30.00
2005	Set of 4 Montreal coins	11,765	99.95	125.00
2005	50¢ Johnny Bower			30.00
2005	50¢ Tim Horton			30.00
2005	50¢ Dave Keon			30.00
2005	50¢ Darryl Sittler			30.00
2005	Set of 4 Toronto coins	included above	99.95	125.00

50 Cents Selective Gold Plating, 2006

Diameter: 27.13 mm; weight: 9.30 grams; finish: Proof;
composition: .925 silver, .075 copper; edge: serrated, selective gold plating

The fourth coin in a series issued with the Annual Reports, leading up to the 100th Anniversary of the Royal Canadian mint in 2008.

DATE		QTY.	ISSUE PRICE	VALUE
2006	50¢ Selective gold plating	4,162	25.95	30.00

50 Cents Holiday Issues, 2007–

Diameter: 35 mm; weight: 12.61 grams; composition: brass plated steel;
edge: plain; finish: obverse is bu, reverse is specimen

DATE		QTY.	ISSUE PRICE	VALUE
2007	50¢ Holiday Ornaments with 3D effect	16,989	25.95	40.00
2008	50¢ Holiday Snowman with 3D effect	21,679	25.95	50.00
2009	50¢ Train - Lenticular (Both views shown)	19,103	25.95	40.00
2010	50¢ Santa and red nosed reindeer - Lenticular (Both views shown)	21,394	26.95	40.00
2011	50¢ Gifts from Santa - Lenticular (Both views shown)	21,837	26.95	30.00

50 Cents NHL Coins
Special Edition Lenticular Coins, 2009

Diameter: 35 mm; weight: 6.9 grams; finish: specimen,
composition: nickel plated steel; edge: plain

These coins are from the 2008-2009 NHL Hockey Pucks. Two images, the old logo and the new logo, appear on each coin when rotated.

DATE		QTY.	ISSUE PRICE	VALUE
2009	50¢ Calgary Flames.	270	24.95	25.00
2009	50¢ Edmonton Oilers.	248	24.95	25.00
2009	50¢ Montreal Canadiens	1,266	24.95	25.00
2009	50¢ Ottawa Senators.	310	24.95	25.00
2009	50¢ Toronto Maple Leafs.	606	24.95	25.00
2009	50¢ Vancouver Canucks	318	24.95	25.00

VANCOUVER 2010 WINTER GAMES MASCOT COINS

Diameter: 35 mm; weight: 12.61 grams; finish: specimen,
composition: nickel plated steel; edge: plain

These coins are issued in collector cards featuring individual Vancouver 2010 mascots on a
50-cent nickel finish coloured coin.

DATE		QTY.	ISSUE PRICE	VALUE
2009	50¢ Ice Hockey Mascot Collector Card - Miga	10,031	9.95	15.00
2009	50¢ Ice Hockey Mascot Collector Card - Quatchi	8,043	9.95	15.00
2009	50¢ Para Sledge Hockey Mascot Collector Card - Sumi	9,513	9.95	15.00
2009	50¢ Figure Skating Mascot collector Card - Quatchi & Miga	8,410	9.95	15.00
2009	50¢ Freestyle Skiing Mascot Collector Card - Miga.	4,807	9.95	15.00

DATE		QTY.	ISSUE PRICE	VALUE
2009	50¢ Skeleton Mascot Collector Card - Miga	4,777	9.95	15.00
2009	50¢ Parallel Giant Slalom Mascot Collector Card - Quatchi	2,524	9.95	15.00
2009	50¢ Alpine Skiing Mascot Collector Card - Miga	3,161	9.95	15.00
2009	50¢ Paralympic Alpine Skiing Mascot Collector Card - Sumi.	2,521	9.95	15.00
2009	50¢ Snowboard Cross Mascot Collector Card - Quatchi	2,396	9.95	15.00
2009	50¢ Speed Skating Mascot Collector Card - Miga	2,552	9.95	15.00
2009	50¢ Bobsleigh Mascot Collector Card - Quatchi & Miga	4,869	9.95	15.00

MONTREAL CANADIENS CENTENNIAL COIN SERIES

1909 - 1910	1910 - 1911	1912 - 1913

1915 - 1916	1945 - 1946	1909 - 2009

These coins are issued in six collector cards on a 50-cent nickel finish coloured coin with the historical logos of the Montreal Canadiens.

DATE		QTY.	ISSUE PRICE	VALUE
2009	50¢ Montreal Canadiens Centennial 1909 - 1910	25,016	59.95(set)	60.00
2009	50¢ Montreal Canadiens Centennial 1910 - 1911	32,967		
2009	50¢ Montreal Canadiens Centennial 1912 - 1913	25,016		
2009	50¢ Montreal Canadiens Centennial 1915 - 1916	25,000		
2009	50¢ Montreal Canadiens Centennial 1945 - 1946	25,000		
2009	50¢ Montreal Canadiens Centennial 1909 - 2009	25,000		

NHL ACTION ON ICE COIN SERIES

Diameter: 35 mm; weight: 6.9 grams; finish: specimen,
composition: nickel plated steel; edge: plain

These coins feature "on ice action" and are package in a tent card format that includes 2008-2009
team stats.

DATE		QTY.	ISSUE PRICE	VALUE
2009	50¢ Calgary	3,518	14.95	15.00
2009	50¢ Edmonton	3,562	14.95	15.00
2009	50¢ Montreal	9,865	14.95	15.00
2009	50¢ Ottawa	3,295	14.95	15.00
2009	50¢ Toronto	5,981	14.95	15.00
2009	50¢ Vancouver	3,563	14.95	15.00

50 Cents Triangle Shape Coins, 2008–2009

Diameter: 34.06 mm; weight: 20 grams; finish: proof,
composition: .925 silver, .075 copper; edge: plain

These coins are designed by the Royal Canadian Mint engravers.

DATE		QTY.	ISSUE PRICE	VALUE
2008	50¢ Milk Delivery, Green enamel effect reverse	24,448	49.95	50.00
2009	50¢ Six String Nation Guitar, Selective hologram centre reverse	13,602	34.95	35.00

50 Cents Lenticular Coin — Dinosaur Series, 2010

Diameter: 35 mm; weight: 12.61 grams; composition: brass plated steel;
edge: plain; finish: obverse is bu, reverse is specimen

The Royal Canadian Mint has teamed up with Canada's museums to create this new series of dinosaur coins, each inspired by a different exhibit.

DATE		QTY.	ISSUE PRICE	VALUE
2010	50¢ Daspletosaurus Torosus - Lenticular (Both views shown)	11,652	24.95	25.00
2010	50¢ Albertosaurus - Lenticular (Both views shown)............	14,325	24.95	25.00
2010	50¢ Sinosauropteryx - Lenticular (Both views shown)	19,865	24.95	25.00

Winnipeg Jets, 2011

Diameter: 27.13 mm; weight: 6.9 grams; composition: nickel plated steel;
edge: reeded; finish: circulation.

This coin depicts the New Winnipeg Jets team to join the NHL since their departure 15 years ago.
Design by William Woodruff.

DATE		QTY.	ISSUE PRICE	VALUE
2011	50¢ Winnipeg Jets.	23,712	14.95	15.00

50 Cents Colourised Silver Plated Copper, 2012

Diameter: 42 mm; weight: 32.82 grams; composition: silver plated copper;
edge: reeded; finish: proof.

R.M.S. Titanic, 2012

The Queen's Diamond Jubilee Emblem for Canada, 2012

DATE		QTY.	ISSUE PRICE	VALUE
2012	50¢ R.M.S. Titanic.	15,000	34.95	100.00
2012	50¢ The Queen's Diamond Jubilee Emblem for Canada	N/A	29.95	30.00

Lenticular Coin — Holiday, 2012

DATE	QTY.	ISSUE PRICE	VALUE
2012 50¢ Santa's Magical Visit - Lenticular (both views shown) 25,000		29.95	30.00

Butterflies of Canada: Canadian Tiger Swallowtail

The Canadian Tiger Swallowtail (*Papilio canadensis*) is one of Canada's most recognizable butterflies. With its broad wingspan of up to ten centimetres and the distinctive yellow and black tiger stripe pattern on its wings and body, the Canadian Tiger Swallowtail is a striking feature of springtime in Canada.

The first coin from the Royal Canadian Mint's new Butterflies of Canada series.

DATE	QTY.	ISSUE PRICE	VALUE
2013 50¢ Canadian Tiger Swallowtail 20,000		34.95	35.00

Snowman — Lenticular Coin, 2013

Watch two enterprising children build a snowman, then enjoy the final result with this beautifully colourful lenticular coin designed to celebrate one of the joys of the Canadian winter holidays. Designer: Tony Bianco.

DATE	QTY.	ISSUE PRICE	VALUE
2013 50¢ Snowman 20,000		29.95	30.00

100 Blessings Of Good Fortune, 2014

Good fortune comes in 100 guises, at times soaring in a cloud of health and prosperity, at times travelling alone. In all of its many forms, may good fortune come to you. Luck arrives where it is welcomed, it pours in from all directions. Like the earth, it comes back to life after even the darkest winter. May abundant happiness reveal itself to you in the progress of each year, in the joy of blessed new unions, in the challenge of rewarding work, in lucky smiles, in the bounty of gaining that which you wish and work for in life. designed by Three Degrees Creative Group.

DATE	QTY.	ISSUE PRICE	VALUE
2014 50¢ 100 Blessings of Good Fortune. 14,888		34.95	35.00

Sinking of the RMS *Empress of Ireland* (1914–2014)

It was the greatest maritime disaster in Canadian history – a tragedy unparalleled by the loss of life and the speed at which the events unfolded. The sinking of RMS *Empress of Ireland* made headlines around the world in 1914; sadly, the onset of the First World War would quickly overshadow the events that transpired in the waters near Rimouski, Que. Designer: Yves Bérubé.

DATE	QTY.	ISSUE PRICE	VALUE
2014 50¢ 100th Anniversary of the Sinking of the RMS *Empress of Ireland* 15,000		34.95	35.00

Lenticular Christmas Tree, 2014

Diameter: 35.0mm; weight: 13.7g; composition: cupronickel; finish: specimen; edge: plain

The magic of the holidays often lies in the traditions that create some of our most treasured memories. And for many Canadians, the selection of a Christmas tree is as much of a time-honoured tradition as decorating one! This stylized lenticular coin follows one tree's journey from the outdoors to an indoor setting, where it plays a central role in one family's joyous holiday celebrations. Designer: Steve Hepburn.

DATE		QTY.	ISSUE PRICE	VALUE
2014	50¢ Christmas Tree................................ 20,000		29.95	30.00

COMMEMORATIVE DOLLARS

Constitution, 1982

For the first time, both a commemorative nickel dollar and a voyageur nickel dollar were struck for circulation in 1982. For collectors, the commemorative dollar honouring the new constitution was also issued in select uncirculated condition, encapsulated and housed in a maroon velvet case.

Jacques Cartier, 1984

As in 1982, two circulating dollars were struck in 1984. The commemorative nickel dollar, struck to celebrate Cartier's landing at Gaspé in 1534, was also issued encapsulated, housed in a green velvet case, in proof quality.

DATE		QTY. (000)	ISSUE PRICE	VALUE
1982	Constitution (Select Uncirculated)	107	9.75	8.00
1984	Jacques Cartier (Proof)	88	9.75	8.00

Aureate Loon Dollar, 1987

Diameter: 26.72 mm; weight: 7.0 grams; thickness: 1.95 mm;
composition: aureate bronze plated on pure nickel; edge: plain

The Loon dollar was not included in any of the collectors' sets issued by the mint in 1987, and was only available as a circulation strike or in proof condition.

DATE		QTY. (000)	ISSUE PRICE	VALUE
1987	Loon reverse, proof	178	13.50	10.00

125th Anniversary of Confederation, 1992

Diameter: 26.50 mm; weight: 7.0 grams; edge: plain;
composition: aureate bronze plated on pure nickel

This is the same as the circulating commemorative aureate dollar, but issued to collectors as a proof coin. The proof coin also appears in the CANADA 125 proof set.

DATE		QTY. (000)	ISSUE PRICE	VALUE
1992	Anniversary of Confederation, proof	24	19.95	15.00

Diameter: 26.5 mm; weight: 7 grams; thickness: 1.90 mm;
composition: nickel plated with bronze, 11-Side plain edges.

National War Memorial, 1994

The Remembrance Proof Dollar is the same design as the circulating commemorative dollar described on page 94, and is also included in the Special Edition 1994 Proof set.

Peacekeeping Monument, 1995

The proof Peacekeeping dollar is the same design as the commemorative circulating dollar.

DATE		QTY. (000)	ISSUE PRICE	VALUE
1994	War Memorial, proof	66	16.95	15.00
1995	Peacekeeping Monument, proof	43	17.95	15.00

Gold Plated Centre Ice Loonie, 2002

Diameter: 26.5 mm; weight: 7 grams;
composition: 22k gold plated nickel, 11-Side plain edges.

This unique centre ice loonie features two loons on the same coin. This special mark is to represent the good luck coin buried at centre ice. Issued as part of the "Going for the Gold Album".

DATE		QTY. (000)	ISSUE PRICE	VALUE
2002	Centre ice loonie, proof, Gold plating	25	54.95	75.00

Lucky Loonie, 2004

Issued to support Canada's Olympic Athletes through the Go Canada Go Program. The 2004 Lucky Loonie celebrates Canada's Olympic athletes and underscores their commitment to excellence. The one-dollar will serve as a good luck charm for the 2004 Canadian Olympic Team.

DATE		QTY. (000)	ISSUE PRICE	VALUE
2004	Lucky Loonie, Uncirculated	20	39.95	70.00

Canadian Goose, 2004

Diameter: 26.5mm; weight: 7 garms;
thickness: 1.90mm; composition: bronze-plated nickel; straight edge with 11 sides.

This special edition of the aureate dollar is a tribute to Jack Miner, one of the world's most influential conservationists, who founded a bird sanctuary in 1904.

2004 Canada Goose, specimen	44	39.95	50.00
2004 Elusive Loon, proof	12	N/A	90.00

Sterling Silver Loon Dollars, 2006–2010

Diameter: 26.5 mm; weight: 7 grams; finish: proof
thickness: 1.90 mm; composition: .925 silver, .075 copper; edge: 11 sided.

Obverse	2006 Lucky Loonie	2006 Lullaby	RCM Logo (L) Obverse

2006 Snowflake	2007 ABC Blocks	2007 Baby Rattle	2007 Wedding

2008 Wedding	2008 Lucky Loonie	2010 Obverse	2010 Lucky Loonie

DATE		QTY. (000)	ISSUE PRICE	VALUE
2006	Lucky Loonie, silver, coloured	20	39.95	45.00
2006	Loon, lullaby, silver	22	29.95	45.00
2006	Snowflake, silver, coloured, Holidays Carols set only.	18	34.95	50.00
2007	ABC Blocks, silver, Baby's Keepsake set only	3	34.95	200.00
2007	Baby Rattle, silver, Baby set only	3	34.95	160.00
2007	Baby Rattle, silver, selective gold plating, Premium Baby set only	2	89.95	200.00
2007	Loon. silver, Premium Wedding set only	1	89.95	90.00
2008	Loon. silver, Premium Wedding or Baby set only.	2	99.95	100.00
2008	Lucky Loonie, silver, coloured.	57	49.95	50.00
2010	Lucky Loonie, silver, coloured.	47	49.95	50.00

Colourised NHL Loon Dollars, 2008

Diameter: 26.5 mm; weight: 6.4 grams; finish: uncirculated
thickness: 1.90 mm; composition: nickel; edge: 11 sided.

DATE		QTY.	ISSUE PRICE	VALUE
2008	Calgary Flames gift set only	314	24.95	25.00
2008	Edmonton Oilers gift set only	1,584	24.95	25.00
2008	Montreal Canadians gift set only	2,659	24.95	25.00
2008	Ottawa Senators gift set only	2,064	24.95	25.00
2008	Toronto Maple Leafs gift set only	835	24.95	25.00
2008	Vancouver Canucks gift set only	2,104	24.95	25.00

DATE		QTY.	ISSUE PRICE	VALUE
2008	Toronto Maple Leafs coin hockey puck only	2,605	15.95	16.00
2008	Montreal Canadiens coin hockey puck only	1,588	15.95	16.00
2008	Montreal Canadiens coin hockey puck only (french text)	174	15.95	16.00
2008	Edmonton Oilers coin hockey puck only	484	15.95	16.00
2008	Ottawa Senators coin hockey puck only	775	15.95	16.00
2008	Vancouver Canucks coin hockey puck only	1,160	15.95	16.00
2008	Calgary Flames coin hockey puck only	1,304	15.95	16.00

Colourised NHL Loon Dollars, 2009

DATE		QTY.	ISSUE PRICE	VALUE
2009	Calgary Flames, gift set only	382	24.95	25.00
2009	Edmonton Oilers, gift set only	472	24.95	25.00
2009	Montreal Canadiens, gift set only	4,857	24.95	25.00
2009	Ottawa Senators, gift set only	387	24.95	25.00
2009	Toronto Maple Leafs, gift set only	1,328	24.95	25.00
2009	Vancouver Canucks, gift set only	794	24.95	25.00

Colourised NHL Loon Dollars, 2009

DATE		QTY.	ISSUE PRICE	VALUE
2009	Calgary Flames, mini stick & coin set only	73	24.95	25.00
2009	Edmonton Oilers, mini stick & coin set only	49	24.95	25.00
2009	Montreal Canadiens, mini stick & coin set only	326	24.95	25.00
2009	Ottawa Senators, mini stick & coin set only	95	24.95	25.00
2009	Toronto Maple Leafs, mini stick & coin set only	199	24.95	25.00
2009	Vancouver Canucks, mini stick & coin set only	101	24.95	25.00

Silver Plated Loon Dollar

Diameter: 26.5 mm; weight: 7 grams;
composition: silver plated bronze plated nickel, 11-Side plain edges.

(SP/PA mark below the Queen denotes silver-plating)

25th Anniversary of the Loonie Coin (1987–2012)

This silver-plated double dated Loonie came with a full colour mini book with illustrations telling the story of the Loonie. Design by Ralph-Robert Carmichael.

DATE		QTY.	ISSUE PRICE	VALUE
2012	25th Anniversary of the Loonie Coin, Uncirculated 7,279		24.95	25.00

CASED SILVER DOLLARS 1971 –

(1971–1978): Diameter: 36.06 mm; weight: 23.3 grams; thickness: 2.84 mm; edge: reeded;
composition: (1971–1991) .500 silver, .500 copper, (1992 –) .925 silver, .075 copper

Obverse 1971–1989

In 1971 the mint began issuing a series of .500 silver dollars in specimen condition for collectors. These were packaged in black leather cases and the coins have been issued encapsulated since 1974. Except for 1977 and 1978, when obverses were designed specifically for the issues, the obverse, with minor revisions, remained the same from 1971 to 1989. It bears the Arnold Machin effigy of Queen Elizabeth II as modified by Patrick Brindley. A new obverse design by Dora de Pédery-HUNT was introduced in 1990 and the composition has been sterling (92% silver) since 1992. From 1981 the dollars have been issued in brilliant uncirculated and proof each year.

In addition to the Canada/USSR hockey commemorative a 10th anniversary Loon dollar was also struck in sterling silver in 1997 and only issued to collectors as a single proof coin. The reverse depicts a loon lifting in flight from the surface of a lake.

1971   1972

British Columbia Centennial, 1971

Commemorating the entry of British Columbia into Confederation in 1871, this was the first non-circulating collectors' dollar ever issued in Canada. The reverse device, based on the provincial arms of B.C., was designed and modelled by Patrick Brindley.

Voyageur Reverse, 1972

The traditional Emanuel Hahn voyageur reverse was modified by Patrick Brindley for the collectors' silver dollar in 1972. The revised reverse design used beads rather than rim denticles. The obverse is similar to the 1971 issue.

DATE		QTY. (000)	ISSUE PRICE	VALUE
1971	British Columbia Centennial	585	3.00	15.00
1972	Voyageur Reverse	341	3.00	15.00

| 1973 | 1974 |

Royal Canadian Mounted Police Centennial, 1973

In addition to the commemorative 25-cent circulation pieces, a collectors' .500 silver RCMP commemorative dollar was struck in 1973. The reverse design was modelled and engraved by Paul Cederberg.

Winnipeg Centennial, 1974

The obverse and reverse designs are the same as the 1974 nickel dollar except that the diameter was increased to 36 mm. The reverse design is by Paul Pederson.

DATE		QTY. (000)	ISSUE PRICE	VALUE
1973	Royal Canadian Mounted Police, Black case 904		3.00	15.00
1973	Blue case with metal coat of arms .... included above			20.00
1974	Winnipeg Centennial 628		3.50	15.00

| 1975 | 1976 |

Calgary Centennial, 1975

The 100th anniversary of the founding of the city of Calgary, Alberta, is commemorated by this issue. Donald D. Paterson designed the reverse, which depicts a rider on a bucking horse with oil wells and the city skyline in the background.

Library of Parliament Centenary, 1976

The reverse design for the 1976 silver dollar commemorates the centenary of the completion of the Library of Parliament building and was modelled principally by Walter Ott.

1975	Calgary Centennial 833	3.50	15.00
1976	Library of Parliament, Black case 484	4.00	15.00
1976	Library of Parliament, Blue leather case .... included above		20.00

1977	1978

Queen Elizabeth II, Silver Jubilee, 1977

The silver dollar issue for 1977 commemorates the 25th anniversary of Queen Elizabeth's accession to the throne. The reverse, designed by Raymond Lee depicts the throne of the Senate of Canada, used for ceremonial events.

11th Commonwealth Games, 1978

The 11th Commonwealth Games, held in Edmonton, Alberta, August 3–12, are commemorated by this silver dollar. The reverse, designed by Raymond Taylor, displays the symbol of the Commonwealth Games, surrounded by designs depicting the ten games involved.

DATE		QTY. (000)	ISSUE PRICE	VALUE
1977	Silver Jubilee, Black case	745	4.25	15.00
1977	Silver Jubilee, Brown velvet case	included above		35.00
1978	11th Commonwealth Games	640	4.50	15.00

1979	1980

Griffon Commemorative, 1979

Diameter: 36.07 mm; weight: 23.33 grams; thickness: 2.66 mm

Recognition of the first voyage on the Great Lakes by a commercial ship was the intent of this commemorative issue. The reverse, which depicts the Griffon, was designed by Walter Schluep.

Arctic Territories, 1980

Diameter: 36.07 mm; weight: 23.33 grams; thickness: 2.74 mm

Celebrating the centenary of the transfer of the Arctic Islands to the Dominion of Canada by the British government, the reverse, by Donald D. Paterson, features a polar bear.

1979	Griffon Commemorative	671	5.50	15.00
1980	Arctic Territories	390	22.00	25.00

1981   1982

Trans-Canada Railway, 1981

Diameter: 36.07 mm; weight: 23.33 grams; thickness: 2.95 mm

The centennial of the construction of the Trans-Canada Railway is commemorated by this reverse design by Christopher Gorey, depicting a steam locomotive with a map of Canada in the background.

Founding of Regina, 1982

The 100th anniversary of the founding of Regina is commemorated by the 1982 silver dollar. The reverse was designed by Huntley Brown.

DATE		QTY. (000)	ISSUE PRICE	VALUE
1981	Trans-Canada Railway, uncirculated	496	14.00	15.00
1981	Trans-Canada Railway, proof	included above	16.00	18.00
1982	Founding of Regina, uncirculated	723	10.95	15.00
1982	Founding of Regina, proof	included above	15.25	15.00

1983   1984

World University Games, 1983

Diameter: 36.07 mm; weight: 23.33 grams; thickness: 2.86 mm

The 1983 silver dollar was issued to commemorate the World University Games, held in Edmonton in July. The reverse was designed by Carola Tietz.

Toronto Sesquicentennial, 1984

The 150th anniversary of the incorporation of the City of Toronto is commemorated by this issue. The reverse design by David Craig depicts a voyageur with the City of Toronto skyline in the background.

1983	World University Games, uncirculated	159	10.85	15.00
1983	World University Games, proof	340	16.15	15.00
1984	Toronto Sesquicentennial, uncirculated	134	11.40	15.00
1984	Toronto Sesquicentennial, proof	571	16.95	15.00

1985   1986

National Parks Centennial, 1985

The 100th anniversary of Canada's National Parks is commemorated by this issue. Designed by Karel Rohlicek, the reverse depicts a moose against a wilderness background.

Vancouver Centennial, 1986

This dollar was issued to commemorate the centenaries of the first transcontinental train crossing and the City of Vancouver. The reverse was designed by Elliot John Morrison.

DATE		QTY. (000)	ISSUE PRICE	VALUE
1985	National Parks Centennial, uncirculated.	163	12.00	15.00
1985	National Parks Centennial, proof	573	17.50	15.00
1986	Vancouver Centennial, uncirculated.	125	12.25	15.00
1986	Vancouver Centennial, proof	496	18.00	15.00

1987   1988

John Davis Expeditions, 1987

Issued for the 400th anniversary of the John Davis expedition in search of the North West Passage. The reverse was designed by Christopher Gorey and modelled by Ago Aarand.

Canada`s Industrial Pioneers, 1988

The 1988 dollar celebrates the 250th anniversary of the Saint-Maurice Ironworks, Canada's first heavy industry. They reverse design was conceived by Robert Ralph Carmichael.

1987	John Davis Expeditions, uncirculated	116	14.00	15.00
1987	John Davis Expeditions, proof	419	19.00	15.00
1988	Canada`s Industrial Pioneers, uncirculated	107	15.00	15.00
1988	Canada`s Industrial Pioneers, proof	255	20.00	18.00

1989

Mackenzie River Bicentennial, 1989

The 1989 silver dollar celebrates Mackenzie's 1789 canoe expedition to the Arctic. The reverse was designed by John Mardon.

DATE		QTY. (000)	ISSUE PRICE	VALUE
1989	Mackenzie River Bicentennial, uncirculated	112	16.25	15.00
1989	Mackenzie River Bicentennial, proof	276	21.75	25.00

1990

Henry Kelsey, 1990

The 1990 silver dollar commemorates the 300th anniversary of Henry Kelsey's 1690 expedition to make peace with remote native tribes and establish trade for the Hudson's Bay Company. The reverse was designed by David Craig.

A new obverse design by Dora de Pédery-HUNT, showing a more contemporary portrait of the Queen wearing a necklace and earrings as well as an elaborate crown last used on Victorian issues, was introduced in 1990. This is the first effigy designed by a Canadian for use on Canadian coins.

DATE		QTY. (000)	ISSUE PRICE	VALUE
1990	Henry Kelsey, uncirculated	99	16.75	15.00
1990	Henry Kelsey, proof	255	22.95	30.00

1991   1992

Steamship Frontenac, 1991

Issued for the 175th anniversary of the Frontenac, the first Canadian-built steamship to operate on Lake Ontario, is commemorated by the 1991 issue. The reverse was designed by David J. Craig.

Kingston-York Stagecoach, 1992

Diameter: 36.07 mm; weight: 25.175 grams; thickness: 2.77 mm;
composition: .925 silver, .075 copper; edge reeded

The 1992 cased silver dollar commemorates the inauguration of the stagecoach service between Kingston and York (now Toronto) in 1817. The reverse was designed by Karsten Smith. This is the first coin of the series to be issued in sterling (92.5% silver); all previous issues having been struck in 50% silver and 50% copper.

DATE		QTY. (000)	ISSUE PRICE	VALUE
1991	Steamship Frontenac, uncirculated	83	16.75	15.00
1991	Steamship Frontenac, proof	223	22.95	40.00
1992	Kingston-York Stagecoach, uncirculated	78	17.50	25.00
1992	Kingston-York Stagecoach, proof	188	23.95	22.00

1993   1994

Stanley Cup, 1993

The reverse of the 1993 cased silver dollar celebrating the 100th anniversary of the Stanley Cup was designed by Toronto artist Stewart Sherwood.

Last Mounted Police Dog Team Patrol, 1994

Issued for the 25th anniversary of the last dog team patrol by the RCMP, was designed by Ian D. Sparkes. The patrol covered 804.5 km on sleds pulled by 21 purebred Siberian huskies.

1993	Stanley Cup, uncirculated	88	17.50	25.00
1993	Stanley Cup, proof	294	23.95	22.00
1994	Last Mounted Police Dog Team Patrol, uncirculated	65	17.50	20.00
1994	Last Mounted Police Dog Team Patrol, proof	178	23.95	35.00

1995 1996

Hudson's Bay Company, 1995

Issue to commemorates the 325th anniversary of the Hudson's Bay Company, and depicts Pierre-Esprit Radisson and Médard Chouart, the Sieur des Groseilliers, the British ketch Nonsuch and the company's first trading post. The reverse was designed by Vincent McIndoe.

McIntosh, 1996

John McIntosh arrived in Canada 200 years ago and is credited with introducing the apple that bears his name. The reverse design by Roger Hill depicts a McIntosh apple and an orchard.

DATE		QTY. (000)	ISSUE PRICE	VALUE
1995	Hudson's Bay Company, uncirculated	62	17.95	20.00
1995	Hudson's Bay Company, proof	166	24.95	35.00
1996	McIntosh, uncirculated	59	19.95	20.00
1996	McIntosh, proof	134	29.95	40.00

1997 1997

Canada / USSR Hockey Series, 1997

Diameter: 36.07 mm; weight: 25.175 grams; thickness: 2.95 mm;
composition: .925 silver, .075 copper; edge reeded

The reverse design, by Walter Burden, depicts the goal scored by Paul Henderson, with 34 seconds left in the final game of the first Canada/USSR Hockey series.

Tenth Anniversary Loon Dollar, 1997

Issued to commemorate the tenth anniversary of the Loon dollar. The reverse, by Jean-Luc Grondin, depicts a loon lifting in flight from the surface of a lake. The same design was used on the reverse of the $1 coins in the "Specimen" and "Oh Canada!" collectors' sets in 1997.

1997	Canada/USSR Hockey, uncirculated	155	19.95	20.00
1997	Canada/USSR Hockey, proof	185	29.95	40.00
1997	Tenth Anniversary Loon dollar, large size silver proof	25	49.95	150.00

1998

Royal Canadian Mounted Police, 1998

The North-West Mounted Police was created in 1873 to maintain law and order in the vast territories with a maximum initial force of 300 men. In 1920 the NWMP and the Dominion Police merged to become the R.C.M.P. The 1998 silver dollar was issued to celebrate the 125th anniversary of the RCMP, The reverse was designed by Adeline Halvorsen.

DATE		QTY. (000)	ISSUE PRICE	VALUE
1998	RCMP, uncirculated	81	19.95	20.00
1998	RCMP, proof	131	29.95	35.00

1999   1999

Sighting of Queen Charlotte Islands, 1999

This coin was issued to celebrate the 225th anniversary of the voyage of Juan Pérez and the first known sighting of the Queen Charlotte Islands by a European. David Craig designed the reverse depicting the Haida paddling out from shore to trade with the Santiago.

International Year of Older Persons, 1999

The United Nations declared 1999 the International Year of Older Persons. The reverse of the silver dollar issued in celebration of Older Canadians was designed by Shelagh Armstrong-Hodgson of Owen Sound and depicts a couple in their golden years travelling the path of life.

1999	Queen Charlotte Islands, uncirculated	68	19.95	20.00
1999	Queen Charlotte Islands, proof	126	29.95	40.00
1999	International Year of Older Persons (IYOP), proof.	25	49.95	50.00

A Voyage of Discovery, 2000

The 2000 cased silver dollar looks to Canada's future as a voyage of discovery into the next millennium. The reverse, by Don F. Warkentine, features "a stylized maple leaf adorned by a crown of lunar phases."

National Ballet of Canada, 2001

The debut performance of the National Ballet occurred in 1951 at the Eaton Auditorium in Toronto. To celebrate the Ballet's 50th anniversary a scene from its first performance, *Les Sylphides*, is depicted on the reverse by Dora de Pédery-HUNT.

DATE		QTY. (000)	ISSUE PRICE	VALUE
2000	A Voyage of Discovery, uncirculated	63	19.95	20.00
2000	A Voyage of Discovery, proof	122	29.95	40.00
2001	The National Ballet, uncirculated	54	20.95	20.00
2001	The National Ballet, proof	89	30.95	25.00

The 1911 dollar remembered, 2001

The reverse side of the mysterious 1911 silver dollar, designed by W. H. J. Blackmore, appears again on the reverse. The date has been changed to 1911–2001 and the obverse features the Dora de Pédery-HUNT effigy of the queen. Only one lead and two silver coins were stuck using the original 1911 dies. The first Canadian dollar coin bore the date 1935 and celebrated the jubilee of King George V.

2001	The 1911 dollar remembered, proof	25	49.95	75.00

Queen Elizabeth II, Golden Jubilee, 2002

To celebrate the 50th anniversary of the Queen's accession to the throne, this dollar has the double date 1952 2002 on the obverse. The reverse depicts the queen and her 1952 coronation coach. The obverse holds the Dora de Pédery-HUNT effigy of the queen and the reverse is by RCM staff.

2002	The Queen and gilded Coach, uncirculated	65.5	20.95	22.00
2002	The Queen and gilded Coach, proof	65	30.95	40.00
2002	The Queen and gilded Coach, proof, gold plated	33	99.95	100.00

The Queen Mother Elizabeth, 2002

This tribute to The Queen Mother Elizabeth (1900–2002) is the first Canadian coin to display two queens: Queen Elizabeth II on the obverse and The Queen Mother Elizabeth on the reverse. The obverse bears the Dora de Pédery-HUNT effigy of the queen.

100th Anniversary of the Cobalt Silver Strike, 2003

Diameter: 36.07 mm; weight: 25.175 grams; thickness: 3.04 mm;
composition: .9999 silver, edge reeded

This is the first 99.99% pure silver commemorative dollar issued by the Royal Canadian Mint. The reverse was designed by John Marden and the obverse bears the Dora de Pédery-HUNT effigy of the queen.

DATE		QTY. (000)	ISSUE PRICE	VALUE
2002	The Queen Mother Elizabeth, proof	10	49.95	225.00
2003	Cobalt Silver Strike, uncirculated	51	28.95	22.00
2003	Cobalt Silver Strike, proof	89	36.95	40.00

New effigy
50th Anniversary of Coronation, 2003

Diameter: 36.07 mm; weight: 25.175 grams; thickness: 3.02 mm;
composition: .9999 silver, edge reeded

The obverse bears the new effigy of Queen Elizabeth II (designed by Susanna Blunt) and the reverse holds the familiar voyageur reverse (by Emanuel Hahn) as it appeared on the first silver dollar in 1935. The coin celebrates the 50th anniversary of the coronation of the queen and the 70th anniversary of the silver dollar.

DATE		QTY. (000)	ISSUE PRICE	VALUE
2003	50th Anniversary of Coronation, proof	30	51.95	50.00

The Poppy, 2004

This Dollar coin features the red poppy, the symbol that pays homage to Canada's men and women who gave their lives for freedom.

400th anniversary of the First
French Settlement in North America (1604-2004)

This dollar was issued to celebrate the establishment of the first French settlement in North America on a small island in the St. Croix River in 1604. The same design with a fleur-de-lis privy mark was included in a 2004 stamp and coin set.

Medal of Bravery, 2006

This medal was established in 1972 as an expression of gratitude to Canada's everyday heroes.

DATE		QTY. (000)	ISSUE PRICE	VALUE
2004	The Poppy	25	49.95	55.00
2004	French Settlement, Uncirculated	42	28.95	25.00
2004	French Settlement, Proof	81	36.95	40.00
2006	Medal of Bravery, Proof	8	34.95	55.00
2006	Medal of Bravery, Proof Enameled	5	99.95	160.00

40th Anniversary of Canada's Flag, 2005

Diameter: 36.07 mm; weight: 25.175 grams; thickness: 3.02 mm; composition: .925 silver, .075 copper; edge: reeded

The 2005 silver dollar celebrates the 40th anniversary of the Canadian flag. The Susanna Blunt effigy of the queen is on the obverse and the reverse was designed by William Woodruff.

DATE		QTY. (000)	ISSUE PRICE	VALUE
2005	Canada's National Flag, Uncirculated	51	24.95	35.00
2005	Canada's National Flag, Proof	95	34.95	45.00
2005	Canada's National Flag, Proof, red enamel	5	99.95	375.00
2005	Canada's National Flag, Proof, selective gold plating	64	N/A	75.00

150th Anniversary of the Victoria Cross, 2006

This dollar coin celebrates the anniversary of the Victoria Cross. Designed by RCM Engravers.

DATE		QTY. (000)	ISSUE PRICE	VALUE
2006	Victoria Cross, uncirculated	27	30.95	30.00
2006	Victoria Cross, proof	56	37.95	45.00
2006	Victoria Cross, proof, selective gold plating	54	N/A	125.00

Thayendanegea, 2007

Thayendanegea was given the christian name of Joseph Brant. As war chief of the six nations and a british military captain, he was respected by both sides. Original drawing by Laurie McGaw.

Celebration of the Arts, 2007

Design features many aspects of the performing arts in a montage, designed by Friedrich Peter.

DATE		QTY. (000)	ISSUE PRICE	VALUE
2007	Thayendanegea, Uncirculated	17	35.95	35.00
2007	Thayendanegea, Proof	33	44.95	45.00
2007	Thayendanegea, Proof selective gold plating (proof set only)	37	89.95	80.00
2007	Thayendanegea, Proof with enamel effect	5	129.95	150.00
2007	Celebration of the Arts, Proof	7	54.95	75.00

Celebrating the 400th Anniversary of Quebec City (1608 - 2008)

Four hundred years ago, Samuel de Champlain built a fur trading post on the St. Lawrence River (Quebec). The location he chose for his "habitation" was a popular spot where the Algonquin people came to fish and to barter. Design by Suzanne Duranceau.

100th Anniversary of the Royal Canadian Mint, 2008

From the beginning, innovation has been the hallmark of the Mint with a revolutionary coin plating process. Design by RCM engravers.

DATE		QTY. (000)	ISSUE PRICE	VALUE
2008	400th Anniv. (1608 - 2008), Uncirculated. 35		34.95	35.00
2008	400th Anniv. (1608 - 2008), Proof 65		42.95	45.00
2008	400th Anniv. (1608 - 2008), Proof, selective gold plating (proof set only) . 39		89.95	90.00
2008	100th Anniversary of the RCM, Proof 15		59.95	100.00
2008	100th Anniversary of the RCM, Proof, selective gold plating . . . . N/A		N/A	200.00

Poppy with Ultra High Relief, 2008

Diameter: 36.15 mm; weight: 30 grams; finish: frosted relief on a proof like field; edge: plain; composition: .925 silver, .075 copper.

This special low-mintage and ultra-high-relief proof silver dollar features a finely sculpted poppy blossom set against a maple leaf with a ribbon of remembrance. Designed by Cosme Saffioti.

DATE		QTY. (000)	ISSUE PRICE	VALUE
2008	Limited Edition Poppy with Ultra High Relief, Proof 5		139.95	225.00

100th Anniversary of Flight in Canada (1909–2009)

Diameter: 36.07 mm; weight: 25.175 grams; thickness: 3.02 mm;
composition: .925 silver, .075 copper; edge: reeded

The coin features a young person running, arms spread out as if in flight. The silhouette echoes the dream with three significant Canadian aviation achievements in the background, the Silver Dart, the Avro Arrow and 431 Bomber Squadron (Snowbird), their formation giving shape to the maple leaf included in this design by Jason Bouwman.

100th Anniversary of the Montreal Canadiens (1909–2009)

Celebrating hockey's greatest dynasty. (1909-2009) Founded on December 4, 1909, eight years prior to the formation of the NHL, the Montreal Canadiens are the oldest and most successful franchise in professional hockey history. Design by RCM engravers. This coin comes with either a clamshell case or an acrylic stand and features selective gold plating.

DATE		QTY. (000)	ISSUE PRICE	VALUE
2009	100th Anniv. of flight in Canada, Uncirculated	13	39.95	40.00
2009	100th Anniv. of flight in Canada, Proof	25	47.95	48.00
2009	100th Anniv. of flight in Canada, Proof selective gold plating (Proof set)	28	99.95	100.00
2009	100th Anniv. of the Montreal Canadiens, Clamshell case	10	69.95	200.00
2009	100th Anniv. of the Montreal Canadiens, Acrylic stand	5	69.95	200.00

The Sun, 2010

Diameter: 36.15 mm; weight: 30 grams; finish: frosted relief on a proof like field; edge: plain; composition: .925 silver, .075 copper.

Since time immemorial, the sun has been a powerful symbol for people through out the world. It has also been a cornerstone in the culture of Canada's many First Nations communities, representing life, abundance, healing and peace. Designed by Xwa lack tun (Rick Harry).

DATE		QTY.	ISSUE PRICE	VALUE
2010	Limited Edition The Sun, Proof	5,000	139.95	230.00

100th Anniversary of the Canadian Navy (1910–2010)

Diameter: 36.07 mm; weight: 25.175 grams; thickness: 3.02 mm; composition: .925 silver, .075 copper; edge: reeded

In 1910, Parliament passed the Naval Service Act to form Canada's navy, a fledgling force that came to fruition during the Second World War when Canada built more than 120 corvettes to guard the North Atlantic. The HMCS Sackville, the last surviving corvette and living memorial to the Canadian Navy, its pennant number (K-181) clearly visible on its hull and its motto (Ready Aye Ready/Prêt Oui Prêt) in morse code. Designer: Yves Bérubé.

DATE		QTY.	ISSUE PRICE	VALUE
2010	100th Anniversary of the Canadian Navy, Uncirculated	12,946	46.95	47.00
2010	100th Anniversary of the Canadian Navy, Proof	29,141	52.95	55.00
2010	100th Anniversary of the Canadian Navy, Proof, Selective GP	32,342	109.95	100.00

Poppy, 2010

A sea of poppies, one enamelled in vibrant colour to represent the individual saga lived by each veteran of war; one of countless stories played out in conflicts around the world—past, present and future. Reverse design by Christine Paquet.

75th Anniversary of the First Canadian Silver Dollar, 2010

This limited edition proof silver dollar shows a voyageur and an algonquin paddling a canoe, inspired by the original design created by Emanuel Hahn. The obverse features the effigy of King George V by Percy Metcalfe.

100th Anniversary of Parks Canada (1911–2011)

The design features four endangered ecological treasures are cradled in the hands of a young Canadian; a Whooping Crane, the Southern Maidenhair Fern, the Western Prairie- Fringed Orchid and a Kentucky Coffee Tree. Reverse design by Luc Normandin.

DATE		QTY.	ISSUE PRICE	VALUE
2010	Poppy, Limited Edition	4,975	139.95	285.00
2010	75th Anniversary of the First Canadian Silver Dollar, Limited Edition.	7,494	69.95	100.00
2011	100th Anniversary of Parks Canada, Uncirculated	12,946	49.95	50.00
2011	100th Anniversary of Parks Canada, Proof	29,142	55.95	60.00
2011	100th Anniversary of Parks Canada, Proof, Selective Gold Plating	32,342	114.95	85.00

Special Edition Proof Silver Dollar

100th Anniversary of the 1911 Silver Dollar, 2011

When the Mint began striking coins in 1908 (then known as the Ottawa Branch of the Royal Mint), a one-dollar coin had not yet entered circulation, but was desperately needed; so in 1911, the Mint struck a trial one dollar coin in lead, while London's Royal Mint struck two trial coins in silver. Reverse design by Royal Canadian Mint engravers. Adaptation of the 1911 coin design originally designed by W.H.J. Blakemore (reverse), Original design by Sir E. B. MacKennal (obverse).

DATE		QTY.	ISSUE PRICE	VALUE
2011	100th Anniversary of the 1911 Silver Dollar, Proof 5,952		64.95	90.00

200th Anniversary of the War of 1812, 2012

A British sergeant, Voltigeur Canadien and Iroquois warrior approach the invader; united in their determination to defend the colonies. Encircling the design are 200 finely struck beads symbolizing the 200th anniversary of the War of 1812. Reverse design by Ardell Bourgeois.

DATE		QTY. (000)	ISSUE PRICE	VALUE
2012	200th Anniversary of the War of 1812, Uncirculated 25		54.95	55.00
2012	200th Anniversary of the War of 1812, Proof 40		59.95	59.00
2012	200th Anniversary of the War of 1812, Proof, Selective Gold Plating 20		224.95	85.00

Two Loons, 2012

The beauty of a pair of loons on a still Canadian lake is captured in this coin, which faithfully reproduces artist Richard Hunt's original limited edition print. The design covers one entire side.

DATE		QTY.	ISSUE PRICE	VALUE
2012	Two Loons, Proof	10,000	179.99	180.00

Lucky Loonie, 2012

DATE		QTY.	ISSUE PRICE	VALUE
2012	Lucky Loonie, Proof	20,000	49.95	50.00

25th Anniversary of the Loonie, 2012

In 2012, the Royal Canadian Mint celebrates the 25th anniversary of the Loonie, the iconic Canadian one-dollar coin bearing the image of this great Canadian symbol. Like its namesake, the Loonie has proven resilient, emblematic, and long-lived. The reverse image, designed by Robert-Ralph Carmichael who designed the original circulation Loonie in 1987, shows two Common Loons swim majestically past one another.

DATE		QTY.	ISSUE PRICE	VALUE
2012	25th Anniversary Loonie	15,000	39.95	40.00

100 Years of the Calgary Stampede, 2012

The reverse image by artist Steve Hepburn centres around a depiction of the wild spirit of the Stampede's bareback bronc rodeo event.

DATE		QTY.	ISSUE PRICE	VALUE
2012	Calgary Stampede, Proof	10,000	109.95	110.00

The 100th Grey Cup, 2012

When the first Grey Cup tournament was played in Toronto in 1909 before 3800 spectators, few could foresee that one day the championship would be watched, celebrated, and obsessed over by millions. The year 2012 marks the 100th Grey Cup tournament, a game celebrated by a 9-day festival in Toronto, Ontario.

DATE		QTY.	ISSUE PRICE	VALUE
2012	100th Grey Cup	10,000	74.95	75.00

250th Anniversary of the end of the Seven Years War, 2013

This coin was designed by Canadian artist Tony Bianco and features a montage of the peoples involved in—and affected by—the Seven Years War. The design represents the British and French soldiers, the First Nations people, and the colonists; and also features a child to symbolize hope for the future.

DATE		QTY.	ISSUE PRICE	VALUE
2013	Seven Years War, Proof	10,000	69.95	70.00

Arctic Expedition, 2013

Designed by Canadian artist Bonnie Ross and draws on photography from the Canadian Arctic Expedition. The coin depicts a group of three men aboard a dogsled, the waiting dog team before them listening for the command to move on across the Arctic tundra.

DATE		QTY.	ISSUE PRICE	VALUE
2013	Arctic Expedition, Proof	40,000	59.95	60.00

60th Anniversary of the Korean Armistice Agreement, 2013

War brings out the worst in humanity–but it can also reveal the best. When the armistice agreement was signed on July 27, 1953, 1,558 Canadians had been injured and another 516 had made the ultimate sacrifice. The Korea Medal was awarded to all the Commonwealth forces that fought in the Korean War. Its design showed Hercules slaying the indomitable hydra-headed monster–an allegory for the perilous struggles of war that have been painstakingly reproduced for this special commemorative coin. A portion of the sales will be donated to support Korean Veteran causes.

DATE		QTY.	ISSUE PRICE	VALUE
2013	Korean Armistice Agreement, Proof	10,000	69.95	70.00

100th Anniversary of the Declaration of the First World War
2014

Train stations across Canada became the stage for tearful goodbyes and lingering embraces. The First World War was a true coming of age for the young nation, and the hope, fear, courage and deep sacrifice Canadians felt 100 years ago remain as poignant and inspiring today. Designer: Bonnie Ross.

DATE	QTY.	ISSUE PRICE	VALUE
2014 100th Anniversary of the Declaration of the First World War 20,000		54.95	55.00

75th Anniversary of the Declaration of the Second World War
2014

Right from its onset, the Second World War ushered in a new era for Canadians. Women helped build the Allied war effort, they turned their nation into an economic power, and forever transformed their role in society—and at war. The image shows women building an Avro 683 Lancaster X.

DATE	QTY.	ISSUE PRICE	VALUE
2014 75th Anniversary of the Declaration of the Second World War 7,500		69.95	70.00

2015 Big Coin Series

Diameter: 65.25mm; weight: 157.6g; composition: 99.99% pure silver; finish: proof with selective gold plating; edge: serrated; ; images reduced by 50%

Part of a six-coin set featuring 5¢, 10¢, 25¢, 50¢, $1, and $2 values.

DATE		QTY.	ISSUE PRICE	VALUE
2014	$1 Loon (September 2014) - Robert-Ralph Carmichael 1,500		549.95	550.00

50th Anniversary of the Canadian Flag, 2015

Diameter: 36.07mm; weight: 23.17g; composition: 99.99% pure silver; finish: proof; edge: serrated

No other symbol is as synonymous with Canada as its distinctive red-and-white flag. To Canadians at home and abroad, the red maple leaf unites us and instills a sense of belonging regardless of our different cultures, languages and beliefs. Designer: John Mantha.

DATE		QTY.	ISSUE PRICE	VALUE
2015	50th Anniversary of the Canadian Flag. 20,000		59.95	60.00

Diameter: 36.07mm; weight: 23.17g; composition: 99.99% pure silver; finish: brilliant; edge: serrated

DATE		QTY.	ISSUE PRICE	VALUE
2015	50th Anniversary of the Canadian Flag. 15,000		54.95	55.00

2 DOLLARS PROOF

Diameter: 28.0 mm; weight: 7.3 grams; thickness: 1.80 mm; edge: interrupted serration; composition (outer ring): nickel, (centre): aluminum bronze, .92 copper, .06 aluminum, .02 nickel (diameter: 16.8 mm)

Polar Bear, 1996

The uncirculated two dollar coin was issued in a presentation folder and was also sold, with a two dollar note from the final issue, in a presentation folder protected in a matching sleeve.

The coin was issued encapsulated and housed in a black display case in a protective sleeve. The coin was also issued with an uncirculated replacement two dollar banknote.

The Polar Bear reverse was designed by Brent Townsend of Campbellford, Ontario. Both the uncirculated and proof editions have the same composition.

Nunavut, 1999

Diameter: 28 mm; weight: 8.83 grams (Ring: 5.86 grams, core: 2.97 grams) thickness: 1.9 mm; edge: interrupted serrations; composition (outer ring): .925 silver, .075 copper; (centre): .925 silver, .075 copper (24 karat gold plated)

Canada's first commemorative circulating two dollar coin was released in 1999 to celebrate the end of the second millennium and the creation of Nunavut, Canada's newest territory. Designed by Inuit artist Germaine Arnaktauyok, the reverse, depicts an Inuit performing the historic Drum Dance.

The Nunavut coin was included in the 1999 Uncirculated and Specimen sets and was sold singly in proof (cased) in .925 silver.

DATE		QTY. (000)	ISSUE PRICE	VALUE
1996	$2 Polar Bear, uncirculated, in presentation folder 75		10.95	10.00
1996	$2 Polar Bear, cased proof 67		24.95	15.00
1999	$2 Nunavut, silver proof, cased 40		24.95	20.00

A Path of Knowledge, 2000

The reverse which features a mother Polar Bear and her two new cubs on an early-summer ice floe, was designed by Tony Bianco. The design suggests the importance of knowledge passes from generation to generation. Patrick Brindley's modification of the Arnold Machin effigy of the queen on obverse.

2000	$2 A Path of Knowledge, silver proof 40		24.95	20.00

Individual Coins Individual uncirculated coins were released in three different forms: (1) in a "standard" black case with red interior; (2) encapsulated with no case; and (3) some individual coins were released through the banks at face value (without encapsulation) to monetize the issue.

YOUNG WILDLIFE — SPECIMEN, 2010–

Diameter: 28.0 mm; weight: 7.3 grams; edge: interrupted serration; composition (outer ring): nickel,
(centre): aluminum bronze, .92 copper, .06 aluminum, .02 nickel (diameter: 16.8 mm)

These coins are issued in a special Specimen set with designs featuring young wildlife. Reverse
by Christie Paquet.

DATE		QTY.	ISSUE PRICE	VALUE
2010	$2 Young Lynx	15,000	49.95	50.00
2011	$2 Elk Calf	15,000	49.95	50.00
2012	$2 Wolf Cubs, designed by Emily Damstra	15,000	49.95	50.00
2013	$2 Black Bear Cubs, designed by Glen Loates	17,500	49.95	50.00
2014	$2 Baby Rabbits, designed by Pierre Leduc	17,500	49.95	50.00

STERLING SILVER 3 DOLLARS

Size: 27 mm square; weight: 11.72 grams; finish: specimen;
composition: 92.5% silver, 7.5% copper, plated in gold

The Beaver, 2006

Canada's cherished beaver poised above its harvest of logs, surrounded by an elaborate guilloche pattern. Reverse by Cosme Saffioti.

DATE		QTY.	ISSUE PRICE	VALUE
2006	$3 Square Sterling Silver coin—The Beaver	20,000	45.95	250.00

Canada's Wildlife Species, 2010–2011

Size: 27 mm square; weight: 11.8 grams; finish: specimen;
composition: 92.5% silver, 7.5% copper, plated in gold

This series with its uncommon square shape provides a setting to showcase the modern style to depict an endangered species of Canada's treasured wildlife. Designs by Jason Bouwman.

DATE		QTY.	ISSUE PRICE	VALUE
2010	$3 Barn Owl	10,578	59.95	75.00
2010	$3 Polar Bear	8,344	59.95	65.00
2011	$3 Urca Whale	10,698	62.95	65.00
2011	$3 Black Footed Ferret	8,237	62.95	75.00

FINE SILVER — SWAROVSKI CRYSTALS — 3 DOLLARS
Birthstones, 2011

Diameter: 27 mm, weight: 7.96 grams; edge: reeded;
composition: .9999 silver, finish: proof.

The design features a Swarovski crystal that glitters from a whirl of flower petals. This new series of pure silver coins provides the perfect setting to showcase gem-inspired Swarovski elements—one for every birthstone of the year. Each coin is a unique keepsake to celebrate a person's individuality, crafted in the Mint's world-renowned tradition of excellence. Reverse designed by the RCM Engravers.

| January - Garnet | February - Amethyst | March - Aquamarine | April - Diamond |
| Constancy & Loyalty | Sincerity & Peace | Courage & Health | Innocence & Love |

| May - Emerald | June - Alexandrite | July - Ruby | August - Peridot |
| Happiness & Fertility | Balance & Joy | Nobility & Beauty | Felicity & Protection |

| September - Sapphire | October - Tourmaline | November - Topaz | December - Zircon |
| Wisdom & Calmness | Balance & Endurance | Friendship & Strength | Wisdom & Wealth |

DATE		COST	VALUE
2011	$3 Birthstones - 12 different issues	64.95	65.00

Quantity

January - 2,534	February - 2,571	March - 2,560	April - 2,528
May - 2,915	June - 2,724	July - 3,073	August - 2,673
September - 2,717	October - 2,593	November - 2,870	December - 2,879

Birthstones, 2012

| January - Garnet | February - Amethyst | March - Aquamarine | April - Diamond |
| Constancy & Loyalty | Sincerity & Peace | Courage & Health | Innocence & Love |

| May - Emerald | June - Alexandrite | July - Ruby | August - Peridot |
| Happiness & Fertility | Balance & Joy | Nobility & Beauty | Felicity & Protection |

| September - Sapphire | October - Tourmaline | November - Topaz | December - Zircon |
| Wisdom & Calmness | Balance & Endurance | Friendship & Strength | Wisdom & Wealth |

DATE		QTY.	COST	VALUE
2012	$3 Birthstones - 12 different issues	N/A	64.95	65.00

Hummingbird and Morning Glory, 2013

The hummingbird and the Morning Glory are two perennially beautiful fixtures of the Canadian garden in summer. Here, they are joined in exquisite harmony around a sparkling red Swarovski crystal element.

DATE		QTY.	COST	VALUE
2013	$3 Hummingbird and Morning Glory	20,000	59.95	60.00

Animal Architects Series, 2013–

Diameter: 27.0mm; weight: 7.96g; composition: .9999 fine silver; finish: proof; edge:serrated

Thanks to the Entomological Society of Canada for assistance with this coin series and congratulations on celebrating 150 years of entomological science and services in Canada.

DATE		QTY.	COST	VALUE
2013	$3 Bee & Hive, design by Yves Bérubé 10,000		69.95	70.00
2014	$3 Spider & Web, design by Yves Bérubé .10,000		69.95	70.00
2014	$3 Caterpillar and Chrysalis, design by Trevor Tennant. 10,000		69.95	70.00

Fishing, 2013

The reverse design by Canadian artist John Mantha portrays an uncomplicated yet evocative moment between father and child. Sitting with their back to the viewer on a long dock that spans the width of the reverse field, a father and child are joined by their young dog.

DATE		QTY.	COST	VALUE
2013	$3 Fishing 15,000		34.95	35.00

Maple Leaf Impression, 2013

Valour, perseverance, diversity: the maple leaf is a powerful symbol of Canadian identity and values. Internationally recognized, the maple leaf has been a Canadian emblem for almost three hundred years. The reverse image by Royal Canadian Mint engraver José Osio features the impression of a hidden maple leaf amongst much smaller maple leafs.

DATE		QTY.	COST	VALUE
2013	$3 Maple Leaf Impression	10,000	59.95	60.00

Martin Short Presents Canada, 2013

Martin Short consulted extensively with Canadian artist Tony Bianco to create this coin to express what Canada means to him. It features Short's summer home in the Muskoka of northern Ontario.

DATE		QTY.	COST	VALUE
2013	$3 Martin Short Presents Canada	15,000	49.95	50.00

Life in the North, 2013

Diameter: 27.0mm; weight: 7.96g; composition: .9999 fine silver; finish: matte proof; edge:serrated

From 1913 to 1916, two teams of scientists took part in an unprecedented exploration of the Arctic region that was known as the First Canadian Arctic Expedition. This striking coin commemorates the centennial of the First Canadian Arctic Expedition by bringing a contemporary perspective to life in the Arctic. Designer: Tim Pitsiulak.

DATE		QTY.	ISSUE PRICE	VALUE
2013	$3 Life in the North	10,000	34.95	35.00

Jewel of Life, 2014

Diameter: 27.0mm; weight: 7.96g; composition: fine silver;
finish: proof with selective gold plating and Swarovski® crystals; edge: serrated

An original design by celebrated Quebec actor and singer Caroline Néron who has also made her mark as a jewellery designer. Caroline finds much of her inspiration in classic designs and reinvents them for the modern woman, often incorporating Swarovski crystals to capture the added beauty of reflected light and to convey a sense of elegant confidence.

DATE		QTY.	ISSUE PRICE	VALUE
2014	$3 Jewel of Life. 15,000		59.95	60.00

SELECTIVE GOLD PLATING
FINE SILVER 3 DOLLARS

Diameter: 27 mm; weight: 7.96 grams; finish: proof with selective gold plating on the reverse;
composition: .9999 fine silver; edge: serrated.

These pure silver coins feature selective gold plating in pink and yellow gold with aboriginal based themes.

DATE		QTY.	ISSUE PRICE	VALUE
2010	$3 Return of the Tyee (Salmon), by Jody Broomfield. 8,301		54.95	65.00
2011	$3 Family Scene (Mother & child), by Andrew Qappik. 6,687		64.95	65.00

Wait for Me, Daddy, 2014

Diameter: 27.0mm; weight: 7.96g; composition: 99.99% pure silver; finish: matte proof; edge: serrated

It is perhaps the most famous photograph taken in Canada during the Second World War: a five-year-old boy breaks away from his mother's grasp to run after his father as he marches off to war. Taken in New Westminster, B.C. in the fall of 1940, by photographer Claude Dettloff, "Wait for Me, Daddy" continues to resonate as a snapshot of the war's impact on Canadians and the personal sacrifices they made.

DATE	QTY.	ISSUE PRICE	VALUE
2014 $3 Wait for Me, Daddy. 15,000		44.95	45.00

50th Anniversary of the Canadian Flag, 2015

Diameter: 27.0mm; weight: 7.96g; composition: fine silver (99.99% pure); finish: proof; edge: serrated

With its bright red maple leaf, the famous red-and-white flag stands as a proud symbol for Canadians. As our national banner, it speaks of our sense of belonging to a broader community, one that is a growing, vibrant mosaic of different cultures, languages and beliefs. It also represents our history and our identity within the international community as we work together to shape a future for ourselves, and for generations to follow.

DATE	QTY.	ISSUE PRICE	VALUE
2015 $3 50th Anniversary of the Canadian Flag .15,000		29.95	30.00

FINE SILVER 4 DOLLARS

Diameter: 34 mm; weight: 15.87 grams; finish: proof with selective aging on the reverse;
composition: .9999 fine silver; edge: serrated.

Dinosaur Series, 2007–2010

This collection, designed by Kerri Burnett, features dinosaurs with variations in tone and colour
that make each unique. This series was originally intended to be a 4 coin series and was then
extended due to popular demand.

DATE		QTY.	ISSUE PRICE	VALUE
2007	$4 Parasaurolophus	14,946	39.95	225.00
2008	$4 Triceratops	13,046	39.95	200.00
2009	$4 Tyrannosaurus rex	13,752	42.95	85.00
2010	$4 Dromaeosaurus	8,982	42.95	80.00
2010	$4 Euoplocephalus tutus	6,256	49.95	70.00

Hang the Stockings, 2009

Diameter: 34 mm; weight: 15.87 grams; finish: proof,
composition: .9999 fine silver; edge: serrated.

The link between stockings and Christmas began to emerge with the legend of Saint Nicholas.
Centuries later, Clement Moore (1779–1863) penned his famous words "...The stockings were
hung by the chimney with care..." and stockings became a Holiday fixture—one that endures to
this day.

DATE		QTY.	ISSUE PRICE	VALUE
2009	$4 Hanging the stockings	6,011	42.95	55.00

Welcome to the World, 2011

The design features baby feet and toes, encircled with the words "Born in 2011" to commemorate the year of a baby's birth. Includes a full-colour Certificate of Authenticity with space to add a personalized message. Reverse designed by RCM Engravers.

DATE		QTY.	ISSUE PRICE	VALUE
2011	$4 Welcome to the World	7,059	59.95	60.00

Heroes of 1812, 2012–2013

DATE		QTY.	ISSUE PRICE	VALUE
2012	$4 Chief Techumseh.	10,000	49.95	50.00
2012	$4 Sir Isaac Brock	10,000	49.95	50.00
2013	$4 Charles Michel de Salaberry	10,000	49.95	50.00
2013	$4 Laura Secord.	10,000	49.95	50.00

5 DOLLARS SPECIAL EDITIONS
"The Driver", 2004

Diameter: 38 mm; weight: 28 grams; edge: reeded;
composition: .9999 silver

Issued as part of the 2004 Open Championship 0f Canada Commemorative Frame. Also included was the 10 cent silver coin "The Putter" and a divot repair kit.

DATE		QTY. (000)	ISSUE PRICE	VALUE
2004	$5 silver proof "The Driver" 25		49.95	50.00

Alberta Centennial (1905–2005)

Diameter: 36 mm; weight: 25.2 grams; edge: reeded;
composition: .9999 silver

Two special coins were struck in celebration of the Alberta's 100th anniversary as a province. The special reverse was designed by Michelle Grant and also adorns the special issue Alberta Centennial twenty-five cent coin.

Saskatchewan Centennial (1905–2005)

Saskatchewan's centennial is being celebrated by the issue of two special coins. The reverse, designed by Paulett Sapergia, also appears on the special Saskatchewan Centennial twenty-five cent coin.

DATE		QTY. (000)	ISSUE PRICE	VALUE
2005	$5 Alberta Centennial, Proof 20		45.95	50.00
2005	$5 Saskatchewan Centennial, Proof 20		49.95	50.00

60th Anniversary
The End of the Second World War, 2005

Diameter: 38 mm; weight: 31.5 grams; edge: reeded;
composition: .9999 silver

This coin was struck to recognize the members of all three of our military services who served so well during the Second World War.

DATE		QTY. (000)	ISSUE PRICE	VALUE
2005	$5 silver specimen	25	39.95	70.00
2005	$5 with maple leaf privy mark	10	N/A	150.00

Breast Cancer, 2006

Diameter: 36.07 mm; weight: 25.175 grams; edge: reeded,
composition: .9999 silver

Features the iconic pink ribbon, the symbol of hope and awareness in the effort to create a future without breast cancer. Designed by Christie Paquet.

Snowbirds, 2006

This coin features the Canadian armed forces famous Snowbirds with a double hologram effect. Designed by Jianping Yan.

DATE		QTY.	ISSUE PRICE	VALUE
2006	$5 Breast Cancer, proof, coloured ribbon	11,048	59.95	60.00
2006	$5 Snow Birds, proof, double hologram	10,034	59.95	60.00

80th Anniversary of Diplomatic Relations
Between Canada and Japan (1929–2009)

Diameter: 36.07 mm; weight: 25.175 grams; edge: reeded,
composition: .925 silver, .075 copper

This coin features flora and fauna of both countries. A white
tail deer with maple leaf foliage, along with a shika deer and
cherry blossoms. The Japanese character "wa" accentuates
harmony. 35,000 of these coins will be used in Japanese mint
sets and the remaining 5,000 made available in Canada. This is
the first joint venture with Japanese mint and the RCM

DATE		QTY.	ISSUE PRICE	VALUE
2009	$5 80th Anniversary of Canada and Japan Diplomatic Relations 27,872		47.95	50.00

Fine Silver $5 Coin
25th Anniv. of the Rick Hansen Man-In-Motion Tour, 2012

Diameter: 36.07 mm; weight: 23.17 grams; edge: reeded,
composition: .9999 silver.

This year marks the 25th anniversary of the completion of the Man-In-Motion World Tour. The
majority of the field of the coin is filled with finely engraved lines that visually represent the new
paths Hansen laid to cut through limiting perceptions of physical disability and his key principles:
"journey, inspire, dream, together, involvement," and, of course, "anything is possible." Design
by Chris Reid and Rosina Li.

DATE		QTY.	ISSUE PRICE	VALUE
2012	$5 25th Anniv. of the Rick Hansen Man-In-Motion Tour........... 7,500		69.95	70.00

STERLING SILVER & NIOBIUM 5 DOLLARS
Full Moon Series, 2011–2013

Diameter: 28 mm; weight: 8.5 grams; edge: segmented reeding; finish: proof;
composition: ring .925 silver .750 copper, reverse core niobium, obverse core .925 silver .750 copper.

Based on Algonquin tradition to mark time by the moon, this series involves a distinct and innovative minting process. A Niobium insert is struck into the core of a sterling silver coin and then selectively colored through a unique oxidation process made possible by the special properties of this metal. Designed by John Mantha.

DATE		QTY.	ISSUE PRICE	VALUE
2011	$5 Buck Moon	6,412	121.95	130.00
2011	$5 Hunter's Moon	5,446	121.95	130.00
2012	$5 Wolf Moon	7,500	121.95	130.00
2013	$5 Full Pink Moon	7,500	121.95	130.00

Georgina Pope, 2012

This special coin celebrates the legacy and achievements of Georgina Fane Pope, a pioneer of Canadian nursing whose work helped to pave the way for Canadian women in the military.

DATE		QTY.	ISSUE PRICE	VALUE
2012	$5 Georgina Pope	10,000	69.95	70.00

Tradition of Hunting Series, 2013–2014

Diameter: 36.07mm; weight: 23.17g; composition: fine silver; finish: proof; edge: serrated

Countless Inuit legends passed down through generations of oral storytelling reflect the profound understanding that all of humanity is irrevocably reliant on the earth. Many stories speak of mystical beings who oversee people's activities to ensure nature's laws are respected.

DATE		QTY.	ISSUE PRICE	VALUE
2013	$5 Deer - Darlene Gait	10,000	69.95	70.00
2013	$5 Bison - Darlene Gait	10,000	69.95	70.00
2014	$5 The Seal - Darlene Gait	10,000	69.95	70.00
2014	$5 Canada Goose - Tim Whiskeychan	10,000	69.95	70.00

Contemporary Aboriginal Art Series, 2013–

Diameter: 28.0mm; weight: 8.5g; composition: fine silver (99.99% pure) with niobium; finish: proof; edge: interrupted serrations

The reverse design is by Inuit artist Ulaayu Pilurtuut. Pilurtuut's design shows a joyous mother celebrating her latest catch with her baby in her amautik.

DATE		QTY.	ISSUE PRICE	VALUE
2013	$5 Aboriginal Art	6,500	139.95	140.00
2013	$5 Ice-Fishing Father	6,500	139.95	140.00

Canadian Bank Note Series, 2013–2015

Diameter: 36.07mm; weight: 23.17g; composition: fine silver; finish: proof; edge: serrated

When paper money first appeared in North American even then counterfeiting was a concern. As paper money evolved over the centuries so did the need to make it increasingly difficult to copy. Art proved to be the perfect strategy-the more detailed and elaborate the better.

DATE		QTY.	ISSUE PRICE	VALUE
2013	$5 Canadian Bank Of Commerce's 1888 $20 Bank Note	8,500	69.95	70.00
2014	$5 Saint George Slaying The Dragon	8,500	69.95	70.00
2014	$5 Lion on the Mountain	8,500	69.95	70.00
2015	$5 Canadian Bank Note Vignette	8,500	69.95	70.00

25th Anniversary of the Silver Maple Leaf 2013 Piedfort Coin

Diameter: 34.0mm; weight: 31.39g; composition: fine silver; finish: proof; edge: serrated

In French, "piedfort" literally means "strong foot." Today, this centuries-old term indicates that a coin is thicker than usual-like this 25th anniversary issue!

DATE		QTY.	ISSUE PRICE	VALUE
2013	$5 Silver Maple Leaf, artist Jean-Louis Sirois	10,000	99.95	100.00

Devil's Brigade, 2013

Diameter: 36.07mm; weight: 23.17g; composition: fine silver; finish: proof; edge: serrated

During World War II, Canada joined forces with the United States to create the First Special Service Force—the first and only time both nations would be seamlessly combined in training, equipment and uniform. Although it was only operational for two years, this elite combat unit demonstrated the power of united national forces against a common foe—and consequently became the forerunner to distinguished Canadian and U.S. units including Canada's Joint-Task-Force 2 and the United States' Navy Seals, Delta Force and Green Berets. Design by Ardell Bourgeois.

DATE	QTY.	ISSUE PRICE	VALUE
2013 $5 Devil's Brigade 20,000		59.95	60.00

Royal Infant with Toys, 2013

Diameter: 36.0mm; weight: 23.17g; composition: 99.99% pure silver with selective gold-plating; finish: proof; edge: serrated

The announcement that the Duke and Duchess of Cambridge are expecting a baby in July 2013 threw their adoring public into a frenzy, eager for the exact date and news whether it will be a boy or a girl, and what its name will be. Designed by Laurie McGaw.

DATE	QTY.	ISSUE PRICE	VALUE
2013 $5 Royal Infant with Toys 15,000		74.95	75.00

Peregrine Falcon, 2014

Diameter: 38.0mm; weight: 31.39g; composition: fine silver; finish: proof; edge: serrated; 1 ounce

Revered since the Middle Ages, the peregrine falcon is one of the most striking, beautiful, graceful aerial predators in the world. Known for its breathtaking displays of flight agility, the bird can reach speeds over 300km/h while stooping, making it the fastest animal in the world. Designer: Emily Damstra.

DATE	QTY.	ISSUE PRICE	VALUE
2014 $5 Peregrine Falson.................................20,000		89.95	90.00

Arctic Fox, 2014

Diameter: 38.0mm; weight: 31.39g; composition: fine silver; finish: proof; edge: serrated; 1 ounce

Just slightly larger than the average housecat, Vulpes lagopus—the Arctic fox—is a silent and prolific hunter. The pelt of the Arctic fox is unmatched for warmth, sustaining it at temperatures below -50° Celsius. Its fur is brown, grey-brown, blue-grey, or dark blue-grey in the warmer months. In the long Arctic winter, most turn pure white, although some populations show lighter blue-grey through the winter phase. The fox's thick fur covers its small rounded ears and even the pads of its feet, for optimum warmth. Designer: Maurice Gevais.

DATE	QTY.	ISSUE PRICE	VALUE
2014 $5 Arctic Fox...7,500		89.95	90.00

Maple Leaf Bullion Replica, 2014

Diameter: 38.0mm; weight: 31.39g; composition: fine silver; finish: reverse proof; edge: serrated; 1 ounce

In the world of investments, precious metals are traded in the form of coins, wafers or bars know as "bullion".

DATE		QTY.	ISSUE PRICE	VALUE
2014	$5 Bullion Replica 20,000		79.95	80.00

Alice Munro, 2014

Diameter: 36.07mm; weight: 23.17g; composition: fine silver; finish: proof; edge: serrated

For more than four decades, Canadian author Alice Munro has delighted readers with her engaging storytelling and profound "slice of life" narratives. As the recipient of the 2013 Nobel Prize in Literature, Munro holds the added distinction of being the first Canadian woman to win this remarkable accolade. Designer: Laurie McGaw.

DATE		QTY.	ISSUE PRICE	VALUE
2014	$5 Alice Munro 7,500		69.95	70.00

First World War — Canadian Expeditionary Force, 2014

Diameter: 36.07mm; weight: 23.17g; composition: fine silver (99.99% pure); finish: proof ; edge: serrated

The Canadian Expeditionary Force (CEF) is the designation for the Canadian forces that served overseas during the First World War. Far from their homeland, they helped build Canada's international reputation and contributed to Canada's coming of age as a nation. Designer: Scott Waters.

DATE	QTY.	ISSUE PRICE	VALUE
2014 $5 First World War — Canadian Expeditionary Force 10,000		64.95	65.00

Five Blessings, 2014

Diameter: 38mm; weight: 31.39g; composition: 99.99% pure silver; finish: proof with colour application; edge: serrated

Blessings are an integral element of Chinese culture. This coin features a beautifully engraved design conferring upon its owner blessings of happiness, success, long life, joy, and good fortune.

DATE	QTY.	ISSUE PRICE	VALUE
2014 $5 Five Blessings 8,500		99.95	100.00

Flowers in Canada Series, 2014

Diameter: 28mm; weight: 9g; composition: 99.99% pure silver with niobium core; finish: proof; edge: interrupted serrations

First coin in a new series of 3 showcasing Canada's favourite flowers. Canada's gardens are filled with a tremendous variety of flowers, but a few of them remain all-time favourites that always capture more admiring gazes than all the others. Designer: Bert Liverance.

DATE		QTY.	ISSUE PRICE	VALUE
2014	$5 Tulip	6,000	139.95	140.00
2014	$5 Rose	6,000	139.95	140.00
2014	$5 Poinsettia	6,000	139.95	140.00

Princess to Monarch, 2014

Diameter: 36.07mm; weight: 23.17g; composition: fine silver (99.99% pure); finish: proof; edge: serrated

Design is Canadian artist Trevor Tennant's interpretation of a photograph.

DATE		QTY.	ISSUE PRICE	VALUE
2014	$5 Princess to Monarch	15,000	64.95	65.00

Bald Eagle, 2014

Diameter: 38.0mm; weight: 31.39g; composition: 99.99% pure silver; finish: proof; edge: serrated

When it comes to hunting, the bald eagle's most important assets are its eyes, its talons and its exceptional diving speed. Designer Emily Damstra.

DATE	QTY.	ISSUE PRICE	VALUE
2014 $5 Bald Eagle 7,500		89.95	90.00

Polar Bear and Cub, 2015

Diameter: 38.0mm; weight: 31.39g; composition: 99.99% pure silver; finish: proof; edge: serrated

A symbol of the power and vastness of Canada's northern landscape, the Polar Bear is an iconic animal for Canadians. In a nation dominated by weather extremes, the Polar Bear's ability to survive and thrive in the harshest climate reflects Canadians' stalwart pragmatism and spirit of adventure. Designer: Germaine Arnaktauyok.

DATE	QTY.	ISSUE PRICE	VALUE
2015 $5 Polar Bear and Cub. 7,500		89.95	90.00

Artwork by Cornelius Krieghoff, 2015

Diameter: 36.07mm; weight: 23.17g; composition: 99.99% pure silver; finish: proof; edge: serrated

Cornelius Krieghoff is one of Canada's most well-known and celebrated artists of the nineteenth century. His iconic images of life among the French-Canadian habitants and First Nations peoples of Quebec helped to shape Canada's early visual identity and captured an important moment in the history of the nation.

DATE		QTY.	ISSUE PRICE	VALUE
2015	Artwork by Cornelius Krieghoff (set of 3)...........................7,000		199.95	200.00
	$5 Hunter in Winter, c. 1855-1865			
	$5 Indian Wigwam in Montagnais, 1848			
	$5 Moccasin Seller Crossing the St. Lawrence at Quebec City, c. 1853-1863			

Year of the Sheep, 2015

Diameter: 36.07mm; weight: 23.17g; composition: 99.99% pure silver; finish: proof with colour; edge: serrated

The year 2015 is ruled by the Sheep. The creative Sheep personality embodies wealth, warmth and loveliness. Good things seem to come to the Sheep naturally because of its irresistibly good nature. The Sheep rarely speaks its mind. It will go with the flow and only object when things aren't going its way. Push too hard and it will react—decisively! The gregarious Sheep is an eternal romantic. It adores being showered with love and attention. Designer: Simon Ng.

DATE		QTY.	ISSUE PRICE	VALUE
2015	$5 Year of the Sheep......................................8,888		74.95	75.00

SILVER 5 AND 10 DOLLARS
OLYMPICS, 1973–1976

$5: Diameter: 38.00 mm; weight: 24.30 grams; composition: .925 silver, .075 copper; edge: reeded
$10: Diameter: 45.00 mm; weight: 48.60 grams; composition: .925 silver, .075 copper; edge: reeded

$5 Obverse $10 Obverse

Struck by the Royal Canadian Mint at its satellite mint in Hull, Quebec, these coins were intended to help finance the XXI Olympiad, in Montreal in 1976. In total twenty-eight silver coins were issued in 7 series of four coins each from 1973 to 1976. Each series of four coins (two $5 and two $10), was issued in both uncirculated and proof condition, in a variety of packaging. The numismatic program for the 1976 olympics also included two $100 gold pieces.

Deluxe Proof Set Proof silver coins were issued only in these sets, consisting of the four proof coins for the series in a case made of Canadian white birch with a tanned steer-hide cover and black insert.

Prestige Set This set was comprised of the four uncirculated coins for the series in a black leatherette case with matte finish and blue insert.

Custom Set The Custom set also contained the four uncirculated coins for the series in a black gold-trimmed case with red insert.

	ISSUE PRICE	VALUE		ISSUE PRICE	VALUE
$5 Uncirculated			**Custom Sets**		
Encapsulated Series I	6.50	20.00	(two $5 and two $10 coins)		
Encapsulated Series II	7.50	20.00	Series I	45.00	120.00
Encapsulated Series III-VII	8.00	20.00	Series II-VII	55.00	120.00
			Prestige Sets		
$10 Uncirculated			(two $5 and two $10 coins)		
Encapsulated Series I	12.00	40.00	Series I	50.00	120.00
Encapsulated Series II	15.00	40.00	Series II-VII	60.00	120.00
Encapsulated Series III-VII	15.75	40.00			
			Deluxe Proof Sets (two $5 and two $10 coins)		
Total quantities minted (1973–1976)			Series I	72.50	130.00
$5.00 – 12,733,789; $10.00 – 12,458,048			Series II-VI	82.50	130.00
			Series VII	82.50	130.00

Series I: Geographic, 1973

Release date: December 13, 1973; Designer: (by invitation) Georges Huel;
Modellers: $5 and $10 Map issues – None (designs photographically etched)
Kingston – Terrence Smith; Montreal – Ago Aarand.

$5 Landmarks of Kingston

$5 Map of North America

$10 Montreal Skyline

$10 Map of the World

Series II: Olympic Motifs, 1974

Release date: September 16, 1974.

Designer: (winner of invitational competition) Anthony Mann.

Modellers: Head of Zeus and Athlete with Torch – Patrick Brindley;
Olympic Rings and Temple of Zeus – Walter Ott.

$5 Athlete with Torch

$5 Olympic Rings and Wreath

$10 Head of Zeus $10 Temple of Zeus

Series III: Early Canadian Sports, 1974

Release date: April 16, 1975; Designer: (winner of invitational competition) Ken Danby.

Modellers: Canoeing – Patrick Brindley; Lacrosse – Walter Ott;

Others: combined work of Brindley, Ott, Smith and Aarand.

$5 Canoeing $5 Rowing

$10 Cycling $10 Lacrosse

Series IV: Olympic Track and Field Sports, 1975

Release date: August 12, 1975; **Designer:** (winner of invitational competition) Leo Yerxa

All designs include stylized Algonquin quill-work.

Modellers: $10 issues – Patrick Brindley; $5 issues – Walter Ott.

$5 Marathon Runner $5 Women's Javelin

$10 Women's Shot Put $10 Men's Hurdles

Series V: Olympic Water Sports, 1975

Release date: December 1, 1975; **Designer:** (winner of open national competition) Lynda Cooper.

Modellers: None (designs were photographically etched).

$5 Diver $5 Swimmer

$10 Sailing $10 Paddler

Series VI: Olympic Team Sports and Body Contact Sports, 1976

Release date: March 1, 1976. **Designer:** (winner of open international competition) Shigeo Fukada.

Modellers: None (designs were photographically etched).

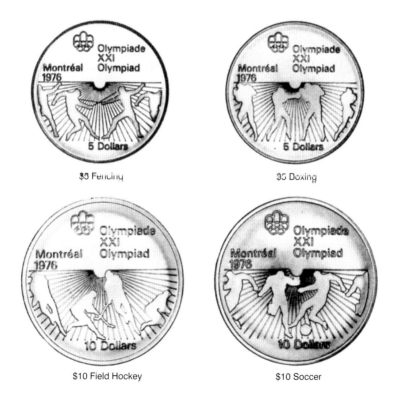

$5 Fencing $5 Boxing

$10 Field Hockey $10 Soccer

Series VII: Olympic Souvenir Issue, 1976

Release date: June 1, 1976. Designer: (winner of invitational competition among several Canadian design houses) Elliot Morrison, using architectural drawings by Roger Taillibert for the $10 pieces.

Modellers: Village – Sheldon Beveridge; Flame – Walter Ott (principally) and Patrick Brindley; Stadium – Ago Aarand; Velodrome – Terrence Smith.

$5 Olympic Village $5 Olympic Flame

$10 Stadium $10 Velodrome

2005 SILVER 8 DOLLARS

Diameter: 40 mm; weight: 32.15 grams; finish: proof;
composition: .9999 fine silver, inner core: gold plated; edge serrated

The Commemoration of
Chinese Railway Workers

120th Anniversary - The Canadian
Pacific Railway (1885-2005)

The first of the two coins in this set, commemorates the thousands of Chinese immigrants who laboured to build the Canadian Pacific Railway. The reverse image, designed by Eldon Garnet, depicts the memorial to these workers in Toronto. The reverse of the second coin was adapted from a photograph in the CPR archives and displays a ballast train and workers on the railbridge spanning the Fraser River.

DATE		QTY. (000)	COST	VALUE
2005	Two-coin set, proof 20		120.00	120.00

2007 SILVER 8 DOLLARS

Diameter: 36.07 mm; weight: 25.175 grams; finish: proof;
composition: .9999 fine silver; edge: serrated.

Maple of Long Life

Chinese Coin
Reverse

Chinese Coin
Obverse

The Maple of Long Life coin is an asian inspired coin with a selective hologram. The second coin, is the first coin ever produced by the RCM with a square hole centre.

DATE		QTY.	COST	VALUE
2007	$8 Maple of Long Life, design by Jianping Yan 12,472		49.95	55.00
2007	$8 Chinese coin, design by Harvey Chan 19,996		49.95	60.00

STERLING SILVER 8 DOLLARS

Diameter: 36.07 mm; weight: 25.3 grams; finish: proof;
composition: .925 silver, .075 copper; edge: serrated.

Maple of Wisdom, 2009

The reverse design depicts a dragon clutching a symbolic "hologram" with a shimmering maple leaf; a red CRYSTALLIZED™ - Swarovski Element embedded in the centre of the coin symbolizes joy and good fortune. The dragon also represents good fortune as well as success, prosperity and wisdom.

Maple of Strength, 2010

Design features five horses parade around a colourful hologram featuring a sprig of two maple leaves. With a decorative pattern in the background, the overall design of this coin echoes the ornate art typical of Chinese pottery, embroidery and sculpture.

DATE		QTY.	COST	VALUE
2009	$8 Maple of Wisdom, design by Simon Ng	7,273	88.88	110.00
2010	$8 Maple of Strength, design by Simon Ng	5,138	88.88	100.00

STERLING SILVER 10 DOLLARS

Diameter: 40 mm; weight: 27.78 grams;
composition: .925 silver, .075 copper; finish: proof; edge: serrated

Blue Whale, 2010

The blue whale (Balaenoptera musculus) is the largest animal ever known to inhabit the earth. It can grow up to 33 m (108 ft) long and can weigh up to 180 metric tons (198 tons). Reverse designed by Pierre Leduc.

DATE		QTY.	COST	VALUE
2010	$10 Blue Whale (Silver Coin & Stamp Set)	9,717	79.95	80.00

FINE SILVER 10 DOLLARS

Diameter: 36.07 mm; weight: 21.475 grams;
composition: .9999 silver; finish: proof; edge: serrated

Pope John Paul II (1920–2005)

One of two coins struck by the Royal Canadian Mint to honour the memory of the first and only Pope ever to visit Canada. Both the silver and gold coins bear the same obverse and reverse designs. The obverse features the uncrowned effigy of Queen Elizabeth II, designed by Susanna Blunt; the reverse design, by Susan Taylor, features the signature wave of Ioannes Paulus PP.II.

Year of the Veteran, 2005

The design depicts the profiles of two veterans from different generations, joined by their love of country.

Fortress of Louisbourg, 2006

Commemorating the Fortress of Louisbourg historical site, which is the largest reconstruction in Canada.

DATE		QTY.	COST	VALUE
2005	$10 Pope John Paul II.	24,725	49.95	55.00
2005	$10 Year of the Veteran	6,549	49.95	50.00
2006	$10 Fortress of Louisbourg	15,000	49.95	50.00

75th Anniversary of the First Bank Notes, 2010

Diameter: 34 mm; weight: 15.87 grams;
composition: .9999 silver; finish: proof; edge: serrated

The Bank of Canada began operating 75 years ago in 1935 and was given responsibility to regulate the country's money supply and to "promote the economic and financial welfare of Canada." Accordingly, it was given the exclusive right to issue Canada's bank notes.

DATE		QTY.	COST	VALUE
2010	$10 75th Anniversary of the First Bank Notes, By RCM Engravers	6,818	54.95	55.00

Highway of Heroes, 2011

The design features an overpass along the Highway of Heroes as viewed from the perspective of the mourning family as they accompany their lost loved one along the route.

DATE		QTY.	COST	VALUE
2011	$10 Highway of Heroes	7,732	69.95	70.00

Canadian Wilderness Series, 2011

2011 was the International Year of Forests, a time to reflect on the significant role the wilderness plays in reducing global warming and preserving the earth's environmental balance. Design by Corrine Hunt.

DATE		QTY.	COST	VALUE
2011	$10 Boreal Forest	3,286	69.95	70.00
2011	$10 Wood Bison	3,053	69.95	70.00
2011	$10 Orca Whale	3,131	69.95	70.00
2011	$10 Peregrine Falcon	3,014	69.95	70.00

Maple Leaf Forever, 2011 & 2012

The designs (relief or raised area) includes both brilliant and mirrored surfaces and the background (field) are striated using laser etching that results in a matte finish. 2011 design by Debbie Adams. 2012 designed by Luc Normandin.

DATE		QTY.	COST	VALUE
2011	$10 Maple Leaf Forever, specimen	41,694	34.95	35.00
2012	$10 Maple Leaf Forever, specimen	100,000	34.95	35.00

10 DOLLARS — FESTIVE SEASON, 2011

These silver coins capture the spirit of the festive season with touches of red and green. Design by Virginia Boulay

DATE		QTY.	COST	VALUE
2011	$10 Little Skaters, proof	3,663	69.95	70.00
2011	$10 Winter Town, proof	4,103	69.95	70.00

Welcome to the World, 2012–

The design features a reverse-proof finish of a baby's feet to commemorate the birth of a new baby. Design by the RCM engravers.

DATE		QTY.	COST	VALUE
2012	$10 Welcome to the World, reverse proof	10,000	59.95	60.00
2013	$10 Welcome to the World, reverse proof	15,000	59.95	60.00

Year of the Dragon, 2012

The design features a four-clawed dragon that stretches along the outer edge of the coin; its lines and contours full of fiery character; with a Chinese character and clouds representing its good fortune. Design by Three Degrees Creative Group Inc.

DATE		QTY.	COST	VALUE
2011	$10 Year of the Dragon, specimen 588,888		29.95	30.00

R.M.S. Titanic, 2012

Design features the words "R.M.S. Titanic" and a map of the Canadian Atlantic coast and the nautical coordinates at which Titanic sank, by Yves Bérubé.

DATE		QTY.	COST	VALUE
2012	$10 R.M.S. Titanic, proof................................ 20,000		64.95	90.00

Praying Mantis, 2012

With its front legs bent forever in seeming supplication, this carnivorous insect's predatory ferocity is easy to underestimate. Engraved from photographer Robert Ganz's award-winning Canadian Geographic wildlife photograph.

DATE		QTY.	COST	VALUE
2012	$10 Praying Mantis 7,500		69.95	70.00

HMS Shannon, 2012

The War of 1812 was a fundamental turning point in Canada's history, a struggle from which some of Canada's earliest unifying moments emerged. These stories—including that of the Leda-class frigate, HMS Shannon—have become important chapters in the narrative of Canada's evolution from colony to sovereign nation.

DATE		QTY.	COST	VALUE
2012	$10 HMS Shannon, Proof............................... 10,000		64.95	65.00

Year of the Snake, 2013

This coin celebrates the unique heritage and ancient culture of Chinese Canadians. The reverse image of the ½ oz. silver proof is designed by Canadian artist Simon Ng features a coiling snake with spots on its body forming the Chinese character for "snake".

DATE		QTY.	COST	VALUE
2013	$10 Year of the Snake, Proof (½ oz. silver).................... 18,888		43.88	44.00
2013	$10 Year of the Snake, Specimen (Fine silver)................. 88,888		39.95	40.00

Winter Scene, 2013

The reverse image by Canadian artist Remi Clark features a colourful painted winter scene. In the foreground, stylized figures—including parents, grandparents, and small children—skate and sled across a frozen pond.

DATE		QTY.	COST	VALUE
2013	$10 Winter Scene, Proof................................ 8,000		69.95	70.00

O Canada 12-coin series, 2013

Diameter: 34.0mm; weight: 15.87g; composition: fine silver; finish: matte proof; edge: serrated

Everything about Canada is rich with variety—its landscape, wildlife, cities, towns and the people

who live in them. And while much that defines Canada is elusive, its geography, fauna and flora, and social and political institutions have come to symbolize its national identity—and evolve along with it.

DATE		QTY.	COST	VALUE
2013	$10 Inukshuk (January) by Tony Bianco	40,000	39.95	40.00
2013	$10 The Beaver (February) by Perre Leduc	40,000	39.95	40.00
2013	$10 Royal Canadian Mounted Police (March) by Janet Griffin-Scott	40,000	39.95	40.00
2013	$10 The Polar Bear (April) by Tony Bianco	40,000	39.95	40.00
2013	$10 Canadian Summer Fun (May) by Claudio D'Angelo	40,000	39.95	40.00
2013	$10 The Wolf (June) by Perre Leduc	40,000	39.95	40.00
2013	$10 Niagara Falls (July) by Emily Damstra	40,000	39.95	40.00
2013	$10 Caribou (August) by Piere Leduc	40,000	39.95	40.00
2013	$10 Hockey (September) by Tony Bianco	40,000	39.95	40.00
2013	$10 Orca (October) by Pierre Leduc	40,000	39.95	40.00
2013	$10 Maple Leaf (November), in colour by Emily Damstra	40,000	39.95	40.00
2013	$10 Holiday (December) by Doug Geldart	40,000	39.95	40.00

The Maple Leaf (November) was $54.95 to non-subscribers of the complete set.

Dragonflies of Canada Series, 2013–

Diameter: 34.0mm; weight: 15.87g; composition: fine silver; finish: proof; edge: serrated

The Royal Canadian Mint's exciting Dragonflies series features painted Canadian dragonfly species set against hologram images of their natural habitat! The hologram technology, representing the water, is used on the coin to capture the full rainbow spectrum of color from any light source as you tilt your coin back and forth. Designer: Celia Godkin.

DATE		QTY.	COST	VALUE
2013	$10 Dragonfly	10,000	79.95	80.00
2014	$10 Green Darner	10,000	79.95	80.00
2015	$10 The Pygmy Snaketail	10,000	79.95	80.00

Dream Catcher, 2013

The dreamcatcher is an iconic identifying symbol of First Nations culture, designed to trap bad dreams and thoughts, and let good dreams pass through the hole at the web's centre, into the mind of the dreamer. Designer: Darlene Gait.

DATE		QTY.	COST	VALUE
2013	$10 Dream Catcher	10,000	74.95	75.00

Ducks of Canada Series, 2013–2015

Diameter: 34.0mm; weight: 15.87g; composition: fine silver; finish: proof; edge: serrated

Celebrating 75 Years of Ducks Unlimited Canada. Designer: Trevor Tennant.

DATE		QTY.	COST	VALUE
2013	$10 Mallard Ducks	10,000	69.95	70.00
2013	$10 Wood Ducks	10,000	69.95	70.00
2014	$10 Pintail Ducks	10,000	69.95	70.00
2014	$10 Harlequin Duck.....................................	10,000	69.95	70.00
2015	$10 Cinnamon Teal	10,000	69.95	70.00

Maple Leaf, 2013

The reverse image by Canadian artist Pierre Leduc features two Sugar Maple leaves.

DATE		QTY.	COST	VALUE
2013	$10 Maple Leaf, Specimen	50,000	39.95	40.00

Vintage Superman, 2013

Diameter: 27.0mm; weight: 7.96g; composition: pure silver (99.99% pure); finish: proof; edge: serrated

A vintage Superman breaking free from chains of bondage. Illustrated by Canadian co-creator Joe Shuster.

DATE		QTY.	ISSUE PRICE	VALUE
2013	$10 Vintage Superman	15,000	44.75	45.00

Holiday Candles, 2013

Diameter: 34.0mm; weight: 15.87g; composition: fine silver; finish: proof; edge: serrated

Candles have been cherished for thousands of years for their ability to light the darkness. At no other time was this more important than the darkest days of winter. Designer: Claudio D'Angelo.

DATE		QTY.	ISSUE PRICE	VALUE
2013	$10 Holiday Candles	10,000	74.95	75.00

A Partridge In A Pear Tree, 2013

Diameter: 34.0mm; weight: 15.87g; composition: fine silver; finish: proof; edge: serrated

A well known lyrical phrase from the Classic Christmas Carol "The Twelve Days of Christmas" Designer: Risto Turunen.

DATE		QTY.	ISSUE PRICE	VALUE
2013	$10 A Partridge in a Pear Tree 10,000		64.95	65.00

O Canada 10–Coin Series, 2014

Diameter: 34.0mm; weight: 15.87g; composition: fine silver; finish: matte proof; edge: serrated

Canada is a country of incredible diversity—its landscapes, its fauna and flora, its people. And while most Canadians live in urban centres, images and icons of this land's wild nature resonate with each and every one of us. An exciting O Canada series featuring iconic images celebrating all that makes Canada unique.

DATE		QTY.	ISSUE PRICE	VALUE
2014	$10 The Igloo (January) by Yves Bérubé	40,000	39.95	40.00
2014	$10 The Grizzly Bear (February) by Glen Loates	40,000	39.95	40.00
2014	$10 Skiing Canada's Slopes (March) by Kendra Dixson	40,000	39.95	40.00
2014	$10 The Moose (April) by Claudio D'Angelo	40,000	39.95	40.00
2014	$10 Down by the Old Maple Tree (May) by Claudio D'Angelo	40,000	39.95	40.00
2014	$10 The Canada Goose (June) by Jean Charles Daumas	40,000	39.95	40.00
2014	$10 The Canadian Cowboy (July) by Bernie Brown	40,000	39.95	40.00
2014	$10 The Bison (August) by Trevor Tennant	40,000	39.95	40.00
2014	$10 The Northern Lights (with colour) (October) by Julius Csotonyi	40,000	39.95	40.00
2014	$10 Canadian Holiday Scene (November)	40,000	39.95	40.00

The Northern Lights was $54.95 for non-subscribers.

Year of the Horse, 2014

Diameter: 34.0mm; weight: 15.87g; composition: fine silver; finish: specimen; edge: serrated

2014 is the Year of the Horse, a sign in the Chinese lunar calendar known for its sunny disposition, and kind and forgiving ways. Designer: Simon Ng.

DATE		QTY.	ISSUE PRICE	VALUE
2014	$10 Year of the Horse	58,888	39.95	40.00

2014 FIFA World Cup

Diameter: 34.0mm; weight: 15.87g; composition: fine silver; finish: proof; edge: serrated

'Football' is arguably the most popular sport on the planet. Almost one million Canadians play the game. Share the excitement of soccer's premier international championship that's held every four years. Designer: Greg Banning.

DATE		QTY.	ISSUE PRICE	VALUE
2014	$10 2014 FIFA World Cup	10,000	54.95	55.00

Welcome to the World, 2014

Diameter: 34.0mm; weight: 15.87g; composition: fine silver; finish: matte proof; edge: serrated

Few things are as endearing as baby's tiny toes. A cherished keepsake of baby's first months of hugs and discoveries.

DATE		QTY.	ISSUE PRICE	VALUE
2014	$10 Welcome to the World	15,000	59.95	60.00

100th Anniversary of the Declaration of the First World War: The Mobilisation of our Nation, 2014

Diameter: 34.0mm; weight: 15.87g; composition: fine silver; finish: matte proof; edge: serrated

Tens of thousands of fathers, sons, husbands and brothers made their way up roped gangways to steel ships that would take them, along with 7,000 horses and critical munitions and supplies, to England. Designer: Maskull Lasserre.

DATE		QTY.	ISSUE PRICE	VALUE
2014	$10 The Mobilisation of our Nation 40,000		44.95	45.00

Skating In Canada, 2014

Diameter: 34.0mm; weight: 15.87g; composition: fine silver; finish: proof; edge: serrated

The Canadian winter is a time of celebration and outdoor fun. Canadian artist Tony Harris captures the joy of a Canadian rite of passage: learning to skate on one of the country's thousands of outdoor rinks.

DATE		QTY.	ISSUE PRICE	VALUE
2014	$10 Skating in Canada. 10,000		64.95	65.00

Pope John Paul II, 2014

Diameter: 36.07mm; weight: 23.17g; composition: fine silver; finish: proof; edge: serrated

Since the birth of the Holy Roman Church nearly 2,000 years ago, the Roman Catholic pope has been a powerful political influencer on the world stage. Unlike any leader of the Roman Catholic Church before him, the 264th pope, Pope John Paul II took proactive control of this global influence in order to criticize and combat political oppression. Designer: Trevor Tennant.

DATE		QTY.	ISSUE PRICE	VALUE
2014	$10 Pope John Paul II 8,500		69.95	70.00

Silver Maple Leaves, 2014

Diameter: 34.0mm; weight: 15.87g; composition: fine silver; finish: specimen; edge: serrated

The maple leaf has long been an internationally recognized emblem of Canada, its people and the land itself. There are more than 150 different species of maple trees in the world – of the 13 species found in North America, 10 are native to Canada. And at least one type of maple grows naturally in each of Canada's 10 provinces! Designer: Pierre Leduc.

DATE		QTY.	ISSUE PRICE	VALUE
2014	$10 Maple Leaf 50,000		39.95	40.00

First Nations Art: Salmon, 2014

Diameter: 34.0mm; weight: 15.87g; composition: 99.99% pure silver; finish: proof; edge: serrated

Original artwork by Darlene Gait that pays tribute to the salmon — a fish that has long been revered by the First Nations people of Canada's West Coast.

DATE		QTY.	ISSUE PRICE	VALUE
2014	$10 Salmon	10,000	74.95	75.00

Wait for Me, Daddy, 2014

Diameter: 34.0mm; weight: 15.87g; composition: 99.99% pure silver; finish: proof; edge: serrated

It is perhaps the most famous photograph taken in Canada during the Second World War: a five-year-old boy breaks away from his mother's grasp to run after his father as he marches off to war. Taken in New Westminster, B.C. in the fall of 1940, by photographer Claude Dettloff, "Wait for Me, Daddy" continues to resonate as a snapshot of the war's impact on Canadians and the personal sacrifices they made.

DATE		QTY.	ISSUE PRICE	VALUE
2014	$10 Wait for Me, Daddy	10,000	59.95	60.00

Year of the Sheep, 2015

Diameter: 34.0mm; weight: 15.87g; composition: 99.99% pure silver; finish: specimen; edge: serrated

The year 2015 is ruled by the Sheep. The creative Sheep personality embodies wealth, warmth and loveliness. Good things seem to come to the Sheep naturally because of its irresistibly good nature. The Sheep rarely speaks its mind. It will go with the flow and only object when things aren't going its way. Push too hard and it will react—decisively! The gregarious Sheep is an eternal romantic. It adores being showered with love and attention. Designer: Simon Ng.

DATE	QTY.	ISSUE PRICE	VALUE
2015 $10 Year of the Sheep 22,888		39.88	40.00

Adventure Canada Series, 2015 –

Diameter: 34.0mm; weight: 15.87g; composition: 99.99% pure silver; finish: matte proof; edge: serrated

For enthusiasts who enjoy the great outdoors.

DATE	QTY.	ISSUE PRICE	VALUE
2015 $10 Windsurfing 20,000		44.95	45.00
$10 Whitewater rafting 20,000		44.95	45.00
$10 Mountain biking 20,000		44.95	45.00
$10 Ice climbing 20,000		44.95	45.00
$10 Dog sledding 20,000		44.95	45.00

Winter Scene, 2015

Diameter: 34.0mm; weight: 15.87g; composition: 99.99% pure silver; finish: proof; edge: serrated

Since the earliest days of settlement, tobogganing has been an integral part of surviving the long Canadian winter. Forget about frozen fingers and toes; this endearing design will lure everyone outdoors for fun-filled adventure, laughter, spills and thrills! Designer: Louise Martineau.

DATE		QTY.	ISSUE PRICE	VALUE
2015	$10 Winter Scene 8,000		64.95	65.00

Welcome to the World, 2015

Diameter: 34.0mm; weight: 15.87g; composition: 99.99% pure silver; finish: reverse proof; edge: serrated

Hold on to today's quiet moments; bask in his softness, delight in her newness. Though time draws us swiftly on, once engraved in your heart and mind, these inexpressible moments are yours to keep forever. Welcome, new one. May you find in this world a life as special and precious as you are.

DATE		QTY.	ISSUE PRICE	VALUE
2015	$10 Welcome to the World 15,000		59.95	60.00

Canadian Maple Leaf, 2015

Diameter: 34.0mm; weight: 15.87g; composition: 99.99% pure silver; finish: specimen; edge: serrated

Designer: Celia Godkin.

DATE		QTY.	ISSUE PRICE	VALUE
2015	$10 Canadian Maple Leaf 25,000		29.95	30.00

200th Anniversary of the Birth of Sir John A. Macdonald, 2015

Diameter: 34.0mm; weight: 15.87g; composition: 99.99% pure silver; finish: proof; edge: serrated

Sir John A. Macdonald gazes charismatically out from the image—taking much the same pose he would have stood for in Prime Ministerial photos of his day. In his right hand he holds a sheet of paper, showing that he is hard at work tackling the task of nation-building. His left hand rests casually on the table top beside him. Designer: Joel Kimmel.

DATE		QTY.	ISSUE PRICE	VALUE
2015	$10 200th Anniversary of the Birth of Sir John A. Macdonald 10,000		69.95	70.00

National Hockey League's® Canadian Franchises, 2015

Diameter: 34.0mm; weight: 15.87g; composition: 99.99% pure silver; finish: reverse proof; edge: serrated

DATE		QTY.	ISSUE PRICE	VALUE
2015	$10 Vancouver Canucks	6,000	74.95	75.00
2015	$10 Edmonton Oilers	5,000	74.95	75.00
2015	$10 Calgary Flames	5,000	74.95	75.00
2015	$10 Winnipeg Jets	5,000	74.95	75.00
2015	$10 Toronto Maple Leafs	6,000	74.95	75.00
2015	$10 Ottawa Senators	5,000	74.95	75.00
2015	$10 Montreal Canadiens	6,000	74.95	75.00

First Nations Art: Mother Feeding Baby, 2015

Diameter: 34.0mm; weight: 15.87g; composition: 99.99% pure silver; finish: proof; edge: serrated

Crafting a wonderful story about a family of eagles nurturing, loving and growing. Within this narrative lies the call for all parents to cherish their young, just as eagle parents work tirelessly to nurture their young; for therein lies the future of the world. Design by Kwaguilth artist Richard Hunt.

DATE	QTY.	ISSUE PRICE	VALUE
2015	$10 First Nations Art: Mother Feeding Baby 10,000	79.95	80.00

"Canoe Across Canada" Series, 2015

Diameter: 34.0mm; weight: 15.87g; composition: 99.99% pure silver; finish: proof; edge: serrated

Paddling a canoe along a tree-lined shore in the heart of the wilderness: it's an iconic Canadian moment that captures Canada's unique history and Canadians' connection to their vast land.

DATE	QTY.	ISSUE PRICE	VALUE
2015	$10 The Wondrous West 20,000	44.95	45.00
2015	$10 Splendid Surroundings 20,000	44.95	45.00
2015	$10 Magnificent Mountains 20,000	44.95	45.00
2015	$10 Serene Scene 20,000	44.95	45.00
2015	$10 Mirror, Mirror 20,000	44.95	45.00
2015	$10 Exquisite Ending 20,000	44.95	45.00

Colourful Songbirds of Canada Series, 2015–

Diameter: 34.0mm; weight: 15.87g; composition: 99.99% pure silver; finish: proof (with sheer effect); edge: serrated

DATE		QTY.	ISSUE PRICE	VALUE
2015	$10 The Northern Cardinal - design by Derek C. Wicks	15,000	64.95	65.00
2015	$10 The Magnolia Warbler - design by Hélène Girard	15,000	64.95	65.00
2015	$10 The Blue Jay - design by Derek C. Wicks	15,000	64.95	65.00
2015	$10 The Baltimore Oriole - design by Hélène Girard	15,000	64.95	65.00
2015	$10 The Violet-green Swallow - design by Derek C. Wicks	15,000	64.95	65.00

SILVER 15 DOLLARS 1992

Diameter: 40.0 mm; weight: 33.63 grams; thickness: 3.1 mm;
composition: .925 silver, .075 copper; edge: lettered, Proof

To celebrate the centennial of the modern olympics, the IOC commissioned five national mints to produce a fifteen-piece set of gold and silver commemorative coins from 1992 to 1996, the centennial year. All fifteen coins in the set will bear the five olympic rings and the dates 1896–1996, with the olympic motto CITIUS, ALTIUS, FORTIUS on the coin edge.

DATE		QTY.	ISSUE PRICE	VALUE
1992	$15 Speed Skater, Pole Vaulter & Gymnast, by David Craig	106,000	46.95	30.00
1992	$15 Spirit of the Generations, by Stewart Sherwood	incl. above	46.95	30.00

15 DOLLARS, CHINESE LUNAR CALENDAR
Proof Sterling Silver

Diameter: 40 mm, weight: 34 grams; edge: reeded; composition: .925 silver, .075 copper.
Cameo (octagonal): diameter: 17.5 mm, covered with 24 karat gold

Each of the twelve years in the Chinese lunar calendar is represented by a different animal. These are shown on the reverse of each coin in the series, positioned like numbers on a clock dial while the animal representing the year of issue is featured as the device displayed on the gold-covered octagonal cameo in the middle of the reverse.

The obverse is common to all twelve coins in the series, except for the changed date, and features the familiar Dora de Pédery-HUNT effigy of the queen and the legend 15 DOLLARS CANADA (DATE) ELIZABETH II. Canadian artist Harvey Chan designed the reverse. Each coin is housed in an embossed red velvet box with gold moiré sides. A collectible box designed to hold all twelve $15 coins and a silver medallion featuring the mint's logo is also available. The box and medallion were offered free when subscribing for coins 2–6 in the series.

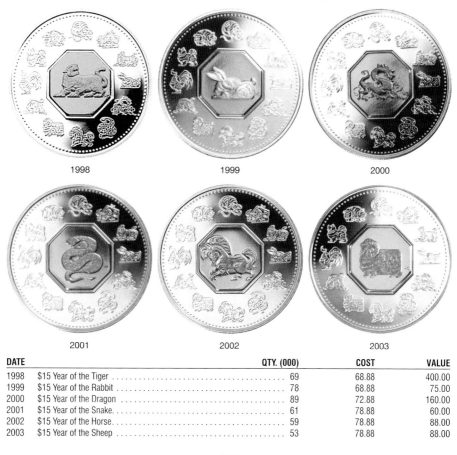

DATE		QTY. (000)	COST	VALUE
1998	$15 Year of the Tiger	69	68.88	400.00
1999	$15 Year of the Rabbit	78	68.88	75.00
2000	$15 Year of the Dragon	89	72.88	160.00
2001	$15 Year of the Snake.	61	78.88	60.00
2002	$15 Year of the Horse.	59	78.88	88.00
2003	$15 Year of the Sheep	53	78.88	88.00

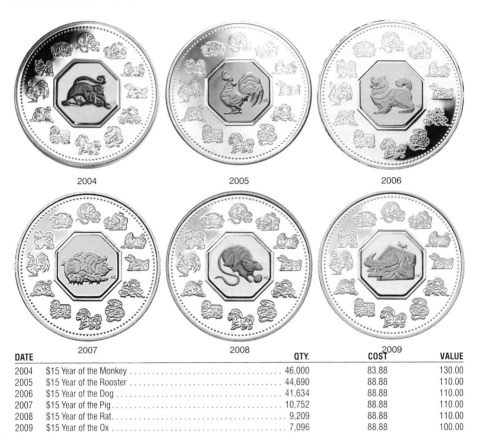

| | 2004 | 2005 | 2006 |
| 2007 | 2008 | 2009 | |

DATE		QTY.	COST	VALUE
2004	$15 Year of the Monkey	46,000	83.88	130.00
2005	$15 Year of the Rooster	44,690	88.88	110.00
2006	$15 Year of the Dog	41,634	88.88	110.00
2007	$15 Year of the Pig	10,752	88.88	110.00
2008	$15 Year of the Rat	9,209	88.88	110.00
2009	$15 Year of the Ox	7,096	88.88	100.00

$15 FINE SILVER — PLAYING CARD SERIES

Dimensions: 49.8 x 28.6 mm rectangle; weight: 31.56 grams; composition: .9999 fine silver; edge: plain.
finish: proof with selective colour and gold plate on the edge.

This series showcases the history of playing card money in Canada. Features an unique rectangular shape and combines colour and selective gold plating for the first time by the Royal Canadian Mint. Design by Henri Beau.

DATE		QTY.	ISSUE PRICE	VALUE
2008	$15 Jack of Hearts	11,362	89.95	95.00
2008	$15 Queen of Spades	8,714	89.95	95.00
2009	$15 Ten of Spades	5,921	94.95	110.00
2009	$15 King of Hearts	5,798	94.95	110.00

$15 STERLING SILVER — VIGNETTES OF ROYALTY

Diameter: 36.15 mm, weight: 30 grams; finish: frosted relief on a proof like field;
edge: plain; composition: .925 silver, .075 copper.

This series of coins showcased the effigies of the five monarchs that have appeared on Canada's circulation coins. These coins are struck 4 times and are designed by the RCM engravers.

DATE		QTY.	COST	VALUE
2008	$15 Queen Victoria	3,442	99.95	100.00
2008	$15 King Edward VII	6,261	99.95	100.00
2008	$15 King George V	11,871	99.95	100.00
2009	$15 King George VI	N/A	99.95	110.00
2009	$15 Queen Elizabeth II	2,643	104.95	110.00

$15 ULTRA HIGH RELIEF STERLING SILVER
Continuity of the Crown Series, 2011

Diameter: 36.16 mm, weight: 28.57 grams; finish: proof like;
edge: plain; composition: .925 silver, .075 copper.

The continuity of the crown has been of paramount importance, every king and queen contributing to the adaptability that has enabled their institution to survive. These coins are crafted in the ultra-high relief of ancient medallic art. Designed by Laurie McGaw.

DATE		QTY.	COST	VALUE
2011	$15 H.R.H. Prince Henry of Wales (Prince Harry)	10,000	109.95	110.00
2011	$15 H.R.H. Prince William of Wales	10,000	109.95	110.00
2011	$15 H.R.H. The Prince of Wales (Prince Charles)	10,000	109.95	110.00
2011	Set of all 3, Continuity of the Crown		329.85	330.00

$15 STERLING SILVER — LUNAR LOTUS, 2010–

Diameter: 38 mm; weight: 26.29 grams; finish: proof;
composition: .925 silver, .075 copper; edge: plain, shape; 8 scallop.

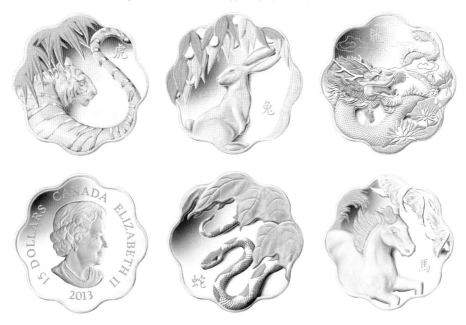

These 8 scallop coins have a shape reminiscent of a lotus flower. Design by Three Degrees Creative Group Inc.

DATE		QTY.	COST	VALUE
2010	$15 Lunar Lotus – Year of the Tiger	10,268	88.88	90.00
2011	$15 Lunar Lotus – Year of the Rabbit	19,888	98.88	100.00
2012	$15 Lunar Lotus – Year of the Dragon	48,888	98.88	100.00
2013	$15 Lunar Lotus – Year of the Snake	28,888	98.88	100.00
2014	$15 Lunar Lotus – Year of the Horse	28,888	98.88	100.00
2015	$15 Lunar Lotus – Year of the Sheep	18,888	98.88	99.00

$15 FINE SILVER — CHINESE LUNAR CALENDAR, 2010–

Diameter: 38 mm; weight: 31.39 grams; finish: proof; composition: 99.99 silver; edge: reeded.

In 1998, the Lunar Cameo Coin Series was launched and has inspired the introduction of a new series celebrating zodiacs from the Chinese Lunar calendar. Design by Aries Chung.

DATE		QTY.	COST	VALUE
2010	$15 Fine Silver – Year of the Tiger	4,344	88.88	90.00
2011	$15 Fine Silver – Year of the Rabbit	9,999	98.88	100.00
2012	$15 Fine Silver – Year of the Dragon	19,098	98.88	100.00
2013	$15 Fine Silver – Year of the Snake	28,888	98.88	100.00
2014	$15 Fine Silver – Year of the Horse	28,888	98.88	100.00
2015	$15 Fine Silver – Year of the Sheep	18,888	98.88	99.00

$15 Hologram Maple Series, 2011–

Diameter: 38 mm; weight: 31.39 grams; finish: proof;
composition: 99.99 silver; edge: reeded.

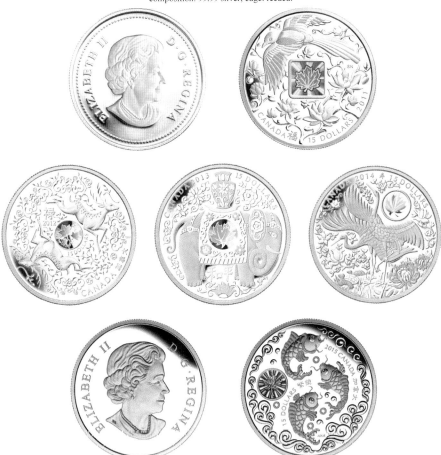

Celebrate the rich cultural heritage of Chinese Canadians A series of Asian-inspired coins that bear a hologram of a maple leaf. Unique selective hologram and captivating style. Designer: Simon Ng.

DATE		QTY.	COST	VALUE
2011	$15 Maple of Happiness	8,888	98.88	99.00
2012	$15 Maple of Good Fortune	8,888	98.88	99.00
2013	$15 Maple of Peace	8,888	98.88	99.00
2014	$15 Maple of Longevity	8,888	98.88	99.00
2015	$15 Maple of Prosperity	8,888	98.88	99.00

Modern Day Superman, 2013

Diameter: 34.0mm; weight: 15.87g; composition: pure silver; finish: matte proof; edge: serrated

Dynamic and exciting with the Man of Steel as seen in his most modern uniform. Rejuvenated and ready for action. Includes Superman's native Kryptonian language, as created by DC Comics, and reads "75 Years of Superman" in English and French.

DATE	QTY.	ISSUE PRICE	VALUE
2013 $15 Modern Day Superman. 15,000		69.75	90.00

Exploring Canada 10–Coin Series, 2014–2015

Diameter: 36.07mm; weight: 23.17g; composition: fine silver (99.99% pure); finish: matte proof; edge:serrated

As long as there have been people on Earth, there have been explorers—pioneering individuals with one eye trained on the horizon, eager to know what lies beyond and always ready to break a new trail towards the future. But their adventure never ends, because every destination inspires another. Exploration—that irrepressible spirit of discovery—fuels the life and passion of individuals. It drives the evolution of their community, and ultimately shapes the future of their nation.

DATE		QTY.	COST	VALUE
2014	$15 The Voyageurs by John Mantha	15,000	54.95	55.00
2014	$15 The Gold Rush	15,000	54.95	55.00
2014	$15 The Arctic Expedition	15,000	54.95	55.00
2014	$15 The Vikings	15,000	54.95	55.00
2014	$15 The West Coast Exploration	15,000	54.95	55.00
2014	$15 Pioneering Mapmakers	15,000	54.95	55.00
2015	$15 The Wild Rivers Exploration	15,000	54.95	55.00
2015	$15 Building the Canadian Pacific Railway	15,000	54.95	55.00
2015	$15 Scientific Exploration	15,000	54.95	55.00
2015	$15 Space Exploration	15,000	54.95	55.00

Artwork by Franklin Carmichael, 2015

Diameter: 36.07mm; weight: 23.17g; composition: 99.99% pure silver; finish: proof; edge: serrated

As the youngest member of Canada's famed Group of Seven, Franklin Carmichael (1890-1945) helped to define a new "Canadian" style of landscape art in the 1920s and '30s—one that conveyed a deep love for the natural beauty of the rugged Canadian landscape.

DATE		QTY.	ISSUE PRICE	VALUE
2015	Artwork by Franklin Carmichael (set of 3)	7,000	199.95	200.00
	$15 The Upper Ottawa, near Mattawa (c. 1924)			
	$15 Cranberry Lake (c. 1934)			
	$15 Gift of Mary Mastin, Toronto 1996			

OLYMPICS, 1985–1988
SILVER 20 DOLLARS

Diameter: 40 mm; weight: 34.107 grams; thickness: 3.00 mm;
composition: .925 silver, .075 copper; edge: lettered

To assist in financing the XV Winter Olympic Games in Calgary, Alberta in 1988, the mint issued a series of ten commemorative sterling silver coins in proof quality only. With the release of the first pair of coins in September, 1985, it was announced that 250,000 complete sets of ten coins would be struck, with a maximum total production of five million coins.

Each obverse bears the Arnold Machin effigy of the Queen and the year of issue. The reverse designs all bear the date of the games, 1988. The legend XV WINTER OLYMPIC GAMES • XVES JEUX OLYMPIQUES D'HIVER appears on the edge of each coin in the series.

1985 Issues

Downhill Skiing   Speed Skating

1986 Issues

Hockey   Biathlon

Cross-country Skiing   Free-style Skiing

1987 Issues

Figure Skating   Curling

Ski Jumping   Bobsled

DESCRIPTION	DESIGNER	ISSUE DATE	QTY. (000)	ISSUE PRICE	VALUE
$20 Downhill Skiing	Ian Stewart	Sept. 1985	351	37.00	30.00
$20 Speed Skating	Friedrich Peter	Sept. 1985	312	37.00	30.00
$20 Hockey	Ian Stewart	Feb. 1986	345	37.00	30.00
$20 Biathlon	John Mardon	Feb. 1986	280	37.00	30.00
$20 Cross-country Skiing	Ian Stewart	Sept. 1986	268	37.00	30.00
$20 Free-style Skiing	Walter Ott	Sept. 1986	264	37.00	30.00
$20 Figure Skating	Raymond Taylor	Mar. 1987	284	37.00	30.00
$20 Curling	Ian Stewart	Mar. 1987	253	37.00	30.00
$20 Ski Jumping	Raymond Taylor	Sept. 1987	247	37.00	30.00
$20 Bobsled	John Mardon	Sept. 1987	217	37.00	30.00

CANADIAN AVIATION
20 Dollars Sterling Silver
Part I: The First Fifty Years (1990–1994)

Diameter: 38.0 mm; weight: 31.103 grams; thickness: 3.5 mm;
composition: .925 silver, .075 copper; gold insert: 0.8 grams; edge; interrupted serration

This series salutes Canadian aviation achievements and heroes. Part I commemorates the first fifty years of powered flight in Canada (1900–1949) with 2 coins struck each year over a 5-year period. Each sterling silver coin contains 1 Troy ounce of silver, with a 24-carat-gold covered cameo, and is issued encapsulated in proof finish only.

Each coin is housed in an aluminum case in the shape of an airplane wing with a propeller design on the lid. A larger case of similar design houses these first ten coins in the series.

All coins feature an interrupted reeded edge, with alternate sections reeded and smooth.

The Dora de Pédery-HUNT effigy of the Queen appears on the common obverse.

Anson & Harvard / Robert Leckie   Lancaster 683 AVRO / John Emilius Fauquier

Harvard & Anson / Robert Leckie

The reverse design, by Nova Scotia artist Geoff Bennett, depicts a Harvard in flight while, on the ground, two pilots are boarding an Anson.

Cameo: Air Marshal Robert Leckie, who was instrumental in setting up schools for the British Commonwealth Air Training Plan. Leckie served as RCAF Chief of the Air Staff from 1944 until his retirement in 1947.

Lancaster 683 AVRO / John Emilius Fauquier

The reverse, designed by Ontario artist Robert Ralph Carmichael, depicts a Lancaster 638 AVRO bomber in flight.

Cameo: John Emilius Fauquier, one of Canada's pre-eminent aviators to be associated with the Lancaster bomber. Often decorated during his three tours of duty, Fauquier is probably best known as the commanding officer of No. 617 "Dambuster" squadron.

DATE		QTY. (000)	ISSUE PRICE	VALUE
1990	$20 Harvard & Anson / Robert Leckie	42	55.50	50.00
1990	$20 Lancaster 683 AVRO / John Emilius Fauquier	44	55.50	120.00

Silver Dart / John McCurdy & F.W. Baldwin   The de Havilland Beaver / Phillip Clarke Garratt

Curtiss JN-4 Canuck / Sir Frank Wilton Bailie   The de Havilland Gypsy Moth / Murton A. Seymour

Silver Dart / John A.D. McCurdy & F.W. (Casey) Baldwin

The reverse, showing the Silver Dart on a test flight, was designed by Quebec artist George Velinger. The Dart made the first powered, heavier-than-air flight in Canada in 1909.
Cameo: John A.D. McCurdy (left), principal designer and pilot of the Silver Dart, and F.W. (Casey) Baldwin, first Canadian to fly previous prototypes.

The de Havilland Beaver / Phillip Clarke Garratt

The Beaver, one of Canada's most famous bush planes, was introduced in 1947 and is still used in more than sixty countries. The reverse design is by Ontario artist Peter Mossman.
Cameo: Aviator Phillip Clarke Garratt who joined de Havilland Aircraft of Canada in 1936 and was instrumental in the development of the Beaver.

Curtiss JN-4 Canuck / Sir Frank Wilton Baillie

The reverse, by George Velinger of Quebec, depicts a Curtiss JN-4 (Canadian) above Camp Borden, Ontario. Nicknamed the Canuck, it was the first aircraft mass produced in Canada.
Cameo: Sir Frank Wilton Baillie, president of Canadian Aeroplanes Limited, the most efficient aircraft manufacturer in North America during WWI.

de Havilland Gypsy Moth / Murton A. Seymour

The reverse, by John Mardon, shows a Gypsy Moth in flight. The Gypsy Moth was the standard of most of the world's flying clubs during the late 1920s.
Cameo: Aviator Murton A Seymour was the first pilot trained by the Aero Club of British Columbia in 1915. He became president of the Canadian Flying Club Association in 1939.

DATE		QTY. (000)	ISSUE PRICE	VALUE
1991	$20 Silver Dart / A.D. McCurdy & F.W. (Casey) Baldwin	35	55.50	45.00
1991	$20 The de Havilland Beaver / Phillip Clarke Garratt	36	55.50	45.00
1992	$20 Curtiss Canuck / Sir Frank Wilton Baillie	33	55.50	45.00
1992	$20 de Havilland Gypsy Moth / Murton A. Seymour	33	55.50	45.00

The Fairchild 71C / James A. Richardson   Lockheed 14 Super Electra / Zebulon Lewis Leigh

Curtiss HS-2L / Stewart Graham   Canadian Vickers Vedette / Wilfred T. Reid

The Fairchild 71C / James A. Richardson

The reverse, by Robert R. Carmichael, shows a Fairchild 71C landing on a northern lake. The aircraft served as a freighter in Northern Canada.

Cameo: James A. Richardson's extensive contribution to the Canadian air transport industry led him to become director of Fairchild Aerial Surveys Limited of Canada.

Lockheed 14 Super Electra / Zebulon Lewis Leigh

This aircraft was developed in 1937 for passenger and cargo transportation service. Robert R. Carmichael's reverse shows a Lockheed 14 in front of the Malton Terminal in Ontario

Cameo: Zebulon Lewis Leigh was awarded the Trans Canada Trophy in 1946 for his exceptional achievement in both civil and military aviation.

Curtiss HS-2L / Stewart Graham

The reverse was designed by John Mardon. The Curtiss HS-2L became an important bush aircraft in Canada.

Cameo: Stewart Graham was the world's first bush pilot and a member of Canada's Aviation Hall of Fame.

Canadian Vickers Vedette / Wilfred T. Reid

The reverse was designed by Robert Ralph Carmichael. The Canadian Vickers Vedette was the first aircraft manufactured in Canada for commercial operations.

Cameo: Wilfred T. Reid created the Reid Aircraft Company.

DATE		QTY. (000)	ISSUE PRICE	VALUE
1993	$20 The Fairchild 71C / James A. Richardson	33	55.50	45.00
1993	$20 Lockheed 14 Super Electra / Zebulon Lewis Leigh	32	55.50	45.00
1994	$20 Curtiss HS-2L / Stewart Graham	31	55.50	45.00
1994	$20 Canadian Vickers Vedette / Wilfred T. Reid	31	55.50	45.00

Part II: Beyond World War II (1995–1999)

Part II honours Canada's contribution to aviation from 1950 to the present with two proof coins struck each year over a 5-year period.

Fleet 80 Canuck / J. Omer (Bob) Noury   DHC-1 Chipmunk / W/C Russell Bannock

Avro Canada CF-100 Canuck   Avro Canadian CF-105 Arrowv
Janus Zurakowski   James A. Chamberlin

Fleet 80 Canuck / J. Omer (Bob) Noury

The reverse design by Robert Bradford features the Fleet Canuck C-FEAI in flight.
Cameo: J. Omer (Bob) Noury who designed the Noury N-75, which became the Fleet 80 Canuck in 1945.

de Havilland DHC-1 Chipmunk / W/C Russell Bannock D.S.O., D.F.C. and Bar

The reverse, also by Robert Bradford, shows a de Havilland DHC-1 Chipmunk.
Cameo: W/C Russell Bannock joined de Havilland Canada in 1946 as chief test pilot.

Avro Canada CF-100 Canuck / Janus Zurakowski

The reverse, designed by Calgary artist Jim Bruce, depicts two Mk. 4B Canucks.
Cameo: Janus Zurakowski, the first man to exceed Mach 1 in a straight wing aircraft.

Avro Canadian CF-105 Arrow / James A. Chamberlin

The reverse, also by Jim Bruce, features two Avro Arrows soaring through the clouds.
Cameo: James A. Chamberlin whose contribution to the Arrow project was invaluable.

DATE		QTY. (000)	ISSUE PRICE	VALUE
1995	$20 Fleet 80 Canuck / J. Omer (Bob) Noury	17	57.95	45.00
1995	$20 de Havilland DHC-1 Chipmunk / W/C Russell Bannock	18	57.95	45.00
1996	$20 Avro Canada CF-100 Canuck / Janus Zurakowski	19	57.95	65.00
1996	$20 Avro Canadian CF-105 Arrow / James A. Chamberlin	27	57.95	135.00

Canadair F-86 Sabre / Fern Villeneuve   Canadair CT-114 Tutor / Edward Higgins

Canadair CP-107   Canadair CL-215
Argus / William S. Longhurst   Waterbomber / Paul Gagnon

Canadair F-86 Sabre / The Golden Hawks / Fern Villeneuve

The F-86 Sabre jet fighter was one of the top military aircraft in Europe in the 1950s. The reverse, by Ontario artist Ross Buckland shows a Sabre with four more from The Golden Hawks aerobatics team in the background.
Cameo: Fern Villeneuve, the first leader of the Canadian Golden Hawks.

Canadair CT-114 Tutor / The Snowbirds / Edward Higgins

This reverse is also by Ross Buckland. A Tutor trainer is shown with nine of the Canadian Armed Forces Snowbirds aerobatics team and the Snowbirds squadron crest.
Cameo: Edward Higgins, former vice-president of Canadair.

Canadair (Bombardier) CP-107 Argus / William Sydney Longhurst

Designed for anti-submarine warfare, the Argus was one of the most sophisticated combat aircraft of its time (1958–1991). The reverse is by Toronto artist Peter Mossman.
Cameo: William S, Longhurst piloted the maiden test flight of the Argus prototype in 1957.

Canadair (Bombardier) CL-215 Waterbomber / Paul Gagnon

The CL-215 is the only aircraft in the world specifically designed to fight forest fires.
Cameo: Paul Gagnon, a pilot and aviation consultant was involved in the development and launching of the Waterbomber as Director of Air Services for Quebec in 1962.

DATE		QTY. (000)	ISSUE PRICE	VALUE
1997	$20 Canadair F-86 Sabre Jet / Fern Villeneuve 16		57.95	55.00
1997	$20 Canadair CT-114 Tutor / Edward Higgins 18		57.95	55.00
1998	$20 Canadair (Bombardier) CP-107 Argus / William S. Longhurst 15		57.95	75.00
1998	$20 Canadair (Bombardier) CL-215 Waterbomber / Paul Gagnon 15		57.95	90.00

de Havilland DHC-8
Dash 8 / Robert H. Fowler, OC

de Havilland DHC-6
Twin Otter / George A. Neal

de Havilland DHC-6 Twin Otter / George A. Neal

Developed primarily for the bush plane market between 1965 and 1988, more than 600 Twin Otters worldwide were still in service in 1990. The reverse was designed by Neil Aird.

Cameo: George A. Neal, Chief Test Pilot and Flight Operations Director with de Havilland.

de Havilland DHC-8 Dash 8 / Robert H. Fowler, OC

The Dash 8 is a fast, quiet high-winged commuter turboprop aircraft capable of taking off and landing on shorter runways (STOL). The reverse was designed by Neil Aird.

Cameo: Robert H. Fowler, OC who joined de Havilland in 1952 as a test pilot and later helped develop the flight control and propeller systems which made the company a world leader in STOL aircraft. Mr. Fowler piloted the first flights of the Dash 8.

DATE		QTY. (000)	ISSUE PRICE	VALUE
1999	$20 de Havilland DHC-6 Twin Otter / George A. Neal	14	57.95	100.00
1999	$20 de Havilland DHC-8 Dash 8 / Robert H. Fowler, OC	14	57.95	125.00

CANADIAN TRANSPORTATION
20 Dollars Sterling Silver Proof

Diameter: 38.0 mm; weight: 31.103 grams; thickness: 3.5 mm;
composition: .925 silver, .075 copper; gold insert: 0.8 grams; edge; interrupted serrations

This series celebrates Canada's achievements in transportation, with coins depicting Canadian vehicles for sea, rail and land. Each coin has a gold holographic cameo and is sold singly in a charcoal-coloured anodized aluminum case with the Royal Canadian Mint logo on the cover. The year 2000 issues were the first Canadian coins ever issued with a gold holographic cameo.

2000 Issues

Obverse	The BlueNose

The Toronto	The H.S. Taylor Steam Buggy

The Bluenose, Sea

The Bluenose was the Canadian-built fishing schooner which won the first International Fishermen's Race trophy in 1921 and retained the title for another 18 years. The reverse for this coin was designed by J. Franklin Wright.

The Toronto, Rail

The first locomotive to be constructed in Canada was the Toronto, which was built in the city of the same name in 1853. The reverse design featuring the Toronto was designed by John Mardon.

The H.S. Taylor Steam Buggy, Land

The H.S. Taylor Steam Buggy was built in 1867 and is considered to be the first Canadian automobile. The reverse of this coin was also designed by John Mardon.

DATE		QTY. (000)	ISSUE PRICE	VALUE
2000	$20 proof, The Bluenose	78	59.95	200.00
2000	$20 proof, The Toronto	incl. above	59.95	60.00
2000	$20 proof, The H.S. Taylor Steam Buggy	incl. above	59.95	60.00

2001 Issues

The Marco Polo

The Scotia   The Russell "Light Four"

The Marco Polo, Sea

To celebrate the 150th anniversary of the *Marco Polo*, which was known as the *Queen of the Seas* from 1851-1883, its image graces the reverse designed by J.Franklin Wright.

The Scotia, Rail

The Scotia, built in Hamilton, Ontario, was the first Canadian-built locomotive equipped with a steel boiler. The reverse was designed by Don Curley.

The Russell "Light Four" Model L Touring Car, Land

This was the first mass-produced Canadian car with a Canadian-built engine and chassis. The reverse was designed by John Mardon.

DATE		QTY. (000)	ISSUE PRICE	VALUE
2001	$20 The Marco Polo	42	59.95	60.00
2001	$20 The Scotia	incl. above	59.95	60.00
2001	$20 The Russell "Light Four"	incl. above	59.95	60.00

2002 Issues

William D. Lawrence

Canadian Pacific D10 Locomotive
Engine No. 926

The Gray-Dort Model 25-SM

The William D. Lawrence (1874) Sea

The reverse was designed by Bonnie Ross and features the largest ship ever built in the Maritimes. This three-masted square rigger reached speeds of 14 knots.

Canadian Pacific D10 Locomotive, Engine No. 926 (1911) Rail

The D10 was an extremely versatile and highly successful "10-wheeler" used by Canadian Pacific from 1905 unit the end of WWII. The reverse was designed by Dan Fell.

The Gray-Dort Model 25-SM (1916) Land

The Canadian-built Gray-Dort was produced 1916–1924 and became one of Canada's most popular cars. Only about 50 of the 26,000 produced remain today. The reverse was designed by John Mardon.

DATE		QTY. (000)	ISSUE PRICE	VALUE
2002	$20 The William D. Lawrence	35	59.95	60.00
2002	$20 The Canadian Pacific D10 Locomotive	incl. above	59.95	60.00
2002	$20 The Gray-Dort Model 25-SM	incl. above	59.95	60.00

2003 Issues

The HMCS Bras d'or (PHE400)

Canadian National FA-1
Diesel-electric locomotive – number 9400

The Bricklin SV-1

The HMCS Bras d'or (FHE400) Sea

The reverse was designed by Donald Curley and features the hydrofoil ship designed for hunting down and sinking submarines. The ship was retired before seeing active military service.

Canadian National FA-1
Diesel-electric locomotive – number 9400 Rail

The FA-1 diesel-electric locomotive changed the Canadian railway industry by supplying the power needed for transporting heavy loads of bauxite and paper up steeper grades. The reverse design is by John Mardon.

The Bricklin SV-1 Land

The Canadian-built Bricklin, a radical, safety-conscious sports car was produced during the 1970s in New Brunswick. Only 2,854 units were produced. The reverse was designed by Brian Hughes.

DATE		QTY. (000)	ISSUE PRICE	VALUE
2003	$20 The HMCS Bras d'or (PHE400) 30		59.95	60.00
2003	$20 FA-1 Diesel-electric locomotive . . . . incl. above		59.95	80.00
2003	$20 The Bricklin SV-1. . . . . incl. above		59.95	70.00

20 DOLLARS SILVER

Diameter: 38 mm; weight: 31.39 grams; composition: .9999 pure silver; obverse: proof.
The reverse of each coin displays a colourised, holographic or selectively gold-plated image.

NATURAL WONDERS, 2003–2005

| 2003 OBVERSE | NIAGARA FALLS, 2003 | CANADIAN ROCKIES, 2003 |

| 2004 OBVERSE | NORTHERN LIGHTS, 2004 | ICEBERG, 2004 |

| HOPEWELL ROCKS 2004 | 2005 OBVERSE | LAC DE GRAS DIAMONDS, 2004 |

DATE		QTY. (000)	ISSUE PRICE	VALUE
2003	$20 Niagara Falls, hologram, by Gary Corcoran	30	59.95	95.00
2003	$20 Canadian Rockies, colourised, by Jose Osio	29	59.95	60.00
2004	$20 Northern Lights, double image hologram, by Gary Corcoran	34	79.95	80.00
2004	$20 Iceberg, colourised, by Royal Canadian Mint staff	25	69.95	60.00
2004	$20 The Hopewell Rocks, selectively gold plated, by Stan Witten	17	69.95	70.00
2005	$20 Lac de Gras Diamonds, double image hologram, by José Osio	35	69.95	70.00

The first three coins could be purchased for the sum of $179.85.

TALL SHIPS COLLECTION, 2005–2007

Diameter: 38 mm; weight: 31.39 grams;
composition: .9999 pure silver; edge serrated: finish: hologram (reverse), proof (obverse).

| 2005 Three-masted ships | 2006 Ketch | 2007 Brigantine |

Each twenty-dollar coin in this series features a tall sailing ship, and each will display a unique hologram effect.

DATE		QTY.	ISSUE PRICE	VALUE
2005	$20 Three-masted ships, designed by Bonnie Ross	18,276	69.95	70.00
2006	$20 The Ketch, designed by John M. Horton	10,299	69.95	70.00
2007	$20 Brigantine, designed by Bonnie Ross	7,935	74.95	75.00

CANADIAN ARCHITECTURAL TREASURES, 2006–

| Notre Dame Basilica | CN Tower | Pengrowth Saddledome |

Notre Dame Basilica of Montreal, 2006

The Notre Dame Basilica is a masterpiece of guilded statues and handcrafted ornamentation. Its two towers of its façade stand vigil over Notre Dame Street. Reverse by Jianping Yan.

CN Tower, 2006

Toronto's defining landmark, the CN Tower, is the tallest building in the world. Reverse by Jianping Yan.

Pengrowth Saddledome, 2006

The fact that Alberta is undoubtedly "saddle country" is reflected in the saddle-shaped architecture of the award-winning Pengrowth Saddledome. Reverse by Jianping Yan.

DATE		QTY.	ISSUE PRICE	VALUE
2006	$20 Notre Dame Basilica	30,906	69.95	70.00
2006	$20 CN Tower	included above	69.95	70.00
2006	$20 Pengrowth Saddledome	included above	69.95	70.00

NATIONAL PARKS AND RESERVES, 2005–

Diameter: 38 mm; weight: 31.39 grams;
composition: .9999 pure silver; edge serrated; finish: proof.

North Pacific Rim   Mingan Archipelago

North Pacific Rim National Park Reserve, 2005

The first coin in this series is the Pacific Rim National Park Reserve of Canada. The obverse holds the Susanna Blunt effigy of Queen Elizabeth. The reverse was also designed by Susanna Blunt.

Mingan Archipelago National Park Reserve, 2005

Treasure Islands Mingan Archipelago National Park Reserve of Canada is a group of some forty islands lying along the North shore of the Gulf of St. Lawrence. The reverse was Pierre Leduc.

Georgian Bay Islands   Nahanni   Jasper

Georgian Bay Islands National Park, 2006

Poised on the edge of the Canadian Shield, the Georgian Bay Islands testify to the power of the glaciers that carved out this region during the last Ice Age.

Nahanni National Park Reserve, 2006

North of the 60th parallel in the Northwest Territories flows one of the most spectacular wilderness rivers in the world. It is the backbone of Nahanni National Park Reserve of Canada.

Jasper National Park Reserve, 2006

This coin features Mount Edith Cavell, one of the park's most recognized peaks as well as a favoured way to explore the backcountry on horseback. Reverse by Michelle Grant.

DATE		QTY.	ISSUE PRICE	VALUE
2005	$20 North Pacific Rim 21,695		69.95	100.00
2005	$20 Mingan Archipelago . . . . included above		69.95	100.00
2006	$20 Georgian Bay Islands. 20,218		69.95	100.00
2006	$20 Nahanni . . . . included above		69.95	100.00
2006	$20 Jasper . . . . included above		69.95	100.00

STERLING SILVER 20 DOLLARS
Special Edition - Swarovski Crystal, 2007

Diameter: 38 mm; weight: 49.456 grams;
composition: .925 silver, .075 copper; edge serrated; finish: proof.

Blue Snowflake   Iridescent Snowflake

These coins featuring Swarovski Crystals, were designed by Konrad Wachelko.

DATE		QTY.	ISSUE PRICE	VALUE
2007	$20 Swarovski Crystal, Blue Snowflake	4,989	94.95	500.00
2007	$20 Swarovski Crystal, Iridescent Snowflake	4,980	94.95	500.00

International Polar Year, 2007

Diameter: 40 mm; weight: 27.78 grams;
composition: .925 silver, .075 copper; edge serrated; finish: proof.

Obverse   Regular   Plasma

This coin pays tribute to the visionary scientists who established an international collaboration to study the earth's polar regions 125 years ago.

DATE		QTY.	ISSUE PRICE	VALUE
2007	$20 International Polar Year, regular	9,164	64.95	80.00
2007	$20 International Polar Year, plasma	3,005	249.95	250.00

STERLING SILVER 20 DOLLARS

Diameter: 40 mm; weight: 27.78 grams;
composition: .925 silver, .075 copper; edge serrated; finish: proof; artist: Marcos Hallam

NHL Team Goalie Mask Coins, 2009

DATE		QTY.	ISSUE PRICE	VALUE
2009	$20 Calgary Flames Goalie Mask	10,000	74.95	80.00
2009	$20 Edmonton Oilers Goalie Mask	10,000	74.95	80.00
2009	$20 Montreal Canadiens Goalie Mask	10,000	74.95	80.00
2009	$20 Ottawa Senators Goalie Mask	10,000	74.95	80.00
2009	$20 Toronto Maple Leafs Goalie Mask	10,000	74.95	80.00
2009	$20 Vancouver Canucks Goalie Mask	10,000	74.95	80.00

Winter Scene, 2011

When faced with the challenges of winter, early settlers demonstrated boundless fortitude and adaptability. Design by Rémi Clark.

DATE		QTY.	ISSUE PRICE	VALUE
2011	$20 Winter Scene	5,287	69.95	70.00

Fine Silver 20 Dollars
HISTORICAL TRADE AND COMMERCE, 2008–2009

Diameter: 38 mm; weight: 31.39 grams;
composition: .9999 silver, edge serrated; finish: proof.

Agriculture Trade

The reverse design by John Mardon, is based on the theme of sowing the seeds of trade. This is the first coin in this series based on historical commerce.

Coal Trade

The reverse design by John Mardon, is based on the theme of the coal trade.

DATE		QTY.	ISSUE PRICE	VALUE
2008	$20 Agriculture Trade, proof	5,802	69.95	80.00
2009	$20 Coal Trade, proof	3,349	74.95	90.00

Holiday Issues, 2007–2008

The reverse designs are by Tony Bianco and are based on Christmas themes.

DATE		QTY.	ISSUE PRICE	VALUE
2007	$20 Holiday Sleigh Ride, proof	6,804	69.95	75.00
2008	$20 Holiday Carols, proof	5,224	69.95	75.00

GREAT CANADIAN LOCOMOTIVES, 2008–2011

The reverse designs are adapted by RCM engravers from images provided by the Canadian Pacific Railway Archives. Plain edge with lettering.

DATE		QTY.	ISSUE PRICE	VALUE
2008	$20 The Royal Hudson, proof	8,350	69.95	70.00
2009	$20 Jubilee, proof	6,036	74.95	75.00
2010	$20 Selkirk, proof	5,874	79.95	80.00
2011	$20 D-10, proof	8,662	79.95	80.00

Summer Moon Mask, 2009

These coins were inspired by an original red cedar mask carved by renowned Canadian artist Jody Broomfield of the Squamish Nation, Coast Salish people.

DATE		QTY.	ISSUE PRICE	VALUE
2009	$20 Summer Moon Mask, proof	2,834	69.95	100.00

Swarovski Crystal Snowflakes, 2008–2010

DATE		QTY.	ISSUE PRICE	VALUE
2008	$20 Swarovski Crystal, Amethyst, by Konrad Wachelko 7,230		94.95	160.00
2008	$20 Swarovski Crystal, Sapphire, by Konrad Wachelko. 7,765		94.95	350.00
2009	$20 Swarovski Crystal, Pink, by Konrad Wachelko 7,004		94.95	150.00
2009	$20 Swarovski Crystal, Blue, by Konrad Wachelko 7,477		94.95	150.00
2010	$20 Swarovski Crystal, Tanzanite, by Konrad Wachelko 7,241		99.95	120.00
2010	$20 Swarovski Crystal, Blue, by Konrad Wachelko 7,390		99.95	120.00

75th Anniversary of the First Bank Notes, 2010

For almost 200 years, Canadian paper money existed in a variety of forms until the first national bank notes were issued on March 11, 1935. Each denomination featured a member of the royal family or former Canadian prime minister on the front with an allegorical figure on the back. Reverse design by RCM Engravers.

DATE		QTY.	ISSUE PRICE	VALUE
2010	$20 75th Anniversary of the First Bank Notes 6,720		79.95	100.00

Swarovski Crystal Rain Drop, 2008–2012

DATE	QTY.	ISSUE PRICE	VALUE
2008	$20 Crystal Rain Drop, by Celia Godkin 13,122	89.95	150.00
2009	$20 Autumn Showers, by Celia Godkin 9,998	94.95	150.00
2010	$20 Maple Leaf Crystal Raindrop, by Celia Godkin 9,659	94.95	95.00
2011	$20 Bigleaf Maple Crystal Raindrop, by Celia Godkin 9,594	109.95	110.00
2012	$20 Sugar Maple Crystal Raindrop, by Celia Godkin 10,000	119.95	120.00

Holiday Issues, 2010

The Holidays are a time of garlands and wreaths filled with evergreen boughs and pine cones, a tradition that dates back to ancient times. Designed by Susan Taylor.

DATE	QTY.	ISSUE PRICE	VALUE
2010	$20 Ruby Holiday Pine Cones 4,907	99.95	100.00
2010	$20 Moonlight Holiday Pine Cones 4,758	99.95	100.00

Painted Wildflowers, 2010–

Diameter: 38.0mm; weight: 31.39g; composition: fine silver (99.99% pure); finish: proof; edge:serrated

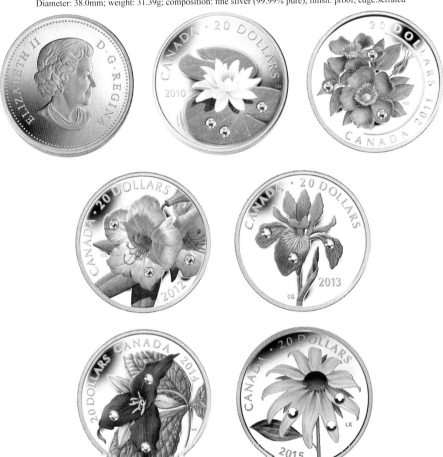

To render the image even more beautiful, three glittering Swarovski "dew drops" nestle among the delicate petals and leaves

DATE		QTY.	ISSUE PRICE	VALUE
2010	$20 Water Lily, by Claudio D'Angelo	9,990	104.95	105.00
2011	$20 Wild Rose, by Margaret Best	9,989	109.95	110.00
2012	$20 Rhododendron, by Claudio D'Angelo	10,000	119.95	120.00
2013	$20 Blue Flag Iris, by Celia Godkin	10,000	119.95	120.00
2014	$20 Red Trillium, by Margaret Best	10,000	119.95	120.00
2015	$20 Black-eyed Susan, by Laurie Koss	10,000	119.95	120.00

H.R.H. Prince William of Wales
and Miss Catherine Middleton, 2011

A Swarovski element glittering in sapphire is breathtaking against pure silver as it echoes Catherine Middleton's engagement ring. The names of the bride and groom laser-engraved along the coin's edge. Designed by Laurie McGaw.

DATE		QTY.	ISSUE PRICE	VALUE
2011	$20 H.R.H. Prince William of Wales and Miss Catherine Middleton . .	24,858	104.95	105.00

Venetian Glass Series, 2011–2015

Diameter: 38.0mm; weight: 31.39g; composition: 99.99% pure silver; finish: proof; edge: serrated

DATE		QTY.	ISSUE PRICE	VALUE
2011	$20 Tulip with Venetian Glass Ladybug, by RCM Engravers	4,985	139.95	900.00
2012	$20 Aster with Venetian Glass Bumble Bee, by Maurice Gervais	10,000	139.95	300.00
2013	$20 Purple Coneflower with Venetian Butterfly, by Maurice Gervais . . .	10,000	149.95	150.00
2014	$20 Water Lily with Venetian Leopard Frog, by Maurice Gervais	12,500	149.95	150.00
2015	$20 Broadleaf Arrowhead Flower with Venetian Turtle, by Maurice Gervais. .."		149.95	150.00

Chrismas Tree, 2011

The design features a traditional star-topped Christmas tree wrapped in fluffy garlands and studded with five SWAROVSKI® ELEMENTS "lights". Reverse design by Tony Bianco.

DATE		QTY.	ISSUE PRICE	VALUE
2011	$20 Christmas Tree, proof	7,974	114.95	115.00

Winnipeg Jets, 2011

This coin celebrates the Jets' hockey franchise return to Winnipeg. Reverse design by William Woodruff.

DATE		QTY.	ISSUE PRICE	VALUE
2011	$20 Winnipeg Jets, proof	5,506	94.95	95.00

Swarovski Crystal Snowflakes, 2011

DATE		QTY.	ISSUE PRICE	VALUE
2011	$20 Hyacinth Red Small Crystal Snowflake, by Konrad Wachelko 5,660		114.95	115.00
2011	$20 Montana Blue Small Crystal Snowflake, by Konrad Wachelko. . . . 5,822		114.95	115.00
2011	$20 Emerald Crystal Snowflake, by Konrad Wachelko. 6,586		114.95	115.00
2011	$20 Topaz Crystal Snowflake, by Konrad Wachelko, all 4 proof 6,041		114.95	115.00

The Queen's Diamond Jubilee, 2012

The year 2012 marks a historic occasion that has not been celebrated in over 100 years—the Diamond Jubilee for Britain's reigning monarch. The previous and only British monarch to reach this milestone was Queen Victoria in 1897. Reverse design by Laurie McGaw.

DATE		QTY.	ISSUE PRICE	VALUE
2012	$20 The Queen's Diamond Jubilee, with crystal 10,780		104.95	105.00

Royal Cypher, 2012

A royal cypher is a monarch's identifier, much like a coat of arms. Cyphers have been used by British royals since the time of Henry VIII. They generally feature the monarch's initial and titles, often beneath a symbol of rule, such as a crown. Unlike monograms that interweave letters, royal cyphers display each letter distinctly. Design by the RCM engravers.

Queen Elizabeth II & Prince Phillip, 2012

Queen Elizabeth II and Prince Philip have four children and eight grandchildren, and continue their lifelong partnership of mutual support and service to the United Kingdom, the Commonwealth, and numerous individual organizations and charities. Design by Laurie McGaw.

DATE		QTY.	ISSUE PRICE	VALUE
2012	$20 Royal Cypher.	3,568	84.95	85.00
2012	$20 Queen Elizabeth II & Prince Phillip	5,627	84.95	85.00

Queen's Visit to Canada, 2012

The design features the Royal Canadian Mounted Police presenting thehe Queen with a prized horse from its musical ride. Reverse design by Bonnie Ross.

DATE		QTY.	ISSUE PRICE	VALUE
2012	$20 Queen's Visit to Canada, proof.	25,000	89.95	90.00

Ultra High Relief $20 Coin — The Queen's Portrait, 2012

Diameter: 36 mm; weight: 30.75 grams;
composition: .9999 silver; edge: plain; finish: proof.

The reverse effigy is struck 4 times in ultra high relief long associated with ancient medallic art. Reverse design by Laurie McGaw.

DATE		QTY.	ISSUE PRICE	VALUE
2012	$20 The Queen's Portrait	200,000	20.00	22.00

Holiday Swarovski Crystal Coins, 2012

DATE		QTY.	ISSUE PRICE	VALUE
2012	$20 Holiday Snowflake with Clear Arctic Ice Swarovski Crystal Gemstone, Proof.	10,000	114.95	115.00
2012	$20 Holiday Snowstorm with three Opalescent White Swarovski Crystal Gemstones, Proof	10,000	114.95	115.00
2012	$20 Three Wise Men with golden shadow Swarovski Elements crystal, Proof	10,000	114.95	115.00

Commemorative Coin, 2011–2014

Diameter: 27 mm; weight: 7.96 grams;
composition: .9999 silver; edge: serrated; finish: reverse proof.

These silver commemorative coins are legal tender with a value of $20.00 and available for the official price of $20.00.

DATE		QTY.	ISSUE PRICE	VALUE
2011	$20 Maple Leaves, by Cosme Saffioti	244,000	20.00	50.00
2011	$20 Canoe, by Jason Bouwman	198,000	20.00	35.00
2012	$20 Polar Bear, by Emily S. Damstra	250,000	20.00	35.00
2012	$20 Diamond Jubilee, by Laurie McGaw	250,000	20.00	35.00
2013	$20 Wolf, by Glen Loates	250,000	20.00	20.00
2013	$20 Iceberg, by Emily Damstra	250,000	20.00	20.00
2013	$20 Hockey, by Greg Banning	250,000	20.00	20.00
2013	$20 Santa, by Jesse Koreck	225,000	20.00	20.00
2014	$20 Canada Goose, by Trevor Tennant	225,000	20.00	20.00
2014	$20 Bobcat, by Ken Ryan	225,000	20.00	20.00
2014	$20 Summertime, by John Mantha	200,000	20.00	20.00

Canadian Art by the Group of Seven, 2012–2013

Diameter: 38 mm; weight: 31.39 grams; composition: .9999 silver; edge: plain; finish: proof.

DATE		QTY.	ISSUE PRICE	VALUE
2012	$20 F. H. Varley, Stormy Weather.	7,000	89.95	85.00
2012	$20 Arthur Lismer, Nova Scotia Fishing Village	7,000	89.95	85.00
2012	$20 Franklin Carmichael, Houses, Cobalt	7,000	89.95	85.00
2013	$20 Lawren S. Harris, Toronto Street, Winter Morning	7,000	89.95	85.00
2013	$20 Franz Johnston, The Guardian of the Gorge.	7,000	89.95	85.00
2013	$20 J.E.H. Macdonald, Sumacs.	7,000	89.95	85.00
2013	$20 A. Y. Jackson, Saint-Tite-des-Caps (1930)	7,000	89.95	90.00

The Moose Family – Robert Bateman, 2012

Diameter: 38mm; weight: 31.39g; composition: .9999 silver; 1 troy ounce

The year 2012 marks the 50th anniversary of the Canadian Wildlife Federation (CWF), an organization that has achieved exceptional results in conserving Canadian wilderness and Canadians about environmental issues that concern us all. Robert Bateman, the coin designer, is a world-renowned wildlife artist and an unflagging proponent of wildlife conservation and education. The reverse image features a detail from Robert Bateman's painting, *The Moose Family*.

DATE		QTY.	ISSUE PRICE	VALUE
2012	$20 The Moose Family, Proof	7,500	149.99	150.00

Untamed Canada, 2013–

Diameter: 40mm; weight: 28.02g; composition: .9999 silver; 0.9 troy ounce

Designed by Canadian artist Tivadar Bote, the coin features a fox sitting serenely in the foreground of the image, looking toward the left side of the field.

DATE		QTY.	ISSUE PRICE	VALUE
2013	$20 Arctic Fox	8,500	84.95	85.00
2013	$20 The Pronghorn	8,500	89.95	90.00
2014	$20 The Wolverine	8,500	89.95	90.00

Canadian Coast Guard (1962–2012)

The year 2012 marks the 50th Anniversary of the Canadian Coast Guard. This important Canadian marine service was created in 1962 to support mariners in Canadian waters, conduct search and rescue services, maintain Canada's sovereignty in the Arctic and in coastal waters, respond to technical advances in its domain, and address issues associated with growing vessel traffic.

DATE	QTY.	ISSUE PRICE	VALUE
2012 $20 Canadian Coast Guard.............................. 7,500		129.95	130.00

World Baseball Classic, 2013

DATE	QTY.	ISSUE PRICE	VALUE
2013 $20 Runner 7,500		114.95	115.00
2013 $20 Hitter.. 7,500		114.95	115.00
2013 $20 Pitcher 7,500		114.95	115.00
2013 $20 Fielder.. 7,500		114.95	115.00

Canada's Maple Canopy Series, 2013–

Diameter: 38mm; weight: 31.39g; composition: .9999 silver; 1 troy ounce

The reverse design by Canadian artist Emily Damstra presents the classic Canadian maple from a novel angle, looking upward at the trunk and tree canopy from below.

DATE		QTY.	ISSUE PRICE	VALUE
2013	$20 Canadian Maple Canopy (Spring) 7,500		99.95	100.00
2013	$20 Canadian Maple Canopy (Autumn), design by Margaret Best 7,500		99.95	100.00
2014	$20 Spring Splendour, design by Margaret Best 7,500		99.95	100.00
2014	$20 Maple Canopy:Autumn Allure, design by Emily Damstra 7,500		99.95	100.00

Butterflies of Canada, 2013–

Diameter: 40mm; weight: 28.02g; composition: .9999 silver; 0.9 troy ounce

DATE		QTY.	ISSUE PRICE	VALUE
2013	$20 Canadian Tiger Swallowtail 10,000		99.95	100.00
2014	$20 Red-Spotted Purple 10,000		99.95	100.00

The Bald Eagle Portrait of Power, 2013

The amazing bald eagle is Canada's largest bird of prey and the only eagle exclusive to North America. A potent symbol of vision, power and stoicism, this impressive bird's wingspan can stretch more than two metres in length. Designer: Claudio D'Angelo.

DATE		QTY.	ISSUE PRICE	VALUE
2013	$20 Bald Eagle	7,500	99.95	100.00
2013	$20 Bald Eagle: Lifelong Mates	7,500	99.95	100.00
2013	$20 Bald Eagle: Returning from the Hunt	7,500	99.95	100.00
2013	$20 Bald Eagle: Mother Protecting Her Eaglets	7,500	99.95	100.00

The Beaver, 2013

The reverse design by Canadian artist Glen Loates features an adult beaver felling a tree. Occupying the centre of the image, a large beaver stands amid the leaves and grasses lining the bank of a waterway, hard at work chewing the trunk of a tree with its sharp incisors.

DATE		QTY.	ISSUE PRICE	VALUE
2013	$20 Beaver	8,500	119.95	120.00

Canadian Dinosaur Series, 2013–2015

Diameter: 38.0mm; weight: 31.39g; composition: fine silver; finish: proof ; edge: serrated

Coins that feature lifelike prehistoric animals and dinosaurs discovered in Canada. Designer: Julius Csotonyi.

DATE		QTY.	ISSUE PRICE	VALUE
2013	$20 Bathygnathus Borealis	8,500	89.95	90.00
2014	$20 Scutellosaurus	8,500	89.95	90.00
2014	$20 Xenoceratops Foremostensis	8,500	89.95	90.00
2015	$20 Albertosaurus	8,500	89.95	90.00

300th Anniversary of Louisbourg, 2013

Laying the foundation for a nation: The 300th Anniversary of Louisbourg. The reverse image by Canadian artist John Horton commemorates the 300th anniversary of the settlement of Louisbourg, and the community that developed there. The edge lettering on the side of the coin reads "Louisbourg 300" and a repeating symbolic pattern of an anchor, fleur de lys, and maple leaf.

DATE		QTY.	ISSUE PRICE	VALUE
2013	$20 Settlement of Louisbourg	8,500	89.95	90.00

A Story Of The Northern Lights Series, 2013–

Diameter: 38.0mm; weight: 31.39g; composition: fine silver; finish: proof; edge: serrated

That is the magic of the northern lights, and if you've ever experienced them firsthand, you know this incredible phenomenon is really beyond words; shimmering waves of light that can leave you breathless. Designer: Nathalie Bertin.

DATE		QTY.	ISSUE PRICE	VALUE
2013	$20 The Great Hare 8,500		109.95	110 .00
2013	$20 Howling Wolf 8,500		109.95	110 .00

Autumn Nature Series, 2013–

Diameter: 38.0mm; weight: 31.39g; composition: fine silver; finish: proof; edge: serrated

When it comes to creating a breathtaking display of colour, autumn is unmatched. The bright reds, oranges and purples of various maple species; the yellows of poplars; and the golden-browns of oaks and beeches. People flock to the countryside to enjoy the fiery spectacle, where still waters of a lake will double the pleasure. Designer: Tony Bianco.

DATE		QTY.	ISSUE PRICE	VALUE
2013	$20 Autumn Bliss 7,500		99.95	100.00
2014	$20 Autumn Falls 7,500		99.95	100.00

Man of Steel™, 2013

Diameter: 38.0mm; weight: 31.39g; composition: pure silver; finish: proof; edge: serrated

Superman stands guard heroically over the city of Metropolis, displaying the iconic Daily Planet in the background. Includes Superman's native Kryptonian language, as created by DC Comics, and reads "75 Years of Superman" in French and English.

One of the most recognized logos in the world, in any industry, the Superman S-shield is an icon for the ages. After 75 years, this symbol is recognizable on every continent and transcends languages and culture. Includes Superman's native Kryptonian language, as created by DC Comics, and reads "75 Years of Superman" in French and English.

For 75 years, Superman has been the protector of the city of Metropolis. With the Daily Planet dominating its cityscape, it's not uncommon to also see the Man of Tomorrow flying overhead. The Royal Canadian Mint, Official Licensee of DC Comics, introduces the first struck achromatic hologram coin in the world. Includes Superman's native Kryptonian language, as created by DC Comics, and reads "75 Years of Superman" in French and English.

DATE		QTY.	ISSUE PRICE	VALUE
2013	$20 Superman: Man Of Steel	10,000	109.75	110.00
2013	$20 Superman: The Shield	10,000	119.75	120.00
2013	$20 Superman: Metropolis	10,000	129.75	130.00

Canadian Contemporary Art, 2013

Diameter: 38.0mm; weight: 31.39g; composition: fine silver; finish: proof; edge: serrated;

Today's artists have access to more sources of inspiration than ever before. Carlito Dalceggio's artwork *Harmony* expresses his roots, his country and its relationships from a higher level of consciousness. Ancestors merge with the future in this round, tribal design that has no starting point because the "fountain of life" never ends.

DATE	QTY.	ISSUE PRICE	VALUE
2013 $20 Canadian Contemporary Art 7,500		89.95	90.00

Maple Leaf Impression, 2013

iameter: 38.0mm; weight: 31.39g; composition: fine silver; finish: proof; edge: serrated

For almost 300 years, the red maple leaf has symbolized Canadian identity and values. Celebrating the robust Canadian spirit, a flurry of maple leaves falls in perfect formation to create the impression of a larger maple leaf. Engraver José Osio.

DATE	QTY.	ISSUE PRICE	VALUE
2013 $20 Maple Leaf Impression with enamel 10,000		114.95	115.00

Holiday Candy Cane, 2013

Diameter: 38.0mm; weight: 31.39g; composition: fine silver
finish: proof (with colour and Venetian glass candy cane on the reverse); edge: serrated

Poinsettias, stars, ornaments, sweets–and the minty taste of a candy cane, usually the first flavour
to mark the start of the holiday season. Designer: Maurice Gervais. Hand-crafted Venetian holiday element created by Cortella & Ballarin s.n.c.

DATE	QTY.	ISSUE PRICE	VALUE
2013 $20 Holiday Candy Cane 10,000		149.95	150.00

Winter Snowflake, 2013

Diameter: 38.0mm; weight: 31.39g; composition: fine silver; finish: proof; edge: serrated

The Snowflake is the source of winter fun–snowballs, snow forts and exciting downhill slides.
Beneath all that joy lies a crystalline sculpture of such remarkable beauty and complexity.

DATE	QTY.	ISSUE PRICE	VALUE
2013 $20 black snowflake-shaped Swarovski crystal by Konrad Wachelko. 10,000		114.95	115.00

Swavorski Crystal Coins, 2013

Diameter: 38.0mm; weight: 31.39g; composition: fine silver; finish: proof; edge: serrated

Historically, people decorated their homes with evergreen boughs to preserve nature's vibrant green during December's fading light. Today, holiday wreaths are decorated with anything that delights the eye. Designer: Maurice Gervais.

DATE		QTY.	ISSUE PRICE	VALUE
2013	$20 Holiday Wreath. 10,000		114.95	115.00

Legend Of Nanaboozhoo, 2014

Diameter: 38.0mm; weight: 31.39g; composition: fine silver (99.99% pure) with selective gold plating (Thunderbird) finish: proof; edge: serrated

Storytelling has long been a rich oral tradition for Aboriginal cultures. It is said that from the first snowfall to the first clap of thunder, elders impart history, traditions and life lessons to the younger generation through rich narratives filled with allegories and imagery. For the Anishinaabe, an important cultural character is Nanaboozhoo; as a shape-shifting spirit, he teaches right from wrong through his adventures while offering lessons on how to live in harmony with the natural world. Designed by Cyril Assiniboine, a renowned self-taught Ojibwa artist and a pow-wow dancer.

DATE		QTY.	ISSUE PRICE	VALUE
2014	$20 Legend of Nanaboozhoo 8,500		99.95	100.00
2014	$20 Nanaboozhoo and the Thunderbird 8,500		114.95	115.00
2014	$20 Nanaboozhoo and the Thunderbird's Nest. 8,500		89.95	90.00

50th Anniversary Of Canadian Peacekeeping In Cyprus, 2014

Diameter: 38.0mm; weight: 31.39g; composition: fine silver; finish: proof with blue enamel; edge: serrated

Canada is celebrated worldwide as a defender of peace. Today, tens of thousands of peacekeepers are serving in more than 40 missions worldwide, including the organization's inaugural mission in Cyprus. Designer: Silvia Pecota.

DATE		QTY.	ISSUE PRICE	VALUE
2014	$20 50th Anniversary of Canadian Peacekeeping in Cyprus 8,500		114.95	115.00

Bathymetric Maps Of The Great Lakes Series, 2014–2015

Diameter: 38.0mm; weight: 31.39g; composition: fine silver; finish: proof ; edge: serrated

The Great Lakes are the world's largest system of fresh surface water. It's five lakes–Superior, Huron, Erie, and Ontario–are visible from the moon and hold about 20% of the world's freshwater supply. Designer: Susanna Blunt.

DATE		QTY.	ISSUE PRICE	VALUE
2014	$20 Lake Superior. 10,000		114.95	115.00
2014	$20 Lake Ontario. 10,000		114.95	115.00
2014	$20 Lake Erie 10,000		114.95	115.00
2015	$20 Lake Michigan 10,000		114.95	115.00
2015	$20 Lake Huron 10,000		114.95	115.00

Majestic Animals, 2014–2015

Diameter: 38.0mm; weight: 31.39g; composition: 99.99% pure silver; finish: proof; edge: serrated

DATE		QTY.	ISSUE PRICE	VALUE
2014	$20 Iconic Polar Bear	8,500	99.95	100.00
2014	$20 The Woodland Caribou	8,500	99.95	100.00
2015	$20 The Majestic Moose - Claudio D'Angelo	7,500	99.95	100.00
2015	$20 Big-Horned Sheep - Maurade Baynton	6,500	99.95	100.00
2015	$20 Majestic Elk - Maurade Baynton	6,500	99.95	100.00
2015	$20 Misty Morning Mule Deer - Trevor Tennant	6,500	99.95	100.00
2015	$20 Imposing Alpha Wolf - Maurade Baynton	6,500	99.95	100.00
2015	$20 Snowy Owl	6,500	99.95	100.00

100th Anniversary of the Royal Ontario Museum, 2014

Diameter: 38.0mm; weight: 31.39g; composition: fine silver; finish: proof ; edge: serrated

For 100 years, the Royal Ontario Museum (ROM) in Toronto, Ontario, has connected visitors with the natural world around them, as well as the many cultures that have shaped human history.

DATE		QTY.	ISSUE PRICE	VALUE
2014	$20 100th Anniversary of the Royal Ontario Museum.	8,500	114.95	115.00

The Bison Series, 2014

Diameter: 38.0mm; weight: 31.39g; composition: fine silver; finish: proof ; edge: plain with edge lettering

The bison is the largest land animal in North America: a symbol of strength, and an important part of the history of the Prairies region of Canada. Until the late 1800s, the bison reigned as the dominant land-grazing animal throughout Canada's grassland regions, from Manitoba to Alberta. Its unique shoulder hump, shaggy mane and are just some of the physical attributes that contribute to the bison's reputation as a symbol of strength.

DATE		QTY.	ISSUE PRICE	VALUE
2014	$20 The Bison: A Portrait by Doug Comeau.	7,500	99.95	100.00
2014	$20 The Bull and His Mate by Trevor Tennant.	7,500	99.95	100.00
2014	$20 Bison: The Fight by Claudio D'Angelo	7,500	99.95	100.00
2014	$20 Bison: A Family at Rest by Claudio D'Angelo.	7,500	99.95	100.00

Stained Glass Series, 2014–

Diameter: 38.0mm; weight: 31.39g; composition: fine silver; finish: proof ; edge: serrated

 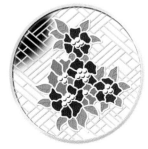 

From coast to coast, many of Canada's public buildings are adorned with these artistic creations. This coin offers a reproduction of one of the breathtaking stained glass windows that can be found at Craigdarroch Castle in Victoria, B.C.

DATE		QTY.	ISSUE PRICE	VALUE
2014	$20 Stained Glass: Craigdarroch Castle......................7,500		129.95	130.00
2014	$20 Stained Glass: Casa Loma 7,500		129.95	130.00

100th Anniversary of the Lost of the RMS *Empress of Ireland*, 2014

Diameter: 38.0mm; weight: 31.39g; composition: fine silver; finish: proof ; edge: plain with edge lettering

It was the greatest maritime disaster in Canadian history—a tragedy unparalleled by the loss of life and the speed at which the events unfolded. The sinking of RMS *Empress of Ireland* made headlines around the world in 1914; sadly, the onset of the First World War would quickly over-shadow the events that transpired in the waters near Rimouski, Que. Designer: John Horton.

DATE		QTY.	ISSUE PRICE	VALUE
2014	$20 100th Anniversary of the Lost of the RMS *Empress of Ireland*....7,000		109.95	110.00

75th Anniversary of the First Royal Visit, 2014

Diameter: 38.0mm; weight: 31.39g; composition: fine silver; finish: antique; edge: serrated

History was made when King George VI and Queen Elizabeth visited Canada in 1939. It was the first time a reigning monarch had ever traveled to North America, and for a young nation eager to flex its muscles of independence, the royal tour provided the perfect opportunity.

DATE		QTY.	ISSUE PRICE	VALUE
2014	$20 75th Anniversary of the First Royal Visit 5,000		139.95	140.00

Maple Leaf Impression, 2014

Diameter: 38.0mm; weight: 31.39g; composition: fine silver (99.99% pure); finish: proof; edge:serrated

From backpackers in Berlin to peacekeepers in Pakistan, Canadians are immediately identifiable by a singular image they faithfully sport on pins, badges, and appliqués: the red maple leaf. Designed by José Osio.

DATE		QTY.	ISSUE PRICE	VALUE
2014	$20 Maple Leaf Impression 7,500		114.95	115.00

Canada Baby Animals Series, 2014–

Diameter: 38.0mm; weight: 31.39g; composition: fine silver (99.99% pure); finish: proof; edge:serrated

Canada is a vast territory that is home to an incredibly diverse wildlife! A Series showcasing Canada's young wildlife depicted by baby animals in their natural setting.

DATE		QTY.	ISSUE PRICE	VALUE
2014	$20 Beaver, design by Glen Loates 7,500		99.95	100.00
2014	$20 Atlantic Puffin, design by Glen Loates 7,500		99.95	100.00
2015	$20 Burrowing Owl, design by Arnold Nogy. 7,500		99.95	100.00
2015	$20 Black Bear, design Clinton Jammer 7,500		99.95	100.00
2015	$20 Mountain Goat, design Glen Loates. 7,500		99.95	100.00
	$20 Deer			
	$20 Porcupine			

Woolly Mammoth, 2014

Diameter: 38.0mm; weight: 31.39g; composition: fine silver (99.99% pure); finish: proof; edge:serrated

Despite the species' extinction 10,000 years ago, the woolly mammoth continues to inspire and intrigue many who identify it with the last glacial period. Design by Michael Skrepnik.

DATE		QTY.	ISSUE PRICE	VALUE
2014	$20 Woolly Mammoth (from a set) 3,000			

Only available as a subscription with the $5 Woolly Mammoth gold coin at $369.90 per set.

Seven Sacred Teachings Series, 2014

Diameter: 40.0mm; weight: 31.83g; composition: fine silver (99.99% pure) with selective gold plating
finish: proof; edge:serrated

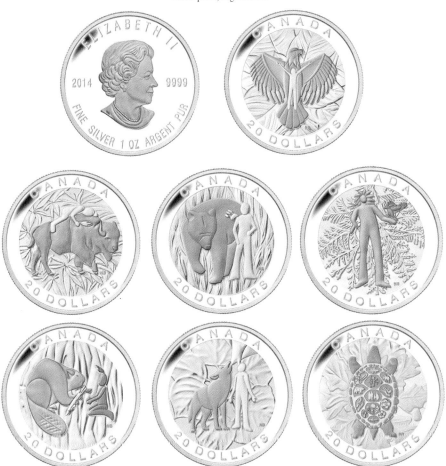

Seven Sacred Teachings honour the traditional concepts of respect and sharing that are the corner-
stones of Aboriginal life. While variations of these teachings do exist throughout North America,
this diversity only enriches them and underscores the universality of their wisdom. Designed by
Métis artist Nathalie Bertin.

DATE		QTY.	COST	VALUE
2014	$20 Love (April) 7,000		109.95	110.00
2014	$20 Respect (May) 7,000		109.95	110.00
2014	$20 Courage (June) 7,000		109.95	110.00
2014	$20 Honesty (July) 7,000		109.95	110.00
2015	$20 Wisdom (August) 7,000		109.95	110.00
2015	$20 Humility (September) 7,000		109.95	110.00
2015	$20 Truth (October) 7,000		109.95	110.00

River Rapids, 2014

Diameter: 38.0mm; weight: 31.39g; composition: fine silver; finish: proof ; edge: serrated

Algonquin Provincial Park in autumn is one of Canada's most beautiful visual treats. In the land that inspired world-renowned Canadian landscape painters Tom Thomson and the Group of Seven, nature shows itself to those who are observant. Designer: Robert Ross.

DATE		QTY.	ISSUE PRICE	VALUE
2014	$20 River Rapids.........................7,500		99.95	100.00

75th Anniversary of The Royal Winnipeg Ballet, 2014

Diameter: 40.0mm; weight: 31.60g; composition: fine silver (99.99% pure); finish: proof; edge: serrated

To commemorate the 75th anniversary of the Royal Winnipeg Ballet. This overhead view features six dancers from the Royal Winnipeg Ballet's lavish production of The Sleeping Beauty. The fairytale-like image is protected by a customized case that plays Sleeping Beauty (Valse) melody by Tchaikovsky when opened. The image is an engraved rendition of a photograph by one of Canada's foremost dance photographers, David Cooper.

DATE		QTY.	ISSUE PRICE	VALUE
2014	$20 75th Anniversary of The Royal Winnipeg Ballet..............7,500		114.95	115.00

Chickadee with Swarovski™ Winter Berry Elements, 2014

Diameter: 38.0mm; weight: 31.39g; composition: 99.99% pure silver; finish: proof; edge: serrated

A common sight from Newfoundland to British Columbia, the beloved black-capped chickadee delights observers with its friendly, inquisitive nature. Its sudden appearance adds a delightful burst of energy to the quiet, snow-covered landscape, and creates a brief enchanting moment that adds to the magic of the holiday season in Canada. Designer: Steve Hepburn.

DATE		QTY.	ISSUE PRICE	VALUE
2014	$20 Chickadee with Swarovski™ Winter Berry Elements 7,500		114.95	115.00

Interconnections Series, 2014

Diameter: 38.0mm; weight: 31.39g; composition: 99.99% pure silver; finish: proof; edge: serrated

Canada's three natural realms of land, sky, and sea mingle in a landscape of unmatched grandeur. Similarly, its people—First Nations and modern inhabitants alike—though culturally distinct, overlap within this landscape in a unique experience of shared history and nationhood. Designer: Andy Everson.

DATE		QTY.	ISSUE PRICE	VALUE
2014	$20 Interconnections: Land - The Beaver. .7,500		114.95	115.00
2014	$20 Interconnections: Air - The Thunderbird 7,500		114.95	115.00
2014	$20 Interconnections: Sea - The Orca 7,500		114.95	115.00

Royal Generations: Her Majesty Queen Elizabeth II, Prince Charles, Prince William and Prince George (2014)

Diameter: 38.0mm; weight: 31.39g; composition: 99.99% pure silver; finish: proof; edge: serrated

On July 22, 2013, His Royal Highness Prince George Alexander Louis became the newest member of Canada's royal family. Third in line for the throne, and prince of the hearts of royal watchers everywhere, young George's birth was met with all of the joy and fanfare that accompanies such a happy event. Canadian artist Cathy Sabourin's interpretation of a photograph by Camera Press.

DATE		QTY.	ISSUE PRICE	VALUE
2014	$20 Royal Generations	10,000	89.95	90.00

Cougar, 2014

Diameter: 38.0mm; weight: 31.39g; composition: 99.99% pure silver; finish: proof; edge: serrated

The cougar is one of Canada's most powerful, elusive and beautiful predators.

DATE		QTY.	ISSUE PRICE	VALUE
2014	$20 Cougar: Atop a Mountain - Artist Glen Loates	8,500	89.95	90.00
2014	$20 Cougar: Perched On a Maple Tree - Artist Glen Loates	8,500	99.95	100.00
2014	$20 Cougar: Pouncing in the Snow - Artist Maurade Baynton.	8,500	114.95	115.00

Majestic Maple Leaves, 2014

Diameter: 38.0mm; weight: 31.39g; composition: 99.99% pure silver; finish: proof; edge: serrated

The maple leaf is a powerful national symbol—one with a distinct and elegant shape that captures much of Canada's nature—winters that have influenced the way the world views this land and its people; breathtaking autumn colours that have captured the hearts of artists for centuries—but most of all, it symbolizes a land of opportunity to build a new life and enjoy the prosperity of free enterprise. Designer: Pierre Leduc.

DATE		QTY.	ISSUE PRICE	VALUE
2014	$20 Majestic Maple Leaves	8,500	89.95	90.00
2014	$20 Majestic Maple Leaves with Colour	8,500	99.95	100.00
2014	$20 Majestic Maple Leaves with Jade	8,500	114.95	115.00

Maple Leaves Glow-in-the-Dark, 2014

Diameter: 38.0mm; weight: 31.39g; composition: 99.99% pure silver; finish: proof; edge: serrated

The maple leaf has long been an internationally recognized emblem of Canada, its people and the land itself. But there are multiple species of maples, making it as diverse as the population it is often used to represent. Designer: Celia Godkin.

DATE		QTY.	ISSUE PRICE	VALUE
2014	$20 Maple Leaves, Glow-in-the-Dark. 7,500		104.95	105.00

Bald Eagle 3–Coin Subscription, 2014

A day in the life of the Bald Eagle is filled with activity from dusk until dawn and beyond. From the moment it awakens, the eagle is at work—tending to its nest, soaring high, hunting, feeding its young, and taking pause to eat and rest. Designer: Claudio D'Angelo.

DATE		QTY.	ISSUE PRICE	VALUE
2014	$20 Bald Eagle with Fish. 8,500		89.95	90.00
2014	$20 Soaring Bald Eagle.		99.95	100.00
2014	$20 Perched Bald Eagle.		114.94	115.00

The White-Tailed Deer, 2014

Diameter: 38.0mm; weight: 31.39g; composition: 99.99% pure silver; finish: proof; edge: plain with edge lettering

DATE	QTY.	ISSUE PRICE	VALUE
2014	$20 The White Tailed Deer: Portrait - Desmond McCaffrey 7,500	99.95	100.00
2014	$20 White-Tailed Deer: A Challenge - Desmond McCaffrey 7,500	99.95	100.00
2014	$20 The White-Tailed Deerr: Mates - Claudio D'Angelo 7,500	99.95	100.00
2014	$20 White-Tailed Deer: A Doe and Her Fawns - Trevor Tennant 7,500	99.95	100.00

70th Anniversary of the End of the Italian Campaign, 2015

Diameter: 38.0mm; weight: 31.39g; composition: 99.99% pure silver; finish: proof; edge: serrated

The Italian Campaign was Canada's first full-scale ground operation of the Second World War. By the summer of 1943, the Allies were revitalised by victories in North Africa and were seeking to open up a second battlefront by invading Germany's Axis ally, Italy. On the morning of July 10, 1943, Canada joined its allies in the planned invasion of Sicily. Designed by Canadian illustrator Joel Kimmel.

DATE	QTY.	ISSUE PRICE	VALUE
2015	$20 70th Anniversary of the End of the Italian Campaign 10,000	109.95	110.00

First World War Battlefront Series, 2015

Diameter: 38.0mm; weight: 31.39g; composition: 99.99% pure silver with selective gold plating; finish: proof; edge: serrated

"Our men in the trenches describe this fire as being the most tremendous both on point of noise and in actual effect they have ever seen or heard." -- Ernest Swinton.

DATE		QTY.	ISSUE PRICE	VALUE
2015	$20 The Battle of Neuve-Chapelle, by Joel Kimmel.	10,000	109.95	110.00
2015	$20 The Second Battle of Ypres, by Silvia Pecota.	10,000	109.95	110.00

Second World War Battlefront Series, 2015

Diameter: 38.0mm; weight: 31.39g; composition: 99.99% pure silver; finish: proof; edge: serrated

By the summer of 1940, much of continental Europe was occupied by Nazi Germany, which had turned its sights across the English Channel to Great Britain. As a precursor to a possible invasion, the Luftwaffe began a series of aerial attacks on Britain's coastal defences in a battle for superiority in the skies.

DATE		QTY.	ISSUE PRICE	VALUE
2015	$20 The Battle of Britain - Ardell Bourgeois	10,000	89.95	90.00
	$20 The Battle for Hong Kong	10,000	89.95	90.00
	$20 The Battle of Dieppe	10,000	89.95	90.00
	$20 The Bombing War.	10,000	89.95	90.00
	$20 The Battle of the Atlantic	10,000	89.95	90.00
	$20 The Battle for Sicily	10,000	89.95	90.00
	$20 Juno Beach on D-Day	10,000	89.95	90.00
	$20 The Battle of the Scheldt.	10,000	89.95	90.00
	$20 The Liberation of the Netherlands	10,000	89.95	90.00
	$20 Victory Day	10,000	89.95	90.00

Canadian Home Front Series, 2015

Diameter: 38.0mm; weight: 31.39g; composition: 99.99% pure silver; finish: proof; edge: serrated

Highlights the war effort on the Canadian home front across the country.

DATE		QTY.	ISSUE PRICE	VALUE
2015	$20 Transcontinental Railroad - David A. Oram 7,500		89.95	90.00
	$20 Canada's First Submarines 7,500		89.95	90.00
	$20 British Commonwealth Air Training Program 7,500		89.95	90.00
	$20 U-Boat 7,500		89.95	90.00

North American Sportfish, 2015

Diameter: 38.0mm; weight: 31.39g; composition: 99.99% pure silver; finish: proof; edge: plain with edge lettering

For the anglers and sports lovers alike. Designer: Curtis Atwater.

DATE		QTY.	ISSUE PRICE	VALUE
2015	$20 Largemouth Bass 6,500		99.95	100.00
2015	$20 Northern Pike 6,500		99.95	100.00
2015	$20 Rainbow Trout 6,500		99.95	100.00
2015	$20 Walleye 6,500		99.95	100.00

Maple Leaf Reflection, 2015

Diameter: 38.0mm; weight: 31.39g; composition: 99.99% pure silver; finish: proof; edge: serrated

No season announces its arrival quite as flamboyantly as autumn. Trees dress for the occasion, turning their leaves to vibrant yellows, reds and golds before tossing them into the air. Those who venture into the forest are treated to a close-up view of the stunning canopy overhead, dancing leaves drifting on the wind, and perhaps coming to rest on a babbling brook where they drift away like little boats. Designer: Lilyane Coulombe.

DATE		QTY.	ISSUE PRICE	VALUE
2015	$20 Maple Leaf Reflection 8,500		99.95	100.00

Forests of Canada Series, 2015

Diameter: 38.0mm; weight: 31.39g; composition: 99.99% pure silver; finish: proof; edge: serrated

With permafrost in the north, deserts to the south, and an ever-changing geography from coast to coast, Canada is home to an amazing array of forests, each with its own distinct flora and fauna.

DATE		QTY.	ISSUE PRICE	VALUE
2015	$20 Carolinian Tulip-Tree, by Julius Csotonyi 8,500		99.95	100.00
2015	$20 Coast Shore Pine, by Margaret Best 8,500		99.95	100.00

200th Anniversary of the Birth of Sir John A. Macdonald, 2015

Diameter: 38.0mm; weight: 31.39g; composition: 99.99% pure silver; finish: proof; edge: serrated

Celebrate the 200th anniversary of the birth of the nation's primary architect and first Prime Minister: Sir John A. Macdonald. Designer: William Lazos.

DATE		QTY.	ISSUE PRICE	VALUE
2015	$20 200th Anniversary of the Birth of Sir John A. Macdonald 8,500		89.95	90.00

Sir George-Étienne Cartier, 2015

Diameter: 38.0mm; weight: 31.39g; composition: 99.99% pure silver; finish: proof; edge: serrated

Celebrate Sir George-Étienne Cartier, one of Canada's most important architects of Canadian Confederation. A French-Canadian lawyer he was one of the most important political figures of Confederation and a key influencer of French-Canadian support for Canadian union. Designer: William Lazos.

DATE		QTY.	ISSUE PRICE	VALUE
2015	$20 Sir George-Étienne Cartier 8,500		89.95	90.00

Wedding, 2015

Diameter: 40.0mm; weight: 31.83g; composition: fine silver (99.99% pure) with selective gold plating; finish: proof; edge: serrated

Some traditions may differ between cultures or change across the generations, but the idea of marriage still "rings" true today as it did in the past: it is about two individuals celebrating their commitment to one another, and the deeper connection they share. Hand in hand, they mark their love with a celebration in which they vow to love one another, to be joined as one to face together life's agonies, joys, challenges and tender rewards—for these are the moments that help write the chapters of each couple's love story. Designer: Joel Kimmel.

DATE	QTY.	ISSUE PRICE	VALUE
2015 $20 Wedding. 10,000		109.95	110.00

Beaver at Work, 2015

Diameter: 38.0mm; weight: 31.39g; composition: 99.99% pure silver; finish: proof; edge: serrated

The beaver is one of Canada's most beloved and iconic animals, one that is forever tied to Canada's early history. Known for its persistence, resourcefulness and hard work, the beaver has endeared itself to Canadians. Designer: John Mardon.

DATE	QTY.	ISSUE PRICE	VALUE
2015 $20 Beaver at Work. 7,500		99.95	100.00

Ice Dancer, 2015

Diameter: 38.0mm; weight: 31.39g; composition: 99.99% pure silver; finish: proof; edge: serrated

From our first glide across the ice, we're hooked. Faster than our feet alone can carry us, we chase, explore, and spend laughing moments with our friends and family. There will be bumps, bruises, and wobbly knees, but before we know it, the hands once occupied in helping us up off the ice will clap as we glide along unaided. Based on an original painting by Douglas R. Laird.

DATE	QTY.	ISSUE PRICE	VALUE
2015	$20 Ice Dancer 7,000	99.95	100.00

UNESCO at Home and Abroad, 2015–

Diameter: 38.0mm; weight: 31.39g; composition: 99.99% pure silver; finish: proof; edge: serrated

Some of Canada's most stunning World Heritage properties with other properties around the world to illustrate how two sites of global importance share similarities while being so different. Designer: Trevor Tennant.

DATE	QTY.	ISSUE PRICE	VALUE
2015	$20 Mount Fuji & The Canadian Rockies - Trevor Tennant 7,500	89.95	90.00
2015	$20 Wood Buffalo National Park and Sichuan Giant Panda Sanctuary Lauren Cramshaw. 7,500	89.95	90.00

The Wolf, 2015

Diameter: 38.0mm; weight: 31.39g; composition: 99.99% pure silver; finish: proof; edge: serrated

Some experts believe that howling—that eerie hallmark of this unique species—is a key element of territory establishment, acting both as a warning to other packs and a call to gathering among pack members. Designer: Pierre Leduc.

DATE		QTY.	ISSUE PRICE	VALUE
2015	$20 The Wolf 7,500		99.95	100.00

100th Anniversary of *In Flanders Fields*, 2015

Diameter: 38.0mm; weight: 31.39g; composition: 99.99% pure silver; finish: proof; edge: serrated

It has become part of our collective memory of the First World War, a hauntingly beautiful poem that gives one voice to the thousands of fallen soldiers. Inspired by the tragic death of a friend during the Second Battle of Ypres in May 1915, *In Flanders Fields* by Canadian physician Lieutenant Colonel John McCrae emerged as the most popular poem of the First World War—one that is still recited around the world each year—and inspired an international effort to remember those who made the ultimate sacrifice. Designer: Laurie McGaw.

DATE		QTY.	ISSUE PRICE	VALUE
2015	$20 100th Anniversary of *In Flanders Fields* 10,000		89.95	90.00

Looney Tunes™, 2015

Diameter: 40.0mm; weight: 31.83g; composition: 99.99% pure silver; finish: proof; edge: serrated

From 1942 until the late 1960s, Looney Tunes were the most popular animated shorts to be shown in film theatres. But as the golden era wound down, television would be the one to keep the laughs going by introducing the characters and their (mis)adventures to new generations. Designer: Warner Bros.

DATE		QTY.	ISSUE PRICE	VALUE
2015	$20 Tweety Bird	12,500	109.95	110.00
2015	$20 Sylvester The Cat	12,500	109.95	110.00
2015	$20 Daffy Duck	12,500	109.95	110.00
2015	$20 Bugs Bunny	12,500	109.95	110.00

Polar Bear: Canadian Icon, 2015

Diameter: 38.0mm; weight: 31.39g; composition: 99.99% pure silver; finish: proof with jade; edge: serrated

DATE		QTY.	ISSUE PRICE	VALUE
2015	$20 Polar Bear, with jade	8,500	114.95	115.00

Looney Tunes™: Merrie Melodies, 2015

Diameter: 38.0mm; weight: 31.39g; composition: 99.9% pure silver; finish: proof; edge: serrated

Bugs Bunny stands in the centre in a true entertainer's pose, while below him sits the Tasmanian Devil. Peering over Bugs' shoulder is the amorous skunk, Pepé Le Pew and Pussyfoot. Also appearing over Bugs' shoulder is Daffy Duck and Sylvester, both bearing wide smiles. Last but not least is Tweety. Designer: Warner Bros.

DATE	QTY.	ISSUE PRICE	VALUE
2015　$20 Looney Tunes™: Merrie Melodies 12,500		109.95	110.00

Prehistoric Animals: American Scimitar Sabre-Tooth Cat, 2015

Diameter: 38.0mm; weight: 31.39g; composition: 99.99% pure silver; finish: proof; edge: serrated

The scimitar cat (Homotherium serum) is arguably one of the most awe-inspiring animals of theIce Age. Famous for its knife-like fangs, the scimitar cat's teeth were shorter than those of the better known sabre-tooth cat, Smilodon fatalis, but were equally lethal: its sabres were coarsely serrated, just like a steak knife, making them perfectly suited for slicing through the soft flesh of its prey. Designer: Julius Csotonyi.

DATE	QTY.	ISSUE PRICE	VALUE
2015　$20 Prehistoric Animals: American Scimitar Sabre-Tooth Cat　. 7,500		89.95	90.00

TORONTO 2015™ Pan Am and Parapan Am Games: United We Play!™, 2015

Diameter: 38.0mm; weight: 31.39g; composition: 99.99% pure silver; finish: proof; edge: serrated

Just as the TORONTO 2015 Pan Am/Parapan Am Games will bring together different cultures under its motto United We Play!, the coin's reverse features the symbolic representation of this theme. Each of these coins is unique as they were crafted with mokume gane*! This ancient Japanese sword-making technique was considered impossible for coins—until now! Designed by Christi Belcourt.

*Mokume Gane is an intricate, labour-intensive process that requires a high level of craftsmanship and metallurgical expertise. To achieve this effect, different metal alloys are layered and fused together to produce a mixed-metal composite; skillful manipulation then creates the distinctive patterns for which mokume gane is renowned.

DATE		QTY.	ISSUE PRICE	VALUE
2015	$20 United We Play.	8,500	139.95	140.00

TORONTO 2015™ Pan Am and Parapan Am Games: In the Spirit of Sports, 2015

Diameter: 38.0mm; weight: 31.39g; composition: 99.99% pure silver; finish: proof; edge: serrated

TORONTO 2015 will be the largest international multi-sport Games ever held on Canadian soil. From July 10 to 26 and August 7 to 15, 2015, Toronto and the Greater Golden Horseshoe region will be brimming with energy and excitement as they play host to athletes from 41 countries and territories, all brought together under the motto, United We Play!

DATE		QTY.	ISSUE PRICE	VALUE
2015	$20 In the Spirit of Sports, with hologram	8,500	124.95	125.00

Iconic Superman™ Comic Book Covers, 2015

Diameter: 38.0mm; weight: 31.39g; composition: 99.99% pure silver; finish: proof; edge: serrated

From the moment Superman first appeared in 1938, comic book covers have played a key role in telling his story. Millions of readers and moviegoers have been captivated by his adventures.

DATE		QTY.	ISSUE PRICE	VALUE
2015	$20 *Action Comics #1*	10,000	109.95	110.00
2015	$20 *Superman Unchained #2*	10,000	109.95	110.00
2015	$20 *Superman #28*	10,000	109.95	110.00

25 DOLLARS VANCOUVER 2010 WINTER GAMES

Diameter: 40 mm; weight: 27.78 grams;
composition: .925 silver, .075 Copper; edge serrated; finish: proof.

This series of 15 holographic coins will be issued five times a year in 2007, 2008 and 2009, leading up to the Vancouver 2010 Olympic Winter Games. Theme, issue date and artist are listed below each coin.

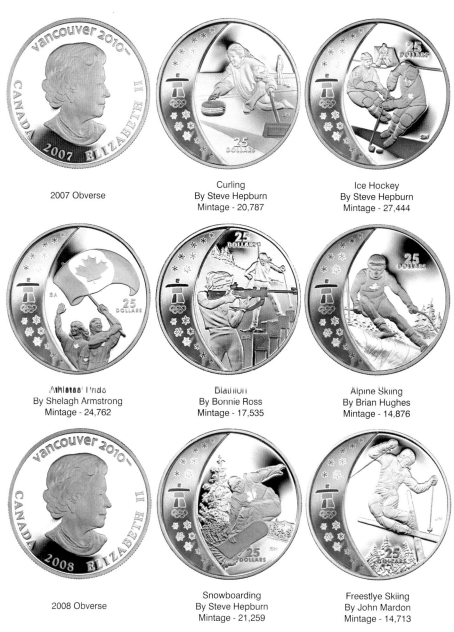

2007 Obverse	Curling By Steve Hepburn Mintage - 20,787	Ice Hockey By Steve Hepburn Mintage - 27,444
Athletes' Pride By Shelagh Armstrong Mintage - 24,762	Biathlon By Bonnie Ross Mintage - 17,535	Alpine Skiing By Brian Hughes Mintage - 14,876
2008 Obverse	Snowboarding By Steve Hepburn Mintage - 21,259	Freestlye Skiing By John Mardon Mintage - 14,713

Home of the Winter Games	Figure Skating	Bobsleigh
By Shelagh Armstrong	By Steve Hepburn	By Bonnie Ross
Mintage - 15,973	Mintage - 21,661	Mintage - 11,264

	Speed Skating	Cross Country Skiing
2009 Obverse	By Tony Bianco	By Brian Hughes
	Mintage - 17,152	Mintage - 16,730

Olympic Spirit	Skeleton	Ski Jumping
By Shelagh Armstrong	By Tony Bianco	By John Mardon
Mintage - 15,057	Mintage - 13,593	Mintage - 15,351

DATE		ISSUE PRICE	VALUE
2007	$25 All five designs (Artist and Mintage are listed below each coin)	69.95	75.00
2008	$25 All five designs (Artist and Mintage are listed below each coin)	69.95	75.00
2009	$25 All five designs (Artist and Mintage are listed below each coin)	69.95	75.00

FINE SILVER HOLOGRAM 25 DOLLARS

Diameter: 38 mm; weight: 31.39 grams;
composition: .9999 silver; edge: reeded; finish: proof.

Wayne & Walter Gretzky, 2011

As a child, Wayne Gretzky practiced for hours on end, spending every available moment skating, shooting and practicing his stick-handling. When he was six years old, his father built him a skating rink in the backyard. Reverse design by Glen Green.

DATE		QTY.	ISSUE PRICE	VALUE
2011	$25 Wayne & Walter Gretzky	6,715	99.99	100.00

O CANADA, Iconic Images, 2013-2014

DATE		QTY.	ISSUE PRICE	VALUE
2013	$25 Beaver	8,500	89.95	90.00
2013	$25 Polar Bear	8,500	89.95	90.00
2013	$25 Wolf	8,500	89.95	90.00
2013	$25 The Caribou	8,500	89.95	90.00
2014	$25 Orca	8,500	89.95	90.00

Moon Mask, 2013–2014

Diameter: 36.15mm; weight: 30.76g; composition: fine silver; finish: proof ; edge: plain

First Nations culture is rich with profound wisdom that eloquently expresses the inter-connectedness between humanity and all of nature. The terms "Mother Earth" and "Grandmother Moon" clearly reflect the similarities that First Nations people see between these two spheres and the foundational and nourishing role women play in their communities.

DATE		QTY.	ISSUE PRICE	VALUE
2013	$25 Grandmother Moon Mask................................6,000		164.95	165.00
2014	$25 Matriarch Moon Mask....................................6,000		149.95	150.00

Canada: An Allegory, 2013

The reverse image by Canadian artist Laurie McGaw features an iconic rendering of a new Canada allegory for modern-day Canada. Seated on the "throne" of the Canadian Shield, this classically dressed, seated female figure occupies the centre of the reverse field.

DATE		QTY.	ISSUE PRICE	VALUE
2013	$25 Canada: An Allegory....................................8,500		89.95	90.00

O Canada Series, 2014

Diameter: 38.0mm; weight: 31.39g; composition: fine silver; finish: proof; edge: serrated

Canada spans an entire continent and is bordered by oceans on three sides. Its landscapes, fauna and flora are incredibly diverse, as are the people who live here.

DATE		QTY.	ISSUE PRICE	VALUE
2014	$25 The Igloo (January) by Yves Bérubé 8,500		89.95	90.00
2014	$25 Scenic Skiing in Canada (March) by Kendra Dixson 8,500		89.95	90.00
2014	$25 Under the Maple Tree (May) by Claudio D'Angelo 8,500		89.95	90.00
2014	$25 Cowboy in the Canadian Rockies (July) by Bernie Brown 8,500		89.95	90.00
2014	$25 The Arctic Fox and the Northern Lights (October) 8,500		89.95	90.00

75th Anniversary of the First Royal Visit, 2014

Diameter: 38.0mm; weight: 38.70g; composition: fine silver; finish: proof; edge: plain

History was made when King George VI and Queen Elizabeth visited Canada in 1939. It was the first time a reigning monarch had ever traveled to North America, and for a young nation eager to flex its muscles of independence, the royal tour provided the perfect opportunity.

DATE		QTY.	ISSUE PRICE	VALUE
2014	$25 75th Anniversary of the First Royal Visit 6,000		149.95	150.00

Canada Lynx, 2014

Diameter: 36.15mm; weight: 30.76g; composition: 99.99% pure silver; finish: proof; edge: plain

Native to the boreal forests that stretch from Yukon to Newfoundland-and-Labrador, the Canada lynx (Lynx canadensis) is one of the most common wild cats in Canada. Yet, encounters with this stealthy, agile predator remain rare. Designer: Pierre Leduc.

DATE		QTY.	ISSUE PRICE	VALUE
2014	$25 Canada Lynx 6,000		149.95	150.00

Christmas Ornament, 2014

Diameter: 36.15mm; weight: 30.76g; composition: 99.99% pure silver; finish: proof; edge: plain

Bring a sparkle to someone's holiday season with all the beauty and magic of a traditional holiday ornament. Designer: Three Degrees Creative Group.

DATE		QTY.	ISSUE PRICE	VALUE
2014	$25 Christmas Ornament. 6,000		129.95	130.00

Star Charts, 2015

Diameter: 40.0mm; weight: 31.83g; composition: 99.99% pure silver; finish: proof; edge: serrated

The seven stars that make up the Big Dipper are arguably one of the most recognized formations in the night sky. They are visible year-round from northern latitudes, and have inspired countless legends around the globe. Designed by Western Ojibwa artist Cyril Assiniboine.

DATE		QTY.	ISSUE PRICE	VALUE
2015	$25 The Quest	7,500	104.95	105.00
2015	$25 Wounded Bear	7,500	104.95	105.00
2015	$25 Great Ascent	7,500	104.95	105.00
2015	$25 Eternal Pursuit	7,500	104.95	105.00

Singing Moon Mask, 2015

Diameter: 36.07mm; weight: 30.76g; composition: 99.99% pure silver; finish: proof; edge: plain

Singing is an integral part of First Nations cultures throughout North America—so integral in fact, that many Aboriginal languages don't have a word for "music." People sing day or night to thank Mother Earth for all her gifts; to express love; to heal the sick; to ask for a successful hunt; to seek guidance. Designer: Andy Everson.

DATE		QTY.	ISSUE PRICE	VALUE
2015	$25 *Singing Moon* Mask - Set (proof, antique and enamel)	3,000	359.95	360.00

Canada Flag, 2015

Diameter: 27mm; weight: 0.256 troy ounces; composition: 99.99% pure silver; finish: specimen

50th anniversary of the National Flag of Canada. This is the very first $25 coin offered at face value

DATE		QTY.	ISSUE PRICE	VALUE
2015	$25 Canada Flag	225,000	25.00	25.00

STERLING SILVER 30 DOLLARS

Diameter: 40 mm; weight: 31.5 grams;
composition: .925 silver, .075 copper; edge serrated; finish: proof

Totem Pole	National War Memorial	Canadarm
Beaumont Hamel	Dog Sled Team	National Vimy Memorial
Panoramic Camera - Niagara Falls	Imax - Canadian Achievements	International Year of Astronomy

DATE		QTY.	ISSUE PRICE	VALUE
2005	$30 Totem Pole, by Dr. Richard Hunt	10,000	79.95	80.00
2006	$30 National War Memorial, by Vernon March	8,876	79.95	120.00
2006	$30 Canadarm, by Cecily Mok	9,357	79.95	100.00
2006	$30 Beaumont Hamel, by RCM Engravers	5,654	79.95	120.00
2006	$30 Dog Sled Team, by Arnold Nogy	7,384	89.95	150.00
2007	$30 National Vimy Memorial, by RCM Engravers	5,336	79.95	90.00
2007	$30 Panoramic Camera Niagara Falls, by Chris Jordison	5,702	84.95	90.00
2008	$30 Imax, final in Canadian achievements series	3,861	84.95	90.00
2009	$30 International Year of Astronomy, by Colin Mayne	7,174	89.95	95.00

Canadian Contemporary Art, 2014

Diameter: 54.0mm; weight: 62.7g; composition: fine silver; finish: proof ; edge: serrated

Explore Canada as you've never seen it before with this captivating coin that draws you in to discover more than 50 images that are Canadian icons in their own right, or reflective of the artist's personal Canadian experiences—like time spent under the Yukon's midnight sun, as shown within the centre of this coin. Designer: Tim Barnard, and is titled "Canada Through the Eyes of Tim Barnard."

DATE		QTY.	ISSUE PRICE	VALUE
2014	$30 Canadian Contemporary Art	5,000	169.95	170.00

Canadian Machine Gunner in Training - 75th Anniversary of the Declaration of the Second World War, 2014

Diameter: 54.0mm; weight: 62.67g; composition: 99.99% pure silver; finish: proof; edge: serrated

The economic hardships of the Great Depression had left Canada's military undermanned and unprepared for the onset of war, and its equipment was at risk of being outdated. Thanks to a national recruitment drive, over 58,000 men and women enlisted by the month's end. In December, units of the 1st Canadian Infantry Division set sail from Halifax to Britain–the first wave of Canadians who would serve overseas until the war's end in 1945. Designer: Silvia Pecota.

DATE		QTY.	ISSUE PRICE	VALUE
2014	$30 Second World War	5,000	169.95	170.00

Grand Trunk Pacific Railway, 2014

Diameter: 54.0mm; weight: 62.67g; composition: 99.99% pure silver; finish: proof; edge: serrated

A century ago, the transcontinental railway enabled the settlement of western Canada. The Grand Trunk Pacific Railway—a massive early twentieth-century engineering feat that linked eastern Canada to the Pacific. Designer: Joel Kimmel.

DATE		QTY.	ISSUE PRICE	VALUE
2014	$30 Grand Trunk Pacific Railway	5,000	169.95	170.00

Canadian Monuments: National Aboriginal Veterans Monument, 2014

Diameter: 54.0mm; weight: 62.67g; composition: 99.99% pure silver; finish: proof; edge: serrated

The National Aboriginal Veterans Monument, located in Ottawa's Confederation Park, pays tribute to the military contributions that Canadian Aboriginal men and women have made throughout Canadian history. Designer: Noel Lloyd Pinay.

DATE		QTY.	ISSUE PRICE	VALUE
2014	$30 Canadian Monuments: National Aboriginal Veterans Monument	5,000	169.95	170.00

Glow-in-the-Dark Coin – Moonlight Fireflies, 2015

Diameter: 54.0mm; weight: 62.7g; composition: 99.9% pure silver; finish: proof; edge: serrated

They are mysterious, elusive, almost magical; when twilight descends, these little creatures suddenly make their presence known as they fly lazily in the hot summer air, flickering and twinkling like miniature shooting stars that seem to be within reach. Fireflies (Lampyridae) prefer to live in moist environments, which is why many cherish childhood memories of trying to catch them while camping in forested areas or spending time near Canada's many lakes and rivers. Designer: Ervin Molnar.

DATE	QTY.	ISSUE PRICE	VALUE
2015 $30 Moonlight Fireflies 4,000		189.95	190.00

Canada's Merchant Navy in the Battle of the Atlantic, 2015

Diameter: 54.0mm; weight: 62.7g; composition: 99.99% pure silver; finish: proof; edge: serrated

"The Battle of the Atlantic was not won by any navy or air force, it was won by the courage, fortitude and determination of the British and Allied merchant navy." – Rear Admiral Leonard Murray, Commander-in-Chief Canadian North Atlantic. Designer: Ervin Molnar.

DATE	QTY.	ISSUE PRICE	VALUE
2015 $30 Canada's Merchant Navy in the Battle of the Atlantic 5,000		169.95	170.00

SILVER 50 DOLLARS

Diameter: 65 mm; weight: 155.5 grams;
composition: .9999 silver; edge serrated; finish: proof
Images reduced by 25%

The Four Seasons, 2006

The Four Seasons — winter, spring, autumn and summer — are most evident in the north and south temperate zones where the changing climate creates vastly different worlds that define the way people live. Reverse by Tony Bianco.

Queen's Diamond Wedding 60th Anniversary, 2007

This 5 ounce fine silver coin was issued in commemoration of the Queens diamond wedding 60th anniversary, with reverse design by Steve Hepburn.

DATE		QTY.	ISSUE PRICE	VALUE
2006	$50 Four Seasons	1,999	299.95	600.00
2007	$50 Diamond Wedding Anniversary	1,945	299.95	400.00

SILVER 50 DOLLARS

Diameter: 65 mm; weight: 157.77 grams;
composition: .9999 silver; edge serrated; finish: proof
Images reduced by 25%

100th Anniversary of the Royal Canadian Mint, 2008

This 5 ounce fine silver coin was issued in commemoration of the 100th Anniversary of the Royal Canadian Mint, with reverse design by the RCM engravers.

150th Anniversary - Construction of the Parliament Buildings Begins, 2009

Issued in commemoration of the 150th Anniversary of the start of construction of the Parliament buildings, with reverse design by the RCM engravers.

75th Anniversary of the First Bank Notes, 2010

The Bank of Canada's inaugural notes were introduced on March 11, 1935 and included denominations of $1, $2, $5, $10, $20, $50, $100, $500 and $1,000 with a $25 note issued later that year to commemorate the silver jubilee of King George V. Reverse design by the RCM engravers.

DATE		QTY.	ISSUE PRICE	VALUE
2008	$50 150th Anniversary of the RCM	2,078	369.95	400.00
2009	$50 150th Anniversary - Construction of the Parliament Buildings	910	459.95	500.00
2010	$50 75th Anniversary of the First Bank Notes	1,991	389.95	500.00

Calgary Stampede (1912–2012)

Diameter: 65.25 mm; weight: 157.6 grams; composition: .9999 silver; 5 troy ounces

The Stampede is known around the world as "The Greatest Outdoor Show on Earth". A cowboy on a bucking bronco, set amidst lavishly engraved western details.

DATE	QTY.	ISSUE PRICE	VALUE
2012 $50 Calgary Stampede	1,500	495.95	500.00

Queen's Coronation, 2013

Diameter: 65.25 mm; weight: 157.6 grams; composition: .9999 silver; 5 troy ounces

This is the first ever coloured five ounce pure silver coin issued by the Royal Canadian Mint, and the Mint's largest coloured coin ever issued in Canada. The image used on this coin is the official coronation photograph taken by Cecil Beaton on June 2, 1953.

DATE	QTY.	ISSUE PRICE	VALUE
2013 $50 Queen's Coronation	1,500	524.95	525.00

HMS *Shannon* & USS *Chesapeake*, 2013

Diameter: 65.25 mm; weight: 157.6 grams; composition: .9999 silver; 5 troy ounces

The reverse image depicts the final moments of the famous battle of HMS *Shannon*, pictured on the right, and the battle-worn USS *Chesapeake*, pictured on the left with its decks ablaze and gun-ports destroyed.

DATE		QTY.	ISSUE PRICE	VALUE
2013	$50 HMS *Shannon* & USS *Chesapeake* 1,500		499.95	500.00

25th Anniversary of the Silver Maple Leaf Coin, 2013

Diameter: 65.25 mm; weight: 157.6 grams; composition: .9999 silver; 5 troy ounces

This coin was designed by Arnold Nogy and features a variation on the original Silver Maple Leaf bullion coin. The design depicts two small sugar maple leaves overlapping the bottom lobes of one large sugar maple leaf.

DATE		QTY.	ISSUE PRICE	VALUE
2013	$50 Silver Maple Leaf...................................... 2,500		499.95	500.00

25th Anniversary Of The Silver Maple Leaf, 2013

Diameter: 65.25mm; weight: 157.6g; composition: fine silver
finish: matte proof with selective gold plating; edge: serrated

When the first Silver Maple Leaf bullion coin was introduced in 1988, the coin's beauty and purity made it an instant success. Since that first release, the Silver Maple Leaf bullion coin has been minted annually with one troy ounce (31.1 grams) of 9999 fine silver and a face value of 5 dollars—the highest face value on the market for any comparable silver bullion coin. Designer: Jean-Louis Sirois.

DATE		QTY.	ISSUE PRICE	VALUE
2013	$50 25th Anniversary of the Silver Maple Leaf	2,000	549.95	550.00

Maple Leaves, 2014

Diameter: 65.25mm; weight: 157.6g; composition: fine silver; finish: proof; edge: serrated

As a symbol of Canada, the maple leaf evokes freedom for people around the world. It's an ideal that has lured untold multitudes across great open waters to a New World; its vast, unknown and untamed nature diminished by the people's resolution to start anew, to turn a new leaf. Designer: Luc Normandin.

DATE		QTY.	ISSUE PRICE	VALUE
2014	$50 Maple Leaves	2,500	519.95	520.00

$50 for $50 Coins

Diameter: 34.0mm; weight: 15.87g; composition: fine silver; finish: matte proof ; edge: serrated

DATE		QTY.	ISSUE PRICE	VALUE
2014	$50 Polar Bear by Emily Damstra	100,000	50.00	50.00
2014	$50 Snowy Owl by Trevor Tennant	90,000	50.00	50.00
2015	$50 Beaver by Emily Damstra		50.00	50.00

Swimming Beaver, 2014

Diameter: 65.0mm; weight: 157.6g; composition: fine silver; finish: proof; edge: serrated

Castor canadensis played a major role in Canada's colonial history, becoming one of the primary motivators for the European explorers of the 17th century to forego their search for a passage to Asia and focus instead on the natural resources offered by the North American continent. With fur at its zenith in European fashions, beaver pelt hats became a product lucrative enough to feed settlement of the "new" continent by England and France. Designer: Emily Damstra.

DATE		QTY.	ISSUE PRICE	VALUE
2014	$50 Swimming Beaver	1,500	519.95	520.00

The Legend of the Spirit Bear, 2014

Diameter: 65.25mm; weight: 157.6g; composition: fine silver; finish: proof; edge: serrated

An original work by Coast Salish First Nation's artist Darlene Gait that recounts the fascinating legend of Spirit Bear.

DATE		QTY.	ISSUE PRICE	VALUE
2014	$50 The Legend of the Spirit Bear 1,500		499.95	500.00

100th Anniversary of In Flanders Fields, 2015

Diameter: 65.25mm; weight: 62.7g; composition: 99.99% pure silver; finish: proof; edge: serrated

The year 2015 marks the 100th anniversary of the poem In Flanders Fields, which was written by Canadian physician Lieutenant Colonel John McCrae amid the horrors of the Second Battle of Ypres in May 1915. Through his hauntingly poignant poem, McCrae succeeded in giving a voice to the 60,000 Canadians who would lose their lives in the First World War, and ignited an international effort to keep their legacy alive. Designer: Tony Bianco.

DATE		QTY.	ISSUE PRICE	VALUE
2015	$50 100th Anniversary of In Flanders Fields. 1,500		519.95	520.00

Lustrous Maple Leaves, 2015

Diameter: 65.25mm; weight: 157.6g; composition: 99.99% pure silver; finish: proof; edge: serrated

Every nation has symbols that convey its character to the world, but one symbol usually dominates over all the others. For Canada, that symbol is the maple leaf. Designer: Michelle Grant.

DATE		QTY.	ISSUE PRICE	VALUE
2015	$50 Lustrous Maple Leaves (hologram)...........................1,500		519.95	520.00

50th Anniversary of the Canadian Flag Rectangular Coin, 2015

Size: 49.8 x 28.8mm; weight: 47.34g; composition: 99.99% pure silver; finish: proof; edge: serrated

With its bright red maple leaf, the famous red-and-white flag stands as a proud symbol for Canadians. As our national banner, it speaks of our sense of belonging to a broader community, one that is a growing, vibrant mosaic of different cultures, languages and beliefs!

DATE		QTY.	ISSUE PRICE	VALUE
2015	$50 50th Anniversary of the Canadian Flag 10,000		159.95	160.00

SILVER 100 DOLLARS
Wildlife in Motion Series, 2013–
$100 for $100 Coins
Diameter: 40 mm; weight: 31.6 grams; composition: .9999 silver; 1 troy ounce

Reverse images by Canadian artist Claudio D'Angelo.

DATE		QTY.	ISSUE PRICE	VALUE
2013	$100 Bison Stampede	50,000	100.00	100.00
2014	$100 Majestic Bald Eagle	50,000	100.00	100.00
2014	$100 The Grizzly	50,000	100.00	100.00
2014	$100 Rocky Mountain Big Horned Sheep	50,000	100.00	100.00
2015	$100 Canadian Horse	45,000	100.00	100.00

100th Anniversary of the Declaration of the First World War, 2013

Diameter: 76.20mm; weight: 311.5 grams; finish: proof; composition: .9999 silver; edge: serrated

100th anniversary of the declaration of the First World War. The reverse image is an emotional tribute to those who left their homeland–and their loved ones–to serve as part of the First Contingent of the Canadian Expeditionary Force. Design by Yves Bérubé.

DATE	QTY.	ISSUE PRICE	VALUE
2014 $100 100th Anniversary of the Declaration of the First World War 1,000		899.95	900.00

Majestic Maple Leaves, 2014

Diameter: 76.25mm; weight: 311.5g; composition: 99.99% pure silver; finish: proof; edge: serrated

The maple leaf is a powerful national symbol—one distinct and elegant shape that captures much of Canada's nature—winters that have influenced the way the world views this land and its people; breathtaking autumn colours that have captured the hearts of artists for centuries and continue to lure people into the forest; a land of opportunity to build a new life and enjoy the prosperity of free enterprise. Designer: Pierre Leduc

DATE	QTY.	ISSUE PRICE	VALUE
2014 $100 Majestic Maple Leaves 2,000		899.95	900.00

SILVER 125 DOLLARS
Howling Wolf, 2014

Diameter: 85.0mm; weight: 500.0g; composition: fine silver; finish: proof ; edge: serrated; illustration at 50%

Some experts believe that howling—that eerie hallmark of this unique species—is a key element of territory establishment, acting both as a warning to other packs and a call to gathering among pack members. Designer: Pierre Leduc.

DATE		QTY.	ISSUE PRICE	VALUE
2014	$125 Howling Wolf 1,000		1,099.95	1,100.

Growling Cougar, 2015

Diameter: 85.0mm; weight: 500.0g; composition: 99.99% pure silver; finish: proof; edge: serrated ; illustration at 50%

Across the wilds of western North and South America stalks the world's fourth-largest cat: the cougar. Found in remote areas from southern Canada to Patagonia, the elusive Puma concolor enjoys the greatest range of any large wild animal in the entire Western hemisphere. This massive tawny cat—about the size of a leopard—stalks the landscapes where its prey lives: from the seaside to the Rocky Mountains, from deserts to boreal forests. Designer: Pierre Leduc.

DATE		QTY.	ISSUE PRICE	VALUE
2015	$125 Growling Cougar 1,000		1,099.95	1,100

Canadian Horse, 2015

Diameter: 85.35mm; weight: 500.00g; composition: 99.99% pure silver; finish: proof; edge: serrated ; illustration at 50%

The year 2015 marks the 350th anniversary of the introduction of the Canadian horse. Robust, resilient, and good natured it has survived near extinction to emerge as one of Canada's official national symbols. Designer: Michelle Grant.

DATE		QTY.	ISSUE PRICE	VALUE
2015	$125 Canadian Horse 1,000		1,099.95	1,100

SILVER 200 DOLLARS
"Landscapes of the North" Series, 2015

Diameter: 50.00mm; weight: 63.07g; composition: 99.99% pure silver; finish: matte proof; edge: serrated

DATE		QTY.	ISSUE PRICE	VALUE
2014	$200 Towering Forests - Ellen Cowie	20,000	200.00	200.00
2015	$200 Coastal Waters Ellen Cowie	25,000	200.00	200.00

SILVER 250 DOLLARS — FINE SILVER KILO COIN
Diameter: 101.6 mm; weight: 1000 grams;
composition: .9999 silver; edge: plain; finish: proof.
Images reduced by 60%

Vancouver 2010 Olympic Winter Games, 2007-2010

These coins are struck in ultra high relief and are the first one kilo silver coins ever produced by the RCM.

DATE		QTY.	ISSUE PRICE	VALUE
2007	$250 Early Canada, by Stanley Witten	2,450	1,299.95	1,500
2008	$250 Towards Confederation, By Susan Taylor	282	1,299.95	1,500
2009	$250 Surviving the Flood, By Xwa Lack Tun	874	1,599.95	1,600
2009	$250 The Canada of Today, By design team of the Vancouver Org.	985	1,599.95	1,600
2010	$250 The Eagle, proof, by Xwa Lack Tun	634	1,649.95	1,750
2010	$250 The Eagle, antiqued, by Xwa Lack Tun	203	1,649.95	1,750
2010	$250 The Eagle, enamel, by Xwa Lack Tun	431	1,649.95	1,750

125th Anniversary of Banff National Park, 2010

Diameter: 101.8 mm; weight: 1000 grams; composition: .9999 silver; edge: plain; finish: proof.
Images reduced by 60%

The reverse design of this coin features a montage depicting the history and development of Banff National Park set among the park's majestic mountains and lakes. Reverse designed by Tony Bianco.

DATE		QTY.	ISSUE PRICE	VALUE
2010	$250 125th Anniversary of Banff National Park 525		1,649.95	1,750

Maple Leaf Forever, 2011–

Diameter: 102.1mm; weight: 1000.0g; composition: 99.99% fine silver; finish: proof ; edge: serrated

A trilogy of maple leaves inspired by the design of Canada's one cent circulation coin since 1937. Reverse designed by Debbie Adams.

DATE		QTY.	ISSUE PRICE	VALUE
2011	$250 Maple Leaf Forever 997		2,195.95	2,200
2012	$250 Maple Leaf Forever 1,200		2,249.95	2,250
2013	$250 Maple Leaf Forever 600		2,249.95	2,250
2014	$250 Maple Leaf Forever with coloured enamel, by Pierre Leduc 600		2,299.95	2,300
2015	$250 Maple Leaf Forever by Celia Godkin 500		2,299.95	2,300

375th Anniversary of Lacrosse, 2011

Lacrosse is sport, legend, culture and history combined, a unique feature of the Canadian identity that emerged when European colonists encountered First Nations society. Reverse designed by Steve Hepburn.

DATE		QTY.	ISSUE PRICE	VALUE
2011	$250 375th Anniversary of Lacrosse 591		2,195.95	2,200

Chinese Lunar Calendar, 2012–

Diameter: 102.1mm; weight: 1000.0g; composition: fine silver; finish: proof ; edge: serrated

Reverse designed by Three Degrees Creative Group Inc.

DATE		QTY.	ISSUE PRICE	VALUE
2012	$250 Year of the Dragon 1,579		2,195.95	2,200
2013	$250 Year of the Snake 888		2,249.95	2,250
2014	$250 Year of the Horse 388		2,249.95	2,250
2015	$250 Year of the Sheep 388		2,288.88	2,289

The Moose Family – Robert Bateman, 2012

Diameter: 102.1mm; weight: 1000g; composition: .9999 silver; 32.15 troy ounces

The year 2012 marks the 50th anniversary of the Canadian Wildlife Federation (CWF), an organization that has achieved exceptional results in conserving Canadian wilderness and Canadians about environmental issues that concern us all. Robert Bateman, the coin designer, is a world-renowned wildlife artist and an unflagging proponent of wildlife conservation and education. The reverse image features a detail from Robert Bateman's painting, *The Moose Family*.

DATE	QTY.	ISSUE PRICE	VALUE
2012 $250 The Moose Family, Proof 1,000		2,249.95	2,250

Canada's Arctic Landscape, 2013

The reverse design by Canadian artist W. David Ward presents a highly detailed portrait of the north shore of Baffin Island, overlooking Lancaster Sound, at the mouth of the Northwest Passage.

DATE	QTY.	ISSUE PRICE	VALUE
2013 $250 Canada's Arctic Landscape 750		2,249.95	2,250

250th Anniversary of the end of the Seven Years War, 2013

Canadian artist Luc Normandin designed the reverse which features a period map inspired by Didier Robert de Vaugondy, a renowned map maker of the mid 1700's.

Battle of Chateauguay, 2013

Reproduction of the illustration Bataille de Chateauguay (Battle of Chateauguay) by celebrated Canadian artist Henri Julien.

The Caribou, 2013

The reverse image by Canadian artist Trevor Tennant features a male and a female caribou standing together on the grassy bank of a broad river.

DATE		QTY.	ISSUE PRICE	VALUE
2013	$250 Seven Years War	500	2,249.95	2,250
2013	$250 Battle of Chateauguay	500	2,249.95	2,250
2013	$250 The Caribou	500	2,249.95	2,250

In The Eyes Of The Snowy Owl, 2014

Diameter: 102.1mm; weight: 1,000.0g; composition: fine silver; finish: proof ; edge: serrated

Few animals can match the owl for the intensity of its gaze. Unlike other birds, an owl's eyes are located on the front of its head, an adaptation that heightens its depth perception for targeting prey, which it can spot over tremendous distances. Designer: Arnold Nogy.

DATE		QTY.	ISSUE PRICE	VALUE
2014	$250 In the Eyes of the Snowy Owl	500	2,299.95	2,300

The Battle of Lundy's Lane, 2014

Diameter: 102.1mm; weight: 1,000g; composition: fine silver (99.99% pure); finish: proof ; edge: serrated

As the War of 1812 waged on, American and British North American forces continued to battle one another for territorial gains. On July 25, 1814, troops from both sides came face-to-face in an explosive encounter that would bring an end to one last attempted invasion of Upper Canada.

DATE		QTY.	ISSUE PRICE	VALUE
2014	$250 The Battle of Lundy's Lane	400	2,249.95	2,250

In the Eyes of the Cougar, 2015

Diameter: 102.1mm; weight: 1,000.0g; composition: 99.99% pure silver; finish: proof; edge: serrated

Few would contest the cougar's reputation as a stealthy hunter that relies on its keen senses to survive in remote areas of western Canada. Its exceptional vision is uniquely adapted to allow the cougar to hunt its prey during any time of day. Designer: Glen Loates.

DATE		QTY.	ISSUE PRICE	VALUE
2015	$250 In the Eyes of the Cougar	500	2,299.95	2,300

SILVER 500 DOLLARS — FINE SILVER 5KG COIN
The Spirit of Haida Gwaii, 2012

Diameter: 180 mm; weight: 5000 grams;
composition: .9999 silver; edge: plain; finish: proof

Coin features 'The Spirit of Haida Gwaii' design from the masterpiece by Bill Reid, one of Canada's most accomplished and renowned artists.

DATE		QTY.	ISSUE PRICE	VALUE
2012	$500 The Spirit of Haida Gwaii 100		9,999.95	10,000

Great Canadian Artists:
Emily Carr's Tsatsisnukomi, B.C. (1912), 1913

Diameter: 180.0mm; weight: 5,000.0g; composition: fine silver; finish: proof ; edge: serrated

Emily Carr (1871-1945) was and internationally renowned artist at a time when women had few opportunities. With a profound love of nature and a deep respect and understanding of British Columbia's First Nation cultures, Carr produced a groundbreaking body of work that captivates and enlightens to this day.

DATE		QTY.	ISSUE PRICE	VALUE
2013	$500 Emily Carr's Tsatsisnukomi, B.C., 1912 100		10,500.00	10,500

Canadian Monuments: National Aboriginal Veterans Monument, 2014

Diameter: 180.00mm; weight: 5,000.00g; composition: 99.99% pure silver; finish: proof; edge: serrated

The National Aboriginal Veterans Monument, located in Ottawa's Confederation Park, pays tribute to the military contributions that Canadian Aboriginal men and women have made throughout Canadian history. Designer: Noel Lloyd Pinay.

DATE		QTY.	ISSUE PRICE	VALUE
2014	$500 Canadian Monuments: National Aboriginal Veterans Monument. . .	150	10,500.00	10,500

PLATINUM 5 Dollars
Portrait of Nanaboozhoo, 2014

Diameter: 16.0mm; weight: 3.13g; composition: 99.95% pure platinum; finish: proof ; edge: serrated

Actual size

Storytelling has long been a rich oral tradition for Aboriginal cultures. It is said that from the first snowfall to the first clap of thunder, elders impart history, traditions and life lessons to the younger generation through rich narratives filled with allegories and imagery. For the Anishinaabe, an important cultural character is Nanaboozhoo; as a shape-shifting spirit, he teaches right from wrong through his adventures while offering lessons on how to live in harmony with the natural world. Designed by Cyril Assiniboine, a renowned self-taught Ojibwa artist and a pow-wow dancer.

DATE	QTY.	ISSUE PRICE	VALUE
2014 $5 Portrait of Nanaboozhoo.............................3,000		299.95	300.00

Cougar, 2014

Diameter: 16.0mm; weight: 3.13g; composition: 99.95% platinum; finish: proof; edge: serrated

Actual size

The cougar is one of Canada's most powerful, elusive and beautiful predators. The animal's powerful, intimidating golden eyes ringed in dark tones, blunt muzzle spiked with long whiskers, short round ears, and dense fur are presented in full detail, bringing the intensity of the moment fully to life. Glen Loates (reverse), Susanna Blunt (obverse)

DATE	QTY.	ISSUE PRICE	VALUE
2014 $5 Cougar...3,000		299.95	300.00

Overlaid Majestic Maple Leaves

Diameter: 16.0mm; weight: 3.13g; composition: 99.95% platinum; finish: proof; edge: serrated

Actual size

The maple leaf is a powerful national symbol—one with a distinct and elegant shape that captures much of Canada's nature—winters that have influenced the way the world views this land and its people; breathtaking autumn colours that have captured the hearts of artists for centuries—but most of all, it symbolizes a land of opportunity to build a new life and enjoy the prosperity of free enterprise. Designer: Pierre Leduc.

DATE	QTY.	ISSUE PRICE	VALUE
2014 $5 Overlaid Majestic Maple Leaves 3,000		299.95	300.00

Bald Eagle, 2014

Diameter: 16.0mm; weight: 3.13g; composition: 99.95% platinum; finish: proof; edge: serrated

Actual size

The great Bald Eagle is an amazing predator whose image has become synonymous with the notions of freedom, majesty, strength and individualism in North America. Designer: Derek Wicks.

DATE	QTY.	ISSUE PRICE	VALUE
2014 $5 Bald Eagle 3,000		299.95	300.00

Platinum 300 Dollars Coin, 2007–2010

Diameter: 30 mm; weight: 31.16 grams; composition: .9995 platinum;
finish: proof; edge: reeded

Woolly Mammoth, 2007

The first coin in an upscale series featuring prehistoric animals, this series provides an opportunity to collect a 1 oz platinum coin independent of a set. The reverse was designed by the engravers of the Royal Canadian Mint.

Scimitar Cat, 2008

With large, razor-sharp fangs, the scimitar cat (Homotherium serum) is arguably one of the most awe-inspiring animals of the Ice Age. Image courtesy of Tyrell Museum.

Steppe Bison, 2009

The Steppe Bison lived on the plains of Eastern Beringia, a large tract of land that emerges between Alaska and Northeast Siberia whenever an Ice Age locks much of the earth's seawater in ice sheets on land. Palaeontologists estimate it died out about 11,000 years ago. Image courtesy of the Canadian Museum of Nature.

Ground Sloth, 2010

The ground sloth is one of North America's most unusual prehistoric animals. Its peculiar bones are an intriguing and welcome find for paleontologists; so remarkable that President Thomas Jefferson felt compelled to present specimens he had received to Philadelphia's American Philosophical Society in 1797. This discussion inspired vertebrate paleontology in North America and the species Megalonyx jeffersonii is named for the third President. Designed by Kerri Burnett.

DATE		QTY.	ISSUE PRICE	VALUE
2007	$300 Woolly Mammoth	287	2,995.95	3,500
2008	$300 Scimitar Cat	200	3,419.95	4,000
2009	$300 Steppe Bison	197	2,995.95	3,500
2010	$300 Ground Sloth	189	2,995.95	3,500

Cougar, 2011

Cougars are known to disperse up to 1,000 km from their natal territory to establish their own hunting domains. Predators of elk, deer, sheep, young moose, and a range of smaller and domesticated animals, their biggest requirements when choosing a home are good cover, access to prey, and the privacy that allows the cougar to live the solitary life it enjoys. Design by Emily Damstra.

DATE	QTY.	ISSUE PRICE	VALUE
2011 $300 Cougar 183		2,999.95	3,000

Maple Leaf Forever, 2012–

Diameter: 30.0mm; weight: 31.16g; composition: 99.95% pure platinum; finish: proof ; edge: serrated

For much of Canada's history, a singular image has symbolized this land and its people: the maple leaf. Popularized in songs and stories, on pins, flags, arms, badges, banknotes and coins.

DATE	QTY.	ISSUE PRICE	VALUE
2012	$300 Maple Leaf Forever by Luc Normandin. .250	2,999.95	3,000
2013	$300 Maple Leaf, 25th anniversary. 250	2,999.95	3,000
2014	$300 Maple Leaf Forever by Lilyane Coulombe. 250	2,999.95	3,000

Bull Moose – Robert Bateman, 2012

Diameter: 30mm; weight: 31.16g; composition: .9995 platinum; 1 troy ounce

The year 2012 marks the 50th anniversary of the Canadian Wildlife Federation (CWF), an organization that has achieved exceptional results in conserving Canadian wilderness and Canadians about environmental issues that concern us all. Robert Bateman, the coin designer, is a world-renowned wildlife artist and an unflagging proponent of wildlife conservation and education. The reverse image features a detail from Robert Bateman's original lithograph, *Bull Moose*.

DATE	QTY.	ISSUE PRICE	VALUE
2012 $300 Bull Moose, Proof 250		2,999.95	3,000

HMS *Shannon* & USS *Chesapeake*, 2013

Diameter: 30mm; weight: 31.16g; composition: .9995 platinum; 1 troy ounce

The reverse image depicts the final moments of the famous battle of HMS *Shannon*, pictured on the right, and the battle-worn USS *Chesapeake*, pictured on the left with its decks ablaze and gun-ports destroyed.

DATE	QTY.	ISSUE PRICE	VALUE
2013 $300 HMS *Shannon* & USS *Chesapeake* 250		2,999.95	3,000

Fighting Bison, 2014

Diameter: 30.0mm; weight: 31.6g; composition: 99.95% pure platinum; finish: proof ; edge: serrated

From the time of the Ice Age until the late 1800s, the magnificent plains bison (Bison bison) reigned as the dominant land-grazing animal throughout Canada's grassland regions, from Southern Manitoba to Alberta. Moving across the landscape in large, free-roaming herds, their numbers and impressive physical attributes contributed to their widely-held reputation as a symbol of strength. Designer: Claudio D'Angelo.

DATE		QTY.	ISSUE PRICE	VALUE
2014	$300 Fighting Bison	200	2,999.95	3,000.00

Grizzly Bear, 2015

Diameter: 30.0mm; weight: 31.16g; composition: 99.95% pure platinum; finish: reverse proof; edge: serrated

The grizzly bear is one of the strongest mammals to inhabit Canada's western provinces. As a symbol of Canada's wilderness, it is an imposing animal that has been both feared and revered throughout history. Designer: Emily Damstra.

DATE		QTY.	ISSUE PRICE	VALUE
2015	$300 Grizzly Bear	250	2,999.95	3,000.00

North American Sportfish: Rainbow Trout, 2015

Diameter: 30.0mm; weight: 31.16g; composition: 99.95% pure platinum; finish: proof; edge: serrated

Known for its penchant to leap and fight on the line, the rainbow trout is one of Canada's most popular fish species among anglers. Designer: Curtis Atwater.

DATE		QTY.	ISSUE PRICE	VALUE
2015	$300 North American Sportfish: Rainbow Trout.................	200	2,999.95	3,000.00

Maple Leaf Forever, 2015

Diameter: 30.0mm; weight: 31.16g; composition: 99.95% pure platinum; finish: proof with selective gold plating; edge: serrated

For much of Canada's history, a singular image has symbolized this land and its people: the maple leaf. Popularized in songs and stories, on pins, flags, arms, badges, banknotes and coins, the glorious maple leaf. Designer: Michelle Grant.

DATE		QTY.	ISSUE PRICE	VALUE
2015	$300 Maple Leaf Forever....................................	250	2,999.95	3,000.00

BRONZE 3 DOLLARS
Canada: An Allegory, 2013

Diameter: 35.75 mm; weight: 19.2 grams; composition: bronze (95% copper, 5% tin); finish: proof

The reverse image by Canadian artist Laurie McGaw features an iconic rendering of a new Canada allegory for modern-day Canada. Seated on the "throne" of the Canadian Shield, this classically dressed, seated female figure occupies the centre of the reverse field.

DATE	QTY.	ISSUE PRICE	VALUE
2013 $3 Canada: An Allegory 15,000		34.95	35.00

UNCIRCULATED GIFT SETS

All coins have the same composition as the circulation coins.

The OH CANADA! set was introduced in 1994 and the BUNDLE OF JOY was first issued in 1995. Each set comprised 6 circulation coins (1 cent through 1 dollar) until 1997 when the two-dollar polar bear was added. Sets are sealed in pliofilm and presented in colourful display folders. In 1998 a display case was introduced to replace the folder and the name changed from BUNDLE OF JOY to TINY TREASURES.

 Coins struck at the Winnipeg mint for the 1998 and 2000 OH CANADA! and TINY TREASURES coin sets bear a **W** mint mark on the obverse. These sets are listed with a W added to the date.

Oh Canada! (1994–)

DATE	QTY. (000)	ISSUE PRICE	VALUE
SIX-COIN SETS			
1994 Loon	19	16.95	10.00
1995 Peacekeeping	51	18.95	10.00
1996 Loon	31	19.95	13.00
2012 Loon, Polar Bear	N/A	19.95	20.00
SEVEN-COIN SETS			
1997 Flying Loon, Polar Bear	84	21.95	38.00
1998 Loon, Polar Bear	84	21.95	16.00
1998W Loon, Polar Bear .. inc. above		21.95	28.00
1999 Loon, Polar Bear*	83	21.95	13.00
2000 Loon, Polar Bear*	108	21.95	13.00
2000W Loon, Polar Bear* incl. above		21.95	13.00
2001P Loon, Polar Bear	67	22.95	13.00
2002P Loon, Polar Bear	61.5	21.95	17.00
2003P Loon, Polar Bear	51	23.95	28.00
2004P Loon, Polar Bear	53	19.95	20.00
2005P Loon, Polar Bear	40	19.95	20.00
2006P Loon, Polar Bear	28	19.95	20.00
2007 Loon, Polar Bear	24	19.95	20.00
2008 Loon, Polar Bear	31	19.95	20.00
2009 Loon, Polar Bear	25	19.95	20.00
2010 Loon, Polar Bear	20	19.95	20.00
2011 Loon, Polar Bear	22	19.95	20.00
FIVE-COIN SETS			
2013 Loon, Polar Bear	N/A	19.95	20.00
2014 Loon, Polar Bear	N/A	19.95	20.00

Bundle of Joy (1995–1997)
Tiny Treasures (1998–2003)

DATE	QTY. (000)	ISSUE PRICE	VALUE
SIX-COIN SETS			
1995 Loon	36	19.95	20.00
1996 Loon	57	19.95	15.00
SEVEN-COIN SETS			
1997 Loon, Polar Bear	55	21.95	16.00
1998 Loon, Polar Bear	62	21.95	16.00
1998W Loon, Polar Bear incl. above		21.95	28.00
1999 Loon, Polar Bear*	68	21.95	14.00
2000 Loon, Polar Bear*	83	21.95	13.00
2000W Loon, Polar Bear* incl. above		21.95	14.00
2001P Loon, Polar Bear	52	22.95	13.00
2002P Loon, Polar Bear	51.5	22.95	22.50
2003P Loon, Polar Bear†	43	23.95	25.00

During the transition year 2001, some coins (1 cent to 50 cents) were struck on the new plated steel blanks while the coins in other sets were struck on the metal blanks used previously. All collectors sets for 2001 contain coins struck on the new steel blanks for the 1¢ through 50¢ values as indicated by a P mint mark on the obverse.

1997 UNC Set

A special 10th anniversary edition of the Loon dollar was struck in 1997 but was only available in the **SPECIMEN** and **OH CANADA!** sets. The reverse depicts a loon lifting in flight from the surface of a lake. No circulation loon dollars were struck for the years 1997–2000.

*In 1999 and 2000 the caribou design was available only on the reverse of the 25-cent piece in the five collectors' sets.

†A Tiny Treasures coin set was also sold with a Teddy Bear for 39.95. A mail-in card was included in both sets for a special gift from the mint.

GIFT SETS

In 2004 the Royal Canadian Mint introduced a series of brilliant uncirculated, seven-coin sets designed for the gift market. Each set features packaging designed especially for the market for which it is intended.

2004 Baby gift set

2004 Congratulations Gift Set

2004 Wedding Gift Set

2004 Holiday Gift Set

DATE		QTY. (000)	ISSUE PRICE	VALUE
2004P	Baby gift set	53.7	19.95	20.00
2004P	Birthday gift set	N/A	19.95	20.00
2004P	Congratulations gift set	22	19.95	20.00
2004P	Holiday gift set, with colourised 25¢ Santa Claus	62.7	19.95	40.00
2004P	Wedding gift set	18.6	19.95	20.00

2005 Holiday Gift Set

DATE		QTY.	ISSUE PRICE	VALUE
2005P	Baby gift set	42,245	19.95	20.00
2005P	Birthday gift set	20,227	19.95	20.00
2005P	Congratulations gift set	12,411	19.95	20.00
2005P	Holiday gift set, with colourised 25¢ Christmas Stocking	72,831	19.95	20.00
2005P	Wedding gift set	11,597	19.95	20.00

2006 Baby Gift Set   2006 Congratulations Gift Set   2006 Birthday Gift Set

2006 Wedding
Gift Set

2006 Quebec Winter
Carnival Gift Set

DATE		QTY.	ISSUE PRICE	VALUE
2006P	Baby gift set 33,786		19.95	20.00
2006P	Birthday gift set 11,984		19.95	20.00
2006P	Congratulations gift set 9,428		19.95	20.00
2006P	Quebec Winter Carnival gift set, with colourised 25¢ Bonhomme 8,200		19.95	30.00
2006P	Wedding gift set 8,012		19.95	20.00
2006P	Holiday gift set, with colourised 25¢ Santa sled and reindeer. 99,258		19.95	20.00
All sets from 2007 to 2010 include colourised 25 cent coins.				
2007	Baby gift set, 25¢ Rattle 30,726		19.95	150.00
2007	Birthday gift set, 25¢ Balloons 13,423		19.95	20.00
2007	Congratulations gift set, 25¢ Fireworks 9,671		19.95	20.00
2007	Wedding gift set, 25¢ Bouquet 10,687		19.95	20.00
2007	Holiday gift set, 25¢ Christmas tree. 66,267		19.95	20.00
2008	Baby gift set, 25¢ Teddy bear 29,819		19.95	30.00
2008	Birthday gift set, 25¢ Party hat 11,376		19.95	20.00
2008	Congratulations gift set, 25¢ Trophy 6,821		19.95	20.00
2008	Wedding gift set, 25¢ Cake 7,404		19.95	20.00
2008	Holiday gift set, 25¢ Santa 42,344		19.95	20.00
2009	Baby Gift Set, 25¢ Night time Teddy Bear .25,000		19.95	100.00
2009	Birthday Greeting Card and Coin, 25¢ Party Favours 14,000		19.95	20.00
2009	Congratulations Greeting Card and Coin, 25¢ Fireworks. 8,000		19.95	20.00
2009	Wedding Greeting Card and Coin, 25¢ Birds 11,000		19.95	20.00
2009	Thank You Greeting Card and Coin, 25¢ Flower 10,000		19.95	20.00
2010	Baby Gift Set, 25¢ Stroller. 27,048		19.95	30.00
2010	Birthday Greeting Card and Coin, 25¢ Gift Box 8,751		19.95	20.00
2010	Congratulations Greeting Card and Coin, 25¢ 4 Stars. 5,693		19.95	20.00
2010	Wedding Greeting Card and Coin, 25¢ Heart 8,194		19.95	20.00
2010	Thank You Greeting Card and Coin, 25¢ Flowers 5,932		19.95	20.00

 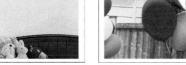  

2012 Baby Gift Set   2012 Birthday Gift Set   2012 Wedding Gift Set   2012 Tooth Fairy Gift Card

DATE		QTY.	ISSUE PRICE	VALUE
2011	Baby gift set, with special 25¢ Feet	38,576	19.95	20.00
2011	Birthday gift set, with special 25¢ Balloons	21,173	19.95	20.00
2011	Wedding gift set, with special 25¢ Wedding Bands	20,046	19.95	20.00
2011	Holiday gift set, with special 25¢ Snowflake	41,666	19.95	20.00
2011	Tooth Fairy gift card, with special 25¢ Fairy	38,200	9.95	10.00
2012	Baby Gift Set, 25¢ Toy by Gary Taxali	N/A	19.95	20.00
2012	Birthday Gift Set, 25¢ Cake by Gary Taxali	N/A	19.95	20.00
2012	Wedding Gift Set, 25¢ Wedding Bands by Gary Taxali	N/A	19.95	20.00
2012	Tooth Fairy Gift Card, 25¢ Tooth Fairy by Gary Taxali	N/A	9.95	10.00
2012	Canadian Coast Guards, 25¢ Coast Guards	N/A	24.95	25.00
2012	O Canada Gift Set, 25¢ Maple Leaf by Gary Taxali	N/A	19.95	20.00
2012	Holiday Gift Set, 25¢ Ornaments by Gary Taxali	N/A	19.95	20.00

2013 Baby Gift Set   2013 Birthday Gift Set   2013 O Canada Gift Set   2013 Wedding Gift Set

DATE		QTY.	ISSUE PRICE	VALUE
2013	Baby Gift Set, 25¢ Baby Feet	N/A	19.95	20.00
2013	Birthday Gift Set, 25¢ Cake	N/A	19.95	20.00
2013	O Canada Gift Set, 25¢ Maple Leaf	N/A	19.95	20.00
2013	Wedding Gift Set, 25¢ Wedding Bands	N/A	19.95	20.00
2013	Holiday Gift Set, 25¢ Wreath	N/A	19.95	20.00
2013	Royal Infant Gift Set, 25¢ Baby Carriage	N/A	24.95	25.00
2013	The Maple Leaf Tartan: Everyday, 50¢	N/A	14.95	15.00
2013	The War of 1812 Commemorative Gift Set	N/A	19.95	20.00

DATE		QTY.	ISSUE PRICE	VALUE
2014	Baby Gift Set, 5-coin, $1 Stork	N/A	19.95	20.00
2014	Happy Birthday Gift Set, 5-coin, $1 Gifts	N/A	19.95	20.00
2014	Wedding Gift Set, 5-coin, $1 Doves	N/A	19.95	20.00
2014	O Canada, 5-coin, $1 Maple Leaf	N/A	19.95	20.00

DATE		QTY.	ISSUE PRICE	VALUE
2015	O Canada, 5-coin, $1 Maple Leaf	N/A	19.95	20.00
2015	Married in 2015 Gift Set, 5-coin, $1 Swans	N/A	19.95	20.00
2015	Born in 2015 Gift Set, 5-coin, $1 Teddy Bear	N/A	19.95	20.00
2015	Happy Birthday Gift Set, 5-coin, $1 Balloons	N/A	19.95	20.00

HOCKEY GIFT SETS

DATE		QTY.	ISSUE PRICE	VALUE
2006P	Montreal Canadians gift set, with colourised 25¢ Montreal 69,697		24.95	25.00
2006P	Ottawa Senators gift set, with colourised 25¢ Ottawa . . . . . . .included above		24.95	25.00
2006P	Toronto Maple Leafs gift set, with colourised 25¢ Toronto . . . .included above		24.95	25.00

DATE		QTY.	ISSUE PRICE	VALUE
2007	Calgary Flames gift set with colourised 25¢ .1,082		24.95	25.00
2007	Edmonton Oilers gift set with colourised 25¢. 2,214		24.95	25.00
2007	Montreal Canadiens gift set with colourised 25¢ 4,091		24.95	25.00
2007	Montreal Canadiens gift set with colourised 25¢ (French text) 687		24.95	25.00
2007	Ottawa Senators gift set with colourised 25¢. 2,474		24.95	25.00
2007	Toronto Maple Leafs gift set with colourised 25¢. 5,365		24.95	25.00
2007	Vancouver Canucks gift set with colourised 25¢ 1,526		24.95	25.00
2008	Calgary Flames gift set with colourised nickel loon $. 314		24.95	25.00
2008	Edmonton Oilers gift set with colourised nickel loon $ 1,584		24.95	25.00
2008	Montreal Canadiens gift set with colourised nickel loon $ 2,659		24.95	25.00
2008	Ottawa Senators gift set with colourised nickel loon $ 2,064		24.95	25.00
2008	Toronto Maple Leafs gift set with colourised nickel loon $ 835		24.95	25.00
2008	Vancouver Canucks gift set with colourised nickel loon $ 2,104		24.95	25.00
2009	Calgary Flames gift set with colourised nickel loon $. 382		24.95	25.00
2009	Edmonton Oilers gift set with colourised nickel loon $ 472		24.95	25.00
2009	Montreal Canadiens gift set with colourised nickel loon $ 4,857		24.95	25.00
2009	Ottawa Senators gift set with colourised nickel loon $ 387		24.95	25.00
2009	Toronto Maple Leafs gift set with colourised nickel loon $ 1,328		24.95	25.00
2009	Vancouver Canucks gift set with colourised nickel loon $ 794		24.95	25.00

COLLECTORS' SETS
PROOF-LIKE SETS AND DOLLARS

The Numismatic Section of the Royal Canadian Mint was established in 1949. Prior to this the Ottawa branch of the Bank of Canada had accepted orders for Uncirculated sets of the coinage for the current year (and sometimes the previous year) at face value plus postage. The sets were shipped in cellophane envelopes until 1953 and in white cardboard holders enclosed in cellophane envelopes from 1953 to 1960. Most of the coins in the year sets of this period were regular production strikes but some of the coins for at least the period 1951–53 possessed a markedly superior finish. In 1954 dealer J.E. Charlton coined the term "proof-like" to describe one such 1953 set. These coins represented the modest beginnings of attempts by the mint to produce superior quality coins for collectors.

From 1961 to the present, all "uncirculated" or "select uncirculated" year sets sold by the mint have been of proof-like quality (although difficulty was experienced in producing a good surface on the coins in 1965 and again in 1968–69) and sealed in pliofilm or polyester film.

Most years it was possible to order proof-like dollars separately. These were not officially issued in 1953 or 1965–67, but are available from broken sets. Proof-like dollars were issued separately in separate cases from 1970 to 1976 but have been available only as part of complete proof-like year sets since that time.

Proof-like Sets 1954–1980

DATE		QTY. (000)	ISSUE PRICE	PL-65
1954	No shoulder fold 1¢	7	2.50	2,200
1954	Shoulder fold 1¢ . incl. above		2.50	750.00
1955	....	6	2.50	475.00
1955	Arnprior .... incl. above		2.50	575.00
1956	....	6.5	2.50	285.00
1957	....	12	2.50	180.00
1958	....	18	2.50	150.00
1959	....	32	2.50	80.00
1960	....	64	2.60	70.00
1961	....	98	3.00	60.00
1962	....	201	3.00	45.00
1963	....	673	3.00	35.00
1964	....	1,653	3.00	35.00
1965	Pointed 5 dollar ...	2,904	4.00	35.00
1965	Blunt 5 dollar ... incl. above		4.00	35.00
1966	....	673	4.00	35.00
1967	....	964	4.00	35.00
1968	....	522	4.00	3.50
1968	No Island .... incl. above		4.00	20.00
1968	Extra Waterlines . .incl. above		4.00	50.00
1969	....	326	4.00	3.50
1970	....	349	4.00	6.00
1971	....	253	4.00	4.00
1972	....	224	4.00	5.00
1973	Small bust 25¢	244	4.00	5.00
1973	Large bust 25¢ .. incl. above		4.00	300.00
1974	....	214	5.00	6.00
1975	....	197	5.00	5.00
1976	....	172	5.25	5.00
1977	Normal Waterlines dollar	225	5.25	5.00
1977	Short Waterlines . .incl. above		5.25	10.00
1978	Square Jewels 50c	260	5.25	5.00
1978	Round Jewels .... .incl. above		5.25	25.00
1979	Type I - (Type II $6.00)..	188	6.25	8.00
1980	....	169	8.00	7.00

Proof-like Dollars 1954–1976

DATE		QTY. (000)	ISSUE PRICE	PL-65
1954	....	1	1.25	325.00
1955	....	6	1.25	225.00
1955	Arnprior .... incl. above		1.25	350.00
1956	....	6	1.25	140.00
1957	....	4	1.25	90.00
1958	....	15	1.25	60.00
1959	....	14	1.25	60.00
1960	....	19	1.25	50.00
1961	....	23	1.25	30.00
1962	....	48	1.25	25.00
1963	....	291	1.25	15.00
1964	....	1,209	1.25	15.00
1965	Pointed 5	—		15.00
1965	Blunt 5	—		15.00
1966	....	—		15.00
1967	....	—		15.00
1968	....	885		2.00
1969	....	211		2.00
1970	....	298		3.00
1971	....	181		3.00
1972	....	143		3.00
1973	....	175		3.00
1974	....	106		3.00
1975	....	88		3.00
1976	....	74		3.00

Nickel dollars from 1970 to 1976 were cased individually and were also in proof-like sets. After 1976, all proof-like dollars have been available only in proof-like or uncirculated sets.

UNCIRCULATED SETS, 1981–2000

In 1981 the mint began issuing the year's decimal coinage in three distinct qualities (Proof, Specimen and Uncirculated) for collectors. The uncirculated sets replace the proof-like sets of previous years and are similarly packaged. Except in 1987, when a nickel voyageur dollar was substituted for the loon dollar, these sets contain one of each denomination of the year's circulation coinage. In 1996 a new finish for the uncirculated sets was introduced: frosted relief on a linen-textured background and in 1997 a seventh coin ($2 Polar Bear) was added.

Uncirculated Sets 1981–2001

	QTY. (000)	ISSUE PRICE	VALUE
SIX-COIN SETS			
1981	186	5.00	6.00
1982	203	5.00	5.00
1983	191	5.40	8.00
1984	181	6.65	8.00
1985	174	6.95	10.00
1986	167	6.95	9.00
1987 Voyageur dollar*	212	6.95	7.00
1988 Loon dollar	182	7.25	7.00
1989	159	7.70	10.00
1990	171	7.70	10.00
1991	148	8.50	30.00
1992	218	9.50	15.00
1993	172	9.50	6.00
1994	142	9.75	9.00
1995	144	9.75	9.00
1996	120	11.95	30.00
SEVEN-COIN SETS			
1997 Loon $1†	Ottawa 175	13.95	25.00
1997(W)Loon $1†	incl. above	13.95	12.00
1998 Loon $1†	145	13.95	25.00
1998W Loon $1†	incl. above	13.95	25.00
1999 Polar Bear $2	117	13.95	12.00
1999 Nunavut $2	75	13.95	15.00
2000 Polar Bear $2	187	15.95	14.00
2000W Polar Bear $2	incl. above	15.95	14.00

Dollars 1981–1989

DATE	VALUE
1981	5.00
1982	4.00
1983	7.00
1984	5.00
1985	6.00
1986	8.00
1987 Voyageur	7.00
1988 Loon	7.00
1989	7.00

Coins struck at the Winnipeg mint for the 1997 Uncirculated coin sets bear no mint mark but have a different finish than those struck in Ottawa [indicated by (W)]. Coins struck at the Winnipeg mint for the 1998 and 2000 Uncirculated coin sets bear a "W" mint mark on the obverse side, and are listed with a W added to the date.

Uncirculated Seven-coin Sets, 2001–2012

Beginning with 2001, all coins from 1¢ to 50¢ have been struck on plated steel blanks manufactured at the Winnipeg mint. The plated coins bear a "P" mint mark below the queen's effigy on the observe. In 2007, a stylized RCM Logo "L" was introduced.

2001P	Loon $1, Polar Bear $2	116	15.95	15.00
2002P	Loon $1, Polar Bear $2	100	15.95	15.00
2003P	Dora de Pédery-Hunt effigy of the queen on all coins	94	15.95	25.00
2004P	Loon $1, Polar Bear $2	97	15.95	25.00
2005P	Loon $1, Polar Bear $2	114	15.95	14.00
2006P	Loon $1, Polar Bear $2	93	15.95	14.00
2007	Loon $1, Polar Bear $2 (curved 7 / small RCM logo on 10c)	116	21.95	24.00
2007	Loon $1, Polar Bear $2 (straight 7 / large RCM logo on 10c)	incl.	21.95	100.00
2008	Loon $1, Polar Bear $2	43	21.95	22.00
2009	Loon $1, Polar Bear $2	38	22.95	25.00
2009	World Money Fair, Berlin issue	1	50.00	70.00
2010	Loon $1, Polar Bear $2	43	22.95	50.00
2011	Loon $1, Polar Bear $2	38	23.95	25.00
2012	Loon $1, Polar Bear $2	75	23.95	50.00

Uncirculated Six-coin Sets, 2013–2015

2013	Loon $1, Polar Bear $2	61	24.95	24.00
2014	Loon $1, Polar Bear $2	75	24.95	25.00
2015	Loon $1, Polar Bear $2	60	24.95	25.00

The round voyageur nickel dollar was issued in all three collectors' sets in 1987. This dollar was never issued as a circulation dollar.
† There were no circulation loon dollars minted for 1997–2001. The common loon dollar was available only in the Uncirculated set and the "Baby" set in 1997, and in all five collectors' sets for 1998–2000.

SPECIMEN SETS

From the early days of the 19th century, mints around the world have struck small quantities of coins in superior quality for presentation to visiting dignitaries, etc. In some years these "specimen" sets were made available to the general public to add to their collections. These coins are from immaculately treated dies and planchets and are struck on slow-moving presses under higher than normal pressure. The coins so produced all have unusually sharp details and sharp edges. Although the device is usually frosted, the fields can be either frosted or mirror-like. Specimen coins from the 1858 Province of Canada and the 1870 Dominion of Canada issues were made available to collectors. Since its inception in 1908, the Royal Canadian Mint, Ottawa has produced in most years a small number of specimen sets, although sets were offered for sale to the public only in the years 1908, 1911 and 1937. The appearance of some specimen pieces of Canadian coins has rivalled that of coins produced as "proof" in the United States, but the Royal Canadian Mint has never considered them to be of the superlative quality of Royal Mint (London) proofs. Hence Canada's strikings prior to 1980 have been officially designated as specimen quality. In 1981, the Royal Canadian Mint began offering proof quality coins as well as Specimen sets.

DATE		CASE	MS-65
1858	Victoria 1¢, 5¢ (small date), 10¢, 20¢	None	30,000
1858	Victoria 1¢, 5¢ (large date), 10¢, 20¢	None	34,000
1858	Victoria double set – 2 each 1¢, 5¢ (small date), 10¢, 20¢	Leather pouch	60,000
1870	Victoria 5¢, 10¢, 25¢, 50¢	None	50,000
1870	Victoria double set – 2 each 5¢, 10¢, 25¢, 50¢	Leather	100,000
1902	Edward VII 1¢, 5¢, 10¢, 25¢	None	30,000
1908	Edward VII 1¢, 5¢, 10¢, 25¢, 50¢	Leather	4,500
1911	George V 1¢, 5¢, 10¢, 25¢, 50¢	Leather	10,000
1911–12	George V 1¢, 5¢, 10¢, 25¢, 50¢, £1, $5, $10	Leather	85,000
1921	George V 1¢, 5¢, 10¢, 25¢, 50¢	None	175,000
1929	George V 1¢, 5¢, 10¢, 25¢, 50¢	None	30,000
1930	George V 1¢, 5¢, 10¢, 25¢	None	15,000
1934	George V 1¢, 5¢, 10¢, 25¢, 50¢	None	30,000
1936	George V 1¢, 5¢, 10¢, 25¢, 50¢	None	25,000
1937	George VI 1¢, 5¢, 10¢, 25¢, 50¢, $1.00 (mirror finish)	Leather	3,500
1937	George VI 1¢, 5¢, 10¢, 25¢, 50¢, $1.00 (mirror finish)	Cardboard	3,250
1937	George VI 1¢, 5¢, 10¢, 25¢, 50¢, $1.00 (matte finish)	Cardboard	1,500
1937	George VI 1¢, 5¢, 10¢, 25¢ (mirror finish)	Leather	3,500

DATE	DESCRIPTION	CASE	MS-65
1938	George VI 1¢, 5¢, 10¢, 25¢, 50¢, $1.00 .... Leather		25,000
1944	George VI 1¢, 5¢, 10¢, 25¢, 50¢ .... None		25,000
1945	George VI 1¢, 5¢, 10¢, 25¢, 50¢, $1.00 .... Leather		11,000
1946	George VI 1¢, 5¢, 10¢, 25¢, 50¢, $1.00 .... Leather		11,000
1947	George VI 1¢, 5¢, 10¢, 25¢, 50¢, $1.00 .... Leather		22,500
1947ML	George VI 1¢, 5¢, 10¢, 25¢, 50¢, $1.00 (50¢ curved right) .... Leather		15,000
1947ML	George VI 1¢, 5¢, 10¢, 25¢, 50¢, $1.00 (50¢ curved left) .... Leather		15,000
1948	George VI 1¢, 5¢, 10¢, 25¢, 50¢, $1.00 .... Leather		13,500
1949	George VI 1¢, 5¢, 10¢, 25¢, 50¢, $1.00 .... Leather		11,000
1950	George VI 1¢, 5¢, 10¢, 25¢, 50¢, $1.00 .... Leather		5,000
1951	George VI 1¢, 5¢ (both types), 10¢, 25¢, 50¢, $1.00 .... None		5,500
1952	George VI 1¢, 5¢, 10¢, 25¢, 50¢, $1.00 (water lines) .... Leather		7,500
1953	Elizabeth II 1¢, 5¢, 10¢, 25¢, 50¢, $1.00 (no shoulder fold) .... Leather		2,750
1953	Elizabeth II 1¢, 5¢, 10¢, 25¢, 50¢, $1.00 (shoulder fold) .... Leather		1,250
1964	Elizabeth II 1¢, 5¢, 10¢, 25¢, 50¢, $1.00 .... Leather		1,500
1965	Elizabeth II 1¢, 5¢, 10¢, 25¢, 50¢, $1.00 .... Leather		1,200

Specimen Custom Sets, 1971–1980

In 1971 the mint began offering three coin sets of different qualities to the public. In addition to the popular Proof-like sets which had been issued in a sealed pliofilm pack since 1961, the mint now offered Custom and Prestige sets.

Custom set This set has one piece of each denomination 1¢ to $1 (nickel), plus an extra cent to show the obverse, packaged in a square, vinyl covered box. The quality was proof-like from 1971 to 1976 and specimen from 1977 to 1980.

DATE	QTY. (000)	COST	MS-65	DATE	QTY. (000)	COST	MS-65
SEVEN-COIN SETS (Proof-like)				**SEVEN-COIN SETS (Specimen)**			
1971	 34	6.50	4.00	1977	 44	8.15	4.00
1972	 38	6.50	4.00	1978	 41	8.75	4.00
1973	25¢ large bust 49	6.50	350.00	1979	 31	10.75	5.00
1973	25¢ small bust... above	6.50	6.00	1980	 41	12.50	8.00
1974	 44	8.00	4.00				
1975	 37	8.15	4.00				
1976	 28	8.15	4.00				

Specimen Sets, 1981–1996

In 1981 the Royal Canadian Mint began producing sets of specimen and proof quality to replace the previous Custom and Prestige sets.

Specimen set One encapsulated coin of each of the six denominations produced for circulation in that year, all of specimen quality, displayed in a blue box.

1981–1995: Coins had a brilliant relief on a brilliant background.

1996: Coins had a brilliant relief on a parallel lined background.

DATE	QTY. (000)	COST	VALUE	DATE	QTY. (000)	COST	VALUE
SIX-COIN SPECIMEN SETS				**SIX-COIN SPECIMEN SETS**			
Brilliant relief; brilliant background				Brilliant relief; brilliant background			
1981	 71	10.00	12.00	1989	 75	16.95	15.00
1982	 62	11.50	12.00	1990	 77	17.95	15.00
1983	 60	12.75	12.00	1991	 69	17.95	35.00
1984	 60	12.75	12.00	1992	 78	18.95	20.00
1985	 62	12.95	12.00	1993	 77	18.95	15.00
1986	 67	13.50	12.00	1994	 76	19.25	15.00
1987	(Voyageur dollar) 77	11.00	12.00	1995	 77	19.25	15.00
1988	(Loon dollar) 70	14.75	12.00	Brilliant and frosted relief; parallel lined background.			
				1996	 62	24.95	25.00

Specimen Sets, 1997 –

	QTY. (000)	COST	VALUE
SEVEN-COIN SPECIMEN SETS			
The two dollar Polar Bear was added in 1997			
Brilliant and frosted relief; parallel lined background.			
1997 $1 flying Loon, ...	98	26.95	40.00
1998 $1 Loon, $2 Polar Bear . .	68	26.95	20.00
1999 $1 Loon, $2 Polar Bear . .	47	26.95	20.00

	QTY. (000)	COST	VALUE
SEVEN-COIN SPECIMEN SETS			
Brilliant and frosted relief; parallel lined background.			
1999 $2 Nunavut	45	26.95	20.00
2000 $1 Loon, $2 Polar Bear . .	88	34.95	20.00
2000 $2 Bear family . . . inc. above		34.95	20.00

Beginning in 2001, the 1¢ through 50¢ coins in the collectors' sets were all struck on plated steel blanks manufactured at the Winnipeg mint, as indicated by a "P" mint mark on the observe. In 2007, a stylized RCM Logo "L" was introduced.

	QTY. (000)	COST	VALUE
SEVEN-COIN SPECIMEN SETS			
Brilliant and frosted relief; parallel lined background.			
2001P	57	34.95	20.00
2002P (1952-2002)	67.5	39.95	40.00
2003P	42	39.95	30.00
2004P $1 Canada Goose. . .	47	39.95	50.00
2005P $1 Tufted Puffin	40	39.95	60.00
2006P $1 Snowy Owl	40	39.95	60.00
2007 $1 Trumpeter Swan .	27	45.95	50.00
2008 $1 Common Eider . .	41	45.95	50.00
2009 $1 Great Blue Heron .	22	47.95	50.00
2010 $1 Northern Harrier .	21	49.95	50.00
2011 $1 Great Grey Owl . .	26	49.95	50.00
2012 $1 25th Anniv. Loon	35	49.95	50.00
2013 $1 Arctic	20	99.95	100.00
SIX-COIN SPECIMEN SETS			
2014 $1 Ferruginous Hawk	50	49.95	50.00
2015 $1 Blue Jay	30	49.95	50.00

	QTY. (000)	COST	VALUE
YOUNG WILDLIFE $2 SPECIMEN SETS			
2010 $2 Young Lynx	15	49.95	50.00
2011 $2 Elk Calf	15	49.95	50.00
2012 $2 Wolf Cubs	15	49.95	50.00
2013 $2 Black Bear Cubs	17.5	49.95	50.00
2014 $2 Baby Rabbits. . .	17.5	49.95	50.00

Specimen Set Dollars

The tenth anniversary loon dollar depicts a Loon rising flight from the surface of a lake. It appeared only in the Specimen and Oh Canada sets for 1997.

The 2002 loon dollar had a reverse designed by Jean-Luc Grondin which depicted a Loon Family in their natural habitat. The reverse was to celebrate the 15th anniversary of the Loon dollar.

On the 2004 aureate dollar, the loon reverse was replaced by a Susan Taylor creation of a Canada Goose in flight and was only available in the Specimen Set. This change was made as a tribute to Jack Miner. The coin only appeared in the 2004 Specimen set.

The Tufted Puffin was selected for the reverse of the aureate dollar in the 2005 Specimen Set. The Tufted Puffin is only available in this set.

The largest bird species in the arctic, Nyctea scandiaca (Snowy Owl) is also one of the most beautiful birds in North America. It is featured on the 2006 Specimen Set.

The 2007 set features the Trumpeter Swan, a native of North America's coastlines and major waterways, found as far inland as Alberta.

The Common Eider is the largest duck in the northern hemisphere. It can be found virtually anywhere along Canada's eastern and northern coasts and is featured in the 2008 Specimen Set.

The Great Blue Heron is featured in the 2009 Specimen Set. Designed by Chris Jordison.

The Northern Harrier appears on the 2010 Specimen Set to pay tribute to Canada's diverse avian residents. Designed by artist Arnold Nogy.

The Common Loon is one of the signature sights and sounds of the great Canadian wilderness. Celebrates the 25th anniversary of the Loonie. Designed by artist Arnold Nogy.

The 2011 design features the Great Gray Owl. Designed by artist Arnold Nogy.

Double Dollar Prestige Sets 1971–1980

Prestige set This set consists of one piece of each denomination 1¢ to $1 (nickel) plus the silver commemorative dollar (except in 1971 and 1972 when the extra dollar was nickel), issued in a rectangular black leather case. The coin quality was specimen. From 1974 to 1980 the coins were mounted in a plastic page frame.

DATE	QTY. (000)	COST	MS-65	DATE	QTY. (000)	COST	MS-65
SEVEN-COIN SPECIMEN SETS				**SEVEN-COIN SPECIMEN SETS**			
Brilliant relief; brilliant background.				Brilliant relief; brilliant background.			
1971	67	12.00	30.00	1976	88	16.00	30.00
1972	36	12.00	60.00	1977	143	16.00	30.00
1973 25¢ large bust	120	12.00	350.00	1978	147	16.50	30.00
1973 25¢ small bust	above	12.00	30.00	1979	156	18.50	30.00
1974	85	15.00	30.00	1980	163	36.00	30.00
1975	97	15.00	30.00				

Proof Sets, 1981–1996

Proof set This set consists of one encapsulated coin of each of the six denominations produced for circulation plus the commemorative silver dollar for each year. All coins are of proof quality and the set is issued in a black leather case.

SEVEN-COIN PROOF SETS				**SEVEN-COIN PROOF SETS**			
Frosted relief; mirror background.				Frosted relief; mirror background.			
1981	199	36.00	35.00	1989	171	46.95	40.00
1982	181	36.00	30.00	1990	158	48.00	40.00
1983	167	36.00	30.00	1991	132	48.00	85.00
1984	162	40.00	35.00	1992	147	49.75	50.00
1985	154	40.00	35.00	1993	143	49.75	45.00
1986	176	40.00	30.00	1994	104	50.75	50.00
1987 (voyageur dollar)	184	43.00	30.00	1995	102	50.75	50.00
1988 (Loon dollar)	175	45.00	35.00	1996	113	64.95	65.00

Proof Sets, 1997–2002

Since 1996, Proof Sets contain 5¢, 10¢, 25¢ and 50¢ coins struck in .925 silver to match the commemorative silver dollar included in the sets. In 1997, the two-dollar Polar Bear was added to all collectors' sets issued by the mint. In the Proof Set, the Polar Bear coin is sterling silver, with the centre core plated in gold. **EIGHT-COIN PROOF SETS**

Year	Description	QTY	COST	MS-65
1997	Loon, Hockey, Polar Bear	114	75.95	60.00
1998	Loon, R.C.M.P., Polar Bear	89	75.95	80.00
1999	Loon, Queen Charlotte Islands, Polar Bear	95	75.95	120.00
2000	Loon, Voyage of Discovery, Polar Bear	98	75.95	100.00
2001	Loon, National Ballet of Canada, Polar Bear	74	81.95	80.00
2002	Loon, Golden Jubilee, Polar Bear (coins dated 1952 2002)	65	81.95	80.00

Silver Proof Sets, 2003 –

In 2003, the Royal Canadian Mint issued the first Canadian dollar ever struck in .9999 silver and this is included in the Proof Set. The set also contains a 5-, 10-, 25- and 50-cent coin struck in .925 silver, a 1-cent piece struck in copper, and the Loon dollar in nickel and bronze. The two-dollar Polar Bear coin is sterling silver, with the centre core plated in gold.

Year	Description	QTY	COST	MS-65
2003	proof 8-coin set	62	81.95	82.00
2004	proof 8-coin set	51	81.95	100.00
2005	proof 8-coin set	64	81.95	110.00
2005	proof 8-coin set CNA issue.	197 sets	N/A	200.00
2006	proof 8-coin set with $1 Victoria Cross-Selective Gold Plating.	54	84.95	110.00
2007	proof 8-coin set with $1 Thayendanegea	37	89.95	110.00
2008	proof 8-coin set with $1 400th Anniv. of Quebec.	39	89.95	110.00
2009	proof 8-coin set with $1 100th Anniv. of Flight in Canada (1909 - 2009)	28	99.95	110.00
2010	proof 8-coin set with $1 100th Anniv. of the Navy (1910 - 2010)	32	109.95	110.00
2011	proof 8-coin set with $1 100th Anniv. of Parks Canada (1911 - 2011)	33	114.95	115.00
2012	proof 8-coin set with $1 200th Anniv. of the War of 1812 (1812 - 2012).	40	99.95	100.00
2013	proof 7-coin set with $1 100th Anniv. of World War I		229.95	230.00

SPECIAL ISSUES

Centennial (Proof-Like) Presentation Set, 1967

In 1967, the Mint produced two special cased coin sets to celebrate the 100th anniversary of Confederation. The Gold Presentation set, containing 1¢ to $1 and a $20 gold coin, was sold to the public for $40. The coins were contained in a black leather box and were of specimen quality.

In addition to the Gold Presentation set, a special set was offered in a red presentation case containing the 1¢ to $1 plus a sterling silver medallion designed by Thomas Shingles. The coins were all of proof-like quality.

DATE		QTY. (000)	ISSUE PRICE	VALUE
1967	specimen quality gold set	338	40.00	750.00
1967	medallion set	72.463	12.00	50.00

Specimen V.I.P. Presentation Sets, 1969–1976

A very limited number of cased Specimen sets were produced by the Mint beginning in 1969 for presentation to dignitaries visiting the Royal Canadian Mint or other parts of Canada. (A small quantity of 1970 cased Specimen sets were sold to the public for $13 each.) The coins, 1¢ to $1 were cased in long narrow leather cases (black and other colours).

DATE	QTY. ISSUED	VALUE	DATE	QTY. ISSUED	VALUE
1969	2 known	3,000	1973	26	1,750
1970	100	1,200	1974	72	1,750
1971	69	1,750	1975	94	1,750
1972	25	1,750	1976	Unknown	1,750

There may be sets dated 1977 to date (no information available).

125th Anniversary of Confederation, 1992

(Aureate Dollar): Diameter: 26.50 mm; weight: 7.0 grams; edge: plain;
composition: aureate bronze plated on pure nickel
(25¢ sterling): Diameter: 23.88 mm; weight: 6.0 grams; edge: reeded;
composition: .925 silver, .075 copper

For the 125th anniversary of Confederation, the Royal Canadian Mint issued a different 25¢ piece each month during 1992 to represent the ten provinces and two territories. On July 1st, a commemorative aureate dollar was issued, representing the country as a whole.

The CANADA 125 proof set consists of one each of the 25-cent pieces, struck in .925 silver, housed together with the commemorative aureate dollar in a flocked royal blue case.

The commemorative sterling silver 25¢ pieces were also offered singly in display cases.

The CANADA 125 uncirculated set is comprised of one each of the circulating 25-cent pieces struck in nickel and the commemorative aureate dollar mounted in a coloured map of Canada. The coins are in brilliant uncirculated condition.

DATE		QTY. (000)	PRICE	VALUE
1992	CANADA 125 set (13 coins) proof	84	129.45	125.00
1992	CANADA 125 set (13 coins) uncirculated	448	17.25	10.00
1992	Commemorative 25¢ (cach) proof	65	9.95	8.00

Special Edition Proof Sets, 1994, 1995

In 1994 and 1995, the mint issued a Special Edition Proof Set as well as the traditional Proof Set because a commemorative circulation dollar was minted in addition to the aureate (Loon) dollar. The aureate (Loon) dollar appears in the regular Proof Set but the commemorative dollar is in the Special Edition Proof Set.

1994	National War Memorial Proof Set	49	64.95	55.00
1995	Peacekeeping Monument Proof Set	50	66.95	55.00

Proof Piedfort $2 Coin and Bank Notes Set, 1996

Diameter: 28.0 mm; weight: 25 grams; thickness: 4.5 mm; edge: interrupted serration;
composition (outer ring): .925 silver, (inner core): .925 silver covered with 24-karat gold

Limited to 15,000 sets worldwide, this set includes the first piedfort coin issued by the Royal
Canadian Mint. The set consists of a proof encapsulated Piedfort $2 coin and two uncut Bank of
Canada BRX banknotes. Banknotes with an "X" as the third letter in the serial number are used to
replace defective notes before shipments are made to the various banks, thus maintaining correct
count for the regular serial numbers.

DATE		QTY. (000)	ISSUE PRICE	VALUE
1996	Proof $2 Piedfort and Banknotes set, in blue case	12	179.95	90.00

$2 Coin and $2 Bank Note Sets, 1996

To introduce the $2 Polar Bear coin as a replacement for the old $2 bank note, the mint offered
sets consisting of a $2 coin and a $2 note. The proof coin is paired with a replacement note (third
letter X in the serial number), while the uncirculated coin is paired with one of the final notes
printed for the Bank of Canada.

1996	$2 Polar Bear, uncirculated, with $2 bank note	91	29.95	15.00
1996	$2 Polar Bear, proof, with $2 bank note	27	79.95	40.00

90th Anniversary Royal Canadian Mint, 1998

All coins are sterling silver: .925 silver, .075 copper; edges: 5¢–50¢–reeded, 1¢–plain;
Diameters (mm): 50¢–29.72, 25¢–23.62, 10¢–18.034, 5¢–15.494, 1¢–25.4;
weights (grams): 50¢–11.62, 25¢–5.81, 10¢–2.32, 5¢–1.167, 1¢–5.67.

For its 90th anniversary, the Royal Canadian Mint minted a reproduction of the coins issued in
1908. All five coins are 92.5% silver and the large cent is also copper plated. The 1908 dates have
been changed to 1908–1998. The common obverse features the Dora de Pédery-HUNT effigy of
the queen. Initially sets were struck with an antique finish and issued in a burgundy leather display
case. After much criticism by numismatists a proof version of the set was issued.

The antique finish large cent does not display the inscription CANADA on either side. The
inscription was added to the obverse die for the large cent in the proof set.

DATE		QTY. (000)	ISSUE PRICE	VALUE
1998	1908–1998 silver coin set, antique finish, in burgundy leather case	25	99.00	50.00
1998	1908–1998 silver coin set, proof finish, in burgundy leather case	10	99.00	60.00

Uncirculated "Test Coin" Set, 1999

In 1999 the mint issued sets of nickel-plated steel coins (1¢ through 50¢ denominations) to the
vending industry on a deposit basis, for the purpose of testing the proposed new coins in machines. After some sets fell into the hands of collectors, the mint issued sets of the five denominations plus a medallion, sealed in pliofilm.

DATE		QTY. (000)	ISSUE PRICE	VALUE
1999P	5 coin "Test coinage" set	20	99.95	70.00

5 and 10 Dollar Gold Commemorative, 2002

Diameter: 21.59/26.92 mm; weight: 8.36/16.72 grams; composition: .900 gold, .100 copper; edge: reeded

Issued for the 90th anniversary of Canada's first five and ten dollar gold coins in 1912, these are double-dated 1912-2002 coins.

DATE		QTY. (000)	ISSUE PRICE	VALUE
2002	$5 Gold Commemorative	—	—	350.00
2002	$10 Gold Commemorative	—	—	700.00
2002	$5 & $10 Set	1,998	749.95	1,100

Special Limited Editions Proof Sets, 2002, 2003

1952-2002 Proof Set contains a commemorative silver dollar and gold plated 50-cent coin. The balance of the coins are the regular proof set issue of 2002.

Proof Set 1953-2003 has the portrait of Queen Elizabeth II, first issued in 1953. It commemorates Queen's coronation and her jubilee with double dates 1953-2003.

GOLDEN JUBILEE
Special Edition Proof Sets, 2002–2003

Special 50¢ Obverse   Reverse of gold-plated Silver Dollar

A Special Edition Proof Set was issued to celebrate the Golden Jubilee of Queen Elizabeth II. The set is similar to the regular 2002 Proof Set except for the introduction of a redesigned 50¢ piece which bears an effigy portraying the queen as she appeared fifty years prior. Also unique to this set is the 24-karat gold plating on the 50-cent cent and dollar coins.

DATE		QTY. (000)	ISSUE PRICE	VALUE
2002	Loon, Golden Jubilee, Polar Bear (coins dated 1952 2002)	33	99.95	100.00
2002	Loon, Accession	33	99.95	110.00
2003	Loon, Coronation	21	99.95	110.00

In 2003, the tiara portrait of Elizabeth II which had been used since 1990, was replaced with the new uncrowned portrait designed by Susanna Blunt.

SPECIAL EDITIONS
Uncirculated Seven-coin Set

The 2002 special edition is similar to the regular 7-coin uncirculated set except for the 25¢ and 50¢ coins. The 25¢ coin is replaced with the Canada Day version showing a large maple leaf being held in place by five figures. The re-designed Golden Jubilee 50¢ coin shows an earlier effigy of the queen on the obverse, with the double date 1952 2002 on the reverse.

All seven coins in the 2003 Special Edition Uncirculated Set bear the new effigy of the Queen designed by Susanna Blunt and each coin also bears a "W" (Winnipeg mint). The 1¢ through 50¢ coins also bear the mint mark P indicating plated coins (WP).

DATE	QTY. (000)	PRICE	VALUE
2002P With special 25-and 50-cent coins 50		15.95	15.00
2003WP Susanna Blunt effigy of the queen on all coins 71		17.95	15.00

SPECIAL EDITION SET
CORONATION DATED 1953 AND 2003

The six coins in this special edition set bear the portrait of Queen Elizabeth as it appeared on coins struck at the beginning of her reign in 1953. The dates 1953 and 2003 appear on each side of the portrait. The 1 cent coin is copper, the dollar is 99.99% silver, and the 5 cents, 10 cents, 25 cents and 50 cents coins are 92.5% silver. The reverse of the silver dollar shows the Voyageur design.

DATE	QTY. (000)	PRICE	VALUE
2003 Set dated 1953 and 2003, silver and copper	68	99.95	80.00

VANCOUVER 2010 OLYMPIC WINTER GAMES
Special Edition Uncirculated Sets, 2007 - 2009

These special edition sets include the annual issue commemorative 25 cents coins as part of the uncirculated set containing all denominations for each year of 2007, 2008 & 2009. Each set contains a total of 11 coins.

DATE	QTY.	PRICE	VALUE
2007	 28,904	23.95	24.00
2008	 18,147	23.95	24.00
2009	 12,383	23.95	24.00
2010	 29,996	23.95	24.00
2011	 19,233	23.95	24.00

Selectively Gold Plated O Canada Set, 2013

Diameter: 34mm; weight: 15.87g; composition: 99.99% pure silver with selective gold plating; finish: matte proof

Everything about Canada is rich with variety–its landscape, wildlife, cities, towns and the people who live in them.

DATE		QTY.	ISSUE PRICE	VALUE
2013	$10 12-Coin Series–O Canada	1,500	899.95	900.00

Royal Infant 3-Coin Set, 2013

Diameter: 38mm; weight: 31.39g; composition: 99.99% fine silver; finish: proof; edge: serrated

A trilogy of parental delights: Sweet dreams: Tender bonds: A hopeful future. The Duke and Duchess of Cambridge may have centuries of royal traditions behind them, but as they welcome their first-born into their arms, their love, devotion and aspirations will be universally linked to the thoughts and emotions that have defined parenthood throughout the ages and around the world. Designed by Canadian artist Laurie McGaw.

DATE		QTY.	ISSUE PRICE	VALUE
2013	$20 Royal Infant 3-Coin Set.	7,500	249.95	250.00

COIN and STAMP SETS

Special collector sets containing a Royal Canadian Mint coin and a pair of corresponding postage stamps from Canada Post — one stamp is mint and the other cancelled.

1 Dollar Loon Coin and $1 Stamp Set, 2004

Diameter: 26.5 mm; weight: 7 grams; thickness: 1.90 mm;
composition: nickel plated with bronze; 11-Sides, plain edges; finish: proof

This image of an elusive loon resting among the reeds is repeated on the dollar stamp in this set. The dollar coin is only available in this set and features a maple leaf privy mark below CANADA.

2 Dollar Proud Polar Bear Coin and $2 Stamp Set, 2004

Diameter: 27.95 mm; weight: 8.82 grams, thickness: 1.7 mm; edge: interrupted serrations; finish: proof

Issued jointly by the Royal Canadian Mint and Canada Post, the two dollar Polar Bear Stamp and Coin Set contains the first single metal two dollar Canadian coin.

DATE		QTY. (000)	ISSUE PRICE	VALUE
2004	Elusive Loon: $1 Stamp and $1 Coin set, boxed 25		25.11	100.00
2004	Polar Bear: $2 Stamp and $2 Coin set, boxed 25		29.22	40.00

5 Dollar Moose Coin and $5 Stamp Set, 2004

Diameter: 38 mm; weight: 28 grams; composition:. 9999 silver; edge: reeded

This stamp and coin set, issued in a wooden display case, includes a booklet concerning the moose's history on stamps and coins.

DATE		QTY. (000)	ISSUE PRICE	VALUE
2004	Moose: $5 Stamp and $5 Coin set, boxed........................25.5		39.95	200.00

DATE		QTY.	ISSUE PRICE	VALUE
2005	Deer: $1 Stamp and $5 Coin set, boxed 6,439		49.95	50.00
2005	Walrus: $1 Stamp and $5 Coin set, boxed. .5,519		49.95	50.00
2006	Falcon: $2 Stamp and $5 Coin set, boxed 7,226		49.95	50.00
2006	Sable Horse: $2 Stamp and $5 Coin set, boxed. 10,108		49.95	50.00

8 Dollar Grizzly Bear Coin and $8 Stamp Set, 2004

Diameter: 40 mm; weight: 28 grams; composition:. 9999 silver; edge: reeded

Issued jointly by the Royal Canadian Mint and Canada Post, the eight dollar Grizzly Bear Stamp and Coin Set contains the first eight dollar Canadian coin. Issued in a presentation case with two eight dollar Grizzly Bear stamps, one mint and one cancelled.

DATE		QTY. (000)	ISSUE PRICE	VALUE
2004	Bear: $8 Stamp and $8 Coin set, boxed. 26		48.88	75.00

Coronation Stamp and Coin Set, 2003

A joint venture of the Royal Canadian Mint and Canada Post, this stamp and coin set was issued to celebrate the 50th anniversary of the reign of Queen Elizabeth II. The boxed set includes a full colour booklet displaying the queen's presence on Canada's stamps and coins and the set of four stamps and four coins as follows:

Two 48-cent Golden Jubilee stamps from 2002, one in mint condition and one cancelled;
Two 48-cent Coronation stamps from 2003, one in mint condition and one cancelled;
One 1-cent circulation coin from 1953;
One 50-cent circulation Golden Jubilee coin from 2002;
One 1-cent and one 50-cent coin, both uncirculated, from 2003 bearing the Susanna Blunt effigy of the queen.

DATE	QTY. (000)	ISSUE PRICE	VALUE
2003 Queen Elizabeth II Coronation Stamp and Coin set.................15		22.95	27.00

Calgary Stampede Stamp and Coin Set, 2012

Included in this set is a souvenir sheet that features a PERMANENT™ domestic stamp featuring a horse with classic western riding gear and a U.S.A. stamp showcasing the 2012 Calgary Stampede belt buckle, the much prized trophy awarded to the winners.

DATE	QTY.	ISSUE PRICE	VALUE
2012 Souvenir sheet and 25¢ Calgary Stampede coin		29.95	30.00

CFL Teams Stamp and Coin Sets, 2012

Each set has a fold out history card with coloured photographs, two stamps and a coloured 25 cent coin celebrating your team.

DATE		QTY.	ISSUE PRICE	VALUE
2012	Two stamps and 25¢ British Columbia Lions coin		25.95	26.00
2012	Two stamps and 25¢ Edmonton Eskimos coin		25.95	26.00
2012	Two stamps and 25¢ Calgary Stampeders coin		25.95	26.00
2012	Two stamps and 25¢ Saskatchewan Roughriders coin		25.95	26.00
2012	Two stamps and 25¢ Winnipeg Blue Bombers coin		25.95	26.00
2012	Two stamps and 25¢ Hamilton Tiger-Cats coin		25.95	26.00
2012	Two stamps and 25¢ Toronto Argonauts coin		25.95	26.00
2012	Two stamps and 25¢ Montreal Alouettes coin		25.95	26.00

NHL Teams Stamp and Coin Sets, 2014

DATE		QTY.	ISSUE PRICE	VALUE
2014	25¢ Vancouver Canucks coin and two stamps	6,000	29.95	30.00
2014	25¢ Calgary Flames coin and two stamps	6,000	29.95	30.00
2014	25¢ Edmonton Oilers coin and two stamps	6,000	29.95	30.00
2014	25¢ Winnipeg Jets coin and two stamps	6,000	29.95	30.00
2014	25¢ Toronto Maple Leafs coin and two stamps	6,000	29.95	30.00
2014	25¢ Ottawa Senators coin and two stamps	6,000	29.95	30.00
2014	25¢ Montreal Canadiens coin and two stamps	6,000	29.95	30.00

Superman Stamp and Coin Set, 2013

Superman through the ages–from his spectacular debut beginnings in 1938 to his modern day interpretation.

DATE		QTY.	ISSUE PRICE	VALUE
2013	Superman: Then and Now, 50¢-coin and stamp set.		29.75	30.00

Silver Six Coin Coronation Set Dated 1953 2003

The six coins in this cased special edition set feature the laureate effigy of Queen Elizabeth as it appeared on the first Canadian coins minted during her reign in 1953. Two dates, 1953 and 2003 appear one on either side of the effigy. The 1-cent is copper and the dollar is 99.99% silver while the 5-, 10-, 25- and 50-cent coins are all 92.5% silver. The silver dollar displays the Voyageur reverse.

2003	Dated 1953 2003, silver and copper cased set	N/A	99.95	100.00

1 Dollar, Ile Sainte-Croix, 1604–2004

Canadian Specifications - Diameter: 36.07 mm; weight: 25.175 grams; edge: reeded;
composition:. 9999 silver; .finish: brilliant uncirculated

This venture involved The Royal Canadian Mint, Canada Post, La Monnaie de Paris and La Poste
(France) in celebrating the 400th anniversary of the founding of the settlement at Ile Sainte-Croix.
The set includes two silver coins (Canadian dollar, French 1/4 Euro) and four postage stamps, two
Canadian and two French. One of each pair is mint and one is cancelled.

DATE		QTY.	ISSUE PRICE	VALUE
2004	$1 Ile Sainte-Croix, etc., brilliant uncirculated 8,315		99.95	125.00

5 Dollar Snowbirds, 2006

Specifications - same as above except the finish is proof, with double hologram on reverse

The set includes the $5 Snowbirds coin and two postage stamps (in a souvenir sheet) issued by
Canada Post. The souvenir sheets were flown onboard two Snowbirds Tutor jets on March 27,
2006 at Moose Jaw, Saskatchewan.

2006	$5 coin and 51¢ stamp set, silver metal box 2,138	59.95	60.00

50 Cents 100th Anniversary of the RCM, 1908-2008

Specifications - Diameter:29.72 mm; weight: 11.62 grams; edge: serrated;
composition:. 9999 silver; .finish: proof.

The set includes the silver commemorative 50 cents coin dated 1908 - 2008 and postage stamp
issued by Canada Post, celebrating the 100th anniversary of the Royal Canadian Mint.

2008	50 cents coin and 52¢ stamp set, wooden box 3,248	44.95	60.00

5 DOLLARS SILVER — SPECIAL PROOF SETS
Norman Bethune, 1998
CANADA / CHINA

CANADIAN SPECIFICATIONS:
Diameter: 38 mm; weight: 31.39 grams; thickness: 3.3 mm; edge: reeded;
composition: .9999 fine silver; finish: proof

Canada's first joint venture with a foreign mint, this two-coin set celebrating the 60th anniversary of Dr. Bethune's arrival in China. The set was issued in a two-coin case protected by an outer box covered in Chinese brocade fabric. The obverse of the Canada coin bears the familiar Dora de Pédery-HUNT effigy of the queen and the Canadian reverse was designed by Harvey Chan.

DATE		QTY. (000)	ISSUE PRICE	VALUE
1998	$5 Dr. Norman Bethune, two-coin proof set 61		98.00	60.00

5 DOLLARS BRONZE
Arrival of the Vikings, 1999
CANADA / NORWAY, 2 coins

Canadian Specifications - Diameter: 27.5 mm; weight: 9.9 grams; edge: smooth;
composition: .81 copper, .09 nickel, .10 zinc; finish: proof

This set commemorates the arrival of the Vikings in North America. The Canadian coin depicts a Viking ship nearing l'Anse-aux-Meadows, Newfoundland, the only authenticated Viking settlement in North America. The reverse design is by Donald Curly. The reverse of the Norwegian 20 Krone coin, by Nils As, depicts the frontal view of a Viking ship and bears the legend *Mot ukjent land* (towards unknown land).

Both coins were struck on Norwegian 20 Krone blanks and are offered only as a set. The Canadian coin is proof; the Norwegian coin is Brilliant Uncirculated.

DATE		QTY. (000)	ISSUE PRICE	VALUE
1999	$5 Arrival of the Vikings, two-coin proof set . . . . N/A		39.95	40.00

CANADA / ENGLAND
Guglielmo Marconi, 2001
5 Dollars, silver
Canadian Specifications - Diameter: 28.14 mm; weight: 15.98 grams; edge: reeded;
composition:. 925 silver, .075 copper; Cameo: 24 karat gold;

The Canadian coin depicts the flow of the first telegraph signals from England to Canada accompanied by a 24 karat gold cameo of Marconi.

The two coins are offered only as a set. The Canadian coin has a proof finish, the British is a reverse proof.

DATE	QTY. (000)	ISSUE PRICE	VALUE
2001 $5 Two coin Marconi set .... N/A		99.95	50.00

F.I.F.A. 2006 World Cup, 2003
Diameter: 38.1 mm; weight: 31.3 grams, thickness: 3.1 mm;
composition: .9999 fine silver; finish: proof

The Royal Canadian Mint struck this coin to celebrate the "2006 FIFA World Cup Germany". The Canadian Soccer Association, founded in 1912, has been affiliated with the Fédération International de Football Association (FIFA) since 1913. Germany hosted the 2006 FIFA World Cup.

DATE	QTY. (000)	ISSUE PRICE	VALUE
2003 $5 Soccer... 50		39.95	50.00

BULLION ISSUES

Gold Maple Leaf, 1979-

The gold Maple Leaf was introduced in 1979 as a bullion coin for investors, each coin containing one Troy ounce of gold. In 1982 the mint raised the fineness from .999 to .9999 and began issuing maple leaf bullion coins in two smaller sizes, $5 (¹/₁₀ ounce) and $10 (¼ ounce). The $20 (½ ounce) size was added in 1986. The $1 (¹/₂₀ ounce) size was added in 1993 and the $2 (¹/₁₅ ounces) in 1994.

In 1988 the Mint introduced five additional maple leaf coins, one in silver (1 Troy ounce) and four in platinum (¹/₁₀, ¼, ½ and 1 Troy ounce). The ¹/₁₅ ounces platinum coin was introduced in 1994. The fineness of the silver maple leaf is .9999, while the platinum issues have a fineness of .9995.

All maple leaf bullion coins bear the same obverse and reverse designs, differing only in date, fineness, size (¼ oz., 1 oz., etc.) and metal specified in the legends.

The obverse bore the Arnold Machin effigy of the Queen until 1989 and has since shown the more mature Dora de Pédery-HUNT effigy, with the simple legend ELIZABETH II above and the nominal value and date beneath. An uncrowned portrait of Elizabeth II by Susan Blunt has been used since 2004 on the obverse. The reverse device, a single maple leaf, was designed by Walter Ott. The reverse legend includes the fineness of the coin and the word CANADA.

To mark the 20th anniversary of the gold Maple Leaf issues, the mint added a privy mark to each gold Maple Leaf value in 1999. The mark consists of "20 years/ans" within an oval and appears below the right half of the leaf.

GOLD MAPLE LEAF COINS
Maple Leaf 50 Dollars, 1979 –
ONE TROY OUNCE GOLD
Diameter 30.00 mm; weight: 31.150 grams; thickness: 2.80 mm;
fineness for all issues (1979–1982): .999 gold, (1983 –): .9999 gold

DATE	QTY. (000)	DATE	QTY. (000)	DATE	QTY. (000)	DATE	QTY. (000)
1979	1,000	1988	801	1997	478	2006	210
1980	1,215	1989	856	1998	594	2007	189
1981	863	1990	815	1999	627	2008	711
1982	883	1991	290	2000	86	2009	1,011
1983	843	1992	369	2001	139	2010	1,037
1984	1,068	1993	321	2002	345	2011	1,108
1985	1,908	1994	180	2003	195	2012	N/A
1986	779	1995	209	2004	254	2013	N/A
1987	1,119	1996	144	2005	282		

Maple Leaf 20 Dollars, 1986 –

ONE-HALF TROY OUNCE GOLD
Diameter 25.00 mm; weight: 15.584 grams; thickness: 2.30 mm

DATE	QTY. (000)	DATE	QTY. (000)	DATE	QTY. (000)	DATE	QTY. (000)
1986	529	1993	99	2000	24	2007	13
1987	384	1994	105	2001	27	2008	34
1988	522	1995	103	2002	29	2009	29
1989	259	1996	66	2003	23	2010	34
1990	174	1997	63	2004	13	2011	32
1991	96	1998	65	2005	20	2012	N/A
1992	116	1999	65	2006	21	2013	N/A

Maple Leaf 10 Dollars, 1982 –

ONE-QUARTER TROY OUNCE GOLD
Diameter 20.00 mm; weight: 7.797 grams; thickness: 1.70 mm

DATE	QTY. (000)	DATE	QTY. (000)	DATE	QTY. (000)	DATE	QTY. (000)
1982	184	1990	254	1998	85	2006	26
1983	309	1991	166	1999	99	2007	17
1984	242	1992	180	2000	32	2008	34
1985	620	1993	158	2001	35	2009	71
1986	915	1994	157	2002	43	2010	42
1987	437	1995	128	2003	23	2011	36
1988	380	1996	89	2004	18	2012	N/A
1989	329	1997	98	2005	26	2013	N/A

Maple Leaf 5 Dollars, 1982 –

ONE-TENTH TROY OUNCE GOLD
Diameter 16.00 mm; weight: 3.131 grams; thickness: 1.22 mm

DATE	QTY. (000)	DATE	QTY. (000)	DATE	QTY. (000)	DATE	QTY. (000)
1982	246	1990	476	1998	302	2006	41
1983	304	1991	322	1999	710	2007	21
1984	—	1992	384	2000	53	2008	39
1985	398	1993	249	2001	63	2009	227
1986	530	1994	313	2002	45	2010	111
1987	529	1995	294	2003	27	2011	81
1988	412	1996	179	2004	33	2012	N/A
1989	539	1997	189	2005	30	2013	N/A

Maple Leaf 2 Dollars, 1994 & 1996

ONE-FIFTEENTH TROY OUNCE GOLD
Diameter 15.00 mm; weight: 2.070 grams; thickness: 0.98 mm

DATE	QTY. (000)	DATE	QTY. (000)
1994	4	1996	120*

*Number of pieces issued.

Maple Leaf 1 Dollar, 1993 –

ONE-TWENTIETH TROY OUNCE GOLD
Diameter 14.10 mm; weight: 1.566 grams; thickness: 0.92 mm

DATE	QTY. (000)	DATE	QTY. (000)	DATE	QTY. (000)	DATE	QTY. (000)
1993	37	1999	63	2005	10	2011	19
1994	79	2000	31	2006	19	2012	N/A
1995	86	2001	20	2007	18	2013	N/A
1996	57	2002	17	2008	15		
1997	60	2003	15	2009	39		
1998	44	2004	20	2010	9		

1/25 Troy Ounce Gold - Special Gold Maple Leaf

Diameter: 13.92 mm; weight: 1.27 grams;
composition: .9999 gold; finish: proof.

Images x 1.5

DATE		QTY.	ISSUE PRICE	VALUE
2004	50¢ Majestic Moose, by Cosme Saffioti	24,991	69.95	200.00
2005	50¢ Voyageur, by Emanuel Hann	13,993	69.95	125.00
2005	50¢ Voyageur, in capsules	11,000	69.95	125.00
2006	50¢ Cowboy, by Michelle Grant	13,524	69.95	125.00
2006	50¢ Cowboy in capsules	7,160	69.95	175.00
2007	50¢ Wolf, by William Wood	12,514	81.95	125.00
2008	50¢ de Havilland Canada Beaver, by Peter Mossman	13,526	81.95	125.00
2009	50¢ Red Maple, by RCM Engravers	11,854	99.95	150.00
2010	50¢ RCMP, by Janet Griffin-Scott	9,594	99.95	150.00
2011	50¢ Geese, by Emily Damstra	7,498	109.95	110.00
2012	50¢ Bluenose, by Philip MacCready	15,000	129.95	130.00

GOLD 50 DOLLARS, 1997

ONE TROY OUNCE – GUARANTEED VALUE

Shape: 10-sided; diameter: 30 mm; weight: 1 Troy oz.;
thickness: 3.25 mm; edge: plain; purity: .9999 gold

The Royal Canadian Mint introduced this 10-sided gold coin with a guaranteed value of US$310 until January 1, 2000. After that date it will trade at the price of gold bullion. The obverse features the Dora de Pédery-HUNT effigy of the queen circumscribed by a circle. The legend ELIZABETH II [date] D. G. REGINA, with 50 DOLLARS at the bottom, is inscribed around the circumference of the circle. The legend 310$US GARANTIS PAR LA MRC JUSQU'AU 1er JANV. 2000 • US$310 GUARANTEED BY THE RCM TO JAN. 1st 2000 • is inscribed between the rim and the inner circle. The coin was sold for a higher premium than other bullion issues.

DATE		QTY.	ISSUE PRICE	VALUE
1997	$50 with guaranteed value until Jan. 1, 2000	13,000	N/A	1,700

50 Dollars Gold Maple Leaf - 25th Anniversary (1979–2004)

2005

The reverse was designed by the Walter Ott of the Royal Canadian Mint to commemorate the 25th anniversary of the gold Maple Leaf. In 2005, a special .99999 fine maple leaf was released.

DATE		QTY.(000)	ISSUE PRICE	VALUE
2004	$50 1979 - 2004 25th Anniversary............................ 10		N/A	1,700
2005	$50 .99999 fine gold ....400 pieces		N/A	2,500

50 Dollars Gold Maple Leaf
Winter Olympic Games - Vancouver 2010

Diameter: 30 mm; weight: 31.1035 grams;
composition: .9999 gold; finish: bullion.

DATE		QTY.(000)	ISSUE PRICE	VALUE
2008	$50 Vancouver 2010......................................76		N/A	1,500
2008	$50 Vancouver 2010 Coloured ....N/A		N/A	1,500
2009	$50 Vancouver 2010......................................74		N/A	1,500
2009	$50 Vancouver 2010 Coloured ....N/A		N/A	1,500
2010	$50 Vancouver 2010.................................. 6 pieces		N/A	1,500
2010	$50 Vancouver 2010 Coloured ....N/A		N/A	1,500

200 Dollars Gold Maple Leaf, 2007–2010

Diameter: 30 mm; weight: 31.15 grams;
composition: .99999 gold; finish: bullion

Privy mark

DATE		QTY.(000)	ISSUE PRICE	VALUE
2007	$200	31	N/A	1,500
2007	$200 with privy mark	595 pieces	1,899.95	1,500
2008	$200	27	N/A	1,500
2009	$200	14	N/A	1,500
2010	$200	23	N/A	1,500

200 Dollars Gold Maple Leaf, 2011

The reverse features a Royal Canadian Mounted Police officer riding a horse at full gallop, surrounded by a circle of maple leaves, in a classic 1997 design by former Master Engraver Ago Aarand.

DATE		QTY.(000)	ISSUE PRICE	VALUE
2011	$200 RCMP	8.4	N/A	1,500

One Troy Ounce Gold Wafer, 1998

Width: 24.2 mm; length: 40.20 mm; weight: 31.160 grams;
thickness: 1.717 mm; purity .9999 gold

The rectangular wafer was introduced in 1998 as an alternative to the Maple Leaf coins for investors. The Royal Canadian Mint's Hallmark is displayed at the top of the obverse with the legend 1 OZ / .999 / FINE GOLD / OR PUR in four lines below. The Royal Canadian Mint logo is repeated 45 times (9 horizontal rows of 5) on the reverse of the wafer.

DATE		QTY. (000)
1998	One Troy ounce wafer	N/A
1999	One Troy ounce wafer	N/A

1,000,000 Dollars Gold Maple Leaf

Diameter: 500 mm; weight: 100 kilos (3215 troy oz.);
thickness: 30 mm; composition: .99999 gold; finish: polished casting.

Image reduced to 10%

DATE		QTY.	ISSUE PRICE	VALUE
2007	1,000,000 Dollars.	2 pieces	BV	5,475,000
2008	1,000,000 Dollars.	2 pieces	BV	5,475,000

MAPLE LEAF PROOF SETS
AND SINGLES
Tenth Anniversary of Maple Leaf Coins, 1989

In 1989, for the tenth anniversary of the maple leaf coins, commemorative sets and singles were issued in proof only. All coins were encapsulated and single coins and sets were packaged in solid maple cases with brown velvet liners.

Physical specifications and composition remain the same as other issues.

ITEM		QTY. (000)	ISSUE PRICE	VALUE
1989	Gold 4-coin set (¹/₁₀, ¼, ½ and 1 Troy ounce)	7	1,395.00	3,150
1989	Platinum 4-coin set (¹/₁₀, ¼, ½ and 1 Troy ounce)	2	1,995.00	3,150
1989	Combination set, 3 coins, 1 Troy ounce each			
	(1 gold, 1 platinum and 1 silver)	4	1,795.00	3,150
1989	Combination $5 set (gold ¹/₁₀ oz., platinum ¹/₁₀ oz.			
	and silver 1 oz. maple leaf coins)	10	195.00	500.00
1989	Single gold 1 Troy ounce maple leaf	7	795.00	1,700
1989	Single silver 1 Troy ounce maple leaf	30	39.00	45.00

GOLD MAPLE LEAF HOLOGRAM SET, 1999 & 2001

In the 1999 & 2001 the Mint issued a set of 5 coins, ranging from 1/20 to 1 full Troy ounce of .9999 gold. The reverse, designed by the Royal Canadian Mint Engraving Department, features three maple leaves on a branch. The image is also a hologram: The obverse features the Dora de Pédery-HUNT effigy of Queen Elizabeth II. All coins have a brilliant relief on a matte field. The edge of each coin is reeded. The 2001 1/4 oz. ($10) coin was also issued singly.

PHYSICAL SPECIFICATIONS

FACE	TROY (OZ.)	DIAMETER (MM)	WEIGHT (GRAMS)	FINENESS
$50	1	30	31.150	.9999
$20	1/2	25	15.584	.9999
$10	1/4	20	7.797	.9999
$5	1/10	16	3.131	.9999
$1	1/20	14.1	1.581	.9999

DATE	QTY.	ISSUE PRICE	VALUE
1999 Gold hologram set	500	1995.95	3,500
2001 Gold hologram set	600	1995.95	3,500

GOLD & SILVER PIEDFORT MAPLE LEAF COIN SET, 2010

Diameter: 16 mm; weight: 6.25 grams; composition: .99999 gold; edge: reeded; thickness: 2 mm; finish: reverse proof.

Diameter: 34 mm; weight: 31.39 grams; composition: .9999 silver; edge: reeded; thickness: 3.84 mm; finish: reverse proof.

Piedfort coins, whose name comes from the French for "heavy measure", originated in medieval Europe. Coin-makers deliberately made their die templates thick and heavy to ensure they would not be confused with regular coins. Traditionally, a piedfort is a piece struck of a planchet that is thicker than normal. Reverse by the RCM engravers.

DATE	QTY.	ISSUE PRICE	VALUE
2010 Gold & Silver piedfort maple leaf set	1,264*	679.95	680.00

*6,843 Silver maple leafs were issued individually.

GOLD MAPLE LEAF SET, 2011

In 1911, the Royal Canadian Mint (then known as the Ottawa Branch of Britain's Royal Mint) opened its much-anticipated refinery in Ottawa. The need for such a facility had been growing for years; fuelled by the gold that was being mined in British Columbia and the Yukon; and the increasing demand for gold coins—a need that also required the complex task of refining raw ore to gold coinage standards. Currently, the Royal Canadian Mint's refinery is recognized as one of the world's largest with a production capacity of 5 million Troy ounces per year.

FACE	TROY (OZ.)	DIAMETER (MM)	WEIGHT (GRAMS)	FINENESS
$50	1	30	31.15	.9999
$10	1/4	20	7.80	.9999
$5	1/10	16	3.13	.9999
$1	1/20	14.1	1.58	.9999

DATE	QTY.	ISSUE PRICE	VALUE
2011 Gold maple leaf set, 100th Anniversary of Refinery	479	3,739.95	3,500

5th Anniversary of the Million Dollar Coin, 2012

The world's first million-dollar coin celebrates its fifth anniversary. This set features Royal Canadian Mint engraver Stan Witten's three-leaf design from the original million-dollar coin.

FACE	TROY (OZ.)	DIAMETER (MM)	WEIGHT (GRAMS)	FINENESS
$50	1	30	31.15	.9999
$10	1/4	20	7.80	.9999
$5	1/10	16	3.13	.9999
$1	1/20	14.1	1.58	.9999
50¢	1/25	13.92	1.27	.9999

DATE	QTY.	ISSUE PRICE	VALUE
2012 Gold maple leaf set, 5th Anniversary of the Million Dollar Coin	N/A	3,999.95	3,750

2012 Year of the Dragon Pure Gold Fractional Set

Symbol of prosperity and leadership, the Dragon is said to be embodied by the Emperor on Earth. A fiery, enthusiastic, captivating, and fiercely loyal creature, the Dragon brings its influence to the events and conditions of the year that carries its name.

FACE	TROY (OZ.)	DIAMETER (MM)	WEIGHT (GRAMS)	FINENESS
$50 1	30	31.16	.9999
$20 . . . . 1/2			.9999
$10 . . . . 1/4	20	7.80	.9999
$5 . . . . 1/10	16	3.14	.9999

DATE	QTY.	ISSUE PRICE	VALUE
2012 Gold Year of the Dragon set 500			

2013 The Maple Leaf Pure Gold Fractional Set

Well before the coming of the first European settlers, Canada's aboriginal peoples had discovered the food properties of maple sap, which they gathered every spring. Today the sugar maple is one of the most important Canadian trees, the major source of sap for making maple syrup. Canada produces more than 80 percent of the world's maple syrup.

FACE	TROY (OZ.)	DIAMETER (MM)	WEIGHT (GRAMS)	FINENESS
$50 1	30	31.16	.9999
$10 . . . . 1/4	20	7.80	.9999
$5 . . . . 1/10	16	3.14	.9999
$1 . . . . 1/20	14.1	1.58	.9999

DATE	QTY.	ISSUE PRICE	VALUE
2013 Gold The Maple Leaf set 600			

2014 The Maple Leaf Pure Gold Fractional Set

The leaf of the strong, resilient and bountiful sugar maple has long been a symbol of Canada. Beloved Acer saccharum, found readily across this land's rugged northeastern forests, has something to offer all year long, from the shade provided by its broad leaves in summer and the glory of its vibrant red, purple, and orange leaves in autumn to the delicious wonder of its sap in springtime.

FACE	TROY (OZ.)	DIAMETER (MM)	WEIGHT (GRAMS)	FINENESS
$50 1		30	31.16	.9999
$10 . . . . .1/4		20	7.80	.9999
$5 . . . . .1/10		16	3.14	.9999
$1 . . . . .1/20		14.1	1.58	.9999

DATE	QTY.	ISSUE PRICE	VALUE
2014 Gold The Maple Leaf set 600		3,999.95	4,000.00

2015 The Maple Leaf Pure Gold Fractional Set

The silver maple, scientifically known as Acer saccharinum, is a species of maple tree native to eastern North America. Though it requires a more sunlight than other maple trees, it is highly adaptable.

FACE	TROY (OZ.)	DIAMETER (MM)	WEIGHT (GRAMS)	FINENESS
$50 1		30	31.16	.9999
$10 . . . . .1/4		20	7.80	.9999
$5 . . . . .1/10		16	3.14	.9999
$1 . . . . .1/20		14.1	1.58	.9999

DATE	QTY.	ISSUE PRICE	VALUE
2015 Gold The Maple Leaf set 600		3,999.95	4,000.00

2014 The Maple Leaf Pure Silver Fractional Set

The strong, resilient, and bountiful sugar maple has long been a symbol of Canada. Beloved Acer saccharum, found readily across this land's rugged northeastern forests, has something to offer all year long, from the shade provided by its broad leaves in summer and the glory of its vibrant red, purple, and orange leaves in autumn to the delicious wonder of its sap in springtime, which makes the best maple syrup on the planet. Artist Arnold Nogy.

FACE	TROY (OZ.)	DIAMETER (MM)	WEIGHT (GRAMS)	FINENESS
$5 1		38	31.39	.9999
$4 ....1/2		34	15.87	.9999
$3 ....1/4		27	7.96	.9999
$2 ....1/10		20	3.23	.9999
$1 ....1/20		16	1.62	.9999

DATE	QTY.	ISSUE PRICE	VALUE
2014 Silver The Maple Leaf set 9,999		249.95	250.00

2015 The Maple Leaf Pure Silver Fractional Set

Artist Lilyane Coulombe.

DATE	QTY.	ISSUE PRICE	VALUE
2015 Silver The Maple Leaf set 9,999		224.95	225.00

2015 Bald Eagle Pure Silver Fractional Set

The amazing bald eagle—Haliaeetus leucocephalus—is Canada's largest bird of prey and the only eagle exclusive to North America. An apex predator with no natural enemies, the bald eagle has long been a potent symbol of vision, power, and stoicism. Designed by award-winning artist Derek C. Wicks.

FACE	TROY (OZ.)	DIAMETER (MM)	WEIGHT (GRAMS)	FINENESS
$5	1	38	31.39	.9999
$4	1/2	34	15.87	.9999
$3	1/4	27	7.96	.9999
$2	1/10	20	3.23	.9999

DATE	QTY.	ISSUE PRICE	VALUE
2015 Silver Bald Eagle set	7,500	199.95	200.00

5 DOLLARS
Silver Maple Leaf, 1988 –
ONE TROY OUNCE SILVER

Diameter: 38 mm; weight: 31.390 grams;
thickness: 3.21 mm, composition: .9999 silver

DATE	QTY. (000)	DATE	QTY. (000)	DATE	QTY. (000)	DATE	QTY. (000)
1988	1,062	1995	326	2002	576	2009	9,727
1989	3,332	1996	250	2003	685	2010	17,800
1990	1,709	1997	101	2004	681	2011	23,130
1991	644	1998	591	2005	956	2012	N/A
1992	344	1999	1,229	2006	2,465	2013	N/A
1993	890	2000	404	2007	3,526		
1994	1,134	2001	399	2008	7,909		

5 DOLLARS SILVER PROOF
Diameter: 38 mm; weight: 31.110 grams; thickness: 3.29 mm, composition: .9999 silver

Maple Leaf Coloured Coin, 2001–2004

2001

2002

2003

2004

The coins in this series are designed to portray the seasons of the year. The first three coins bear the Dora de Pedery-HUNT effigy on the obverse while the 2004 coin shows the Susanna Blunt design

DATE		QTY.	ISSUE PRICE	VALUE
2001	$5 Autumn Maple Leaf reverse by Debbie Adams	50,000	34.95	70.00
2002	$5 Spring Maple Leaf	29,000	34.95	75.00
2003	$5 Summer Maple Leaf reverse by Stan Witten	29,416	34.95	70.00
2004	$5 Winter Maple Leaf reverse by Stan Witten	26,848	34.95	85.00

5 DOLLARS
SILVER MAPLE LEAF WITH HOLOGRAM
Silver Maple Leaf of Hope, 2001–2005
Diameter: 38 mm; weight: 31.39 grams; thickness: 3.15 mm;
fineness: .9999 silver, edge: reeded; finish: reverse proof

| 2001 | 2003 | 2005 |

The first Silver Maple Leaf coin with a hologram had a privy mark on the reverse which included Chinese characters meaning "Maple of Hope." Subsequent issues have also incorporated the Chinese "Maple of Hope" into the privy mark on the reverse. The first two coins bear the Dora de Pedery-HUNT effigy on the obverse while the 2005 coin shows the Susanna Blunt design

DATE		QTY.	ISSUE PRICE	VALUE
2001	$5 Maple Leaf of Hope	30,000	59.95	100.00
2003	$5 Maple Leaf of Hope	29,731	39.95	80.00
2005	$5 Maple Leaf of Hope	19,888	39.95	90.00

5 DOLLARS SILVER
SILVER MAPLE LEAF WITH HOLOGRAM
15th Anniversary of the Loon Dollar, 2002

The Dora de Pedery-HUNT adorns the obverse and the reverse was designed by the staff of the Royal Canadian Mint for this anniversary salute to the popular Loon Dollar.

DATE		QTY.	ISSUE PRICE	VALUE
2002	$5 15th Anniversary Loon, Hologram	30,000	59.95	125.00

5 Dollars Silver Maple Leaf Coloured Coin, 2005-2007

Diameter: 38 mm; weight: 31.39; edge: serrated;
composition: .9999 pure silver; finish: bullion.

2005	2006

2007 Obverse	2007

Found throughout southwestern British Columbia the Big Leaf (or Broadleaf) Maple's leaves can grow to 30 cm (1 foot) wide. The obverse (by Susanna Blunt) has a brilliant effigy on a bullion background. The reverse was designed by Stan Witten.

DATE		QTY.	ISSUE PRICE	VALUE
2005	$5 Big Maple Leaf	21,233	39.95	70.00
2006	$5 Silver Maple Leaf.	14,157	45.95	135.00
2007	$5 Sugar Maple Leaf	11,508	49.95	135.00

20th Anniversary of the Silver Maple Leaf (1988–2008)

DATE		QTY.	ISSUE PRICE	VALUE
2008	$5 Silver Maple Leaf, bullion finish	9,998	74.95	100.00

5 Dollars Silver Maple Leaf
Winter Olympic Games — Vancouver 2010

Diameter: 38 mm; weight: 31.39 grams;
composition: .9999 silver; finish: bullion.

DATE		QTY. (000)	ISSUE PRICE	VALUE
2008	$5 Vancouver 2010.	938	N/A	100.00
2009	$5 Vancouver 2010.	569	N/A	100.00
2010	$5 Vancouver 2010.	79	N/A	100.00
2010	$5 Vancouver 2010, Gold plated	N/A	N/A	100.00

5 Dollars Silver Maple Leaf — Wildlife Series, 2011

Diameter: 38 mm; weight: 31.39 grams;
composition: .9999 silver; finish: bullion.

DATE		QTY. (000)	ISSUE PRICE	VALUE
2011	$5 Wolf.	1,000	BV	45.00
2011	$5 Grizzly bear, by William Woodruff	1,000	BV	45.00

Wildlife Series, 2012

DATE		QTY.	ISSUE PRICE	VALUE
2012	$5 Cougar	N/A	BV	50.00
2012	$5 Moose	N/A	BV	50.00

Wildlife Series, 2013

DATE		QTY.	ISSUE PRICE	VALUE
2013	$5 Antelope	N/A	BV	50.00
2013	$5 Wood Bison	N/A	BV	50.00

25th Anniversary of Silver Maple Leaf, 2013

Designed by Canadian artist Jean-Louis Sirois, this coin's reverse "Shadowleaf" image features an original and highly creative take on the perennial Canadian maple leaf design present on all Silver Maple Leaf bullion coins.

DATE		QTY.	ISSUE PRICE	VALUE
2013	$5 Silver Maple Leaf	10,000		

20 DOLLARS SILVER PROOF

Diameter: 38 mm; weight: 31.39 grams;
composition: .9999 silver; finish: proof.

CANADIAN LIGHTHOUSES
Sambro Island Lighthouse, 2004

The first lighthouse in North America, Sambro Island Lighthouse was built in 1758 and still serves today as a life-saving beacon in the Port of Halifax, Nova Scotia. The reverse was adapted from a photograph by Hedley Doty.

Toronto Island Lighthouse, 2005

The Toronto Island Lighthouse was built in 1808 and is the oldest existing lighthouse on the Great Lakes.

DATE		QTY.	ISSUE PRICE	VALUE
2004	$20 Sambro Island Lighthouse	17,515	69.99	60.00
2005	$20 Toronto Island Lighthouse	14,006	69.99	60.00

50 DOLLARS - (TEN TROY OUNCES SILVER)
Silver Maple Leaf, 1998

Diameter: 65 mm; weight: 311.04 grams; thickness: 11 mm, composition: .9999 silver.
Certificate of authenticity: .925 silver (sterling), .075 copper

Issued for the tenth anniversary of the Silver Maple Leaf bullion coin, this is the largest legal tender Canadian coin ever produced. The edge bears the inscription "10th Anniversary / 10e anniversaire" and each coin is accompanied by a certificate of authenticity in the form of a sterling silver plaque engraved by the engravers at the Royal Canadian Mint. The coin was issued encapsulated and accompanies the Certificate of Authenticity in a black leather display case with black ultrasuede lining.

DATE	QTY.	ISSUE PRICE	VALUE
1998 $50 Silver Maple Leaf, 10 Troy ounces 14,000		199.99	600.00

SILVER MAPLE LEAF HOLOGRAM SET, 2003

The Royal Canadian Mint produced its first full set of fractional silver Maple Leaf Hologram coins in 2003. The set introduced $3 and $4 coins to Canadian denominations.

PHYSICAL SPECIFICATIONS

FACE	WEIGHT	DIAMETER (mm)	WEIGHT (grams)	FINENESS
$5	1 Troy Ounce (Maple)	38	31.39	.9999
$4	½ Troy Ounce	34	15.87	.9999
$3	¼ Troy Ounce	27	7.96	.9999
$2	¹⁄₁₀ Troy Ounce	20	3.23	.9999
$1	¹⁄₂₀ Troy Ounce	16	1.63	.9999

CANADIAN SILVER WILDLIFE COLLECTION
Arctic Fox, 2004

Artist: Claude D'Angelo

Canadian Lynx, 2005

Artist: Michael Dumas

DATE		QTY.	ISSUE PRICE	VALUE
2003	Silver Hologram proof set	28,947	149.95	150.00
2004	Arctic Fox, proof set of 4 coins	13,694	89.95	90.00
2005	Canadian Lynx, proof set of 4 coins	7,942	89.95	90.00

PLATINUM MAPLE LEAF 50 DOLLARS, 1988-

ONE TROY OUNCE PLATINUM

Diameter 30.00 mm; weight: 31.160 grams; thickness: 2.52 mm; purity: .9995 platinum

DATE	QTY. (000)	DATE	QTY. (000)	DATE	QTY. (000)	DATE	QTY. (000)
1988	26	1992	41	1996	62	2009	33
1989	10	1993	18	1997	25	2010	0
1990	15	1994	36	1998	10	2011	5
1991	32	1995	26	1999	3		

Maple Leaf 20 Dollars, 1988 – 1999

ONE-HALF TROY OUNCE PLATINUM

Diameter 25.00 mm; weight: 15.590 grams; thickness: 2.02 mm; purity: .9995 platinum

1988	24	1991	6	1994	7	1997	4
1989	5	1992	13	1995	6	1998	5
1990	3	1993	6	1996	5	1999	1

Maple Leaf 10 Dollars, 1988 – 1999

ONE-QUARTER TROY OUNCE PLATINUM

Diameter 20.00 mm; weight: 7.800 grams; thickness: 1.50 mm; purity: .9995 platinum

1988	87	1991	7	1994	9	1997	5
1989	3	1992	12	1995	7	1998	4
1990	2	1993	8	1996	6	1999	2

Maple Leaf 5 Dollars, 1988 – 1999

ONE-TENTH TROY OUNCE PLATINUM

Diameter 16.00 mm; weight: 3.132 grams; thickness: 1.01 mm; purity: .9995 platinum

1988	46	1991	13	1994	19	1997	7
1989	18	1992	16	1995	9	1998	6
1990	9	1993	14	1996	9	1999	4

Maple Leaf 2 Dollars, 1994–1997

ONE-FIFTEENTH TROY OUNCE PLATINUM

Diameter 15.00 mm; weight: 2.070 grams; thickness: 0.94 mm; purity: .9995 platinum

1994	135*	1995	1	1996	120*	1997	—

Maple Leaf 1 Dollar, 1993 – 1999

ONE-TWENTIETH TROY OUNCE PLATINUM

Diameter 14.10 mm; weight: 1.558 grams; thickness: 0.92 mm; purity: .9995 platinum

1993	2	1995	460*	1997	1	1999	4
1994	4	1996	2	1998	2		

*Number of pieces issued.

The Royal Canadian Mint did not produced platinum maple leaf bullion coins from 2000 to 2008. In 2009, a one ounce coin was struck.

PLATINUM PROOF SETS, 1990–2004

In 1990 the mint began issuing four-coin proof sets struck in platinum. Each set features a different animal or bird as its reverse theme and is housed in a burled walnut case lined with black ultra suede. The mintage of each set is restricted to 3,500 sets worldwide.

The common obverse features the new portrait of Queen Elizabeth II by Canadian artist Dora de Pédery-HUNT.

CANADIAN WILDLIFE
Physical Specifications

	BULLION CONTENT	DIAMETER (MM)	WEIGHT (GRAMS)	FINENESS
$300	1 Troy ounce	30.00	31.1035	.9995
$150	½ Troy ounce	25.00	15.552	.9995
$75	¼ Troy ounce	20.00	7.776	.9995
$30	1/10 Troy ounce	16.00	3.111	.9995

Polar Bear, 1990
The reverse designs are by Robert Bateman.

DATE		QTY.	ISSUE PRICE	VALUE
1990	Polar Bears – Proof set of 4 coins	3,000	1,990	4,000

Snowy Owl, 1991
The reverses designs are by Glen Loates.

DATE		QTY.	ISSUE PRICE	VALUE
1991	Snowy Owls – Proof set of 4 coins	1,000	1,990	4,000

Cougar, 1992

The reverse designs are by George McLean.

DATE		QTY.	ISSUE PRICE	VALUE
1992	Cougars – Proof set of 4 coins	1,000	1,955.00	4,000

Arctic Fox, 1993

The reverse designs are by Claudio D'Angelo.

DATE		QTY.	ISSUE PRICE	VALUE
1993	Arctic Fox – Proof Set of 4 coins	1,000	1,955.00	4,000

Sea Otter, 1994

The reverse designs are by Ron S. Parker, of British Columbia.

DATE		QTY.	ISSUE PRICE	VALUE
1994	Sea Otter– Proof Set of 4 coins	766	1,955.00	4,000

Canadian Lynx, 1995
The reverse designs are by Michael Dumas.

In 1995 the mintage for the Platinum Proof set was restricted to 1,500 sets worldwide and the encapsulated $30 and $150 coins were also sold singly, accompanied by a certificate of authenticity and housed in a case.

DATE		QTY.	ISSUE PRICE	VALUE
1995	Canadian Lynx – Proof set of 4 coins	569	2,095.95	4,000
1995	$30 Lynx (1/10 oz.) in burgundy case	523	159.95	475.00
1995	$150 Lynx (½ oz.) in mahogany case	193	599.95	2,400

Peregrine Falcon, 1996
The reverse designs are by Dwayne Harty.

1996	Peregrine Falcon – Proof set of 4 coins	675	2,095.95	4,000
1996	$30 Peregrine Falcon (1/10 oz.) in burgundy case	910	159.95	475.00
1996	$150 Peregrine Falcon (½ oz.) in mahogany case	196	599.95	2,400

Wood Bison, 1997
The reverses are the designs of Chris Bacon.

1997	Wood Bison – Proof set of 4 coins	616	2,095.95	4,000
1997	$30 Wood Bison (1/10 oz.) in burgundy case	740	159.95	475.00
1997	$150 Wood Bison (½ oz.) in mahogany case	184	599.95	2,400

Gray Wolf, 1998

The reverses are the designs of Kerri Burnett

DATE		QTY.*	ISSUE PRICE	VALUE
1998	Gray Wolf – Proof set of 4 coins	661	2,095.95	4,000
1998	$30 Gray Wolf (¹/₁₀ oz.) in burgundy case	664	179.95	475.00
1998	$150 Gray Wolf (½ oz.) in mahogany case	194	599.95	2,400

Musk-ox, 1999

The reverses are the designs of Mark Hobson

DATE		QTY.	ISSUE PRICE	VALUE
1999	Musk-ox – Proof set of 4 coins	495	2,095.95	4,000
1999	$30 Musk-ox (¹/₁₀ oz.) in burgundy case	999	179.95	475.00

Number of sets or pieces issued.

Pronghorn Antelope, 2000

The reverses are the designs of Mark Hobson

DATE		QTY.	ISSUE PRICE	VALUE
2000	Pronghorn Antelope – Proof set of 4 coins	599	2,095.95	4,000

Harlequin Duck, 2001

The Harlequin Duck, endangered in eastern Canada, is featured on the reverse of each coin. The designs are by Royal Canadian Mint's engravers.

DATE		QTY.*	ISSUE PRICE	VALUE
2001	Harlequin Duck – proof set of 4 coins	448	2,395.95	4,000

Great Blue Heron, 2002

The reverse designs are by Jean-Luc Grondin.

DATE		QTY.	ISSUE PRICE	VALUE
2002	Great Blue Heron – proof set of 4 coins	344	2,495.95	4,000

*Number of sets or pieces issued.

Atlantic Walrus, 2003

The reverse designs are by Jean-Luc Grondin.

DATE		QTY.	ISSUE PRICE	VALUE
2003	Atlantic Walrus – proof set of 4 coins	700	2,995.95	4,000

Grizzly Bear, 2004

The reverse designs are by Kerri Burnett.

DATE		QTY.	ISSUE PRICE	VALUE
2004	Grizzly Bear – proof set of 4 coins	376	2,995.95	4,000

PALLADIUM MAPLE LEAF 50 DOLLARS, 2005-

ONE TROY OUNCE PALLADIUM

Diameter 30.00 mm; weight: 31.15 grams; thickness: 2.91 mm; purity: .9995 palladium

DATE	QTY. (000)	DATE	QTY. (000)	DATE	QTY. (000)	DATE	QTY. (000)
2005	63	2007	15	2009	40	2011	0
2006	69	2008	10	2010	25		

Special Test Issue, 2005

Two types were struck to test two different planchets of different manufacturers. Privy marks "A" & "B" were used to distinguish those types. The reverse was designed by the Walter Ott.

DATE		QTY.	ISSUE PRICE	VALUE
2005	$50 test maple leaf - privy mark "A"	146	1,300.00	3,100
2005	$50 test maple leaf - privy mark "B"	144	1,300.00	3,100

50 Dollars - Big and Little Bear Constellations, 2006

Diameter: 34 mm; weight: 31.15 grams; thickness: 2.91 mm;
fineness: .9995 palladium, edge: reeded; finish: specimen with laser effect.

Obverse	Spring

Summer	Autumn	Winter

DATE	QTY.	ISSUE PRICE	VALUE
2006 Spring	300	849.95	1,000
2006 Summer	300	849.95	1,000
2006 Autumn	300	849.95	1,000
2006 Winter	300	849.95	1,000

THE FRENCH REGIME

None of the coins of the French regime is strictly Canadian. All were general issues for the French colonies of the New World. The coinage of 1670 was authorized by an edict of Louis XIV dated February 9, 1670, for use in New France, Acadia, the French settlements in Newfoundland and the French West Indies. The copper of 1717 to 1722 was authorized by edicts of 1716 and 1721 for use in New France, Louisiana, and the French West Indies.

Issue of 1670

The coinage of 1670 consisted of silver 5 and 15 sols. A copper 2 deniers was also authorized but never struck. A total of 200,000 of the 5 sols and 40,000 of the 15 sols was struck at Paris. Old copper coin was to have been melted down at Nantes, but this was not done; the reasons for this may never be known, since the archives of the Nantes mint before 1700 were destroyed. The only known specimen is a pattern struck at Paris. The coins were not popular in New France. The silver coins were raised in value by a third in 1672 to keep them circulating, but in vain. They rapidly disappeared, and by 1680 none was to be seen. Later they were restored to their original value.

Note: Silver pieces similar to the 5 and 15 sols, with other dates and inscribed SIT NOMEN DOMINI BENEDICTUM were struck for use in France. Their use in the colonies was not intended at first. Most of the pieces are much more common than the colonial issue of 1670.

Copper

DATE AND VALUE	VG	F	VF	EF
Double or 2 Deniers 1670			(Unique)	

Silver

DATE AND VALUE	VG	F	VF	EF
5 sols 1670	800.00	1,300	2,250	3,500
15 sols 1670	20,000	35,000	50,000	75,000

Coinage of 1717–1720

The copper 6 and 12 deniers of 1717, authorized by an edict of Louis XV dated December 1716, were to be struck at Perpignan. The order could not be carried out because the supply of copper was too brassy. A second attempt in 1720 also failed, probably for the same reason. All these coins are extremely rare, the 6 deniers of 1720 probably being unique.

Copper

DATE AND VALUE	VG	F	VF	EF
6 deniers 1717	2,750	3,750	6,500	
6 deniers 1720				Unique
12 deniers 1717	2,750	3,750	6,500	

Coinage of 1721–1722

The copper coins of 1721–1722, authorized by an edict of Louis XV dated June 1721, were struck on copper blanks imported from Sweden. Rouen and La Rochelle struck pieces of 9 deniers in 1721 and 1722. New France received 534,000 pieces, mostly from the mint of La Rochelle, but only 8,180 were successfully put into circulation as the colonists disliked copper. In 1726 the rest of the issue was sent back to France.

Copper

DATE AND VALUE	VG	F	VF	EF
9 deniers 1721B	275.00	400.00	550.00	750.00
9 deniers 1721H	100.00	140.00	200.00	275.00
9 deniers 1722H, 2 over 1	120.00	225.00	300.00	450.00
9 deniers 1722, normal date	100.00	140.00	200.00	275.00

French Billon Coins Used In Canada

Almost every type of French coin minted between 1600 and 1759 sooner or later found its way into Canada. To enumerate all these would be unwise, therefore we have confined the listings to the billon coinages, large shipments of which were known to have been sent to Canada. There are several types which were brought to New France. They are:

(a) The countermarked douzains of 1640. In 1640 all old douzains in France were stamped with a fleur de lys in an oval and re-issued at 15 deniers.

(b) The douzain of 1658. This was issued at 12 deniers, but raised to 15 deniers four months later.

(c) The 15 deniers of 1692–1707.

(d) The mousquetaire of 30 deniers 1709–1713, with its half, already listed.

(e) The 23 deniers of 1738–1760 and its half, already listed.

The John Law Coinage. At the instigation of John Law, many changes were made in the French coinage. Copper pieces of 3, 6 and 12 deniers were introduced in 1719 and 1720 and coined till 1724. A coinage of silver ecus, halves, thirds, sixths, and twelfths was introduced in 1720 and coined till 1724. The petit Louis d'argent of 3 livres was coined in 1720, and a pure silver livre was also coined. Gold Louis and halves were coined from 1720 to 1723.

Date and value	VG	F	VF	EF
15 deniers 1710–1713AA	200.00	330.00	460.00	800.00
30 deniers 1709–1713AA	175.00	230.00	330.00	525.00
30 deniers 1709–1713D	155.00	230.00	290.00	525.00

Date and value	VG	F	VF	EF
Half sol marque 1738–54	175.00	225.00	300.00	500.00
Sol marque 1738–1760*	60.00	85.00	150.00	400.00

The piece of 30 deniers was called a "mousquetaire," and was coined at Metz and Lyons. The 15 deniers was coined only at Metz. The sol marque and half were coined at almost every French mint, those of Paris being most common.

Specimens of the sol marque dated after 1760 were not used in Canada, which by then was firmly in British hands.

Mint marks on French Regime coins:

Paris – A; Metz – AA; Rouen – B; Lyons – D; LaRoche – H; Perpignan – Q.

Playing Card Money

In the early days of New France the first ship arriving from France in the spring of each year carried a supply of coins to be used for paying the troops and purchasing furs and other raw products. Everything that New France could not produce for itself had to be imported from France, with payment in cash. Taxes were also paid in cash. In spite of a rich trade in furs, New France imported more than it exported with the result that most of the coinage received from France was shipped back (sometimes on the next ship) in payment to France. The resultant shortage of coins (particularly in winter when no ships would arrive from France) caused considerable inconvenience.

In 1685 the Intendant, Jacques de Meulles, decided to introduce an emergency issue of paper money for paying the troops. There were no printing presses in New France and the only available paper was writing paper which was not durable enough to be used as currency. Playing cards were plentiful in New France and made to be handled repeatedly, so de Meulles issued the first such notes on the backs of playing cards.

The first series of playing card money was issued in three denominations; four livres (equivalent to four English pounds) written on an entire card; two livres written on half a card; and 15 sols (the sol or sou being considered equivalent to the English shilling) written on a quarter card.

The measure adopted by de Meulles brought only temporary relief and the need for card money was met in the same manner by successive Governors and Intendants. Each new issue replaced the previous issue and stiff penalties were imposed on anyone keeping old cards after new ones were issued. It is for this reason that not a single specimen of the first eight issues of card money is known to exist today. After the first five issues, plain card was used rather than the backs of playing cards and a few of these can be found today in museum collections.

From 1685 to 1760 there were no fewer than 22 issues of card money used in New France. In the latter part of this period the supply of card money was supplemented by the issue of ordonnances (notes drawn on the treasury of Quebec) which were printed and written on ordinary paper. Although the issuance of card money was originally intended as a temporary expedient, the economy of New France was run almost entirely on locally produced paper money of this nature for a period of seventy-five years (two and a half generations).

All playing card money is very rare and is now protected from export from Canada by the Heritage and Culture Act.

COLONIAL TOKENS
MAGDALEN ISLANDS

The penny token was issued by Isaac Coffin, who planned to rule the islands like a feudal baron. At this time the islands belonged to the colony of Lower Canada. Coffin soon learned that he did not have the powers of a colonial governor, but his pennies must have circulated for a long time, since they are rather rare in very fine or better condition. The islands had been granted to Coffin, but were taken from him and put under the direct administration of Lower Canada, now the province of Quebec. There is evidence that this token was used in Halifax, Nova Scotia after being rejected by the Magdalen Islanders, and that it circulated in Halifax to a considerable extent at one time.

1

	BRETON		G	VG	F	VF	EF
1	520	Penny token 1815	70.00	125.00	225.00	475.00	1,300

NEWFOUNDLAND

Newfoundland was discovered by John Cabot in 1497 and claimed for England. The city of St. John's dates from about 1500. English authority was firmly established by Sir Humphrey Gilbert in 1583. Further settlements took place after 1600, but the French planted some colonies along the south coast, at and near Placentia. These were ceded to the British in 1710.

Rutherford Tokens

There was no coinage specifically for Newfoundland until 1841, when the first copper tokens issued by R. & I.S. Rutherford of St. John's appeared. The Rutherford family arms on the reverse contains the Latin phrase PER MARE PER TERRAS, meaning "by sea, by land."

2-3 obv   *2 rev.*   *4 rev.*

	BRETON		G	VG	F	VF	EF
2	952	RUTHERFORD etc., reverse no date	4.50	8.00	20.00	70.00	225.00
3		Same, 1841	4.50	8.00	20.00	75.00	225.00

The second Rutherford tokens were issued by Rutherford Bros. of Harbour Grace. These latter pieces were struck by Ralph Heaton & Sons, whose initials RH appear above the date. Eventually the Rutherford tokens became too plentiful and fell into discredit.

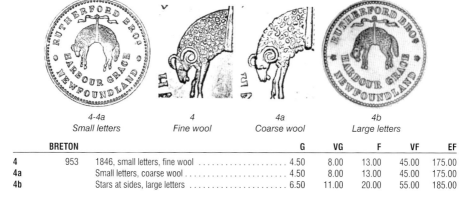

| | 4-4a | 4 | 4a | 4b |
| | Small letters | Fine wool | Coarse wool | Large letters |

BRETON			G	VG	F	VF	EF
4	953	1846, small letters, fine wool	4.50	8.00	13.00	45.00	175.00
4a		Small letters, coarse wool	4.50	8.00	13.00	45.00	175.00
4b		Stars at sides, large letters	6.50	11.00	20.00	55.00	185.00

M'Auslane Token

Number 5, of farthing size, appeared about 1845. It was not a farthing but an advertising piece issued by Peter M'Auslane, a general merchant whose business at St. John's was destroyed by fire shortly afterward. He then quit the island and settled in Ontario.

| 5 | 956 | PETER M'AUSLANE etc., brass .... Extremely Rare |

Anonymous Issues

At this time lightweight halfpennies were being brought over by the barrel from Prince Edward Island, and in 1851 and 1860, the government had to forbid their further importation and use. The rare ship token of 1858 was struck by Heaton and issued anonymously at St. John's. According to Breton, it had been faked, but the fakes were easily exposed.

The FISHERY RIGHTS token of 1860 commemorates the signing of a treaty by the major fishing nations to regulate the fisheries. Shore limits were fixed, the rights of local fishermen were recognized, and steps were taken for controlling the behaviour of foreign seamen whose vessels had to use local harbours for shelter or repairs.

BRETON			VG	F	VF	EF
6	954	Ship, 1858	1,000	1,500	2,200	3,000
7	955	FISHERY RIGHTS etc., 1860	75.00	150.00	200.00	450.00

Prince Edward Island

Prince Edward Island was colonized by France and originally named Isle St-Jean. Acquired by Great Britain in 1758, it was governed from Nova Scotia until 1770, when it was given the status of separate colony. In 1794 the island was given its present name in honour of Edward, Duke of Kent, the father of Queen Victoria.

The "Holey Dollar" and "Plug" of 1813

In 1813 the newly-arrived governor found a serious commercial crisis resulting from a lack of coined money on the island. His solution was to issue mutilated Spanish-American "dollars" (8 reales pieces), as was being done in some of the colonies in the West Indies and elsewhere. He directed that up to 1,000 dollars would be perforated, forming "plugs" (the discs punched out of the centre) and "holey dollars" (the rings that remained). The plugs were to pass for 1 shilling and the rings for 5 shillings; this over-rating (the whole dollars went for only 5 shillings), plus the mutilation was believed to be sufficient to keep these pieces in circulation.

Unfortunately, some individuals saw a chance to make a quick profit, and soon the colony was plagued with additional holey dollars (and plugs?) privately issued in imitation of those officially issued by the government treasury. This forced the recall of the official issue in 1814. Interestingly, the merchants then agreed to continue accepting the imitations in trade, thus raising them to the status of tokens.

Although we know of no documentary evidence regarding how the official issues were marked, purely circumstantial evidence points to a counterstamp of 10 triangles arranged in a circle, resembling a rayed sun. Furthermore, it is quite possible that the countermark was applied such that it overlapped the King's forehead on the dollars and his throat on the plugs.

There is presently no way of positively authenticating the supposed government counterstamp punch (or punches). The official and imitation issues are listed together for that reason.

Unfortunately, the situation is further complicated by the fact that later forgeries have been produced to deceive collectors. Some are complete fabrications which can be easily detected; however, others are made from genuine Spanish-American dollars and can be very difficult to differentiate from the pieces that circulated in P.E.I. Needless to say, great caution should be exercised in purchasing a purported P.E.I. "holey" dollar or "plug."

	VG	F	VF	EF	UNC
Holey dollar, original or contemporary imitation	2,500	3,000	4,000	5,000	—
Plug, original or contemporary imitation	2,500	3,500	4,500	—	—

Ships, Colonies & Commerce Tokens

The inscription on these pieces is an allusion to a remark made by Napoleon at the battle of Ulm. Ships, colonies, and commerce, he said, were the three British advantages that would defeat him in the end. The first tokens came out about 1829, and were struck in New York by Wright & Bale, and bear a striped flag superficially resembling the United States flag. These pieces were popular, and later issues were imported from England. Most of them were designed by Thomas Halliday. The two brass pieces dated 1815 were struck after 1830, being antedated to evade laws against anonymous tokens. The reverse of No. **9** is that of a private token of the Isle of Man.

BRETON			VG	F	VF	EF	UNC
8	995	ONE HALFPENNY TOKEN, 1815 . . . . 25.00		55.00	115.00	300.00	650.00
9	996	FOR PUBLICK ACCOMMODATION, 1815 . . . . 30.00		60.00	175.00	350.00	750.00

LEES			VG	F	VF	EF	UNC
10	2	Ship with U.S. flag 12.00		22.00	75.00	175.00	550.00
10a	1	Same with W & B N.Y. 22.00		45.00	150.00	325.00	850.00

It is doubtful if Number **11** (Breton's No. 999) will ever be positively identified. Its obverse, as drawn by Breton, shows a small ship very much like that of such Nova Scotia tokens as the Starr & Shannon pieces. Its reverse die has yet to be identified. The high poopdeck variety (**12**) has been said to be Breton 999, but this is not so. Judge Lees, who published these pieces in The Numismatist in 1926, made this point very clear.

11		Small ship . . . . Existence doubted		
12	5a	High poopdeck, blank flag . . . . Extremely Rare		

Tokens **10–12** *are also known to have been used in Lower Canada.*

The next three varieties bear the same reverse, characterized by very large, bold lettering. The first, Lees 5b, is very rare. It has been called fraudulent, and its status is still in question.

13   13a   13b

LEES			VG	F	VF	EF	UNC
13	5b	Long, low hull, no poopdeck	(Only Two Known)			. . . .	Extremely Rare
13a	6	Short, choppy waves	18.00	40.00	115.00	150.00	525.00
13b	7	Long, running waves	10.00	20.00	45.00	100.00	450.00

Tokens 13–13b are also known to have been used in Lower Canada.

The following tokens, numbered 997 by Breton, have over forty minor die varieties, some of which are very rare. They were struck in Birmingham and designed by Thomas Halliday. Most of the varieties are in the reverse inscription. For example, four styles of "&" are found on varieties of **14, 14b** and **14c**. The varieties of **14a** all have the "&" ending in a short horizontal bar.

14a

14	23–33	Raised H on exergue line	7.00	12.00	20.00	60.00	275.00
14a	9–13	No H on exergue line	12.00	25.00	65.00	150.00	600.00

14b   14c

14b	14–22	Two guys at top of spritsail	35.00	80.00	150.00	250.00	650.00
14c	34–46	H on exergue line and in water	10.00	20.00	50.00	125.00	375.00

The next three pieces are all characterized by ships having a drooping flag at the stern. Numbers **15** and **15a**, which correspond to Lees 3, are from complete dies in which all of the design (including rim beads) is present. There are thick (presumably struck first) and thin varieties. Lees 4, a lightweight piece of "blacksmith-like" character, was produced from the obverse die of **15, 15a** and a reverse die lacking rim beads. Care should be taken not to confuse worn lightweight specimens of Lees 3 (**15a**) for Lees 4 (**15b**).

15-15b obv.	15-15a rev.	15b rev.

LEES			AVERAGE CONDITION
15	3	Drooping flag, beads on both sides, thick	150.00
15a	3	Same, lightweight	225.00
15b	4	Same, no beads on reverse	2,000

Numbers 15, 15a and 15b are also known to have been used in Lower Canada.

Local Tokens, 1840–1858

Local tokens appeared first in 1840, the rarest being the sheaf of wheat halfpenny. It was struck by James Milner of Charlottetown with dies and machinery imported from the United States. The "SUCCESS TO THE FISHERIES" tokens (**17–17c**) were issued by E. Lydiard and F. Longworth of Charlottetown. Those with a clevis to the plow were issued in 1840, and those with a hook in 1857. The large tail to the fish fillet is well struck up, while the small tail is weak. These and all later tokens were struck by Ralph Heaton & Sons.

16

	BRETON		VG	F	VF	EF	UNC
16	916	Sheaf of wheat 1840	2,000	2,500	3,500	6,000	—

Clevis   Hook

17   Weak Tail   Bold Tail

17	917	Clevis, weak tail	10.00	15.00	40.00	100.00	600.00
17a		Clevis, bold tail	12.00	20.00	50.00	120.00	650.00
17b		Hook, weak tail	7.00	10.00	25.00	75.00	450.00
17c		Hook, bold tail	8.00	12.00	27.00	90.00	475.00

The Cent of 1855 was issued by James Duncan, a hardware merchant who moved to Charlotte-town from Montreal. This is the first Canadian decimal piece. It is doubtful if it was accepted as a hundredth of a dollar, for it weighed the same as the other tokens which were halfpennies and which went at 150 to the Spanish dollar. Specimens on thicker flans may have been an attempt to pass them as cents by increasing the weight.

The token showing the paddle steamer was issued in 1858, probably by James Duncan, though this has never been established. Early writers attributed it to Newfoundland.

18   19

BRETON			VG	F	VF	EF	UNC
18	920	One cent 1855	5.00	10.00	20.00	90.00	400.00
19	921	Paddle steamer	10.00	18.00	35.00	95.00	525.00

The tokens inscribed SELF GOVERNMENT AND FREE TRADE were issued by Henry Haszard and George and Simeon Davies. Numerous minor varieties are known. The most noticeable differences are in the island name and the style of 5 in the date. The first issues have the name rendered as PRINCE EDWARD'S ISLAND, and have 5s with short, thick tops. Later issues show first a change to 5s with longer, thinner tops, followed by a change to PRINCE EDWARD ISLAND.

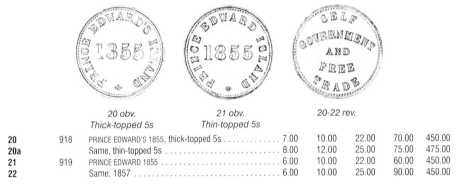

20 obv.   *21 obv.*   *20-22 rev.*
Thick-topped 5s *Thin-topped 5s*

20	918	PRINCE EDWARD'S 1855, thick-topped 5s	7.00	10.00	22.00	70.00	450.00
20a		Same, thin-topped 5s	8.00	12.00	25.00	75.00	475.00
21	919	PRINCE EDWARD 1855	6.00	10.00	22.00	60.00	450.00
22		Same, 1857	6.00	10.00	25.00	90.00	450.00

Nova Scotia

Nova Scotia was colonized for the first time in 1604 by Sieur de Monts, who claimed the land for France under the name of Acadia. Captured several times by the British, it was always returned to France, but in 1713 it passed permanently into British hands and was renamed Nova Scotia.

Very little coined money was available in the early days under the British. Some Spanish dollars and occasional shipments of British halfpennies and farthings were almost the only coins to be had. The Spanish dollar was accepted in Halifax at five shillings, which rating became legal by 1758. Halifax Currency, as this rating was called, was destined to become the standard of all the Canadian colonies.

Trade & Navigation Tokens, 1812–1814

After 1800 the shortage of copper began to become serious, and about 1812 local merchants started to import tokens from England and Ireland. The first were the "Trade & Navigation" tokens, struck over the tokens of Samuel Guppy of Bristol. The farthing is known to have been imported by a Halifax merchant named Haliburton.

For many years there have been reports of a penny bearing the date 1812, but in recent years none has been found. Early auction sales record specimens dated 1812, but none has been traced.

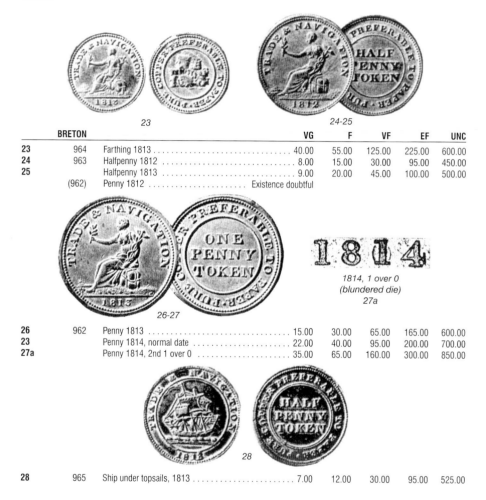

23   24-25

BRETON			VG	F	VF	EF	UNC
23	964	Farthing 1813 . . . . 40.00	55.00	125.00	225.00	600.00
24	963	Halfpenny 1812 . . . . 8.00	15.00	30.00	95.00	450.00
25		Halfpenny 1813 . . . . 9.00	20.00	45.00	100.00	500.00
	(962)	Penny 1812 . . . . Existence doubtful				

1814, 1 over 0
(blundered die)
27a

26-27

26	962	Penny 1813 . . . . 15.00	30.00	65.00	165.00	600.00
23		Penny 1814, normal date 22.00	40.00	95.00	200.00	700.00
27a		Penny 1814, 2nd 1 over 0 . . . . 35.00	65.00	160.00	300.00	850.00

28

28	965	Ship under topsails, 1813 . . . . 7.00	12.00	30.00	95.00	525.00

Broke Token of 1814

The Broke tokens were struck in honour of Captain P.B. Vere Broke, who commanded H.M.S. Shannon and captured U.S.S. Chesapeake in 1813. This was the first British naval victory in the War of 1812.

29

BRETON			VG	F	VF	EF	UNC
29	879	Broke, 1814	12.00	22.00	65.00	200.00	600.00

Local Merchants' Tokens, 1814–1820

In 1814 merchants began to issue tokens of their own design, a few being issued anonymously. There was a great variety of these pieces issued from 1814 to 1816, and in 1817 the government ordered their removal from circulation within three years because they had become too plentiful. Most were struck in England.

31   32

			VG	F	VF	EF	UNC
31	880	FOR TRADE, 1814	45.00	90.00	200.00	375.00	900.00
32	881	CARRITT & ALPORT, 1814	18.00	35.00	95.00	250.00	700.00

Tokens **33** to **38** were engraved and struck by Thomas Halliday of Birmingham. The smaller pieces (**34–37**) show a close relationship through the use of common obverse dies.

33

33	882	HOSTERMAN & ETTER, 1814	12.00	25.00	50.00	10.00	500.00

34-37
Typical obv.

Hosterman rev.	*Barry rev.*	*British Copper rev.*	*Halifax rev.*			
BRETON			**VG**	**F**	**VF**	**EF**	**UNC**

			VG	F	VF	EF	UNC
34	883	HOSTERMANN & ETTER, 1815 . . . . 8.00	15.00	40.00	95.00	450.00
35	891	JOHN A. BARRY, 1815 . . . . 9.00	15.00	45.00	125.00	600.00
36	886	GENUINE BRITISH COPPER, 1815 . . . . 8.00	12.00	35.00	125.00	600.00
37	889	HALIFAX, 1815 . . . . 6.00	15.00	35.00	85.00	275.00

38

39

			VG	F	VF	EF	UNC
38	888	SUCCESS TO NAVIGATION & TRADE, 1815 . . . . 8.00	20.00	65.00	160.00	600.00
39	887	GENUINE BRITISH COPPER, 1815 . . . . 35.00	65.00	160.00	325.00	900.00

The crude pieces **41** and **42** were made, probably locally, for a merchant J. Brown, and the bust and harp piece (**40**) may also have been made for him. All are of a "blacksmith-like" character.

Bust obv.	*Harp in wreath rev.*	*Warehouse obv.*	*JB rev.*
BRETON			**AVERAGE CONDITION**

			AVERAGE CONDITION
40	—	Bust, 1815, harp in wreath . . . . Extremely Rare
41	—	Warehouse, harp in wreath . . . . Extremely Rare
42	—	Warehouse, script JB 2,500

The halfpenny of J. Brown (**43**) was once attributed to Scotland because of its design. It has an obverse with a thistle and the Latin legend NEMO ME IMPUNE LACESSIT. The translation is "No one may hurt me with impunity."

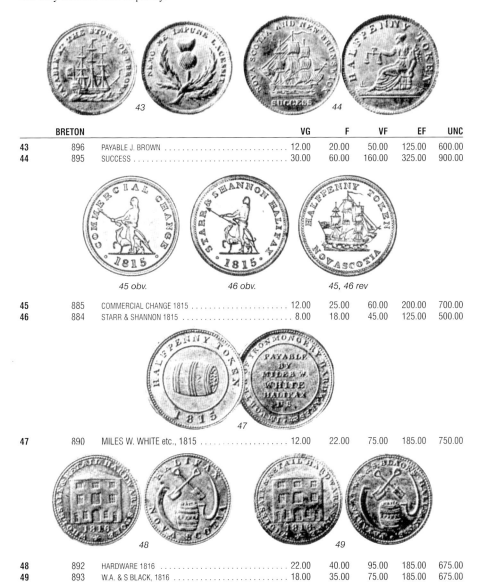

BRETON			VG	F	VF	EF	UNC
43	896	PAYABLE J. BROWN	12.00	20.00	50.00	125.00	600.00
44	895	SUCCESS	30.00	60.00	160.00	325.00	900.00

45 obv.   _46 obv._   _45, 46 rev_

45	885	COMMERCIAL CHANGE 1815	12.00	25.00	60.00	200.00	700.00
46	884	STARR & SHANNON 1815	8.00	18.00	45.00	125.00	500.00

_47_

47	890	MILES W. WHITE etc., 1815	12.00	22.00	75.00	185.00	750.00

_48_   _49_

48	892	HARDWARE 1816	22.00	40.00	95.00	185.00	675.00
49	893	W.A. & S BLACK, 1816	18.00	35.00	75.00	185.00	675.00

The TRADE AND NAVIGATION tokens of 1820 are attributed to Nova Scotia because of the inscription. Since they are dated 1820, they would have been issued in violation of the law, for by 1820 all private tokens were to be out of circulation as required by a law passed in 1817. A variety with two shamrocks growing under the harp has been reported, but none has been seen in Canada.

50

BRETON			VG	F	VF	EF	UNC
50	894	TRADE & NAVIGATION, 1820 copper	12.00	22.00	65.00	200.00	700.00

SEMI-REGAL TOKENS, 1823–1843

The withdrawal of private tokens after 1817 created a fresh shortage of small change which by the early 1820s became quite serious. Because British regal coppers could not be obtained, the provincial government made arrangements with a private coiner in England to provide coppers that were slightly lesser in weight than the corresponding official coins. This was done without the knowledge of the British government, who would surely not have allowed such a local issue at that time. These coppers are therefore best described as semi-regal tokens, as they lacked the authority of the home government.

George IV Thistle Tokens, 1823–1832

The first government of semi-regal tokens were issued in 1823. These and the later issues through 1843 are known as the Thistle Tokens because of their reverse design. All the issues were struck in Birmingham. There was an issue of 400,000 halfpennies in 1823 and in 1824 there was an issue of 217,776 pennies and 118,636 halfpennies.

In 1832 there was an issue of 200,000 pennies and 800,000 halfpennies bearing the bust of George IV, although coined two years after his death. Presumably the order for coins "similar in design" to those of 1824 was taken too literally.

	51 obv.	*51a obv.*			*Typical rev.*		
51	867	Halfpenny 1823	7.00	15.00	40.00	115.00	500.00
51a		Same, no hyphen in NOVA SCOTIA	12.00	22.00	75.00	225.00	700.00
52	869	Halfpenny 1824	10.00	20.00	50.00	125.00	750.00
53	871	Halfpenny 1832	6.00	9.00	30.00	60.00	375.00

54-55

BRETON			VG	F	VF	EF	UNC
54	868	Penny 1824	9.00	22.00	50.00	125.00	800.00
55	870	Penny 1832	9.00	18.00	40.00	110.00	600.00

Imitations of George IV Thistle Tokens

Among the products of the clandestine "mints" of Lower Canada in the 1830's were struck imitations of the 1832 thistle tokens. They were shipped to Nova Scotia and for a time circulated along with the government issue. One much prized variety of the imitation halfpenny has the date 1382, resulting from a blundered die. This was apparently soon discovered, for a second variety with the date altered to 1832 exists. Pieces from this altered die at first glance appear to be dated 1882. Fakes have been made of the 1382 variety in order to deceive collectors; these, however, have a round topped 3 in the date as opposed to a flat topped 3 on the true 1382s.

Imitation Halfpennies

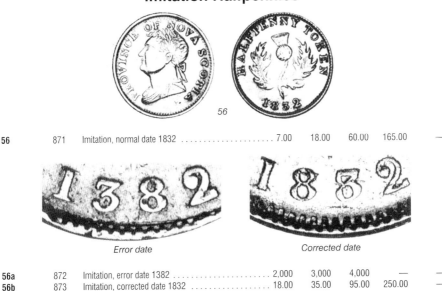

56

56	871	Imitation, normal date 1832	7.00	18.00	60.00	165.00	—

Error date   *Corrected date*

56a	872	Imitation, error date 1382	2,000	3,000	4,000	—	—
56b	873	Imitation, corrected date 1832	18.00	35.00	95.00	250.00	—

Imitation Penny

57

BRETON			VG	F	VF	EF	UNC
57	870	Imitation penny 1832	9.00	18.00	50.00	185.00	—

Victoria Thistle Tokens, 1840–1843

On the 1840 and 1843 issues of thistle tokens the portrait was that of the current British monarch, Victoria. The coiners attempted to copy William Wyon's beautiful bust used on the British regal coinage, but were not very successful. The weight and size of Victorian thistles, particularly the 1840 halfpennies, is somewhat variable. The quantities issued were 300,000 halfpennies and 150,000 pennies of each date. Very rare cast imitations of the 1840 halfpenny are known.

58

1840 0 varieties

Large 0   Medium 0   Small 0

58	874	Halfpenny 1840, large 0	9.00	20.00	70.00	225.00	650.00
58a		Same, medium 0	7.00	15.00	45.00	95.00	500.00
58b		Same, small 0	8.00	18.00	55.00	125.00	600.00
59		Halfpenny 1843	7.00	15.00	40.00	115.00	450.00

60

60	873	Penny 1840	7.00	15.00	40.00	115.00	750.00
61		Penny 1843, 3 over 0	100.00	165.00	450.00	800.00	—
61a		Penny 1843, normal date	9.00	20.00	45.00	115.00	750.00

Imitations of Victoria Thistle Tokens

62

BRETON			AVERAGE CONDITION
62	874	Imitation halfpenny 1840	Very Rare

PRE-DECIMAL COINAGE
Mayflower Coinage, 1856

By the 1850s the attitude in Great Britain was more favourable toward the issue of local coppers in British North America and the Nova Scotia government applied for a coinage of halfpennies and pennies. Their application was accepted and the first true coins were struck for this province. They are popularly known as the Mayflower coppers because of their reverse designs and are among the most beautiful of all Canadian colonial coppers. The master tools were engraved by Leonard C. Wyon, using his own design for the obverse and that of Halifax botanist John S. Thompson for the reverse. The halfpennies with L.C.W. under the bust exist only in proof and are most likely patterns; hence, they are not listed here (see comments in the Introduction). The coinage was executed by Heaton's Mint in Birmingham because the Royal Mint in London was too busy with the Imperial Coinage at the time. Most of the pieces were struck in bronze, although the halfpenny is also known in brass.

63   64

BRETON			VG	F	VF	EF	UNC
63	876	Halfpenny 1856, bronze 6.00		8.00	19.00	70.00	325.00
63a		Same, brass 165.00		250.00	500.00	825.00	—
64	875	Penny 1856, L.C.W. under bust 6.50		12.00	25.00	75.00	525.00
64a		Same, no L.C.W. 7.00		15.00	30.00	80.00	600.00

New Brunswick

New Brunswick was claimed by France as part of Acadia. It was not settled until 1631, when a fort was built at the mouth of the St. John River. When Acadia was ceded to Great Britain in 1713, the French continued to dispute the British claim to New Brunswick, but gave up all claims in 1763.

Under British rule it was governed from Nova Scotia until 1784, when it was detached from Nova Scotia at the request of the inhabitants. New Brunswick was not as seriously short of coin as were the other colonies. Brisk trade with Nova Scotia kept the colony supplied to a limited extent with copper. The need for copper was not serious before 1830, at which time a halfpenny was issued anonymously at Saint John.

Miscellaneous Tokens, ca. 1830–1845

The first piece was not issued because the name of the city was spelled incorrectly. Saint John is the largest city of New Brunswick, St. John's is the capital city of Newfoundland. Evidently this rarity was made by the manufacturers of the almost equally rare Montreal Ropery halfpenny.

The second piece appeared about 1830. Its reverse die was used also for an anonymous token issued at the same time in Lower Canada (**101**).

65   66

	BRETON		VG	F	VF	EF	UNC
65	—	ST. JOHN'S . . . TOKEN. . . . . . .Extremely Rare (only two known)					
66	913	FOR PUBLIC ACCOMMODATION. 12.00	25.00	65.00	160.00	550.00	

Semi-regal Tokens, 1843

In 1841 the provincial government took steps to solve their growing shortage of copper currency by importing £3000 worth of British Imperial pennies and halfpennies. Being sterling, these coins were worth a fraction more in local currency than their face value. The government soon found that they could circulate them only at 1d and d local currency, because there was no way to make change for small numbers of pieces.

Only about £150 worth of the Imperial coppers had been put into circulation when the New Brunswick government decided to return the unissued remainder to England and obtain in their place tokens payable in local currency. The government entered into a contract with Mr. William Hammond of Halifax to choose the designs and make the other necessary arrangements for obtaining the new coppers. When the British government was informed of the colony's plan, it was furious. Thus rebuked, the colonial government informed the Colonial Office in London that the contract with Hammond had been cancelled and plans for the new coinage shelved.

The subsequent events are most interesting. The evidence at hand suggests that the New Brunswick government quietly went ahead with their plans and obtained coppers from Boulton & Watt of Soho. The British government knew nothing about them until 1853, when application was made for a fresh coinage of coppers by the unknowing successor of the Lt. Governor under whom the 1843s had been obtained.

BRETON		VG	F	VF	EF	UNC
67	910	Halfpenny 1843 .... 6.00	12.00	25.00	80.00	525.00

| 68 | 909 | Penny 1843 .... 7.00 | 15.00 | 40.00 | 115.00 | 525.00 |

PRE-DECIMAL COINAGE, 1854

By 1853, when a fresh coinage of pennies and halfpennies was required by the New Brunswick government, the climate in the Colonial Office was more favourable for the issue of local coinages by the British North American colonies. The master tools from the 1843 tokens were forwarded from New Brunswick to the Royal Mint, where they were used as a source of modified designs. These alterations, probably by L.C. Wyon, consisted of the substitution on the obverse of William Wyon's portrait for the British shilling on the halfpenny and that for the British halfpenny on the penny. Also, the word CURRENCY was used in place of TOKEN on the reverse. The use of CURRENCY indicated the official nature of the issue and also implied Halifax Currency, the standard at the time. Due to a heavy schedule at the Royal Mint, the new dies were sent to the Heaton Mint, where 480,000 pieces of each denomination were struck.

| 69 | 912 | Halfpenny 1854 .... 6.00 | 12.00 | 25.00 | 80.00 | 525.00 |

70

BRETON			VG	F	VF	EF	UNC
70	911	Penny 1854	7.00	15.00	40.00	115.00	500.00

Lower Canada

New France was conquered by the British in 1760 and ceded to Great Britain in 1763. It was known as the colony of Quebec until 1791. Originally the colony included the St. Lawrence basin and the Great Lakes region, and large areas of territory extending south to the Ohio River. In 1783 the Great Lakes and the upper St. Lawrence became the boundary with the United States. In 1791 the Great Lakes area was separated from Quebec, which now became the colony of Lower Canada. Lower Canada was predominantly French, and was the largest and most populous of the Canadian colonies.

Wellington Tokens

No special coinage was struck for Lower Canada until 1837. About 1813 anonymous tokens began to appear. The earliest were the Wellington tokens, brought over by British troops sent to Canada to fight the Americans in 1814. These tokens depicted a bust of the Duke of Wellington, and were very popular. They were often struck over other tokens. Some of them are antedated in order to evade laws passed in 1825 against private tokens.

In 1808 Napoleon sent an army into Spain and Portugal, deposed the king of Spain, and placed his brother Joseph on the Spanish throne. In the same year the British invaded Portugal and won major victories at Vimeira, Talavera, Busaco and Almeida, finally driving the French out in 1811. The action in Spain continued until 1813. Major British victories were scored at Ciudad Rodrigo, Badajoz, Salamanca, Madrid, San Sebastian, Vitoria and Pamplona. Wellington commanded the British forces during most of the period of conflict.

The Wellington pieces dated 1805 and 1811 are of questionable connection to British North America. The reverse of the 1805 token would seem to be the work of Peter Wyon for an Irish piece (also see No. **237**).

In honour of the Peninsular campaigns J.K. Picard of Hull had the battle tokens (**73–75**) struck by Sir Edward Thomason of Birmingham. Specimens in silver were struck for presentation at Court, Picard having been invited by the Prince Regent to come to London and shows his coppers. They are halfpenny size, but there is no expression of denomination, perhaps because they were initially intended to be more in the nature of medalets. In any case they were ultimately used as halfpenny tokens and there was even a brass imitation of one of the varieties which circulated in Canada. Note that only on 74b is the Spanish word ciudad (city) spelled correctly.

Numbers **76–79, 81–89** were all designed by Thomas Halliday, the Cossack penny being considered an example of his best work. Of these pieces, most varieties of **76–79, 85–86** were struck over Guppy tokens of Bristol. Specimens of **86** were overstruck with other designs for use in England, proving that not all the anonymous Wellington tokens of these listed types were sent to Canada.

71

72

BRETON			VG	F	VF	EF	UNC
71	976	WELLINGTON, HIBERNIA, 1805	25.00	40.00	80.00	200.00	500.00
72	977	TRADE & COMMERCE, 1811	50.00	75.00	125.00	300.00	750.00

73

73b

73	987	CUIAD &c.&c.&c, copper	7.00	11.00	25.00	55.00	240.00
73a		Same, silver	700.00	900.00	1,500	2,000	2,500
73b		Imitation No. 73, brass	50.00	100.00	220.00	365.00	—

74 obv.

74 rev.

74b rev.

74	986	CUIAD MADRID, copper	7.00	12.00	30.00	60.00	300.00
74a		Same, silver	700.00	900.00	1,500	2,000	2,500
74b		CIUDAD (correct spelling), copper	12.00	25.00	50.00	105.00	330.00

75

75	988	SALAMANCA PAMPLUNO	15.00	35.00	65.00	150.00	525.00

Halfpennies

All of the undated halfpennies with HALFPENNY TOKEN on the reverse were produced by Thomas
Halliday of Birmingham and most (if not all) were struck over halfpennies of Samuel Guppy.

	BRETON		VG	F	VF	EF	UNC
76	972	Undated, trident 5.00		8.00	25.00	65.00	300.00
76a		Undated, spear 20.00		35.00	70.00	150.00	400.00

77	971	Undated, large letters 5.00		8.00	20.00	60.00	300.00

The next three pieces, showing Britannia surrounded by a continuous wreath on the reverse, are
lightweight and are believed to have been struck by Thomas Halliday on Canadian order. They are
linked to the Britannia-eagle tokens of Lower Canada through their reverses.

	Field Marshall obv.	Halfpenny obv.	Clockwise wreath	Counterclockwise wreath

78	973	FIELD MARSHALL, clockwise wreath .... Extremely Rare				
78a		Same, counterclockwise wreath .... Extremely Rare				
79	980	HALFPENNY, counterclockwise wreath 85.00	175.00	400.00	725.00	—

The Marquis Wellington halfpenny was struck by Isaac Parkes of Dublin. It is antedated, since Wellington did not become a marquis until 1814. The tokens of 1814, struck on Canadian order, also were antedated to evade the law against private tokens.

80

BRETON			VG	F	VF	EF	UNC
80	978	MARQUIS WELLINGTON, 1813	15.00	30.00	50.00	150.00	450.00

The other halfpennies dated 1813, including the lightweight one dated 1814, were produced by Thomas Halliday. The 1813s were struck over Guppy halfpennies and the 1814 was probably struck on Canadian order.

		81-81a			82		
81	969	1813, plain edge	5.00	10.00	20.00	55.00	240.00
81a		1813, engraved edge	8.00	15.00	30.00	77.00	275.00
82	979	Wellington 1814	8.00	15.00	30.00	75.00	350.00

The halfpenny tokens dated 1816 are lightweight pieces struck by Halliday on Canadian order about 1830.

		83			84		
83	981	WATERLOO 1816	5.00	12.00	30.00	65.00	350.00
84	531	MONTREAL 1816	7.00	15.00	45.00	160.00	500.00

Pennies

In most cases the pennies produced by Thomas Halliday of Birmingham were struck over penny tokens of Samuel Guppy. It is questionable whether any of the Wellington pennies, particularly the "Cossack" penny (see below), circulated to a large degree in British North America.

		Obverse	85		86		
BRETON			**VG**	**F**	**VF**	**EF**	**UNC**
85	970	Undated, no wreath on reverse 75.00	110.00	200.00	325.00	850.00
86		Undated, wreath on reverse 40.00	55.00	125.00	175.00	600.00

The following three pennies form a group called the Peninsular Pennies because they were struck for use by Wellington's troops in Portugal and Spain. They were specially designed so that they could not be mistaken for British, Spanish or Portuguese copper coins. The "Cossack" piece is a tribute to the Russian Cossacks, who gave Napoleon's Grande Armée such an uncomfortable time in Russia in 1812 and 1813. All these pieces were struck by Sir Edward Thomason, undoubtedly from dies made by Halliday.

87	985	COSSACK PENNY TOKEN 25.00	50.00	70.00	120.00	450.00

88	974	1813 under bust 45.00	75.00	150.00	300.00	650.00

BRETON		VG	F	VF	EF	UNC
89	984 1813 on reverse	25.00	50.00	85.00	175.00	500.00

Anonymous Tokens

Until the mid-1830s when some of the banks began issuing tokens of their own, the copper currency was provided by merchants and other individuals. It consisted largely of anonymous halfpenny tokens. Some were brought into the colony from the other British North American provinces or from the British Isles in the pockets of immigrants or visitors. Others were surreptitiously imported in quantity and still others were produced locally. The imported tokens were often English or Irish types which had circulated in the British Isles; however, some were new designs struck on Canadian order.

In 1825 the governments of Upper and Lower Canada passed laws forbidding the further importation of private tokens. Due to a loophole in the wording, it was not illegal to import coppers that lacked a date or bore a date prior to 1825. The laws were never corrected and the way was paved for the importation of undated or antedated pieces.

The first anonymous halfpenny attributable to Lower Canada is No. **90**, the VICTORIA NOBIS EST token. It was produced by Birmingham coiner Thomas Halliday and the stylistic relationship to the Wellington is unmistakable. Indeed its reverse die is that of the Wellington halfpenny No. **76a**. The bust is thought to be that of Lord Nelson and the Latin legend means, "Victory is ours!." Most of this issue was struck over Guppy tokens.

			VG	VF	EF	UNC
90	982	VICTORIA NOBIS EST 7.00	15.00	35.00	80.00	350.00

Britannia/Eagle Tokens
Original Issue, 1813

The original Britannia-eagle tokens of 1813 were struck over Guppy tokens of Bristol, probably for a Boston merchant who settled in Montreal in 1813. Other lightweight pieces dated 1813–1815 are believed to have been struck much later than the dates they bear. Aside from the difference in weight, the original 1813 issue can be distinguished from the later strikings having the same date by the larger reverse lettering on the later strikings. Most of the 1815s were discovered in 1867 still in mint state in a barrel in a warehouse.

BRETON			VG	F	VF	EF	UNC
91	994	Eagle 1813 . . . . 8.00		15.00	40.00	90.00	350.00

Lightweight Antedated Issues, 1813–1815

	Counterclockwise wreath	Clockwise wreath	Reverse

			VG	F	VF	EF	UNC
91a	994	Eagle 1813 . . . . 8.00		18.00	40.00	90.00	350.00
92		Same 1814 . . . . 8.00		18.00	40.00	90.00	350.00
93		Same 1815, counterclockwise wreath 8.00		18.00	35.00	80.00	325.00
93a		Same 1815, clockwise wreath 6.00		15.00	20.00	45.00	200.00

The following group of lightweight halfpennies presumably all come from the same coiner, as they stem from a small number of dies used in various combinations. Some of these combinations were quite inappropriate because the dies were originally designed for coining various size pieces. For example, the small bust obverse appears to have been made for use with the COMMERCIAL CHANGE reverse; when it was used with the larger SHIPS COLONIES & COMMERCE reverse, a very broad rim resulted on the obverse. Conversely, the large bust obverse, when used with the smaller COMMERCIAL CHANGE reverse, produced a piece that had little or no rim design on the obverse.

These pieces were imported about 1830. Their linkage with Lower Canada is unmistakable, since they were later found in hoards in the province of Quebec. It is interesting to note that among the tokens in one large hoard was a variety of the Ships Colonies & Commerce token, 13a, which has always been considered a variety of Breton 997, but portrays a very different ship. The hull is much shorter than on the varieties of Breton 997, and the water is very rough.

Obverses

Ship	Large bust	Medium bust

Small bust | Military bust (open sleeve) | Military bust (closed sleeve)

Reverses

WELLINGTON WATERLOO | SHIPS, etc. | COMMERCIAL CHANGE | TRADE

BRETON			VG	F	VF	EF	UNC
94	1003	Ship, rev. WELLINGTON WATERLOO 1815 . . . . 12.00	18.00	35.00	100.00	375.00
95	1006	Large bust, rev. WELLINGTON WATERLOO 1815. . . . . 15.00	30.00	50.00	125.00	350.00
96	1002	Large bust, rev. SHIPS, etc. 12.00	22.00	40.00	85.00	350.00
96a		Medium bust, rev. SHIPS, etc. 25.00	40.00	75.00	150.00	400.00
96b		Small bust (broad rim), rev. SHIPS, etc. 125.00	200.00	350.00	550.00	—
97	1007	Large bust, rev. COMMERCIAL CHANGE (no rim)	1,000	2,000	3,000 . . . . .Very Rare		
97a		Small bust, rev. COMMERCIAL CHANGE 9.00	18.00	35.00	85.00	400.00
98	992	Large bust, rev TRADE 1825 . . . . Extremely Rare				
98a		Military bust (open sleeve), rev. TRADE 1825 . . . . 7.00	15.00	40.00	100.00	275.00
98b		Same, closed sleeve 100.00	175.00	350.00	500.00	—

Other Anonymous Issues

99

100

99	1011	Bust 1820, rev. "Commerce" 9.00	18.00	40.00	100.00	400.00
100	1001	Ship, rev. "Commerce" . . . . 10,000 . . . . Extremely Rare			

The halfpennies inscribed FOR PUBLIC ACCOMMODATION were issued about 1830. They were struck with the same reverse die used for 66, the token of Saint John, New Brunswick.

101

BRETON		VG	F	VF	EF	UNC
101	533	FOR PUBLIC ACCOMMODATION 8.00	15.00	35.00	100.00	350.00

The seemingly anonymous "Canada" tokens of 1830 and 1841, are known to have been issued by James Duncan, a hardware merchant of Montreal. He later settled in Charlottetown, Prince Edward Island, where he circulated these pieces until issuing his "cents" in 1855 (Nos. **18–22**).

102

102	532	CANADA 1830 .... 8.00	18.00	40.00	125.00	400.00
103		CANADA 1841 .... 8.00	18.00	40.00	125.00	400.00

Private Tokens
Bearing the Issuer's Name

The private tokens bearing their issuer's names are extremely variable in weight and quality. The only really honest token in this regard is the Molson halfpenny of 1837. The Montreal Ropery halfpenny was issued about 1824, shortly before the firm changed hands. The Mullins token was issued in anticipation that the son would enter into partnership, but this did not happen.

104   *105*

104	564	R.W. OWEN ROPERY	13,000	18,000	25,000.....	Extremely Rare
105	563	FRANCIS MULLINS & SON MONTREAL 18.00	30.00	65.00	165.00	525.00

T.S. Brown, the issuer of **106**, was a hardware merchant who took up arms in the Rebellion of 1837, and had to flee to the United States when the rebellion was put down. He remained there until amnesty was granted in 1844.

John Shaw's halfpenny was issued at Quebec in 1837, Shaw withdrew his tokens when the Quebec Bank issued its Habitant tokens the following year.

BRETON			VG	F	VF	EF	UNC
106	561	T.S. BROWN . . . MONTREAL	8.00	18.00	45.00	125.00	425.00
107	565	J. SHAW . . . QUEBEC	12.00	22.00	60.00	125.00	425.00

The Molson halfpenny was struck in Montreal by Jean Marie Arnault, who also engraved the dies, probably from designs submitted by the Company. The obverse is a copy in reverse of that of a halfpenny token issued in Perth, Scotland, in 1797.

108	562	MOLSON, Copper	500.00	800.00	1,200	1,800	6,000
108a		Same, silver (not struck for circulation)	—	—	—	8,000	12,000

The Roy token was issued in 1837. Specimens on thin flans were made by a journeyman employed by the manufacturer. This individual would run off a few extra specimens from the dies whenever he needed money for liquor. The appearance of these lightweight sous forced Roy to withdraw his tokens to avoid discredit.

109	671	J. ROY, thick flan	50.00	100.00	200.00	600.00	3,000
109a		Same, thin flan	50.00	100.00	200.00	600.00	3,000

The Bust and Harp Tokens, 1820–1825

These halfpennies first appeared in Lower Canada about 1825. Their design was undoubtedly inspired by the Irish regal halfpennies. The originals were struck in Dublin and are dated 1825. They have denticles at the rims. A second pair of dies, with the reverse also dated 1825 but without rim denticles, was prepared. It is assumed that upon instructions from those who ordered the tokens, the date on this second die was altered to 1820 and pieces struck. One may further assume the purpose in overdating was to antedate the tokens so they would not be excluded from importation by the law passed in Lower Canada in 1825. A non-overdated 1820 reverse dies was also used.

Originals

			VG	F	VF	EF	UNC
		1820 – 0 over 8		*Normal date*			
BRETON							
110	1012	Bust and harp 1825 2,000		3,000	4,000	6,000	
111		Same, 1820, 0 over 5 4,500		8,500	12,000	16,000	
111a		Same, 1820 normal date 30.00		55.00	110.00	225.00	—

Imitations

Vast quantities of imitations (mostly in brass) of the bust and harp halfpennies were locally produced, probably about 1837. The next two tokens were very likely the product of the same "mint." No. **112** is of moderately good quality and is by far the most common today. No. **113** is noticeably cruder, almost of "blacksmith" style (see No. 259).

112   *113*

			VG	F	VF	EF	UNC
112		Bust and harp imit., good quality dies 5.00		8.00	15.00	50.00	175.00
113		Same, "blacksmith-like" 450.00		700.00	1,000	—	—

The next piece is perhaps Lower Canadian, but its attribution to British North America is hardly firm. Considered by some to be part of the "blacksmith" series, its uncertain status dictates that it should be listed here temporarily until conclusive evidence can be found. Note that the bust faces right.

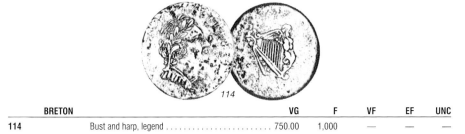

114

BRETON		VG	F	VF	EF	UNC
114	Bust and harp, legend 750.00	1,000	—	—	—

The Tiffin Tokens

About 1832 a Montreal grocer named Joseph Tiffin imported copper halfpennies from England, the design of which was a copy of pieces which had circulated twenty years earlier in Great Britain (and perhaps to a much lesser degree in British North America as well). The original pieces had been struck by Birmingham coiner Thomas Halliday. These are of good weight, have an engrailed edge and bear Halliday's "H" on the truncation of the bust of George III. Collectors have come to call "Tiffins" any tokens of the bust and commerce 1812 design, whether or not they are the variety issued by him.

The pieces actually circulated by Tiffin appeared later (see below).

Halliday Copper Originals

115

| 115 | 960 | Halfpenny 1812, with H . . . . | 6.00 | 11.00 | 25.00 | 65.00 | 300.00 |

116 Obv.

116, 117 Rev.

117, 118 Obv.   *116, 117 Rev.*

116	959	Penny, 1812 on reverse.	8.00	20.00	50.00	150.00	510.00
117	957	Penny, 1812 on both sides	10.00	20.00	50.00	120.00	525.00
118	958	Penny, 1812 on obverse	10.00	20.00	44.00	90.00	350.00
119	958	Penny, 1813 on obverse	20.00	30.00	66.00	150.00	510.00

Halfpennies Probably Circulated by Tiffin

Writings of R.W. MacLachlan suggest that the tokens ordered by Joseph Tiffin in 1832 were halfpennies of the kind shown below. These are of medium weight, well executed and struck in copper. They are most easily separated from the original strikings by their plain edge and lack of the letter "H" on the truncation.

BRETON			VG	F	VF	EF	UNC
120	960	Halfpenny 1812, no H 4.00		7.00	20.00	50.00	270.00

Lightweight Imitations in Copper Alloys

Like the bust and harp halfpennies, Tiffin's pieces were soon buried by a vast quantity of light-weight, poorly executed imitations. Various copper alloys were used, so the colour of the imitations varies from brassy yellow to the brown of nearly pure copper. These pieces were quite probably produced by the same "mint" that was responsible for the bust and harp imitations. There were two basic obverse designs (wreath running counterclockwise or clockwise) and two reverses (legend and date or date only).

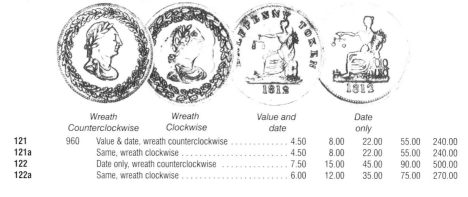

			Wreath Counterclockwise	Wreath Clockwise	Value and date	Date only
121	960	Value & date, wreath counterclockwise 4.50	8.00	22.00	55.00	240.00
121a		Same, wreath clockwise 4.50	8.00	22.00	55.00	240.00
122		Date only, wreath counterclockwise 7.50	15.00	45.00	90.00	500.00
122a		Same, wreath clockwise 6.00	12.00	35.00	75.00	270.00

The Vexator Canadiensis Tokens

These pieces appeared perhaps in the mid-1830s and are close relatives of the "blacksmiths" (see Nos. **261** and **262**) in that their devices, though very crudely executed, resemble those on the British regal halfpennies. The "classical" Vexators, Breton 558 and 559, have legends which are satirical and at the same time cleverly designed to evade the laws against forgery, sedition and the issue of private tokens.

To ensure that they would be accepted in change, the tokens bore a bust on the obverse and a seated female figure on the reverse, thus superficially resembling English regal copper. To avoid being prosecuted for forgery, the issuers made use of inscriptions quite different from those seen on regal copper.

They are satirical pieces in that the types are caricatures and the legends are definitely provocative. The obverse legend as usually read means "The Tormentor of Canada." The reverse legend means, "Wouldn't you like to catch them." and could allude to those who put the coins into circulation. However, the toils of the law were foreseen here and cleverly avoided. The third letter in the obverse legend is very vague in form, and could as easily be an N as an X. The word could then be read as VENATOR and the legend translated as "A Canadian Trapper." The bust is very shaggy and appears to be wearing a fur cap such as trappers wore in those days. The reverse legend could as easily have referred to fur-bearing animals as to the issuers of the tokens. Thus, if caught, the issuers could plead that the pieces were really medalets honouring the fur trade, of which Montreal was in those days an important centre.

The date 1811 is clearly an antedate. After going to all the trouble to evade prosecution for forgery and sedition, the issuers were not going to run afoul of the law of 1825 against private tokens. This method of evasion was very easy. The light and variable weight of these tokens also indicates that they were antedated, for nothing as light as these would have been acceptable in 1811.

Who was the "Tormentor of Canada?" Since the tokens are antedated, it certainly was not Sir James Craig, autocratic though he was. It probably was King William IV, whose attitude toward colonies, especially those acquired from other countries in warfare, was very harsh. Almost any of the governors of Lower Canada from 1830 to 1838, or some particularly obnoxious local officials of the period, also could have qualified for this dubious title.

The fur-trade aspect of these tokens is the fruit of brilliant reasoning by Dr. J.P.C. Kent of the British Museum and R.H.M. Dolley of Belfast. The evasion of the laws against forgery was suggested to the author by R.C. Bell of Newcastle-on-Tyne, who pointed out that it was in the technique of the makers of the old English "Bungtown" tokens. It has been known since the time of R.W. McLachlan that these pieces were antedated, but the fact had been almost forgotten in recent years.

There are two very rare Vexators in addition to the "classical" ones. The first is from the reverse die of Breton 558, but has a new obverse, apparently with only the date 1810 and the crude bust. The second is from entirely new dies. There seems to be only a bust on the obverse. The so-called "variety" of Breton 559 with an ML in the obverse legend is not a variety at all. The ML simply doesn't show on many of the pieces; they were all struck from the same obverse die.

BRETON			AVERAGE CONDITION
123	558	VEXATOR CANADIN SIS 1811	1,750
124		Obverse dated 1810, but no legend	Extremely Rare

BRETON			VG	F	VF	EF	UNC
125	559	VEXATOR ML. CANADIENSIS 1811					1,500
126		No (?) obverse legend or date					Unique

THE FIRST BANK TOKENS, 1835–1837
Bank of Montreal

In 1835 the banks refused to take any more anonymous brass pieces and other metallic trash except by weight. To supply a copper coinage, the Bank of Montreal began issuing halfpenny tokens of good weight. The value was inscribed in French on the reverse, but was incorrectly expressed by the plural form SOUS rather than SOU. This did not hinder their circulation at all. In 1836 the bank received government authority to supply copper, and added its name to the reverse inscriptions, but did not correct the value, for the error was taken by everyone as a guarantee of authenticity. The Bank of Montreal sous were struck in Birmingham. Each year there was an issue of about 72,000.

			VG	F	VF	EF	UNC
127	713	BANK TOKEN MONTREAL	7.00	15.00	35.00	85.00	350.00
128	714	BANK OF MONTREAL TOKEN.	7.00	15.00	35.00	110.00	450.00

Banque du Peuple

The first sou of the Banque du Peuple was the so-called "Rebellion Sou," issued in 1837. It received its name because of the addition of a small star and a liberty cap on the reverse, said to have been done at the instigation of an accountant who favoured the cause of the rebels of 1837. It was soon discovered, and the token was replaced with another type in 1838. The Rebellion Sou was engraved by Jean Marie Arnault of Montreal, who struck about 12,000 pieces. There is considerable variation in size and weight.

The second sou of the Banque du Peuple (**130**) was issued in 1838 to replace the Rebellion sou. About 84,000 were struck in Belleville, New Jersey.

BRETON		VG	F	VF	EF	UNC
129	716 "Rebellion" sou	10.00	25.00	60.00	125.00	375.00
130	715 BANQUE DU PEUPLE, "oak" wreath	5.00	7.00	15.00	60.00	270.00

BOUQUET SOUS

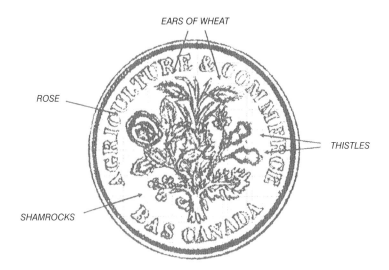

The Bouquet Sous are imitations of the Bank of Montreal tokens. The latter were so popular that lightweight imitations soon appeared, bearing a similar obverse bouquet of roses, thistles, shamrocks, and wheat. Inscriptions were entirely in French, however (with the words AGRICULTURE and COMMERCE the same in both languages), and the value was correctly rendered in the singular.

Because of the wide usage of the Bouquet Sous, they became the first series to achieve great popularity with collectors. They have been more thoroughly studied than other colonial issues, and it has been traditional to collect them by die variety.

Bouquet Sous are most easily identified by first counting the number of leaves in the reverse wreath. This number will serve to locate a general area in one of the groups below, after which details may be compared with the notes below the illustrations. Such points as the number and location of shamrocks and relative position of letters, berries, and leaves will serve as guides to identification. To illustrate, an enlarged bouquet token (in this case No. **157**) is shown with arrows pointing to the shamrocks, roses, thistles and ears of wheat on obverse. The number of leaves on the wreath can be counted.

I. Belleville Issues

The Belleville mint was a private company in Belleville, New Jersey, whose production was mainly American tokens.

Sixteen leaves in reverse wreath:

| *Rev. A: no berry* | *Rev. B: no berry* | *Rev. C: berries* |
| *left of bow* | *right of bow* | *each side of bow* |

| *Obv. 1: dots for* | *Obv. 2: shamrock and* | *Obv. 3: stalk between* |
| *stops in legend* | *large leaf lower left* | *thistles at left* |

| *Obv. 4: high bow, shamrock* | *Obv. 5: 2 horizontal thistles;* | *Obv. 6: bent stalk* |
| *between thistles; thin stops* | *2 shamrocks lower right* | *under UL* |

	BRETON		VG	F	VF	EF	UNC
131	680	Rev. A, obv. 1	15.00	30.00	90.00	200.00	550.00
132		Same, obv. 2					Unique
133	678	Same, obv. 3	6.00	12.00	40.00	120.00	475.00
134	679	Same, obv. 4	5.00	10.00	22.00	60.00	200.00
135		Same, obv. 5	—	—	—	—	—
136	681	Rev. B, obv. 5	175.00	250.00	500.00	—	—
137	682	Same, obv. 6	8.50	20.00	50.00	100.00	300.00
138	675	Rev. C, obv. 2					Very Rare
139	677	Same, obv. 3					Rare
140	676	Same, obv. 6	15.00	30.00	65.00	120.00	400.00

Seventeen leaves in reverse wreath:

Rev D: 17 leaves	Obv. 7: rose flanked by 2 pairs of stalks

BRETON			VG	F	VF	EF	UNC
141	683	Rev. D, obv. 1	7.50	18.00	45.00	100.00	350.00
142		Same, obv 5					Extremely Rare
143		Same, obv. 7					Unique

Eighteen leaves in reverse wreath, no bow:

Rev. E: UN close together	Rev. F: berry left of bottom N	Rev. G: berry over bottom N	Obv. 8: similar to obv. 4 thick stops

			VG	F	VF	EF	UNC
144	—	Rev. E, obv.5					Extremely Rare
145	688	Same, obv, 7	7.50	15.00	45.00	160.00	400.00
146	687	Same, obv. 8	7.50	15.00	35.00	130.00	375.00
147	685	Rev.F, obv. 5	9.00	20.00	50.00	130.00	375.00
148	686	Rev. G, obv.	8.00	20.00	45.00	130.00	400.00

Eighteen leaves in reverse wreath, with bow:

Rev. H:	Rev. J:	Rev. K:

			VG	F	VF	EF	UNC
149	696	Rev. H, obv. 1	20.00	40.00	100.00	220.00	500.00
150	691	Rev. J, obv. 9	5.00	8.00	15.00	50.00	225.00
151	695	Rev. K, obv. 1	10.00	30.00	60.00	110.00	300.00
152	692	Same, obv. 4	5.00	8.00	12.00	50.00	250.00

Rev. L: leaf tip
above centre of M

Rev. M:
SOU very low

Obv. 9: colon stops;
S-C closely spaced

Obv. 10: colon stops;
S-C widely spaced

Obv. 11: shamrock, small leaf
above ribbon ends

Obv. 12: rose at
left; no punctuation

Obv. 13: "broken"
leaf at top left

Obv. 14: 1 large, 2 small
leaves above ribbon ends

Obv. 15:
ribbon ends left;
bouquet base over A

Obv. 16:
ribbon ends left;
bouquet base over N

	BRETON		VG	F	VF	EF	UNC
153	693	Same, obv. 7	11.00	22.00	55.00	110.00	475.00
154	694	Same, obv. 10	5.00	7.00	17.00	66.00	325.00
155	697	Rev. L, obv. 11	11.00	18.00	40.00	60.00	325.00
156	698	Same, obv. 12	18.00	35.00	77.00	145.00	475.00
157	699	Rev. M, obv. 12	8.50	18.00	44.00	85.00	400.00
158	703	Same, obv. 13	750.00	1,500	3,300	—	—
159	702	Same, obv.14	5.50	12.00	28.00	60.00	300.00
160	700	Same, obv. 15	6.00	12.00	33.00	70.00	325.00
161	701	Same, obv. 16	13.00	30.00	77.00	170.00	450.00

Twenty leaves in reverse wreath:

Obv. 17: 2 shamrocks lower right	Rev. N: small bow		Obv. 18: no shamrocks lower right	Rev. P: large bow

	BRETON		VG	F	VF	EF	UNC
162	704	Rev. N, obv. 17 .... 4.50	7.50	17.00	50.00	175.00
163	705	Rev. P, obv. 18 .... 6.00	12.00	28.00	110.00	275.00

II. Birmingham Issues

The sous numbered **164** through **169** were struck in Birmingham, England by the same firm that produced the early sous of the Bank of Montreal. These issues can be readily distinguished by the large number of leaves (**32–42**) in the wreath on the reverse. The bouquet sou assigned number 712 by Breton was exposed as fraud by McLachlan, who described how it was made. All specimens of this variety seen by the authors are fabrications. It is therefore not assigned a number in this catalogue.

Rev. R: 32 leaves

Obv. 19: no shamrocks at lower left	Obv. 20: 1 shamrock at lower left	Obv. 21: 2 shamrocks at lower left	Obv. 22: English legend; 2 roses

Thirty-two leaves in reverse wreath:

164	706	Rev. R, Obv. 19 .... 18.00	35.00	95.00	145.00	600.00
165	707	Same, obv. 20 .... 5.00	10.00	22.00	60.00	200.00
166	708	Same, obv. 21 .... 18.00	30.00	50.00	120.00	400.00
167	709	Same, obv. 22 .... 25.00	40.00	66.00	145.00	450.00

Forty-two leaves in reverse wreath:

		Rev. S: 42 leaves	Obv. 23a: 1 shamrock right, 2 left	Obv.23: 1 large, 2 small shamrocks at lower left			

	BRETON		VG	F	VF	EF	UNC
168	710	Rev. S, obv. 21 .... 20.00	40.00	95.00	180.00	450.00
169	712	Same, obv. 23 .... Very Rare
—	712	Same, obv. 23a .... Authenticity questionable

III. Montreal Issues

Several varieties of the bouquet sous were produced in Montreal by Jean Marie Arnault. Nos. **171** and **172** were routinely struck over other tokens withdrawn from circulation, quite possibly in 1837. No. **170** was long thought to be No. **171** struck over an Upper Canada sloop token (No. **199**); however, closer examination shows that neither of the dies used for the overstriking was that of No. **171** or any other catalogued sou. The lettering is quite small and the bouquet clearly different from that on Nos. **173, 174**. It is very possible that the "small letters" sou was a prototype for sou No. **171** and that the dies were created in both cases for the purpose of overstriking other tokens.

The last two varieties, which share the same obverse, were postulated by Courteau to have been "patterns" for a coinage of sous for one of the Montreal banks, perhaps the City Bank. As this is far from proven, we list these pieces here.

Obv. 24: small letters in legend	Rev. T: small letters in legend	Obv. 25: 1 shamrock right, 4 left	Rev. U: 16 small leaves

170		Rev. T, Obv. 24 .... Unique
171	674	Rev. U, obv. 25 .... 9.50	25.00	60.00	150.00	425.00
172	684	Rev. V, obv. 26 .... 5.50	12.00	33.00	100.00	350.00

Obv. 27:	Rev. W:	Rev. X:
English legend	½ penny token 1837	½ penny bank token

	BRETON		VG	F	VF	EF	UNC
173	672	Rev. W, obv. 27					Unique
174	673	Rev. X, obv. 27					Extremely Rare

IV. Miscellaneous Issues

The first two varieties probably never circulated; both were unknown until at least the 1860s and do not come in well worn condition. The dies and a few "original" specimens of No. **175** were found in Montreal. A small number of restrikes were struck in various metals after the dies had been fitted with a collar. Most specimens of No. **176** are know as "proofs" and were found in Boston. For that reason this variety has been called the "Boston" sou.

Number **177** is a heavy piece which could well have circulated more in the United States than it did in Canada. Its reverse is thought to have been originally intended for a token for Belleville butcher T.D. Seaman. The U was deliberately added so the name would read DUSEAMAN to facilitate passing these pieces off as anonymous cents in the United States.

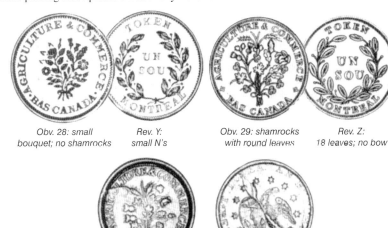

Obv. 28: small	Rev. Y:	Obv. 29: shamrocks	Rev. Z:
bouquet; no shamrocks	small N's	with round leaves	18 leaves; no bow

			VG	F	VF	EF	UNC
175	689	Rev. Y, obv. 28, Original, struck without collar					Extremely Rare
175a	(689)	Same, restrike, struck with collar ....—	—	165.00	275.00	600.00	
176	690	Rev. Z, obv. 29 ....—	—	165.00	300.00	650.00	
177	670	Rev. DUSEAMAN, obv. 5 .... 12.00	30.00	50.00	110.00	450.00	

LATER BANK TOKENS
Habitant Tokens

The Habitant tokens, so called because they show on the obverse a Canadian habitant in traditional winter costume, were struck by Boulton & Watt and released early in 1838. The Bank of
Montreal, the Quebec Bank, the City Bank, and the Banque du Peuple participated in the issue,
with the bank name appearing on the reverse ribbon. The Bank of Montreal issued 240,000 pennies and 480,000 halfpennies; the others issued 120,000 pennies and 240,000 halfpennies each.

	BRETON		VG	F	VF	EF	UNC
178	522	Halfpenny, CITY BANK 3.50	7.00	17.00	45.00	160.00
179		Same, QUEBEC BANK 3.50	7.00	17.00	45.00	175.00
180		Same, BANQUE DU PEUPLE 6.00	12.00	33.00	70.00	275.00
181		Same, BANK OF MONTREAL 6.00	12.00	33.00	65.00	275.00

			VG	F	VF	EF	UNC
182	521	Penny, CITY BANK 4.00	8.00	20.00	45.00	250.00
183		Same, QUEBEC BANK 4.00	8.00	20.00	45.00	250.00
184		Same, BANQUE DU PEUPLE 12.00	22.00	66.00	100.00	400.00
185		Same, BANK OF MONTREAL 7.00	15.00	40.00	70.00	425.00

Side View Tokens

The "Side View" tokens, so called because they show a corner view of the Bank of Montreal
building, were struck by Cotterill, Hill & Co. of Walsall, England. In 1838 the coiners shipped
120,000 pennies and 240,000 halfpennies to Montreal. The bank returned the coins because the
workmanship was far inferior to that of the Habitant tokens, and the copper was brassy. The most
probable point of objection on the obverse is the trees, which appear "frizzy." The reverse is
considerably more crude than that for the Habitant pieces. In 1839 another 120,000 pennies and
240,000 halfpennies arrived, but these were also returned with the complaint that they were even
worse than the shipment of 1838.

The reverse of the 1839s is an improvement over the 1838 issue. The fault is in the obverse,
which has the bank building rendered in atrocious perspective. Note the portico, for example.
These tokens are more expensive than rare today.

	BRETON		VG	F	VF	EF	UNC
186	524	Halfpenny 1838	1,000	2,000	3,000	4,000	8,500
187		Halfpenny 1839	1,000	2,000	3,500	4,500	11,000
188	523	Penny 1838	2,000	3,500	6,000	10,000	20,000
189		Penny 1839	2,000	3,500	6,000	10,000	20,000
190		Penny 1839, BANQUE DU PEUPLE					Very Rare

Upper Canada

In 1791 the Great Lakes region was detached from Quebec and organized as the colony of Upper Canada. It is now the Province of Ontario. Very little coined money was in use before 1800. A few of the Wellington tokens trickled in from Lower Canada after 1814, and local tokens appeared about 1812.

The Brock Tokens

The Brock tokens were struck about 1816 to honour one of the heroes of the War of 1812, Major General Sir Isaac Brock, who was commander of the British troops in Upper Canada. In July of 1812 he captured Detroit and on 13 October of that year successfully repulsed an American invasion attempt at Queenstown (near Niagara Falls), although Brock himself was killed in the battle. The tokens are light in weight. They soon became too plentiful and fell into discredit. Note the spelling blunder on **191** (Brook instead of Brock). No. **193** is a mule struck from very worn dies.

		Ship obverse	Monument obverse	Text reverse	1816 reverse		
191	723	Ship, text	12.00	25.00	66.00	180.00	475.00
192	724	Monument, 1816	6.00	12.00	28.00	80.00	300.00
193	725	Ship, 1816	40.00	70.00	132.00	360.00	—

The Sloop Tokens

These tokens feature on their obverses a sloop, which was in those days the chief means of transportation on the Great Lakes. This obverse was the work of John Sheriff of Liverpool. The tokens are heavier, as Upper Canada by this time was using Halifax Currency. Most of them are antedated to evade the law against private tokens enacted in 1825. As this law became a dead letter, later issues bore the actual date of issue. The "hunter" piece (**198**) is a mule struck from very worn dies. Its reverse die was used previously to strike one of the Nova Scotia tokens (**45**).

Antedated Issues

Obverse   Anvil reverse   Upper Canada reverse

Jamaica reverse   Plow reverse   Hunter reverse

	BRETON		VG	F	VF	E	UNC
194	727	Anvil, 1820	6.00	12.00	25.00	50.00	225.00
195	728	UPPER CANADA on cask, 1821	55.00	110.00	225.00	410.00	850.00
196	729	JAMAICA on cask, 182	450.00	600.00	1,200	—	—
197	730	Plow, 1823	6.50	15.00	30.00	75.00	300.00
198	726	Hunter, 1815	35.00	60.00	250.00	550.00	—

Contemporaneously Dated Issues

199   200

199	730	Plow 1833	6.00	12.00	25.00	50.00	200.00
200	731	Tools 1833, brass	10.00	20.00	40.00	110.00	400.00

The Lesslie Tokens

The tokens were issued by a drug and book firm with shops in Toronto, Dundas, and Kingston. The first halfpennies were issued from 1824 to 1827 and have a plain edge. Note the use of York, which was the old name for Toronto; the change took place in 1834. A second issue of halfpennies (1828–1830) has an engrailed edge and a comma after YORK. The twopence was engraved by Thomas Wells Ingram and was struck at least as early as 1827. A specimen was found in the cornerstone during the demolition of the old Courthouse of Hamilton, Ontario, which was built in that year. Because of its size, the twopence was never popular and many became washers.

Both Lesslie denominations are unique in being the only Upper Canada issues with French in their inscriptions. They have the phrase, LA PRUDENCE ET LA CANDEUR, meaning "wisdom and honesty."

201

	BRETON		VG	F	VF	EF	UNC
201	718	LESSLIE & SONS, halfpenny, plain edge 7.50	15.00	45.00	110.00	400.00
201a		Same, engrailed edge 10.00	20.00	50.00	110.00	400.00
202	717	Twopence 1822 .... 200.00	400.00	900.00	1,500	2,500

202

Miscellaneous Tokens

About 1830 tokens inscribed NO LABOUR NO BREAD were imported into Toronto by Perrins Bros., a dry goods firm. Because of the act outlawing private tokens, however, the pieces were seized by the Customs Dept. and ordered to be melted down. A large number of the coppers "fell to the floor" as it has been so quaintly said, and so escaped the melting pot and entered circulation. They were occasionally found in change as late as 1837.

In 1832 a halfpenny token (**204**) was issued of honest size and weight. It was struck in Birmingham by the firm which struck the thistle tokens of Nova Scotia. Like the Nova Scotia issues of 1832, this piece shows the bust of George IV, even though it was then two years after his death. It is not yet known whether this token is semi-regal or private.

203   *204*

203	1010	NO LABOUR, NO BREAD......................... 5.00	10.00	28.00	70.00	400.00
204	732	Halfpenny, George IV 1832 .... 12.00	25.00	50.00	145.00	525.00

The Northwest
Fur Trade Tokens

What was loosely termed "the Northwest" in colonial times included all of British North America north and west of colonial Canada to the Pacific coast and the Arctic Archipelago. This vast region was the preserve of the Hudson's Bay Company. No settlement took place anywhere in this region before Lord Selkirk opened up the valley of the Red River, later to become the province of Manitoba. Beyond this area the only permanent establishments were the trading posts of the Hudson's Bay Company and its rival, the Northwest Company. After years of bitter strife the two companies merged in 1821.

On the west coast, Vancouver Island was detached from the Company and set up as a Crown Colony. The British Columbia mainland was separated in 1858 as a second Crown Colony. The two colonies united in 1866 and the united colony entered the Dominion of Canada in 1871. The remainder of the territory of the Hudson's Bay Company was acquired by the Dominion of Canada in 1869.

Northwest Company Token, 1820

The Northwest Company token was struck in Birmingham in 1820. It is not known by whom, but its style suggests that it may have been struck by the makers of Nova Scotia coinage of 1823–1843. Many known specimens of this piece were found in the lower valley of the Columbia River in Oregon, which is now in the United States. For this reason it is sometimes considered an American piece. It is also thought of as Canadian because it was issued by a Canadian firm. All but one of the known specimens is holed. It is believed that they were issued holed to facilitate wearing them as medalets or attaching them to garments.

205

	BRETON		VG	F	VF	EF	UNC
205	925	NORTHWEST COMPANY, copper	3,000	4,500	6,500	—	—
205a		Same, brass	3,500	5,500	8,000	—	—

Hudson's Bay Company Tokens

The brass tokens of the Hudson's Bay Company were issued around 1854. At the top of the reverse is the Company's HB monogram, below which are the initials EM for the East Main district, south and east of Hudson Bay. The tokens have been found in northern Quebec and Ontario, and as far west as Manitoba. They are erroneously valued in "new beaver." The unit of the fur trade was the "made beaver," which is an adult beaver skin in prime condition. It was never cut up, so the Company thought that tokens would be the ideal way in which to express fractions of the made beaver. The indians, however, preferred to trust the Company accounts rather than take the tokens, which were easily lost. For this reason the pieces never circulated in large quantities. When it was decided to redeem them, the tokens were punched on the reverse at the top to show that they had been redeemed and cancelled. The number of unpunched pieces available now suggests that they were not all presented to be redeemed, or that not all company offices punched them as they were redeemed.

206 *207*

208 *209*

BRETON			VG	F	VF	EF	UNC
206	929	1/8 made beaver	125.00	225.00	350.00	500.00	750.00
207	928	1/4 made beaver	125.00	225.00	350.00	500.00	750.00
208	926	1/2 made beaver	125.00	225.00	350.00	500.00	750.00
209	926	1 made beaver	125.00	225.00	350.00	500.00	750.00

Province of Canada
Bank of Montreal
"Front View" Tokens, 1842–1845

In 1841 Upper and Lower Canada were reunited to form the colony of Province of Canada. The Bank of Montreal was given the right to coin copper, and issued 240,000 pennies and 480,000 halfpennies in 1842. A further issue of 1,440,000 halfpennies was released in 1844. The tokens were struck by Boulton & Watt. A halfpenny die was prepared in 1845, and two tokens struck, but the bank did not issue any tokens dated 1845.

In addition to the normal 1842 front view penny, a mule exists with the Habitant reverse of 1837 (with CITY BANK on the ribbon). It has long been known that dies and other tools connected with the Habitant and front view tokens later fell into the hands of an unscrupulous die sinker named W.J. Taylor and that he used them to produce proofs for sale to collectors. It is also believed that Taylor produced a number of mules which had never been issued for circulation. Many people have generally believed the front view 1837 mule pennies to be just such a concoction. Nevertheless, some pieces recently examined are clearly circulation strikes and are presumably originals produced by Boulton & Watt. Such pieces seem to be inadvertent mules. Because of the relative commonness of the Taylor restrikes compared with the originals, both are listed here.

210 *213*

	BRETON		VG	F	VF	EF	UNC
210	527	Halfpenny 1842	6.50	12.00	22.00	55.00	250.00
211		Halfpenny 1844	4.00	7.00	17.00	35.00	150.00
212		Halfpenny 1845					Extremely Rare
213	526	Penny 1842	5.00	8.00	20.00	50.00	325.00
213a	526a	Mule penny: CITY BANK 1837; rev. original	100.00	150.00	220.00	360.00	775.00
213b	—	Same, Taylor restrike	—	—	—	—	550.00

Quebec Bank Tokens, 1852

In 1852 the Quebec Bank was allowed to issue pennies and halfpennies because of a serious shortage of copper in Quebec. The Bank of Upper Canada coinage was supposed to be enough for the whole province, but the first two issues of this bank were not delivered until 1853, and the Quebec Bank was desperate. With government sanction the bank issued 240,000 pennies and 480,000 halfpennies in 1852. A request for permission to issue more was turned down on the grounds that a change to decimal currency was under contemplation, which occurred in 1858. The Quebec Bank pieces were struck by Ralph Heaton & Sons, and are among the most attractive Canadian colonial issues. The obverse features the familiar "habitant" device and the reverse shows the coat of arms of Quebec City.

214   215

			VG	F	VF	EF	UNC
214	529	Quebec Bank halfpenny 1852	4.00	7.00	17.00	45.00	200.00
215	528	Quebec Bank penny 1852	5.00	9.00	20.00	55.00	450.00

Bank of Upper Canada Tokens, 1850–1857

The Bank of Upper Canada received the right to issue copper in 1850, after the capital was transferred to Toronto from Montreal. An order was placed at the Royal Mint that same year for halfpennies and pennies. The Province of Canada's agent for coinage was the British firm of Rowe, Kentish and Co. The obverse device is the popular St. George and the Dragon motif and the reverse shows the then obsolete arms of Upper Canada. The master tools were engraved by John Pinches of London, but it is Rowe, Kentish's RK & Co. that appears on the ground line on the obverse.

The pieces dated 1850 were struck at the Royal Mint in 1851 and did not reach Canada until 1852. Some of the pennies have a dot between the cornucopia tips on the reverse. Although this dot seems to have been deliberately added, its significance is not known.

In 1852 a second order was placed. The Royal Mint began the coinage, but was unable to complete it because of more pressing demands. The remaining blanks were transferred to Heaton's Mint in Birmingham where the remainder of the order was struck. The Royal Mint striking probably have the die axes ↑↑ (medal struck), while the Heaton's pieces have the dies ↑↓ (coinage struck).

The 1854 and 1857 issues were also produced by Heaton's. No further orders were placed because of the change to the decimal system of currency in 1858.

In 1863 the Bank complained to the government that because of the introduction of the decimal coins it had not been possible to put much of the final order of their tokens into circulation. The government agreed to purchase the tokens and they were stored in Montreal for a number of years. It seems that, through some irregularity (after the Bank had closed in 1867), a portion of the tokens were circulated. The tokens were moved to Toronto early in the 1870s, sold as copper bullion and melted under government supervision in 1873.

216

BRETON			VG	F	VF	EF	UNC
216	720	Halfpenny 1850	4.00	6.00	12.00	28.00	175.00
217		Halfpenny 1852, dies ↑↑	4.00	6.00	12.00	28.00	140.00
217a		Same, dies ↑↓	4.00	6.00	12.00	28.00	140.00
218		Halfpenny 1854, plain 4	4.00	6.00	12.00	28.00	140.00
218a		Same, crosslet 4	25.00	35.00	55.00	135.00	400.00
219		Halfpenny 1857	3.00	5.00	10.00	22.00	140.00

220

220a
Dot between cornucopiae tips

220	719	Penny 1850	5.00	8.00	18.00	35.00	165.00
220a		Same, dot between cornucopiae tips	6.00	12.00	30.00	65.00	250.00
221	719	Penny 1852, Dies ↑↑	5.00	8.00	15.00	35.00	140.00

Plain 4   Crosslet 4

221a		Same, dies ↑↓	5.00	7.00	12.00	28.00	140.00
222		Penny 1854, plain 4	5.00	8.00	12.00	33.00	140.00
222a		Same, crosslet 4	10.00	15.00	30.00	77.00	275.00
223		Penny 1857	4.00	7.00	12.00	28.00	110.00

Anonymous and Miscellaneous Tokens

This section contains various kinds of tokens which are not included in the sections dealing specifically with tokens of the individual colonies, provinces or geographical regions.

With the exception of the "blacksmith" tokens, most of the pieces are of Irish or English origin, some of which had been used in the British Isles before being sent to Canada. Those of light weight were probably struck on Canadian order. A few, such as the North American token, circulated to a limited extent in the United States near the Canadian border.

The North American Token

The North American token was struck in Dublin long after 1781. It was dated 1781 to evade Canadian laws against the importation of anonymous tokens after 1825. To add to the illusion of age, the token was struck without a collar.

224

BRETON			VG	F	VF	EF	UNC
224	1013	NORTH AMERICAN TOKEN, copper	20.00	35.00	80.00	150.00	450.00

The Success to Trade Token

Number 225 is an anonymous English piece with altered legends: SUCCESS TO TRADE was punched over George III Rules, and Commerce was punched over Britannia.

225

225	983	SUCCESS TO TRADE	25.00	40.00	90.00	225.00	450.00

Other Issues

Pieces **226** through **231** were engraved by Thomas Halliday and struck in Birmingham. The "Irish" piece, number **226**, evidently was used in Ireland before being sent to Canada, as specimens have been found there.

226   227

	BRETON		VG	F	VF	EF	UNC
226	1009	Irishman in wreath	6.00	12.00	28.00	80.00	400.00
227	996	FOR GENERAL ACCOMMODATION	6.00	12.00	28.00	70.00	325.00

The RH tokens have sometimes been attributed to Richard Hurd of Montreal but, in light of available evidence, it is more reasonable to consider them English. Even if Hurd also ordered pieces of this design, it is likely that only the halfpenny on the thin flan was involved.

228   229   230

228	991	RH farthing	30.00	40.00	83.00	160.00	525.00
229	990	RH halfpenny, thick flan	10.00	15.00	33.00	70.00	325.00
229a		RH halfpenny, thin flan	15.00	25.00	55.00	120.00	450.00
230	989	RH penny	25.00	40.00	110.00	240.00	675.00

The ship tokens, **231** through **233**, are lightweight tokens, probably struck on Canadian order. The reverse of **232** is that of a halfpenny token of Shaw, Jobson & Co. of Roscoe Mills, Sheffield, England, whose initials S.J & Co. can be seen on the bale. The ship on this piece flies a pennant from the mainmast.

A second variety dated 1812 appears to be a direct copy by another coiner and can be distinguished by the presence of a pennant flying from the foremast (the Halliday variety has none). The 1815 issue was by Halliday, using the same obverse die as in 1812 and a new reverse die.

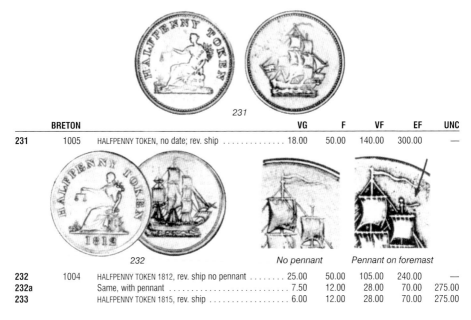

231

BRETON			VG	F	VF	EF	UNC
231	1005	HALFPENNY TOKEN, no date; rev. ship	18.00	50.00	140.00	300.00	—

232 *No pennant* *Pennant on foremast*

232	1004	HALFPENNY TOKEN 1812, rev. ship no pennant	25.00	50.00	105.00	240.00	—
232a		Same, with pennant	7.50	12.00	28.00	70.00	275.00
233		HALFPENNY TOKEN 1815, rev. ship	6.00	12.00	28.00	70.00	275.00

The anchor and H halfpennies are rather crudely made. It has been said that they were issued in Halifax, Nova Scotia, but this has not yet been proved. An 1814 date has been reported but cannot be confirmed.

234

234	Anchor and H, 1816 . . . . Baker Sale 1987: $3,500

235 *236*

Doubtful Pieces

The five tokens listed here have been traditionally included in Canadian collections but are more properly placed in the English or Irish category. While they may have circulated in British North America in very small quantities, none was specifically imported.

The BRITISH COLONIES tokens were originally sent to Jamaica for circulation as pennies. No. **236** was issued for use in British Guiana.

	BRETON		VG	F	VF	EF	UNC
235	993	TO FACILITATE TRADE 1825.	7.50	15.00	45.00	75.00	275.00
236	967	TRADE & NAVIGATION 1838	5.00	10.00	22.00	90.00	400.00

The Hibernia penny (**237**) is an anonymous Irish token designed by Peter Wyon.

237

237	975	HIBERNIA 1805, penny	20.00	40.00	83.00	265.00	650.00

The two pennies with the "Tiffin" obverse and the inscription COMMERCE on the reverse are English tokens, produced by Thomas Halliday.

239

238		COMMERCE	35.00	75.00	110.00	200.00	500.00
239		COMMERCE 1814	20.00	50.00	95.00	170.00	425.00

The "Blacksmith" Tokens

This fascinating group of tokens derives its name from a quaint legend that attributes their origin to a Montreal blacksmith, who made them to pay for liquor. Whatever their origin, it is clear that the blacksmith tokens were not produced by a single source and arose over a period of some years. They could have appeared as early as about 1820, when the tokens then in circulation had been largely decried and the only acceptable coppers were the battered, worn out old British and Irish regal halfpennies of George III. In any case they were still being introduced as late as 1837. The blacksmiths were initially copper, but the late issues tended to be brass.

In a traditional sense the blacksmiths have been defined as specially produced imitations of worn British and Irish regal halfpence. The first blacksmiths were that, but the series grew more complex with the passage of time. Later issues imitated popular tokens in circulation at the time and yet other pieces were of "original" designs resulting from the muling of various dies or the use of dies that were not copying anything.

The blacksmith technique was to leave the designs unfinished and to engrave in very low relief. The devices were often reversed compared to those being copied and usually there was no legend or date. To further heighten the appearance of age and wear, the copper pieces were darkened by heating before being passed into circulation.

The series was almost completely ignored by the earlier writers, Breton including only two in his work. They were described in detail by Howland Wood, whose 1910 monograph is still the standard reference.

The nature of blacksmiths makes them difficult to grade and, in any case, most pieces fall within a rather narrow range of condition. Therefore, the prices for pieces in this series are given for "Average Condition" only. Some of the extremely rare varieties are not priced.

Imitations of British Regal Halfpennies

Obverses:

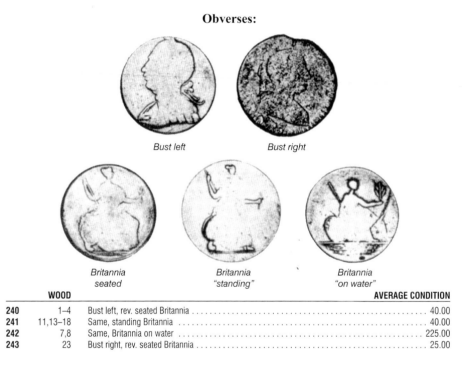

| *Bust left* | *Bust right* |

| *Britannia seated* | *Britannia "standing"* | *Britannia "on water"* |

WOOD			**AVERAGE CONDITION**
240	1–4	Bust left, rev. seated Britannia	40.00
241	11,13–18	Same, standing Britannia	40.00
242	7,8	Same, Britannia on water	225.00
243	23	Bust right, rev. seated Britannia	25.00

The next two pieces are of a rather complex nature. There is a group of tokens generally considered U.S., called "bungtowns." These are imitations of British and Irish halfpence, where the legend has deliberately been garbled to circumvent the laws against counter- feiting. The first piece (**244**) could well be a U.S. "bungtown" shipped to Lower Canada. (So many of them have been found in Canada that there can be no doubt of their right to be called Canadian.) The legends are GLORIOUS III • VIS (instead of GEORGIUS III REX) on the obverse and BITIT • (instead of BRITANNIA) on the reverse. It was thought by Wood to be an imitation of a bungtown; however, the relatively high quality of the lettering leads us to believe it to be a U.S. product.

The legend on the second piece (**245**) is much cruder and more difficult to read. The letters which show suggest that this token is a copy of the "bungtown" issue.

	244		245
WOOD			**AVERAGE CONDITION**
244	33	Bust right, GLORIOUS III • VIS	25.00
245	34	Bust left, GLORIOUS III • III VIS (?)	575.00

Imitations of Irish Regal Halfpennies

In addition to a plain harp on the reverse there are some curious pieces with a harp surrounded on the sides and bottom by a non-descript design. This design has generally been believed to have resulted from deterioration of the die, but this is only partially correct. Much of it was engraved.

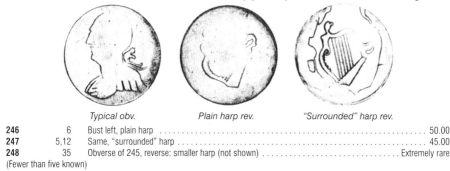

	Typical obv.		*Plain harp rev.*		*"Surrounded" harp rev.*
246	6	Bust left, plain harp			50.00
247	5,12	Same, "surrounded" harp			45.00
248	35	Obverse of 245, reverse: smaller harp (not shown)			Extremely rare

(Fewer than five known)

Imitations of Regal Halfpennies
With Only a Bust

This is group consisting of uniface strikings from the obverse dies for some of the preceding pieces, but mostly from dies apparently intended to be used alone. Most were unknown to Wood and all are extremely rare and hence not priced.

	250		251		252
249	(34)	Obverse of 245			600.00
250	42	Bust left, single ribbon end			—
251	—	"Horned" bust left			—
252	39	Bust left, X behind			Extremely rare

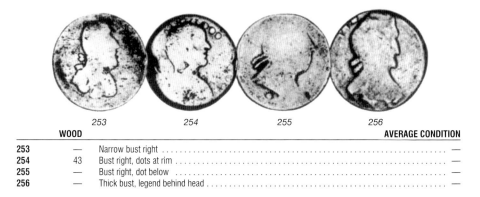

| | 253 | 254 | 255 | 256 |

WOOD			AVERAGE CONDITION
253	—	Narrow bust right	—
254	43	Bust right, dots at rim	—
255	—	Bust right, dot below	—
256	—	Thick bust, legend behind head	—

Imitations of Ships, Colonies
and Commerce Tokens

The next two pieces, not found in Wood, are rare and have both been included in Lees under 5. Recently, however, their obverses have been shown to be from different dies. The first (**257**) has faint rim beads on the obverse, a distinct ball at the top of each mast and a thin line extending back from between the two waves just below the ship's stern. The classical Lees 5 (**258**) lacks rim beads, has indistinct mast tops and no line between the waves at the rear. In addition all known examples are from a badly cracked die.

| | 257 | | 258 |

LEES			AVERAGE CONDITION
257	5	Drooping flag, incomplete ship.	Extremely Rare
258	5	Same, no beads either side	Extremely Rare

Other Imitating Designs

| | 259 | | 260 |

WOOD			VG	F
259	21,22	"Bust-Harp-like" 1820		Extremely Rare
260	19	"Tiffin-like" 1820	250.00	400.00
260a	20	Same, brass		Extremely Rare

261   262

WOOD			VG
261	"Vexator-like" 1811 (?), uniface		Extremely Rare
262	Same, no date (?), uniface		Extremely Rare

263

| **263** | 31 | "Sloop-like"' wreath .... | Unique |

Miscellaneous "Original" Designs

Some of the tokens in the blacksmith series fall into a category which can be called original designs. The dies, individually or in combination, did not copy an existing design. The first two pieces are from one die for an imitation of a regal halfpenny, and the other for an imitation of the SHIPS COLONIES & COMMERCE tokens. The reverse die of **264** is the same as the obverse die for **258**.

264   265

| **264** | 9 | Bust, ref. ship .... | Extremely Rare |
| **265** | 10 | SHIPS COLONIES etc., rev. "surrounded" harp .... | .400.00 |

The reverses of **266** and **267** are said to be from very worn reverse dies for standard type tokens. In the first case it is the Upper Canada Sloop **197** to **199** and in the second it is a U.S. "hard times" token (Low 19). The obverse of **267** also strongly resembles that of **98a**. Whether the dies which struck these blacksmith issues are really those that struck the tokens they resemble is not yet established.

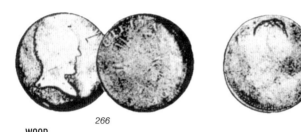

266   267

WOOD			AVERAGE CONDITION
266	45	Bust rev. TO FACILITATE TRADE	Extremely Rare
267	46	Bust, rev. U.S. "hard times" token	Extremely Rare

The "Mexican" bouquet sou has what appears to be a copy of a State of Chihuahua copper coin (1833–1856), depicting a standing Indian, for its reverse design. The obverse is probably a copy of a bouquet sou die, rather than a deteriorated original die.

268

268	"Mexican" bouquet sou	Extremely Rare

The next group of "original" designs stems from five kinds of dies used in various combinations. The RISEING SUN TAVERN piece has been tentatively linked to a tavern in Toronto; however, this is not certain. It is interesting that two of the dies are apparently discarded reverse dies from metallic store cards of N.S. Starbuck & Son and J. & C. Peck, both of Troy, New York.

Bust obv.   Eagle obv./rev.

RISEING SUN TAVERN rev.   STARBUCK rev.   PECK rev.

WOOD			F
269	24	Bust, RISEING SUN TAVERN	400.00
270	26	Bust, eagle	775.00
271	25	Bust. STARBUCK	500.00
272	27	Eagle, STARBUCK	Extremely Rare
273	28	Eagle, PECK	700.00
274	30	Eagle, EAGLE	300.00
275	29	STARBUCK, PECK	125.00

The following three tokens are of completely new designs, but nevertheless are generally considered to be part of the blacksmith series.

276

277

WOOD			AVERAGE CONDITION
276	—	Windmill, rev. NO CREDIT	(Fewer than ten known) 1,800
277	32	Anchor, rev. shield	1,750

278

278	—	Balance, rev. tools and star	Extremely rare

A Guide For Attributing Tokens

The listings of tokens in the main body are arranged according to the colony for which they were struck or where they were most used. Many of the pieces bear some indication of the colony of issue, in the form of either a city in the colony or the colony name itself. However, others do not, and as an aid to finding such pieces in the catalogue listings, the table below was constructed. To find a given token the following rules should be noted:

1. Pieces with the name of a city or the colony are NOT included in this list if they are listed under the expected colony.

2. If one or both sides of the token has a legend, consult the lists of legends.

3. Where a token has two legends on the same side – one around the outside and the second (usually the value) in a circle in the centre – the legends are listed separately.

4. When there is no legend or the legend is indistinct, the lists of designs should be consulted.

Pieces Without Legend

DESIGN	HAXBY-WILLEY TOKEN NOS.	DESIGN	HAXBY-WILLEY TOKEN NOS.
Anchor / shield	277	Bust in wreath / seated female 1812	122–122a
Balance scale / tools and star	278	Bust / eagle	270
Bouquet / dancing Indian	268	Bust / harp	113–114, 246–248
Bust left (uniface)	249–52, 262	Bust / harp 1820	111–112, 259
Bust right (uniface)	253–256	Bust / harp 1825	110
Bust 1811? (uniface)	261	Bust / ship	264
Bust / seated female	240, 242–243	Eagle / eagle	274
Bust / standing female	241	Ship / 1858	6
Bust 1820 / seated female	99	Ship / seated female	100
Bust / seated female 1820	260–260a	Sloop in wreath / anvil, shovels in wreath	263

Pieces With Legends

AGRICULTURE & COMMERCE • BAS CANADA	117	GLORIOUS III • VIS	245, 248–249
BRITISH COLONIES	235	H	234
BRITIT	244	HALFPENNY OR HALF PENNY	40–42, 102–103
CANADA 1830	102	HALFPENNY OR HALF PENNY TOKEN:	
1841	103	(undated)	19, 24–25, 28, 39, 76–77, 90, 227, 231
CANADA HALF PENNY TOKEN	101	1812	24, 115, 120–121a, 232
COMMERCE (undated)	80, 224	1813	25, 28, 82–81a, 91–93a
1814	239	1814	31, 229–229a
COMMERCE RULES THE MAIN	225	1815	36, 38, 40, 233
COMMERCIAL CHANGE	97–97A	1816	84, 234
COSSACK PENNY TOKEN	87	HB EM 1/8 (1/4, 1/2 or 1) NB	206–209
EXECUTIVE EXPERIMENT	267	HIBERNIA 1805	71,237
FARTHING TOKEN 1812	228	HISPANIUM ET LUSITANIUM RESTITUIT	
FIELD MARSHALL WELLINGTON		WELLINGTON	73–75
(undated)	71, 76–78A, 81–81A, 85–86	JB (script)	42
1813	88	MACHINE SHOP, etc.	271–272, 275
FISHERIES AND AGRICULTURE	18–19	MAGDALEN ISLAND TOKEN	1
FOR GENERAL ACCOMMODATION	227	MARQUIS WELLINGTON 1813	80
FOR PUBLIC ACCOMMODATION	101, 237	NEMO ME IMPUNE LACESSIT	43
FOR PUBLICK ACCOMMODATION	9	NO CREDIT	276
FOR THE CONVENIENCE OF TRADE	31	NO LABOUR NO BREAD	203
GENUINE BRITISH COPPER (undated)	36	NORTH AMERICAN TOKEN 1781	224
1815	39	NORTH WEST COMPANY	205–205a
GLO III • VIS (?)	244	ONE CENT 1855	18

Pieces with Legends (Continued)

TRADE, ADVERTISING AND TRANSPORTATION TOKENS

Trade and advertising tokens appeared in the developing portions of the Dominion after 1880. They were issued by rural storekeepers and city firms in the West and in the north of Ontario as a means of enticing customers to return to their place of business. Given out in change, they could only be redeemed in the locality or at the shop of the issuer. In many cases they augmented the local supply of cash. Saskatchewan saw an enormous quantity and variety of these pieces in use, in denominations ranging from one cent to ten dollars. Large numbers were issued in Manitoba, Alberta, and British Columbia.

There was also a great variety of tokens issued which were redeemable in goods or services. Cordwood tokens, pool checks, hotel and restaurant tokens, barber shop tokens, cigar store tokens, dairy tokens, and bread tokens abound in all provinces. A special class of tokens good for some service are transportation tokens. These were issued to pay the fare by bus, street car or ferry in various localities, or to pay tolls for the use of bridges and tunnels. The famous Bout de l'Isle tokens are an example of tokens issued to pay tolls, in this case over a series of bridges near Montreal. One of the earliest fare tokens is the Montreal & Lachine Railroad token.

Trade Tokens

Another item now becoming very popular is the trade or souvenir coin. This is a sort of cross between a trade token and a commercial medal, for it is issued by a local organization or municipality for temporary use as money within the limits of a municipality, and commemorates or honours some important local event or historical personage. Usually these pieces are issued with a value of one dollar, and collectors have called them trade dollars, but their appearance in other denominations necessitates their being called by some other name, for by no conceivable stretch of the imagination ought a fifty-cent trade coin be called a trade dollar.

One of the earliest of these pieces was the dollar struck in 1960 for the golden jubilee of the founding of Prince Rupert, British Columbia, They have been most widely used in Western Canada, but have recently spread into the East.

Dairy token   Bread token

Barber shop token   Ferry token

Montreal and Lachine Railroad Token

It was found that ordinary railway tickets were not convenient for use among the Indians and workmen on the Lachine Canal, who formed the bulk of third class travel on the Montreal & Lachine Railroad Company.

These tokens were therefore imported from Birmingham, England. The tokens were strung on a wire as they were collected by the conductor.

Article reprinted from An Introduction to Coin Collecting *with the kind permission of the Canadian Numismatic Association.*

COLONIAL DECIMAL ISSUES
NEW BRUNSWICK
Victoria, Half Cent
1861

Diameter: 20.65 mm; weight: 2.835 grams;
composition: .950 copper, .040 tin, .010 zinc; edge: plain

G: Hair over ear worn through
VG: Little detail to hair over ear or braid
F: Strands of hair over ear begin to merge; braid is worn
VF: Hair over ear is worn; braid is clear but no longer sharp
EF: Slight wear on hair over ear; braid that holds knot in place
is sharp and clear

In 1860 New Brunswick adopted a monetary system consisting of dollars and cents, with the dollar equal to the United States gold dollar. This made the British shilling worth slightly more than 24 cents and the 6d slightly more than 12 cents. Consequently, it was not necessary for the province to issue half cents to make change for the 6d. The Royal Mint nevertheless struck over 200,000 New Brunswick half-cents. The mistake was soon discovered and most of the coins melted. The only ones to escape were a few proofs and an unknown number of business strikes (perhaps in the hundreds) that were mixed with the Nova Scotia half-cents and sent to Halifax.

The obverse design is identical to that used for the Nova Scotia half-cents and is one of those used for the British bronze farthing (Peck's obv. 3).

The reverse is similar to that for the Nova Scotia half cent.

DATE	Qty. (000)	G-4	VG-8	F-12	VF-20	EF-40	Brown AU-50	UNC-60	Red/Brown BU-63
1861	223	150.00	225.00	300.00	375.00	500.00	700.00	1,000	1,600

Victoria, Large Cents
1861–1864

Diameter: 25.53mm; weight: 5.670 grams;
composition: .950 copper, .040 tin, .010 zinc; edge: plain

Short tip 6   Long tip 6

The obverse is the same as the Nova Scotia coins of the same denomination and is one of those used for the British halfpenny (Peck's obv. 6). Designed and engraved by L.C. Wyon.

The reverse design is very similar to that used for the Nova Scotia issue; the wreath differs only in minor respects. The design was adapted from a model by C. Hill.

1861	1,000	3.00	6.00	9.00	15.00	25.00	70.00	175.00	750.00
1864 short tip 6	1,000	4.00	8.00	11.00	20.00	45.00	115.00	265.00	1,250
long tip 6	incl. above	6.00	11.00	15.00	30.00	70.00	150.00	400.00	—

Victoria, 5 Cents Silver
1862–1864

Diameter: 15.49 mm; weight: 1.162 grams; composition: .925 silver, .075 copper; edge: reeded

G: Braid around ear worn through
VG: No details in braid around the ear
F: Segments of braid begin to merge into one another
VF: Braid is clear but not sharp
EF: Braid is slightly worn but generally sharp and clear

The obverse, designed and engraved by L.C. Wyon, has a portrait of Victoria that would later be used on the Dominion of Canada five cents of 1858.

DATE	QTY. (000)	G-4	VG-8	F-12	VF-20	EF-40	AU-50	UNC-60	BU-63
1862 100		60.00	120.00	180.00	350.00	800.00	1,750	3,250	6,000

Small 6   Large 6

1864 small 6 100		60.00	120.00	180.00	350.00	800.00	1,750	3,500	7,500
large 6 . . . . incl. above		115.00	225.00	350.00	650.00	1,500	3,200	4,500	9,000

Victoria, 10 Cents Silver
1862–1864

Diameter: 17.91 mm; weight: 2.324 grams; composition: .925 silver, .075 copper; edge: reeded

The obverse is virtually identical to and was derived from Portrait No. 6 of the Canadian 10-cent piece. (This particular Canadian obverse existed long before it appeared on the issues of 1892.) The designer and engraver was L.C. Wyon.

The reverse design, the device of which is a wreath of maple surmounted by the St. Edward's crown, is identical to that used for the Province of Canada ten cents of 1858.

Normal 2 Double-punched 2

1862 normal date 150		55.00	110.00	180.00	350.00	750.00	1,500	2,500	5,000
double-punch 2 . . . . . incl. above		100.00	200.00	300.00	600.00	1,250	2,500	4,500	12,500
1864 150		55.00	110.00	180.00	350.00	750.00	2,000	4,500	10,000

Victoria, 20 Cents Silver
1862–1864

Diameter: 22.99 mm; weight: 4.648 grams; composition: .925 silver, .075 copper; edge: reeded

The obverse, designed and engraved by L.C. Wyon, has a portrait similar to that on the Province of Canada 20-cent issue.

DATE	QTY. (000)	G-4	VG-8	F-12	VF-20	EF-40	AU-50	UNC-60	BU-63
1862	150	25.00	50.00	75.00	175.00	400.00	900.00	2,000	6,000
1864	150	25.00	50.00	75.00	175.00	425.00	1,100	2,500	7,500

Newfoundland

In an act of 1863 Newfoundland turned to decimal currency and adopted the Spanish dollar as its unit. This made the British shilling equivalent to 24 cents and the sixpence to 12 cents.

Victoria, Large Cents
1865–1896

Diameter: 25.33 mm; weight: 5.670 grams; composition: .950 copper, .040 tin, .010 zinc; edge: plain

G: Hair over ear worn through
VG: Little detail to hair over ear or braid
F: Strands of hair over ear begin to merge, braid is worn
VF: Hair over ear is worn, braid is clear but no longer sharp
EF: Slight wear on hair over ear, braid that holds knot in place is sharp and clear

The obverse, designed and engraved by L.C. Wyon, is unusual in two respects. First, the portrait was one of those used for the British halfpence (Peck's obv. 6) and second, the lettering is in simple, very bold type.

The reverse was engraved by Wyon's assistant, T.J. Minton, from a design by Horace Morehen. The wreath consists of pitcher plant and oak.

1880 date varieties. Two styles for the 0 are known, narrow and wide. The position of the wide 0 also varies, these positional differences, however, are considered trivial and will not be perpetuated here.

Die axis varieties. With the exception of the 1872H, all of the Victorian Newfoundland cents were medal-struck (die axes arranged ↑↑). The opposite alignment (die axes arranged ↑↓) of the 1872H is probably because the alignment was not specified and Heaton's assumed it was to be the same as on the silver coins.

DATE	Qty. (000)	G-4	VG-8	F-12	VF-20	EF-40	AU-50	Brown UNC-60	Red† MS-63
1865	240	3.00	6.00	9.00	18.00	50.00	120.00	300.00	1,250
1872H	200	3.00	5.00	7.00	14.00	35.00	80.00	150.00	400.00
1873	200	3.00	7.00	11.00	27.00	85.00	225.00	600.00	2,600
1876H	200	3.00	6.00	11.00	27.00	90.00	225.00	650.00	2,250

† 70% lustre

Narrow 0 Wide 0

DATE	Qty. (000)	G-4	VG-8	F-12	VF-20	EF-40	AU-50	Brown UNC-60	Red† BU-63
1880 narrow 0 400		125.00	250.00	400.00	650.00	1,150	2,100	3,500	8,000
wide 0 .... incl. above		3.00	4.50	7.00	14.00	36.00	90.00	225.00	850.00
1885 40		25.00	45.00	70.00	120.00	275.00	550.00	1,000	4,200
1888 50		25.00	50.00	80.00	135.00	325.00	750.00	1,500	–
1890 200		3.00	5.00	9.00	25.00	75.00	175.00	400.00	2,100
1894 200		3.00	5.00	9.00	22.00	70.00	165.00	350.00	1,900
1896 200		3.00	4.50	7.00	14.00	35.00	100.00	200.00	800.00

† 70% lustre

Edward VII, Large Cents
1904–1909

Diameter: 25.53 mm; weight: 5.670 grams; composition: .950 copper, .040 tin, .010 zinc; edge: plain

G: Band of crown worn through
VG: Band of crown is worn through at highest point
F: Jewels in band of crown will be blurred
VF: Band of crown is still clear but no longer sharp
EF: Band of crown slightly worn but generally sharp and clear

The obverse was derived from a portrait model by G.W. De Saulles; the portrait is unusually large for the size of the coin.

The reverse design is the same as used for the Victoria series, except for the substitution of the Imperial State crown for the St. Edward's crown. The modification was made by W.H.J. Blakemore.

1904H 100		6.00	11.00	20.00	35.00	80.00	200.00	550.00	1,600
1907 200		2.50	4.00	7.00	15.00	50.00	140.00	350.00	1,350
1909 200		2.50	4.00	6.00	10.00	30.00	75.00	150.00	300.00

George V, Large Cents
1913–1936

Diameter: (1913, 1929, 1936) 25.53 mm, (1917–20) 25.40 mm; weight: 5.670 grams;
composition: (1913–20) .950 copper, .040 tin, .010 zinc, (1929–36) .955 copper, .030 tin, .015 zinc; edge: plain

G: Band of crown worn through
VG: Band of crown is worn through at highest point
F: Jewels in band of crown will be blurred
VF: Band of crown is still clear but no longer sharp
EF: Band of crown slightly worn but generally sharp and clear

The obverse, from a portrait model by Sir E.B. MacKennal (B.M. on truncation), is identical to that for the Canadian issues of the same denomination.

The reverse is a continuation of the design introduced in the Edward VII series.

1913 400		1.25	2.00	3.00	4.00	10.00	35.00	70.00	150.00
1917C 702		1.25	2.00	3.00	4.00	9.00	35.00	125.00	450.00
1919C 300		1.25	2.00	3.00	5.00	15.00	60.00	250.00	850.00

DATE	Qty. (000)	G-4	VG-8	F-12	VF-20	EF-40	AU-50	Brown MS-60	Red† MS-63
1920C	302	1.25	2.00	3.00	7.00	25.00	100.00	400.00	2,000
1929	300	1.25	2.00	3.00	4.00	8.00	35.00	100.00	200.00
1936	300	1.25	2.00	2.50	3.00	6.00	20.00	50.00	125.00

George VI, Small Cents
1938–1947

Diameter: 19.05 mm; weight: 3.240 grams; composition: .955 copper, .030 tin, .015 zinc; edge: plain

VG: Band of crown almost worn through; little detail in hair
F: Band of crown considerably worn; strands of hair begin to merge together
VF: Wear extends along band of crown; hair is clear but no longer sharp
EF: Band of crown shows slight wear; hair is sharp and clear

Because of the need to have new obverses for the George VI coinage, the government of Newfoundland considered the question of changing to smaller one-cent and larger five-cent pieces, similar to those already in circulation in Canada and the U.S. Despite the economic advantages of such a change, there was a strong conservative element in favor of retaining the old sizes. The final decision was to alter only the one-cent size.

The obverse for the small cent was derived from a portrait model for British colonial coinages by Percy Metcalfe (P.M. below neck). The reverse device is the insectivorous pitcher plant, Sarracenia purpurea, which is native to the island. The die was engraved by W.J. Newman, a senior engraver at the Royal Mint, from designs sent from Newfoundland.

The 1938 issue was produced in London. Due to the danger of loss of trans-Atlantic shipments during World War II, all later coinages were struck at the Royal Canadian Mint in Ottawa. The C mint mark was inadvertently omitted in 1940 and 1942.

1938	500	.25	.50	1.00	1.50	4.00	10.00	25.00	85.00
1940(C)	300	1.00	1.50	2.50	5.00	15.00	45.00	100.00	750.00
1941C	828	.25	.50	.75	1.50	3.00	10.00	30.00	300.00
1942(C)	1,997	.25	.50	.75	1.00	3.00	15.00	45.00	300.00
1943C	1,240	.25	.50	.75	1.00	3.00	10.00	25.00	125.00
1944C	1,329	1.00	2.00	3.00	10.00	40.00	125.00	350.00	2,500
1947C	314	.50	1.00	1.50	5.00	20.00	50.00	110.00	750.00

† 70% lustre

Victoria, Five Cents Silver
1865–1896

Diameter: 15.49 mm; weight: 1.178 grams; composition: .925 silver, .075 copper; edge: reeded

G: Braid around hair worn through
VG: No detail in braid around ear
F: Segments of braid begin to merge into one another
VF: Braid is clear but not sharp
EF: Braid slightly worn but generally sharp and clear

The initial obverse was derived from that used for New Brunswick by modifying the legend. Periods are present on both sides of NEWFOUNDLAND. A second variety lacks the periods. On the final obverse the Queen has more aged facial features with repressed upper lip and recessed forehead, and the period after NEWFOUNDLAND was restored (closer to the D).

Two noteworthy reverses are known for this series. The first has a Roman I in the date, while the second has the more conventional Arabic 1.

The first and probably all later obverse and reverse varieties were designed and engraved by L.C. Wyon.

The weights of the silver denominations were made proportional to those of the equivalent values in English silver coin; that is, 5.6552 grams per shilling (12 pence). The value of the 5 cents was 2½ d.

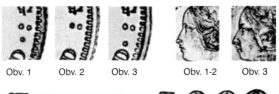

| Obv. 1 | Obv. 2 | Obv. 3 | Obv. 1-2 | Obv. 3 |

Roman "I"      Arabic "1"

DATE	QTY. (000)	G-4	VG-8	F-12	VF-20	EF-40	AU-50	MS-60	MS-63
Roman "I" Reverse (1865)									
1865 obv........1, 2 80		30.00	60.00	100.00	225.00	450.00	900.00	2,000	4,000
Arabic "1" Reverse (1870–1896)									
1870 .... obv. 1, 2 40		70.00	125.00	250.00	500.00	1,000	1,700	3,000	5,500
1872H........ obv. 2 40		30.00	55.00	100.00	200.00	400.00	800.00	1,500	2,750
1873 .... obv. 2 39		150.00	325.00	500.00	1,100	2,600	5,000	–	–
1873H........ obv. 2 .... est. 1		800.00	1,500	2,200	3,500	6,500	11,000	–	–
1876H........ obv. 2 20		125.00	225.00	350.00	600.00	1,000	1,500	2,500	4,750
1880 .... obv. 2 40		45.00	80.00	125.00	275.00	600.00	1,250	2,500	4,500
1881 .... obv. 2 40		45.00	80.00	125.00	275.00	600.00	1,250	3,000	4,800
1882H........ obv. 3 60		25.00	50.00	80.00	150.00	350.00	750.00	2,000	3,500
1885 .... obv. 2 16		165.00	300.00	475.00	850.00	1,800	3,200	5,250	8,500
1888 .... obv. 2, 3 40		40.00	85.00	170.00	350.00	850.00	1,800	4,900	9,000
1890 .... obv. 3 160		9.00	18.00	35.00	75.00	200.00	800.00	2,500	5,000
1894 .... obv. 3 160		9.00	18.00	35.00	75.00	175.00	600.00	2,500	4,500
1896 .... obv. 3 400		5.00	9.00	15.00	35.00	125.00	500.00	2,000	4,000

Edward VII, Five Cents Silver
1903–1908

Diameter: 15.49 mm; weight: 1.178 grams; composition: .925 silver, .075 copper; edge: reeded

G: Band of crown worn through
VG: Band of crown worn through at highest point
F: Jewels in band of crown will be blurred
VF: Band of crown still clear but no longer sharp
EF: Band of crown slightly worn but generally sharp and clear

The obverse, designed and engraved by G.W. De Saulles (DES. below bust), is identical to that for the Canadian issues.

The reverse was also the work of De Saulles.

1903 100	3.50	6.00	12.00	30.00	75.00	200.00	500.00	1,750
1904H...................... 100	3.00	4.00	8.00	20.00	50.00	100.00	250.00	475.00
1908 400	3.00	4.00	8.00	20.00	50.00	125.00	300.00	1,200

George V, 5 Cents Silver
1912–1929

Diameter: (1912–19) 15.49 mm, (1929) 15.69 mm; weight: (1912) 1.178 grams, (1917–29) 1.166 grams;

composition: .925 silver, .075 copper; edge: reeded

G: Band of crown worn through
VG: Band of crown worn through at highest point
F: Jewels in band of crown will be blurred
VF: Band of crown still clear but no longer sharp
EF: Band of crown slightly worn but generally

The obverse bears a portrait which was derived from a model by Sir E.B. MacKennal (B.M. on truncation) and is identical to that for the Canadian issues.

The reverse is as for the Edward VII series.

DATE	QTY. (000)	G-4	VG-8	F-12	VF-20	EF-40	AU-50	MS-60	MS-63
1912	300	2.00	3.00	4.00	8.00	25.00	65.00	150.00	300.00
1917C	300	2.00	3.00	5.00	10.00	30.00	125.00	400.00	1,500
1919C	101	3.00	7.00	12.00	30.00	125.00	500.00	1,500	4,000
1929	300	2.00	2.50	3.50	5.00	17.00	75.00	200.00	450.00

George VI, 5 Cents Silver
1938–1947

Diameter: (1938) 15.69 mm, (1940–47) 15.49 mm; weight: 1.166 grams;

composition: (1938–44) .925 silver, .075 copper, (1945–47) .800 silver, .200 copper; edge: reeded

VG: Band of crown almost worn through
F: Band of crown considerably worn; strands of hair begin to merge together
VF: Wear extends along band of crown; hair is clear but no longer sharp
EF: Band of crown shows slight wear; hair is sharp and clear

The obverse is derived from a portrait model by Percy Metcalfe (P.M. below neck) intended for English colonial coinages.

The reverse is as for the Edward VII and George V issues.

1938	100	–	–	2.00	4.00	9.00	35.00	125.00	350.00
1940C	200	–	–	2.00	4.00	9.00	35.00	125.00	400.00
1941C	613	–	–	2.00	3.00	5.00	10.00	25.00	40.00
1942C	298	–	–	2.00	3.00	6.00	15.00	35.00	65.00
1943C	352	–	–	2.00	3.00	6.00	12.00	25.00	50.00
1944C	287	–	–	2.00	3.00	10.00	25.00	75.00	175.00
1945C	204	–	–	2.00	3.00	5.00	10.00	25.00	40.00
1946C	2	300.00	500.00	700.00	850.00	1,100	1,800	2,600	3,500
1947C	38	2.00	4.00	6.00	8.00	20.00	55.00	120.00	275.00

Victoria, 10 Cents Silver
1865–1896

Diameter: 17.98 mm; weight: 2.356 grams;
composition: .925 silver, .025 copper; edge: reeded

G: Braid around ear worn through
VG: No details in braid around ear
F: Segments of braid begin to merge together
VF: Braid is clear but not sharp
EF: Braid slightly worn but generally sharp and clear

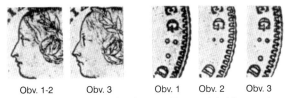

Obv. 1-2   Obv. 3   Obv. 1   Obv. 2   Obv. 3

The initial obverse was derived from that for the New Brunswick 10-cent piece by modifying the legend. A second variety lacks the period following the word NEWFOUNDLAND. A third variety has the period restored (but closer to the D) and depicts the Queen with more aged facial features. Two noteworthy reverses are known for this series. The first has Roman Is in the I0 and date, while the second has the more conventional Arabic 1s. There are also slight differences in the devices and rim denticles.

Roman "I"   Arabic "1" (note 2nd 8 over 7)

1871H Newfoundland / Canada mule. Quite possibly the result of an inadvertent muling of a Canadian 1871H reverse with a Newfoundland obverse. The two known examples of this interesting and extremely rare variety are in well circulated condition, adding credence to the proposition that it is not a pattern.

1880 2nd 8 over 7. All of the 10- and 50-cent pieces of 1880 examined have the second 8 in the date punched over a 7. By the latter part of the 1870s, the dies for these denominations were sunk from reverse punches bearing the partial date 187–; the final digit was hand punched into each die. In 1880, then, the Mint was faced with either making new punches or using the old ones and correcting the 7 in each die, in addition to adding the final digit. The latter course of action was chosen in 1880, probably because of a lack of time and the small number of dies which had to be made for Newfoundland in that year. The reverse punches for the other denominations lacked both the third and the fourth digits, so this problem did not arise for them.

DATE	QTY. (000)	G-4	VG-8	F-12	VF-20	EF-40	AU-50	MS-60	MS-63
Roman "I" Reverse (1865–1870)									
1865 . . . . obv. 1 80		25.00	50.00	80.00	150.00	350.00	750.00	2,000	3,750
1870 . . . . obv. 1, 2 30		175.00	325.00	475.00	700.00	1,400	2,250	4,000	6,500
Arabic "1" Reverse (1872–1896)									
1872H . . . . bv. 2 40		20.00	40.00	60.00	125.00	300.00	700.00	1,500	2,500
1873 . . . . obv. 1, 2 20		60.00	120.00	250.00	500.00	1,200	3,000	–	–
1876H . . . . obv. 2 10		60.00	120.00	250.00	425.00	875.00	1,700	2,700	4,000
1880 . . . . obv. 2 10		50.00	100.00	180.00	350.00	800.00	1,600	3,000	4,500
1882H . . . . obv. 3 20		35.00	75.00	110.00	225.00	800.00	2,500	7,000	–
1885 . . . . obv. 3 8		110.00	200.00	300.00	650.00	1,200	2,000	4,000	6,500
1888 . . . . obv. 3 30		40.00	80.00	125.00	350.00	1,300	3,000	7,000	–
1890 . . . . obv. 3 100		8.00	18.00	30.00	70.00	350.00	1,000	3,500	–
1894 . . . . obv. 2, 3 100		8.00	15.00	25.00	50.00	200.00	650.00	2,000	4,500
1896 . . . . obv. 3 230		6.00	12.00	20.00	40.00	175.00	700.00	3,500	6,000

Edward VII, 10 Cents Silver
1903–1904

Diameter: 17.96 mm; weight: 2.356 grams; composition: .925 silver, .025 copper; edge: reeded

G: Band of crown worn through
VG: Band of crown worn through at highest point
F: Jewels in band of crown will be blurred
VF: Band of crown still clear but no longer sharp
EF: Band of crown slightly worn but generally sharp and clear

The obverse, designed and engraved by G.W. De Saulles (DES. below bust), is identical to that for the Canadian issues.

The reverse was also done by De Saulles.

DATE	QTY. (000)	G-4	VG-8	F-12	VF-20	EF-40	AU-50	MS-60	MS-63
1903 100		6.00	12.00	35.00	95.00	2750.00	750.00	3,000	7,500
1904H 100		4.00	7.00	15.00	40.00	125.00	225.00	400.00	750.00

George V, 10 Cents Silver
1912–1919

Diameter: (1912) 17.96 mm, (1917, 1919) 18.03 mm; weight: (1912) 2.356 grams,
(1917, 1919) 2.333 grams; composition: .925 silver, .075 copper; edge: reeded

G: Band of crown worn through
VG: Band of crown worn through at highest point
F: Jewels in band of crown will be blurred
VF: Band of crown still clear but no longer sharp
EF: Band of crown slightly worn but generally sharp and clear

The obverse bears a portrait derived from a model by Sir E.B. MacKennal (B.M. on truncation) and is identical to that for the Canadian issues.

The reverse is identical to that of the Edward VII series.

1912 150		3.00	4.00	7.00	15.00	50.00	125.00	250.00	400.00
1917C 251		3.00	4.00	6.00	15.00	50.00	200.00	500.00	1,500
1919C 54		3.00	5.00	10.00	25.00	75.00	150.00	275.00	400.00

George VI, 10 Cents Silver
1938–1947

Diameter: 18.03 mm; weight: 2.333 grams; composition: (1938–44) .925 silver, .075 copper,
(1945–47) .800 silver, .200 copper; edge: reeded

G: Band of crown worn through
VG: Band of crown worn through at highest point
F: Jewels in band of crown will be blurred
VF: Band of crown still clear but no longer sharp
EF: Band of crown slightly worn but generally sharp and clear

The obverse is derived from a portrait model by Percy Metcalfe (P.M. below neck) intended for English colonial coinages.

The reverse is as for the Edward VII and George V issues.

DATE	QTY. (000)	VG-8	F-12	VF-20	EF-40	AU-50	MS-60	MS-63
1938 100		3.00	5.00	9.00	35.00	120.00	325.00	1,250
1940(C) 100		3.00	3.50	5.00	15.00	50.00	125.00	425.00
1941C 484		–	3.00	3.50	8.00	20.00	55.00	135.00

DATE	QTY. (000)	VG-8	F-12	VF-20	EF-40	AU-50	MS-60	MS-63
1942C	293	–	3.00	3.50	8.00	25.00	75.00	250.00
1943C	105	–	3.00	3.50	10.00	35.00	300.00	1,000
1944C	151	3.00	4.00	12.00	30.00	75.00	300.00	1,500
1945C	176	–	3.00	3.50	8.00	25.00	125.00	500.00
1946C	38	4.00	5.00	10.00	35.00	70.00	150.00	350.00
1947C	62	3.00	4.00	8.00	22.00	50.00	125.00	400.00

Victoria, 20 Cents Silver
1865–1900

Diameter: 23.19 mm; weight: 4.713 grams;
composition: .925 silver, .075 copper; edge: reeded

G: Braid around ear worn through
VG: No details in braid around ear
F: Segments of braid begin to merge together
VF: Braid is clear but not sharp
EF: Braid is slightly worn but generally clear and sharp

The first obverse was derived from the New Brunswick 20-cent obverse by modifying the legend. A second design, derived from the first, shows the Queen with more aged facial features: slight double chin, repressed upper lip and recessed forehead.

The reverses for the 1865 and 1880 issues have a Roman "I" in the date; later issues have the more conventional Arabic "1" in the date.

The weights of the silver denominations were made proportional to those of the equivalent values in English silver coins; that is, 5.6552 grams per shilling (12 pence). The value of the 20 cents was 10d.

	Obv. 1	Obv. 2		Roman I	Arabic 1			

DATE	QTY. (000)	G-4	VG-8	F-12	VF-20	EF-40	AU-50	MS-60	MS-63
Roman "I" Reverse (1865–1880)									
1865 . . . . obv. 1 100		15.00	25.00	50.00	110.00	400.00	900.00	2,100	4,000
1870 . . . . obv. 1 50		15.00	35.00	70.00	150.00	600.00	1,100	2,600	4,000
1872H . . . . obv. 1 90		11.00	20.00	35.00	70.00	325.00	700.00	1,700	3,000
1873 . . . . obv. 1 46		20.00	40.00	100.00	250.00	900.00	3,000	9,000	–
1876H . . . . obv. 1 50		20.00	40.00	75.00	160.00	500.00	1,000	2,500	3,750
1880 . . . . obv. 1 30		20.00	45.00	85.00	175.00	600.00	1,250	3,000	5,000
Arabic "1" Reverse (1881–1900)									
1881 . . . . obv. 1 60		12.00	25.00	50.00	120.00	500.00	1,100	2,500	4,500
1882H . . . . obv. 2 100		11.00	18.00	30.00	70.00	400.00	850.00	2,500	5,000
1885 . . . . obv. 1 40		16.00	30.00	60.00	150.00	600.00	1,500	4,000	–
1888 . . . . obv. 2 75		12.00	22.00	40.00	85.00	400.00	1,100	4,000	–
1890 . . . . obv. 2 100		10.00	18.00	30.00	85.00	350.00	1,100	4,000	–
1894 . . . . obv. 1, 2 100		0.00	18.00	30.00	60.00	300.00	700.00	1,750	4,000
1896 small 96 . . . . . . obv. 2 125		9.00	14.00	24.00	50.00	300.00	900.00	3,200	–
1896 large 96 . . . . obv. 1 . .incl. above		10.00	18.00	30.00	70.00	300.00	900.00	3,000	–
1899 small 99 . . . . . . obv. 2 125		25.00	50.00	100.00	220.00	850.00	1,800	–	–
1899 large 99 . . . . obv. 2. incl. above		8.00	12.00	18.00	35.00	200.00	700.00	3,500	8,500
1900 . . . . obv. 2 125		8.00	12.00	18.00	35.00	150.00	550.00	1,600	5,000

Edward VII, 20 Cents Silver
1904

Diameter: 23.19 mm; weight: 4.713 grams; composition: .925 silver, .075 copper; edge: reeded

G: Band of crown worn through
VG: Band of crown worn through at highest point
F: Jewels in band of crown will be blurred
VF: Band of crown still clear but no longer sharp
EF: Band of crown slightly worn but generally sharp and clear

The obverse was derived from a portrait model by G.W. De Saulles (DES. below bust).
The reverse was designed and engraved by W.H.J. Blakemore.

DATE	QTY. (000)	G-4	VG-8	F-12	VF-20	EF-40	AU-50	MS-60	MS-63
1904H	75	15.00	22.00	40.00	70.00	325.00	1,000	2,800	7,500

George V, 20 Cents Silver
1912

Diameter: 23.19 mm; weight: 4.713 grams; composition: .925 silver, .075 copper; edge: reeded

G: Band of crown worn through
VG: Band of crown worn through at highest point
F: Jewels in band of crown will be blurred
VF: Band of crown still clear but no longer sharp
EF: Band of crown slightly worn but generally sharp and clear

The obverse was derived from a portrait model by Sir E.B. MacKennal (B.M. on truncation).
The reverse was a continuation of that used for the Edward VII series.

1912	350	6.00	8.00	10.00	20.00	80.00	200.00	400.00	800.00

George V, 25 Cents Silver
1917–1919

Diameter: 23.62 mm; weight: 5.32 grams; composition: .925 silver, .075 copper; edge: reeded

G: Band of crown worn through
VG: Band of crown worn through at highest point
F: Jewels in band of crown will be blurred
VF: Band of crown still clear but no longer sharp
EF: Band of crown slightly worn but generally sharp and clear

Because of continuing public confusion between Canadian 25-cent and Newfoundland 20-cent pieces, the latter denomination was discontinued and a 25-cent piece was struck instead. The obverse, from a portrait model by Sir E.B. Mackennal (B.M. on truncation), is identical to that for the Canadian issues of the same denomination.

W.H.J. Blakemore designed and engraved the reverse.

1917C	465	6.00	8.00	10.00	13.00	20.00	60.00	225.00	450.00
1919C	164	6.00	8.00	11.00	20.00	40.00	150.00	500.00	2,500

Victoria, 50 Cents Silver
1870–1900

Diameter: 29.85 mm; weight: 11.782 grams;
composition: .925 silver, .075 copper; edge: reeded

G: Braid around ear worn through
VG: No details in braid around ear
F: Braid segments begin to merge together
VF: Braid is clear but not sharp
EF: Braid slightly worn but
generally sharp and clear

This denomination bears a laureate bust, distinctly different from the crowned effigy on the Canadian 50-cent issues. There are two portrait varieties; the first is a youthful effigy with prominent upper lip, while the second, derived from the first, is a more aged representation with repressed upper lip, a drooping mouth and a longer depression over the eye.

The initial reverse is characterized by the presence of thick loops near the rim denticles. A second design has thin loops.

L.C. Wyon was the designer and engraver of the first and probably the later designs as well.

The weights of the silver denominations were made proportional to those of the equivalent values in English silver coins; that is, 5.6552 grams per shilling (12 pence). The value of the 50 cents was 2s. 1d.

1880 2nd 8 over 7. See 10-cent copy for details.

	Thick Loops		Thin Loops			Obv. 1		Obv. 2	

DATE	QTY. (000)	G-4	VG-8	F-12	VF-20	EF-40	AU-50	MS-60	MS-63
Thick Loops Reverse (1870–1880)									
1870 . . . . .obv. 1 50		25.00	45.00	80.00	200.00	800.00	2,000	6,000	–
1872H . . . . .obv. 1 48		19.00	33.00	65.00	140.00	600.00	1,100	3,000	–
1873 . . . . .obv. 1 32		40.00	75.00	140.00	300.00	1,250	3,000	–	–
1874 . . . . .obv. 1 80		25.00	50.00	90.00	200.00	800.00	3,000	–	–
1876H . . . . .obv. 1 28		30.00	65.00	125.00	275.00	900.00	1,850	4,000	–
1880 2nd 8 over 7 . obv. 1 24		35.00	75.00	150.00	450.00	1,500	3,500	9,000	–
Thin Loops Reverse (1881–1900)									
1881 . . . . .obv. 1 50		23.00	45.00	75.00	225.00	900.00	2,000	5,000	–
1882H . . . . .obv. 2 100		19.00	33.00	55.00	140.00	600.00	1,200	3,500	–
1885 . . . . .obv. 1 40		27.00	50.00	100.00	275.00	900.00	2,000	6,000	–
1888 . . . . .obv. 1 20		30.00	65.00	125.00	350.00	1,500	5,500	20,000	–
1894 . . . . .obv. 1 40		12.00	22.00	45.00	120.00	725.00	1,500	5,000	–
1896 . . . . .obv. 1, 2 60		12.00	20.00	35.00	100.00	500.00	1,500	7,500	–
1898 . . . . .obv. 1, 2 77		12.00	17.00	25.00	75.00	250.00	1,200	5,000	–

Narrow, bold 9s  Wide, delicate 9s

DATE	QTY. (000)	G-4	VG-8	F-12	VF-20	EF-40	AU-50	MS-60	MS-63
1899 narrow 9s... obv. 2 150		12.00	17.00	25.00	75.00	250.00	1,000	4,000	–
wide 9s .... incl. above		12.00	17.00	25.00	85.00	350.00	1,500	7,500	–
1900 .... obv. 2 150		12.00	17.00	25.00	65.00	225.00	900.00	3,500	–

Edward VII, 50 Cents Silver
1904–1909

Diameter: 29.85 mm; weight: 11.782 grams; composition: .925 silver, .075 copper; edge: reeded

G: Band of crown worn through
VG: Band of crown worn through at highest point
F: Jewels in band of crown will be blurred
VF: Band of crown still clear but no longer sharp
EF: Band of crown slightly worn but generally sharp and clear

The obverse, designed and engraved by G.W. De Saulles (DES. below bust), is identical to that used for the Canadian issues.

The reverse was designed by W.H.J. Blakemore.

1904H...................... 140		12.00	15.00	17.00	25.00	75.00	200.00	400.00	1,250
1907 100		12.00	15.00	17.00	30.00	90.00	250.00	500.00	1,500
1908 160		12.00	15.00	17.00	25.00	70.00	150.00	350.00	1,000
1909 200		12.00	15.00	17.00	30.00	80.00	175.00	400.00	1,250

George V, 50 Cents Silver
1911–1919

Diameter: (1911) 29.85 mm, (1917–19) 29.72 mm; weight: (1911) 11.782 grams,
(1917–19) 11.664 grams; composition: .925 silver, .075 copper; edge: reeded

G: Band of crown worn through
VG: Band of crown worn through at highest point
F: Jewels in band of crown will be blurred
VF: Band of crown still clear but no longer sharp
EF: Band of crown slightly worn but generally sharp and clear

The obverse was derived from a model by Sir E.B. MacKennal (B.M. on truncation) and is identical to that used for the 1912–36 Canadian issues. It should be noted that the legend contains DEI GRA : (by the Grace of God), a feature which was absent on the 1911 Canadian issue of the same denomination.

The reverse is as for the Edward VII series.

1911 200		12.00	15.00	17.00	20.00	55.00	120.00	325.00	900.00
1917C 376		12.00	15.00	17.00	20.00	45.00	90.00	200.00	600.00
1918C 295		12.00	15.00	17.00	20.00	45.00	90.00	200.00	600.00
1919C 306		12.00	15.00	17.00	20.00	50.00	125.00	325.00	1,250

Victoria, 2 Dollars Gold
1865–1888

Diameter: 17.983 mm; weight: 3.328 grams; composition: .917 gold, .083 copper; edge: reeded

F: Segments of braid begin to merge together
VF: Braid is clear but not sharp
EF: Braid slightly worn but generally sharp and clear

This series of "double dollars" as they were sometimes called, gives Newfoundland the distinction of being the only English colony with its own issue of gold.

This denomination is the same diameter as the 10-cent piece, and obverses in both cases were derived from the same matrices and punches (and perhaps dies). See the 10-cent description for details on the three obverse varieties.

The reverse was designed and engraved by L.C. Wyon.

DATE	QTY. (000)	VF-20	EF-40	AU-50	MS-60	MS-63
1865 . . . . obv. 1	10	375.00	500.00	675.00	2,000	15,000
1870 . . . . obv. 1, 2	10	375.00	500.00	750.00	2,000	12,000
1872 . . . . obv. 2	6	475.00	650.00	1,000	3,500	15,000
1880 . . . . obv. 2	2	1,800	3,000	3,100	6,500	25,000
1881 . . . . obv. 2	10	310.00	375.00	550.00	1,750	12,000
1882H . . . . obv. 3	25	310.00	325.00	375.00	700.00	2,250
1885 . . . . obv. 2	10	310.00	350.00	425.00	900.00	3,500
1888 . . . . obv. 2, 3	25	310.00	325.00	375.00	700.00	2,500

Nova Scotia

In 1859 Nova Scotia adopted a monetary system of dollars and cents, but set its dollar at the rate of $5 per £ sterling. This enabled the province to utilize British silver (the shilling was equal to 25 cents and the 6d to 12½ cents); however, it necessitated the issue of a half-cent piece to make change for the 6d.

Only cents and half cents were issued prior to Confederation in 1867.

Victoria, Half-Cent
1861–1864

Diameter: 20.65 mm; weight: 2.835 grams; composition: .950 copper, .040 tin, .010 zinc; edge: plain

G: Hair over ear worn through
VG: Little detail in hair over ear or braid
F: Strands of hair over ear begin to merge; braid is worn
VF: Hair over ear is worn; braid is clear but no longer sharp
EF: Slight wear on hair over ear; braid that holds knot in
    place is harp and clear

The obverse, with a laureated bust of Victoria, is identical to the New Brunswick coins of the same denomination and is one of those used for the British bronze farthing (Peck's obv. 3). The designer and engraver was L.C. Wyon.

The original pattern for the issue had a reverse device of the Imperial crown and a wreath of roses and rose leaves. However, as a result of a propaganda campaign led by J.S. Thompson (father of Sir John Thompson), the wreath of the adopted issue consisted of both roses and mayflowers. The mayflower, Epigea repens, being the provincial flower of Nova Scotia.

DATE	Qty. (000)	G-4	VG-8	F-12	VF-20	EF-40	AU-50	Brown UNC-60	Red† BU-63
1861	400	4.00	7.00	10.00	15.00	25.00	60.00	120.00	550.00
1864	400	4.00	7.00	10.00	15.00	25.00	50.00	100.00	400.00

Victoria, Large Cent
1861–1864

Diameter: 25.53 mm; weight: 5.670 grams;
composition: .950 copper, .040 tin, .010 zinc; edge: plain

The obverse is identical to that used for the New Brunswick coins of the same denomination and is one of those used for the British bronze halfpence (Peck's obv. 6). Two reverses, stemming from different matrices, are known. The first was used only for some of the 1861 issue. The crown is very detailed and a rosebud at the lower right is large. The second reverse saw use in 1861–64 and has a somewhat plainer crown with a thinner headband and a smaller rosebud at the lower right; and a repositioned inner circle and NOVA SCOTIA. All designs were by L.C. Wyon, the reverses being adapted from a model by C. Hill.

Large bud

Small bud

Note position of I, relative to ribbon tip.

1862 issue. Although the reported mintages for the 1861 and 1862 cents were 800,000 and 1,000,000 respectively, the latter date is very scarce. Some, probably most, of the 1862 strikings are believed to have been made with dies dated 1861. Consequently, the figures have been combined for these two years.

DATE	Qty. (000)	G-4	VG-8	F-12	VF-20	EF-40	AU-50	Brown UNC-60	Red† BU-63
Large Rosebud Reverse (1861)									
1861 large rosebud	1,800	2.50	5.00	7.50	11.00	22.00	60.00	150.00	650.00
Small Rosebud Reverse (1861–1864)									
1861 small rosebud	incl. above	6.00	9.00	15.00	25.00	50.00	125.00	250.00	1,200
1862	incl. above	45.00	85.00	140.00	250.00	500.00	1,000	2,000	–
1864	800	4.00	7.00	10.00	15.00	35.00	85.00	190.00	1,000

† 70% lustre

Prince Edward Island
Victoria, Large Cent
1871

Diameter: 25.40 mm; weight: 5.670 grams;
composition: .950 copper, .040 tin, .010 zinc; edge: plain

G: Hair over ear worn through
VG: No details in hair over ear
F: Strands of hair over ear begin to merge
VF: Hair and jewels no longer sharp, but clear
EF: Hair over ear sharp and clear; jewels in diadem must show sharply and clearly

In 1871 the island adopted a decimal system with a dollar equal to the U.S. gold dollar, as in Canada. Only the 1-cent denomination was issued prior to entry into Confederation in 1873.

The obverse was designed and engraved by L.C. Wyon, based on a portrait model by William Theed, and is identical to that for the Jamaica halfpenny of the same year.

The reverse was adapted by L.C. Wyon from the Government seal of the island. The device is composed of a large oak tree (representing England) sheltering three oak saplings. (representing the three countries of the island); beneath these is the Latin phrase PARVA SUB INGENTI (The small beneath the great).

The issue is distinctive in that it was struck at the Heaton Mint in Birmingham, but lacks the familiar H mint mark and has English titles rather than Latin on the obverse.

DATE	Qty. (000)	G-4	VG-8	F-12	VF-20	EF-40	AU-50	Brown UNC-60	Red† BU-63
1871	2,000	2.00	4.00	6.00	10.00	25.00	60.00	120.00	250.00

† 70% lustre

CANADIAN BANK NOTES

DOMINION OF CANADA
1867–1935

Transitional Issues

The newly formed government of the Dominion of Canada decided to utilize the large stockpiles of Province of Canada notes which had only been in circulation for a short time. These notes were not withdrawn from circulation and became the first issue of Dominion notes. In addition to the Province of Canada type notes payable at Toronto or Montreal the newly formed Dominion government had to prepare notes payable in the Maritimes. Notes prepared for New Brunswick were overprinted with a horizontal blue ST. JOHN in addition to the regular vertical green markings PAYABLE AT TORONTO (on $1 to $50 notes). Nova Scotia notes were specially prepared ($5 note only) with a green PAYABLE AT HALIFAX ONLY appearing vertically at each end of the face.

As the types payable only at Toronto or Montreal were previously issued by the Province of Canada, they will not be listed here. All notes have the engraved signature of T.D. Harington at the right and the manuscript signature or various individuals at the left. After 1871 all Provincial issue notes were withdrawn and replaced by Dominion of Canada notes.

Toronto / St. John issue

	VG	F	VF
Province of Canada Type Payable at:			
$5 payable at Halifax 12,000		18,000	25,000
$1 overprinted ST. JOHN 6,000		10,000	17,000
$2 overprinted ST. JOHN 7,000		11,500	18,000
$5 overprinted ST. JOHN 12,000		18,000	25,000
$10, $20 or $50 overprinted ST. JOHN . . . . .No notes known to exist			

25 CENTS
(Shinplasters)

The first issue of 25¢ notes was an emergency issue to halt large amount of U.S. silver coinage circulating at par in Canada. At that time the U.S. dollar was valued at only 80¢ Canadian and was discounted 20% at banks in Canada, with the result that individuals had to bear the loss. The Canadian government hoped to replace the need for U.S. silver with an issue of Canadian coins. In order to fill the time delay required to produce the large quantity of Canadian coins needed, it was decided to meet the shortage by issuing 25¢ notes. These were never intended to be more than a temporary issue but they proved so popular with the public that the government was forced to produce further issues in 1900 and 1923.

The expression "shinplaster" has been attributed to the use of such low denomination notes by soldiers of the Revolutionary war period as a lining to protect their ankles and shins from chafing by their boots.

1870 Issue

Vignette: Britannia; signatures: right T.D. Harington (engraved), left W. Dickinson (engraved). There were three series: the A series (1870), the B series (1871–ca. 1885) and the no letter or "plain" series (ca. 1885–1900). The series letter, is located at the lower left just below the 0 of 1870.

Series letter location

VARIETY / SIGNATURES	G	VG	F	VF	EF	UNC
25¢ A series 125.00		250.00	400.00	475.00	950.00	3,250
B series 30.00		55.00	90.00	150.00	375.00	2,500
"Plain" series 25.00		35.00	60.00	120.00	200.00	1,500

1900 Issue

Vignette: Britannia; signature (engraved): various (see below).

25¢	J.M. Courtney 10.00	15.00	22.00	30.00	110.00	550.00
	T.C. Boville 8.00	12.00	18.00	25.00	100.00	450.00
	J.C. Saunders 10.00	15.00	22.00	40.00	125.00	650.00

1923 Issue

Vignette: Britannia; signatures (engraved); various (see below). The first printing displays AUTHORIZED BY R.S.C. CAP. 31. above the signature at the left and a red check letter A, B, C, D, E, H, J, K, L or M to the left of the number. Later printings lack this statement, and a black check letter (to the left of the left 25) replaces the red one. All notes bear the seal of the Department of Finance at the right.

VARIETY / SIGNATURE AT LEFT	G	VG	F	VF	EF	UNC
25¢ With AUTHORIZED, etc.						
G.W. Hyndman	10.00	20.00	30.00	45.00	135.00	750.00

VARIETY / SIGNATURE AT LEFT	G	VG	F	VF	EF	UNC
25¢ Without AUTHORIZED, etc.						
G.W. Hyndman 12.00	20.00	30.00	50.00	135.00	650.00
S.P. McCavour 8.00	12.00	18.00	25.00	75.00	275.00
C.E. Campbell 8.00	12.00	18.00	25.00	75.00	275.00

ONE DOLLAR
1870 Issue

Vignette: Jacques Cartier (left) and "Canada" (right); signatures: T.D. Harington (engraved at right), W. Dickinson (engraved at left) and one of various others written vertically (positioned at one end, usually the left). The city payable is indicated on the back of each note. In addition the extremely rare notes issued in Manitoba have a black MANITOBA stamped vertically on the face at the right end of PAYABLE AT MONTREAL or TORONTO varieties.

The Toronto issue was heavily counterfeited. The counterfeits can be most easily recognized by the presence of D4 (check letter D, plate number 4) twice on their face and a crude black dot for Cartier's eye.

VARIETY	G	VG	F	VF	EF	UNC
$1 1870 Back reads Payable at:						
Montreal 500.00	1,000	2,200	4,200	6,500	15,000
Toronto 550.00	1,000	2,200	4,200	6,500	15,000
MANITOBA stamped on either of above 6,000	9,000	16,000			
Halifax.............................2,000	4,000	6,500	10,000	15,000	—
St. John 2,000	4,000	6,500	10,000	15,000	—
Victoria 6,000	11,000	19,000	—	—	—

1878 Issue (Dufferin)

Vignette: The Countess of Dufferin, wife of the Governor General, and on the back the Great Seal of Canada; signatures: T.D. Harington (engraved at right) and one of various others (written at left). The city payable is indicated on both the face (lower left) and the back. The initial issue had a frame (border) consisting of a scallop-like design with a large "scallop" in each corner. It was replaced in 1881 with a modified design due to some notes of the original issue being altered to $4s. The frame of the new design contains 1 ONE DOLLAR repeated with a 1 in each corner, plus other differences.

Scalloped Frame   Lettered Frame

VARIETY / SIGNATURE	G	VG	F	VF	EF	UNC
$1 1878 Scalloped Frame on Face — Back reads Payable at:						
Montreal 350.00	800.00	1,400	3,000	5,000	10,000	
Toronto 350.00	800.00	1,400	3,000	5,000	10,000	
Halifax 1,250	2,800	4,000	6,000	12,000	—	
St. John 1,250	2,800	4,000	6,000	12,000	—	
$1 1878 Lettered Frame on Face — Back reads Payable at:						
Montreal 125.00	300.00	750.00	1,600	3,000	6,500	
Toronto 135.00	300.00	750.00	1,800	3,250	6,500	
Halifax 1,200	3,000	5,000	7,500	12,000	—	
St. John 1,200	3,000	5,000	7,500	12,000	—	

1897 and 1898 (Aberdeen)

Vignettes: The Countess of Aberdeen, the Earl of Aberdeen (Governor General 1893–1898), a logging scene and on the back the centre block of the Parliament buildings in Ottawa; signatures: J.M. Courtney (later T.C. Boville) engraved at the right and one of various persons written at the left.

The face tint (background colour) on the 1897 issue is green and the design on the back contains a large 1 at each end. Probably to better distinguish it from the $2 of 1897, the colour of the face tint on the $1 was changed to brown and the notes redated 1898. It had also been found that the large 1s on the back of the original design tended to disfigure the portraits on the face (by showing through the paper), so the 1898 issue has a modified back where three small counters replace each of the large 1s. The initial 1898 back has the small ONE at each end curving inward; this was later changed to have the ONEs curving outward.

These issues mark the termination of domiciling for this denomination.

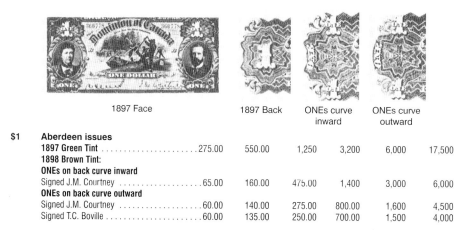

| 1897 Face | 1897 Back | ONEs curve inward | ONEs curve outward |

	G	VG	F	VF	EF	UNC
$1 Aberdeen issues						
1897 Green Tint 275.00	550.00	1,250	3,200	6,000	17,500	
1898 Brown Tint:						
ONEs on back curve inward						
Signed J.M. Courtney 65.00	160.00	475.00	1,400	3,000	6,000	
ONEs on back curve outward						
Signed J.M. Courtney 60.00	140.00	275.00	800.00	1,600	4,500	
Signed T.C. Boville 60.00	135.00	250.00	700.00	1,500	4,000	

1911 Issue (Grey)

Vignettes: The Earl of Grey (Governor General 1904–1911) and the Countess of Grey; back design: the same as the second design for the 1898 issue; signatures: T.C. Boville (engraved at right) and one of various persons (written at left).

The first notes of this issue had a green signature pane across the bottom. On later printings a black line was added along the top edge of the panel.

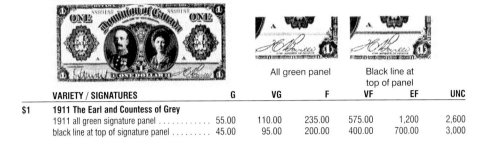

| | | | All green panel | | Black line at top of panel | | |
VARIETY / SIGNATURES	G	VG	F	VF	EF		UNC
$1 1911 The Earl and Countess of Grey							
1911 all green signature panel 55.00		110.00	235.00	575.00	1,200		2,600
black line at top of signature panel 45.00		95.00	200.00	400.00	700.00		3,000

1917 Issue (Princess Pat)

Vignettes: Princess Patricia of Connaught and on the back the centre block of the original Parliament buildings. The first printings have a plain green ONE on each side of the portrait on the face side, have the written signatures of various persons at the left and the engraved signature or T.C. Boville (later J.C. Saunders) at the right. In 1922 the government switched over to countersigning the notes by printing; as a security device the seal of the Department of Finance was added with the second signature. The initial printings involving machine countersigning were with the notes of the original design (ONE at right), so a transitional variety with the seal over the ONE was created. The final issue lacks the ONE at the right, allowing the Finance Department seal to be more easily seen.

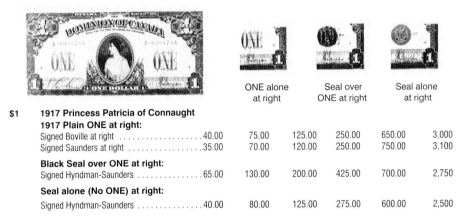

ONE alone at right   Seal over ONE at right   Seal alone at right

	G	VG	F	VF	EF	UNC
$1 1917 Princess Patricia of Connaught						
1917 Plain ONE at right:						
Signed Boville at right 40.00	75.00	125.00	250.00	650.00		3,000
Signed Saunders at right 35.00	70.00	120.00	250.00	750.00		3,100
Black Seal over ONE at right:						
Signed Hyndman-Saunders 65.00	130.00	200.00	425.00	700.00		2,750
Seal alone (No ONE) at right:						
Signed Hyndman-Saunders 40.00	80.00	125.00	275.00	600.00		2,500

1923 Issue (George V)

Vignette: King George V and on the back the Library of Parliament; signatures: various, all engraved. On this issue the seal of the Department of Finance comes in various colours, the purpose of which was to aid in sorting the notes when they came back in for destruction.

SEAL COLOUR / SIGNATURE	G	VG	F	VF	EF	UNC
$1 **Black Seal at right:**						
Hyndman-Saunders 30.00	70.00	100.00	250.00	875.00	2,750
McCavour-Saunders 22.50	45.00	60.00	130.00	400.00	2,100
Campbell-Sellar 20.00	35.00	45.00	80.00	220.00	875.00
Campbell-Clark 18.00	30.00	40.00	70.00	175.00	625.00
Red Seal at right:						
McCavour-Saunders 25.00	60.00	90.00	225.00	700.00	2,300
Blue Seal at right:						
McCavour-Saunders 25.00	60.00	100.00	225.00	875.00	2,900
Green Seal at right:						
McCavour-Saunders 22.50	45.00	75.00	160.00	450.00	2,300
Purple-Brown Seal at right:						
McCavour-Saunders 22.50	45.00	75.00	160.00	450.00	2,300
Lilac Seal at right:						
McCavour-Saunders 85.00	175.00	350.00	775.00	1,600	5,000
Campbell-Sellar 250.00	450.00	775.00	1,300	2,500	8,000

All of the scarce lilac seal notes have a C prefix in the note number and have a small C-1 to the right of the seal. Purple-brown seal notes do not come with this letter.

TWO DOLLARS
1870 Issue

Vignettes: Generals Wolfe and Montcalm, the ill-fated commanders of the British and French forces in the Battle of the Plains of Abraham at Quebec City in 1759, and "civilization" (centre); signatures: T.D. Harington (engraved at right), W. Dickinson (engraved at left) and that of various persons (written, vertically positioned at one end, usually the left). The city payable is indicated on the back of each note. In addition, the extremely rare notes issued in Manitoba have a black MANITOBA stamped vertically on the face at the right end of PAYABLE AT MONTREAL or TORONTO varieties.

VARIETY	G	VG	F
$2 **1870 Back reads Payable at:**			
Montreal 1,900	4,200	6,500
Toronto 1,900	4,200	6,500
MANITOBA overprint 6,000	12,000	22,000
Halifax 3,500	8,000	12,000
St. John 3,250	6,000	10,000
Victoria . . . . No notes known to exist		

1878 Issue (Dufferin)

Vignettes: The Earl of Dufferin, Governor General 1872–1878 and on the back the Great Seal of Canada; signatures: T.D. Harington (engraved at right) and that of various persons (written at left). The city payable is indicated on both the face (lower left) and the back. Both the Montreal and Toronto issues were heavily counterfeited; which is likely the reason for the early retirement of the whole issue compared to the corresponding $1 issue. The counterfeits have a rather inferior portrait and all known examples have at least a single 1 in the serial number. The counterfeits have curved-topped 1s, while genuine notes have flat-topped 1s. Most of the surviving notes of the Toronto and Montreal varieties are the counterfeits.

	Flat topped 1 (Genuine)	Curved top 1 (Counterfeit)	
	G	VG	F

		G	VG	F
$2	1878 Back reads Payable at:			
	Montreal	1,500	3,000	6,000
	Toronto	1,500	3,000	6,000
	Halifax	3,500	7,000	10,000
	St. John	3,500	7,000	11,000

1887 Issue (Lansdowne)

Vignettes: the Marchioness of Lansdowne, the Marquis of Lansdowne (Governor General 1883–1888) and on the back "Quebec!," showing Jacques Cartier and his men aboard ship. The back is bi-coloured for security reasons—the only Dominion note to have such a back.

		G	VG	F	VF	EF	UNC
$2	1887 (Lansdowne)	400.00	950.00	1,600	3,200	6,000	N/A

1897 Issue (Princee of Wales)

Vignettes: Edward, Prince of Wales (later King Edward VII), men cod fishing from a boat and on the back field workers harvesting grain; signatures: J.M. Courtney (later T.C. Boville) engraved at the right and that of various persons written at the left. The first printings have a red-brown back; this was soon revised to dark brown.

		G	VG	F	VF	EF	UNC
$2	1897 Prince of Wales						
	Red-brown coloured back						
	Signed J.M. Courtney	3,300	5,500	8,500	16,000	22,000	35,000
	Dark brown coloured back						
	Signed J.M. Courtney	190.00	400.00	1,000	2,500	5,500	14,000
	Signed T.C. Boville	160.00	350.00	900.00	1,900	4,500	11,000

1914 Issue (Connaught)

Vignettes: The Duke of Connaught (Governor General 1911–1916), the Duchess of Connaught and on the back the Canadian coat-of-arms, along with those of the provinces; signatures: the initial design has the statement WILL PAY TO THE BEARER ON DEMAND in a curved line over the large **2** counter in the centre of the face. On later printings this statement is in a straight line. Initially the notes also have an olive **TWO** on each side of the portrait on the face side, have the written signature of various persons at the left and the engraved signature of T.C. Doville (later J.C. Saunders) at the right. In 1922 the government switched over to countersigning the notes by printing; as a security device the seal of the Department of Finance was added with the second signature. The first printings involving machine countersigning were with notes of the second design (straight WILL PAY, etc. and **TWO** at the right), so a transitional variety was created. The final issue lacks the TWO at the right, allowing the Finance Department seal to be more easily seen.

| | Curved WILL PAY, etc. | | Straight WILL PAY, etc. | | | |

VARIETIES / SIGNATURE	G	VG	F	VF	EF	UNC
$2 1914 Duke and Duchess of Connaught						
Plain TWO at right						
Curved WILL PAY etc.:						
signed Boville	60.00	125.00	250.00	600.00	2,000	7,000
Straight WILL PAY, etc.:						
Signed Boville	100.00	200.00	400.00	950.00	2,800	9,000
Signed Saunders	75.00	150.00	300.00	650.00	2,000	6,500
Black seal over TWO at right						
Straight WILL PAY, etc.:						
Signed Saunders	125.00	225.00	500.00	1,000	3,000	9,000
Seal alone (no TWO) at right						
Straight WILL PAY, etc:						
Signed Saunders	125.00	225.00	500.00	1,000	3,000	9,000

1923 Issue (Prince of Wales)

Vignettes: Edward, Prince of Wales (later King Edward VIII) and on the back the coat of arms of Canada; signatures: various, all machine signed, (see below). On this issue the seal of the Department of Finance comes in various colours, the purpose of which was to aid in sorting the notes when they came back in for destruction.

VARIETY / SIGNATURES	G	VG	F	VF	EF	UNC
$2 **Black Seal at right:**						
Hyndman-Saunders	55.00	110.00	165.00	350.00	1,150	3,250
McCavour-Saunders	45.00	90.00	150.00	330.00	1,100	2,750
Campbell-Sellar	50.00	100.00	150.00	330.00	650.00	2,200
Campbell-Clark	40.00	90.00	135.00	330.00	650.00	2,200
Red Seal at right;						
McCavour-Saunders	45.00	90.00	150.00	350.00	1,100	2,850
Blue Seal at right:						
McCavour-Saunders	55.00	125.00	200.00	450.00	1,400	4,000
Campbell-Sellar	60.00	120.00	190.00	375.00	1,100	3,100
Green Seal at right:						
McCavour-Saunders	55.00	110.00	180.00	325.00	1,150	3,300
Purple-Brown Seal at right:						
McCavour-Saunders	60.00	120.00	200.00	350.00	1,100	3,100

Four Dollars
1882 Issue (Lorne)

Vignette: The Marquis of Lorne (Governor General 1878–1883); signatures: J.M. Courtney engraved at the right and that of various persons written at the left. As a security device the notes were printed on watermarked paper (they were the only Dominion notes that were) and bear an orange Great Seal of Canada at the right on the face side. The colour of the seal is sometimes brown due to oxidation of the ink.

$4 1882	600.00	1,400	3,000	8,000	15,000	N/A

1900 and 1902 Issues (Minto)

Vignettes: The Countess of Minto, the Earl of Minto (Governor General 1898–1904), the locks at Sault Ste. Marie, connecting Lakes Superior and Huron and on the back Parliament Hill as seen from the Ottawa River to the east; signatures: J.M. Courtney (1900 and the 1902 issue with the 4s at the top) or T.C. Boville (1902 issue with the **FOUR**s at the top) engraved at the right and that of various persons written at the left. On the initial printings (dated 1900) the U.S. side of the locks was portrayed. This error was corrected in 1902 and the design redated. In 1911, on the eve of the introduction of the $5 notes and the withdrawal of the $4s a third variety (with **FOUR**s at the top for easier recognition of the denomination) was issued because of a pressing need for paper money.

| 1900 Issue | Back (all issues) |

| 1902 Issue (FOURs at top) | 1902 Issue (4s at top) |

VARIETY / SIGNATURES	G	VG	F	VF	EF	UNC
$4 1900 . . . . .400.00	850.00	1,600	3,500	6,500	16,000
1902 Large 4s at top:						
Signed J.M. Courtney 600.00	1,500	2,800	4,500	6.500	20,000
Large FOURs at top:						
Signed T.C. Boville .375.00	750.00	1,500	3,000	5,500	14,500

Five Dollars
1912 Issue (Train)

Vignette: The "Maritime Express" travelling through the Wentworth Valley in Nova Scotia and on the back a large Roman numeral V in the centre. The first printings have a counter on each side of the vignette on the face, the written signature of various persons at the left and the engraved signature of T.C. Boville at the right. In 1922 the government switched over to countersigning the notes by printing; as a security device the seal of the Department of Finance was added with the second signature. The first printings involving machine countersigning were with notes of the original design (FIVE at the right), so transitional notes with the seal over the FIVE were created. A signature change also occurred at this time. The final issue lacks the FIVE at the right, allowing the Finance Department seal to be more easily seen.

| FIVE alone at right | Seal over FIVE at right | Seal alone at right |

VARIETY / SIGNATURES	G	VG	F	VF	EF	UNC
$5 **Plain FIVE at right:**						
Signed T.C. Boville at right 450.00	850.00	1,200	1,650	2,400	6,500
Blue Seal over FIVE at right:						
Signed T.C. Boville at right 450.00	850.00	1,250	1,900	2,900	6,500
Signed J.C. Saunders at right 550.00	1,000	1,500	2,200	3,200	9,000
Seal alone (No FIVE) at right:						
Signed Hyndman-Saunders 450.00	850.00	1,200	1,650	2,400	6,500
Signed McCavour-Saunders 7,000	10,000		40,000		

1924 Issue (Queen Mary)

Vignettes: Queen Mary, wife of King George V and on the back the east block of the Parliament buildings; signatures: W. Sellar at the right and C.E. Campbell at the left, both printed on with the Department of Finance seal after the rest of the note had been printed. Although they were dated 1924, these notes were not issued until 1934, just before the withdrawal of the Dominion notes and the introduction of the Bank of Canada notes. Because of this, the notes of this issue are often encountered in high grade.

VARIETY / SIGNATURES	G	VG	F	VF	EF	UNC
$5	1924	2,500	4,250	6,500	7,750	13,000	25,000

Higher Denominations

The Dominion government also issued $50, $100, $500 and $1000 notes for circulation, although the two higher denominations were used almost exclusively in transactions between banks. The earliest issues were domiciled: The $50 and $100 notes came payable at Montreal or Toronto and the $500 and $1000 of 1871 came payable at Montreal, Toronto, Halifax, St. John, Victoria, Charlottetown or Winnipeg.

		G	VG	F	VF	EF	UNC
$50	1872 Only proof known to exist					3,500	
$100	1872 Only proof known to exist					3,500	
$500	1871 Only proof known to exist					4,000	
	1911 Two known to have survived	100,000	250,000	350,000	—	—	—
	1925	20,000	35,000	40,000	70,000	100,000	—
$1000	1871 Only proof known to exist					4,500	
	1911	50,000	125,000	175,000	250,000	—	—
	1925	25,000	40,000	50,000	85,000	125,000	—

Bank of Canada 1935 –

Introduction

The Bank of Canada was created by the Central Bank Act of 1934. Under this Act, the Bank was given sole responsibility for the issuance and management of Canadian paper money as well as being responsible for the national debt and giving advice to the government on monetary policy. The Bank of Canada while dealing directly in ordinary banking, would loan money to the chartered banks as well as accept deposits from them.

Commencing business on March 11th, 1935, the Bank of Canada assumed responsibility for all Dominion of Canada notes still in circulation, which would be replaced with the new Bank of Canada 1935 issue notes. Although chartered banks were allowed to continue issuing their own notes into the mid 1940s, they had to drastically reduce their note circulation and in fact the last date on a chartered bank issue was 1943 (Royal Bank of Canada $5). During the latter part of the 1940s, the chartered banks actively withdrew their notes and in 1950 transferred to the Bank of Canada a sum of money equal to the face value of their notes outstanding as of December 31, 1949 ($13,302,046.60). As of January 1st, 1950 the Bank of Canada assumed responsibility for redeeming these notes.

All Bank of Canada notes have been printed on blank note paper containing randomly scattered green planchettes (tiny discs of green paper embedded in the white paper during its manufacture as an anti-counterfeiting device). Two security printers in Ottawa produce the notes: the British American Bank Note Company, Ltd., and the Canadian Bank Note Company, Limited.

1935 Issue

Face side with portrait at left   Back with allegorical vignette

The Bank of Canada's first issue of notes was put into circulation early in 1935. The official changeover date from Dominion notes to Bank of Canada notes was March 11, 1935 and thereafter the Dominion notes were rapidly retired. The new Bank of Canada notes were small size (about 152 x 72 mm) to decrease printing costs. They consisted of two separate emissions, one English and one French, for each denomination making 18 different notes in all. The portrait on the face is positioned at the left end.

Design Details

	BASIC COLOUR	PORTRAIT	BACK DESIGN
$1	Green	King George V	Allegorical figure of Agriculture
$2	Blue	Queen Mary	Mercury with implements of transportation
$5	Orange	Prince of Wales, later Edward VIII, then Duke of Windsor	Allegorical figure of Power
$10	Purple	Princess Royal	Allegorical figure of Harvest
$20	Rose Pink	Princess Elizabeth, now Elizabeth II	Worker showing produce to Agriculture
$50	Brown	Duke of York later George VI	Allegorical figure of Invention with radio
$100	Dark Brown	Duke of Gloucester	Allegorical scene of Shipping with industry
$500	Tan	Sir John A. Macdonald first Prime Minister of the Dominion in 1867	Allegorical scene showing Produce
$1000	Olive Green	Sir Wilfrid Laurier, Prime Minister 1896–1911	Allegorical figure of Security

Dates, Signatures and Numbering

All notes of this issue bear the legend ISSUE OF 1935 (or its French equivalent), the facsimile signatures of Deputy Governor (of the Bank) J.A.C. Osborne and Governor G.F. Towers, and at the right the seal of the Bank. The numbering system was the same as that used for the final issues of Dominion notes. That is, the notes were numbered in groups of four; each note within a given group received the same series letter and number (in red at top). The individual notes within a group were differentiated from each other by a black check letter, A, B, C or D. All notes of the French issue were series F, while those of the English issue were series A (except that B was also used for the $1 because the A series was completed). Within each series the numbers could go from 1 (preceded by various amounts of 0s) to 1000000.

DENOMINATION		G	VG	F	VF	EF	UNC
English Issues:							
$1	....	30.00	45.00	60.00	120.00	235.00	800.00
$2	....	38.00	70.00	120.00	275.00	725.00	2,200
$5	....	50.00	100.00	165.00	425.00	950.00	4,000
$10	....	60.00	110.00	185.00	450.00	950.00	3,500
$20	Large Seal	400.00	700.00	1,400	2,750	5,500	14,000
	Small Seal	220.00	600.00	975.00	2,200	4,200	11,000
$50	....	1,000	1,700	2,750	4,400	7,000	15,000
$100	....	500.00	1,300	1,800	2,650	4,000	11,000
$500	....	17,000	35,000	45,000	60,000	80,000	—
$1000	....	—	3,500	4,500	5,500	7,000	18,500
French Issues:							
$1	....	35.00	75.00	110.00	220.00	375.00	1,225
$2	....	120.00	250.00	550.00	1,500	3,300	10,000
$5	....	75.00	150.00	325.00	950.00	2,400	6,500
$10	....	90.00	175.00	375.00	800.00	1,500	5,700
$20	....	450.00	1,000	2,000	4,500	7,500	22,000
$50	....	1,500	2,200	4,200	8,250	11,000	22,000
$100	....	1,200	2,500	4,000	7,500	11,000	30,000
$500	....	—	—	—	—	—	—
$1000	....	—	5,500	7,500	10,500	14,500	32,500

George V
Silver Jubilee Commemorative, 1935

In addition to the regular denominations, the Bank of Canada issued $25 notes to mark the 25th anniversary of the accession of George V. There were separate English and French issues like the notes of the Bank's first issue; however, the $25 notes were strictly a special commemorative issue and were not part of the first issue. This is emphasized by the different issue date on the notes (May 6, 1935) and the date span 1910–1935 at the top. The portraits of King George V and Queen Mary are shown in the centre on the face and a view of Windsor Castle appears on the back. The face tint and back colour is royal purple. The signatures and numbering are as for the regular 1935 issue.

DENOMINATION		G	VG	F	VF	EF	UNC
$25	English issue	1,250	2,400	3,500	6,000	7,750	15,000
	French issue	1,900	3,000	5,000	7,000	12,000	23,000

1937 Issue

The preparation of new issue of Bank of Canada notes was begun under King Edward VIII. Upon Edward's abdication in December 1936, the portrait of his brother, the Duke of York, was substituted and work continued on the new issue. The portrait of the new monarch, King George VI, had already been used on the $50 1935 notes when he was the Duke of York. A number of major changes took place from the previous issue. The King's portrait is in the centre of the face side and was used on all denominations from $1 to $50. The $100 note has Sir John A. MacDonald (same portrait as on the 1935 $500 note) and the $1000 denomination once again had Sir Wilfrid Laurier. The $500 denomination was discontinued. The use of one bilingual note rather than two monolingual notes for each denomination was instituted, as the cost of preparing separate English and French issues had simply been too high. The text and denominations are in French on the right side and English on the left.

Back Design Details

All the allegorical back designs of the 1937 notes were the same as those used in 1935, although they did not necessarily appear on the same denominations as previously. The backs were also made bilingual and small changes in the design were made. Several denominations also changed colour from the 1935 issue.

DENOM.	BASIC COLOUR	BACK DESIGN	DENOM.	BASIC COLOUR	BACK DESIGN
$1	Green	Same as 1935	$20	Olive Green	As $500,1935
$2	Dull Red	As $10, 1935	$50	Orange	Same as 1935
$5	Blue	Same as 1935	$100	Brown	Same as 1935
$10	Purple	As $2, 1935	$1000	Pink	Same as 1935

Dates, Signatures and Numbering

All notes bear the date January 2, 1937 but only the denominations $1 to $100 were released at that time. The $1000 note was not released by the Bank of Canada until the early fifties although the Osborne-Towers signatures indicate that they were printed much earlier. All notes bear the fac-simile signature of Governor G.F. Towers at the right. Three different Deputy Governors served during the period of these notes: J.A.C. Osborne, D. Gordon and J.E. Coyne. The numbering system was changed beginning with the 1937 issue. The serial number of each note consists of a two-letter prefix, expressed as a fraction, followed by a number. The lower letter in the fraction is the denominational letter (a given letter was used on only one denomination) and the upper letter is the series letter (which could be used on any denomination). Within each series the numbers could go from 0000001 to 10000000 with the number printed twice on the face of each note.

DENOMINATION		G	VG	F	VF	EF	UNC
Notes signed J.A.C. Osborne at left:							
$1		14.00	25.00	35.00	50.00	120.00	350.00
$2		25.00	50.00	90.00	180.00	350.00	1,700
$5		55.00	125.00	200.00	325.00	1,000	9,000
$10		45.00	80.00	125.00	250.00	500.00	2,600
$20		50.00	80.00	140.00	275.00	700.00	3,000
$50		200.00	400.00	800.00	2,000	5,000	15,000
$100		—	300.00	500.00	700.00	1,200	4,500
$1000		—	2,500	3,500	4,500	6,000	17,500
Notes signed D. Gordon at left:							
$1		—	8.00	10.00	15.00	22.00	65.00
$2		—	18.00	25.00	45.00	85.00	210.00
$5		—	18.00	25.00	45.00	85.00	235.00
$10		—	20.00	30.00	40.00	60.00	140.00
$20		—	30.00	40.00	50.00	100.00	275.00
$50		—	80.00	120.00	160.00	375.00	1,050
$100		—	140.00	175.00	225.00	325.00	1,000
Notes signed J.E. Coyne at left:							
$1		—	8.00	10.00	15.00	22.00	65.00
$2		—	18.00	25.00	45.00	85.00	210.00
$5		—	18.00	25.00	45.00	85.00	235.00
$10		—	20.00	30.00	40.00	60.00	140.00
$20		—	30.00	40.00	50.00	100.00	275.00
$50		—	80.00	120.00	160.00	375.00	1,050
$100		—	140.00	175.00	225.00	325.00	1,000

1954 Issue

Upon the death of George VI in 1952, a new issue of Canadian paper currency was prepared for the incoming monarch, Elizabeth II with a number of marked departures from previous issues. The portrait of the Queen was positioned at the right end of the face for all denominations, where it would get less wear by folding than the centred portraits of the 1937 issue. The face tint (background colour) was more complex than previous notes and the allegorical vignettes on the backs of the 1937 issue were replaced by Canadian scenes.

This issue was withdrawn beginning in 1970 because the prefix letters were almost entirely used up. There was also a large number of counterfeits appearing on this issue, particularly on the higher $50 and $100 denominations. The later signature varieties of these denominations were replaced quickly and are relatively scarce today.

Back Design Details

The colours for all denominations were carried over from the previous issue.

DENOM.	BACK DESIGN	DENOM.	BACK DESIGN
$1	Western prairie and sky	$20	Laurentian hills in winter
$2	Country valley in Central Canada	$50	Atlantic seashore
$5	Northern stream and forest	$100	Mountain, valley and lake
$10	Rocky Mountain peak	$1000	Village, lake and hills

Date, Signatures and Numbering

All notes of the first issue of Elizabeth carry the designation OTTAWA, 1954. There are five signature combinations in this issue.

> J.E. Coyne and G.F. Towers (all with "Devil's Face")
> J.R. Beattie and J.E. Coyne (with and without "Devil's Face")
> J.R. Beattie and L. Rasminsky
> G. Bouey and L. Rasminsky
> R.W. Lawson and G. Bouey

For denominations of $5 and up, some of the later signature combinations were not printed.

The numbering on the notes is as previously described on the 1937 issue except that after 1968 the number range in any given series was changed to run from 0000000 to 9999999, the zero note being removed and destroyed prior to issue. Each denomination letter was used for up to 250,000,000 notes and eventually every possible denomination letter except Q was used.

Varieties

Asterisk note (replacement)

Prior to the 1954 issue, replacement notes (to replace ones that were spoiled during printing) were individually made up with exactly the same serial numbers as those that were spoiled. In order to eliminate the nuisance of preparing new notes, a new system was devised for use with the 1954 issue. The Bank of Canada began printing series of independently numbered notes with an asterisk (*) preceding the serial number to replace defective notes. No asterisk notes were printed for the $50, $100 or $1000 denominations.

Shortly after the 1954 issue notes appeared in circulation it was noticed that certain highlighted portions of the queen's hair created the illusion of a devil's face peering out from behind her ear. This was not an "error," nor was it the result of a prank, but was simply the faithful copying of the original photograph used as the model. The "Devil's Face" portrait created enough controversy that it was decided to modify the queen's hair thereby creating two varieties of the queen's portrait on this issue.

Devil's Face Portrait

"Devil's face"   Modified hair
in Queen's hair

DENOM.	SIGNATURES	VG	F	VF	EF	UNC.

Regular Issue

DENOM.	SIGNATURES	VG	F	VF	EF	UNC.
$1	Coyne-Towers	13.00	17.00	24.00	40.00	140.00
	Beattie-Coyne	7.00	10.00	15.00	25.00	120.00
$2	Coyne-Towers	25.00	25.00	65.00	100.00	350.00
	Beattie-Coyne	15.00	20.00	30.00	70.00	275.00
$5	Coyne-Towers	30.00	45.00	70.00	120.00	350.00
	Beattie-Coyne	20.00	25.00	50.00	90.00	275.00
$10	Coyne-Towers	20.00	25.00	40.00	70.00	300.00
	Beattie-Coyne	20.00	25.00	40.00	70.00	275.00
$20	Coyne-Towers	40.00	50.00	70.00	120.00	425.00
	Beattie-Coyne	30.00	35.00	50.00	80.00	375.00
$50	Coyne-Towers	90.00	115.00	200.00	400.00	1,800
	Beattie-Coyne	100.00	120.00	200.00	600.00	2,400
$100	Coyne-Towers	—	165.00	200.00	300.00	1,150
	Beattie-Coyne	—	175.00	225.00	375.00	1,650
$1000	Coyne-Towers	—	—	4,000	5,750	14,500

Asterisk Issue

DENOM.	SIGNATURES	VG	F	VF	EF	UNC.
$1	Coyne-Towers	800.00	1,050	1,800	2,500	6,000
	Beattie-Coyne	600.00	800.00	1,200	1,800	4,800
$2	Coyne-Towers	1,200	1,600	2,700	4,000	9.500
	Beattie-Coyne	850.00	1,200	1,950	2,800	7,500
$5	Coyne-Towers	4,000	6,500	7,500	12,000	22,000
	Beattie-Coyne	2,250	2,800	3,750	7,000	15,000
$10	Coyne-Towers	1,200	1,600	2,800	4,000	10,000
	Beattie-Coyne	900.00	1,300	1,900	2,800	8,000
$20	Coyne-Towers	3,000	5,000	7,000	9,000	20,000
	Beattie-Coyne	2,000	4,000	6,000	8,000	14,000
$50	Coyne-Towers					Not Printed
	Beattie-Coyne					Not Printed
$100	Coyne-Towers					Not Printed
	Beattie-Coyne					Not Printed
$1000	Coyne-Towers					Not Printed

Modified Portrait

DENOM.	SIGNATURES	F	VF	EF	UNC.

Regular Issue

DENOM.	SIGNATURES	F	VF	EF	UNC.
$1	Beattie-Coyne	1.25	2.25	4.50	14.00
	Beattie-Rasminsky	—	2.25	3.25	11.00
	Bouey-Rasminsky	—	2.25	3.25	11.00
	Lawson-Bouey	—	2.25	3.25	12.00
$2	Beattie-Coyne	6.00	9.00	15.00	45.00
	Beattie-Rasminsky	—	2.50	5.00	14.00
	Bouey-Rasminsky	—	2.50	5.50	16.50
	Lawson-Bouey	—	2.75	5.50	16.50
$5	Beattie-Coyne	9.00	15.50	22.00	65.00
	Beattie-Rasminsky	—	11.00	16.50	40.00
	Bouey-Rasminsky	—	11.00	16.50	40.00
$10	Beattie-Coyne	12.00	15.00	22.00	65.00
	Beattie-Rasminsky	—	15.00	22.00	55.00
$20	Beattie-Coyne	—	27.50	40.00	130.00
	Beattie-Rasminsky	—	22.00	35.00	90.00
$50	Beattie-Coyne	—	70.00	95.00	360.00
	Beattie-Rasminsky	—	70.00	110.00	250.00
	Lawson-Bouey	60.00	85.00	110.00	300.00
$100	Beattie-Coyne	—	—	140.00	385.00
	Beattie-Rasminsky	—	—	135.00	275.00
	Lawson-Bouey	—	—	135.00	360.00
$1000	Beattie-Coyne	—	—	—	3,400
	Beattie-Rasminsky	—	—	—	2,300
	Bouey-Rasminsky	—	—	—	2,300
	Lawson-Bouey	—	—	—	1,875
	Thiessen-Crow	—	—	—	2,500

Asterisk Issue

DENOM.	SIGNATURE	VG	F	VF	EF	UNC.
$1	Beattie-Coyne	5.00	10.00	20.50	40.00	125.00
	Beattie-Rasminsky	—	—	3.25	5.50	16.50
	Bouey-Rasminsky	—	—	3.25	5.50	16.50
	Lawson-Bouey	5.00	8.00	11.00	27.50	90.00
$2	Beattie-Coyne	35.00	45.00	80.00	160.00	500.00
	Beattie-Rasminsky	—	—	6.50	11.00	22.00
	Bouey-Rasminsky	—	—	12.00	20.00	75.00
	Lawson-Bouey	—	—	11.00	22.00	70.00
$5	Beattie-Coyne	25.00	45.00	100.00	200.00	600.00
	Beattie-Rasminsky	—	12.00	16.50	35.00	140.00
	Bouey-Rasminsky	—	9.00	13.00	22.00	140.00
$10	Beattie-Coyne	—	100.00	150.00	300.00	850.00
	Beattie-Rasminsky	—	11.00	16.50	35.00	110.00
$20	Beattie-Coyne	—	80.00	160.00	325.00	1,000
	Beattie-Rasminsky	—	80.00	120.00	275.00	900.00
$50	Beattie-Coyne					Not Printed
	Beattie-Rasminsky					Not Printed
	Lawson-Bouey					Not Printed
$100	Beattie-Coyne					Not Printed
	Beattie-Rasminsky					Not Printed
	Lawson-Bouey					Not Printed
$1000	Beattie-Coyne					Not Printed
	Beattie-Rasminsky					Not Printed
	Bouey-Rasminsky					Not Printed
	Lawson-Bouey					Not Printed

Centennial of Confederation, 1967

$1 – 1967 Commemorative (1867 1967 collectors' issue)

As part of the 1967 Centennial celebration, special $1 notes were issued. The face remained the same as that of the 1954 issue, except for the addition of the maple leaf symbol for Confederation and some wording changes. However, the prairie scene on the back of the $1 in 1954 was replaced with a view of the first Parliament buildings. This vignette was originally engraved in 1872 and saw use on the face of the $100 Dominion notes. For the 1967 Bank of Canada notes certain portions (e.g. the sky) were re-engraved.

In addition to the regular serial number and asterisk issues released for circulation, a special collectors issue was prepared with the dates 1867 1967 replacing the serial numbers and were available only from the Bank of Canada at face value (although many later entered circulation). The collectors issue has remained very common, as they were hoarded by the public. The regular serial number issue are not nearly as common. All notes are signed J.R. Beattie/ L. Rasminsky and bear the date OTTAWA 1967.

		EF	UNC
$1	1967 Confederation, regular serial number	$2.00	6.00
	Confederation, Asterisk Issue	5.00	35.00
	Confederation, Collector's Issue 1867 1967	1.50	4.00

Multicoloured Issue, 1969–1975

Face side with portrait at right   Back with Canadian scene

In 1969 the release of a completely new and more modern series of Canadian notes began. The Bank of Canada, because of the increased circulation of counterfeit notes of the 1954 series, was concerned with producing notes which would be virtually impossible to counterfeit. The most advanced security features available were incorporated into the new designs while maintaining a high artistic standard. The updated style of this series includes multicoloured printing with deeper engravings to give the notes more of a "feel."

The face of each denomination displays the multicoloured Canadian coat of arms and a red serial number on the left half, while a black portrait is on the right with the serial number repeated in blue. For the first time since the 1937 issue, portraits of former Canadian Prime Ministers replace that of the ruling British monarch on some denominations. All denominations from $1 to $100 were released.

Design Details

DENOM.	BASIC COLOUR	PORTRAIT	BACK DESIGN
$1	Black	Queen Elizabeth	Ottawa River and Parliament Buildings
$2	Terra cotta	Queen Elizabeth	Eskimos preparing for a hunt
$5	Blue	Sir Wilfrid Laurier	Fishing boat on the west coast
$10	Purple	Sir John A.Macdonald	Oil refinery
$20	Olive Green	Queen Elizabeth	Rocky Mountains and lake
$50	Bright red	W.L. McKenzie King	Dome formation from R.C.M.P. "Musical Ride"
$100	Dark Brown	Sir Robert L. Borden	Maritimes dock scene

Dates, Signatures and Numbering

For the first time, because of the length of time required for design and preparation of each denomination, the various notes of a Bank of Canada issue do not bear the same date. The year shown on the notes and the actual month and year of issue for each are as follows:

$1 1973 (June, 1974)	$10 1971 (Nov., 1971)	$100 1975 (May, 1976)
$2 1974 (Aug., 1975)	$20 1969 (June, 1970)	
$5 1972 (Dec., 1972)	$50 1975 (Mar., 1975)	

The check letter system for numbering is as on the previous issue, except that the two letters are beside each other instead of in the form of a fraction. The left letter signifies denomination and the right letter indicates the series. Within each series the numbers go from 0000000 to 9999999, the zero note being removed and destroyed prior to issue. Since the series letters may include all letters from A to Z (except I, O or Q), each denomination can use 23 different series, or 230,000,000 notes. In 1981 a triple letter prefix was introduced to provide a wider range of series to be used to meet future demand.

There are four signature combinations on this issue:

J.R. Beattie and L. Rasminsky   G.K. Bouey and L. Rasminsky
R.W. Lawson and G.K. Bouey   J.W. Crow and G.K. Bouey

Replacement of defective notes by asterisk notes was continued with the multicoloured issue on all denominations but was discontinued when the new triple letter prefix notes were introduced. Replacement notes are now indicated by using the letter **x** for the third letter of the prefix.

DENOM.	SIGNATURE / VARIETY	REGULAR ISSUE UNC.	REPLACEMENT NOTE ISSUE* UNC.
$1	Lawson-Bouey / 2 letter prefix	5.50	20.00
	Lawson-Bouey / 3 letter prefix	4.50	30.00
	Crow-Bouey / 3 letter prefix	4.50	16.50
$2	Lawson-Bouey / 2 letter prefix	17.50	65.00
	Lawson-Bouey / 3 letter prefix	15.50	275.00
	Crow-Bouey / 3 letter prefix	15.50	450.00
$5	Bouey-Rasmminsky / 2 letter prefix	55.00	170.00
	Lawson-Bouey / 2 letter prefix	45.00	190.00
$10	Beattie-Rasminsky / 2 letter prefix	95.00	275.00
	Bouey-Rasminsky / 2 letter prefix	80.00	260.00
	Lawson-Bouey / 2 letter prefix	55.00	300.00
	Lawson-Bouey / 3 letter prefix	50.00	1,750
	Crow-Bouey / 3 letter prefix	50.00	225.00
	Thiessen-Crow / 3 letter prefix	45.00	160.00
$20	Beattie-Rasminsky / 2 letter prefix	135.00	425.00
	Lawson-Bouey / 2 letter prefix	105.00	525.00
$50	Lawson-Bouey / 2 letter prefix	200.00	1,100
	Lawson-Bouey / 3 letter prefix	200.00	3,500
	Crow-Bouey / 3 letter prefix	150.00	375.00

DENOM.	SIGNATURE / VARIETY	REGULAR ISSUE UNC.	REPLACEMENT NOTE ISSUE* UNC.
$100	Lawson-Bouey / 2 letter prefix 300.00		1,500
	Lawson-Bouey / 3 letter prefix 200.00		3,000
	Crow-Bouey / 3 letter prefix 175.00		450.00

Replacement notes using 2-letter prefixes have an asterisk preceding the serial number.
Replacement notes with 3-letter prefixes are designated by the use of an "X" as the third letter of the prefix.

Black Serial Number Issue, 1979

In 1979 the Bank of Canada released $5 and $20 notes in a new format. The basic style of the multicoloured issue was retained but there were several changes. In order to make it easier to distinguish the $20 from the $1 note, the orange and pink colours on the $20 note were strengthened while the green tones were diminished, creating a greater colour contrast between the two denominations.

The major change in the design was the removal of **BANK OF CANADA – BANQUE DU CANADA** from below the vignette on the back. New black serial numbers were put in this position replacing the red and blue serial numbers on the note faces.

These notes were introduced as an experiment to produce notes that would be machine readable but the experiment was unsuccessful and no further denominations were made in this series.

Dates, Signatures and Numbering

The black eleven-digit serial numbers differ from those of previous issues in that no letters are used as identification prefix. The first digit indicates the denomination, digits two through four indicates the series, and the remaining seven digits are the sequential note numbers from 0000000 to 9999999 as in the past. The $20 note was first issued in December 1978 and the $5 note in October 1979.

DENOM.	DATE SIGNATURE	REGULAR ISSUE UNC.	REPLACEMENT NOTE ISSUE* UNC.
$5	1979 Lawson-Bouey 35.00		500.00
	1979 Crow-Bouey 40.00		900.00
$20	1979 Lawson-Bouey 100.00		1,250
	1979 Crow-Bouey 40.00		275.00
	1979 Thiessen-Crow 40.00		140.00

Bar Code Issue, 1986–2000

In March 1986, the Bank of Canada introduced the first of a new series of notes, completely redesigned to assist the visually impaired, increase efficiency of high speed sorting equipment, and provide improved security against counterfeiting. The $1 note was not included in the new series and manufacture of $1 notes ceased as of July 1, 1988, this denomination being replaced by the new Loon dollar coin.

Security elements include the use of microprinting. A background rainbow of wavy lines on the face of the note is composed entirely of microprinted digits corresponding to the value of the note, while the fine horizontal lines through the centre portion of the note face are actually a repeated microprinted legend (**BANK OF CANADA 2 BANQUE DU CANADA** on the $2 note), in which the numeral corresponds to the denomination of the note. The much larger denomination numerals and portrait are intended to assist the visually impaired and are readable by a new portable electronic device being developed for the blind.

The reverse features native Canadian birds. The serial number appears in black on each half of the reverse at the bottom of the note. A bar code is included at the bottom of the reverse side to be read by high speed sorting equipment at the Bank of Canada. The serial number consists of a three-letter prefix and a seven-digit serial. Replacement notes are identified by the letter **X** as the third letter of the prefix.

The notes are the same size as the previous series and are printed on the same stock. The face of the note is printed using the intaglio process combined with lithography and the reverse using lithography and letterpress.

Design Details

	BASIC COLOUR	PORTRAIT	BACK DESIGN
$2	Terra Cotta	Queen Elizabeth	Two Robins
$5	Blue	Sir Wilfrid Laurier	Belted Kingfisher
$10	Purple	Sir John A. Macdonald	Osprey in flight
$20	Green	Queen Elizabeth	Common Loon
$50	Red	William Lyon Mackenzie King	Snowy Owl
$100	Brown	Sir Robert Borden	Canada Goose
$1000	Reddish purple	Queen Elizabeth	Pine Grosbeak

Dates, Signatures and Numbering

The year shown on the note and the actual month and year of issue for each denomination are as follows:

DENOM.	YEAR DATED	ISSUE DATE	SIGNATURE	REGULAR ISSUE UNC.	REPLACEMENT NOTE ISSUE UNC.
$2	1986	September, 1986	Crow-Bouey	8.00	50.00
	1986		Thiessen-Crow	8.00	25.00
	1986		Bonin-Thiessen	5.00	5.00
$5	1986	April, 1986	Crow-Bouey	35.00	350.00
	1986		Thiessen-Crow	10.00	30.00
	1986		Bonin-Thiessen	10.00	150.00
$10	1989	June, 1989	Thiessen-Crow	25.00	80.00
	1989		Bonin-Thiessen	20.00	300.00
	1989		Knight-Thiessen	15.00	—
$20	1991	June, 1993	Thiessen-Crow	65.00	100.00
	1991		Bonin-Thiessen	35.00	100.00
	1991		Knight-Thiessen	25.00	300.00
$50	1988	December, 1989	Thiessen-Crow	140.00	200.00
	1988		Knight-Thiessen	85.00	300.00
$100	1988	December, 1990	Thiessen-Crow	225.00	450.00
$1000	1988	May, 1992	Thiessen- Crow	1,600	2,500

Canadian Journey, 2001–2013

This issue celebrates Canadian history, culture and achievements in its reverse designs.

The new notes are the same size and retain the same dominant colours as previous bank note series. The Queen and the prime ministers shown on the new series are depicted on the same denominations. However, new portraits were engraved for both security and aesthetic purposes.

Notes in the new series are distinguished by new and enhanced security features to help fight counterfeiting and a tactile feature to help the blind and visually impaired identify the different denominations.

The $10 note features an iridescent image of three gold maple leaves used to discourage counterfeiting. Other security devices appearing on the note's face include a large image of the Coat of Arms with **DIX·TEN** above and **BANK OF CANADA BANQUE DU CANADA** in six lines below, which can be seen only under ultraviolet light. Micro printing is also used for security.

For those with impaired vision, the denomination is embosed in Braille-like characters on the upper right corner of the note's face while the numerals representing the denomination are much larger than previous and appear on a white background. A hand-held device for reading the denomination of the new notes is being developed.

The new $50 note was unveiled on 13 October 2004. It went into circulation on 17 November 2004. It is the fifth and last bank note of the Canadian Journey series and celebrates Nation Building, with an emphasis on the shaping of the political, legal, and social structures for democracy and equality.

Design Details

	BASIC COLOUR	PORTRAIT	BACK DESIGN
$5	Blue	Sir Wilfrid Laurier	Children at play
$10	Purple	Sir John A. Macdonald	Remembrance and Peacekeeping
$20	Green	Queen Elizabeth	Arts and Culture
$50	Red	William Lyon Mackenzie King	Nation Building
$100	Brown	Sir Robert Borden	Exploration and Innovation

Dates, Signatures and Numbering

The serial number, consisting of a three-letter prefix and a 7-digit number, appears twice on the back of the note. The year the note was printed appears in the middle at the bottom on the note's back while the year of issue is shown on the lower right corner of the note face.

DENOM.	YEAR PRINTED	ISSUE DATE	SIGNATURES	UNC
$5	2001	27 Mar 2002	M. D. Knight / D. A. Dodge	22.00
	2004		W. P. Jenkins / D. A. Dodge	25.00
	2005	15 Nov 2006	W. P. Jenkins / D. A. Dodge	30.00
	2006		W. P. Jenkins / M. J. Carney	
$10	2000	17 Jan 2001	M. D. Knight / G. G. Thiessen	20.00
	2001		M. D. Knight / D. A. Dodge	18.00
	2004		W. P. Jenkins / D. A. Dodge	20.00
	2005	18 May 2005	W. P. Jenkins / D. A. Dodge	20.00
	2006		W. P. Jenkins / M. J. Carney	
$20	2004	29 Sep 2004	W. P. Jenkins / D. A. Dodge	25.00
$50	2004	17 Nov 2004	W. P. Jenkins / D. A. Dodge	65.00
$100	2003	17 Mar 2004	W. P. Jenkins / D. A. Dodge	125.00

Frontier (Polymer Banknotes), 2011–

Beginning in 2011, the Bank of Canada introduced a new series of polymer banknotes.

These are the first Canadian notes produced on polymer. In place of a watermark are two visual features: a translucent maple leaf and a transparent window. The leaf includes a security feature that, when viewed close to the eye with a single-point light source behind, produces a circular image displaying the note's denomination. The window is fringed by maple leaves; at its top is a smaller version of the portrait, and at its bottom a light-refracting metallic likeness of an architectural feature from the parliament buildings. The portraits on the face are more centred on the note. The backs of the notes introduce new cultural and thematic imagery, but the literary quotation is not continued. The polymer notes continue the tactile feature, from the Canadian Journey series.

Design Details

	BASIC COLOUR	PORTRAIT	BACK DESIGN
$5	Blue	Sir Wilfrid Laurier	Canadarm2, Dextre and a Canadian astronaut
$10	Purple	Sir John A. Macdonald	The Canadian train; a map of passenger railways in Canada
$20	Green	Queen Elizabeth II	Canadian National Vimy Memorial; poppies
$50	Red	William Lyon Mackenzie King	CCGS Amundsen in arctic waters; a map of Canada's North; 'Arctic' in Inuktitut
$100	Brown	Sir Robert Borden	Medical research; DNA double helix; vial of insulin

Dates, Signatures and Numbering

The serial number, consisting of a three-letter prefix and a 7-digit number, appears twice on the back of the note.

DENOM.	ISSUE DATE	SIGNATURES	UNC
$5	Nov 2013	T. Macklem / M. J. Carney T. Macklem / S. Poloz C. Wilkins / S. Poloz	
$10	Nov 2013	T. Macklem / M. J. Carney T. Macklem / S. Poloz C. Wilkins / S. Poloz	
$20	7 Nov 2012	T. Macklem / M. J. Carney T. Macklem / S. Poloz C. Wilkins / S. Poloz	
$50	26 Mar 2012	T. Macklem / M. J. Carney T. Macklem / S. Poloz C. Wilkins / S. Poloz	
$100	14 Nov 2011	T. Macklem / M. J. Carney T. Macklem / S. Poloz C. Wilkins / S. Poloz	

BULLION VALUES

A worn or damaged coin, regardless of extreme age, can be worth less as a collectible piece than it is for the value of the precious metal it contains. Often, collectors are confused about determining the value of the gold or silver in coins. The following table indicates the bullion weight, in troy ounces, of the gold or silver contained in most of the coins in this catalogue.

The value for gold or silver, multiplied by the bullion weight in troy ounces, will produce the "melt" or bullion value of the piece. The spot value for gold and silver can be obtained from the business or financial section of most newspapers from the business reports given on radio and television newscasts, or from your dealer, and are usually expressed as dollars per troy ounce of the refined metal.

Dealers will purchase bullion coins for 15%–25% less than the current "melt" value. Because refineries will not accept shipments below their minimum weight requirement, and have fee scales which reduce with increasing weight, the dealer must accumulate bullion coins, jewellery, etc. until he has sufficient to ship to the refinery. The costs of, storage, security, shipping, and a reasonable profit must be covered by the 15%–25% discount from the final "melt" value.

The following will explain how to determine the "melt" value of a coin if the weight and fineness are known.

Fineness

The fineness is the percentage of a coin's weight that can be refined out as silver or gold, and in this catalogue is expressed as a decimal number. For example, all of the 25¢ pieces from the reign of King George V (1911–1936) have the same diameter (23.62) and weight (5.83 grams) but were 92½% silver (.925) until 1919, and only 80% silver (.800) thereafter. The earlier issues are said to be .925 fine silver and the later issues are only .800 fine silver.

The purety (fineness) of gold in coins, jewellery, etc., is often expressed in karats, pure gold is 24 karat. Because of the presence of trace elements, 24 karat gold is usually considered as .999 fine. Whenever the gold content of a piece is given in karats, it can be converted to a decimal by dividing the number of karats by 24. Some of the finenesses more commonly expressed as karats are:

24 karat	22 karat	18 karat	14 karat	10 karat
.999 fine	.916 fine	.750 fine	.585 fine	.417 fine

Weight

Throughout this catalogue, the weight of a coin is expressed in grams. Precious metals, however, are valued in dollars per troy ounce. The following table lists most of the coins appearing in the catalogue, with the weight of gold or silver in both grams and troy ounces. Multiplying the spot price for gold or silver by the number of troy ounces (under bullion) will produce the "melt" value of the piece.

For determining the "melt" value of other coins, jewellery, etc., the following information might prove useful.

Sometimes the weight of a gold piece might be expressed in pennyweights. Twenty pennyweights (based on the old English penny) equal 1 troy ounce. To convert pennyweights to troy ounces, divide by 20.

One troy ounce = 31.103 grams, and hence 1 gram = .032 troy ounces.

To convert any weight (in grams) to troy ounces, multiply by .032. After the weight of the piece has been converted to troy ounces, the weight of the precious metal (bullion weight) can be found by multiplying the troy ounces by the fineness of the coin. These calculations have been done for the following table.

Bullion Value of Canadian Coins

DENOMINATION	DATES	COIN WEIGHT GRAMS	TROY OZ.	FINENESS	BULLION WEIGHT GRAMS	TROY OZ.

GOLD
Canada

DENOMINATION	DATES	GRAMS	TROY OZ.	FINENESS	GRAMS	TROY OZ.
£1 sovereign	1908C–1919C	7.99	0.26	.917	7.33	0.24
5 dollars	1912–1914	8.36	0.27	.900	7.52	0.24
10 dollars	1912–1914	16.72	0.53	.900	15.05	0.48
20 dollars	1967	18.27	0.59	.900	16.44	0.53
100 dollars (14k)	1976	13.34	0.43	.583	7.78	0.25
100 dollars (22k)	1976–1986	16.96	0.54	.917	15.56	0.50
100 dollars	1987 to date	13.34	0.43	.583	7.78	0.25
200 dollars	1990 to date	17.11	0.55	.917	15.69	0.50

Maple Leaf Issues

DENOMINATION	DATES	GRAMS	TROY OZ.	FINENESS	GRAMS	TROY OZ.
50 dollars	1979 to date	31.15	1.00	.999	31.12	1.00
20 dollars	1986 to date	15.58	0.50	.9999	15.58	0.50
10 dollars	1982 to date	7.80	0.25	.9999	7.80	0.25
5 dollars	1982 to date	3.13	0.10	.9999	3.13	0.10
1 dollar	1993 to date			.9999		0.05

Newfoundland

DENOMINATION	DATES	GRAMS	TROY OZ.	FINENESS	GRAMS	TROY OZ.
2 dollars	1865–1888	3.33	0.11	.917	3.05	0.10

SILVER
Canada

DENOMINATION	DATES	GRAMS	TROY OZ.	FINENESS	GRAMS	TROY OZ.
5 cents	1858–1919	1.17	0.04	.925	1.08	0.04
5 cents	1920–1921	1.17	0.04	.800	0.94	0.03
10 cents	1858–1919	2.32	0.07	.925	2.15	0.06
10 cents	1920–1966	2.33	0.07	.800	1.86	0.06
10 cents	1967–1968	2.33	0.07	.500	1.16	0.04
20 cents	1858	4.67	0.15	.925	4.32	0.14
25 cents	1870–1910	5.81	0.18	.925	5.37	0.17
25 cents	1911–1919	5.83	0.19	.925	5.39	0.18
25 cents	1920–1966	5.83	0.19	.800	4.66	0.15
25 cents	1967–1968	5.83	0.19	.500	2.92	0.10
50 cents	1870–1919	11.62	0.37	.925	10.75	0.34
50 cents	1920–1967	11.66	0.37	.800	9.33	0.30
1 dollar	1935–1967	23.33	0.75	.800	18.66	0.60
1 dollar†	1971–1991	23.33	0.75	.500	11.66	0.38
1 dollar†	1992 to date	25.18	0.80	.925	23.29	0.74
5 dollars‡	1973–1976	24.30	0.78	.925	22.48	0.72
10 dollars‡	1973–1976	48.60	1.56	.925	44.96	1.44
20 dollars‡	1985–1988	34.11	1.09	.925	31.55	1.01

Maple Leaf Issue

DENOMINATION	DATES	GRAMS	TROY OZ.	FINENESS	GRAMS	TROY OZ.
5 dollars	1988 to date	31.39	1.00	.9999	31.39	1.00

New Brunswick

DENOMINATION	DATES	GRAMS	TROY OZ.	FINENESS	GRAMS	TROY OZ.
5 cents	1862–1864	1.16	0.04	.925	1.08	0.04
10 cents	1862–1864	2.32	0.07	.925	2.15	0.06
20 cents	1862–1864	4.65	0.15	.925	4.30	0.14

Newfoundland

DENOMINATION	DATES	GRAMS	TROY OZ.	FINENESS	GRAMS	TROY OZ.
5 cents	1865–1912	1.18	0.04	.925	1.09	0.04
5 cents	1917–1944	1.17	0.04	.925	1.08	0.04
5 cents	1945–1947	1.17	0.04	.800	0.94	0.03
10 cents	1865–1912	2.36	0.08	.925	2.18	0.07
10 cents	1917–1944	2.33	0.07	.925	2.15	0.06
10 cents	1945–1947	2.33	0.07	.800	1.86	0.06
20 cents	1865–1912	4.71	0.15	.925	4.36	0.14
25 cents	1917–1919	5.32	0.17	.925	4.92	0.16
50 cents	1870–1911	11.78	0.38	.925	10.90	0.35
50 cents	1917–1919	11.66	0.37	.925	10.78	0.34

† Collectors' issues.
‡ Olympic issues.

GLOSSARY

ALLOY: Mixture of more than one metal, usually preceded by the name of the most predominant or most important metal in the mix, such as nickel alloy.

ASSAY: The analytical test to determine the purity and weight of metal.

BAGMARKS: Slight scratches and nicks acquired by coins in contact with others in a mint bag. Most common on large and heavy silver and gold coins.

BILLON: A low-grade alloy used for some minor coin issues consisting usually of a mixture of silver and copper, and sometimes coated with a silver wash.

BLANKS: Flat round metal discs or planchets from which the coins are made.

BROCKAGE: Formerly any misstruck coin, now specifically refers to a coin having one side normal and the opposite side having the same design only as an incuse "mirror image."

BULLION: Uncoined gold or silver in the form of bars, ingots and plates. Bullion value is a term used in reference to the value of the metal content in gold and silver coins.

BUSINESS STRIKE: Any coin struck with the intention of circulating.

CAMEO-EFFECT: A description of the appearance of certain gold and silver proof coins which have frosted devices on highly polished fields.

CLASHED DIES: Damaged dies caused by the absence of a planchet at the time of striking. Each die retains a portion of its opposite's design, in addition to its own. The resulting coins show a partial impression of the reverse design on the obverse and/or vice versa.

CLIPPED PLANCHET (CLOSE PLANCHET): A planchet less than fully round, having been punched too closely to the edge of the metal sheet, or due to the adjacent planchet having been punched too closely.

DEBASEMENT: Debasement of a coin takes place when the issuing authority reduces the purity of the metal, lowering the intrinsic value of the coin but circulating it at par with the previous coins of the original purity.

DENTICLES: Tooth-like projections running inside the rim of a coin.

DEVICE: Any design feature appearing on the obverse, reverse or edge of a coin.

DIADEMED: A coin where the portrait head has a headband or fillet as a sign of royalty.

DIE: Engraved metal pieces used to impress the design of a coin on a blank planchet.

DIE AXIS: The vertical axes of the two dies when striking a coin or medal are indicated by arrows; with the obverse die assumed to be upright and the relative position of the reverse die indicated by a second arrow. Medal struck pieces have both dies upright (↑↑); coin struck, the reverse appears upside down (↑↓).

DIE CRACK: A stress crack on a die producing a raised line on the pieces struck.

DIE POLISHING LINES: Minute scratches on the die from polishing which produce very fine raised lines on some well struck coins.

ESSAI: A trial piece from dies already accepted for regular coinage. It may bear a date or mint mark other than on the coins issued for circulation or it may be a different metal.

EXERGUE: The lower part of a coin or medal which is usually divided from the field by a line under which is contained the date, place of minting or engraver's initials.

FIELD: Areas on either side of a coin not occupied by portrait, design or description.

FLAN: See BLANKS.

GEM: A relatively flawless piece of superlative quality.

HAIRLINES: Minute lines or scratches on a coin caused by cleaning or polishing.

HIGH POINTS: The highest points on the design of a coin. The first points to show wear.

INCUSE: Coins with either obverse or reverse design sunk below the coin's surface.

IRIDESCENT: Multi-coloured blending or toning usually found in older uncirculated coins.

KARAT: The degree of fineness of gold. Pure gold is 24 karats and most gold coins have a fineness of 22 karats.

LAMINATED PLANCHET: A "peeling off" of a top layer of the metal of a planchet.

LEGEND: The principal inscription on a coin.

LUSTRE: The sheen on the surface of an uncirculated coin caused by the centrifugal flow of metal on striking. Mint lustre (bloom) is somewhat frosty in appearance as opposed to the mirror-like fields of a proof. An important indicator of a coin's condition, lustre is worn through with the slightest circulation. Chemical cleaners can destroy it. Once gone, lustre cannot be restored.

MAJOR VARIETY: A coin of the same date, mint mark and denomination as another, but struck from another pair of dies and having at least the major device added, removed or redesigned.

MATTE PROOF: A proof coin for which the planchet is treated in a manner other than polishing. A dull and grainy finish is achieved.

MEDAL: A commemorative metal piece in honour of a person or event. Not money.

MEDALET: A small medal, usually smaller in diameter than a fifty-cent piece.

MILLED EDGE: [1] Prior to use of collar dies the edge design was milled onto the blank before minting; [2] using collar dies, flan edges are milled so that the border or design will be adequately raised when struck.

MINOR VARIETY: A minor variety is one with all major devices the same as another, but with some easily recognizable variation.

MINT ERROR: An incorrectly struck or defective coin produced by a mint.

MINT MARK: Letter designation for a branch mint product.

MULE: A coin struck from dies not designed to be used together.

OBVERSE: The "face-up" side of the coin, regarded as more important than the reverse side and usually bearing the portrait of the monarch.

OVERDATED: The date made by an engraver at the mint punching one or more numbers on a previously dated die.

OVERSTRIKE: A coin where part of the design, particularly the date, appears over another design or date.

PATINA: Originally: a green or brown surface film (from oxidation) found on ancient copper and bronze coins; now refers to toning on any coin.

PATTERN: A design suggested for a new coinage, struck in a few examples but not adopted. If adopted for regular coinage with the same date, the piece ceases to be a pattern.

PIEDFORT: A type of pattern struck on a thick flan. Probably, piedforts were struck for use by coiners as models when making actual coins.

PLANCHET: See BLANKS.

PROOF: [1] A special striking of a coin, produced to show to those who have the right to choose the design at its best. Proofs are carefully struck by gentle pressure, usually at least twice, from carefully polished dies, on polished flans. The minutest details of the design are thus made clear. The term does NOT refer to the condition of the coin. [2] A bank note or other form of paper money specially printed as a sample or specimen but not intended for circulation.

REEDED EDGE: Minted vertical serrations on the edge of a coin.

RELIEF: Where the lettering and design are raised above the surface of the coin.

RESTRIKE: Any coin struck later than the date appearing on the coin.

REVERSE: Opposite from obverse. The back or "tails" side of a coin.

ROTATED DIE: Dies are positioned and locked on a coining press by means of a key. When these keys come loose, rotation can occur resulting in the next coin being struck with the obverse and reverse dies rotated. Coins struck from rotated dies are errors.

SPECIMEN: [1] A coin or bank note prepared, often with special care, as an example of a given issue. Sometimes, particularly with bank notes, surcharged SPECIMEN or a similar word. [2] A synonym for a numismatic item, e.g., a very rare specimen.

SPURIOUS: A false piece made to deceive, often an original creation rather than a copy of a known item. Not genuine, counterfeit, false.

TOKEN: Usually a piece of durable material appropriately marked and unofficially issued for monetary, advertising, services or other purposes.

TRADE DOLLAR: A token used by a municipality primarily as a tourism promotion, and redeemable in most stores in the issuing municipality.

VIGNETTE: A pictorial element of a bank note design that shades off gradually into the surrounding unprinted paper or background rather than having sharp outlines or a frame.

WIRE EDGE: Slight flange on coins or medals caused by heavy striking pressure, often characteristic on Proof coins (also KNIFE EDGE). The metal is squeezed up the side of the die faces by the collar die.

WORKING DIE: Used to strike coins. Not a master die, etc.

UNITRADE
ASSOCIATES

UNI-SAFE

CANADA

Blue vinyl covers with silver coloured stamping. Each folder has four clear vinyl pages with pockets to completely cover coin for ultimate protection while leaving both sides of the coin in view. The inside cover of each folder has a listing for the appropriate denomination.

Retail 4.95   each

141	Canada Cents	1858–1920
142	Canada Cents	1920–Date
142B	Canada Cents	Blank
143	Canada 5 Cents	1922–Date
143B	Canada 5 Cents	Blank
144	Canada 10 Cents	1920–Date
144B	Canada 10 Cents	Blank
132	Canada 25 Cents	2000 –Date
145	Canada 25 Cents	1937–1999
145B	Canada 25 Cents	Blank
146	Canada 50 Cents	1937–1983
146B	Canada 50 Cents	Blank
148	Canada 50 Cents	1984–Date
147	Canada Dollars	1935–1986
147B	Canada Dollars	Blank
149	Canada Dollars	1987–Date
131	Canada Two Dollars	1996–Date

COINS OF THE WORLD

As above folders but covers are in brown vinyl with gold and silver coloured stamping. Each folder contains 6 pages with a total of 142 pockets - 24 for large coins, 48 for medium coins and 70 for small coins.

#130 For assorted coins   each 4.95

Tel: 416. 242.5900 Fax: 416.242.6115
99 Floral Parkway, Toronto, M6L 2C4
unitrade@rogers.com   www.unitradeassoc.com

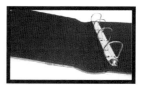

NOTES

NOTES